The Barbarian Invasions

Other Volumes of Delbrück's *History of the Art of War*
Available in Bison Book Editions

*Warfare in Antiquity,* Volume I
*Medieval Warfare,* Volume III
*The Dawn of Modern Warfare,* Volume IV

# The Barbarian Invasions

## HISTORY OF THE ART OF WAR
### VOLUME II

By Hans Delbrück

*Translated from the German by Walter J. Renfroe, Jr.*

University of Nebraska Press
Lincoln and London

First Bison Book printing: 1990
Most recent printing indicated by the last digit below:
10 9 8 7 6 5 4

Library of Congress Cataloging-in-Publication Data
Dulbrück, Hans, 1848–1929.
[Geschichte der Kriegskunst im Rahmen der politischen Geschichte.
Volume I–II. English]
History of the art of war / by Hans Delbrück: translated from the
German by Walter J. Renfroe, Jr.
p.   cm.
Translation of: Geschichte der Kriegskunst im Rahmen der
politischen Geschichte, v. I–II.
Contents: v. I. Warfare in antiquity—v. II. The barbarian invasions.
ISBN 0-8032-6584-0 (set).—ISBN 0-8032-9199-X (v. I).—
ISBN 0-8032-9200-7 (v. II)
1. Military art and science—History. 2. Naval art and science—
History. 3. War—History. I. Title.
U27.D34213   1990
355'.009—dc20
89-24980 CIP

Reprinted by arrangement with Greenwood Press, Inc.

Originally titled HISTORY OF THE ART OF WAR WITHIN THE FRAMEWORK
OF POLITICAL HISTORY, by Hans Delbrück, Volume II, THE GERMANS.
Translated from the German by Walter J. Renfroe, Jr., and published as part of the
Greenwood Press Series, Contributions in Military History, Westport, CT. Maps
drawn by Edward J. Krasnoborski. Originally published in German under the title
GESCHICHTE DER KRIEGSKUNST IN RAHMEN DER POLITISCHEN GES-
CHICHTE. Copyright © 1980 by Walter J. Renfroe, Jr. All rights reserved.

# Table of Contents

## BOOK III
Emperor Justinian and the Goths

## BOOK IV
The Transition to the Middle Ages

# List of Illustrations

# Translator's Foreword

This translation into English of the second volume of Hans Delbrück's *Geschichte der Kriegskunst im Rahmen der politischen Geschichte* is based on the third edition of that volume, which was published in Berlin in 1921. It is a continuation of my translation of Delbrück's four volumes, the first of which was published by Greenwood Press in 1975.

As in the first volume, I have adhered as closely as possible to the original, both in spirit and style, without adding notes or comments.

The Greek and Latin quotations included by Delbrück throughout his text have been treated in the same way as in Volume I. Each Latin quotation has been retained, with the English translation normally following it in parentheses. In some cases, because of the length of the quotation, the Latin and English have been shown in parallel columns, and four passages were so long as to warrant separate placement in an appendix. In the latter cases, only the English translation is given in the body of the text. Greek passages appearing in Delbruck's text are given in the English translation only, with an asterisk following the final quotation mark to indicate this fact. Occasionally, where the interpretation of a Greek word or expression is vital to Delbrück's argument, a transliteration of the expression has been included.

In some cases where Delbrück quotes the Latin or Greek passage of one of the sources, he has incorporated the German translation in his text, and his words have been translated into English in the running text. In most cases, however, the translations into English from Greek and Latin have been provided by Dr. Everett L. Wheeler, Department of Classical Studies, Duke University, to whom I am greatly indebted for his important contribution to the overall work. Dr. Wheeler points out that, while some of the passages quoted by Delbrück have been revised in more recent editions of the original source material, he has based his translations on the readings appearing in Delbrück's text. In cases where a quoted passage lends itself to varying interpretations, Dr. Wheeler has given the interpretation that supports Delbrück's argument.

As in Volume I, distances are shown in kilometers in those passages

where Delbrück used that unit of measure and in English miles in cases
where Delbrück used German miles.

Delbrück's page references to Volume I have been changed so as to
reflect the pagination of the Greenwood translation of 1975.

Once again I am pleased to express my appeciation and that of Greenwood Press to Frau Helene Hobe-Delbrück, daughter of Hans Delbrück,
for kindly granting permission for this translation.

# Preface to the Third Edition

This third edition differs from the second, which appeared in 1909, only in a series of minor additions and improvements, such as, for example, the military institutions of the Visigoths. My overall concepts have remained unchanged, and not only have I found no basis for modifying my accounts of detailed points which have been challenged by my critics, but I have even been able to reinforce them with new arguments. This applies, for example, to my concept of the Germanic wedge (*Keil*) formation and the siting of the fort of Aliso on the hill where the Paderborn Cathedral now stands.

In the meantime, the fourth and last volume of this work, which covers the period up to Napoleon and Clausewitz, has been published (1920). Now that an Austrian critic has stated that the two most basic points established in the work are the reduction of the huge army strengths and the clarification of the differences between the strategies of annihilation and attrition, one might conclude from that statement that the first and fourth volumes are the two most important ones. My own feeling is that, rather, the second one is the most important. This volume affects most deeply of all four our inherited concepts of world history, through its elimination of the legendary ideas on the fall of the ancient world and on the migrations of the peoples (*Völkerwanderung*), as well as its positive contributions, especially those concerning the substantiation of the alliance between Constantine and the Christian Church as postulate of the changed military system and institutions and the clarification of the system of feudal institutions and of knighthood. Basic to all of this is the polarity between individual combatants and tactical bodies in the system of warriorhood, the development of which forms the substance of the third volume.

*Grunewald, 29 July 1921*

Hans Delbrück

# BOOK I

## The Conflict Between the Romans and the Germans

# Chapter I

# The Early Germanic Nation

In order to understand the military institutions and deeds of the Germans, we must first become acquainted with the political-social organization of this people.

The Germans, like the Gauls, did not have political unity; they were divided into tribes (*Völkerschaften; civitates*), each of which possessed an area averaging some 2,000 square miles. Because of the danger of enemy raids, the border regions of the area were not inhabited, so that it was possible to travel in a single day's march from the most distant settled localities to a centrally located assembly point.

Since a very large part of the land was covered by forests and swamps and the inhabitants cultivated only a small area, living principally on milk, cheese, and meat, the average population cannot very well have amounted to more than 11 or 12 persons per square mile. The tribe therefore normally had about 25,000 souls, with the larger tribes numbering up to 35,000 or 40,000. That gives between 6,000 and 10,000 men, a number which, even in the largest case, after deducting 1,000 to 2,000 absentees, could still be reached by a speaker and which could therefore still form a unified consultative assembly. The highest sovereign power was exercised by this general assembly of the tribe.

The tribes were composed of clans or "Hundreds." These groupings were called clans because they were not arbitrarily composed but were held together in the natural relationship of procreation. There did not exist any cities to which portions of each younger generation could go streaming away, there to form new associations. Each person remained in the group into which he was born. But the clans are also referred to as Hundreds because they numbered about 100 households or warriors,[1] a number which, of course, may well have been often far exceeded in practice, for the Germans used the word "hundred" in the sense of a rather large round number in a general way. This numerical designation existed alongside the patriarchal one because the actual familial relationships between the members of the clan were after all only very tenuous. The clans cannot have originated through a situation where originally a number of couples lived close together, developing over a few centuries into a large clan, but rather only from the fact that clans which became too large to feed themselves in one location split up. Consequently, a certain size, a certain number — about 100 — formed the constitutive element of the group, just as much as did its origin; the name, therefore, depended as much on the former as on the latter. Clan (*Geschlecht*) and Hundred (*Hundertschaft*) are identical.

The clan or Hundred, whose number we may hereafter assume as being from 400 to 1,000 souls, and possibly on occasion as high as 2,000, controlled an area of some 20 square miles or possibly several times that size, the district, and lived together in one village. The Germans did not build their huts side by side, gable to gable, but wherever the particular site, forest, or spring pleased the individual. Nevertheless, this is not to be understood in the sense of individual farms, such as are found today in many parts of Westphalia, but of a loose-knit general settlement built in a stretched-out style. The cultivation of the soil, which was carried out principally by the women and those men unfit for hunting and fighting, was very meager. In order to till fresh, fertile soil, the location of the settlement within the district was changed quite often. Even at a later period, Germanic law did not consider the house as real estate but rather as movable property. Since, as we have seen, there were 11 or 12 persons on the average to each square mile, so that a village of 750 souls had a corresponding area of some 60 square miles,[2] it would have been impossible to utilize very much tillable land in any way except through these periodic displacements. Even if they were no longer nomads, the Germans still felt only a very loose tie to the land.

The members of the clan, who were at the same time inhabitants of the same village, together formed a single unit in time of war. Hence, even today, in Norse, a body of troops is called a *thorp* and in Switzerland the word *Dorf* is used for a group and *dorfen* means to hold an assembly. In fact, our German word *Truppe* (troop) is of the same derivation and, carried along by the Franks to the Latins and thence back to us, it preserves a recollection of our forbears out of times to which no written source reaches back. The group that moved out to war together as a unit and that together inhabited a settlement was the same; for that reason, there developed from the same word an indication of a place of residence, village (*Dorf*), and of soldiers, troops (*Truppe*).[3]

The Old German community was, consequently, a village insofar as the manner of settling was concerned, a district with respect to its area, a Hundred as judged from its size, and a clan in the matter of its mutual interrelationship. Land was not private property but belonged in common to this close-knit community. It formed, according to the expression of a later period, a communal march.

The Romans had no words which completely described this entire phenomenon, and so they had to resort to circumlocutions. The Roman *gens*, the word which would have come closest, had become an almost meaningless form and no longer had any true significance for a Latin. Consequently, Caesar called the Germanic clans *"gentes cognation-esque hominum, qui una colerunt"* ("clans and families of men who lived together"), in order to express the idea that a true blood relationship existed in these settlements. Tacitus says that the *"familiae et propinquitates"* ("households and their relatives") stood side by side in the field and that the "communities" (*universi*) possessed the cultivated land. Paulus Diaconus, too, felt that the Germanic situation could not really be expressed by a Latin word, and in his book written in the Latin language, he retained the German word *fara*, "family" (of the same derivation as *pario* [I give birth to], *peperi* [I gave birth to]), while adding three translations: *generationes* (races, families), *lineas* (lineages), and *prosapias* (families).[4] The same confusion existed in the case of the word for the village. The Roman *vicus* (village) was small and was built in close-knit fashion like a city. In order to give an idea of the more loosely constructed and stretched-out settlements of the Germans, Tacitus used the expression *"vici pagique"* ("villages and rural districts").

At the head of each community was an elected official, who was called either *Altermann* (elder) or *hunno*, just as the community was called both clan and Hundred. Ulfilas calls the centurion in the Bible Hunda-faths. Among the Anglo-Saxons we find the *Ealdorman*, in Norway the *Herredskönige* or *Hersen*. In Germany, the *hunno* continued to exist in many areas throughout the Middle Ages as village magistrate under the names *Hunne*, *Hun*, and *Hundt*, and even today he exists in Siebenburgen in the form of *Hon*.

The elders or *hunni* were the governors and leaders of the communities in peace and commanders of the men in war. But they lived with and among the people; socially, they were common citizens, like all the others. Their authority was not great enough to enable them to maintain the peace in case of serious disputes or crimes. Their station was not high enough nor their perspective broad enough for them to be able to exercise political guidance and leadership. In each tribe there stood, high above the common citizens, one or several noble families which, elevated above the masses, enjoyed their own special status and traced their descent from the gods. From among them the general assembly elected several "princes" or "most outstanding men" (*principes*) who traveled through the districts (*per pagos vicosque:* "through rural districts and villages") to hold court, treated with foreign powers, conferred together on public affairs, possibly also in consultation with the *hunni*, in order to pass their proposals on to the general assembly, and one of whom, in war, exercised the high command as duke.

What in the eyes of the Germans amounted to great wealth resided in the princely families as a result of the sharing of booty, tribute, gifts, prisoners of war who worked for them, and favorable marriages.[5] This wealth enabled them to maintain a retinue of free men, the bravest warriors, who pledged their loyalty to their lord, even to death, and as his dining companions lived in his presence, providing ceremony in peacetime, protection and help in wartime (*in pace decus, in bello praesidium:* "in peace his honor, in war his guard"). Wherever the prince appeared, the men of his retinue lent authority and force to his word.

There certainly did not exist any specific law to the effect that only the scion of one of the noble families could be elected as prince. In practice, however, these families had become so definitely separated from the mass that it was not easy for a commoner to cross over into this elite circle. Why should the assembly have chosen as prince a man from the mass who was no more important than any other man? Nevertheless, it may not have been such a rare thing for *hunni* whose families had held that office for several generations and had thereby acquired a special prestige and even wealth to be absorbed into the class of princes. In fact, it was probably precisely in this way that the formation of the noble families themselves had taken place; the natural advantage that the sons of distinguished fathers enjoyed in elections of officials gradually turned into a custom of electing, in place of a deceased official, and assuming qualification for the position, the son of the deceased. The advantages of the position, in turn, tended to raise the family so far above the common mass that it became less and less possible for others to compete. If today we detect rather weak effects of this psychological-social process in public life, that is because other forces are strongly at work against such a natural development of a prestige class. There is no doubt that, in Germanic antiquity, an hereditary status developed from the originally elected officialdom. On the territory of conquered Britain the princes of the older order became kings and the aldermen earls. During the period with which we are dealing here, these relationships were still in the process of development. No doubt, the princely class had already risen as a group above the mass, but the *hunni* still belonged to the mass and on the continent they never did arrive at the special status of a separate class.

The assembly of the Germanic princes with the *hunni* was, it seems, designated by the Romans as the senate of the Germanic tribes. The sons of the most distinguished families were accorded the princely dignity while still quite young and they were taken along to the discussions of the senate. Otherwise, it was the retinue of a prince that served as school for those youths who were striving for more unusual things than the everyday life of a freeman.

The government by the princes was transformed into a kingdom whenever only one prince was on hand or one of them eliminated or suppressed the others. The basis and the spirit of the system was, of itself, not yet changed because of this, since the highest, final jurisdiction still remained, as previously, the general warrior assembly. The difference between a princedom and a kingdom was so slight that the Romans on one occasion even used the title of king when there was not just one prince but two of them at hand.[6] And the kingship, too, just like the princely position, was not passed on by heredity from one incumbent to the next, but the most highly qualified man was elevated to this position by the vote and the call of the people. In this procedure, a physically or mentally incompetent heir could and would be passed over. If then the kingship and the princeship at first differed only on a quantitative basis, there was naturally still a very great difference if the leadership and direction were in the hands of a single person or several people. The possibility of opposition, of weighing various plans in the general assembly and making various proposals, was for all practical purposes completely eliminated by the kingship. The sovereign power of the general assembly gradually changed to a simple role of acclamation; but this still remained indispensable, even for the king. Even in the king's presence the German retained the pride and the questioning spirit of the free man. "They were kings," Tacitus says (13. 54), "to the extent that Germans ever let themselves be ruled" ("*in quantum Germani regnantur*").

The relationship of the district to the state was a rather loose one. It could happen that, by moving its settlement somewhat farther away, a district would gradually separate itself from the state to which it previously belonged. Attendance at the general assemblies would become more complicated and less frequent; the two groups no longer had common interests. At this point the district was tied to the state only through a kind of alliance relationship, and in time, as the clan grew larger, it formed a new state of its own. The previous *hunno* family became a princely family. Or in other cases it happened that, when districts were allocated to the various princes as their administrative regions, these princes united the regions under them, developed a kingship, and broke off from the mother state. This is not directly proven in the sources, but it is reflected in the uncertainty inherent in the terminology of the sources that have been handed down. The Cherusci and the Chatti, who appear to us as tribes in the sense of nations (*civitates*), had such an extensive area that we may actually see in them primarily an alliance of states. Of many tribal names it may be doubtful whether they are not simple names of districts. In turn, the name "district" (*Gau: pagus*) may often have been used in referring not to a Hundred but to the region of a prince that was made up of several Hundreds. The firmest relationship was the cohesiveness of the Hundred, the clan, which lived together half communistically and could not easily be dissolved through either external or internal factors.

## EXCURSUS

My concept of the political-social organization of the Germans, which indeed differs significantly from the generally accepted beliefs, I first explained and thoroughly justified in the 81st volume of the *Preussische Jahrbücher* 3 (1895). Let me once again present here the most important factors of my proof.

The decisive point is the identity of clan and Hundred.

In my opinion, the fact that the Hundred is the same as the district has already been satisfactorily demonstrated by Waitz. More recent scholars — Sybel, Sickel, Erhardt, Brunner, Schröder — have accepted, instead of this concept, one in which the district is a region of at least 2,000 warriors. This conception is not justifiable, however. The word *pagus*, which is primarily at the center of the question, is in the Roman sense quite generally a region of land, the subdivision of a country or a region of indefinite size. Caesar has the Helvetii occupying four *pagi;* it is clear that these *pagi* not only were not Hundreds but also must even have been considerably larger than Thousands. We must assume that the Helvetii, who had become too numerous to govern themselves any longer through a single popular assembly, split up into four communities bound together through ties of allegiance. Since these four communities continued to act as a unit in their external affairs, the Romans referred to them as simple *pagi* of the nation of the Helvetii. In our particular case, this kind of *pagi* can be eliminated from the start, just like the *pagi* of the Middle Ages, which corresponded somewhat to the old tribes.

The largest unit that can be considered as coming under the German *pagi* of the earliest period was the Thousand. We could consider this possibility just as long as we had no definite concept of the population density, the number of members of a Germanic tribe. If it is correct, however, that under conditions of culture and agriculture like those of ancient Germany not more than 11 or 12 souls, on the average, can live on a square mile, we must abandon the idea of a Thousand. We can no doubt imagine that a tribe which had three or four princes would assign to each of them as judge a region which counted some 1,200 to 2,000 warriors, and it is possible that such a region, too, was sometimes called a *pagus*.[7] If, however, we have first gained a clear insight into the nature of the Hundred and the appearance of its settlement, there can then be no doubt that the Romans, when they spoke of Germanic *pagi*, were thinking primarily of these Hundreds. And since the Saxons used the word *Go* in this sense until the late Middle Ages, we are justified in using this word in the technical sense for the Hundreds, even in the earliest period, without denying the possibility that the Germans may also have used it in the general sense, as we use "district" (Bezirk) today.

It is therefore a question of the Hundred. Brunner's latest hypothesis, which has also been accepted by Richard Schröder, is that the Hundred was a personal unit, a subdivision of an army under a chief, which to be sure did not always stay exactly at a strength of 100, since whole clans were supposed to remain together, but which was adjusted from time to time for the sake of its military objective.

The following considerations militate against this hypothesis. It is definitely established that the Germans moved into battle in clan groups. There was no reason at all for uniting these clans artificially into Hundreds (assuming that they were smaller than that number). A city-state like Rome had to organize its warriors arbitrarily into "centuries" for the maintenance of good order, since there did not exist any useful natural units. Clans, however, that after all could not have been so very small under any circumstances — and if they had been too small, then the villages at any rate — gave the Germans such excellent subordinate units for the army that it is impossible to see why, on a continuing and general basis applying to all the Germans and lasting through many centuries, an artificially contrived assignment of personnel by Hundreds should have sprung up and been maintained.

That is all the more unlikely when we see that it is precisely the leader of this band, the *hunno*, who is a functionary whom we find again and again and who was apparently the real leader at the lower level, a position stemming from ancient times. How would that have been possible if he had stood at the head of a simple unit whose personnel kept changing, if the Hundred itself had not been an extremely fixed and lasting unit, and if in this unit the true corporate life had not pulsated in the unit itself but in the subordinate units, the families?

Finally, the completely decisive point: the idea that several clans together formed a Hundred is impossible, because the clan was much too large for that concept. Dio Cassius (71. 11) reports to us that the Germans made peace with Marcus Aurelius partly by clans, partly by tribes. These "clans" (*Geschlechter*) cannot possibly have been small groupings of ten to twenty individual families. The same conclusion results from the account in Paulus Diaconus (2. 9) cited above. If we must imagine the clans (*Geschlechter*) themselves, however, as units of 100 warriors, and often of several hundred, then it naturally follows that the Hundred, once again, cannot have been a subordinate unit of the clan (*Geschlecht*) and that the clan and the Hundred were identical. Precisely through this concept, and through it alone, can we clarify the widespread and continuing position of the *hunno* among all the Germanic tribes, that is, that he was the leader of the clan, the *Altermann*.

By proceeding from the economic conditions we arrive at the same result. It is definite that it was the clans that occupied the land in common and assigned plots to individuals, but without having that lead to private ownership. Even leaving aside the testimony presented by Dio Cassius and Paulus Diaconus, it is clear that it would not have been possible for several clans to occupy a single village. That would have made of each of them not only a superfluous intermediate unit between the individual family and the village, but also an intolerable one. Still rather late in our early documents we find villages referred to as *genealogiae*;[8] in Old High German *tribus* is translated as *chuni*, and *contribules* as *chunilinga* (relatives, family members).[9] Among the Anglo-Saxons the word *maegd* (equivalent of *gens*) has precisely the meaning of *territorium, provincia, patria*. Clan and village were therefore identical, a situation which does not eliminate the possibility that apparently from time to time several settlements existed at quite some distance from each other. For practical reasons even that probably happened only seldom, since from the viewpoint of mutual assistance the settlements could not be too small; under any circumstances, politically there existed only a single unit, the one that regarded itself as master of the region and divided this up among individuals.

This unit, this village, must have had a head for its economic leadership, a chief who was a very important, authoritative personality, because the public fields, the pastures, the forest, the herding and protection of the animals, sowing and harvesting, protection against fires, and mutual help constantly demanded his attention. Not only is it nowhere proven that there existed an official below the *hunno*, but it is even fully clear that the leader of the village, which was at the same time the clan, was a much too important personality to have a *hunno* directly over him, who, after all, did not himself stand high on the social ladder as yet. The clan patriarch and village chief would necessarily have dispossessed the *hunno*. The two positions would have stood too closely to one another to allow room for both, and it is clear that the *hunno* would have been the weaker. This division is therefore an impossible one. A military leader who from time to time would have exercised command over several villages or clans would be conceivable, but the *hunno*, who continued as a common Germanic phenomenon over many centuries and shows up again and again, was nothing of a transitory nature but must have stood in a very definite relationship to an inherently firm corporate body. Consequently, he cannot possibly have existed in addition to the village chief and clan patriarch, who was the leader of the economic unit, but was identical with him. And the identity of these officials leads to the identity of the corporate bodies: the clan is the village and the village is the Hundred.

THE DENSITY OF POPULATION IN GERMANY

Today it is no doubt recognized that the figures given by the Romans for the peoples of Germany, which until recently were repeated without any questioning, are worthless. How extraordinarily difficult it is, leaving aside completely any tendentious exaggeration, to estimate tribal populations we have learned from the reports from those countries which only now have moved into the cognizance of the civilized world.

In the Urundi region, Stanley had estimated the population density at 75 persons to the square kilometer; later, Baumann estimated it at 7. For Uganda, Reclus believed himself justified in estimating 230 souls to the square mile (much denser than in France). Ratzel reduced the 230 to 31, and Jannasch once explained that, despite all his careful efforts, he had found it completely impossible to arrive at a reasonably reliable estimate of the population of a region in Africa. If, despite this, Vierkandt estimates for the westerly regions of Central Africa population densities from 0.85 up to 6.5 per square kilometer, and, on the average, for an area of 5,010,000 square kilometers a density of 4.74 per square kilometer (some 11 to 12 per square mile), he is able to do that only with the help of very numerous and mutually verifying figures and actual reliable counts.[10] How could it be possible for us to arrive at even a roughly trustworthy estimate of the ancient Germans, for whom we do not have a single reliable count, one that could be interpreted with certainty?

This estimate is nevertheless possible, since today we have at our disposal something about which there was no definite idea a generation ago, that is, certain measures of the food production of all countries in various stages of cultural development, measures that provide us with very definite points of reference for many places, even if not everywhere. These measures leave no doubt that the Germans, who still had no cities, cultivated the soil but little, and lived principally on milk, cheese, meat, the fruits of the hunt and fishing, in a country consisting mostly of forest and swamp, can only have been very thinly spread.

E. Mor. Arndt, in Schmidt's *Zeitschrift für Geschichtliche Wissenschaft* 3: 244, at one time estimated that the population of Germany was between 37 and 46 souls per square mile, but on the condition that the Romans' accounts of the Germans' limited agriculture were untrue. Today scholars agree that the descriptions of German agriculture in Caesar and Tacitus are true, and along with this condition, which does full honor to the healthy, natural perceptiveness of the veteran author in question, there also collapses the resulting conclusion, the large population, the great masses of people that the Romans loved to tell about. On the basis of a comparison with Beloch's figures for Gaul, I estimated, in the cited essay in the *Preussische Jahrbücher*, a density of 4 to 5 per square kilometer (11 to 12 per square mile). Since then, the basis for these figures has been shaken somewhat, inasmuch as in the meantime I have abandoned my belief in the figures Caesar gives for the Helvetii, figures that Beloch used as his point of departure. Nevertheless, we can hold fast to the estimate itself.

The comparative figures which we can use as a base in order to gain first of all an approximate foothold are now to be found admirably assembled in Schmoller's *Fundamentals of Political Economy (Grundriss der Allgemeinen Volkswirtsohaftslehre)* 1: 158 ff., especially p. 183. Schmoller arrives at a figure for Germany at the time of Christ's birth of 5 to 6 persons per square kilometer. At another place in his work (p. 169), he states the belief that my estimate of 25,000 souls for the tribe (4 to 5 per square kilometer) seems to him rather too high than too low. That is not a real contradiction, since here, after all, it can only be a question of very general estimates. Whether it was a density of 4 or 6 souls per square kilometer, the number of Germans between the Rhine and the Elbe fluctuated somewhere around a figure of not more than a million; we are able to pin that down still more narrowly, with the help of figures for the extension and the constitution of the individual tribes.

We know the geography of northwest Germany accurately enough to determine that the region between the Rhine, the North Sea, the Elbe, and a line drawn from the Main in the vicinity of Hanau to the confluence of the Saale with the Elbe was inhabited by 23 [sic] Germanic tribes: two of Friesians, the Canninefates, Batavians, Chamavi, Ampsivarii, Angrivarii, Tubantes, two Chauci, Usipetes, Tencteri, two Bructeri, Marsi, Chasuarii, Dulgibini, Lombards, Cherusci, Chatti, Chattuarii, Inneriones, Intverges, and Calucones.[11] The entire region has an area of about 50,000 square miles, so that, on the average, each tribe had an area of about 2,170 square miles. The sovereign power in each of these tribes lay in the general assembly of the people or the warriors. That was also true of Athens and Rome, but in those developed states the working population played only a minor role in the popular assemblies. We may assume that with the Germans very often practically the entire body of warriors was actually present. For this very reason, their states covered no great area, because if the distance from the more distant villages to the central point had been greater than a long day's march, it would no longer have been possible to hold truly general assemblages, and just as an area of some 2,200 square miles corresponds precisely to this concept, so too is an assembly of from 6,000 to 8,000 men at most the largest one that can be conducted in a fairly orderly manner. If that was the maximum, the average size could not have been significantly higher than 5,000, and that leads us to a population figure of about 25,000 for a tribe, or between 11 and 12 to the square mile (4 to 5 per square kilometer). First of all, let it be noted that that is the maximum, the upper limit. But to put the figure significantly lower than this is not possible, for another reason, the military one. The military accomplishments of the Germans against the Roman Empire and its battle hardened legions were so great that they appear unthinkable without a certain mass of men, and in comparison with these accomplishments even 5,000 warriors in each tribe seems such a small figure that no one will be inclined to lower it further.

Consequently, here we have a case in which, despite the complete lack of useful, positive information, we are still able to state definite figures with great certainty. The relationships are so simple, and the economic and military, geographical and political facts so closely interlaced that with today's perfected methods of scientific research we are able to fill in the missing parts of the source accounts and to estimate the numbers of Germans better than the Romans could when they saw them before their very eyes and had daily dealings with them.

Sering estimates that the population density in the estate districts of the East Elbe region was as low as 4 souls to the square kilometer.

PRINCES AND *HUNNI*

The fact that the system of Germanic officials fell into two different classes can be concluded just as well from the nature of things, the political organization, and the composition of the tribe as it is attested to directly from the sources. Caesar (*Bell. Gall.* 4. 13) recounts that the "princes and elders" ("*principes majoresque natu*": "chieftains and elders") of the Usipetes and Tencteri came to him. To the Ubii, in addition to the princes, he attributes (4. 11) a senate ("*principes ac senatus*"), and he says that the senate of the Nervii, who, even though they were not Germans, surely had an organization very similar to that of the Germans, had 600 members. Leaving aside the exaggeration in the number, it is still clear that a Roman could use the word "senate" only in speaking of a rather large consultative assembly. That cannot have been composed exclusively of the princes but must have been a rather large body. Consequently, among the Germans, in addition to the princes, there existed still another category of public officials.

Also in regard to the agrarian organization of the Germans, Caesar not only speaks of the princes, but he also says that the "*magistratus et principes*" ("magistrates and chieftains") allocated the tillable land. To understand the additional word *magistratus* as a mere pleonasm is hardly justifiable in view of Caesar's otherwise concise form of expression. It would have been most unusual if Caesar time and again had made this addition simply for the sake of padding his expression precisely in the case of the clear and simple concept of "princes."

The double category of officials does not appear so clearly in Tacitus as in Caesar, inasmuch as Tacitus, specifically with regard to the concept of the Hundred, was deluded by a fateful misunderstanding that has caused much trouble for scholars. But in the final analysis we can derive this questionable fact with certainty even from Tacitus. If there had been only *one* category of officials among the Germans, this group would at any rate have had to be quite numerous. Now, we are told time after time that in each tribe individual families stood out far above the mass, so far that no other family could compare with them, that the few were plainly referred to as the "*stirps regia*" ("royal family") (Tacitus, *Ann.* 11. 16; *Hist.* 4. 13). Present-day scholars agree that there was no lesser nobility among the original Germans. The *nobilitas* that is constantly referred to is a princely aristocracy. These families traced their origin back to the gods, "*reges ex nobilitate sumunt*" ("They select their kings from the aristocracy") (*Germania* 7).[12] The Cherusci asked Emperor Claudius for Arminius' nephew as the only other person of noble lineage (*Ann.* 11. 16). In the northern nations, there was no nobility except the kingly families. Such a marked distinction between these noble families and the common people could not have existed if there had been a princely family for each Hundred. It is not sufficient to assume that among these numerous chieftains' families a few enjoyed a very special prestige. If it had been nothing more than such a difference of degree, then the position of families that became extinct would simply have been taken by others; a few would not have been designated as "*stirps regia*," and their number could not possibly have been so small. The difference was, of course, not an absolute one; an old *hunno* family could no doubt on occasion move up among the princes. But the difference on that account was still not one of degree, but rather a distinct one: the princely families formed a nobility in which the concept of the official position was very secondary. The *hunni* belonged to the freemen of the community and were significantly raised by their office, which could, after all, also assume a certain hereditary aspect. What Tacitus tells us of the Germanic princely families therefore implies that their number was very small; this small number presupposes, in turn, that there were still lower officials under the princes.

From the military point of view, too, it is obviously necessary that in a rather large army unit there be smaller units of 200 to 300 men at the most under the command of a special superior. A Germanic levy of 5,000 warriors must have had at least 20, and probably more like 50, subordinate leaders. The number of *principes* could not possibly have been so large.

Consideration of the economic life gives the same result. Each village had to have its own chief. It was precisely the agrarian communism and the many precautions that were necessary for driving out and protecting the herds that made this inevitable. As a community, the village had to be ready to act at any moment and could not await the arrival and orders of a *princeps* who lived at quite some distance away. Even if we must imagine the villages as being quite large, still the individual head of each village was only a very minor dignitary. The families whose lineage was regarded as royal must have had a more all-inclusive authority, just as they were much less numerous. We must therefore distinguish between princes and village heads as being functionaries of a significantly different order.

ROTATION OF VILLAGES AND TILLED LAND

I consider Caesar's statement that the Germans *annually* shifted their tilled land as well as their dwelling place to be questionable in a general sense, since I can find no reason for an annual change of dwelling. Even if the hut with its household furnishings, provisions, and animals could easily be shifted, still the establishment of a new residence always required a certain effort, and, with the small number and crude condition of the shovels the Germans had at their disposal, the digging of cellars must have been particularly difficult. Consequently, I have no doubt that the "annual" shifting of the dwelling place, as recounted to Caesar by the Gauls and Germans, was either a gross exaggeration or a misunderstanding.

Tacitus, on the other hand, makes no direct mention of a rotation of dwelling places but speaks only of a shifting of tilled land (*Germania* 26). There has been a tendency to interpret this difference as indicating a higher step in the economic development. I consider that impossible. It is no doubt possible and probable that in Tacitus' time — in fact, even at the time of Caesar — many Germanic villages were fixed settlements, that is, those that had a very fertile and continuous area. In their cases, it sufficed to alternate the tilled land and the fallow areas each year. Nevertheless, those villages whose district consisted principally of forest and swampland or whose soil was less fertile could not make a go of it that way. They had to make use of the individual usable areas of their broad region one after the other, and for this purpose they had to move their village from time to time. As Thudichum has already correctly remarked, Tacitus' descriptions in no way eliminate the possibility of this kind of displacement of dwelling places, and even if they do not expressly state this, it still seems to me quite certain that Tacitus must have had this in mind as he wrote. His words read (*Germania* 26): "agri pro numero cultorum ab universis in vices occupantur, quos mox inter se secundum dignationem partiuntur; facilitatem partiendi camporum spatia prae-bent, arva per annos mutant et superest ager." ("The lands are taken up by all in turn in proportion to the number of cultivators, and then they are mutually divided according to rank. The extent of their fields offers ease of division. They change the fields of cultivation annually and land is still left over.") The remarkable point in this description is the double alternation; first it states that the *agri* (lands) are taken possesion of in turn, and then that the *arva* (cultivated fields) are shifted annually. If it were only a question of the village alternately designating a rather large part of its district as arable land and then within this area alternating annually between tilled and fallow land, the description would be quite elaborate for Tacitus' style, which is elsewhere so terse, and the procedure itself would be too unimportant, so to speak, for so many words. It is quite different, however, if the Roman author had in mind that a community that alternately occupied entire areas and thereupon divided them among its members also shifted its dwelling places with the shifts of arable land. He does not tell us that expressly; considering his succinct style, however, that is not so puzzling. Furthermore, we can by no means assume that all villages acted in this way. Those that possessed only a very small but fertile area did not need to move about.

Consequently, I do not doubt that Tacitus (*Germania 26*), in distinguishing between "*agri in vices occupantur*" ("Lands are taken up in turns") and "*arva per annos mutant*" ("They change fields of cultivation annually"), was not so much desribing a newer level of Germanic economic life but rather quietly correcting Caesar. If we realize that a Germanic village of 750 souls had a district of 64 square miles, then Tacitus' statement is immediately clear. With their inefficient method of cultivation it was necessary to put new land to the plow (hoe) each year, and if the fields near the village were exhausted, it was simpler to move the whole village to another part of the district than to remain in the village and cultivate and guard new fields at a considerable distance. After a number of years and perhaps several moves, they came back again to the original location and could also use the old cellars again.

SIZE OF THE VILLAGES

An important point in my concept is that we must picture the Germanic villages as quite large. One might tend to imagine that the Hundred (the district) consisted of a group of quite small villages. This is no doubt the idea that has been generally accepted until now. Nevertheless, it is not hard to contradict, both through the sources and from an objective viewpoint.

1. In his Book II, Chapter 9, Gregory of Tours recounts that, according to Sulpicius Alexander, the Roman army, when it made an expedition into the land of the Franks in 388, found "*ingentes vicos*" ("immense villages") among them.

2. There can be no doubt that village and clan were identical, and it is positively proven that the clans were quite large (see p. 21 above.)

3. In confirmation of this point, Kiekebusch (see p. 36 n.2), through the resources of prehistory, has estimated the size of a Germanic settlement in the first two centuries after Christ at at least 800 inhabitants. The burial ground at Darzau held some 4,000 urns and was used for 200 years. That amounts to about 20 deaths per year, and this figure leads to a population of at least 800 souls.

4. The shifting of fields and dwelling places, even if reported to us with a certain degree of exaggeration, cannot be without some grain of truth. This shifting of entire arable areas and even of dwelling places is logical only in the case of large villages that possessed a very large region. Small villages whose arable land did not extend so very far had no occasion to effect any shift other than that between tilled and fallow land. Large villages did not have enough arable land nearby to permit this, and so they had to go to the more distant corners of their area, where they took the most convenient alternative of moving their whole village. Hettner reports in "European Russia" ("Das europäische Russland" |*Geographische Zeitschrift* 10.11: 671|) that the villages on the Russian steppes have very extensive communal fields and that consequently, during the farming season, the people leave the village and live in the fields in hastily erected huts.

5. Each village must necessarily have a chief. The communal ownership of the land, the moving and tending of the common herds, the frequent dangers from enemies and wild animals made it indispensable to have a recognized authority on the spot. It is not possible to call for a leader from somewhere else when it is a question of defending against a pack of wolves and pursuing them; of warding off an enemy attack until families and cattle are brought into a protected area; of damming in a flooding brook or extinguishing a fire; of settling the little daily quarrels; of beginning the tilling or the harvesting — the last of which, under conditions of common ownership of the land, must take place uniformly. If all of this is right, then the village necessarily had a community leader, and, since the village was a clan, this leader was the patriarch. But, as we have seen, he must be identical with the *hunno*. Consequently, the village was the Hundred; it had some hundred warriors or more; and it could therefore not be so very small.

6. Smaller villages had the advantage of obtaining their foodstuffs more easily. But the large villages, even though they had to put up with the inconvenience of rather frequent displacements of the village, were still preferable for the Germans because of the constant danger in which they lived. No matter what threat came from wild animals or still wilder men, at least there was always a considerable number of men ready to face the enemy. If in the cases of other barbarian peoples, for example later with the Slavs, we still find small villages, that nevertheless cannot lessen the force of our aforementioned evidence and arguments. For Slavs are not Germans, and the presence of many similar aspects of their circumstances still does not postulate similarity in everything. Furthermore, our evidence on the Slavs is from such a later period that it possibly relates to another stage of development. The large Germanic village, too, did, of course, break up later into groups of smaller villages as the population increased, the cultivation of the land became more intensive, and the shifting of dwelling places came to an end.

THE *TUNGINUS*

My concept of the nature of the *hunno's* office finds its confirmation in the Frankish period. We shall have to come back to this when we observe the dissolution of the original Germanic organization after the *Völkerwanderung*, but let us nevertheless expressly make a few remarks at this point on the question of the *hunno's* office in the later period. In this way, we shall create an important point of support by establishing the continuity, whereas the later discovery of a previously unmentioned contradiction in the characteristics and distinctions of the Frankish offices would necessarily reflect unfavorably on the reliability of our reconstruction of the original period.

If my concept of the *hunno*'s office is correct, then it follows directly that the *centenarius* that is so often mentioned in the popular laws is no other than, as the name indicates, the *hunno*, and that, whenever the formula *"tunginus aut centenarius"* is used, both designations mean the same thing; the one name only clarifies the other. The count is an official of the king; the *centenarius* or *tunginus* is the people's officeholder, he does not possess the prerogative of the threefold *wergeld*, and he is not installed or discharged by the count. Not until the Carolingian period does he become a subordinate of the count. The count has the important functions of the older *princeps*, but he discharges these functions not in accordance with the legal concepts of the ancient period but as an official in the name and service of the newly created king. This king has assumed the dignity of the older principality; of all the ancient *principes* he alone has remained, and more and more tribes have gradually ranged themselves under his authority or subjected themselves and now accept being governed by the counts whom the king has set over them. The older community leaders, however — the *hunni* — continue to exist for many generations as people's officials under the counts, just as they formerly did under the princes. In the Romanic areas, where there were no closed Germanic clan communities, the *centenarius* was from the start, under the name *vicarius*, a subordinate of the count, something that the *centenarius* in the Germanic region did not become until later.

Brunner and Richard Schroder believe that there was a period of transition in which the count was still exclusively an administrative official and the judicial function over the *hunni* was exercised by the *tunginus*. Under this concept, therefore, the *tunginus*, as judge, would in this period have been the older *princeps*, who, elected by the people, exercised authority over a rather large district. It was only later that the count incorporated this function of the *tunginus* in his own position.

Brunner seeks to corroborate this concept through a few provisions of the *lex Salica* (Salic Law); Amira opposed this explanation in the *Göttingische Gelehrte Anzeigen* (1896): 200; Richard Schröder, however, took Brunner's side in the *Historische Zeitschrift* 78: 196-98.

I am not in a position to become involved in the strictly legal aspects of the historical study, but it still seems clear to me that Amira's viewpoint has not been refuted by Schröder's arguments. Schröder himself only arrives at a probability, "that the *mallus publicus legitimus* (common judicial assembly) of the *tunginus*, that was considered as equivalent to the *Curia Regis*, did not coincide with the . . . *mallus* (judicial assembly) which the *tunginus aut centenarius* (*tunginus* or hundred-leader) had as his jurisdiction." Consequently, there is no real counterproof adduced against Amira.

There still remains Brunner's argument that, if the *tunginus* had not been judge of a rather large district, there would have been, aside from the king, only Hundred judges. This argument becomes weak, however, if we consider the chronology more closely.

In the *Historische Zeitschrift* 78: 200, Schröder himself says that "even the first Salic Law, which with the greatest probability can still be ascribed to Clovis himself, no longer recognizes the *tunginus*, but rather the count, as the regular judge for the district." Now since it was Clovis himself who first created the kingly status on such a broad scale that it could no longer personally practice a traveling judgeship, there is absolutely no reason why there should have been, up to that time, a position of judge between the king (as successor of the former princeship) and the *hunno*. Indeed, it even appears impossible that precisely in this period the growing monarchy would have obliged the people, or even allowed them, to choose for themsleves a higher official who would have been, in the county, the natural and inevitable rival of the king's appointed man, the count. We know how Clovis pursued and eliminated the rivals of his power. It seems clear to me that the moment when the counts became the regular judges for the district was the same moment in which Clovis created the real Frankish monarchy, which made impossible any further exercise of the traveling higher judgeship by the king. If not only the need but even the possibility for the existence of an elected district higher judge disappears, then the *tunginus* of the Salic Law cannot have been any other than the *centenarius*, that is, the former *hunno*. The two scholars erred in that they did not attribute enough importance to this position in the older period, and, obsessed with the concept of the Thousand district, they did not correctly appraise the significance and the organization and functioning of the Hundred.

It is a well-known fact that a sure etymological definition of the word *tunginus* has not yet been discovered. In this connection, see the recently published work by van Helten, *Contributions to the History of German Language and Literature (Beiträge zur Geschichte der deutschen Sprache und Literatur)*, published by Sievers, 15: 456 (para. 145). Parallel to the meaning "outstanding," "highly esteemed" (*vortrefflich, angesehen*), van Helten comes to "superior" (*rector*), but against this latter derivation he has practical objections arising from the heretofore accepted concept based on legal history. If the concept I have proposed is correct, then these objections are removed.

RECENT WORKS

In 1906 the second edition of Brunner's *German Legal History (Deutsche Rechtsgeschichte)*, Vol. I, appeared. This book touches on the divergences with my concept of the Germanic organizational conditions in only a few peripheral points, so that the full significance of the difference is not expressed.

In view of the fundamental importance of these differences for the concept and the understanding of European history in the most varied areas, I wish to assemble here, by way of supplement, an overall perspective of the most important points.

Brunner has the Germanic peoples divided into Thousand districts (p. 158); the districts consist of a number of villages; parallel to this organization there exists a simple grouping of persons in Hundreds for military and juridical purposes (p. 159); finally, groups of several families form the very important unit of the clan, which traces its descent back through the male lineage to the same ancestor (p. 111). At the head of the district are district princes, and at the head of the Hundreds are chiefs, who were perhaps already called *hunni* in an early period (p. 163). Nothing whatever is said of the village chiefs, who certainly must have existed, since the villages formed agrarian economic units. Just as little is said of the clan elders, although they, too, in view of the numerous functions the clan had to exercise, could not possibly have been dispensed with, and whose existence was even taken for granted by Brunner himself on occasion (p. 119, conclusion of the first section).

Instead of this complicated organization, with its numerous interwoven areal and personal divisions, I propose a simple division into Hundred districts. Each such district has one large settlement, and the inhabitants trace their descent from one ancestor and are therefore also called a clan or a *Sippe*. The chief of this clan, which is also the village, the district, and the Hundred, is the *hunno* or elder (*Ealdorman*).

I find the proof for my concept in the fact that, first and foremost, village and clan are undoubtedly identical. Brunner himself established the fact (pp. 90, 117) that there was a time when the clan was possessor of the tilled land but when the village also owned the land at the same time. Which one, then, was the owner? The clan or the village? The sources are just as clear and as numerous for the one as for the other. Brunner makes no attempt to clarify the contradiction. There can be no other solution than that village and clan were identical.

Now it is expressly indicated that the villages were very large (see above, pp. 27-28). That this was so is also to be seen, as shown above, from the custom of moving the village from time to time, something that would be purposeless in the case of small villages with small acreage.

Now if the village is very large, it necessarily counts at least on the order of 100 families and must therefore be identical with the Hundred. And with this conclusion we can eliminate the artificial construction of a unit of personnel that does not coincide with the settlements.

The question that arises is whether a further grouping of Thousand districts existed above these Hundreds. This grouping may possibly have existed in individual cases, that is, where the princes who really reigned in common over the entire state divided up the administration — and especially the legal jurisdiction — among themselves in such a way that each one of them had a grouping of Hundreds under him and this grouping then grew into a certain unit. The actual, original division of the tribe, as Brunner conceives it, was not like that, however, and the name "Thousand" was hardly ever used in the early period.

In the question of the relationship between clan and Hundred in the disposition for war, Brunner becomes involved in the same contradiction as in the question of whether the village or the clan is the owner of the land. For him the Hundred is a personnel unit, an organization of 100 (or 120) warriors under the leadership of the head of the Hundred (p. 162). In another place, however (p. 118), the military importance of the clan, even up to the latest period, is documented with a whole array of impressive citations, and from this the conclusion is drawn "that there were certain times and conditions in which the clan fought as a unit in the army under common leadership." That would still not be a contradiction but would fit well into the picture if the clans were the subordinate units of the Hundred. Brunner, however, does not see it in this way at all, but he claims only that (p. 118) "the organization of the army took into consideration the clan units," or (p. 163) that the Hundreds were not of uniform strength, because the clan units were not to be broken up. Our author had to grasp at these indefinite expressions because the enunciation of the sentence that the clans were the subordinate units of the Hundreds would have given his picture of the Hundred a completely different meaning than he intended. There could no longer have been any question of "uniform strength." Either the numerical concept of the Hundred would have had to be completely discarded, or we would have to draw the conclusion that the Hundreds had always carefully been composed of only such clans that were precisely of a strength in warriors as to field approximately 100 of them. Here, too, we can recognize the impossibility, already pointed out above, of conceiving of the clans as parts of the Hundred.

In defense of his concept, Brunner writes (p. 195):

"Whoever makes the claim, in order to support the idea of the Hundred district, that it is the same as the *pagus* must necessarily reject as unreliable the statements of Caesar that point to a more extensive area for the German *pagi*, brand Tacitus' information on the Hundred as misunderstandings, and abandon the conclusions stemming from comparison with the Celtic *pagus*."

To this I can only reply: why not, after all? In order to rescue the concept of the 2,000 warriors that, according to Caesar, each district of Sueves could send forth, Brunner would necessarily first have to reject my explanation of the early Germanic population density. But he has not made even a single attempt to do so. It is obvious that we have here an exaggeration by Caesar — and it is by no means his most flagrant one — perhaps only a tenfold exaggeration, whereas how many times in this work have we proven hundredfold exaggerations!

Furthermore, it has been proven by no less a person than Waitz and accepted by so many scholars that Tacitus' reports on the *centeni* are based on a misunderstanding that that point cannot be considered as absurd even on the face of the matter.

Finally, the analogy with the Celtic *pagus* proves nothing, since the Romans could have used that word in a very flexible manner, just as we do with our word *Bezirk* (district, region).

Brunner objects in the following way to my explanation of the identical nature of the Hundred, district, clan, and village (p. 160, footnote): "In that case, these names and concepts, but for one, would be superfluous. The very fact of their existence speaks for a distinction." I cannot follow this conclusion. If it is said of a man on one occasion that he has a son, at another time that he has a youngster, a third time that he has a kid, and on a fourth occasion that he has a boy — does that mean that he has four male children?

Brunner's principal error is that he claims to interpret the political, social and economic forms without regard for the relationship of sizes. As soon as one realizes how many souls, how many men, and how many square miles, at the maximum, can be attributed to a German tribe, then the decision between the Thousand district and the Hundred district is quickly apparent.

A further error of Brunner's is that he does not distinguish between the clan of the period when it was still an economic unit (common land) and the later clan that was only a legal institution. The latter could be limited from case to case according to the degree of relationship, so that the limit fell between father and son. If compensation for damages was to be paid or received, the degree of kinship was determined in order to establish who was to participate and who would not. Such a transitory method of limitation, however, is impossible for a clan that possesses common land. Let us suppose that the clan extended to the seventh degree; what happens then when the situation is reached where the members are related to each other only in the eighth degree? Do the children from a given generation on no longer belong to the clan? Do they have no claim to the common property, once they have grown up and wish to establish their own household? One needs only to ask this question in order to have the answer immediately apparent — that is, the clan that possessed common land can never have been limited in accordance with a specific number of degrees of relationship (*Knien*).

The clan that possesses common land cannot be divided up in any other way than that the families, the fathers and sons, remain together. The clan that is made up of six or seven branches (*Knien*) is, consequently, somewhat different from the original clan, which still existed at the time of Caesar and Tacitus. Brunner overlooked the fact that in this case there had been a development, and a distinction has to be made between several periods in the concept of the nature of the clan.

This development can now be defined in this way, that the limitation on the older clan was not a genealogical one but rather was established through the actual situation of living together; in other words, the original clan was the village.

In Schmoller's *Yearbook for Legislation (Jahrbuch für Gesetzgebung)* 31: 1739, Rachfahl discussed Brunner, and on p. 1751 of the same work he defended the Hundred district against him, using the same reasons as mine.

There is no real validity in the points that Krammer brings forth in favor of the Thousand in *New Archives of Ancient Historiology (Neues Archiv der älteren Geschichtskunde)* 32 (1907): 538.

In the fifth edition of his *Manual of German Legal History (Lehrbuch der deutschen Rechtsgeschichte)*, 1907, Richard Schröder accepts a threefold organization: Thousand, Hundred, and clan ( = village). Even though for him the clan is identical with the village, nevertheless he believes the Hundred is the lowest community of the public law. As such, it is not supposed to have formed a district, but rather a purely personal unit, with a *hunno* at the head, forming at the same time a military unit and an independent court with definite jurisdiction; not until later were these personnel Hundreds to become physical districts as well. At the head of each Thousand was a prince.

This concept is more closely related to my own than might at first glance be apparent; that is, in (1) the identification of the clan with the village; (2) the distinction between the two categories, *hunni* and princes (*principes*);13 (3) the assumption that a prince stood at the head of a number of Hundreds, a point which, it is true, I do not regard as a basic and significant phenomenon and do not call a Thousand, but which, in practice, I recognize as having existed quite often (see p. 21). In order to reconcile Schröder's concept with mine, it is only necessary to imagine the village as consisting not of from 10 to 30 huts, but of some 100 to 200. Then the "personnel unit" concept of the Hundred, which is otherwise so unclear and difficult to understand, has become superfluous. The village is the Hundred. It is the natural, original settlement. Of the "Thousand" concept there remains only the jurisdictional area of the princes, which varies according to the circumstances.

Writing in the *Savigny-Zeitschrift* 27: 234 and 28: 342, Siegfried Rietschel has once again studied the Thousand and Hundred on the broadest possible basis of the available sources. He, too, has come to the conclusion that the Thousand is not to be regarded as an original Germanic institution but rather that the Hundred must be considered as the initial institution common to the Germans. He also traces the Anglo-Saxon Hundred back to the time of the immigration.

Rietschel's idea of the nature of the clan remains unclear, although he is still far in advance of other scholars, at least in the matter of facing up to the questions. He recognized that, according to the usual concept, which defines the clan simply as the descendants of a single ancestor, there results no unified clan situation but rather, according to the ancestor that one chooses as the point of origin, a larger or smaller unit (pp. 423, 430). This possibility of limiting the size of the clan in quite different ways serves him as an aid in forcing the clans into the numerical scheme of the regular Hundred of 100 hides. He did not realize, however, that in doing so he removes the characteristic of the clan as a legal institution. An organization that here includes only brothers, there cousins, elsewhere cousins of the second, third, fourth, and fifth degrees, cannot possibly be considered as the same institution.

If one agrees with Rietschel's concept of the settlement as determined by specific numbers, then the idea of the clan is necessarily completely eliminated, and there remains only the alternative that, where possible, the agnate relatives were left together when the land was allocated — a practice for which there can no longer be any inherent legal basis. From the point of view of the clan, such a settlement (Hundred) can only be given a legal basis if the entire settlement is regarded as a single clan, and no doubt that is what happened.

At the same time that Rietschel was writing, Claudius Baron von Schwerin was also publishing a defense of the Hundred based on the sources, *The Old Germanic Hundred (Die altgermanische Hundertschaft /Untersuchungen herausgegeben von Gierke 90, 1907/)*. Schwerin places particular emphasis on the point that the Hundred has nothing to do with the number 100 but simply means a large number. His etymological basis may well be erroneous, as Rietschel claims on p. 420 of his work, but he might very well be correct in his conclusion (see p. 15 above), except that he was not justified in leaving the size of the group completely indefinite, so that, for example, it could have been 20 or 10,000. Rather, we are justified and obliged to say that in reality these groups can quite probably be reconciled with the number 100, whether we accept the idea of 100 families or 100 warriors, both of which, as explained on p. 15 above, amount to approximately the same thing.

The errors in Schwerin's study (aside from the fact that he, too, fails to understand the clear concept of the clan) stem from his failure to grasp the relationships of size. Without any attempt to check on my study, he rejects my effort to estimate the numbers in a Germanic tribe and Hundred. I should like to risk making the opposite claim, that a determination of the population made from all the building blocks that we can use for the construction of the early German organization is the most definite and reliable one. Every single bit of information in one of the ancient authors or in the early medieval laws is uncertain and susceptible to various interpretations. One agrees with Caesar on the 2,000 warriors in a Sueves district, while another rejects it. One considers Tacitus' information on the *centeni* to be a misunderstanding, while another does not, and so it goes. It is absolutely indisputable, however, that the region between the Rhine and the Elbe, which I described on p. 24 above, is about 50,000 square miles in area, was shared by some twenty tribes, and was very lightly populated.

If Schwerin had taken into account these facts with all their implications, he could not possibly have equated the *hunno* or elder (p. 109) with the *princeps*, all the less so in that he, too, just as I do, came to the conclusion (p. 128) that the *hunno*, the Frankish *centenarius*, and the *tunginus* are identical.

Schwerin speaks out strongly against the idea of naming the Hundred the district; he claims that that can only confuse the issue (p. 109, note 4). But since he himself proves that the Saxon *Go* is the Hundred and likewise the *pagus*, which we can hardly translate other than "district," then one can hardly object to the application of the word "district" to the Hundred. True enough, the word "district" *(Gau)* later means an area or region *(Bezirk)* of the same size as the older *civitas*, and consequently through the application of this same word to such various sizes confusion can be, and in fact was, created. But the same thing applies to *pagus* (see p. 20 above), and we must accept the fact that no better distinction in terminology has been passed down to us. On one occasion (note 4. 45), Tacitus even uses *pagus* in such a way that, according to the context, it can hardly be translated other than "village." (Cf. Gerber, *Lexicon Taciteum*, p. 1049.)

The first scholar to accept my ideas on the numerical strength of the German tribes in general was Ludwig Schmidt in his "History of German Tribes Up to the End of the *Völkerwanderung*" ("Geschichte der deutschen Stämme bis zum Ausgange der Völkerwanderung"), *Sources and Studies on Ancient History and Geography (Quellen und Forschungen zur alten Geschichte und Geographie)*, published by W. Sieglin. See also in this connection the review of the *History of the Art of War (Geschichte der Kriegskunst)* in the *Historische Vierteljahrsschrift* (1904), p. 66. Schmidt, however, opposes my equating of clan and Hundred and holds to the concept of the Thousand as the original German institution. It seems to me that in doing so he is being inconsistent. If it is true that a Germanic tribe, on the average, numbered no more than 5,000 to 6,000 warriors, and the smaller and smallest ones therefore only 3,000 and even fewer, then it is also beyond question that the people cannot have been organized into basic units of 1,000 warriors, a size that of itself would already have been awkwardly large and would have been so close to the overall strength. Furthermore, the principal argument in favor of the Thousand, the 100 Sueves districts of 2,000 warriors each, of which Caesar speaks, is hereby destroyed.

Schmidt also agrees that village and clan are identical, but he claims that there were small clans (villages) of ten to twenty families. He does not go into the question of why, if the villages and consequently the corresponding lands were so small, the shifting of the village would have been necessary. Although he tries to argue away the positive source materials to the effect that the Germanic villages had a considerable size, he does so in an obviously inadequate manner. He believes that, with the extensive area covered by the villages *(Historische Vierteljahrsschrift*, p. 68), even the villages with their ten to twenty huts appeared to the Romans as "vastly extended," and the clans *(gene)** with which, according to Dio Cassius, the Germans made peace with Marcus Aurelius, were different from what was otherwise known as clans. According to Schmidt, these were too small for a peace treaty to be negotiated with them. Therefore, we must imagine that term as meaning, for example, independent branches of larger stems or noble clans with a numerous retinue of followers and servants. How numerous are we supposed to picture such a following of a noble clan? After all, at the very most, certainly no more than several hundred warriors. That would therefore be about the same number that I imagine a Germanic clan to have been. According to Schmidt himself, then, smallness forms no basis against a literal interpretation of the passage, and since in all the sources passed down to us there is no statement that points to small villages or small clans, it is a completely unmethodical whim that leads to rejection of the so positive statement of Dios, which is supported by Sulpicius Alexander.[14]

I bring these polemic explanations to a close by adding, as I look forward and call the reader's attention to the next chapter, why I place such emphasis in this work on the history of the art of war on establishing — perhaps I should say fighting my way through to — the correct political-historical interpretation. In my opinion, the military accomplishments of the Germans remain completely incomprehensible without this political-legal basis. The savage courage of the individual is all the less sufficient as an explanation when we establish, as we have now done, how small their numbers were. Among these masses there must necessarily also have been a very useful and effective military organization which made possible leadership and control. For this purpose, transitory "personnel units" are completely ineffective, for they are lacking in the cement of discipline. Loose grains of sand produce no solid balls. The identity of the village with the clan, however, of the clan with the Hundred, with their elder *(hunno)* at their head, gives a natural cohesiveness and solidarity that is capable of facing the strongest challenges. In this connection, the reader is asked to compare these points with Chapter V of Book II, below, "The Peoples' Armies in the Migrations," and especially "The Hundred in the *Völkerwanderung.*"

NOTES FOR CHAPTER I

1. According to Caesar (6. 21), the Germans did not marry before their twentieth year; it could not have been much later, however, that they went about establishing a family, since otherwise they would not have been able to maintain their strict custom with respect to chastity. Consequently, in a community of 100 families we must subtract from the 100 heads of families as warriors the aged, invalids, sick, and accidentally crippled, while the quite young men of fourteen to twenty fill the ranks, more or less balancing off the total.

2. The estimate of a Germanic village at a strength of some 750 souls has recently received a noteworthy corroboration in the area of prehis-

toric research. In Albert Kiekebusch's dissertation "The Influence of Roman Culture on the Germanic as Reflected in the Burial Mounds of the Lower Rhine" ("Der Einfluss der römischen Kultur auf die germanische im Spiegel der Hügelgräber des Niederrheins"), Berlin, 1908, on the basis of the graves of Darzau the size of the community that buried its urns here is reckoned at a minimum of 800 souls. This is opposed, it is true, by Kaufmann in *Zeitschrift für deutsche Philologie* (1908), p. 456.

3. Cf. Braune, *Zeitschrift für romanische Philologie* 22: 212.

4. Paulus Diaconus 2. 9: "nisi ei quas ipse eligere voluisset Langobardorum faras, hoc est generationes vel lineas, tribueret. Factumque est, et annuente sibi rege quas obtaverat Langobardorum praecipuas prosapias, ut cum eo habitarent, accepit." (" . . . unless he granted to him those *farae* [that is, races or familial lines] of the Langobards he had wanted to select. And so it happened. With the king's assent he received his wish that the distinguished families of the Langobards which he had chosen should reside with him.")

5. Caesar's claim (*Bell. Gall.* 6. 22) that among the Germans the most powerful man possessed no more than any other is not to be taken literally but is, rather, a rhetorical exaggeration of the impression that the account of the agrarian communism necessarily made on the Roman listener. Princes who had a retinue that they fed and provided with expensive weapons must have had significant means, and men like Ariovistus or Arminius and his brother Flavus, who appeared in Rome as eminent men, are unthinkable without a certain wealth. For all that, however, in the eyes of a prominent Roman they still appeared not much different from a common German. The agrarian communism gave the latter such a great economic support that Caesar could no doubt be permitted to write this rhetorical embellishment without our being justified or obligated to interpret it strictly and base further conclusions on it.

6. Tacitus, *Ann.* 13. 54.

7. Rachfahl is to that extent right when he says, in *Jahrbuch für Nationaloekonomie* 74: 170, note, that by taking my stand in favor of the Hundred district, I am nevertheless indirectly bringing the Thousand district back into Germanic legal history. There is nothing to prevent our assuming that the Romans did not always use the word *pagus* in exactly the same technical sense, just as is the case with our use of the word "district" *(Bezirk)*.

8. Still under Louis the German. Rubel, *The Franks and their Settlements (Die Franken und ihre Siedlungen)*, p. 228.

9. Müllenhoff, *Germania*, p. 202.

10. All of this is taken from Vierkandt, *The Population Density in Western Central Africa (Die Volksdichte im westlichen Zentral-Afrika)*.

11. Cf. in detail on the above, as well as on the Fosi, Sugambri, Danduti, Texuandri, Marsaki, and Sturii, *Preussische Jahrbücher* 81: 478, as well as Much, *Deutsche Stammsitze*. Against this account one could still object that, although the names have come down to us through the sources and can, in general, be definitely established geographically, nevertheless quite a few of the names may not apply to tribes but simply to districts or clans. It certainly happened quite often and easily that individual clans which had had a strong increase broke away from their original stem and formed their own new tribe. But if, for this reason, we should eliminate a few names as being uncertain and therefore establish the size of the average area of a tribe at some 2,600 square miles, our conclusion is still not affected thereby, especially since we can once again establish an offsetting estimate and conceive of some of the named tribes as federated states.

12. Müllenhoff, *Die Germania*, p. 183.

13. On his p. 20, footnote 16, Schröder states quite correctly that, based on the corroborating appearance of the *hunno* in later periods in the most varied tribes, we must conclude that he existed already in the Germanic period. For this reason, I cannot understand why Brunner, on p. 75, places a question mark by the *hunno* in his quotation, especially since I had added "or other leader."

14. I still cannot understand in what way Schmidt cites the *Acta S. Sabae* as an authority for the fact that, with the Goths, the villages were subordinate units of the district. In the report *(Acta Sanctorum*, April-is II, p. 89; the Greek text in the appendix of the same volume, p. 2), it is not stated (as Schmidt, *History of German Tribes /Geschichte der deutschen Stämme/*, p. 93, says it is) that the "members of the clan" sought to protect Saint Sabas, but only that "a few" of the pagans attempted to do this. No conclusion whatever is to be drawn from this statement as to the relationship of clan to village or of village to district.

# Chapter II

# Germanic Warriorhood

As we have seen in the first volume of this work, military accomplishment stems not from one but from two roots of widely differing types. The first of these, which is immediately apparent, is the courage and physical capability of the individual warrior. The other is the firm formation of the cohesiveness among the individual warriors, the tactical body. As different as these two strengths — the effectiveness of the individual and the cohesion of the individuals among themselves — are by their nature, nevertheless the second is in no way to be separated from the first. A unit consisting of nothing but cowards, no matter how well drilled, would be incapable of accomplishing anything. If, however, even a moderate measure of courage is present in the mass and to this is added the second element, the cohesive incorporation, a military power is created that is more effective than all the achievements of personal courage. The knightly courage of the Persians was shattered against the phalanx of Greek citizens, and the development of this tactical unit, the phalanx, into new, refined forms, up to the echelon and cohort tactics, forms the nucleus of the history of the art of war in antiquity. The Romans were victorious again and again, not because they were more courageous than all their opponents but because, thanks to their discipline, they had the firmer tactical unit. From this development we have been able to recognize how important, and yet how difficult, too, it was to move from the original, stiff phalanx to a number of smaller, flexible tactical units.

We need only remember this sequence of development in order to realize at first glance, after learning the Germanic organization, what a mighty military strength must have been inherent in this people. In their raw, barbaric life close to nature, in constant battle with wild animals and neighboring tribes, every single one of them was conditioned to the highest degree of personal courage. The solidarity within itself of each group, which was at the same time clan and neighborhood, economic community and military comradeship, under a leader whose authority in the daily routine of life extended over the entire existence of the group, in peace as in war — the cohesiveness of such a Germanic Hundred under its *hunno* was so tight that even the strictest discipline of a Roman legion could not overcome it. The psychological elements of which a Germanic Hundred and a Roman legion were composed were completely different, but the result was completely similar. The Germans did no training, the *hunno* hardly had any definite power of punishment, and certainly no serious one, and even the concept of real military obedience was unknown to the Germans. But the unbroken unity of the entire existence in which the Hundred was melded together and which is so inherent in it that it is also called community, village, comradeship, and clan in the historical accounts — this natural unity is stronger than the artificial unity that civilized peoples must seek to create through discipline. The Roman centuries no doubt surpassed the Germanic Hundreds in the external compactness of their forming up, their approach march, and their attack, in holding their direction and their alignment; but the inner firmness, the mutual reliance on each other that stems from strength of morale, was strong enough among the Germans to remain unshaken, even under conditions of outer confusion, complete breakup of the unit, and even occasional retreat. Every call of the *hunno* — we shall pass up the word "command" — was followed because each one knew that every other one would follow it. The real weakness of all undisciplined groups of warriors is panic; Germanic Hundreds, however, even in retreat, could be brought to a halt and to a renewed advance by the word of their leader.[1]

Consequently, it was not for nothing that we first established, in the preceding chapter, the identical nature of *hunno* and elder, of district, clan, Hundred, and village. This is not merely a question of a point of contention dealing with a formal political-legal situation, but rather a matter of the discovery of a great and important factor in world history. It is now obvious that the *hunno* was not the leader of a company varying in makeup and formed according to the chances of the situation, who was selected from time to time, but he was the born leader of a natural unit. He had the same name and exercised in war the same functions as the Roman centurion, but he differed from the latter just as nature differs from art. A *hunno* who did not exercise his command as the elder of a clan would have accomplished just as little in war as a centurion without discipline. But since he was the elder of the clan, he attained, without an oath of allegiance, military law, or tight control, the same cohesiveness and a similar degree of obedience as his Roman namesake was able to attain only by means of the most extreme strictness.

If the Romans sometimes spoke of the lack of order among the Germans,[2] or if Germanicus, in order to give courage to his legionaries, tells them of the Germans: *"sine pudore flagitii, sine cura ducum abire"* ("They retreat without the shame of disgrace and with no heed to their leaders"), that is not untrue, measured by Roman standards. But viewed from the other side, it serves as testimony to how strong the inner cohesiveness of the Germans was when they could get along with very little outer appearance of order, temporary withdrawals, and the lack of a real leadership by command without breaking up their formation or even suffering in the matter of energetic battle leadership.

The tactical formation in which the Germanic infantry fought was called *cuneus* by the ancients and has been translated as "wedge" (*Keil*) by more modern scholars. Nevertheless, the word is misleading, just like our expression "column," which, technically, would probably be its most accurate translation. If one wishes to contrast the concepts of "line" and "column," he will point out as a formation in "line" one that is wider than it is deep, and a formation in "column" one that is deeper than it is wide. If, however, from a practical viewpoint, these concepts have gradually tended to become confused, the verbal usage has wandered even further from that basic contrast. For example, we call a formation of only six men in depth and twelve to forty men in breadth a "company column." In like manner, we find among the Romans formations that we must call conceptually "phalanx," "line," actually named *cuneus* (wedge). For instance, in the battle of Cannae, Livy calls the Carthaginian center *"cuneum nimis tenuem"* ("a very shallow wedge"), where it is undoubtedly a question not only of a linear formation but even, according to Livy's own addendum, a rather shallow one. Often *cuneus* even has the meaning of nothing more than "band."[3]

If, consequently, there is no definite meaning to be drawn from the word *cuneus*, nevertheless there is no doubt that, in addition to its general meaning, this word was also used in a specifically technical sense.

We seem to be accurately informed on this technical meaning through a few authors from the period of the *Völkerwanderung*. Vegetius (3. 19) defines *cuneus* as "a mass of men on foot, in a close formation narrower in front, wider in the rear, that moves forward and breaks the ranks of the enemy." Ammianus (17. 13) reports that the Romans — that is, the Roman military units made up of barbarians — attacked, as the *"soldatische simplicitas"* ("soldierly directness") referred to it, in "boar's head formation," "*desinente in angustum fronte*" ("with its front ending in a point"), and Agathias reports that the wedge (*embolon*)* of the Franks in the battle against Narses had the shape of a triangle. Consequently, it has been customary to picture the wedge in this manner: at the head, a single warrior, the most outstanding of all; in the second rank, three; in the third, five, and so forth. If we look more closely, however, we see that this concept is impracticable. No matter how strong and well armed the man at the apex of the wedge might be, while he is defeating his opponent in the enemy front, one of the men next to the latter, on the right or left, will at some point detect a moment when he can strike the enemy from the side. In order to protect the foremost man against this double flank attack, there is no other remedy than for the two flank men of the second rank to spring forward as quickly as possible. But the envelopment repeats itself against them: the three men who now form the point of the wedge are attacked by five. In turn, the flanking men of the third rank must jump forward. In brief, the wedge, instead of penetrating into the enemy front, flattens out at the moment it makes contact and turns about within a very short time. All the flanking men, who have been held back intentionally to keep the form of the wedge, now storm forward; the broad side of the triangle is displaced toward the front and the point toward the rear, since, of course, on the flanks, the men who at first had no man in front of them now have nobody behind them. Consequently, the wedge would not only have failed to accomplish its purpose, but also during the time in which the flanking men of the ranks in the rear would be running to the front, presumably the point, hemmed in as it was, would have suffered the heaviest losses. No formation of a tactical body could be more foolish than this one. A group of men, no matter how firmly holding together, still remains the sum of the individuals, who, no doubt, push forward from the rear but cannot, like a sharpened piece of iron, concentrate the entire flanking pressure in a point or cutting edge.

   The correct description of the wedge is provided for us in two places in the literature of antiquity, in Tacitus and again at the end of the period of the *Völkerwanderung* in the "Strategicon" of Emperor Mauricius or whoever else it was that wrote this book (perhaps in 579 A.D.). "The blond peoples," the Franks, Lombards, and similar ones, says the "Strategicon," attack in groups that are just as wide as they are deep,[4] and Tacitus (*Hist*. 4. 20) says of the *cuneis* of the Batavians: "*densi undique et frontem tergaque ac latus tuti*" ("closely compressed on all sides and secure in front, rear, and flank"). "A closely compressed band that is of equal strength on all sides, not just in the front and rear, but also on the flanks," is a square formation, consequently with a total of 400, 20 deep and 20 wide; with 10,000 men, 100 deep and 100 wide. Such a unit forms no true square, but a rectangle whose front is the narrower dimension, since on the march the interval between ranks is about double that of the interval between files. If a leader or prince with his retinue behind or beside him moves out in front of a column of such depth, that makes it look like a point set out in front of the square mass. This point provides the leadership. From modern situations, we can cite by way of comparison the attack of a cavalry brigade. At the head is the general, with three men behind him — his aide and two buglers — and then the two regimental commanders with their aides and buglers. Then come eight squadron commanders and their buglers, then thirty-two platoon leaders, and then the mass of troopers. That can be described as a triangle, but it is only a parade-ground formation. For the regulations prescribe not a gradual penetration into the enemy front but, in a battle situation, despite the advanced position of the officers, they call for the whole mass to break into the enemy line simultaneously by having the officers overtaken during the charge. The point of the Germanic boar's head formation is to be understood in the same way. When the prince or a Nordic thane, at the head of his retinue, places himself in front of the square of privates, he pulls and encourages, through his advanced position and his charge, the whole mass along with him. The penetration, however, presumably takes place just about simultaneously. The point does not have the mission of boring in first, but at the moment of impact the whole mass, surging forward with the leader, is to give the shock action as a unit. Even without having a point out in front, however, the deep column can resemble a triangle. If such a wedge, let us say of a breadth of 40 men, and consequently of a total strength of 1,600 men, charged against a broader front, the two most threatened positions were those of the flanking men in the first rank, since they had to be prepared at the moment of impact to deal not only with an enemy to their front but also with the latter's adjacent file, who threatened them from the flank. It could result from this that the flanks attacked with a certain caution and held back somewhat, so that the center made the first contact. On the other hand, the outer files of the rear ranks easily surged outward in their attack. The front of the column, which at any rate appeared narrow, therefore gave the impression of being actually pointed. That was, however, no advantage; it was more a deformation than a formation. The more uniformly the whole formation struck the enemy and pushed forward, the better. The more courageous the flankers were, the less could they let the suspicion arise that they were intentionally hanging back. The better the rear ranks covered their files, the sharper was the impact, and the leaders undoubtedly did their best to see that their men struck the enemy with the best possible alignment in breadth and depth.

While the Germanic column charged against the enemy, the warriors sounded the *baritus*, the battle song; as they did, they held their shields in front of their mouths, so that the resonance magnified the volume. "It begins as a dull murmur," Tacitus tells us, "and swells with the heat of battle until it resembles the din of waves crashing against the rocks."[5] Just as we have recognized in the piping that accompanied the march of the Spartan phalanx the evidence of their orderly movement (see Vol. I, p. 58), the *baritus* gives proof of the same thing for the wedge of the Germans.

If a Germanic wedge charges against a similar enemy unit and both sides withstand the impact, then each side wells out from the rear and seeks to envelop the enemy. If the wedge strikes a phalanx, either it breaks through, in which case the enemy gives way probably not only at the point of rupture but all along the line, or the phalanx holds fast and the men of the wedge continue the battle with no alternative than to well out and surge forward from the rear as quickly as possible, broadening their formation likewise into a phalanx.

The Roman centurion took his position and marched in the front line of the phalanx as the right flank man of his company. Only in this position was he able to carry out his functions: maintaining the interval, commanding the launching of the *pilum*-salvo and the short assault thereafter. The Germanic *hunno* strode along at the head of his wedge, and whenever several clans were united in a larger wedge, they stood side by side, each one only two or three files wide, with the *hunno* in front of each one and the prince with his retinue in front of the entire wedge. Here there were no commands for *pilum*-salvos, and here there were no prescribed intervals to be maintained, and the attack became an assault at a much greater distance. The leader did not need to be concerned with adjacent units or to maintain a specific direction, but only to storm forward, taking advantage of the most favorable route and of whatever opportunity offered itself, with his band following him.

The deep column, the squared formation, was the original formation of the tactical body of the Germans, just as the phalanx, the line, was the original formation of the Greeks and Romans. Let us repeat here that the two formations are not absolute opposites. The squared formation does not, after all, need to have exactly as many ranks as files but would still serve its purpose if it had about twice as many files as ranks; for example, a breadth of 140 men and a depth of 70, for a total of 9,800. We would still be allowed, and indeed obliged, to name such a unit a square, since the 70 men give the flanks the strength for independent protection.[6] The unit would still be, according to the expression of Tacitus, *"densus undique et frontem tergaque et latus tutus"* ("closely compressed on all sides and secure in front, rear, and flank"). On the other hand, we have also heard of phalanxes that were drawn up in great depth. Consequently, the formations merge into each other without specific limits. This does not, however, eliminate the theoretical opposition of the two, and the reason why the classical peoples started with the one original formation and the Germans with the other is not difficult to recognize.

The advantage of the phalanx over the wedge is that it brings many more weapons directly into the battle. Ten thousand men in a phalanx of ten ranks have 1,000 men in the first rank; the corresponding wedge, 100 men deep, has only 100 men in its front line. If the wedge does not penetrate the phalanx at once, it will very quickly be enveloped from all sides. The phalanx is capable of outflanking movement.

On the other hand, the phalanx has the weakness of its flanks; a powerful pressure from the side rolls it up and bowls it over. Such pressure from the flanks is particularly easy for cavalry to carry out. But the Germans were strong in their cavalry, while the Greeks and the Romans were not. Consequently, the Germans preferred to take a deep formation, in order to have strong and secure flanks. With the Greeks and the Romans this need was felt to be much less important; they were able to risk a much more shallow formation so that they might have all the more weapons in the front line.

A second motive that must have reinforced these respective tendencies on the two sides probably lay in the fact that the Germans had fewer and poorer protective arms than did the Greeks and Romans, with their developed industries. Therefore, the Germans were inclined to place only their few, best outfitted men in the first rank and sought to get the maximum effect from the pressure of the impact from the depth of their formation, where the inadequate equipment of those in the interior of the wedge did not cause much harm.

Finally, the wedge also has the advantage of being able to move easily and quickly even over broken terrain without falling into disorder. A phalanx can move forward at an accelerated pace only a short distance.

The question is, how large the Germans' square formations were, whether they customarily formed one, several, or many of them, and what their overall formation was.

In the battle against Ariovistus, Caesar says (1. 51) that the Germans formed up by tribes (*generatim*) with equal intervals: Harudes, Marcomanni, Triboci, Vangiones, Nemetes, Seduni, Sueves. Unfortunately, of course, we do not know what the strength of the army was (see Vol. I). Since Caesar probably had 25,000 to 30,000 legionaries in his battle formation and the Germans were, under any circumstances, considerably weaker, we may estimate their number at a maximum of 15,000. Consequently, aside from the cavalry and some light infantry deployed to the front, they would have formed seven wedges of 2,000 men each, some 40 men wide and deep. They struck the Romans with such speed that the centurions did not have time to order the normal salvo of *pila*, so that the legionaries, dropping their *pila*, immediately resorted to the sword. The Germans, Caesar continues, then quickly formed their phalanx, as was their custom ("*Germani celeriter ex consuetudine sua phalange facta impetus gladiorum exceperunt*": "The Germans quickly formed their customary phalanx and received the onslaughts of the Roman swords"). I interpret that in this way: When the squares did not succeed in overrunning and penetrating the Roman line of battle (Caesar naturally had his second echelon immediately close on his first) and the Romans were pushing into the intervals in order to take the wedges from the flanks, the Germans from the rearmost ranks rushed forward to fill the intervals and thus form a phalanx. This cannot have been carried out in a very orderly manner, and in his next sentence Caesar speaks of "phalanxes" in the plural, which we may interpret as meaning that the Germans had not succeeded in forming a single continuous line. This whole pressing forward of the rearmost ranks gives shining evidence of the personal courage of the German warriors, since with the failure of the wedges to break through the Roman phalanx, the real basis for the Germans' strength was already broken and the tactical situation had turned to their disadvantage. All their courage was then to no avail in the face of the steadfast formation and the numerical superiority of the Roman cohorts, which now also had the advantage of better order.[7]

Tacitus' battle accounts are in accord with the picture we get from Caesar's description. According to Tacitus (*Hist.* 4. 16), Civilis draws up his Canninefates, Friesians, and Batavians in separate wedges. Of another battle it is specifically said (5. 16) that the Germans stood not in an extended line, but in wedges ("*haud porrecto agmine, sed cuneis*").

By virtue of their form, the Germanic wedges easily drew together and needed no special practice to be able to move. When Plutarch (*Marius* 19) reports that the Ambrones moved into battle at quick time, beating the cadence on their shields, that is not to be interpreted exactly as a march with parade-ground precision, but it can probably be taken as the result of a natural tendency. On the other hand, the Germans were also capable of easily giving up that outer order and of storming forward or moving quickly backward through forest and field in irregular groups or completely individually. It is nevertheless clear that they retained the spirit of the tactical body: the inner sense of unity, the mutual trust, the consistent conduct, whether prompted by their own instinct or the call of their leaders. As we have seen, everything depends on this; it is much more important than an external show of order and is much harder to attain through the kind of discipline developed on a purely military basis than through the natural organization of a Germanic clan under its born leader, the *hunno* or elder. The Germans, therefore, are competent not only in pitched battle but also particularly in scattered combat, surprise attacks in the forest, ambushes, feigned withdrawals, and guerrilla warfare in every form.

The armament of the Germans was limited and was characterized by their paucity of metal. It is true that they, too, had long since progressed from the Bronze Age to the Iron Age, but they still did not understand, as did the civilized peoples of the Mediterranean or even the Celts, how to stretch their material according to their needs and accordingly how to fashion and form it freely.[8] Surprisingly enough, in some respects we are better informed about the weapons of the Germans than about those of the Romans in the classic period of the republic, because the Germans, like the Celts, placed the weapons with their dead in the graves, which we are now able to excavate, whereas the Romans did not do that. The German and his weapon belong together; it is a part of his person. For the Roman it is a manufactured product, very much in the way he himself, as a warrior, is a unit — we might almost say a number — in the maniple in which his levy authorities have placed him. Consequently, the German also buries the weapon with the man. We can even carry this idea a step further. The weapons in the graves were for the most part made useless by bending. Why? It has been supposed that this was to prevent grave desecrators from stealing them. This explanation might well miss the mark, since mere bending easily lends itself to repair, and furthermore valuable jewelry was also placed in the graves. The reason is this rather: since the man can do nothing more, his weapon is also rendered powerless. Careful investigation and comparison of the contents of graves have led, it is true, to some correcting of the reports of the Romans on the Germans' armament, but in general they have confirmed the reports. Only very few of them, the Romans tell us, had armor or helmets. Their principal piece of protective armament was a large shield of wood or braided material, covered with leather. On their heads they wore a covering of leather or hide. In an harangue that Tacitus (*Annals* 2. 14) has Germanicus giving before a battle, he reports the Roman leader as saying that only the first rank (*acies*) was armed with spears, that the others had only *"praeusta aut brevia tela"* ("weapons with points sharpened by fire or short spears"). Naturally, that is an exaggeration of the speaker encouraging his troops; if the mass of Germans had actually been armed only with sharpened sticks, all their courage would have been to no avail against the Romans, with their head-to-foot protective armor. Tacitus gives us a more accurate report in *Germania* 6, where he likewise says at the start that the Germans had few long spears and but few swords, and then names as their principal weapon the *framea,* which he also mentions quite often elsewhere (*Germania* 6, 11, 13, 14, 18, 24) and describes as a spear of the type of the old Greek hoplite spear. Only later do we find the battle-ax as a weapon.[9]

It appears questionable as to how the long spears were integrated into the wedge formation with the shorter weapons. In his speech already referred to, Germanicus comforts his soldiers with the argument that these spears were not so easy to handle in the forest as were their own *pila* and swords. From this we might conclude that the Germanic spears had the length of *sarissa* and lansquenet spears, and that does not seem impossible.

Since the long spear was wielded with both hands and the warrior consequently could carry no shield, we would have to conclude that it was the men wearing harness who handled these spears. Standing in the first rank, probably mixed in with shield-bearers in order to be somewhat protected by their shields, the long spears formed the point of the assaulting wedge. While they broke through the enemy front with powerful shock action and threw the enemy into disorder, the men equipped with the *framea* pushed forward behind them and moved past them into the openings in the line. Without this close cooperation with a shorter weapon, the long spear would not have been usable in hand-to-hand combat.

Then, too, the spear bearer himself had to have a sword or a dagger as well, as a second weapon, for the continuation and completion of the battle.

The picture becomes simpler if we assume that the accounts of the Romans concerning the gigantic long spears of the Germans were only exaggerations resulting from a comparison with their *pila*. If the spears were only 12 to 14 feet long, so that they could still be manipulated with one hand and the man could also carry a shield, then the difference from the *framea* was not so great as to prevent a mixing of these weapons in the square, as seemed appropriate.

An important question is: the Greeks and Romans, as well as the knights of a later period, provided themselves with good protective equipment for hand-to-hand combat; how could the Germans get along without such equipment? For a long time I believed that they wrapped themselves in hides that rotted away in the graves. But the numerous pictures of Germanic warriors that have come down to us never show that[10], rather, they confirm the statements in our sources that they had hardly any protective equipment other than the shield. The answer probably lies in the fact that the phalanx and the legion were oriented to a much greater degree toward the combat of the individual soldier than was the Germanic formation; the latter was intended to overrun the enemy by virtue of its deep mass. If that succeeded, then it was only a matter of pursuit. Therefore, only the outer ranks needed protective weapons, as we shall also see later in the case of the Swiss. On the other hand, in running, scattered combat, which for the Germans came into question almost even more often than the wedge, lightness of movement was so important that they renounced any protective equipment other than the shield.

The Germans made very frequent use of the javelin. It is noteworthy that they had given up the use of bow and arrow, which they had had during the Bronze period and did not take up again until the third century A.D. The written sources and the archaeological finds agree on this point.[11]

EXCURSUS

THE WEDGE

As early as in the *Portable Library for Officers (Handbibliothek für Offiziere)*, "History of Warfare" ("Geschichte des Kriegswesens") 1 (1828): 97, the triangular formation and the hollow wedge for enveloping action are described, to be sure, but only as a supplement.

These wedge-shaped formations were probably more likely tactical inventions and easy exercises for the drill field rather than for actual use in war, for which there are no examples.

"In general, by 'wedge' the Greeks understood that type of attack mass of greater depth than width. The attack columns of Epaminondas are also included under this heading."

On the other hand, Peucker believes in the triangular form of the Germanic wedge and praises it, in *The German Military System of the Earliest Times (Das deutsche Kriegswesen der Urzeiten)* 2: 237, for the fact that "with it, changes of front were more easily executed." The authority of the Greek writers on tactics, on which he bases his claim, we need not belabor, since they speak only of the cavalry, no more than the example of the flight of the cranes. The alleged easier mobility is, like the entire formation, a theoretical construction.

Peucker, in 2: 245, believes on the other hand that "the wedge-shaped attack column could move without endangering its basic cohesiveness only on firm, open, and level terrain."

The Nordic reports are thoroughly treated in the two studies by G. Neckel, "Hamalt Fylkin" in Braunes, *Contributions to the History of the German Language (Beiträge zur Geschichte der deutschen Sprache)* 40 (1915): 473 and "Hamalt Fylkin and Svinfylkin" in the *Archives for Nordic Philology (Arkiv för Nordisk Filologie)* 34, New Series 30.

By "Hamalt" Neckel understands the square mass, for which he believes the close line of shields to be the main characteristic. The "Hamalt" becomes the "Swinfylking" when a triangle with its apex toward the enemy is formed in front of it. Since we have become convinced that there can be no tactical significance in such a point, I cannot imagine that the poetic sources contain such a sharp and obvious distinction: whether during the approach march, in order to gain easier command control, only one or a few warriors are placed in the first rank and the' closest ones behind them spring up abreast of them only at the moment of contact, or whether the ranks are of equal strength from the start. Even if the commander really intends to move forward and into the assault with a triangular point, that can hardly be carried out in practice, since the overlapping warriors of the second, third, and fourth ranks will find it very hard always to hold back deliberately at one rank's distance behind the warriors of the first rank. The distances between ranks are so small that they are not easy to maintain even during peacetime drills on level terrain, and impossible to hold in the heat of an assault in battle, where each individual does his utmost to accomplish at least as much as his neighbors and perhaps even to surpass them.

To both Agathias and the Nordic poems up to Saxo Grammaticus, who takes his material from them, I attribute much less weight as source evidence than to Neckel. Indeed, I have been careful not to arrive at conclusions on tactical formations even from Homer, as has customarily been done, and Agathias cannot compete with the report in the *Tactics* of Mauricius (p. 42 above).

See also in this connection Volume III, Book III, Chapter 2, Book V, Chapter 4 (last two paragraphs), and Book V, Chapter 8, fifth and sixth paragraphs from end of chapter.

Somewhat in contradiction to my description is Tacitus' account (*Annals* 2. 45) of the battle between Arminius and Maroboduus: "deriguntur acies, pari utrimque spe, nec ut olim apud Germanos, vagis incursibus aut disjectas per catervas: quippe longa adversum nos militia insueverant sequi signa, subsidiis firmari, dicta imperatorum accipere." ("With an equal expectation of victory on both sides they drew up their battle lines, not as the Germans once did with roving assaults or in scattered bands, for they had become accustomed by lengthy military service against us to follow the standards, to support themselves with reserves, and to obey the orders of commanders.") These words are to be interpreted as meaning that the Germans formerly had no tactical formation whatever, but they had learned it from the Romans and had copied their methods by forming a line of battle and supported and secured it by means of reserves, that is, a second or several echelons.

In this description, however, we must be careful to note and discount the rhetorical emphasis. The "old custom" of the Germans, *"vagis incursibus aut disjectas per catervas"* ("with roving assaults or in scattered bands"), of which Tacitus speaks, is therefore nothing other than the attack in massed squares, in wedges, that are accompanied by sharpshooters and can also quickly break up completely. But we can accept for a fact the *"acies subsidiis firmata"* ("battle lines supported by reserves") as an imitation of the Roman formations. From Caesar's time onward, countless Germans, princes as well as privates, were in the Roman service and had become thoroughly acquainted with the Roman system. It is entirely possible that Arminius, like Marobodus, had considered it advantageous to adopt the Roman battle formation. For this purpose, they only needed to order that the individual clans, instead of forming together in large massed squares, should form up one beside the other. A clan, a Hundred, was after all nearly the same thing as a Roman century or a maniple. Even several echelons or a reserve could be formed in this way. There is no contradiction in the fact that the Mediterranean peoples needed several centuries to arrive at such a refined organization, whereas the barbarian Germans were able to copy it without difficulty. The Germans would not have been able to do that on their own; the strength of the obstinate conservatism in the masses and the belief in the inherited formation were too strong for that. No personal authority would have been great enough to overcome the mistrust of the mass of men for such an innovation, especially for the formation of echelons or a reserve. But since each one knew from his own observation or through the accounts of his comrades what success the Romans had attained with these formations, the field commander who made such a proposal in the council of war of the *hunni* was easily able to win approval, and the automatic execution of his orders could not have been so very difficult for the *hunni*, who, of course, had their units in such close control.

The combat methods of the Germans in the Roman style can be explained in about this way. But I would still like to add that the documentary sources for this point seem to me, in the final analysis, to be very questionable. After all, it is probably very doubtful that the Romans really had a trustworthy report on the Germans' battle methods, and it is not at all impossible that we have before us nothing more than a Roman fantasy. In any case, it would only be a question of an incidental account. In the Batavian battles, even those Germans who had been in the Roman service appear in their native combat formation, and in the period of the *Völkerwanderung* we find time and again the Germanic square mass or wedge in the reports. Agathias reports — though in a grotesquely distorted fashion — on the wedge formation of the Frankish-Alamanni army under

Buccelin and Lothar in the battle on the Casilinus (see below, Book III, Chapter 4), and we have already heard that Emperor Mauricius named the square mass as the specific battle formation of the Germans.

### PROFESSIONAL WARRIORS

In *Germania* 30. 31, Tacitus praises the Chatti for their very special military qualities and recounts that many among them possess neither house nor land their whole life long, but simply live the military life. This description is suspect to the extent that it holds up the Chatti much too high above the other Germans. The historical facts never tell us that any one Germanic people accomplished significantly more than any other. True enough, they inflicted defeats mutually the one against the other, and the Cherusci, who at one time stood so high, are said, according to Tacitus' account, already to have declined very strongly by this time. However, we still have no basis for establishing a specific distinction between their warlike qualities, as, for example, between the Spartans and the other Hellenes in the fifth century B.C. Every man in every Germanic people is primarily a warrior; that basic fact dominates every other one. That on the base of this general warriorhood certain individuals developed into special heroes, moving through the various districts as adventurers, robbers, and parasites, founding no families, cultivating no land, and only occasionally returning to their clans, but who, whenever it was a question of a fight, were always on hand and gladly had themselves placed in the first rank of the wedge — we may well believe that such men, who also at one time gladly accepted Roman wages, existed in large numbers in all the Germanic tribes. In designating these ruffians as professional warriors, however, we must be careful not to think of the other Germans as farmers; there is only a difference of degree. All are warriors.

### THE *FRAMEA*

The armament of the Germans is described in the harangue of Germanicus (Tacitus, *Annals* 2. 14) and in *Germania* 6. But both descriptions evoke objections and contradict each other. "*Praeusta aut brevia tela*" ("weapons with points hardened by fire, or short spears"), as Germanicus describes them, is hardly very clear, and even if we accept the fact that a portion of the Germans had only wooden javelins with a point hardened in the fire, the *aut* (or) and the *brevia* (short) furnish neither an explanation nor a contradiction.

In *Germania* it is stated: "Ne ferrum quidem superest, sicut ex genere telorum colligitur: rari gladiis aut majoribus lanceis utuntur; hastas vel ipsorum vocabulo frameas gerunt angusto et brevi ferro, sed ita acri et ad usum habili, ut eodem telo prout ratio poscit, vel comminus vel eminus pugnent." ("Not even iron is abundant, as one infers from their type of weapons. Very few use swords or larger *lanceae* |throwing spears|. They carry *hastae* |thrusting spears| or, according to their term, *frameae* with a short, narrow iron head, but so sharp and easy to use that they fight, as the situation demands, either hand-to-hand or at a distance with the same weapon.")

A *hasta angusto et brevi ferro* is the old hoplite spear, which lends itself to close combat as well as to being thrown. In this description, however, the contrast with the "larger lances," to the extent that it is related to the shortage of iron, is obviously distorted. For the greater or lesser length or strength of the shaft has nothing to do with the blade. We can have quite short javelins with a very long iron part, like the Roman *pilum*, and long spears with a short point. For this reason, Josef Fuchs, in *Historische Vierteljahrsschrift* 4 (1902): 529, claims that *lanceis* should be translated as "lance points." While it is true that this eliminates the really illogical aspect of the question, the expression itself remains strange, and from an objective point of view the long spear, which is testified to in other places, falls completely out of the picture. Furthermore, also striking is the exaggerated manner in which such a normal weapon as the hoplite spear, which was so common with the Romans, is described to us as something extraordinary. Not only here, but also in many other passages, Tacitus calls the Germanic *framea*, as if with reverent respect, "*cruenta victrixque framea*" ("the bloody and victorious *framea*").[12] Consequently, we have come to a completely different interpretation. The excavations of graves have brought to light an unusual instrument from the earliest period, to which the antiquarians have given the invented name "celt."[13] The celts, which are found in stone, bronze, and iron, have the shape of a narrow axe that is placed on the shaft not perpendicularly but in extension of the shaft. It is therefore possible to place a celt on a pole in such a way as to form a spear that has a cutting blade forward instead of a point. Scholars have tended to believe this weapon was the Germanic *framea;* even Jähns, in his *History of the Development of Ancient Offensive Weapons (Entwicklungsgeschichte der alten Trutzwaffen)*, has accepted this interpretation and has given a thorough rationale for it. His main argument is that in this way we have an appropriate use for the celts, which are so very frequently mentioned and yet otherwise so hard to explain. We can thus reconcile findings and historical reports, and furthermore, the emphasis with which Tacitus speaks of the *framea* as a completely unusual weapon would therefore be justified. The *framea* — that is, celt-spear — would then be the weapon of a people lacking in metal who create their weapon in such a way that it serves at the same time every possible purpose, and can be used not only as a weapon but also as a work tool. Its advantage is that one can just as easily jab and strike with it and, when necessary, throw it. Throwing and stabbing are naturally more effective with a spear, since a broad edge does not penetrate as easily and deep as a point, but the man who, in addition to a spear, is without even the service of a sword — and most of the Germans lacked that — will also want to be able to use his spear for striking, and that is effective enough with the sharp edge of the celt. Jähns supports this interpretation by referring to striking weapons with a broad blade, which are also to be found elsewhere, and by referring to the relationship of this development with the Stone Age: in stone they were not able to produce a pointed battle weapon; the stone would have splintered on the enemy's protective gear. Pointed stone weapons are useful only for hunting. Consequently, the original form of the military striking weapon was wide, and they continued to use this proven weapon also in the Bronze Age and even in the Iron Age. Finally, we find that in a glossary of the ninth century *framea* is explained with the word "Ploh" — that is, plow, which leads us to conclude that it was a broad, and not a pointed instrument.

This line of reasoning, while attractive, is certainly false. The celts that have been found — to be sure, very numerous — do not necessarily stem from the

Romanic-Germanic period but are very much older. It is, therefore, not at all necessary to reconcile these finds and the reports of the Roman authors. Even if a few celts have been found that are actually fashioned like a spear — a point that Jähns strongly emphasizes (p. 168) — the celts can generally very well have been attached to an angled piece of wood, so as to be used as a hacking instrument or an axe. A broad blade is so much less effective as a jabbing weapon than a point that it cannot possibly have been intended principally for that purpose. On the other hand, the edge of the celt was much too dull to allow its use as a striking weapon; in this case they would have sharpened a true edge on at least one side. Finally, as far as Tacitus is concerned, he would have omitted precisely the most important characteristic, the blade instead of the point, with his description "*hasta brevi et angusto ferro*" ("a *hasta* with a short, narrow iron head"). If, as Jähns claims, there really are instances elsewhere of jabbing weapons and arrows with a broad blade instead of a point, they may have served a special purpose and cannot contradict the obvious uselessness of the celt for jabbing. The "hands-wide Sachs" (the blade of Siegfried's arrow, referred to in Jähns, p. 174) can also no doubt be interpreted in another way. The "Ploh" of the glossary proves nothing, since the oldest instrument for "plowing" was under any circumstances pointed and not wide. (Cf. in connection with the other pieces of source evidence and comparisons Müllenhoff's review of Lindenschmit's *Manual of German Archaeology: Reviews of German Antiquity [Handbuch der deutschen Altertumskunde: Anzeigen fur deutsches Altertum]* , Vol. VII, reprinted in *German Archaeology [Deutsche Altertumskunde]*, Vol. IV [Die Germania]*, p. 621. Also *Zeitschrift für Ethnologie* 2 (1870): 347.

We must therefore accept the fact that the *framea* is virtually nothing other than the ancient Greek 6- to 8-foot-long hoplite spear. That Tacitus specifically mentions the "short" iron is due to the comparison with the Roman *pilum*. The error in the objective aspect of his description lies in his drawing the long spear into consideration. If we omit this, we have this train of thought: "The Germans have little iron, and so they fight not with swords and *pila*, but with spears, which are used both for close combat and long-range fighting," a very natural statement for a Roman reporter. True enough, Tacitus also distorts the logical continuation: "The weapon is so sharp and useful that it can be used both for close combat and long-range fighting." The two clauses should be joined not by "so that," but simply by "and." Finally, the tone of the entire account is misleading, allowing the *framea* to appear as something quite special, when it actually was a very commonplace weapon of many uses. All of this will disturb us less, however, if we accept the idiosyncrasy of Tacitus' historical style, which is elsewhere already well known to us: for him, it is not so much a matter of the substance itself, but rather of the impression that is to be evoked, and he seeks to add a certain spice to his antitheses by not bringing them directly face to face.

(Added in the 3d edition.) Schubert-Soldern, in the *Zeitschrift für historische Waffenkunde* 3 (1905): 338, has again defended Jähns' interpretation with reasons worthy of consideration. He stresses particularly that under the conditions of shortage of iron available to the Germans, as well as with bronze and stone, the points broke off easily, and as a result the blade could well have been preferred. The word *celtis* he points out as of the late Latin period, with the meaning "chisel."

NOTES FOR CHAPTER II

1. Tacitus, *Germania* 6.
2. Tacitus, *Annals* 2. 45. Mauritius, G. A., 167. Agathias, *Bonn. A.*, p. 81. cit. Müllenhoff, pp. 180-181.
3. Müllenhoff, *Germania*, p. 179.
4. The passage reads (taken from Scheffer, p. 269): "In battles they make the front of their line even and closely packed, and they render their mounted forces or infantry violent and uncontrollable, thinking that only these of all traits keep them from every deed of cowardice."* Müllenhoff, in *Germania*, p. 179, has interpreted that in the completely opposite way, as a phalanx front. In my first edition of this volume and again in the first edition of Vol. III, p. 286, I agreed with him, but now I believe that I have found the correct interpretation. Cf. the passage from Leo's *Tactics*, in Vol. III, Book III, Chap. 2. At Leo's time, whatever it might have been (cf. Vol. III, Book II, Chap. 7), the Germanic square mass no longer existed. His description was only taken over from Mauricius.
5. Tacitus, *Germania* 3. *Historia* 2. 22; 4. 18. Ammianus, 16. 12; 31.
7. Eduard Norden, in *The Early Germanic History in Tacitus' Germania (Die germanische Urgeschichte in Tacitus' Germania)* (1920), p. 125, sees somewhat too much significance in the "Shield song," in my opinion.
6. Plutarch, in *Marius* 25, describing the battle formation of the Cimbri, tells us that it was just as deep as it was wide, and it may be that this serves as the basis for the concept of the German square mass. But since it is also said that this square mass was 30 *stadia* (about 3½ miles) deep and wide and the entire account is also riddled with fables in other places, its validity as evidence is slight.
7. The description in Dio Cassius 38. 49. 50 is purely rhetorical and has no historical worth.
8. According to Kiekebusch in *The Influence of Roman Culture on the Germanic as Reflected in the Burial Mounds of the Lower Rhine (Der Einfluss der römischen Kultur auf die germanische im Spiegel der Hügelgräber des Niederrheins)*, p. 64 (see p. 36 n.2 above), that applies only to the Rhenish Germans. According to him, the Elbe Germans, judging from the grave finds, were rich in iron and generally superior to the Rhenish Germans in their culture.
9. An excellent work is the broad-based study that appeared in 1916 from the Kossinnas Mannus Library, *The Armament of the Ger-*

*mans in the Older Iron Age, from About 700 B.C. to 200 A.D. (Die Bewaffnung der Germanen in der älteren Eisenzeit etwa von 700 v. Chr. bis 200 n. Chr.),* by Martin Jahn (Würzburg, Curt Kabitzsch). In order to determine their possible influence on the Germanic weapons system, the author extends his study to cover those of the Celts and the Romans. According to the grave finds, the shields were so light and thin that they could hardly have withstood a powerful thrust of the lance or blow of the sword. For that purpose, however, they had a metal projection which in its extreme form extended into a rod more than 12 centimeters long. This can hardly be interpreted in any other way than that the Germans not only used the shield for passive parrying, like the Romans, but also brandished it actively and sought not so much to stop the enemy thrusts and slashes but to ward them off, and therefore fought simultaneously with both arms. In this connection, see below, Book III, Chapter 1, the excursus concerning the Herulians. According to information given to me by Jahn in a letter, the battle-ax played hardly any role before 200 A.D., judging from grave finds. It is more often found from the third and fourth centuries on, especially in the graves of the Lusatian region, which at that time was inhabited by the Burgundians.

10. They are collected in the publication *Catalogue of the Castings . . . with German Depictions (Verzeichnis der Abgüsse . . . mit Germanen-Darstellungen),* by K. Schumacher, 2d ed., Mainz, 1910.

11. Martin Jahn, *Bewaffnung der Germanen,* pp. 87, 216.

12. *Germania* 14.

13. The discoverer seems to have been the humanist Konrad Celtis, who translated his name "Pickel" in that way. Olshausen, *Verhandlungen der anthropologischen Gesellschaft,* 1894, p. 353.

# Chapter III

# The Subjugation of Germany by the Romans

As the Romans defeated the Gauls and made the Rhine their border river, they assumed the mission of protecting their new subjects against the Germans. In order to avoid coming under the yoke of these barbarians, the Gauls had, of course, thrown themselves on Caesar's mercy, and the Roman hegemony had started with the expulsion of Ariovistus by the united powers of the Romans and the Gauls. The strife that started there, however, continued. The savage Germanic hordes kept coming back across the Rhine; the more the new province blossomed under the peace of the Roman World Empire, the more the sons of the primeval forest, conscious of their strength, lusted for its booty. It seemed to the Romans, little as they were attracted by the raw, misty country, that the most effective means of confronting this continuously threatening danger was to draw it into their dominion and put an end to the Germanic freedom, just as they had previously done with the Gauls.

After Augustus had brought interior order to the empire, subjugated the Alpine territories, and pushed the borders of the Roman Empire up to the Danube, he first entrusted his younger stepson Drusus, and after the latter's death, Tiberius, with the mission of subduing the peoples from the Rhine to the Elbe. The Romans went systematically about this difficult task.

Although the individual Germanic tribe was very small in numbers and even many tribes together could form only moderately large armies, or, if they did assemble larger ones, could nevertheless not operate with them (see Vol. I, "The Roman Art of War Against the Barbarians") — regardless of this, wherever one turned, each man was a warrior, and in no other way than with large, cohesive armies could the Romans risk opposing these barbarians who scorned death and wounds. But it was a very difficult matter to supply large armies in the interior of Germany. The land itself, with its very limited agriculture, could provide only a little. To move supply columns over long distances overland requires a very strong organization, and, except for the causeways over the swamps, which the Germans laid down with a surprising application of labor and cleverness, there was no question of developed roads. After Drusus was forced to turn back from his first campaign into the interior for lack of food supplies, he created a double base for his advance. The Romans' main garrison on the lower Rhine was the camp of Vetera (Birten) near Xanten, opposite the confluence of the Lippe with the Rhine. In the spring and also for part of the rest of the year, the Lippe can be used for navigation by smaller boats almost to its source. Therefore, Drusus, by moving up along the river, installed at the place where the Paderborn Cathedral stands today the fort of Aliso, which was to serve as a depot (11 B.C.).

Nothing would be more erroneous than to see in the laying out of a fort or a fortress, whether one pictures it as large or small, a means for subduing and establishing hegemony over the neighboring tribe. There are situations and peoples where it is possible to establish control through the emplacement of garrisons or the erection of stations, that is, in those cases where no real war is to be expected or the subjugation has progressed so far that only rebellious elements on a small scale remain to be subdued. Then it is no longer a question of strategy, but of police. The Germans, however, were different from the Negroes of today, for example, who can be held in sway over a wide area by small mobile commands from a fixed station. With the Germans, such a procedure would have brought grief to the Romans. First of all, they had to be conquered in warfare on the grand style, and as long as they were not conquered, the garrison of a fort had no broader mission than to secure and protect itself and the enclosed parcel of earth that it occupied. Of Caesar, too, we do not hear that in Gaul, aside from a fort to protect the Rhine bridge, he had built forts, for they require garrisons, and he always sought, not to split up his troops, but to keep them together, in order to defeat the Gauls in the open field with his absolute superiority and to put them to flight.

Some have also thought that Drusus built the fort on the Lippe in order to have a continuously open and secured river crossing, and consequently they have sought the place farther down on the Lippe. For a medium-sized river like the Lippe, where trails led along each side, even

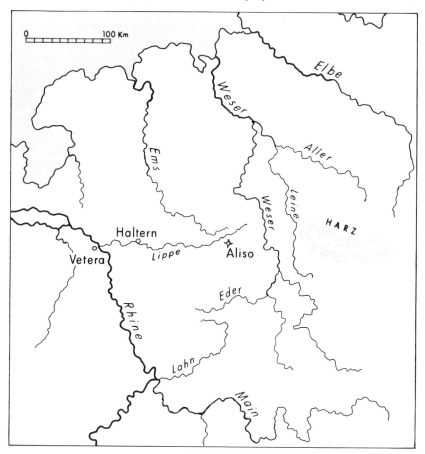

Fig. 1 GERMANY FROM THE RHINE TO THE ELBE

if they were not directly on the banks, that is really no decisive consideration. Even if the Lippe for extended distances cannot often be easily crossed, because of the swampy banks, nevertheless there could practically never have been a question of the Germans blocking the crossing against the Romans, with their numerous means of support and the relatively simple means of detouring. Consequently, the establishment of the Lippe fort cannot even have had the significance of a bridgehead.

It is quite different when one considers the supply situation, which depended on the water route. The water route needed a destination point, a depot, where the boats could unload their provisions and where the supply columns could pick them up for a march farther into the interior. The conduct of war in the interior of Germany was quite different if it was not necessary to carry along the grain or meal from the Rhine, but one needed only to take on these supplies 150 kilometers as the crow flies farther on, along the upper Lippe, and, as the situation demanded, could replenish the supplies here. In Gaul, Caesar had not been obliged to build depots and detach garrison troops for them from the legions. The subjugated peoples and allies, with the support of the Roman suppliers, had to take care of the provisions. In Germany, the Romans necessarily had to deviate from this basic organization. Drusus built Aliso not for the purpose of holding the inhabitants of the surrounding area in check — it would have been a poor means of doing so — but rather in order to form a secure base for the Roman operations in the interior of Germany. (See below, the special study on Aliso.)

Once the fort was there, of course, it served other purposes as well: for example, to receive the sick, to observe the country and its inhabitants, thereby exercising, as far as the Roman power could reach, a certain police function, representing a constant threat to the surrounding tribes, and serving as a place of refuge. The one purpose, however, that gave the character to the whole and necessarily determined the location of the installation was the depot on the water route, with its facility for transferring to land transport.

Besides Aliso, Drusus reportedly built fifty more forts on the Rhine.[1] At first glance, that seems to stand in contradiction to a plan for the conquest of Germany, for the occupation of these fifty strongholds used up a large portion of the available troops, and if the subjugation of the Germans succeeded, the forts were superfluous. The explanation probably is that, whenever the army moved into the field, the militia was to occupy the forts and hold them as a place of refuge for the population, in case the Germans, unable to defend their land against the Romans, sought by means of diversions into the Roman area to relieve the pressure on them. Moreover, field troops were probably held in the large permanent camps in order to bring assistance where it was needed.

In addition to the route leading from the Rhine along the Lippe, there was another route by which an army could penetrate into the interior of Germany. That was by way of the sea and the rivers flowing into it. The first project that Drusus undertook when he took over his command in Germany was the construction of a canal from the Rhine into the Yssel, which gave him the capability of arriving directly on the German coast of the North Sea via the Zuider Zee. There still exists today the *fossa Drusiana* (canal of Drusus), which Suetonius called "*novi et immensi operis*" ("a singular and huge engineering feat") (*Claudius* 1).[2] The Roman trade in the North Sea was not sufficient to justify such an expenditure of effort, but it is understandable from the viewpoint of strategy. When Tiberius made his march to the Elbe in the year 4 A.D., the land army made contact at the mouth of the Elbe with a fleet that "was transporting a huge supply of all things."[3] The Roman ships sailed as far up as Jutland, and on the rivers they engaged the Germans on numerous occasions.[4] Later, in the Civilis War, when the Bructeri captured the Praetorian trireme, the flagship of the Roman admiral, they moved it up the Lippe in order to present it to their priestess and prophetess Veleda.[5]

Already under Drusus forts are said to have been built also at the mouth of the Weser and even of the Elbe, and somewhat later we have definite proof of a Roman garrison at the mouth of the Weser.[6] These installations served as bases for the Roman naval and merchant fleets.[7]

The undertaking of the Romans, carefully prepared in this manner, was crowned with the most complete success. First, Drusus brought the inhabitants of the coastal area, the Friesians and the Chauci, to a recognition of the Roman hegemony, and Tiberius then received the obeisance of all the peoples as far as the Elbe, without the situation having required even fairly large battles. The reason for the surprising ease with which this was accomplished was, according to Ranke's attractive supposition, similar to that which had led the Gauls to join Caesar: precisely in those years Marobodus, prince of the Marcomanni, had established a large Germanic kingdom. Stretching out from Bohemia, it included peoples as far away as the lower Elbe. In order to escape from him, the tribes on the Weser allied themselves with the Romans (in the years 11-7 B.C.).

At first the relationship was still a free alliance, and in winter the Romans regularly withdrew their armies to the Rhine or close to it. It is obvious what a great disadvantage this shift of base was. The Germans could not regard themselves as irreversibly subject to the Romans as long as the Romans did not even risk staying there through the winter. Again, the explanation can be found only in the supply situation.

The voyage through the North Sea and up the Ems, the Weser, and the Elbe was a risk, even in summer, and in winter it was completely abandoned. Thus we hear that now this and now that Germanic tribe had to be subjected anew. It was not until 4 A.D. that Tiberius, sent to the north for the second time, seemed finally to have subdued these rebellious tribes. He took the risk of having his army spend the winter at the source of the Lippe, that is, in the proximity of Aliso. The Romans established towns and marketplaces, and the Germans seemed to adapt themselves to this new life-style, frequenting the markets and entering into trade with the invaders (Dio Cassius 56. 18). Soon the Romans were preparing to subjugate even the Germanic kingdom of Marobodus in Bohemia. The subject tribes on the Main would have provided the base for the campaign. This war was prevented when a large uprising broke out among the peoples south of the Danube, who had recently been conquered in like manner, and it demanded all the forces of the Romans for three years. Even during this period, however, the Germans in North Germany remained completely peaceful.

But finally, when the Romans under their governor, Varus, went seriously about establishing their hegemony, the great, general rebellion of the tribes between the Elbe and the Rhine erupted.

## EXCURSUS

### THE SOURCES

While we can establish a clear and reliable picture of the character, conditions, and activity of the Germans, it is with much less certainty that we can speak of the individual historical events in the earliest period of our history. This is because of the character of our sources. They are numerous and thorough, but will-o'-the-wisps. If we had to treat even Caesar's account of the conquest of the Gauls with caution, since it not only has a strong Roman bias but also cannot be measured against other Roman sources, we are much worse off with respect to the battles of the Romans with the Germans. While it is true that here we have not just one but several sources, almost all of them are second-, third-, or even fourth-hand accounts. Our principal account of the battle in the Teutoburger Forest, that of Dio Cassius, was not written until two centuries after the event, and even Tacitus, after all, lived a century after Germanicus' campaigns, which he describes for us, took place. This weakness, however, is only the smallest of the ones that concern us, since our authors did have available to them good contemporary reports, and we also have in Velleius Paterculus a well-informed contemporary as witness. Complicating this situation is the spirit of the literature of the period, which is completely dominated by rhetoric. These authors have no wish to recount the events as they actually happened or even as they might wish to have the reader believe they happened, but they desire primarily to stir up sensations and to make an impression through the artistry of their language. It seems to me that, in the numerous studies that have been devoted to the battles of Arminius and Germanicus to date, this peculiarity of the nature of our sources, even though frequently mentioned, has been given much less critical consideration than it deserves.

Not even those points that such sources present in specific words are objectively reliable. Hence, there is a much lesser degree of reliability in the indirect conclusions that are to be drawn from their descriptions, for the authors themselves did not intend that their accounts and the related concepts that they created be taken as objective pictures of the realities. Let us now clarify this point with several examples.

According to the account by Dio Cassius, which is supported by Tacitus, Varus' army was suddenly attacked while on the march. According to Florus, however, Varus was conducting a court of justice in his camp when the Germans suddenly burst in. The contradiction in these two accounts is so strong that Ranke came to the conclusion that it could be no other than a question of two different events. He thought that Dio's famous description of the defeat of the legion on the march through forests and swamps in rain and storm must refer only to an individual detached unit, while Varus himself was actually attacked in his camp while holding court. Mommsen rejected this separation of the actions, saying that Florus' account of the eruption in the middle of the court hearing was nothing more than rhetorical exaggeration of the imprudent sense of security into which Varus had been lulled and which had brought on his misfortune. In this respect not only must we agree with Mommsen, but also we must treat the entire substance of the available reports, including Tacitus, with the same critical nitric acid and measure these reports with the same ruler.

Florus writes "*castra rapiuntur, tres legiones opprimuntur*" ("The camps were seized, and three legions were overwhelmed"). It is entirely false to conclude from this sequence of statements by the author that the Germans first captured the camp and then attacked the legions.

Tacitus (*Annals* 1. 61) reports that in the year 15 Germanicus arrived in the area of the Varus battlefield and proceeded to that point in order to bury the dead. He supposedly sent Caecina ahead to reconnoiter the wooded mountain and to set up bridges and causeways through the wet swamps and treacherous fields ("ut occulta saltuum scrutaretur pontesque et aggeres umido paludum et fallacibus campis imponeret"). This has usually been interpreted as meaning that the march must have gone through an impassable area of mountains, forests, and swamps hardly known to the Romans up to that time. But it is not at all impossible that Germanicus used a much-traveled road, possibly even an old Roman army route. In the six years after the fall of the Roman dominion over this region, this army road, however well it might have been developed previously, had naturally fallen into disrepair and was perhaps even intentionally destroyed by the Germans. Germanicus therefore had to restore some bridges and causeways and, since the Germans were in the area, he had to have the stretch of forested mountain bordering the road carefully searched. Nothing more than this is to be concluded from Tacitus' account.

Tacitus goes on to tell us how those accompanying Germanicus had been able to recognize the chain of events: the first camp, suitable for three legions; at the next site a smaller one, corresponding to the reduced number of the hard-pressed survivors, with its fallen wall and shallow ditch. From this it has been customary to conclude that Germanicus had marched in the same direction as Varus, since he first came to the larger camp, then the smaller. But it is very possible, as others have already remarked, that Germanicus came from the opposite direction and that Tacitus blows up the account purely for the sake of the effect.

Dio says (56. 18) that the Germans had lured Varus from the Rhine to the Weser ("They led him on far from the Rhine").* This has been interpreted as meaning that the Germanic conspiracy had been planned long in advance; presumably the Germans themselves, intentionally and craftily, had persuaded Varus to set up his camp deep in the interior of their territory. But nothing prevents us from assuming that we have here only a hyperbolic expression for the dissimulation and cunning of the Germans, which had lulled the Roman leader into a sense of security. If he had not trusted the Germans, he would not have pushed his base camp with all its appendages up to the Weser.

These individual examples probably seem to explain each case, but they give, after all, no true picture of the real situation. The general tendency is to accept as credible each individual phrase in the accounts handed down to us, as long as no positive basis is brought forward to contest them, especially in the case of an historian like Tacitus, whose great authority we cannot deny. But one cannot arrive at the correct understanding of the sources until one is completely determined to *confront every single expression with the most extreme mistrust, even if it appears at first to be in no way suspect.*

Our questioning of each detail does not mean a rejection of the historian himself. We must realize that what is important to us is completely different from what was important to the Roman. The Roman wished to paint the most impressive picture; the individual facts were unimportant to him. We, on the other hand, place the greatest emphasis precisely on these details because we wish to establish from them a new, particular relationship of events, something that Tacitus did not think of at all.

We shall do well to clarify for ourselves, as we have already done quite often, the practical significance of this principle in an example from the most recent historiography. Even though an analogy does not constitute proof, it does provide a measure of it. Whoever works in ancient history, where the control factors are so difficult, would do well, if he wishes to be careful, always to reassure himself again and again with an example from more recent history that the measures with which he judges are still valid.

Among the most magnificent pieces of writing of modern history is the account of the battle of Belle Alliance in Treitschke's *German History (Deutsche Geschichte).*

If no other source had remained, however, it would be very difficult, indeed almost impossible, to determine or reconstruct from it the objective context of the event. Treitschke's whole attention is directed toward depicting the characteristics of the personalities, the peoples, the warriors who fought here, and evoking in the soul of the reader an echo worthy of this gigantic event, making the strongest imaginable impression. In doing so he gives less attention to individual actions and their interrelationships. For the sake of psychological cohesiveness, the chronological relationships, on which everything depends for the overall picture, are pushed into the background.

Wellington's defensive position is described with the adjective "strong" *(fest).* We must be careful not to take the word technically; it is used only as an exaggeration.

"A side road with a deep cut, bordered by hedges, ran across the front." The description applies only to a small section of the front.

When the Prussians began their attack, at 4:30, Wellington supposedly already had his reserve committed "up to the last man." Taken literally, that statement is completely false; even at 8 o'clock in the evening Wellington still had one division completely out of the action (Chassé) and one that had seen very little action (Clinton). As an expression of the tremendous tension of the situation, the effort that it cost Wellington to assert his position — that is, taken symbolically — we may let the sentence stand as it is. It contains a simple exaggeration, such as the "strong" position and the "deeply sunken side road, bordered by hedges, running across the front." If we accept this in a positive manner, however,it becomes incomprehensible how the English battle line could have withstood the impact of Napoleon's Old Guard in the evening.

The main body of the Prussian army is supposed to have been on the St. Lambert ridge at 1 o'clock. St. Lambert is only about 3½ miles away from the edge of the battlefield. If the main body of the Prussian army had already been in that location at 1 o'clock, it would be as inexcusable as it is incomprehensible that Blücher did not enter the battle until such a late moment.

After the abortive attack of the Imperial Guard against the English line is described, the author continues: "In the meanwhile, Blücher had already carried out the blow that decided the destruction of Napleon's army," that is, the storming of Plancenoit.

Whoever interprets the expression "in the meanwhile, Blücher had already . . ." literally must necessarily conclude that Plancenoit was taken while the French and English were still locked in battle. There is all the more reason for arriving at this interpretation in that it is said previously that, even before the attack by the Guard, the batteries of Zieten's Prussian corps "broadly raked the right wing of the enemy, and the panicky word spread to the center of the French formation that there on the right everything was lost."

If another source revealed that Plancenoit was already taken by the Prussians at 6:30, whereas the attack by the Emperor's Guard did not take place until about 8 o'clock, any doubt would appear to be eliminated. Actually, however, after it had fallen once, Plancenoit was once again taken from the Prussians by the French Guard — an intermediate action that Treitschke completely passed over — and the second conquest of the place did not occur until after the failure of the attack by the French Guard against the English. Since Plancenoit lay completely behind the French battle line, it would be impossible to understand how this army could have escaped and was not cut off and captured if Treitschke's account were correct.

The genesis of the historiographic error is obviously this, that the author's only concern was to depict the sudden change of fortune with the strongest possible force and in doing so to emphasize the Prussians' role. The real tactical picture of the overall action is of less importance to him, so that he uses the expression "in the meanwhile, Blücher had already . . ." as a mere conjunctive expression without becoming aware of the factual relationships he was thus establishing.

Now Trietschke is in no way an inaccurate historian; on the contrary, he studied all the sources carefully and critically and paid very close attention to the details. But he has little interest in the sequence of tactical events. This aspect of the situation is not included in his viewpoint, and it is precisely for this reason that the example of his account of the battle of Belle Alliance is so instructive.

Not a single one of the sources that recount the Germanic-Roman wars can even approach Treitschke in factual exactness; on the other hand, their rhetorical impulse is much stronger yet and more broadly impressive, so that we must be careful not to understand the word "rhetoric" simply as "an expression of melodious words." Even if the rhetoric has very often sunk to the level of mere external embellishment, nevertheless here it is intended to mean what it actually should be, the real art of expression, which is the reflection of the strong inner sensitivity, the pathos, of the writer.

Now in no way does this observation permit us to generalize and speak of the unreliability of all historical reports. We must discriminate between many types of historical writings. The accounts of Herodotus, Xenophon, Polybius, and Caesar also have their errors, but they are of a completely different kind and stem from other sources than those of Treitschke or Tacitus. The errors that we have revealed in Treitschke's account of Belle Alliance would not have been made by any of the historians mentioned above, and for our type of study they are fundamental. For Treitschke, in whose view everything depends on characterization and impression, as well as for his readers, they are completely secondary. As well known as the circumstances of this battle are, I am still perhaps the first critic who has been shocked at all by these errors and has noted them, because, fortunately, we are still accustomed to using this book as a work of art and not as a "source." We detract just as little from the peculiar value of Tacitus' work as from Treitschke's if we regard every single expression of his account with skepticism and establish the possibility that he completely ignores connecting links and important relationships.

Scholars heretofore have proceeded from the basis that, insofar as source reliability is concerned, Tacitus' account is a correct and reliable picture of the events and only needs to be correctly and exactly interpreted, or at best to be filled in or corrected here and there. But I wish to state that it is entirely wrong to claim that one can establish real situations from Tacitus' rhetorical descriptions and expressions and that, on the contrary, we may be sure from the start that, in order to arrive at the true cause and effect relationship, his account needs far more completing and correcting than, for example, that of Treitschke in the battle of Belle Alliance.

THE ROMAN POST AT THE MOUTH OF THE WESER

According to Florus 4. 12, Drusus also built forts on the Elbe and the Weser ("*praesidia atque custodias disposuit*": "he stationed garrisons and guardhouses"). In *Annals* 1. 28, Tacitus tells us that on the occasion of the great uprising of the Roman soldiery in the year 14, even the garrison of veterans (*vexillari*) in the area of the Chauci mutinied. That must have been in the Weser fort established by Drusus, that is to say, at the mouth of the river.

According to the usual assumption, the Chauci occupied the area on both sides of the Weser and up to the Ems. But Much, in *Germanic Areas of Origin* (*Germanische Stammsitze*), p. 54, has, for good reasons, placed the Ampsivarii on the lower Ems. Even if that should not be right, and the area of the Chauci began on the right bank of the Ems, the Roman garrison was certainly stationed not here, but at the mouth of the Weser. If, as we may assume, there was also a garrison at the mouth of the Ems, it was located on the left bank and consequently not in the territory of the Chauci but in that of the Friesians. On the right bank, it would have been in a more dangerous location and would have required constant security measures without accomplishing anything, since certainly there was no fixed bridge at hand. A garrison "in the area of the Chauci" served a useful purpose only at the river's mouth, perhaps on a dune-covered island in front of the Weser. In this position, however, if the Romans really wanted forcefully to exercise their hegemony over the Weser region, a fixed post was indispensable.

## NOTES FOR CHAPTER III

1. Florus 4. 12.

2. Ritterling (*Bonner Jahrbücher,* 1906) would substitute here, instead of the Yssel, the Vecht River, which branches off farther away from the Rhine. This difference has no significance for our purposes.

3. Velleius 2. 106.

4. Strabo 7. 1.3. Velleius 2. 121.

5. Tacitus, *Hist.* 5. 22.

6. Florus 4. 12: "Praeterea in tutelam provinciarum praesidia atque custodias ubique disposuit, per Mosam flumen, per Albim, per Visurgim. Nam per Rheni quidem ripam quinquaginta amplius castella direxit." ("Moreover, for the protection of the provinces he stationed garrisons and guardhouses everywhere along the Meuse, Elbe, and Weser rivers. In fact, along the bank of the Rhine he erected more than fifty forts.") Instead of "Mosam," Asbach (*Bonner Jahrbücher* 85 [1888]: 28), probably justifiably, would read "Amisiam." See also in this connection Tacitus, *Annals* 1. 38.

7. It is therefore an erroneous expression when Köpp, *The Romans in Germany (Die Römer in Deutschland),* p. 22, explains that Drusus' advance to the Elbe was only an "isolated, temporary move forward."

# Chapter IV

# The Battle in the Teutoburger Forest

The history of the art of war, as such, does not have a direct interest in establishing the location of the Teutoburger Forest battlefield. If we look into this frequently treated problem, the focus of our study does not lie in the topographical question but, on the contrary, in the development of the general strategic conditions of the Roman-Germanic war, which must serve as a compass in the search for that battlefield.

First, we must establish the location of Varus' summer camp.

We have determined that, as their base of operations, the Romans used the sea on one side and the Lippe route and Aliso on the other. Beyond Aliso they had to cross over the Osning mountain area, which divides the Rhine basin from that of the Weser.

If they wanted to go one stage farther from the Lippe region, the next sector was the Weser, which is some 50 kilometers distant from Aliso as the crow flies. Establishing a post in the mountainous area between Aliso and the Weser would have been worthless. But by means of the camp on the large river they could control the region both upstream and down and could bring up by water at least a portion of the important forage, wood, and supplies provided by the Germans (game, cheese, milk, fish). The Romans' base, therefore, must have been located on the bank of the Weser at a spot situated as close as possible to Paderborn (Aliso) and facilitating good communications.

Since the middle Weser forms a kind of semicircle, all the towns from Bevern to Rehme are about equally distant from the Lippe valley. From the Lippe, therefore, it would not be possible to determine the location of the Roman station on the Weser. But for the Romans on the Weser communications with the North Sea were no less important than com-

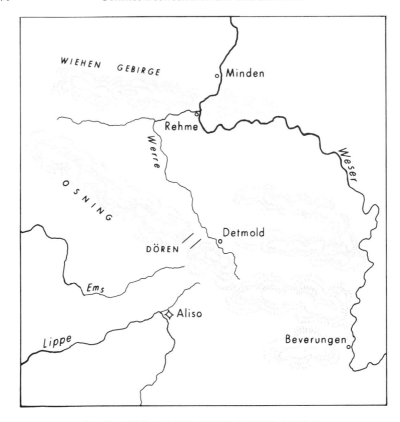

Fig. 2   AREA OF THE TEUTOBURGER BATTLE

munications with the Lippe route. In the area of the Chauci at the mouth
of the Weser they had a garrison, which still held out there after Varus'
defeat until the year 14. Consideration of this communication with the
North Sea forces us to the conclusion that, among the suitable points situated at equal distances from Aliso, only the northernmost one can have
been the site of the camp, the point that at the same time had the
shortest and best possible line of communications with Aliso and lay closest to the mouth of the Weser.

This point is the Porta Westphalica, the Westphalian Gate, at the
southern entrance of which lies the village of Rehme. Not far from its
northern entrance lies the city of Minden.

The straight-line distance from Aliso to Rehme amounts to some 33
miles; the route cuts through the Osning mountain chain in a deep sad-

dle, visible from afar, called the *Döre* (Door), or **Dören** ravine, through which the road ran since time immemorial. The trace of this road is attested to by the numerous cairns that to some extent are still present today and were much more numerous a few generations ago and that stretch out from the valley of the Werre through the Dören ravine, detouring around the deep-cut brooks feeding the Senne, along the edge of the mountains, as far as Aliso. It was customary in the earliest periods to erect burial mounds along the military road. The Romans can have used no other road than this to gain access from the Lippe into the North German Plain.

At the Porta Westphalica their two strategic access routes into the interior of Germany intersected. This was the natural place for a base camp from which they could dominate the Weser region. Here they had the secure, double line of communications homeward, were in the middle of the area of the tribes over which it was important to preserve their dominion, and, if necessary, could operate either upstream or down, could facilitate the forwarding of supplies through use of the river, and, by building a fixed bridge, could move out as necessary either on the right or the left bank. The supposition that Varus' camp was located at this spot has long been expressed, and there can be no doubt that it actually was here. Despite many searches, however, the exact spot has not yet been found. The camp could have been located above or below the Porta Westphalica, on the right or the left bank of the river. But at that time there was no road extending along the river on the right bank. The cliffs of the mountainous area extended right up to the water and only in the seventeenth and eighteenth centuries were they moved back sufficiently, by blasting, to allow the laying out of a road. On the left bank, however, above the Porta, there is a spot near Rehme that seems to have been created for a Roman camp.

Whereas Rehme itself lies in the hollow and consequently offers no advantages for a fortified position, opposite the town, on the north bank of the Werre, in the angle that it forms with the Weser, there rises a flat-topped hill, called the Hahnenkamp, which enjoys all the desirable conditions for a large Roman legion-sized camp. On two sides, south and east, it is protected by the two rivers; on the north the hill falls off toward the Porta, and only toward the west is it joined, by a saddle, to the continuing landscape. Actually, then, only this side is exposed to an attack, and the hill projects close enough to the banks of the two rivers to dominate the waterways, while still leaving enough room for bringing ships ashore or establishing a harbor. Nevertheless, the excavations that have been carried out on the Hahnenkamp have led to the conclusion that, unless great changes took place in the terrain, a Roman camp was not situated here. Not only was there no direct evidence of potsherds or similar objects, but also the cross ditches that were dug at various places in such a way that they would necessarily have intersected the ditches of the Roman camp showed that the dirt lying below the surface here had never been dug up. What instead came to light was, of course, also significant: the first early Germanic village, the small individually laid-out dwelling excavations, as Tacitus describes them, still having the remains of the carbonized corner beams in the post holes.

If Varus' camp was not situated on the Hahnenkamp, it can only be sought downstream from the Porta. With the defile of the Porta behind it, it was, to be sure, less secure there, but all the more suited and all the more imposing for immediate offensives. The Romans may well have secured the defile by means of a fort on Wittekind Mountain, where the monument now stands. But to date no trace has come to light here either, and it is probable — indeed, as good as certain — that it has been eradicated forever because the city of Minden now stands on the spot of the camp, just as does the city of Paderborn on the site of Aliso. It is, of course, quite natural that the locations that seemed suitable for an installation to the Romans were also favored in later centuries and villages or towns were built on them. Consequently, they can no longer be found in our day. The Romans built at least fifty forts and camps in Germany, but only a very few of them have been discovered.

In spite of the favorable double communication lines that the Romans created for their camp near the Porta, they were still unwilling to risk remaining on the Weser in winter, too, but went back to the Rhine, or to Haltern on the Lippe, where the remains of a large camp have been uncovered. Varus' camp was only a summer camp. Even if the Romans immediately took up the improvement of the road, as can be assumed, it ran through a dense forest full of ravines, and a large army that is dependent on a continuous flow of supplies seeks to maintain in winter an absolutely secure tie with its base.

Varus was in his summer camp on the Weser when it was reported to him that rather distant tribes had rebelled. He marched off with his entire army to pacify them, and his column was accompanied by a large train of women, children, slaves, wagons, and pack animals. This convoy shows us with complete certainty the route that the army followed. It is absolutely impossible that Varus, however mediocre a field commander he was, should have taken along such a train for a rather extended distance into the German forests. It was hard enough in the interior of Germany to move and provision the soldiers; it is unthinkable that any Roman general would not have limited his train to the most essential items on such a march. It could be asked if the burden and the delay caused by this convoy might not be rhetorical embellishment and exaggeration by our source, but the entire context attests to the truth of this march. It is a definite fact that the battle took place in autumn; undoubtedly, Varus did not intend to return to the camp at the Porta for the winter. Consequently, by abandoning the camp he also had to take along the train, and it plays such an important role in the account of the battle itself that any question of fiction is eliminated. At the same time, however, the possibility that Varus might have taken a route other than the main road leading to the Lippe and Aliso is also eliminated. Supposedly, the tribe that he was going out to pacify also lived in this direction, south or west of Aliso. Otherwise, since he would have believed himself in friendly territory, he would probably have sent the train toward Aliso with only a covering escort, and he would immediately have headed for his goal with the legions, for which he always had available sufficient supplies and train for a short expedition. However that may be, whether the expedition was directed against the Bructeri, the Marsi, the Chatti, or some other people, there can be no doubt about the route that the army, together with the train, first followed. Up to now, however, many scholars have not realized what this route was, since Dio Cassius reports that the Romans had to move through a wooded mountainous area full of ravines and uneven ground, where, even before the enemy attack, they were kept busy opening up the route, felling trees, and building bridges. It would be wrong, however, to conclude from this description that the route ran through a pure wilderness. It is impossible at the same time to build a road and to march along it. It takes hours to fell an old tree or to build a bridge. If an army is to march through a trackless primeval forest, a detachment has to be sent out in advance to open up the route or build it, while the main body remains in camp and rests. Then the army can advance by stages of a few kilometers each as the opening of the route progresses. Consequently, Dio Cassius' account is in any event a strong exaggeration, and the conclusion that scholars have drawn from it, that the march was over trackless terrain, becomes completely untenable if we once more recall the unusual train that accompanied the army.

If we reduce the rhetorical hyperboles of the account instead of extending them still further, we soon realize that what is being described to us is the route to Aliso. The terrain south of Rehme, the area of the

Lippe, the "Lehmgau" (Lemgo), is a heavy clayey ground which at that time was undoubtedly primeval forest and even today is partially wooded. The route did not follow the Werre valley, which was too swampy, but went directly southward over a hilly area crossed by ravines. A violent storm, with rain and wind, fell upon the marching column, softened the ground and made it slippery. We must picture the route not as a well-developed Roman military road but as an ordinary forest trail that the Romans had improved here and there by building a bridge, throwing up a causeway, or draining off water. In the brief period of their hegemony, they had not yet built a real, firm road even on the Lippe, much less here.[1] The bad weather rendered the road impassable in a number of places, so that here and there they had to make a little detour and probably had to cut down a tree or two. The storm washed away bridges, broke limbs from the trees, and uprooted whole trees which then fell on the marching column. The Germans, for their part, may also have contributed toward holding up the march as much as possible by destroying bridges.

Although he was warned by Segestes, Varus had not taken any special security measures. The soldiers were not ready for battle and the train was somewhere in the middle, without any particular order, between troop units. Suddenly, the Germans broke out of the forest and fell on the long column.

According to the Roman account, the uprising that Varus intended to put down had been deliberately incited by the German conspirators. This has been interpreted to mean that the plan was to entice Varus away from the fixed military road into an area particularly favorable for the ambush.

That is a fictitious concept. Areas suitable for an ambush existed everywhere in Germany; but to lure an enemy army to a definitely specified, distant spot and to have one's own forces on that spot, unnoticed, on the very day that the enemy passes it is simply an unfeasible stratagem. And besides, there could not have been a better terrain for Arminius' plan than the regular road from the Porta to Aliso.

If the conspirators were really connected with that uprising, their purpose probably was not to lure the Romans to a particular area but rather to assemble their own warriors and move them up under the guise of supporting Varus.

The Roman army was composed of three legions, six cohorts of allies, and three squadrons (*alae*) of cavalry. It is expressly added in the sources that the army had been very much weakened by detaching troops for the occupation of individual forts, escorting of trains, executions, and pursuit of robbers. Nevertheless, it is not clear whether this weakening refers to the legions themselves or to the small number of auxiliary troops. Consequently, we are not in position to say more than that the army at the scene of the battle probably numbered between 12,000 and 18,000 combatants, which Varus had intended to reinforce by levying additional Germanic auxiliary troops from the region for the impending campaign. It was precisely these would-be allies who suddenly turned their weapons against their masters and fell upon the column in its disorder.

The column, which, with its entire train and its low degree of march discipline, we can estimate as comprising a total of 18,000 to 30,000 persons spread over a length of some 9 miles, had probably covered between 9 and 12 miles, with its point reaching the "black moor" near Herford or the region of Salzufeln-Schöttmar, when it was attacked.

As soon as the cry rang out that the Germans were attacking, the point naturally halted immediately. A relatively open spot was selected and a fortified camp erected, protected by a wall and a ditch, in which the oncoming troops and columns gradually assembled. Varus may have deliberated as to whether he should not turn back to the summer camp he had just left, where the nature of the camp would naturally have offered much better protection. Probably a garrison had remained behind there for the winter in some kind of fort. But not only might the Germans already have taken possession of the summer camp, despite its defenders, but also there would hardly have been enough provisions on hand for withstanding a long siege. Furthermore, the route forward was no more dangerous than the route back. Consequently, Varus had his men burn all the superfluous baggage and the wagons, and on the following day he marched out in better order than on the first, hoping to reach his destination, Aliso. A certain amount of time was required for rearranging the army and for culling out and burning the superfluous parts of the train, so that they probably did not get started on the march until quite late. The first part of the march was over open terrain, but it was, nevertheless, still not without some losses. The fact that the Romans were able to move forward at all leads us to conclude that the Germans' attack was still weak and that they had little cavalry on hand. Although the sources make no mention of mounted men, still some of them must have been on the scene, for the Germans were, after all, particularly strong in this arm, and the Romans, for their part, had three squadrons of cavalry with them. If the Germans had had no cavalry at all, they would not have been able to get near the column in the open field, since the Roman cavalry would have driven them off. On the other hand, if the Germans had had a strong cavalry force at hand, the Romans would not have been able to move forward at all, for an army cannot fight and march at the same time. We know that from the battle of Carrhae (Vol. I, p. 442) and the engagement at Ruspina (Vol. I, p. 557). For the same reason, the attack of the Germans, too, must still have been very weak on the first day, only a probing one so to speak; otherwise, the long, uncoordinated column would not even have gotten out of the forest.

Under the conditions of caution and closed formation with which the movements of the second day were made, it was possible to move forward only slowly. Finally, they arrived once again in a wooded area, where the troops had little freedom of movement.

Even today we can read from the terrain the alternation that occurred between forest and open country. Near Salzufeln the clayey terrain comes to an end and is replaced by sandy and marshy soils, on which the beech forest, which is prevalent elsewhere, does not grow well and which only here and there offer conditions that allow oaks to thrive. The pine forests that presently cover extensive stretches of the sandy soil are only of rather recent origin. Consequently, the open terrain over which the Romans marched started near Salzufeln. But a short distance before the Osning little shell-lime ridges parallel to the mountain rise up from the sand, and like the ridge of the mountain itself, they too were undoubtedly wooded at that time. We may assume that it was already late in the afternoon when the army, after a march of a good 9 to 10 miles, approached this wood and the Dören ravine, only to find that the passage was blocked and occupied by the Germans. At this point, it would have been best for the Romans immediately to commit all their forces in order to storm the pass and break the obstacle, for the strength of the Germans was increasing continuously, and the night made it possible for them to add further artificial obstacles. But storming of the pass would also call for a flanking movement by means of a detour, all of which required time. It was also impossible to plunge into combat without safeguarding the unarmed train as long as necessary by means of some kind of fortified position.

Let us not imagine, for instance, that the Romans could have stormed through the pass in a closed column, warding off attacks as best they could, come what may. If they had already suffered heavy losses on that day during their march over open country, then a continuation of the march through a pass that was defended by troops on the hills on both

sides was completely out of the question. In order to break through, they
had to drive the enemy away from the pass in a pitched battle, not hindered by an unarmed convoy, in order to penetrate through the enemy
quickly before he had the chance to move up again from the rear. Varus
therefore decided once again to draw up a camp in order to force his way
through the pass on the following day.

We have received only a very skimpy account of the battle that took
place here on the third day. But we already know, from Marathon, that
if we are familiar with the armament and the combat methods of the
opposing armies, then the terrain is such an important and eloquent witness to the nature of a battle that we may risk reconstructing the course
of the battle in its general outline, since, after all, there is no doubt as to
the outcome.

The Dören ravine, a deep saddle in the Osning range, at its narrowest
point is still some 300 paces wide. The mountain chain is made up of cal-
careous ragstone with sand dunes situated on both sides and on the
approaches. The Dören ravine itself is filled principally with deep sand,
which at that time was without trees. The road did not lead through this
sand in the middle of the ravine but along the two sides, close to the rising ground. The dune hills in the ravine and on its approaches are partially overgrown with heather; rather small areas here and there are
clayey. In the ravine itself, which forms a water divide, a small brook
runs off toward the north; there are also some swampy and marshy areas.

Wide as the ravine is, the passage through this terrain form is very difficult; one must pass either through deep sand or over the rises in the
ground. We may assume that from the first day on Arminius had men at
work blocking the pass by felling trees.

On the other hand, we must give the Romans credit for not simply
attacking the pass frontally but assume that they sought to make a
detour over the mountains, which at no place are entirely impassable. As
the historical account tells us, they succeeded in taking by storm the first
dunes at the entrance to the ravine and in driving the Germans down
from them. But behind those hills more and more dunes arose. From the
edge of the open hilly terrain into the narrow pass there is a distance of
about a kilometer and a half, and the farther the Romans pressed forward, the more they exposed themselves to flank attacks downward from
the real mountain ridge. And the warrior strength of the Germans lay
precisely in the fact that they now faced up to the Roman hoplites in
closed groups, despite the meagerness of their protective weapons. Then,
driven back, the Germans broke up their formation but did not fall into

panic. Instead, taking advantage of their lighter armament, they only withdrew from one good position in order to occupy immediately another one just as good as the first a short distance to the rear. The storm had set in again, and it made it hard for the Romans to attack the smooth hills and to move forward on the wet forest floor. The Germanic cavalry, which could not be used in the pass, was probably left outside from the start by Arminius, to harass the enemy in the rear and to hold up enveloping columns. Instead of breaking open the blocking of the pass, the Romans, by moving forward, only felt they were enclosed in it.

And so their attacks were finally stalled. The pouring rain not only hindered them in their movements, but it also depressed their attitude and their morale. As soon as the cohorts took their first step backward, the Germanic Hundreds stormed down from all the heights and drove them completely back into their camp. Any chance of rescue was lost. The cavalry rode away, hoping to be able to cross the mountains at some other point. Varus and a number of the higher officers committed suicide. A standard bearer, unable to save his standard, at least for the honor of his legion, and to prevent its falling into enemy hands, plunged with his eagle into a swamp.

The rest of the army, under the camp prefect Ceionius, finally surrendered unconditionally. During the negotiations for the surrender, Varus' loyal servants had sought to burn their master's body, in order to shield it from desecration, and had finally buried it, half burned. But Arminius had it dug up again and sent the severed head to Marobodus, king of the Marcomanni.

On one occasion, as we are told by a later writer,[2] Arminius had the heads of his fallen enemies placed on spears and carried up to the wall, in order to terrify a Roman garrison. That reference probably cannot apply to the last camp by the Dören ravine, since the troops that were encircled there knew only too well what had happened. However, this account presumably does apply to this campaign, perhaps to the garrison that was left back in the camp by the Porta, perhaps to Aliso.

Those Romans who did succeed in breaking through the ring of Germans and escaping, either through the Dören ravine or over the mountains, fled to Aliso and were besieged there for a long time. When their provisions finally ran out, they tried to outwit the watchfulness of the Germans. On a dark and stormy night, under the leadership of a determined old soldier, the camp prefect and *primus pilus* L. Caedicius, they broke through the encircling force and finally succeeded in eluding their pursuers, with the help of a stratagem. They had the trumpeters blow, thereby causing the Germans to fear a relief force was approaching.[3] In exactly the same manner, more than a thousand years later, the garrisons of the knights' castles that were besieged by the Prussians managed to escape. The garrison of Bartenstein made its way for 70 miles through enemy country and arrived safely at Königsberg (see Vol. III, Book III, Chapter 7). All the other Roman garrisons and detachments that were still spread through the interior of Germany fell into the hands of the insurgents, so that, for all practical purposes, Varus' three legions were completely destroyed.

We know the battle of the Teutoburger Forest only from the reports of the vanquished. Even the name of the battlefield, even though it lies in the middle of Germany, is presumably of Roman rather than German origin. No chronicle, no historical account of the Middle Ages mentions the name of the Teutoburger Forest. It is indicated to us solely by Tacitus, in a single passage (*"saltus Teutoburgiensis,"* Annals 1. 60), and from that it came into modern geography as a result of seventeenth-century scholarship. But today we are in a position to understand it and to clarify its origin.

About 4 miles southeast of the Dören ravine are located two circular walls, a very large one atop the mountain and a small one a few hundred paces downhill, which give the impression of installations from the early Germanic period.[4] The smaller one could have been the seat of a prince, and the larger a place of refuge for the populace, a refuge-keep. Such refuges, which were not normally inhabited but in time of emergency could shelter the inhabitants of the entire region, have been preserved in numerous places. The largest is probably the one on Mount Saint Odile in the Vosges.

In all probability, "Teutoburg" means "people's castle" *(Volksburg)*; the stem is identical with the first syllable of the name of the nearby city Detmold (Tietmallus). Very often individual names have gradually developed from such generic names. In this case, it was perhaps not used by the Germans but by the Romans, who, when they asked the local inhabitants what the large stone wall on the mountain above the prince's castle was, heard "Teutoburg" and also applied that name to the wooded hills through which their military road ran.

Today the Teutoburg is called the Grotenburg; in the middle of the large circular wall stands the Arminius (Hermann) monument.

It stands in the right place; all the more so if, as can be assumed, this was the stronghold of Segestes, from which he fled to the Romans, taking Thusnelda with him.

Two other items from this battle have been preserved. In 1868, that wonderfully beautiful silver treasure which undoubtedly came from Varus' table and constituted a Cheruscian prince's share of the booty was found near Hildesheim, 9 feet underground. And the museum in Bonn houses the gravestone that brotherly reverence set up for the centurion M. Caelius of the eighteenth legion, killed in the "Varian War"; the gravestone is embellished with the likeness of the deceased and his two loyal servants, and bears the inscription that they had not been able to bury his remains.

## EXCURSUS

### 1. THE POSITION OF THE SUMMER CAMP

We have established through purely objective considerations that Varus' camp was situated on the Weser. This is also attested to twice in source documents, but in neither case in such a way as to exclude any other interpretation. Dio Cassius says of the Germans: "They led him on far from the Rhine into the land of the Cherusci and toward the Weser *(kai pros ton Ouisourgon).*"* It is possible to interpret this as "in the direction of the Weser" rather than "to the Weser." In Velleius 2. 105 we read: "Intrata protinus Germania, subacti Caninifati, Attuari, Bructeri, recepti Cherusci gentes et amnis mox nostra clade nobilis transitus Visurgis." ("Immediately after Germany had been entered, the Canninefates, the Attuari, and the Bructeri were subjugated and the nations of the Cherusci occupied. Then the Weser, a river notorious by our defeat, was crossed.") This wording, however, is based on conjecture. The princeps edition and Amerbach show "*inamninus*" instead of "*amnis,*" and the Burer Collection has "*inamminus.*" From these there has been a recent tendency for scholars to read "*gentis ejus Arminius*" ("Arminius of this nation") instead of "*gentes et amnis*" ("nations and river").

On objective grounds, it has been thought that Detmold could be presumed to be the site of the camp, since here, judging from the name (*tietmallus: tiet +* judicial assembly), there was a court of justice. It seems to me out of the question that that would have been a reason for the Romans to establish a camp there. The Roman hegemony could not keep the large, armed peoples' assemblies under police surveillance, so to speak. They either had to prohibit them or, if they did not want to and could not, they had to have such a political relationship with the Germans that they could tolerate the assemblages. But in the latter case they would also have to keep every Roman far away from the area of these passionate and easily excited groups. Nothing would have been more illogical and more dangerous than to allow such a meeting to take place in close proximity to the Roman camp, just as, on the other hand, it would have been an unnecessary provocation to situate a Roman camp at or near a sacred assembly place where the Germans could no longer assemble in the manner of their ancestors.

All these considerations, however, are altogether beside the point, for the only reason that could have determined the choice of the campsite and had to do so was the strategic one, and that called for the river.

On 30 March 1901, along with Museum Director Schuchhardt, I reconnoitered the Rehme area and confirmed the fact that the Hahnenkamp is the appropriate place for a Roman camp in this vicinity. Dr. Huchzermeier, the medical director in Oeynhausen, told us that a Roman gold coin bearing the likeness of an emperor had been found there some fifteen years earlier and had been sold by the finder to a numismatist. Unfortunately, Dr. Huchzermeier could not remember any other details, but he promised us that he would inquire further. Nothing was known of any other finds in that area.

The wells on the hill all have water not far below the surface.

Mr. Schuchhardt also made a special point of the fact that a camp in this location would correspond not only in its size but also in its orientation to the Roman practice by being emplaced principally on the slope of the hill facing southward, toward the sun.

As he further pointed out, a very important reason that the Roman camp could not have been situated farther upstream on the Weser was the fact that the strong rapids close above Rehme would have interfered with navigation to the North Sea.

Nevertheless, my conjecture that Varus' camp had been on the Hahnenkamp was not confirmed by excavations that I, along with Dr. Schuchhardt, had made that same autumn. Not only did we fail to find even the slightest trace of former ditches on the plateau, but it might also be said that, quite to the contrary, the diggings definitely showed that there had been no Roman camp at that site. According to the configuration of the terrain, it could be determined quite accurately where the Romans would have dug their trenches, and since our cross ditches made it clear that the earth at some depth under the surface had never been disturbed, no camp could have existed here.[5]

Instead of what we expected, we found something else, perhaps even more important: Germanic dwelling cellars spread across the entire plateau. This is the first ancient German village to be discovered, and it confirms Tacitus' description: "colunt discreti ac diversi ut fons, ut campus, ut nemus placuit, vicos locant non in nostrum morem conexis et cohaerentibus aedificiis: suam quisque domum spatio circumdat, sive adversus casus ignis remedium, sive inscitia aedificandi." ("They live separated and apart, wherever a spring, a field, a grove catches their fancy. They do not situate their villages as we do with structures connected and adjoined. Each surrounds his home with open ground, either as a safeguard against the incidence of fire or through ignorance of building practices.") This discovery also confirms the theory that this description does not refer to individual farms, as in Westphalia, but to extended, loosely knit villages.

The same types of building excavations were also found on another plateau, the Mooskamp near Babenhausen, somewhat farther up the Weser.

Now if German villages were situated in the two places suitable for a Roman camp directly before the Westphalian Gate, this could well have been the reason why the Romans did not erect their camp precisely in this area.

I next explored further directly across the Weser, on the right bank, but there, too, no trace has been found to date.

It will be a matter for the local authorities to continue the search and also to consider the terrain downstream from the Westphalian Gate. Earlier I was definitely opposed to considering this area because it seemed to me incredible that the Romans should have encamped before the defile instead of behind it. Nevertheless, there is perhaps something to be said for that, especially since the suitable places upstream were already occupied by German villages. That is, if the Romans encamped downstream from the Gate, they would be able there to build and control a fixed crossing over the Weser, which opened up the entire downstream area to them. On the other hand, a bridge near Rehme would have led into a funnel (a point which, once again, brings up the question of how far the route along the right bank was passable). The most effective arrangement, strategically, would have been to establish the camp on the right bank. We could imagine that the bridge would have been secured by a bridgehead and the danger of the defile formed by the Gate lessened by a fort on the Wittekindsberg. However, as I learned through personal reconnaissance, the first little rise in the terrain on the right bank near the village of Neesen, below the Jacob Mountain, is so insignificant that it can hardly be considered a likely site for a Roman camp. Next there came into consideration on the left bank the area near Böhlhorst and Minden itself. In the former case, the Böhlhorst mine and brickyard and in the latter, the city of Minden would have eradicated forever any trace of the camp. From the strictly strategic viewpoint of security, it would, of course, still have been an error to encamp in front of the defile. But the Romans may well have felt that their hegemony in Germany was already so firmly established that they discounted this factor as compared with other advantages.

I have given a more thorough report of the excavations on the Hahnenkamp in the September 1901 issue of the *Preussische Jahrbücher* 105: 555. Mr. Schuchhardt has done likewise in *Zeitschrift für vaterländische Geschichte und Altertumskunde Westfalens* 61: 163. The artifacts have been turned over to the Rektorschule in Oeynhausen.

Later, I also had test diggings carried out at the exit from the Dören defile, near Pivitsheide, and to date these, too, have been fruitless. There is no doubt at all that the Romans must have camped in this general location at some time or other. Whenever they wanted to move from the Lippe area into the North German Plain, which must have been a frequent necessity during the twenty years of their domination and conduct of war in this region, they had to cross the Teutoburger Forest and Wiehen Mountains, and only a very few clearly recognizable passes lead over the two high areas. One crosses the Wiehen Range by going through the Westphalian Gate, and leading through the Teutoburger Forest are the Dören defile and the Bielefeld defile. The numerous megalithic graves found there definitely indicate the Dören defile to be an age-old route. Even if we should eventually succeed in finding traces of Roman camps along this route, that still would not mean that they were associated with Varus' march. The Romans marched through this same area a great deal, and here in the midst of their dangerous allies they everywhere established their march bivouacs with walls and ditches. It is astonishing enough that no traces have yet come to light in this area but hardly credible that we shall never find any. May the local research efforts not be slackened!

## 2. THE DÖREN DEFILE

After Rehme, Mr. Schuchhardt and I also reconnoitered the Dören defile. We were assisted by Professor O. Weerth of Detmold, who proved to be an effective guide, not only because of his knowledge of the locality and of ancient history but also because of his expertise as a naturalist. He pointed out that the geological character of the landscape changes near Salzufeln. He knew (a point he later confirmed for me in the official records of Lippe) that it was not until the eighteenth century that pines were planted in the open sandy areas and moors south of Salzufeln. If this area was still free of forest growth in the eighteenth century and was only then planted with trees in planned fashion, it is not too bold to conclude that it was also open ground in the early ages. From this fact we see the agreement of Dio Cassius' report with the forest conditions between the Westphalian Gate and the Dören defile.

I am also indebted to Mr. Weerth for his information concerning the megalithic graves and their significance as an indication of the age of this route. In the 1820 article by Wilhelm Tappe, "The True Location and Line of Movement of the Three-day Battle with Arminius" ("Die wahre Gegend und Linie der dreitägigen Hermannsschlacht"), we find a map of the graves that were still there at that date.

The descriptions that have heretofore been given in writings on the Dören ravine itself contradict each other in places or give an inaccurate picture, so that I would like to add a few words on that subject.

In addition to this ravine, there is a second route leading from the upper Lippe over Mount Osning to the Westphalian Gate, the Bielefeld defile, through which the railroad now runs. Nevertheless, it does not concern us, since from Aliso the route through the Dören defile is considerably shorter.

Major Dahm, in *The Arminius Battle (Die Hermannsschlacht)*, p. 26, describes the ravines as follows: "Both ravines are equally passable; they form 500-600 paces of broad saddle terrain in which one can pass through the steep mountain chain with hardly any grade." Lieutenant Colonel von Stamford, in *The Battlefield in the Teutoburger Forest (Das Schlachtfeld im Teutoburger Walde)*, pp. 86 and 111, gives a contradictory report. He states that in the Dören pass itself the route rises and descends quite steeply and has one "bad stretch" where the slope is too steep for heavily laden vehicles.

Dahm is not wrong, in that the present paved road on the eastern edge of the ravine has only gentle slopes. In the sandy low area, too, the elevation above the plains south and north of the mountain chain is not exactly great. Stamford's description, however, is the only accurate one, since this road owes its gentle inclines partially to modern changes. The middle of the ravine, because of the sand dunes and small streams, is uneven and very sandy, and consequently is passable only with difficulty.

Knoke says on p. 96: "There can be no question of swamps either inside the Lippe forest or to the north of it." Dahm, too, says something similar on p. 29, although with the more cautious addition, "swamps that could be a hindrance to an army." It is not stated in the sources that the swamps actually formed a direct obstacle for the army (see Eduard Meyer, *Studies on the Battle in the Teutoburger Forest [Untersuchungen zur Schlacht im Teutoburger Walde]*, p. 216). That there are swampy spots throughout the Teutoburger (Lippe) Forest, however, has been established by Stamford and cannot be subject to any doubt. Directly in front of the Dören pass, on the north, lies the Hörste Break, with deep, swampy ravines, and there are also swampy areas in the Dören pass itself (Stamford, pp. 85-86).

The earthen walls that cut across the entire pass somewhat to the north of the most narrow spot, up to the points where the deciduous forest starts on the slopes on both right and left, are presumably of later origin, possibly as late as the Middle Ages.

On a "Chart of the Teutoburger Forest and the Battle with Arminius" ("Charte des Teutoburger Waldes und der Hermannsschlacht"), which was published in 1820 by Prince Friedrich of Lippe, a camp is indicated close to the north of the Dören ravine. Varus' last camp must in fact have been located in this general area. The remains of the walls that come into question here, however, are too close to the entrance of the ravine and have nothing to do with Roman fortifications. According to Mr. Schuchhardt's determinations, these are the remains of a medieval fieldwork. They are situated on the Hammer Moor, on the right of the road that leads from Pivitsheide to Hörste, shortly beyond the road fork, and are now quickly disappearing, since they are being dug up by the farmers. I mention them in order to help future researchers avoid the error of looking for the Roman camp here on the basis of Prince Lippe's map.

Just as the location of the battle of Barenau was sought north of Osnabrück on the basis of the discovery of coins, so in determining our last camp site we feel tempted to give credence to a statement of the very reliable Lieutenant Colonel F. W. Schmidt in the *Zeitschrift für vaterländische Geschichte und Altertumskunde Westfalens* (1859), p. 299. It reads: "In the region of Stapelage, an hour and a half northwest of the Dören ravine, especially in the fields of the large farms of Hunecken and Krahwinkel, frequently Roman coins are plowed up which, with respect to those known to the author, are of no later a period than that of Augustus."

I take this quotation from the study *The Location of the Varus Battle (Die Oertlichkeit der Varusschlacht)* by H. Neubourg, p. 50. Since the coins in question are not at hand, it is no longer possible to verify the decisive point, namely, that they were indeed of no more recent date than the Augustan period. Even if this point is correct, we may still probably conclude nothing further than that it is a question of booty taken from the Teutoburger battle by one of the Cherusci clans that lived in this area. The cited places are situated too far in the mountains for us to assume that the Roman camp itself was located there.

Major General Wolf has occasionally voiced the supposition that no trace of Aliso is any longer to be found in the area of the village Elsen near Paderborn for the reason that the location suitable for it forms a sand dune which has swallowed up everything. The same thing could also have happened in the region in front of the Dören ravine, where the centuries have perhaps worked greater changes in the configuration of the dune terrain than we might suppose from our present-day observation.

### 3. CLOSTERMEIER AND WIETERSHEIM

In general, the accurate account of Varus' march has already been given by Clostermeier in *Where Arminius Defeated Varus (Wo Hermann den Varus Schlug)* Lemgo, 1822. It is only the end of the march that he does not describe quite accurately. He assumes that Varus' camp was near Minden, or somewhat farther downstream near Petershagen, and that the final catastrophe did not take place before the Dören defile but in the valley of the Berlebeke, at the foot of the Grotenburg. According to Clostermeier, Varus actually wanted to take the route through the Dören ravine, but since the Germans had blocked it off, he attempted to escape via the detour through Detmold. That is not possible. If Varus believed he was too weak to open up the Dören pass, then he had all the less reason to hope to escape by marching along the mountain chain through the Lopshorn pass or even across the mountain. The Germans did not lose contact with this long, slow-moving convoy, once they had come in touch with it. The Romans had to take the Dören ravine or die. There was no other option.

Wiitersheim has already very effectively raised these objections to Clostermeier's account in his *History of the Völkerwanderung (Geschichte der Völkerwanderung)*. Consequently, he quite correctly places the final catastrophe in the Dören ravine itself, but he believes Varus' summer camp was much farther upstream on the Weser. Therefore, he did not recognize the correct route or the tactical character of the final battle and, most importantly, he did not achieve a full understanding of the basic strategic elements of warfare in Germany. Otherwise Wietersheim's solution, which comes so close to the truth, would probably have been more highly regarded.

4. THE NUMBER OF DAYS OF MARCHING AND FIGHTING

Historians are not agreed as to whether the Teutoburger battle took place on the same day the Romans marched out from their summer camp or not until later, nor whether the battle itself lasted two or three days.

From the account by Dio Cassius one has the impression, even if it is not stated directly, that Varus peacefully marched several days before the first German attack took place. Knoke based his solution on this impression, up to this point rightfully so. But when Tacitus (1. 58) has Segestes speaking of his vain warning to Varus, "nox mihi utinam potius novissima" ("I wish that night had been my last"), that seems to indicate that the catastrophe followed immediately on the next day. This seems all the more the case in the account of Velleius (2. 118), that after Segestes' warning there was no more time for a second one ("nec diutius post primum indicem secundo relictus locus") ("No longer after the first hint did an opportunity remain for a second"). Wilms has called our attention particularly to this point. However important Velleius' testimony as a contemporary must be considered, in keeping with our basic rules for analyzing the sources, very little weight can be placed on such indirect conclusions. In any case, the source account does not prevent us from concluding that the Germans made their attack on the same day the Romans marched out from their summer camp.

The same situation applies to the question of whether the fighting lasted two or three days. The sources possibly lend themselves to both interpretations. Nevertheless, the most likely interpretation is to be found in the assumption of three days that we stated above.

In Dio Cassius the text is faulty at the decisive point. The manuscript reads as follows, after the battle of the second day is described, "Then the day (*tote gar hēmera*) dawned on them still on the march . . . ."* That makes no sense. The simplest and most natural correction would be "Then on the third day (*tritē t' ar' hēmera*). . . ."*

Nevertheless, those who accept two days on the basis of objective analysis cannot be prevented from making other conjectures, but we must reject the one which supposed that the Romans made a night march. Such a large army as that of Varus cannot, so to speak, slip away. The Germans were not like the Persians under Tissaphernes, who broke off contact with the Greeks near evening in order to establish a secure night camp as far away from them as possible. But if the enemy remained close by, such a march was not possible without a battle. Under the prevailing circumstances, where the morale of the troops was already badly shaken, a night battle would have been the most unfavorable development possible; it would have led to panic and an immediate and complete collapse.

Tacitus says that when Germanicus came through the Teutoburger Forest and looked for the traces and remains of Varus' army, "prima castra lato ambitu et dimensis principiis trium legionum manus ostentabant; dein semiruto vallo, humili fossa accisae jam reliquiae consedisse intellegebantur." ("The first camp with its wide circuit and marked off headquarters area displayed the work of three legions. Then at a half-destroyed rampart and a shallow trench, where the last remnants of them had already fallen, they were thought to have made their last stand.") The tendency has been to understand the *prima castra* as the summer camp. That meaning may not be entirely impossible, though only if we assume that Tacitus deceived his readers in order to stress the contrast. The fact that there was a great difference between a permanent summer camp and a march camp for one night must have been obvious to any Roman.[6] Consequently, Tacitus would not have been able to make any impression on his readers with this contrast. If there had really been only one march camp and Tacitus had wished to point out the contrast between it and the base camp, he would have been truthful enough, with all his rhetoric, to word his antithesis accordingly, which would not have been at all difficult. It is therefore most likely that the expression *prima castra* means the first march camp, which, as Knoke has correctly remarked, had been drawn up according to the regulation plan for three legions, despite the considerable losses of the first day. The conclusive point, however, as soon as we have clearly understood the locality, is determined by the distance. It is some 23 miles from Rehme to the Dören ravine and about 27 miles from Minden to the ravine. Not only is it impossible for an army under such difficult conditions as the Romans faced to cover such a distance in one day, but it is precisely one-half that distance that would be appropriate. In fact, I would not consider it impossible that the Romans, with the large number of wagons, the very difficult route through the forest, over hills and ravines, and the rain that soaked the clayey ground, would have taken even one more day's march and that the battle therefore was fought on the second, third, and fourth days of the march. That Tacitus speaks only of two camps naturally does not contradict this possibility.

Lieutenant Colonel von Stamford, in *The Battlefield in the Teutoburger Forest (Das Schlachtfeld im Teutoburger Walde)*, pp. 105 and 107, reports that he found remains of walls at several places near Schöttmar bei Salzufeln.

### 5. THE FINAL CATASTROPHE
The account I have given above of the actual battle in the Dören defile and the final catastrophe is not based on one of the source accounts, as we know them.

Rather, it is based on the combination of individual details in the reports of Velleius, Tacitus, and Florus with the basic facts given by Dio Cassius, with a filling-in of the remaining lacunae by means of objective analysis as to distances and terrain. This procedure calls for a special justification.

We must start with the fact that the only thorough account of the Teutoburger battle that we have, that of Dio Cassius, while based on a very good report, nevertheless comes to us in a third- or fourth-hand revision. The colorful aspects are naturally more strongly accentuated, and individual points in which Dio Cassius or even his predecessor was less interested or which were only slightly mentioned in the original report, might have been omitted entirely.

The question as to whether the legates were killed in the battle or, following the example of their commander, committed suicide, cannot be dealt with here. On this point there may have been no reliable report in Rome itself, and one person may have reported one thing and another something else.

Dio Cassius recounts the battle as if it ended as it had begun, with the Romans gradually being killed in the repeated attacks by the Germans, while their leaders killed themselves. On the other hand, Velleius reports that one of the camp prefects, Eggius, set a good example, while the other, Ceionius, behaved disgracefully, "qui cum longe maximam partem absumpsisset acies auctor deditionis supplicio quam proelio mori maluit" (" . . . . who, the instigator of surrender, when the battle had taken its toll of the vast majority of the Roman forces, preferred to die by execution rather than in battle"). He goes on to report that the Germans had cut off Varus' head from his half-burned body, a point that can be explained and supplemented from Florus' account that Varus had already been buried and was dug up again. This attempt at a funeral, especially by burning, is unthinkable without an established camp. Troops in the field, faced with the Germans and their particular style of warfare, would probably not have been able to surrender at all. Dio Cassius says nothing of these points. That can be no reason, however, for us to reject as fable such a definite account as that of Velleius, who in other respects is a well-informed contemporary. There is a lacuna in the final part of the text of Dio Cassius' account (perhaps a page was lost), where something further on this subject may have appeared. But even if that were not the case, it might simply be a question of an abbreviation of the text undertaken by the author, since his description of this event was otherwise very detailed. That he expressed himself very briefly at the end is also evident in the fact that he summarily has everything, both man and beast, cut down in the battle, whereas shortly thereafter he speaks of prisoners who were later ransomed by members of their families.

If we now accept Velleius' account of the attempted burial for Varus and the final capitulation, then we must conclude that the battle cannot have taken place in a continuing combination of march and combat but must have ended with a face-to-face, drawn battle. If the Romans had been continually marching, they would have had no camp where they could have attempted to burn Varus' body and in which they finally surrendered.

Militarily — one might say abstractly — this distinction is very important. Therefore, it is psychologically quite understandable that this particular point is missing in Dio Cassius. On the face of it, the final battle may not have appeared so very different from the continuing combats of the preceding day, as they were envisaged by the reporter. Above all, however, we must remember in this respect that we are dealing only with Roman reports. The authors did not feel themselves authorized to emphasize particularly that the Romans were not just attacked while marching but also had finally lost a pitched battle and had failed in an attack. How readily they sought to explain the defeat simply as resulting from treachery and ambush comes through to us in the harangue that Tacitus (*Annals* 2. 46) has Marobodus making to his warriors: "*tres vacuas legiones,*" that is, uncommitted, immobile legions, were defeated by Arminius; and for this reason the success did not call for any great fame. This objection does not appear so very unjustified in the usual account. Therefore, it is doubly important from the viewpoint of military history that it is possible for us to reconstruct the pitched battle at the end which the Romans have so played down.

This concept is also supported by the particular way that Tacitus formulates the antithesis between the two camps, when they were seen by Germanicus and his soldiers: "prima castra lato ambitu . . . . dein semiruto vallo, humili fossa" ("the first camp with its wide circuit . . . then at a half-destroyed rampart and a shallow trench"). The "*semirutum vallum*" is not the wall, which was never high, but a wall which has fallen down again. In keeping with strict logic, there is postulated here as the opposite of the large, regulation-style first camp a smaller one, unfinished and poorly prepared. While Tacitus, as he so often does, states the antithesis so obliquely that the reader must fill in here and there, he nevertheless introduces with the expression *semirutum* the suggestion that this wall was broken down by the assaulting Germans. The eye witness on whom Tacitus' account is based must have had a very strong impression precisely of this condition of the wall and the ditch. From this, he must have seen before his eyes a picture of the last terrible scene, so that the characteristic word *semirutum* was probably not injected by Tacitus but stems from the original report.

Whether one now considers our siting of the battle as really proven or as being only a reasonable probability, in any case the reconstruction of the last battle is not based only on a reconciliation of the external aspects of the reports. But it may be said that, from the objective and documentary approaches, a camp and its final capitulation can be added without difficulty to the account by Dio Cassius.

The correct reconstruction, once found, is confirmed by the fact that other portions of the sources, which are otherwise hard to understand, can now also be explained simply and clearly.

Velleius recounts that in this defeat soldiers who had wished to use their weapons in keeping with traditional Roman practice and Roman courage had been punished. We would place this action rather at the time during which capitulation negotiations were taking place.

According to Dio Cassius, the last battle took place in a narrow area, whereas Tacitus says that Germanicus saw the bleaching bones of the dead lying "*medio campi*" ("in the middle of the field"). This contradiction is now solved. Dio Cassius is speaking of the last real battle, which took place in the Dören ravine itself, but after the Romans had moved back out of the Dören defile, naturally many more of them were killed in the open field in front of the ravine.

Eduard Meyer, in his *Studies on the Battle in the Teutoburger Forest (Untersuchungen zur Schlacht im Teutoburger Walde)*, has already proven through his analysis of the sources that Dio Cassius' report is in itself very good and also lends itself to being reconciled with the details of the other sources. If Meyer's account did not immediately find general agreement, that was probably due only to the fact that his solutions in their small details were quite often inaccurate. Most importantly, the basic strategic conditions of warfare in Germany were not yet recognized, and therefore topographical determinations were not yet correct.

6. THE HYPOTHESES OF MOMMSEN AND KNOKE

We need not go into the details of the controversial hypotheses that seek to place the Teutoburger battlefield near Barenau to the north of Osnabrück or near Iburg to the south, since, according to our concept, the battlefield undoubtedly was located on the route from the Westphalian Gate toward Aliso. If the battle had been in the vicinity of Osnabrück, that would mean that the Romans' main military road had not gone upward through the Lippe valley but from Haltern in the direction Münster-Osnabrück, either to the north or the south of the Wiehen Mountains toward Minden or Rehme. There was most likely a route here as well. We can especially agree with Knoke that a German road ran along between the two mountain chains, the Wiehen and the Osning, at the foot of the hills. We could also imagine that the large amount of supplies that were necessary for Varus' summer camp and would have been very hard to move up along this land route had been brought to Minden by ship through the North Sea. Nevertheless, there can be no doubt that the Romans had a military road along the Lippe and over the Osning Mountain (Dören pass) to the Westphalian Gate. They also had a fortified base along this military road on the upper Lippe, and therefore this was their principal road. One can imagine what a relief it was for the troops marching back and forth to find such a supply base along the way. Without very great preparations and expense, they were never able to separate themselves in Germany from the road leading along the river. Consequently, if Varus himself had had any reason whatever for marching directly from the Westphalian Gate into the Osnabrück area, he would not have taken his train on this route. Rather, since he considered the nearest German tribes to be loyal allies, he would undoubtedly have sent the train directly to the Lippe route.

To all of this can be added the positive statements in Tacitus that Germanicus, after coming up the Ems by ship, had laid waste all the land between the Ems and the Lippe and had come up to the border of the Bructeri into the area of the Teutoburger Forest. Further, after relieving the fort on the Lippe, he had given up the reconstruction of the destroyed gravemound. All of this would be very difficult to reconcile — indeed impossible — with the Osnabrück hypothesis. In this respect, see also below the special study on the location of Aliso.

The great extent to which the basis for the study of these problems has been changed on all sides by recognition of the density of population factor can be measured by reading what Mommsen has to say concerning "the Location of the Varus Battle" ("die Oertlichkeit der Varusschlacht"), p. 10. The German leaders, he stated, had "been able to place their men, who outnumbered the Romans two- or threefold, at every desirable spot, even some out-of-the-way points."

Mommsen's hypothesis is defended by Eduard Bartels, in *The Varus Battle and Its Location* (*Die Varusschlacht und ihre Oertlichkeit*), 1904, where he places particular stress on the fact that the march by Varus' army must have gone along the Wiehen Mountains on the north and not through the forested mountain chain itself. He points out that the region around Barenau conforms so well to the sources because the large swamps present here are not to be found in the Dören ravine. In reply, we can say that the swamps play an important role only in Florus and Velleius and even there it is not impossible that their mention is pure rhetoric, which normally relates swamps to the German landscape. They are not mentioned in Dio Cassius, whose report, after all, is our principal source. Furthermore, the Dören ravine is in no way free of swamps.

Bartels logically places the march route along the northern foot of the Wiehen Mountains, and consequently in the plain instead of the wooded mountain, because he realizes that the army with its train could not have taken the road through the primeval forest. Nevertheless, through this solution he loses something else that is indispensable, that is, the terrain that offered the Germans the opportunity for repeated attacks on the convoy and finally complete blocking of the route.

Bartels believes an important reason that the convoy cannot have moved in the direction toward the Lippe is the fact that the information on the rebellion has come down to us without the name of the rebellious tribe. In his opinion, the tribes along the Lippe and the Ruhr were so well known to the Romans that the names would have been given if the revolt had been in that area. Against this point we might say that the Romans dominated these regions long enough to know equally well the names of all the tribes between the Rhine and the Weser.

Also beside the point is the argument that the route toward the upper Lippe would have been without danger. Whether they marched in the Werre valley or whether, as I believe, they cut across the bend in the river and marched directly to the south, in either case the terrain was more dangerous than that along the northern foot of the Wiehen Mountains. Most important of all, the Dören ravine itself seemed to be created by nature for the plan and the combat methods of the Germans.

## TEXTS OF THE SOURCE REPORTS

In view of the special interest that the battle in the Teutoburger Forest holds for Germany, it will no doubt be useful for many of our readers who do not have access to the ancient authors to be able to read the texts of the original sources, on which our account is based, and to compare that which is specifically reported with our reconstruction.

### DIO CASSIUS

The Romans possessed a number of regions in Germany that were not contiguous but just as they had been conquered, which is why they are not mentioned in history. Their soldiers wintered right there and established towns, and the barbarians soon accommodated themselves to Roman customs, came to the market centers, and carried on peaceful relations with them. Nevertheless, they still could not forget the customs of their ancestors, their local habits, their uninhibited life-style, and their armed power. Up to now, they had supposedly been getting away from these conditions only very gradually and under careful observation, imperceptibly adopting their new way of life without themselves realizing the change that was taking place in them. But when Quinctilius Varus, after his governorship in Syria, was given Germany as his province, he struck too high a tune, wanted to change everything too quickly, treated the province haughtily, and exacted tribute as from subjugated peoples. And this the Germans did not like. The heads of the tribes longed for their former power; the people found their inherited organization better than foreign domination. But because they found the Roman forces too strong for them on the Rhine and in their own regions, at first they did not rebel openly. Instead, they received Varus as if they intended to fulfill all his demands, and they lured him from the Rhine into the area of the Cherusci and up to the Weser. Here they lived with him on a completely peaceful and friendly footing and led him to believe that they would humbly accede to his orders without the force of arms.

And so it happened that Varus did not keep his troops assembled, as he should have done in enemy territory. He sent many of his men out in various directions on the requests of the weaker peoples, here for the protection of certain places, there to seize robbers, elsewhere to protect the movement of supplies. The chiefs of the conspiracy, the treachery, and the war that now developed included Arminius and Segimer, who were always around Varus and often feasted at his table. Varus now became so trusting and saw nothing suspicious in anything, but rather refused to believe those who were concerned and who advised him to be careful, even blaming them for their worry and accusing them of slander. At this point a few distant tribes rebelled. This rebellion was planned with the intention of luring Varus into a trap, so that he would move out against them as if passing through friendly territory on the way and would not take the precautions he would ordinarily have taken if all the tribes had risen up against him simultaneously. And that is the way it happened. They allowed him to move out and accompanied him a certain distance but then remained behind under the pretense of assembling their troops and planning to come help him as fast as possible. With their forces that were already assembled and ready, they fell upon the troops that had been requested earlier and cut them down, whereupon they attacked Varus himself, who had already penetrated into the pathless forests. Now the supposed allies suddenly appeared as enemies and set upon the army relentlessly. The mountains were full of ravines and unlevel areas, and the trees were thick and high so that the Romans, even before the enemy attacks, had their hands full felling trees, opening up a route, and bridging streams when necessary. They also were taking along with them many wagons and pack animals, as in peacetime, and women, children, and servants followed them in large numbers, so that the convoy was necessarily stretched out. A heavy rain and stormy wind came down and spread them out even farther, and the ground, which had become slippery around the roots and trunks of the trees, made their footing uncertain. Tree tops broke off and added to the confusion as they fell. In this emergency, the barbarians fell upon the Romans on all sides out of the thickest forests. Taking advantage of their knowledge of the area, they surrounded them and at first shot at them from a distance, but then, when nobody offered any defense and many had been wounded, they closed in on them. Since the Romans were moving along in no order but with wagons and unarmed persons all mixed together, they could not easily close their ranks. Since their numbers were also inferior to those of the attackers, they suffered heavy losses without being able to harm the enemy.

When they found a suitable place, to the extent that was possible in the wooded mountain, they set up a camp, burned most of the wagons and other equipment that could be spared, or left them behind. Then on the following day they marched on in better order and came into a more open area, but even this did not happen without losses. When they proceeded from there, they came into more woods and fought, of course, against the attackers but in doing so they encountered new misfortunes. When they drew together in the narrow area in order to strike out in closed ranks with cavalry and infantry, their formation became confused because of the limited space and the trees. It was the third (fourth?) day that they moved along in this way; a heavy rain and strong wind came down on them again and prevented them both from marching farther and from finding sure footing. In fact, the elements made it impossible for them to make use of their weapons, for arrows, javelins, and shields were all soaked and unusable. The enemy on the other hand, mostly armed with light weapons, suffered less from these things, since they could move forward and back unhindered. Furthermore, they were far superior in numbers, for now even those who had hesitated earlier had joined their ranks, at least to get in on the booty. They now all the more easily surrounded the weaker Romans, who had already lost many men in the preceding fights, and they cut them down. Varus and the most important leaders, fearful of being taken prisoner alive or being killed at the hands of the most hated enemies (for they were already wounded), reached the sad but, under the circumstances, inevitable decision to fall upon their own swords.

As soon as this word spread, no one continued to fight, even those who still had some strength left. Some imitated the leaders' example, while others threw their arms away and had themselves cut down by the nearest person, for flight was out of the question even if one wanted to flee. Now, without any further risk, the barbarians struck down man and beast.

VELLEIUS PATERCULUS

Hardly had Tiberius ended the Pannonian and Dalmatian war, when five days later the unhappy news arrived from Germany concerning the death of Varus and the annihilation of three legions, as well as many cavalry squadrons and six cohorts. In this matter, fate favored us in only one aspect, so to speak: the commander who was able to avenge such a defeat, namely Tiberius, was at hand. The cause of the disaster and the principal person involved deserve some attention here. Quinctilius Varus, scion of a highly regarded family, though not belonging to the old nobility, was a man of moderate ideas and calm temperament. Somewhat slow in mind and body, he was better suited for quiet camp life than for fighting. How little he scorned money was shown in the fact that when he went to Syria, which he had previously governed, he arrived as a poor man in a rich province, and when he left, he was a rich man leaving behind a poor country. Entrusted with the high command of the army in Germany, he considered the inhabitants to be persons who were human only in their voice and their physical members. He believed that, through the working of Roman law, he could tame those people who could not be controlled by the sword. With this intention he went to Germany as if he were coming to men who enjoyed the blessings of peace, and he spent the time in his summer camp exercising formal judgment from his seat of justice.

But these people, as one could hardly believe who had not had the personal experience, were with all their wildness extremely sly and born liars. They stretched out complicated trials, at times bringing complaints against one another. At other times they thanked Varus because he was deciding with Roman justice and so was tempering their wildness by a new and unknown type of discipline and was replacing might with right. Thus, they lulled Quinctilius into the greatest sense of security, so that he felt as if he were the city praetor meting out justice in the Forum rather than commanding an army in the middle of Germany. At that time among the Germans there was a young man of noble family, of courageous hand, quick mind, and a wisdom such as one would not believe possible of a barbarian. He was named Arminius, a son of Sigimer, one of the princes of that tribe. His fiery spirit shone out from his countenance and his eyes. He had served in our army and had also been awarded Roman citizenship and knightly rank. Now he took advantage of the commander's sluggishness for a dastardly deed, concluding rightly that nobody can be more quickly destroyed than the man who fears nothing, and realizing that a sense of security is very often the beginning of disaster. At first he divulged his plan to only a few and then later to more. He explained to them thoroughly that they were clearly in a position to overcome the Romans. After the decision was made, the execution of the plan was to follow at once, and the time for the attack was definitely established.

This word was brought to Varus by a loyal man of the tribe, Segestes, a member of a prominent family. But Varus' insight had already been blinded and so he was no longer open to wise counsel. And so it happens that usually the gods cloud the wisdom of those whose happiness they wish to destroy and create the effect that, sadly enough, what happens seems to be deserved, and the disaster becomes a fault. Consequently, Varus refused to believe this warning and assured his informant that he would know how to reward this proof of friendship. So after this first warning there was no time left for a second one.

This terrible disaster, the worst that befell the Romans since the defeat of Crassus by foreign tribes, I shall describe thoroughly in a separate book. For the time being, suffice it to treat only the lamentable outcome. This incomparably courageous army, outstanding among Roman warriors for its discipline, courage, and combat experience, because of the incompetence of its leader and the treachery of the enemy, and pursued by the disfavor of fate, was not even able to fight or to break out. Those who wanted to use their Roman weapons and their Roman courage were even punished and, surrounded in forests, swamps, and the enemy ambush, the army was annihilated by the very enemy that it had formerly butchered like cattle, so that life and death now depended on his anger or his mercy. The commander had more courage to die than to fight; he followed the example of his father and his grandfather and fell on his own sword. One of the two camp prefects, Lucius Eggius, set a noble example, while the other, Ceionius, gave an equally disgraceful one, since, after the largest part of the army had fallen in battle, he preferred to die executed rather than fighting, and so surrendered. Vala Numonius, one of Varus' legates, otherwise an intelligent and brave man, set an appalling example by leaving the infantry in the lurch and fleeing with the cavalry in order to reach the Rhine. Nevertheless, fate avenged this conduct, for he did not survive those he had abandoned but died as a deserter. The barbarous enemy tore apart the half-burned body of Varus, cutting off his head and taking it to Marobodus, who sent it to the Emperor so that it could be buried with honor in the family plot.

FLORUS

It is more difficult to hold provinces than to establish them; they are created through force and are held through justice. Consequently, the joy was short-lived. That is, the Germans were more conquered than tamed, and they looked more toward our customs than toward our weapons while under the command of Drusus. After Drusus died, they began to hate the attitude and the haughtiness of Quinctilius Varus no less than his anger. He took the risk of proclaiming an assembly and carelessly boasted that he was capable of controlling the savagery of the barbarians with the lashings of the lictor and the voice of the herald. But the barbarians, who had already sadly watched their swords rusting and their horses unexercised, when they realized that toga and court were worse than weapons, took up their arms under the leadership of Arminius. At the same time, Varus' illusion of the peaceful atmosphere was so great that he did not even take any action when one of the princes, Segestes, divulged the conspiracy to him. So he who could foresee no trouble and feared nothing was attacked unsuspectingly, and while he was citing the law in the court — oh, what a sense of security! — they attacked from all sides. The camp was taken and three legions were overcome. Varus, after losing the camp, followed the example of Paulus on the day of Cannae. Nothing was grimmer than the carnage between swamps and forests; nothing was more intolerable than the scorn of the barbarians, especially against the leaders. They pierced out the eyes of some and cut off the hands of others. In one case, they cut out the man's tongue and stitched his lips together, and the barbarian who held it in his hand shouted at him: "Now, snake, your hissing is finished." Even the body of the Consul, which had been buried by his loyal soldiers, was dug up. The field standards and two eagles are still in the hands of the barbarians today. The third one, before it could be taken by the enemy, was broken off by the standard bearer, who hid it under his clothing and disappeared with it in the blood-red swamp.

Through this defeat it happened that the empire, which had not halted at the edge of the ocean, now had to halt on the banks of the Rhine.

TACITUS

Tacitus does not give us a direct account of the Teutoburger battle, since his account only begins with the death of Augustus. Only indirectly, in connection with the campaigns of Germanicus, especially the account of the visit to the battlefield and the burial of the bones, do we learn something. Elsewhere in Roman literature we also find isolated references here and there. For example, in one of Seneca's letters (*Ep.* 47), it is said that the foremost Romans were taken into slavery by the Germans, and men who might have hoped to enter the Senate someday spent the rest of their lives as shepherds or doorkeepers.

NOTES FOR CHAPTER IV

1. The fact that the road ran over the hill and not along the valley seems curious to us today, but that was almost the general rule with the roads of antiquity. The Roman milestones in the area of the Rhine that have remained until the present day date back only to the time of Trajan.

2. Frontinus, *Strategem.* 2. 9. 4.

3. It is appropriate that the citations in Frontinus, *Strategem.* 3. 15. 4 and 4. 7. 8, Velleius 2. 120, and Dio Cassius' reference to the effect that only *one* Roman fort had held out have been combined. In this connection, see below, the special study on the location of Aliso following Chapter VI.

4. Schuchhardt, "Roman-Germanic Research in Northwest Germany" ("Römisch-Germanische Forschung in Nordwestdeutschland"), extract from *Neue Jahrbücher für das klassische Altertum* (1900), p. 29.

5. I do not wish to fail to remark that Dahm (*Ravensberger Blätter*, Vol. IV |1904|, No. 6) nevertheless holds to the possibility that there had been a camp here. For the opposite opinion, see Schuchhardt *Ravensberger Blätter*, Vol. IV, No. 7/8).

6. Vegetius 3. 8 thoroughly describes the difference between a march camp and a base camp.

# Chapter V

# Germanicus and Arminius

The Romans were not capable of immediately avenging the defeat in the Teutoburger Forest. It is true that Tiberius, the only commander that Rome could have entrusted with such a mission, did hasten to the Rhine, but he was not in a position to plunge into a years-long war. Since it was only through adoption that he had been designated to succeed to the imperial throne ahead of Augustus' grandson, Tiberius had to be on the spot in Rome whenever the old emperor might pass away. Tiberius therefore limited himself to securing the border along the Rhine, bringing the army back to full strength, and reestablishing the morale. It was not until five years later, on the news of the death of Augustus and the assumption of power by Tiberius, that Germanicus, the son of Drusus and nephew and adopted son of Tiberius, began the war of revenge with the objective of once more subjecting the Germanic tribes up to the Elbe.

For the campaigns of Germanicus we are entirely dependent on the report by Tacitus. As thorough as this report is, it still is not sufficient. In addition to the author's flowery rhetoric, which neglects and obliterates the objective coherence of the report, there is a second disturbing characteristic. As thoroughly as Tacitus took pains to describe the Germans, he obviously had very hazy ideas about the geographical conditions of the country. In his *Germania* he has the Chauci, who actually lived at the mouth of the Weser on the North Sea coast, living as neighbors to the Chatti, who were in Hesse, although in addition to other, lesser known tribes, as important a tribe as the Cherusci lived between the two.[1]

In the campaign of the year 15 A.D., Roman troops, which marched back from the Ems along the shore to the Rhine, came to the Weser, according to Tacitus.

In the year 16 A.D., Germanicus landed his army on the bank of the

Ems. Directly after this statement there appears the sentence: "While he was setting up his camp, he received a report of the revolt by the Angrivarii in his rear." But the Angrivarii lived on both sides of the Weser. Scholars have sought to correct this obvious error by changing the text and inserting in the first example, in place of the Weser, a small river in Holland, the Unsingis (Hunze), or by substituting in the second example the Ampsivarii instead of the Angrivarii. But the rest of the context hardly permits these corrections and creates other unsolvable difficulties. We must accept the fact that Tacitus actually did make these errors, and in fact they are, psychologically, not at all incredible. They are closely related to his whole point of view. The actual, objective relationships are not of interest to him, and it makes no difference to him if he occasionally confuses the names of two German rivers or tribes. Of course, this is immediately apparent to us. The tendency has been to accept in the first passage the fact that Tacitus neglected to mention that in the year 15 A.D. the Romans had undertaken a reconnaissance to the mouth of the Weser before their withdrawal to the Rhine. In the second case, from the year 16 A.D., he neglected to recount the march from the Ems to the Weser and back because he felt no unusual events were connected with it. This expedient may not be entirely impossible, but insofar as Tacitus' reliability as a source for military history is concerned, this interpretation offers no better guarantee than the confusion of the names. In fact, it is even worse, for instead of a momentary lapse of attention we have a basic negligence. For a large army, even if it had no fighting at all on the way, a march from the Ems to the Weser and back would always be a very important event, one which an author concerned with the whole strategic situation could never neglect to mention. However this might be, we must from the start approach the treatment of these campaigns with the knowledge that, despite the detailed report by an historian of the first order, we still do not have a reliable, objective account of the events and will not arrive at a coherent understanding without making very strong corrections, if indeed we succeed at all.

In Caesar's case, he had suppressed the revolt of the Gauls, after first having lived with them on a halfway peaceful basis, by defeating them in the open field with the superior strength of his assembled large army and by conquering their towns. The widely cultivated land, in which there were always a few tribes who remained loyal to the Romans, was capable of feeding the Roman troop units on their marches out and back.

In Germany, the task was completely different. The Germans had no towns which, if captured and destroyed, would have made it possible to bring them to reason. Even Caesar had not been able to force Vercingeto-rix directly into battle, and it was much easier for the Germans, in their primeval forests and moors, to avoid an attack by the Romans. For the Romans, however, it was completely impossible to provision a large army off the land itself, a point that we must once again emphasize very strongly. The population was very thinly spread and lived principally from its herds and only to a rather small degree from agriculture. Conse-quently, Germany had no large supplies of grain that could have been either requisitioned or purchased. If the Germans would not accept bat-tle, there was nothing else to do but to seek out their villages and burn them down. But such a loss was not particularly hard on the Germans, who, after all, often moved their dwelling places, providing they had time to move out their household goods in advance. A district suffered the most when the enemy captured its herds. But that was not so easy. The Romans could not break up into small detachments in order to search the forests and find the Germans' hiding places and their proper-ty. Any rather small detachment had to expect to fall into a German ambush. Even units of several thousand men could encounter a superior force and would then be lost in the endless terrain. Consequently, the Romans found themselves facing a strategic task of a completely peculiar type, such as we have never before been confronted with in our passage through the history of warfare.

As early as the fall of the year 14 A.D., Germanicus conducted a wast-ing march through the area south of the Lippe, where the Marsi lived. Since they were attacked completely by surprise, Germanicus risked di-viding his army into four detachments and was consequently able to move through and pillage a region about 45 miles wide, as best we can make out. On the return march, the Roman army was attacked by Bruc-teri, Tubantes, and Usipetes, who had come to the aid of the Marsi. The Romans, however, who were well ordered and prepared for everything, threw back the attack successfully, even though the four legions together were only 12,000 men strong, supported by twenty-six allied cohorts and eight *alae* of cavalry. If we estimate the allies at 8,000 to 10,000 and the cavalry between 1,000 and 1,500 men, the entire army may have been something over 20,000 men strong.

THE SPRING CAMPAIGN OF 15 A.D.

In the spring of the following year (15 A.D.), Germanicus made an incursion into the land of the Chatti and went as far as crossing the Eder.

From Mainz, the base camp of the army of the upper Rhine, from which this movement must have started, to the middle section of the Eder is a straight-line distance of 150 kilometers, or some 90 miles. An army marching through German forests with the strictest security measures, and at the same time carrying out destructive actions, could probably not cover much more than a straight-line distance of 5 miles as a daily average. Therefore, this expedition must have required five to six weeks. The army consisted of four legions and 10,000 support troops, so that, if we consider the legions as not quite full strength, it was some 30,000 combat soldiers strong, or all together, with the trains, nearly 50,000 souls. To transport provisions for five to six weeks for 50,000 persons is as good as impossible; the grain itself would require some 3,000 double-team wagons, which form a march length of 27 miles.[2] We have an indication, however, that Germanicus was able to make use of the water route for this campaign as well. Tacitus reports that at the beginning of the expedition Germanicus reconstructed a fort on the Taunus Mountain that had already been erected by his father and later destroyed. It has been customarily assumed that this fort was the Saalburg, and that is not entirely impossible.

The road at that time probably passed from the Main-Nidda valley into the valley of the Lahn across the Taunus pass, which was protected by this fort. Germanicus may have moved out directly from Mainz with only a part of his army, while the other part accompanied the supply train from Coblenz up the Lahn. Through the approach of the Roman main body over the Taunus this detachment was indirectly protected against an attack by German bands that would have been too large for it; and the Roman units may already have joined forces by the time they reached Weilburg. Now the Romans were able to transport their provisions to Marburg via the Lahn, which is very usable for this purpose, and from the bend of the Lahn north of Marburg it is only 20 more straight-line kilometers to the Eder. The Saalburg on the Taunus, 70 kilometers in a straight line from Mainz, would consequently have been charged with keeping the pass open for the return of the Roman army, with stocking certain supplies, and with making as difficult as possible any future traffic between the Germans north and south of the mountain.

Even if such a sequence is not entirely impossible, it is not exactly probable. There is another place where the establishment of a fort "*in monte Tauno*" ("on Mount Taunus") lends itself much better to the concept of a campaign from Mainz to the Eder. That is the town of Friedberg, which stands on a ridge that can still be considered part of the

Taunus and along which the great Roman high road later ran from Mainz through the Wetterau in the direction of the Eder. Friedberg is situated on a small stream, the Uhse, which has a moderate slope and can be used in the spring by small vessels. Toward the north the ridge has a steep incline, and a castle was situated there in the Middle Ages. Therefore, this stronghold would have been the counterpart to Aliso: the advanced depot still reachable via the water route. It is only some 55 miles from here to the Eder — seemingly only a short distance, but for a large army under the conditions existing in Germany an expedition that could be carried out only with unusual preparations and effort.

While Germanicus overran the Chatti from the southwest, Caecina simultaneously marched with the legions of the lower Rhine from Vetera up the Lippe and prevented the Cherusci from coming to the aid of the Chatti. The Chatti did not risk approaching his army. Caecina fought a battle with the Marsi, whose land had been overrun the previous year.

When he returned from this expedition, Germanicus received emissaries from Segestes, who reported to him that their prince had again dissociated himself from Arminius, who was then besieging him. Segestes requested help from the Romans. The Roman commander set out at once, moved up along the Lippe route again, drove off Segestes' enemies, and escorted him with his followers to the Rhine. Since Tacitus makes no mention of an actual battle with the Cherusci, the stronghold in which Segestes was besieged must have been situated at the very border of the Cherusci territory. If Germanicus had driven more deeply into the wooded mountains of the Cherusci, it is hard to believe that Arminius would have let him return again without a fight. Such an undertaking would also have required very extensive preparations and equipment. Since we hear in the following year that the Germans were besieging Aliso, we must assume that during the year 15 A.D. this stronghold had been reconstructed by the Romans and established as a supply depot, probably while Caecina was in the area and could protect the construction. Without the use of a well-stocked depot on the upper Lippe, such an expedition could not have been improvised at all. The stronghold of Segestes was probably no other than Teutoburg (Grotenburg), no more than 14 miles from Aliso. Consequently, it was no great undertaking, but nevertheless the garrison of Aliso was not sufficient. A real army had to be sent out to scare off the Cherusci, who had their principal area on the far side of the Weser, extending into the Harz Mountains (Hildesheim, Braunschweig).

THE PRINCIPAL CAMPAIGN OF THE YEAR 15 A.D.

The spring campaign had not only sorely beset the German tribes between the Lippe and the Main, but it had also served to prepare for a second, larger campaign by enabling the reconstruction of Aliso. Whereas in that first campaign the two halves of the Roman army had worked together only indirectly, now the entire united Roman power was to fall with crushing effect, first on one of the German tribes, the Bructeri, north of the Lippe, and then to turn against the Cherusci themselves.

Germanicus embarked the smaller half of his army, four legions, and sailed with them through the Drusus Canal into the North Sea and then up the Ems, in order to attack from the north the Bructeri, who lived on both sides of the upper Ems, while Caecina moved out from the Lippe route with the other half of the legions from the south, from Vetera. The cavalry marched along a special route through the region of the Friesians. We have not been given a reason for their not moving with Caecina's legions. At any rate, this separation of forces indicates that the Romans did not expect an attack while west of the Ems. (See Figure 3 on page 104.)

By time and space considerations, it would, of course, have been much more advantageous to have the whole army move out from Vetera in several parallel columns. Since the Germans did not accept battle in the open field and did not allow themselves to be surrounded, it made no real difference whether the Romans all came from one direction or from various sides. But the great advantage of the divided expedition was that Germanicus could take along his provisions by ship. We may assume that, while he was still some distance from the Bructeri, perhaps in the vicinity of Meppen, at the confluence of the Hase and the Ems, he left the major portion of his fleet, together with the provisions necessary for the return, in a fortified camp and took along for the march up the Ems only a number of special flat-bottomed boats, which carried his provisions.

According to Tacitus, the Roman armies now joined forces on the Ems, but we will have to understand this junction only as an establishing of contact and not as a real blending of the two. An actual joining of the armies would have contradicted the purpose of the war. As long as there was no prospect of fixing the Germans for a battle, it was less important to keep the troops together than to spread them out in order to be able to sweep through, destroy, and plunder the widest possible area. The larger the region that was covered, the greater the probability of capturing the

hidden belongings of the enemy. The extended formation not only covered more ground but also increased the effect. The only concern was to
be careful that each column remained strong enough to be able to withstand independently an attack by the Germans. Tacitus goes on to
report that the entire country between the Lippe and the Ems was laid
waste. Here, too, we are not to understand this statement as meaning the
Romans had limited themselves strictly to the area between these two
rivers, for after all, at their sources, the area is hardly 9 miles wide. Tacitus' source probably named the area between the Lippe and the Ems
particularly, since it was principally there that the Bructeri had their
dwelling places, but their area also included the wooded mountains
directly to the north and the valley between them in which Osnabrück is
situated. The Romans probably also combed these regions as best they
could.

As the Roman armies moved through the territory along the Osning
and came to the sources of the Ems and the border of the Bructeri, they
arrived in the vicinity of the Varus battlefield. Germanicus had also
approached very close to this place a few months earlier, when he had
liberated Segestes, but he had not gone all the way to it. The question
has been asked as to why he did not then carry out his act of piety. The
explanation is clear enough. True, the Dören pass is only some 14 miles
from Aliso and only about 5 miles from the Teutoburg, to which the
Romans were very close when they relieved Segestes. In order to carry
out the formal burial completely, however, Germanicus had to go to
Varus' summer camp by the Westphalian Gate. That would have been
three or four days' march from Aliso, since they would have had to move
in that area with extreme precaution. The gathering of the bones and the
formal burial required several days. Consequently, the entire expedition
could not have been carried out in less than ten to twelve days, and for a
large army that would have called for very extensive preparations. Most
of all, however, Germanicus did not wish simply to seek out the scene of
the catastrophe hastily, bury the dead, and retire. More importantly, he
wanted to combine the act of piety with a campaign that through its positive success would once again establish the prestige of the Romans and
wipe out the shame of Varus' defeat. Now, after he had inflicted heavy
punishment on one of the tribes involved and had driven it almost entirely from its territory, he appeared at the scene of death, the conqueror
against whom the Germans no longer risked defending their home territory. He buried the remains of those who had fallen and erected a burial
mound for them.

Fig. 3   LOCATION OF ALISO

Tacitus reports that, when they had arrived at the border of the Bructeri region, Caecina was sent out in advance to reconnoiter the wooded
mountains and to build causeways and bridges through the swamps and
the moors. This account in no way eliminates the possibility that a portion of the Roman army simply marched over the old road from Aliso
through the Dören pass, since the Senne, the stretch of land directly
below the Teutoburger Forest, is heath and moor and at that time was
probably even more swampy than today, and the Germans had probably
destroyed the earlier Roman causeways and bridges. In any case, only a
part of the Roman army followed this route. The northern column prob-

ably moved through the Bielefeld pass, where, for lack of any earlier installations, new works were necessary. It has even been claimed in recent times that traces of Caecina's constructions have been discovered.

Up to now we have heard nothing of Arminius' activity. And if Tacitus goes on to say that Germanicus now followed Arminius into trackless terrain and waged an undecisive battle with him, that still does not tell us much, for he does not indicate the direction in which Arminius retired and the Romans followed him. The only reference point that we have is that Germanicus finally led his army back to the Ems. If the Romans had followed the Cherusci across the Weser, Germanicus would certainly not have withdrawn to the Ems but would have taken the much shorter route to Aliso, where he had his depot and could comfortably move the troops back on the Lippe route to the Rhine. We must assume, then, that it is much more likely, in accordance with their nature, that the Germans did not assemble in front of the Romans but behind them, as they marched through the Teutoburger Forest to the Westphalian Gate. Consequently, from the Westphalian Gate Germanicus turned again to the west and sought to catch Arminius in the Wiehen Mountains and the Osning. Presumably, one portion of the Romans moved between the mountain ranges in the direction from Rehme toward Osnabrück, while another marched north of the mountains in the direction from Minden to Bramsche. When the army had approached Aliso on the march out, the supply columns were probably replenished at that place so that they were able to march a rather long way into the countryside. Nevertheless, Arminius succeeded in evading the Romans, and so in the end, when the supply columns were becoming empty, there was nothing else for Germanicus to do but take up the withdrawal. With half of his army he moved to the Ems and traveled home by ship. Presumably from the camp near Meppen, whether it may have been on the Ems or on the Hase, provisions had already been sent forward for the army. The cavalry, which had crossed through the territory of the Friesians on the march out — possibly on the Emmerich-Rheine or Arnheim-Lingen route — now had to accompany Germanicus' move as far as the point of embarkation because of the proximity of the German forces. Since the ships could not accommodate the cavalry and the direct route homeward was blocked by the Bourtang Moor, the cavalry returned by detouring to the north of this obstacle and moving along the seacoast to the Rhine.[3]

After the Roman army had split up, the other half, under Caecina, took the direct land route to Vetera. Now the moment had come for Arminius to act. Caecina's corps had to cross a very dangerous pass, a causeway or corduroy road leading through wooded hills, which had been built a few years earlier by the Roman commander L. Domitius Aheno-barbus. Every effort has been made to find these long bridges, as the Romans called this route, but without any success to date. There are too many of the old corduroy roads, and such installations have recently been discovered even in West Prussia, where the Romans never penetrat-ed. According to the strict interpretation of Tacitus' text, we would have to assume that the Roman army marched as a whole up to the Ems and did not separate until reaching that point. Following this account, the long bridges must therefore have been situated to the left of the Ems, somewhere near Coesfeld. But, as we have seen, Tacitus does not offer us a firm enough basis for such definite interpretations. It seems in no way impossible that Caecina may already have split off from Germanicus much sooner and that the long bridges were situated near Iburg, south of Osnabrück.[4]

This topographical question is not very important for our understand-ing of military history. The only important point is that Germanicus, with his huge army of eight legions and support troops probably totaling 50,000 men, did not succeed in forcing the Germans to a large-scale tacti-cal decision or in surrounding them. Quite to the contrary, when the Romans were forced to divide their army and start their withdrawal because of supply considerations, Arminius found the right place and the right moment to attack one of the corps, that of Caecina. According to the Romans' own report, Arminius brought them into the most precar-ious situation, and they would have suffered the fate of Varus if the Germans' lack of discipline and their greed had not thwarted Arminius' plan. They allowed themselves to be persuaded by another prince of the Cherusci, Inguiomerus, an uncle of Arminius, to storm the Roman camp. In doing so, they were defeated by Caecina, who, as a veteran soldier, knew what had to be done and made a sortie at the right moment, just as Caesar had done at Alesia. The Germans suffered a serious defeat. Ger-manicus' part of the Roman army on the fleet also suffered considerable losses from storms and bad weather but finally, like Caecina, reached home base successfully.

EXCURSUS

1. The fort "*in monte Tauno*" that, according to Tacitus, *Annals* 1. 56, Germanicus built before he moved out against the Chatti, was the reconstruction of an old installation of Drusus. Now Dio Cassius reports, 54. 33, in the same

sentence in which he recounts the construction of Aliso, that Drusus had erected another fort on the Rhine among the Chatti. This seems to lead to the presumption that this stronghold was precisely the one that Germanicus reconstructed, but in that case, if Dio Cassius is not mistaken, it had to be on the Rhine. For this reason, scholars have recently hit upon Hofheim, 9 miles from Mainz, in the direction of Höchst, somewhat north of the Main, where traces of a very old Roman installation have been discovered. If that is correct, then this stronghold, which was so close to the principal fort, would have had no particular importance. Precisely for this reason, however, it would also probably not have been mentioned in the sources. Furthermore, it cannot even be said that Hofheim is situated on the Rhine. According to his text, we would have to interpret Dio Cassius' reference as applying to a bridgehead, such as Kastell, for example.

I would prefer another interpretation. After all, let us not forget that as a source Dio Cassius is not original but derives from earlier reports. It is entirely possible that in his own source he found that Drusus, after he had returned to the Rhine from his Lippe campaign, during which he built Aliso, also built a fort among the Chatti. From this finding Dio Cassius may have jumped to the conclusion that he had built a fort on the Rhine. Finally, the identification of this fort with the one constructed by Germanicus is, after all, only a supposition.

That Friedberg is really the installation in question is to a degree confirmed through the excavations, since at that point old artifacts of the time of Augustus have been found: coins of that period, potsherds with the stamp of the ceramist Ateius, who worked at that time, a sword scabbard from a factory in Baden in Switzerland, which also was flourishing in the first half of the century. See the article by Eduard Anthes in the *Minutes of the General Meeting of the Union of German Historical Associations (Protokollen der Generalversammlung des Gesamtverbands der deutschen Geschichtsvereine)*, 1900, pp. 65 ff.

If Friedberg is the place we are seeking, the question arises as to why the Romans did not move farther up the Wetter as far as possible into the country, as they did on the Lippe. A combination of factors may have been responsible, but particular note should be taken of the fact that only smaller expeditions were made along this route, whereas the route on which the Romans went farther and over which they intended to conduct their large-scale warfare was the Lippe route. From here they could move into the Weser region, where they could take advantage of the fleet and, with its support, could move on to the Elbe. Consequently, it was here that they were obliged, to the extent that it was at all possible, to move ahead and to accept the risk of the difficulty of relief operations that might be required. The task was easier in the Wetterau because with their advanced post they could remain closer to their base.

2. According to Tacitus, *Annals* 1. 56, while on the move against the Chatti in the year 15 A.D., Germanicus came to the Adrana (Eder), where young German men, after swimming the river, tried in vain to prevent the Romans from building their bridge. Whereas this event is customarily placed in the region of Fritzlar, Knoke would have it take place in the region of Kassel on the Fulda.[5] According to him, the Eder does not contain enough water for such a swim, and the Romans had perhaps considered the Eder as the principal river and had also given the same name to the lower Fulda. In opposition to this viewpoint, we can

argue that the Eder is a river with swift-flowing water, so that at times it has a very great depth. The spring of the year in question was, as Tacitus adds, unusually dry, but it is conceivable, in keeping with his account, that the rain which was expected had actually come before the fight on the Eder.

Finally, here we very possibly have simply a Roman exaggeration. The sense here is that *"quod imbecillum aetate ac sexu"* ("all frail by age or sex") fell into the hands of the Romans and only the *juventus* (youths) had saved themselves by swimming. We may confidently suppose that the river also did not prevent many of the *imbecillum* (frail) of the Chatti from escaping.

3. Tacitus (*Annals* 1. 57) recounts the relief of Segestes in such a way that we can also understand that it happened along the route in the direction from Mainz to the Eder. Not long after the Romans withdrew to the Rhine, he says, the messengers came from Segestes, and Germanicus found it worth the effort to turn around. "Germanicum pretium fuit, converte agmen." ("It was worthwhile for Germanicus to retrace his march.") After we understand how much work it was to march with an army from Mainz to the Eder, it is no longer necessary to prove that Germanicus could not have taken up this route again immediately. Even if Segestes' stronghold had been situated on the Diemel, the Romans could not have brought him relief from Mainz in an improvised campaign. Therefore, Germanicus did not have that portion of the army which he commanded personally up to that point turn about again, but rather Caecina's corps, which, after all, had operated along the Lippe. The supplies stored in the reconstructed base of Aliso enabled the commander to order such a movement without further ado.

Koepp, in *The Romans in Germany (Die Römer in Deutschland)*, 1905, p. 34, believes it possible that Germanicus carried out the relief of Segestes along the route from Mainz. He assumes that the Roman army had not yet returned to the Rhine but had only just started back and was still perhaps on the Eder, whereas Segestes' stronghold was on the Diemel. And so the route to be covered for the relief of his position was perhaps only half as long as the move back to Mainz. According to Koepp, we cannot therefore say the expedition was impossible, and the text of Tacitus' account shows that Germanicus' army and not Caecina's accomplished the relief. Nevertheless, the Roman army had to have something to eat not only on the march out but also on the return march. The march to the Diemel would therefore have required 50 percent more provisions than were planned for the original campaign, completely aside from the fact that it is extremely unlikely that the Cherusci area extended up to the Diemel. Anyone who estimates the importance of the supply factor for the Roman armies in the Germanic campaigns any differently than I do may also believe in the expedition by Germanicus for the relief of Segestes across the Eder. But anyone who, like Koepp, recognizes in principle the decisive importance of the supply factor and has acknowledged it cannot also accept on this point the text of Tacitus' account.

Kessler, in *The Legend of Germanicus (Die Tradition über Germanicus)*, through his source analysis, gives an excellent explanation of how the confusion originated in Tacitus. (See Chapter VI, Excursus 5.)

NOTES FOR CHAPTER V

1. Müllenhoff, in *Germania*, pp. 436 and 545, has sought explanations for such an apparently incredible error and has made various suggestions; nonetheless, he finally arrives at the conclusion that Tacitus had erroneous geographical concepts. Bremer's attempt in his "Ethnography of the Germanic Tribes" ("Ethnographie der germanischen Stämme"), *Pauls Grundriss*, to bring order to this confusion by shifting the peoples has also failed to have any satisfying result.

2. See in the last chapter of this volume "Provisions and Train."

3. Knoke has already correctly explained the sequence of events in this manner.

4. General F. Wolf, in *The Feat of Arminius (Die That des Arminius)*, has determined that the region of Iburg corresponds in every respect to Tacitus' description. Caecina would then have split off from Germanicus near Osterkappeln or Bramsche.

5. *The Campaigns of Germanicus (Die Kriegszüge des Germanicus)*, p. 39.

# Chapter VI

# Climax and End of the War

We have seen what importance the fort of Aliso had for the Romans'
conduct of war. Arminius opened the next campaign in the year 16 A.D.
with an attempt to capture it, but when Germanicus approached with six
legions, Arminius did not stand for a battle. Instead, he gave up the
siege, withdrew, and once again turned over the initiative to the
Romans.

Tacitus' report on this year's campaign is even more uncertain than
the one just described. Indeed, it contains such a strong inherent contradiction that, without a thorough correcting, it has to remain completely
incomprehensible. Tacitus tells us at first quite clearly how Germanicus
judged the strategic situation. In pitched battle and in the open field he
defeated the Germans; they were helped by forests and swamps, the
short summer, and the early winter. The Roman soldier was less vulnera-
ble to wounds than to marches and the loss of materials. Gaul was
becoming tired of providing horses. The endless columns of trains offered
the opportunity for ambushes and were difficult to defend. If one moved
by water, however, one arrived at the desired place suddenly and unexpectedly. One could start the war sooner and transport legions and supplies together; in this way cavalrymen and horses could arrive fresh and
ready for action in the middle of Germany. Taking all these things into
consideration, Germanicus had a fleet of 1,000 ships built. According to
Tacitus, he traveled up the Ems, just as he had done previously, and
moved by land over the long stretch from the Ems to the Weser.[1] The
great difference from the previous campaign would have been that not
just half but the whole army was moved by ship. The Roman army
would not have been able to gain from this change, however, since the
concentration in one spot necessarily made movements much more awk-
ward than in the previous year, when Caecina's corps was based on the

Lippe. In fact, Germanicus' actions become completely incomprehensible when we remember that previously he was already near Aliso with six legions. From here to the Weser he would not have had more than four days' march. And he is supposed to have moved back, embarked on the fleet in order to travel to the Ems, from which, on the north side of the mountain, he had at least eight to ten days' march to the Weser? That would have been an unusual way of sparing the horses and of bringing troops fresh into the middle of Germany.

Furthermore, Tacitus recounts nothing whatever of the march from the Ems to the Weser but has the army arriving at the Weser directly after it supposedly landed on the bank of the Ems.

There can be only *one* explanation that will clear up this confusion: that is, that Tacitus confused the names of the Ems and the Weser. We know that Drusus and Tiberius had already sailed into the Weser and the Elbe. We know, too, that the Chauci at the mouth of the Weser remained loyal to the Romans and that, even after Varus' defeat, until 14 A.D., a Roman garrison remained in their territory (see above, p. 66). In a speech that Tacitus has Arminius making to his compatriots later, he reports him as saying that the Romans had chosen the detour by way of the sea so that nobody could engage them immediately on their arrival and that, if defeated, they could not be pursued. This speech would have made no sense if the Romans had made the long overland march from the Ems. We have already cited above (p. 97) another passage, where it is shown that Tacitus had no concept of the geographical relationship of the German rivers, since he reports an army marching from the Ems to the Rhine as coming to the Weser. There can be no doubt that here, too, there has been a confusing of the rivers. Germanicus did not sail into the Ems but into the Weser and disembarked there, on the immediate border of the Cherusci territory. Certainly, however, it was not the entire Roman army that made this expedition by sea but only a part of it, be it four or even only two legions. Two legions appears a somewhat small number, but it is almost necessarily correct. It would be very hard to understand the effort that would have been required to have even only a part of the six legions at Aliso make the march to the Rhine and then the movement by sea in order to bring them to the Wesphalian Gate via the Weser.[2] For Tacitus, whose entire attention was concentrated on the person of Germanicus, it is not so unreasonable that he neglected to mention the part of the army not under Germanicus' command, which, of course, was the considerably larger one but to which nothing worthy of recounting happened. It is testimony to Germanicus' qualities of leadership that he took upon himself the command of the fleet as the most difficult and most important part of the campaign, even though only the smaller part of the army took this route.

The entire purpose of the seaborne expedition was to bring up a floating supply depot to the Weser. The troops accompanying the expedition were necessary only for security. If there were actually only two legions, it is, of course, possible that precisely these two legions were at full strength and only the six other ones had left behind the necessary garrison troops for the forts and the Rhine border. Furthermore, the two legions may well have had a particularly strong contingent of allies with them, who were joined on the Weser by the Chauci. Later, Tacitus expressly reports (2. 23) that for the return Germanicus sent a part of his army overland to its winter quarters.

I therefore assume that, while Germanicus moved up the Weser with a larger or smaller part of his army, the other part marched toward him over the Aliso-Dören pass route. The two parts of the army joined up somewhere on the middle Weser, perhaps near Minden.

The long time during which the main part of the army remained at Aliso and waited for the fleet to appear on the Weser was used to link this area with the Rhine by means of a firm, direct road and thereby to secure the Aliso region.[3]

If by our correction we have found an obvious and clear basic strategic idea for the campaign, the continuing sequence is in no way clearly recognizable. Tacitus reports that Germanicus defeated the Germans in two great battles, at Idistaviso beside the Weser, and again near the bank that separated the Angrivarii from the Cherusci. Although very good topographical reference points seem to be given here, the interrelationship of the movements is so unclear that scholars do not know whether they should place the battles on the right or the left bank of the Weser and whether the second battle took place on the continuing march forward or on the Romans' march back. The great successes which the Romans claimed to have gained appear extremely questionable, since they brought no benefits. Moreover, according to Tacitus' own later account, Arminius appears in his fight against Marobodus not as a man who had been conquered by the Romans but rather as one who had conquered them. The details of the battle accounts are not only unclear and contradictory but also completely impossible from a tactical standpoint. I shall treat this point in detail later. The battles lose their general interest for us, for from the start I feel obliged to question their very existence.

How in the world is Arminius supposed to have been able to face the united Roman force in a pitched battle? Up to now we have come to know the Cherusci prince as a man who very correctly judged the strengths and weaknesses of the Romans. He avoided open battle and awaited the opportunity for surprise attacks. This analysis still holds true, even if we assume that in the meantime, by diplomatic means, Arminius had greatly extended his confederation and had at his disposal a much larger army than in the previous year. This year the Romans did not have the extremely large train of supply columns that would have facilitated German ambushes. When the Cherusci evaded them, the Romans could do nothing else but move through their territory, to plunder it and lay waste. In order to be able to carry that out with a relative degree of advantage, they had to divide up their army. Under any circumstances, this would have given the Germans more advantageous opportunities to fight than in a defensive battle against the entire Roman army, which, with its large, probably overwhelming, numerical superiority, could have outflanked the Germans wherever they were and perhaps destroyed them.

That the Romans achieved large, decisive victories is impossible from the further sequence of events, which shows nothing of such victories, and also from Tacitus' own later account, in which Arminius continuously appears as an unconquered person.[4] That the Romans were defeated is likewise impossible, since in that case not many of them would have returned to the Rhine. That two great battles were fought but with both remaining undecisive is also impossible. In the first place, indecisive battles, whenever there have been actual large battles on other occasions, have necessarily been very costly in their losses, so costly in fact that this would have had to show somewhere even in a completely one-sided account such as that of Tacitus. Second, a truly large battle in which the Romans were not victorious would have been for them the equivalent of a full strategic defeat. They had their entire force on the spot. Their absolute certainty of victory with this force in pitched battle was the basis not only of their conduct of war but of their entire political posture, not only with respect to the Germans but also, we may say, throughout the world.

I therefore relegate the two great battles of Idistaviso and the Angrivarii bank to the realm of fables. The Roman account is not sufficient to prove it to us credibly, since the results do not confirm it and all objective considerations speak against it. There may have been small fights. The supposition has been expressed that Tacitus' direct or indirect source for this campaign of Germanicus was a poem. I confess that this hypothesis seems to me very probable.[5] The account is full of adventurous episodes and colorful scenes, as would be appropriate for the composer of a war epic: the conversation between Arminius and his brother Flavus across the river; Germanicus' nocturnal stroll through his camp, where he overhears his soldiers speaking his praises; the Odysseyan stories of the return voyage over the sea. On the other hand, the strategic and geographical relationships are neglected in such a way as to appear almost impossible in the writings of a prose reporter.

I therefore discard all these details, but I believe that, despite everything, it is not impossible to arrive at the strategic context and to reconstruct it from analysis of the general situation.

After all, we are not dealing with an improvised stroke that might have been undertaken unthinkingly on the basis of false reports. Rather, we are concerned with a campaign plan which the most expert and experienced men analyzed and established from a broad viewpoint in all its details. Even if Germanicus was a young man whose personal competence may be exaggerated by our sources, there is still no doubt that Augustus and Tiberius, both of whom were keen judges of human nature, provided him a general staff of the most experienced officers. Likewise, there can be no doubt that the war plan was not only agreed on at the army headquarters but was also presented to Tiberius for his approval. But Tiberius was such an oustanding general and had such a good knowledge of Germany that we may assume the war plan was worked out wisely and logically. If on the basis of definitely reported facts various logical possibilities result, then we cannot arrive at a decision. As far as I can see, however, and as far as there has appeared in the various writings to date, only a single possibility can explain the overall context on the assumption of a carefully planned strategy. We must therefore work with this one possibility.

When Segestes went over to the Romans, he suggested to them, according to Tacitus (*Annals* 1. 58), that he might intermediate between them and his fellow countrymen.

Even if we did not have this positive information, we would have to assume that Segestes made that statement. It is a common illusion of *émigrés,* wherever we may find them in history — from Hippias, the tyrant of Athens, up to the French nobility in the Revolution and the German Republicans in 1848 — that they have always lived in exile with the thought that a large body of followers at home was only awaiting their return in order to join them. After Segestes, his brother Sigimer, too, went over to the Romans at the end of 15 A.D. We may believe that these Cherusci princes suggested to Germanicus that if he only appeared on the Weser with an imposing army, they would guarantee that the Cherusci would abandon Arminius and would come over to them and the Romans. In fact, not only *may* we assume that such a factor played a part in Germanicus' campaign plan, but such an assumption is unavoidable. If that had not been the case, the shift of the theater of operations to the territory of the Cherusci would have been an obvious mistake for the Romans. In the years 14 and 15 A.D., the Romans had most severely ravaged the territories of the Marsi, the Bructeri, the Chatti, and presumably also those of the smaller tribes living between them. We can hardly see how the Bructeri could have survived such an overrunning of their territory as in the year 15. If the Romans had repeated these actions several years in sequence, the tribes involved would necessarily have starved or emigrated — or have been subjugated. In this way, the Romans would undoubtedly have moved forward step by step from the Rhine to the Weser. By now allowing these tribes to recover somewhat and join forces with the Cherusci, the Romans were being negligent on both sides — unless they had the prospect of subjecting the Cherusci in a single campaign. It could not be assumed that this could happen as a result of large battles. Germanicus was no more in a position now than in 15 A.D. to force Arminius into battle, and certainly no large battles took place. But in Germanicus' retinue we find Flavus, the brother of Arminius, and as we may conclude, even if Tacitus does not mention it, also Segestes, Arminius' father-in-law, and the latter's brother Sigimer. If these three Cherusci princes should succeed in creating a split in their tribe and in bringing even a part of the tribe over to the side of the Romans, then Arminius could certainly not hold out. He would finally either have been turned over to the Romans or have fled across the Elbe. The Cherusci under other leaders would have been received and pardoned by the Romans, and this success would certainly have affected the tribes between the Weser and the Rhine in favor of the Romans. With a single stroke the Roman hegemony would have been established up to the Elbe.

We may discern a rejection of this policy in the supposed conversation between Arminius and his brother Flavus across the Weser. We should not be led astray by Arminius' alleged assumption of the initiative thereafter; psychologically, that is most unlikely. If the entire story of that conversation is not pure fiction, it is the poetically biased account of the fact that not only was there fighting but also negotiating. We do not know how far these negotiations proceeded, but we may consider it impossible that Segestes should not have made any attempt whatever to carry out his promise of mediation, which would have put him back in power in his own principality. Otherwise no mention of Segestes' proposal would have appeared in the Roman account.

It may seem foolhardy to inject into a campaign an idea which is not mentioned directly in our source. Whoever so wishes may consider it as only an hypothesis. However, only by inserting such a factor does the otherwise obvious error of Germanicus in attacking the Cherusci before finishing off the Marsi and Bructeri disappear. We now, on the other hand, may say: a Roman commander seriously interested in accomplishing great feats could hardly have acted differently than Germanicus did. But since the political prerequisite on which his campaign was based gave way, so too did the great undertaking also have to fail. The Cherusci must have found themselves in rather dire straits and have been strongly tempted, but Arminius' personality was strong enough to keep them on his side and to maintain their morale despite the defection of so many nobles of the tribe. This is a situation similar to Antony's campaign against the Parthians. The Roman armies successfully joined forces at the Westphalian Gate on the Weser and also probably penetrated more deeply into the Cherusci territory and perhaps across the Leine or even as far as the Aller, on which rivers their floating depot once again could rejoin the army. Since the Roman faction among the Chersuci did not show itself or did not accomplish anything and since in fact the Angrivarii, on the middle Weser between the Chauci and the Cherusci, once again rebelled, the Roman armies had to turn back again. As the reason for the withdrawal, Tacitus mentions only the fact that the summer had ended. This reason has been challenged, since Germanicus, as Tacitus reports, still undertook an extensive double expedition against the Chatti and the Marsi in the same fall. If he had really sailed back on the Ems, as has been believed up to now, the suspicion would be justified. If we shift the entire expedition to the Weser, however, then everything straightens out. The Roman commander could not possibly let things reach the point of running into autumn storms on the North Sea with his gigantic transport fleet. Since he nevertheless was exposed to a storm, we may presume that he waited in Cherusci territory somewhat too long in view of the great distance to be covered, perhaps into September, still hoping to tame the Germans. Even if he was back on the Rhine no earlier than the end of September, he could still very well carry out in October the two expeditions against the border tribes.

It seems natural that Tacitus tells us nothing of the political factor in the strategic idea of the campaign if we accept as his source a war epic, with which such an account in prose is at odds from the very start. But even if this hypothesis should be unfounded, the omission is still sufficiently explained through his tendency to glorify Germanicus. By stating that aspect of the situation, he would, of course, also have had to admit the failure. But the war was supposed to appear as a success, and the author did indeed succeed in giving this impression. The Cherusci were supposedly defeated almost to the point of annihilation in two great battles, and the Romans returned to the Rhine only because of the season, which was known to prevent a Roman army's remaining in the interior of Germany.

For our part, here we recognize once again what it meant for a Roman army to take up a position in the interior of Germany. Not even now, after two campaigns successful in the military sense, could Germanicus risk spending the winter, say in Aliso, much less in the Weser region; he had to move back to the Rhine. As long as the Bructeri and Marsi on the north and south of the Lippe had not been subjugated and made to recognize the Roman domination, a winter camp at the sources of the Lippe brought so much danger, discomfort, and small losses that the result was not worth the cost.

## END OF THE WAR

If we survey the results of all of Germanicus' campaigns, it is clear that this last and largest one, even though the Romans held the upper hand militarily, was for the most part a failure. Nevertheless, it was not entirely fruitless. Tacitus reports that the Angrivarii finally submitted to the Romans and, in order to gain the favor of the Romans, even ransomed and brought back Roman prisoners held among other tribes. Since the Friesians and Chauci already were allied with the Romans, the latter would now have had a position on the Weser from which they could exert extreme pressure on the Cherusci. We may be allowed to doubt the subjugation of the Angrivarii. Since the Chauci were already friends of the Romans and occupied the area up to the mouth of the Elbe, it is difficult to see from which tribes the Angrivarii were supposed to have ransomed the shipwrecked prisoners. However this may have been, the Romans had appeared with a powerful force between the Weser and the Elbe, and even if they had suffered losses through shipwreck on the voyage home, they certainly caused much destruction in the territory of the Cherusci. Nothing could prevent them from returning in the following year.

Caesar, once he was in Gaul, did not leave the country again, even when he had suffered defeats. The Romans had to move time and again out of Germany back to the Rhine because they could not feed themselves in this country of forests and pastures. Had they continued the war still further, first they would presumably not have gone back into the Cherusci area but would have thoroughly defeated the Bructeri and Marsi. Of course, that would have called for a very strong effort; only armies of several legions could risk penetrating farther into the Germanic area. But at the end of his campaigns in Gaul Caesar had had at least eleven or twelve legions, whereas Germanicus had only eight. It is difficult to understand why the Roman Empire would not have been able to send a similar or even larger number of legions across the Rhine many years consecutively or how the Germanic border tribes could have defended themselves against such forces. Every expedition was as costly as it was dangerous, but in no way impossible. In the long run, the opponent who is not strong enough to let events lead to a large-scale tactical decision through a battle between the assembled armies is always doomed to defeat. Added to this is the fact that we see in the case of the Germans, just as previously with the Gauls, all kinds of tendencies toward the formation of a faction favorable to the Romans. Already in the autumn of 16 A.D. a Marsi prince, Malovendus, went over to the enemy of his people and disclosed to the Romans where the Marsi had hidden an eagle taken in the Teutoburger battle. Tacitus' report that the Roman soldiers had no doubt that the enemy was already wavering and considering suing for peace, and that the war could be ended in the next summer, may possibly have a grain of truth — even though we have completely eliminated the two great victories of the Romans over the Cherusci.

The explanation is to be sought not only in the theater of war but, as Ranke has already recognized, in the inner relationships of the leading circles of the empire. Tiberius had become emperor only as a result of adoption; he was not a blood relative of Augustus. Germanicus had the same relationship to Augustus as Augustus had to Caesar: he was the grandson of Augustus' sister and he was married to Agrippina, a granddaughter of Augustus; his and her sons were natural descendants of Augustus. Even if by Roman law an adopted son had the same rights as a real son and Tiberius for his part had adopted Germanicus, still there existed between the emperor and this family a tension which was a source of continuous danger to them. For the sake of his own security, Tiberius could not tolerate the development of a relationship between Germanicus and the legions in Germany in a years-long war similar to the relationship between Caesar and the legions of the Roman Republic in Gaul. The battle of the Teutoburger Forest and Germanicus' three campaigns had shown what a frightfully difficult task the subjugation of these obstinate Germanic sons of nature would be. Only a commander of the highest authority, possessing the most extensive means, given a free hand for many years, could have brought this war to a close. Tiberius had no such commander to send out; indeed, he would not allow himself to send one out. For two years he had watched events, and then he recalled Germanicus and the Germans remained free.

No fact could have been more important for posterity than that the Germans remained outside the circle of Roman domination and did not become Romanized, like the Celts. The causality of this fact can be correctly understood only in its double aspect, as Tacitus, with his penetrating regard for everything important, has already correctly seen. In many details his account is not satisfying to us, and the underlying mood is completely subjective in all its accents. Nevertheless, however he may think, he goes to the bottom of the subject. He has rightfully judged on the one hand that the Romans would have been victorious if Tiberius' suspicions had not been responsible for recalling Germanicus, and on the other hand that Arminius was undoubtedly the liberator of Germany.

After the Teutoburger victory, Arminius had sent Varus' head to Marobodus, king of the Marcomanni. This act can be understood in no other way than that it was supposed to be a call to all the tribes for a general Germanic national struggle against the Romans. Marobodus had declined to go along and had sent Varus' head to Augustus for burial. Precisely through this act we learn of the fact, and it is proven to us beyond doubt. It was not long before the Germans on the one side under Arminius and on the other under Marobodus were fighting against each other. No doubt the leader of the Cherusci, who was allied to the Lombards, was victorious, but he himself was finally killed in this civil war through the treachery of his own relatives. He was their liberator, and the barbarians still praise him in their songs, adds the Roman author who described these events a century later. Is it possible that he nevertheless was then so forgotten among his people and was only brought back to new life 1,500 years later as a result of scholarly studies? Philological flair claims to have found a shimmer of this posthumous fame, which can never really be proven but is in itself of such poetic force that it cannot be ignored.

We do not know the German name of the prince of the Cherusci; it has nothing to do with the word "Hermann." Arminius is the Roman name that was given to him when he visited Rome and was honored with knightly rank. His father, however, was named Sigimer, and among the Germans the son's name is often formed in harmony with that of the father. Could it be possible that Arminius was named Siegfried? In the Nibelungenlied Siegfried's father has the name Sigemund. Another prince of the Cherusci, according to Tacitus, was named Segimundus. There is no doubt that this group of names belongs in Arminius' clan. The Siegfried saga goes back to Germanic mythology. It also contains a relationship to the Roman period, for Siegfried's father had his capital in Xanten, which was of significance only when the large Roman base camp of Vetera was there. Like Arminius, Siegfried dies while still young and at the peak of his development, as a result of the envy and the betrayal of his relatives. His wife remains loyal to him and not to her own relatives. Siegfried's murderer, Hagen, has only one eye, a point that is not mentioned in the Nibelungenlied but does appear in another account. We are told the same thing about Flavus, Arminius' brother, who fought on the side of the Romans. The entire princely family of the Cherusci, except for a son of Flavus who was living with the Romans, was wiped out in the struggles following Arminius' death, as were all the Nibelungen princes.

It would be the most noble of all monuments that a people ever erected to its hero if Arminius is Siegfried and the memory of his personality has lived on in the form of this most irreproachable of all men. Indeed, for an historic person of flesh and blood it would probably be too great. For this reason, it is well that we look on it only as a fable through the veil of a supposition.

## EXCURSUS

CONCERNING THE CAMPAIGN OF 16 A.D.

In order to justify further our concept of the value and the character of Tacitus' *Annals* as an historic source, let us test a few details of his account of the campaign of 16 A.D.

1. Immediately after the landing was completed, we are told that the Angrivarii revolted in the rear of the Romans and that Stertinius was sent with a corps to punish them. In the following fight on the Weser, however, as well as in the battle of Idistaviso, which occurred immediately thereafter, Stertinius was also present.

At the end of the campaign, he was again sent off against the Angrivarii and received their submission. This sequence is not entirely impossible, even if it is extremely questionable that Stertinius would return to the main body of the army before he had quelled the uprising in the army's rear. In any case, the historian, even if he is correct, has left a large lacuna in the account.

Shortly thereafter is the account of the conversation between Arminius and Flavus across the Weser. Scholars have already believed it should be assumed that it was another river, since the Weser is rather wide for such a conversation. In reality, the communication of the Cherusci brothers may well be poetic fiction, which, incidentally, is perhaps to blame for the shifting of the expedition to the Ems. In his source, Tacitus may not have found the name of the river into which Germanicus sailed. However, since it is expressly said later that they crossed over the river, that is, to the enemy side, and the conversation of the Cherusci princes, expressly stated to have been across the Weser, followed the crossing by the Romans, the author concluded that they must have landed on the Ems. Actually, this sequence simply reflects a lapse of attention by the poetic reporter, who first had the Romans crossing the river and then told of the brothers speaking to each other from one bank to the other without suspecting that both were already on the same bank.

We are surprised to read the reproach that Tacitus expresses because Germanicus, instead of landing directly on the enemy bank, first had his troops disembark on the other side and lost several days building a bridge. That can hardly have appeared in an epic dedicated to the praise of Germanicus. But once again this matter can be explained quite well through the confusion of the rivers. If Germanicus sailed up the Weser, it was quite natural that he would land first on the left bank, in order to establish contact near Rehme or Minden with the corps marching up from Aliso. But the epic said nothing of this corps, and Tacitus imagined that the army was landed on the Ems. Of course, it was impossible to find any reason for the landing on the left bank. Tacitus measured his source and his hero independently enough and finally decided after all to inject a word of reproach for such a gross error.

In view of the Germanic battle formation on the far side of the Weser, Germanicus did not risk, according to Tacitus, having his legions cross the river without bridges and defensive positions and only sent the cavalry across, via a ford. This procedure is completely incredible. How then was the cavalry alone supposed to take on the Germans? If we wish to make this action credible, we can only assume that it was not the Germanic army but only a rather strong outpost in position on the far bank and that the cavalry had the mission of driving it off so that the construction of the bridge would not be disturbed. The pompous statement: "Caesar nisi pontibus praesidiisque impositis dare in discrimen legiones haud imperatorium ratus" ("The commander considered it a mark of bad generalship to expose legions in battle, unless bridges and defensive positions had been set up") is nothing but a rhetorical flourish. The fact that Tacitus reports two different instances of bridge construction, across the Ems and across the Weser, in no way indicates that two bridges were actually built. Instead, it may be a question of two references to the same event that, as a result of some lack of clarity in the original source, were interpreted as separate actions.

It was reported to Germanicus that the Germans had chosen a position for the battle and that they would attempt to attack the Roman camp at night. The nocturnal attack is fantasy. Germanicus' army was probably no smaller than 50,000 men, and Arminius' army, even though much smaller, was still much too large to be led in the night like a reconnaissance patrol up to the enemy wall and then to be withdrawn.

To this same poetic fiction belongs the story of the German horseman who during the night dashed up to the enemy camp and, speaking Latin, tried to lure the Roman soldiers to desert. He promised them wives, land, and 100 sesterces at once. The fantasy of this Roman poet was apparently quite meager; it is astonishing that Tacitus repeated such nonsense.

The battlefield of Idistaviso is described to us: "is medius inter Visurgim et colles, ut ripae fluminis cedunt aut prominentia montium resistunt inaequaliter sinuatur; pone tergum insurgebat silva, editis in altum ramis et pura humo inter arborum truncos." ("This is the central area between the Weser and the hills winding here and there, as the banks of the river recede and the spurs of the mountains stand against them. In the rear a forest begins to rise with branches reaching to the heights and unobstructed ground between the trunks of the trees.") This description may be appropriate for a landscape but is very poor for a battlefield. It can be understood in no other way than that one flank of the Germans rested on the river and the other on wooded hills, with a high forest behind them. The flank of a battle formation, however, cannot rest on several bends of the river or several hills, which extend into the open field irregularly at different places. For the main battle position there must always be a single specific point on the river and a single definite hill on which it rests.

The Roman battle formation is described as follows: first, the Gallic and Germanic allies in the front, then dismounted archers, then four legions and, with two Praetorian cohorts and selected cavalry, the commander and then four more legions and the lightly armed troops with the mounted archers and the rest of the allies. It is obvious at first glance that this is no battle formation but at most a misunderstood order of march.

The Cherusci were in position on the hills in order to move down from there to attack the Romans, consequently on their flank. While they were dashing down from the hills, Germanicus ordered the cavalry to attack them from two sides, "*ipse in tempore adfuturus*" ("it would be there at the right moment") — a militarily incomprehensible procedure. To what extent was it possible to attack the Cherusci from two sides? Had the Roman army perhaps already marched by their position so that they attacked it from the flank? Or were the Germans, for their part, so poorly defended on their flanks that they could be quickly enveloped, even by cavalry across wooded hills?

At the same time, the Roman infantry attacked, and advanced cavalrymen closed in on the Germans from the flank and the rear. These advanced cavalrymen cannot, however, have accomplished this envelopment on the battlefield itself, which was bounded on one side by the river and on the other by the mountain. If it was intended to mean that Germanicus had sent a part of his cavalry into the rear of the enemy from a more distant position, Tacitus would have had to mention expressly this maneuver, which would have been as unusual as it was effective. But it is obviously completely wrong to interpret such ingenious operations into his text; we are dealing here with the fantasies of a poet.

In the face of the double attack, the enemy fled, their two parts crossing each other in flight. Those who had been in the forest fled into the open field, and those in the field fled into the forest. In an extreme case, we could imagine this by assuming that there was a Germanic reserve in the forest, which was driven by the Romans' attack from the rear toward the Roman front at the same moment when this front itself was already pushing back the Germans of the first ranks. But we realize immediately that it is love's labor lost to try to introduce a military meaning into these shifting pictures, for we hear later that the Cherusci were driven down from their hills into the middle of these fleeing groups. Previously, we had learned that they had stormed down from the hills and that Germanicus had sent the cavalry out against them. This action can only have taken place on a flank, but now the Cherusci are suddenly in the middle and it is the archers that they have attacked. The archers would have been thrown back if the Celtic auxiliaries had not come to their aid. Now we ask, where were the legions? And we ask that all the more specifically when we hear that Arminius himself was perhaps only saved by the fact that the Chauci recognized him and let him pass. As we heard above, the Roman legions were supposed to be in position behind the archers and the Gallic and Germanic allies. Why did they then not capture the enemy commander?

Almost the entire Germanic army is supposed to have covered the battlefield. The chains with which the barbarians had intended to bind the captured Romans were found later in their camp. We quite often hear of these chains in world military history, for example, in the battle of Ceresole in 1544. In the case of a people that was so poor in iron that they could not even manufacture satisfactory weapons, we may either see in these chains a doubly strong indication of their confidence in victory or, on the other hand, a doubly strong reason for considering the story as invented.

A victory symbol that Germanicus set up so angered the Germans that they once again resorted to arms. Again they chose a battle location which was bounded by a river and forests, and the forests were surrounded by a deep swamp. Since we cannot assume that the Germans took position with their backs against a swamp, the swamp must have been situated in front of the forest, so that it served as the base for their flank. Between the river and the swamp there was a narrow plain that was cut off by a dike, the border fortification of the Angrivarii. That would have given a very definite battlefield, but there is not the slightest connection between this battlefield and the account of the battle. We hear of a plain where the Romans easily penetrated; where was it? We hear of cavalry that was sent against the forest. Consequently, the swamp was after all behind the forest and not in front of it, and the Germans had chosen a position offering no opportunity for withdrawal. The Romans, who were supposed to storm the dike, did not penetrate it. Instead of having them move from that plain around the dike, the commander pulled the legions back and had sharpshooters and slingers work the dike over until the Germans withdrew. Now the battle continued in the forest, and we actually hear that the Germans had the swamp in their rear. But this was not so bad for them, since they had the swamp in their rear in the same way the Romans had the river. The author did not mean to say that both commanders were poor tacticians, but he simply wanted to gain a springboard for his rhetoric: *utrisque necessitas in loco, spes in virtute, salus ex victoria.*

(The dispositions on both sides dictated an all-out battle. Hope lay in their courage, their safety in victory.)

And finally, the battle had no end at all. In the evening, the commander withdrew a legion to erect a camp (strange Roman, who goes into such a battle without previously erecting a camp!), and the remaining legions continued to cut down the enemy into the night. Nevertheless, it is admitted that the cavalry battle remained indecisive. After such a battle account, let one read for direct comparison an actual battle account, for example, Caesar's battle at Pharsalus. Then one knows not only that the cavalry battle cannot remain indecisive if the infantry is winning such a decisive victory, but one also knows that there is not a true word in this whole account of the battle at the dike of the Angrivarii.

2. As an analogy to these battles of Germanicus, we can cite Tacitus' account of Agricola's great victories over the Britons and the two battles of Bedriacum.

The account of the victory over the Britons is in general simple and understandable — but for this very reason it is also obvious that an action that was not very important is presented with the pathos of a great victory. Agricola's 8,000 allied troops, together with his cavalry, were enough to conquer the Britons. The legions, standing in the second echelon or in reserve, did not strike a blow. Tacitus gives as the reason "legiones pro vallo stetere, ingens victoriae decus citra Romanum sanguinem bellanti, et auxilium, si pellerentur." ("The legions stood in front of the camp's rampart as a reserve if the auxiliaries were repulsed. Great would be the glory of victory in a battle won without the spilling of Roman blood.") If we were inclined to take that seriously, we would have to say that Agricola was a quite incompetent commander. The account goes on to say that the Britons had a large numerical superiority and for a time the Romans were hard pressed. That would have been avoided if the commander had not held out such a very large reserve but had instead immediately sent a part of his legions into the fight. Actually, this temporary critical situation probably belongs to the embellishment of the story, just like the reason for holding out the legions and the account of the large number of Britons. The Britons were so weak and gave so little resistance that even the approach march of the first Roman echelon was enough to throw them back, and the situation never developed into a real battle.

We learn even less from the two battles of Bedriacum. Tacitus' entire account of the civil war, which rhetorically is so powerful, is almost worthless from the viewpoint of military history.

In the battle in which they conquered Boadicea, the Romans were, according to Tacitus (*Annals*, 14. 34), 10,000 strong and had 400 killed; the Britons lost something like 80,000. According to Dio Cassius 62. 8, the Britons had a strength of 320,000 men. After all, why not? There are still some scholars, critics with very strong backgrounds, who cannot bring themselves to reject the countless numbers composing the Persian armies, or, if they absolutely cannot avoid it, might be willing to strike perhaps one zero from the number but never two at the same time.

3. In his book *Germanicus' Campaigns in Germany (Die Feldzüge des Germanicus in Deutschland)*, Lieutenant Colonel Dahm has attempted to salvage and clarify from the military viewpoint Tacitus' report on the campaign of 16 A.D.[6] In a review in the *Deutsche Literatenzeitung*, No. 3, 17 January 1903, I have given the following opinion on this book:

The author reconstructs Germanicus' main campaign of 16 A.D. in such a way that the Roman army, in accordance with Tacitus, *Annals* 2. 8, sailed into the Ems and established a large depot at Meppen.' From Meppen it then supposedly marched across the plain to the Weser and fought the battle of Idistaviso south of the Westphalian Gate. For purposes of resupply, columns of provisions were constantly under way between the depot and the army. Dahm estimated that the daily requirement of the army of 100,000 was some 200,000 kilograms for men and horses. Therefore, every six days a column of 12,000 pack animals, taking up 17 kilometers in length if they moved in two files, had to reach the army.

This estimate is much too small. In the first place, the route from Meppen to the place where Dahm assumes the battle of Idistaviso took place is close to 200 kilometers. That would not be six days' march but nine, and twelve days with necessary rest stops. Second, Dahm estimates an average ration of only 5 kilograms per horse and assumes that the necessary hay and straw could be taken from the countryside. That would be impossible with such a huge mass moving in close formation. The provisions that might have been found would have been quickly exhausted. Third, Dahm has forgotten to take into account the supplies for the transport columns themselves (25,000 animals with their drivers). If we consider these three factors, the necessary amount increases perhaps sixfold, and the result is that the means of supply accepted by the author is technically impossible. It is also impossible to imagine that such a large mass of animals could have been transported by ship through the North Sea. Finally, it is impossible strategically that a Roman army operating along the Weser could be based on a depot on the Ems. Nothing in the world would have been easier for Arminius than to have one of the long supply columns attacked and destroyed by a strong force of his men. Then Germanicus and his entire army would have been sacrificed through starvation.

The author rejects emphatically (page 97) the explanation that the Roman fleet with the army did not sail into the Ems but into the Weser, since, according to him, Tacitus' report "is beyond any doubt." On page 93 he presents a notable contradiction to this point by referring to another part of Tacitus' report as "nothing more than idle words stemming from Tacitus' obvious lack of knowledge in the geographical and military areas."

Corresponding to this method of arbitrarily accepting a source as absolutely reliable in one case and rejecting it in another is the explanation that the author (page 95) gives of the fact that Tacitus did not report anything of that supposed march from the Ems to the Weser. The author believes that this march was made in order to punish the Chasuarii and Angrivarii, who lived in this region. He says that Tacitus, however, gives no account of this because "it must after all have become too much even for him to recount time and again the cowardly murders and burnings by his hero, which in the case of these allies of the Cherusci certainly reached an inhumane degree." It would be difficult to misjudge Roman ways and Roman concepts more definitely than this.

Dahm's idea of the 16 A.D. campaign is tenable neither from a military-technical viewpoint nor from critical analysis of the sources. He may indeed have correctly recognized — and this is an important contribution — that the salient point for the Roman campaigns in Germany is to be sought in the question of supply, but his scholarly method is not sufficient for a correct solution. Similar errors to those mentioned above are repeated frequently in the other campaigns as well. (See also "Provisions and Train" at the end of this volume.)

4. Koepp, in *The Romans in Germany (Die Römer in Deutschland)*, perspicaciously recognizes Tacitus' campaign report for 16 A.D. as unreliable. However, he remains cooly skeptical of our attempt to recognize and correct the errors through realization of the strategic basis, with the help of our exact knowledge of the geographical conditions, and he admits a lack of understanding. That is a position which would deserve consideration if it were followed consistently, but in numerous other places Koepp himself cannot refrain from coming to the aid of the source by using strategic reasoning (although often not the correct one). The caution by which he apparently intends to be guided — that we should not try to be wiser than Tacitus (page 34) — could easily be turned against Koepp himself. As an answer to this caution, however, I would like to ask the colleague in question if he has followed my advice (see page 64 above) and has tested his measure for Tacitus as a source in military accounts against Treitschke's description of the battle of Belle Alliance. I fear that he has not done it any more than our older historians tested Herodotus against Bullinger and Caesar against Napoleon and Frederick. If he had done so, I am convinced that his book, as handsome and useful as it is, would have been somewhat different in a number of places.

5. Gerhard Kessler, in *The Germanicus Legend (Die Tradition über Germanicus)*, Leipzig dissertation, 1905, has also sought to clarify the Germanic campaigns through the source analysis method. He assumes that Tacitus' main source was a biography of Germanicus that also formed the basis for Dio Cassius' report. The factual events coincide throughout with those presented in this work, particularly on the point that in 16 A.D. the Roman fleet sailed not into the Ems but the Weser. Kessler cleverly proves that a confusion of names was involved in Germanicus' crossing over the Ems and then over the Weser. However, when Kessler states the opinion that the entire eight legions were transported on this fleet (page 51), he does not realize what is involved in having an army of 50,000 combatants make such a long sea voyage. One cannot, for example, base this theory on the fact that in the previous year Germanicus had already moved four legions by ship and that this time, according to Tacitus' detailed report, he had built many new ships and consequently had moved a considerably larger army on them. Two legions with their support troops and the entire stock of provisions and other supplies that the whole army needed for the entire summer campaign, ships that could sail through the North Sea, and auxiliary ships that could sail as far as possible up the rivers — that is such a massive preparation that Tacitus' account seems fully justified. The four legions in the preceding year were probably without support troops, and it is expressly reported that the cavalry moved by land through the area of the Friesians. And too, this expedition had gone only into the Ems and not, as even Kessler assumes for the new one, into the Weser. Therefore, even if the number of ground troops embarked was smaller, the new expedition was still much more important and necessitated the most extensive preparations.

To transport eight legions with support troops, cavalry, and supplies for an entire campaign from the Batavian Islands into the Weser was not only impossible but also completely unnecessary, since the Roman army could much more quickly and conveniently move into the region of the Cherusci by land over the

shorter distance from the Lippe. The purpose of the great fleet was not the transportation of the army but the moving forward of the supplies on a floating depot,
without which the Roman army could not operate in the territory of the Cherusci. The two legions and support troops with the fleet were needed only for security. Kessler did not give sufficient credit to this importance of the supply factor.
As a result, his strategic analysis is thrown off not only here but also elsewhere,
and he has finally been diverted into a completely unjustified and unfounded
judgment of Germanicus' strategic ability and character. We cannot deny Germanicus credit for bringing the most extreme energy to the execution of his mission. Moreover, the means he employed and the various ways he went about his
task were correctly thought out and corresponded well to the circumstances and
conditions. Indeed, it is only with this recognition that Arminius, too, deserves
his position in world history. If Germanicus had been as short-sighted as Kessler
makes him appear, and if Segestes and his clan had been so insignificant, then
Arminius' achievement would not have meant so much. The decisive point, however, is that by all human measurement Germanicus estimated correctly that, if
he appeared on the Weser with his huge army, with the Cherusci princes allied to
him, and with the supply fleet behind him in a position to support the war for the
entire summer, the Cherusci would regard their cause as lost and would accept
the Roman domination. That this did not occur, however, and that the Cherusci
despite everything continued the fight and held fast to their leader proves to us
much more strongly than the battle in the Teutoburger Forest that Arminius was
a truly great man.

6. LIMITES

　　Tacitus, *Annals*, 2. 7, says "cuncta inter castellum Alisonem ac Rhenum novis
limitibus aggeribusque permunita." ("The whole area between the fort Aliso and
the Rhine was completely built up with new roads and embankments.") Until
now, scholars have tended to think of the *limitibus* as border dikes, but that is a
patent impossibility. In which direction are they supposed to have run? What
were they supposed to limit and what did they protect? Where did the troops
come from who were to garrison such lines? We shall have occasion to speak of
this subject again when we consider the later large *limes*. *Limes* means the border, that is, at the same time a border and a road. However, the word is used so
much in the one sense that we tend to think only of the one meaning and the other one disappears completely. For example, "*aperire limites*," in Velleius, 2.
121, means simply "to establish a border," in which sense Seneca also uses the
expression in *de benef.* 1. 14, even in the restrictive sense "*minus laxum limi-
tem aperire*" ("to establish a less lax boundary"). But Livy 31. 39, has King
Philip marching against the enemy "*transversis limitibus*" ("by oblique
routes"); Cicero, *Somn. Scip.* 8 (*de re publ.* 6. 24), says "*bene meritis de
patria quasi limes ad coeli aditum patet*" ("just as a way to the entrance of
heaven lies open for those who have served their country well"); and Ovid,
*Metam.* 8. 558, even says "*solitus fluminis limes*" ("the usual course of the
river"). Here then, as in many other places, it is nothing more than "route." The
idea that the *limes* was related to a fortification or was in fact a border defense is
a much more recent one, probably of completely modern origin. Now once again
it has been gradually given up as a result of the research on the *limes*.

Tacitus uses the expression seven times: in *Germania* 29, and *Agricola* 41, in the sense of "border"; in *Hist*. 3. 21 and 25, on the battle of Cremona, no matter how one understands the rest of the description, the expression is obviously used in the sense of "route." In *Annals* 1. 50, Germanicus moves against the Marsi "silvam Caesiam limitemque a Tiberio coeptum scindit, castra in limite locat." ("He cut through the Caesian Forest and the road begun by Tiberius, and pitched camp on the road.") Germanicus moved out to the north of the Lippe, then turned southward, crossed the Lippe, and thereafter moved through the Caesian Forest and the *limes* of Tiberius. It is completely impossible to imagine a fortress here. On the other hand, the concept of a road that Tiberius started to build south of and approximately parallel to the Lippe and that they now crossed and on which they built the camp fits very well here.

The seventh citation is precisely ours. In this case, the word *limes* can have nothing to do with a "border." The *aggeres*, an expression used in conjunction with the *limites*, are causeways. In addition, in the citation referred to above concerning the battle of Cremona, it is first a question of the *"agger viae"* ("embankment of the road") (*Hist*. 3. 21 and 23). Directly connected with that is the use of *limes* in the sense of "road," and that is probably what it is here. Elsewhere in Tacitus *permunire* means "to fortify," in which *per* only emphasizes the sense and does not change it. "To fortify" in the sense of "entrenching" cannot be intended here. Perhaps it can be translated as "to secure," in which sense *munire* often occurs, as for example in Pliny, *h. nat*. 20. 51, and Lucretius 4. 1256 (Lachmann) *"gnatis munire senectam"* ("to render old age secure with sons"). However, since the expression *"munire viam,"* "to build a road," is also often used, perhaps our sentence can best be translated as follows: "He built through everything between Aliso and the Rhine with new roads and routes," or in a more natural expression: "He built a continuous firm road from Aliso to the Rhine."

Another interpretation, not entirely impossible, that first occurred to me would be to conceive of the *limites* as clearings of the woods along the road in order to make it more difficult for German ambushes. Since the original meaning of *limes* is "border" and whenever a border ran through a forest certainly it was often marked by a cleared space, this concept would probably not be impossible. But since *limes* so very often appears simply as "route" and even with the word *agger*, this latter interpretation is probably also the right one in the passage under consideration. In any case, the sense of the passage is that Germanicus, while the legions at Aliso were remaining in place and were waiting until the commander sailed into the Weser with the fleet, had the time used for improving the connecting route to the Rhine.

* * *

(Added in the second edition.) The concept developed above has been confirmed in an article prepared with the broadest philological scholarship by Oxé in the *Bonner Jahrbücher*, Vol. 114/115. He, too, explains that Tiberius' *limes* was a military road, which the author assumes to have been very straight and very broad. The construction that Germanicus had carried out in 16 A.D. is for Oxé simply the completion of the road begun by Tiberius. In his opinion, both the essence of the matter and the interpretation of the expression *permunire* point to the idea of the completion of the project. If that should be correct, then Tacitus must have drawn that expression from his source, for he himself hardly had so much appreciation of topography and hardly devoted so much attention to the objective possibilities of the sequence of events to allow him to think of the *limes* of Tiberius in his account of the work of Germanicus. See below the discussion of Domitian's *limites*.

NOTES FOR CHAPTER VI

1. Tacitus 2. 6, recounts the fact that unusually shallow-bottomed vessels were also built as if that was done in consideration of the tides. This can probably be more correctly considered, as Knoke does, as referring to the ships that were to be able to navigate as far as possible up the rivers.

2. It would not be impossible to explain the return march of one part of the army as serving Germanicus as a covering force, since he had personally come with his legions to Aliso, where he reconstructed an old altar that had once been erected in honor of his father and had dedicated it with a festival. In such cases, however, a cavalry unit, which can move quickly, is no doubt a better covering force than the slow-moving legions. Furthermore, it still seems more likely that the six legions were left at Aliso and two were moved by sea.

3. This is the sense of the words "cuncta inter castellum Alisonem ac Rhenum novis limitibus aggeribusque permunita." ("The whole area between the fort Aliso and the Rhine was completely built up with new roads and embankments.") In this connection, see paragraph 3 of the Excursus.

4. This is effectively proved by Paul Höfer in *Germanicus' Campaign of 16 A.D. (Der Feldzug des Germanicus im Jahre 16)*, 1885.

5. Paul Höfer, *Germanicus' Campaign of 16 A.D.*

6. Otto Dahm, Lieutenant Colonel, retired, "Germanicus' Campaigns in Germany" ("Die Feldzüge des Germanicus in Deutschland"), *Westdeutsche Zeitschrift für Geschichte und Kunst*, Ergänzungsheft XI.

7. Even Dahm himself did not entirely reject the impression that establishing a depot at Meppen was basically an impossibility. And he belatedly admits the possibility that the Weser may have been used as a supply route, leaving this point at least as an "open question" (page 100), but without drawing any further conclusions from this.

# SPECIAL STUDY ON THE LOCATION OF ALISO

Aliso has become for us almost the central point for the reconstruction of all the Roman-Germanic campaigns. We must therefore undertake a special investigation of the very controversial question as to the location of this fort. This question has best been left until now, since in doing so the general strategic laws and conditions of this theater of operations naturally come into consideration. These conditions will now be more clearly obvious to the reader, after the discussions of the individual campaigns than after an introductory account of a purely theoretical nature.

For our study, two questions are obvious from the start: the first one is whether the Romans established on the upper Lippe a supply depot that served as a base for their operations in the truly interior part of Germany; the other one is whether this place was called Aliso.

The question that is best considered a prerequisite of any study and of a comparison of the sources is a technical one: how far was the Lippe navigable?

On this point I shall give the information that was very kindly furnished to me by technical experts in the field of waterways, Privy Councillors for Construction Röder and Keller II in the Ministry of Public Works, as well as Construction Engineer Röder in Diez, who was formerly in Hamm on the Lippe.

The difficulty of transporting goods by land before definite roads are built is so great that in ancient times even very small water courses were used for transportation. In the fifteenth century, Herford sought to develop the Werre as a water route, as did Braunschweig the Oker.[1] It is, of course, not easy to move a loaded boat upstream before a tow path is built, but still easier than moving a corresponding number of carts over a soft land route. The boats were pulled by men who normally went along in the water close to the bank. If they came to rapids that could not be passed, the goods were brought ashore and carried as far as necessary, and the empty boats were pulled up and over. This is still done today in Africa. Even such a stream spotted with obstacles is more advantageous than a land route. The Lippe does not have this kind of obstacle; today it has a natural navigability up to Lippstadt. Beyond Lippstadt, the navigability is given up because of dams favoring agriculture. By eliminating these obstacles, however, it could immediately be made navigable again up to Neuhaus, where the Pader and the Alme join the Lippe.[2] The slope from Neuhaus to Lippstadt amounts on the average to one foot in 2,000. The cross-section shows a very deep cut and is therefore very favorable. Hence, with the elimination of the obstacles, barges 20 meters long, 4 meters wide, with a draught of 0.75 meters, having a capacity of 45 tons (100,000 pounds) could travel without difficulty. On the average, such barges would be able to move easily 98 days of the year, to move in a limited way for 101 days, and not to move at all for 166 days — 156 because of insufficient water and 10 days because of too much water. We cannot claim that the German rivers must definitely have had more water in ancient times than they have today. Even without that assumption, however, the above figures leave no doubt that in Arminius' time the Lippe was navigable enough up to Neuhaus for the military purposes of the Romans, who, of course, were able to use much smaller vessels than those described above. In the spring, they could ship necessary supplies for the summer campaign almost up to the river's source.

Now there appears to have arisen an opponent to my concept in a study entitled "Was the Lippe a Navigable Route of Considerable Importance in the Middle Ages?" ("War die Lippe im Mittelalter ein Schiffahrtsweg von erheblicher
Bedeutung?"), by Archives Director Ilgen in Düsseldorf. The author was kind
enough, on my request, to make this study available to me before it was pub-
lished.³ In an article of great interest from cultural and historical viewpoints,
Ilgen establishes the fact that from the Middle Ages to the eighteenth century
the Lippe was used but little for transport and offered many natural obstacles to
navigation. Nevertheless, even he leaves enough leeway for my concept, since the
expression "considerable" is very elastic; a moderate degree of navigability is
completely satisfactory for our purposes. Finally, I would like to modify somewhat, not the substance of Ilgen's treatise, which certainly is correct, but a few
details and the tone, so to speak, which has the relative navigability of the river
appear much too small.

According to Ilgen, a technical study in the years 1735 and 1738 determined
that between Wesel and Hamm there were fifty-one sand banks and three rock
ledges in the river. These obstacles cannot, however, have been very important,
since even in the dry season there was still more than 1½ feet of water above
them. More bothersome would have been the six mill dams between Haus Dahl
and Hamm. These mill dams have restricted navigation everywhere since the end
of the Middle Ages, and right up to our time the two interests have been in conflict. In the work *The Oder River (Der Oderstrom)* by the Office of the Water
Commission (Bureau des Wasserausschusses), we read (1: 233): "At the time of
the political decline of Silesia, the local princes gave permission for the construction of mill dams, which interfered very strongly with water transportation."
The increase of navigation on the Oder dates from the elimination of these dams.
And it probably happened in the same way on the Lippe. Ilgen tells us that in
1597 bricks for the construction of the Jesuit church in Münster were moved by
boat only as far as Haltern and from there by land. From this statement, however, we cannot draw any conclusion on shipping above Haltern, since the land
route from about Werne to Münster would not have been significantly shorter
than from Haltern.

We can also draw no more of a conclusion from the fact that the monasteries of
Herford, Corvey, and Liesborn had their Rhine wine transported from Duisburg
by land. September is the month of lowest water in the Lippe, and October is
only very slightly better. But the empty wine casks had to be transported to the
Rhine in September and the full ones returned in October. It was precisely at this
time, however, that the water route could not be used or at least not used with
any degree of certainty. Hereafter, I would like to place less emphasis on the negative points made by Ilgen and concentrate on his positive indications of the
Lippe's navigability.

If the town of Soest wanted to open up a water route to the Lippe in 1486,
using the Soest Creek and the Ahse, and also raised the necessary money for the
work, then that is no doubt a point of proof that the Lippe was not a completely
useless water route. This point is reinforced by the fact that there were toll stations at Dorsten, Haltern, and Ostendorf, and if in the year 1526 there were 225
vessels that passed through the toll station at Dorsten, that is a considerable
number.

The statement by Werner Rolevink (in about 1475) that Westphalia had no navigable rivers is, therefore, to be understood as meaning there were, to be sure, no waterways continuously open, such as the Rhine and the Spree, but that there were, nevertheless, streams that were quite usable at certain times in the year.

Against this point Schuchhardt has argued that they could not have pulled boats up the Lippe because the river bed is slimy.[4] On this point I turned for information to Construction Engineer Röder, formerly of Hamm on the Lippe and now in Diez, who is well acquainted with the conditions on the Lippe from his years of experience with stream control. I received the following reply from him:

> Swampy terrain, that is, moors and bogs, are nowhere to be found along the Lippe; all the way from Wesel upstream to Neuhaus there are sandy areas on both sides of the river. On the other hand, wet and easily flooded low spots are to be found at many places along the banks. In Roman times such spots probably existed even more frequently, but for such a large mass of men, so experienced in constructing routes as were the Roman legions, these areas did not form any serious obstacle to the towing of ships from the bank. Passing over the tributaries must have been more difficult, for there bridges had to be built if they wanted to avoid frequently ferrying the draught horses to the other bank.
>
> For a body of troops like the Romans, with such systematic organization, accustomed to the construction of model highways and ingenious bridges, this cannot have created any significant difficulty.
>
> The wet areas along the banks were crossed with corduroy roads, traces of which are sometimes still found today.

Consequently, Schuchhardt's idea of the impassable "slimy" bottom is incorrect. In fact, I believe that the difficulty caused by the soft bottom can be more easily overcome than is stated in Mr. Röder's letter if the boats are pulled not by horses, but by men. The latter go along over areas where even today there are no tow paths, close to the bank in the water itself. If they come to impassable spots, it is easier to lay down a useful corduroy road along the bank for men than for horses. The crossing of tributaries is also easier for men, and often not even a bridge is necessary.

If these points show that there can be no further doubt that the Lippe was navigable and usable to a sufficient degree as far as Neuhaus, this also definitely establishes that a Roman supply depot was built in this area. We shall need an explanation as to why, of the numerous military scholars studying the Roman campaigns, nobody until now has made this point, but this explanation is not hard to find. Until a short time ago, our scholarly procedures had not yet brought us to the point of questioning the huge numbers in the German armies. Hundreds of thousands of men moved back and forth, and, according to the reports by Tacitus and Suetonius, Tiberius is supposed to have moved 40,000 from the one tribe of the Sugambri alone to the left bank of the Rhine.[5] General von Peucker, in his widely used book *German Warfare in Primeval Times (Das deutsche Kriegswesen der Urzeiten)*, Berlin, 1860, explains (2: 34) how the German commanders' situation was complicated by the great size of their armies. He blithely states:

According to Orosius and Livy, the army of the Teutones approached a strength of 300,000 men; the army of the Cimbri is stated by Livy, Velleius Paterculus, Eutropus, and Orosius as being 200,000 men strong. By Caesar's account, Ariovistus commanded an army of more than 100,000 men; of the armies of the Goths that swept out from the banks of the Black Sea in the third century, the one that was defeated by Emperor Claudius in 269 reached a strength of 320,000 men, according to Trebellius Pollio. At the beginning of the fifth century, Radagaisus led into Italy an army variously estimated as follows: according to Orosius, more than 200,000 men, since it was supposed to have had, in Goths alone, 200,000; according to Jornandes, 200,000; and by Zosimus' figure, 400,000. Attila's army, which fought on the Catalaunian Fields and was comprised principally of German tribes, was 500,000 men strong in the account by Jornandes, and by Paulus Diaconus' account even 700,000.

Where such masses lived and could move about, supply offered no difficulty. Consequently, this question was not brought up at all. Not until we faced the population problem did we arrive at the supply question, and this question had to lead to the conclusion concerning the Lippe fort.

Not far from Paderborn and the confluence of the Lippe and the Alme, on the left bank of the latter stream, stands the village of Elsen. The similarity of this name to Aliso in the vicinity of a place to which so many indications pointed naturally led early in these studies to a simple identification of the name Aliso with Elsen. Even in the first edition of this work, I believed I was justified in placing Aliso in this area because of the name Elsen. In the meantime, however, it has been established (see Fr. Cramer, *Westdeutsche Zeitschrift* 21 |1902|: 254) that place names with this stem are so very frequent that there is no longer any basis for the argument placing Aliso there.

Now let us compare the testimony of the sources:

Dio Cassius tells us (53. 33) that Drusus, in his campaign of 11 B.C., moved into the territory of the Cherusci as far as the Weser, and that he would also have crossed it if he had not been forced to turn back for lack of provisions. On his return march the Germans attacked him in a narrow pass, but they were finally defeated, so that Drusus ventured to erect a fort against them at the confluence of the Lippe and the Elison.

Dio Cassius gives the following verbatim account:

The enemies set up ambushes everywhere and caused Drusus great harm. One time they bottled him up in an area surrounded by hills and accessible only through narrow passes and almost destroyed him. And he would have been lost with his entire army if the enemy, overconfident in the belief that the Romans were already in their power and needed only one more blow of the sword as a finishing touch, had not pushed in on them without any order. In doing so, they were defeated and they no longer dared to move in so boldly but harassed them from afar, without coming close, so that Drusus for his part erected a fort in defiance of them at the place where the Lippe and the Elison run together, and another one among the Chatti on the Rhine.

The overall context shows that the Germans with whom Drusus fought in a pass as he was returning from the Weser can have been no others than the Cherusci. The description of the terrain no longer applies to the flat land along the Lippe but only to the mountainous terrain east (northeast, southeast) of Paderborn. The slopes along the Lippe valley are much too insignificant to have become dangerous for a Roman army. If Drusus established a fort in defiance of the people who had hard pressed him there, he cannot have done that at a distance of a few days' march from them but only either in the enemy territory itself or directly in front of the entrance to this territory, that is, in the Paderborn region. Since the reason for the campaign's lack of success had been the difficulty of supply, then the purpose of the fort was to establish a depot for the future resumption of the war, an installation that belonged at no other place than this one, to which water transportation offered a connection with the Rhine.

In fact, the building of such an installation must have been the principal purpose of this campaign from the start. That is, Dio Cassius tells us that, when Drusus appeared south of the Lippe in the territory of the Sugambri, the latter were engaged against the Chatti in the field just at that time. If the Roman commander had intended to achieve an immediate great success, apparently he could have done nothing better than to drive against the Sugambri with all his power; squeezed between the Romans and the Chatti, they could have been destroyed. At first appearance, it seems quite incomprehensible how Drusus could have allowed this success to escape him. Instead, he used this opportunity only to march unchallenged up the Lippe and to move forward to the Weser. From that point, without any base and with the Sugambri in his rear, he could not possibly accomplish anything. His passing up the success he could have gained over the Sugambri with little effort on his march forward no longer appears to be an error, however, but rather the act of a thoughtful strategist if we see the purpose of this campaign from the start as the reconnoitering of the routes and the construction of the supply base. This installation was more important to him than victory over a single tribe, even over the much-feared Sugambri; for his plans were directed toward the subjugation of all the Germans up to the Elbe. Against this concept one might raise the question of why Drusus did not then erect the fort on his march forward. When he had arrived at the point where the Lippe ceased to be navigable, he was after all at the spot for the installation. It is possible that it really did happen that way. In any case, the Romans had a large part of their provisions follow the army by water (see p. 100 above), and it is practically impossible that they then loaded everything onto pack animals or wagons near the source of the Lippe and moved them up to the Weser and back. But the commander knew from the start that he also would need significant supplies for the march back. Nothing could be more natural — so obvious for Roman concepts that our sources do not even mention it — than that he should stock the necessary supplies for the return march at the end of the waterway and should protect them by a temporary fortification and a garrison. While the army marched on, the engineer of the garrison searched the surrounding area for the most appropriate spot for constructing a permanent fort, and when the army returned, it completed the construction. Whether this installation was new or an extension of the original one, for Dio Cassius it was only natural to relate it in this way: When Drusus came back and had defeated the enemies, he felt strong enough to construct a fort in this area in defiance of them.

With the same purpose for which he built this fort Drusus had already had dug in the previous year the large canal which led from the Rhine into the Yssel and through the Zuider Zee into the North Sea. Anyone who carries out such works is not content with the occasional subjugation of a small border tribe like the Sugambri but has in mind great campaigns, that is, in our case, the area all the way to the Elbe. For this purpose, the strategic means was a supply depot in as advanced a location as possible.

In an article, "Aliso and Haltern," in the *Korrespondenzblatt des Gesamtverbands der deutschen Geschichts—und Altertumsvereine*, 1906, Schuchhardt and Koepp expressed the opinion that locating the fort on the upper Lippe was out of the question, since it would then have had the hostile Sugambri and the Bructeri in its rear. This argument is easily reversed: it was exactly because of this that Aliso, situated in their midst and yet impregnable for them in their stage of knowledge, became a manacle for the defiant Germans. The objection that the Germans could nevertheless have finally captured the stronghold by starving the garrison is also faulty. It would only be correct if we imagine the fort without the Roman army. It falls aside, however, if we consider the fort not as isolated but in the strategic relationship from which and for which it was built. The fort is the base for the field army operating in these regions, and the field army protects the fort. Even if the army returned to the Rhine, it was still close enough in view of the fort's own great strength. If the Germans should seek to overpower it (as Arminius tried in 16 A.D.), it would always be able to hold out long enough for the relieving army to move up and lift the siege. Not until the army was destroyed in 9 A.D. did Aliso fall, and even then it was only after a long siege.

*     *     *

It has been conjectured that a series of intermediate forts were built along the Lippe to the Rhine because otherwise Aliso, at a straight-line distance of 90 miles from Vetera, would have been completely isolated. But the remains of these forts (with the exception of one, which we shall speak of later), which had already presumably been found, have proven to be misleading, and I, too, am inclined to doubt their existence. Certainly, Roman troops did not march along this road without setting up a fortified camp at night, and wherever possible they would use the previously built camps which the Germans had not taken the trouble to level time and again. But to establish permanent garrisons everywhere would have required many soldiers and would still have had only little benefit. Marching troops protected themselves; transport trains moved with a covering force; merchants had to take care of themselves. And forts are not built in order to provide secure night-time billets for couriers, who, after all, could also be attacked on the road. If the Germans attacked the isolated stronghold on the Elison, it had to defend itself until relief came from the Rhine. The garrisons of the intermediate forts would not have been able to help. The critical point was that a report of the siege should reach Vetera. That would necessarily always happen either sooner or later. It was also important that the commander have in his service a few Germans who, in case of necessity, would undertake to slip through their compatriots and bring the news to the headquarters. Consequently, it is in no way unthinkable that there should have been a completely isolated Roman installation at Paderborn. We simply have to keep in mind how incompetent the Germans were to carry out a real siege; they did not even have enough metal for weapons, much less for regular tools. Even after the Teutoburger victory, as high as was their morale and as low as was that of the Romans, the Germans still could not take Aliso by force. And so Drusus, too, was justified in his time to risk building the fort in the middle of enemy territory, beyond the hostile Sugambri, Marsi, and Bructeri. Furthermore, he did not, after all, have a permanent situation in mind, but the Romans hoped within a few years to be masters of the entire land, at least as far as the Weser.

\*     \*     \*

When the news reached Rome that Drusus was on his deathbed, Valerius Maximus tells us (5. 5. 3) that his brother Tiberius hastened to him and had to go far into the interior of Germany. We may combine this report with the account in Tacitus (*Annals* 2. 7) that the Germans, when they besieged the fort on the Lippe in 15 A.D., destroyed an old altar of Drusus, which Germanicus reconstructed after he had relieved the fort with his six legions. It is not easily imaginable that the Romans, if they erected an altar to Drusus in the interior of Germany, would have built it anywhere else but at the place of his death. If they had simply chosen some appropriate place or other, they would at least have built the altar in the vicinity of one of the large permanent camps on the Rhine. If we then find in the one source that the altar to Drusus was located in the vicinity of the Lippe fort and we know from the other source that Drusus died deep in the interior of Germany, the result is that the fort is to be sought not on the lower Lippe but near its head.

\*     \*     \*

In the year 5 A.D., according to Velleius (2. 105), the Romans for the first time took up their winter quarters in Germany "*ad caput Juliae*" ("at the source of the Julia"), as the source reads. Since no river named "Julia" is known to us, Lipsius already in his time substituted *Lupiae* for it, no doubt correctly. Very recently, attention has been drawn to a place called "Jollenbeck"; it is situated on a small stream that flows into the Werre above Rehme. The similarity of the name is there, but this name is to be found quite frequently, and from the critical viewpoint this combination is not acceptable. We can assume neither that Tiberius had taken up his winter quarters on the far side of the mountain, something that even Varus with his trustfulness did not dare to do, nor that, if Tiberius should have done that once, he did not then establish the camp on the Weser. We may therefore accept Lipsius' conjecture, "*ad caput Lupiae*." If only the lower Lippe had been navigable, we would not be able to draw any further conclusion from this piece of information. We would then assume that Tiberius did not shy away from transporting provisions by land up to the source of the Lippe. Since we may in any case accept the fact, however, that the Lippe was navigable high into its upper course, then we may not suppose that Tiberius, simply for the purpose of being situated one or two days' march farther into the country, burdened his staff with the necessity of setting up an extensive land transportation system from the point of debarkation to the camp. The only logical step was to establish the camp right at this natural transfer point.

If it were not for the uncertain text, here we would have absolutely decisive proof for our claim that a strategic point for the Romans was situated close to the sources of the Lippe. Paderborn is no more than a scant 9 miles from the Lippe's sources.

A camp at this place could very well be referred to as situated *"ad caput Lupiae,"* If an advantageous spot for a base camp was to be found so far up the Lippe, then that was also the logical place for a supply depot pushed forward as far as possible. It was an important advance in securing the Roman domination, a point correctly stressed by Velleius, that Tiberius risked establishing his winter camp here, where there had previously been only a stopping point.

\*  \*  \*

When Germanicus in 16 A.D. relieved the Lippe stronghold that was besieged by the Germans, he reconstructed the destroyed altar in honor of Drusus. Tacitus goes on to say that *"tumulum iterare haud visum"* ("he decided not to reconstruct the mound"), the burial mound erected in the previous year to the dead of Varus' army, which had likewise been destroyed by the Germans. If the burial mound had been in a completely different area, this remark would be incomprehensible. We now know very well that Roman campaigns to any desired distant area in Germany could not be improvised. The *"tumulum iterare haud visum"* makes sense only if there really arose the question that the mound was not too very far from the fort. As long as the Teutoburger battle is thought to have been even approximately in the area where we have placed it, it must be assumed that the fort was situated on the upper Lippe and not on its lower or middle course.

\*  \*  \*

The name "Aliso" is not mentioned in any of the citations from the ancient authors that we have referred to so far. We read only about the stronghold at the confluence of the Lippe and the Elison, and of a fort on the Lippe that was besieged by the Germans in 16 A.D. and relieved by Germanicus. With respect to this fort, we have seen that it must have been situated on the upper Lippe. The name "Aliso" is mentioned in three other places, and the question arises as to whether they refer to this same place or another fort.

The geographer Ptolemy (2. 11) places Aleison one-half degree east and one-fourth degree south of Vetera. That does not correspond to our fort, but it proves nothing, since the stated location so far south of Vetera is wrong in any case, and particularly since the estimates of this geographer specifically concerning Germany are known to be very unreliable. We would do well to leave completely out of our consideration his reference to this point as well as the one concerning the *Tropaia Drousou* ("trophies of Drusus").*

There follows the chapter in Tacitus' *Annals* (2. 7) which first gives the accounts of the siege and the relief of the fort on the Lippe, the reconstructed Drusus altar, and the fact that the burial mound was not reconstructed. Finally, it reads: "cuncta inter castellum Alisonem ac Rhenum novis limitibus aggeribusque permunita." ("The whole area between the fort Aliso and the Rhine was completely built up with new roads and embankments.")

The question is whether the fort on the Lippe mentioned at the start of the chapter, which in any case was situated on the upper Lippe, is identical with the place Aliso named at the chapter's end. There is no doubt that Tacitus in his normal style would in this case have given the name at the first mention of the place. But we know his indifference toward geography. It is not at all impossible that in his work the two forts are identical, although he himself probably did not consider it worth the trouble to clarify that point. As he combined the sources he had at hand and reworked them, it is possible that he more or less accidentally overlooked the name in the first passage while finding it useful for his sentence construction in the second case. This assumption becomes highly probable if we realize that the account is in no way suitable for some fort on the lower Lippe. For "cuncta inter castellum Alisonem et Rhenum novis limitibus aggeribusque permunita" means "between Aliso and the Rhine a continuous firm road was built." That cannot have been a work of only a few miles. The length of the entire Lippe, however, is a good 90 miles, and a firm road of such length, with causeways, is a project that the Roman historian was justified in mentioning with some degree of emphasis.

The third passage, in Velleius (2. 120), states in extension of the account of Varus' defeat: "L. Caedici, praefecti castrorum, eorumque qui una circumdati Alisone immensis Germanorum copiis obsidebantur, laudanda virtus est" ("The courage of Lucius Caedicus, prefect of the camp, was praised along with the valor of those surrounded and besieged by vast numbers of Germans at Aliso"), because they saved themselves from the most dangerous situation through their vigilance and determination. This passage is to be combined with one in Dio Zonaras (in Dio Cassius 56. 22), according to which only one Roman fort held out, and with another passage, in Frontinus (3. 15.4), where one finds the mention "*reliqui ex Variana clade cum obsiderentur*" ("when the survivors of the Varian disaster were besieged"). A fourth passage, in Frontinus (4. 7. 8), also speaks of a siege after Varus' defeat, where Caedicus was in command. Since Dio Cassius says that only one fort held out, all four of these accounts refer to the same event. It is not only a question of a siege following Varus' defeat, but the besieged troops were also "*reliqui ex Variana clade*" ("survivors of the Varian disaster") (from the third passage), and the place was named Aliso (from the first passage). That is direct proof from the sources that it was the fort on the upper Lippe that was named Aliso. For the fugitives from the slaughter in the Dören ravine naturally rushed into the nearest stronghold that offered them protection, and that was the fort on the upper Lippe. If they had continued their rush farther, possibly for fear of being surrounded here, they would not have fled into any fort that was still situated on German soil but would have continued right on to the Rhine. Under any circumstances, we would have to presume that there was a Roman fort on the upper Lippe in Varus' time, even if we had no report on that point or if all the reports we have necessarily referred to some other fortification. Under the agricultural conditions existing in Germany, it is completely out of the question that the Romans made their constant marches to the Weser and back without a large supply depot at the point where the Lippe became unnavigable, even for the smallest vessels. This supply depot was naturally fortified, and was therefore a fort. Consequently it was the closest stronghold and refuge for the fugitives from the Teutoburger battle. According to Velleius (2. 120), this fort was named Aliso.

\*    \*    \*

The Germans were not capable of taking the fort by force. They sought to starve it into submission, and since it was well stocked with provisions, the siege lasted a long time. We realize the length of the siege from the fact that the besieged garrison finally heard that Tiberius was approaching with a large army. But at the time of the battle of the Teutoburger Forest Tiberius was in Pannonia, and he first went to Rome before he moved to the Rhine. In this long period, the besieging Germans grew negligent in their watchfulness, so that the besieged troops succeeded in slipping by them and covering the 90-mile route to the Rhine unchallenged. It might perhaps seem strange that the Germans should not have overtaken the fugitives on such a long move. But military history offers very similar analogies to this event, situations attesting to its possibility. The strongholds of the German knights in Prussia were also besieged for a very long time during the Great Rebellion, and they could not be relieved. One of them, Bartenstein, was under siege for four years. Finally, the garrisons did exactly as the Romans in Aliso: they slipped through, and the garrison of Bartenstein got safely away, while those from Kreuzburg were discovered and killed (see Vol. III, Book III, Chapter 7). The flight of the Bartenstein garrison to Elbing was over 70 miles.

\*    \*    \*

Important support is once again being provided for the study of the Roman campaigns in Germany through the excavations that have now been undertaken with the greatest energy. These diggings have already brought very valuable remains and much information to light. But, of course, for the direct knowledge of these wars this activity has so far created more confusion than clarification. Formerly, we did not know very definitely how to distinguish Roman installations from prehistoric or Carolingian ones or even from the simple phenomena of nature. Captain Hölzermann and General von Veith thought they had discovered entire systems of Roman fortifications on the lower Rhine and up the Lippe; these discoveries later proved to be nothing but sand dunes. Real Roman installations of the largest scale are now being identified by the most expert scholars, but their place in history is being erroneously determined. In the twenty years of their hegemony between the Rhine and the Elbe, the Romans must have built hundreds of march camps and dozens of base camps and forts. From all of these there may be some remaining traces, and from many of them there must be such remains. Only a few base camps and forts have yet been found. But with each single discovery the happy explorers have shouted: Aliso! Not only the discoverers, and with them public opinion among those interested in antiquity, but also the most competent scholars in the field have allowed themselves to be carried away by the enthusiasm of the joy of discovery and have agreed with more or less hesitation. As a result, not only has understanding of the overall strategy of the Roman campaigns been disturbed and held up, but also it is still necessary today to pursue in detail the claims of the various areas of discovery to the name Aliso, to test them against the sources, and once again to pronounce the presumed proof as negative.

I think I may ignore Dünzelmann's idea that he has found Aliso on the Hunte, as well as the claim that it was located near Wesel. The sites deserving investigation are the two large, successful excavations at Haltern and Oberaden.[6]

At the small town of Haltern on the Lippe, some 28 miles from its mouth on the Rhine, a Roman fort on St. Anna's Mountain on the north bank has long been known. It has recently been carefully uncovered in its overall outline. One and one-half kilometers upstream from this installation and at a little distance from the Lippe, on a plateau where no remains of any kind were to be found on the surface, a large Roman camp was discovered through excavations in the years 1900, 1901, and thereafter. Directly on the bank of the old bed of the Lippe there have been found, in the third instance, a series of port and storage installations, as well as fortifications. In general, the nature and purpose of these installations need no explanation, even if so many details are doubtful. As we have seen, the Lippe was not navigable up to Aliso for larger vessels even for seven months. Even though for men of antiquity very small vessels were still more advantageous than land transportation, and for this reason we may assume that they used the waterway up to Aliso perhaps eight months a year or even somewhat longer, finally there came a time when this possibility also failed. We may assume, however, that the Lippe was navigable as far as Haltern during the entire year. Therefore, they installed a supply and storage area at that point early in the game, enclosed a ship-docking area with dikes, and built the fort on St. Anna's Mountain for their protection.

The legions also often erected their march camps and their base camp in the vicinity of this harbor. The base camp required the large harbor installations on the Lippe, which, it appears, were securely connected with the camp by long embankments. It has been determined that no fewer than three camp locations were built here one after the other. The innumerable remains that have gradually been found — weapons, coins, pottery, jewelry, tools — prove that the camps were occupied for a long time. Domitius Ahenobarbus may have had his headquarters here when he had the *pontes longos* (long bridges) built; and here the legions may have spent the winter at one time or other during the years 5 to 8 A.D. Whether Germanicus, too, when he again took up the war, restored the fortification must remain unknown; perhaps he used it as a march camp.

Some 19 miles farther up, 1½ kilometers from the Lippe, a similar base camp for a legion was situated on the south side near Oberaden, larger than the largest one of those near Haltern.

Of all these installations, only the stronghold on St. Anna's Mountain near Haltern can be considered as possibly identical with Aliso. The camps are much too large for forts. *Castellum* is the diminutive of *castrum*, and not only because of its name is it limited to a certain size, but also because of the inviolable laws of strategy. Under the military conditions that we find in Germany, strategy requires first that the field army be strong. The commander keeps his troops together by detaching only the smallest possible number of garrisons and by making those that are absolutely unavoidable, that is, the forts, no larger than the situation absolutely requires. If the fortification is too extensive for the size of the garrison, then the place is endangered to the highest degree and a strong defense is not possible. The Aliso that we are seeking can therefore only have had a moderate size, just large enough to accommodate, in addition to the garrison, a few large storage areas and perhaps also a hospital and a few work shops. But the camp near Oberaden occupies an area of more than 35 hectares. The large camp near Haltern covers about 35 hectares, the intermediate one some 20, and the smallest 18.

Let us compare these with a few other Roman installations that are known to us:

|  | Size | Garrisoned by |
|---|---|---|
| Caesar's camp on the Aisne | 41 hectares | 8 legions |
| Caesar's camp before Gergovia | 35 hectares | 6 legions |
| Caesar's camp at Mt. St. Pierre | 24 hectares | 4 legions |
| The camp near Bonn | 25 hectares | 1 legion with support troops |
| The camp near Neuss | 24 hectares | 1 legion with support troops |
| Lambaesis in Africa | 21 hectares | 1 legion |
| Camp of Carnuntum | 14 hectares | 1 legion |
| Kesselstadt | 14 hectares | |
| St. Anna's Mountain | 7¼ hectares | |
| Nieder-Bieber | 5 hectares | 1 cohort and 2 *numeri* |
| Pföring | 4 hectares | 500 men |
| Friedberg | 3 3/4 hectares | 1000 men |
| Saalburg | 3¼ hectares | |
| Weissenburg | 3 hectares | 500 men |

Most of the forts along the *limes*, except for the very small ones, had an area between 1½ and 3½ hectares. The normal garrison was a cohort or a cavalry squadron (*ala*) of 500 men, which was increased to 1,000 men in the most endangered and larger forts in time of war.[7]

If we compare these numbers, we see noticeable variations. In Caesar's camps, each legion was allocated some 6 hectares, and therefore 1,000 men per hectare; in the forts the ratio was threefold, fourfold, and even eightfold. That is quite natural. In a camp in open warfare, the troops are squeezed together as much as possible; in a permanent fort, they spread out more but never any farther than the garrison can defend, and this depends not only on the size, but numerous other circumstances may come into consideration.[8]

If we now limit ourselves to the examples of Bonn, Neuss, and Lambaesis, we can conclude that perhaps one legion sufficed for the defense of a fixed camp of 20 to 25 hectares. Under the conditions at Aliso, however, which was protected by earthworks and located in the most exposed situation, that would have been too small a garrison. Even for the smallest of the camps, of 18 hectares, we could hardly go below one and one-half legions as a permanent garrison.

By speaking of the smallest of the installations, however, we have already granted too much, for it is entirely clear, as even Schuchhardt himself accepts, that we are dealing with a somewhat varied repetition of the same installation. This very repetition, since it is, after all, known to us from Aliso, provides Schuchhardt with an argument for naming the place Aliso. If we assume that the harbor installations and the fort on St. Anna's Mountain were also supposed to be held, it would have required Varus' entire army with its three legions to defend these works, and no field army at all would have been left. By neglecting to clarify this result of his hypothesis, Schuchhardt is himself responsible for the appearance of the camp of Oberaden, of almost 2½ kilometers in circumference, as a possible competitor of his Haltern.

In accordance with the sizes of Caesar's camps given above, there would have been room for three legions even in the smallest of the camps. Since we must think of this camp as a permanent one, presumably a winter camp where the troops are allowed more room and comfort, this smaller camp may have been occupied by only two legions or perhaps even only one. However, the large camp near Haltern and the camp near Oberaden probably sheltered three legions — and the eagerness of the discoverers caused them to consider these camps as forts with a permanent garrison! We hardly need add that, completely aside from the number of garrison troops that it swallowed up, the huge space would have been completely unnecessary. What purpose was it supposed to serve? If the field army arrived, it built its own camp, and the basic law held true for the fort: as tight a circumference as possible around the installation, so that it might more easily be defended. Between a fort and a camp there is not only a distinction of degree but also one of basic principle. In a fort, the garrison is determined by the circumference of the fortification; in a camp, the circumference of the fortification is determined by the size of the army.

The discoveries at Haltern and Oberaden are not forts but winter camps.

When the troops moved out of such a winter camp, it was necessary neither to garrison it nor to destroy it. It was useless for the Germans; if they had wanted to occupy it, they would, thanks to the Roman siegecraft, have fallen to the Romans even more quickly than Vercingetorix in Alesia. If the Romans themselves wished to occupy the same position again and the Germans for their part had taken the trouble to destroy it, the earth works could be built up again quickly enough.

There remains the question of whether the 7¼-hectare fort on St. Anna's Mountain could also be Aliso. It is unnecessary for us to subject this question to the test, since no one any longer makes the claim, strictly speaking. The advocates of Haltern always base their claim specifically on the large camps that, because of the vivid picture of the Roman military system which they offer the

scholar in such colorful completeness, have inspired the fantasy and have continued to maintain it. But in such controversies one must also be flexible. For that
reason, let us not shrink from once again putting to the test all the sources in
which we have already heard above that they are referring to the fort on the
Lippe, to see if they can also be referring to this other place.

When Drusus moved out against the Sugambri, Dio Cassius tells us, he did not
find them in their usual habitat, but they were on the move against the Chatti.
Drusus then moved up to the Weser.

Schuchhardt interpreted that as follows: "As a result of their move against the
Chatti, they avoided at the same time the first blow of the still fresh Roman
troops." So if one is attacked in his own country by an all-powerful enemy, one
"avoids" him by starting as quickly as possible a war against another enemy, and
the attacker is so kind as to respect this stratagem and for his part, instead of
striking with full vigor, he first goes off somewhere else? And with it all, the
entire territory of the Sugambri was certainly not much broader than 45 miles.

From the two things, one point emerges: either Drusus intended to fight
against only the Germanic border tribes — and in that case it would be incomprehensible why he did not grasp the opportunity against the Sugambri — or he
planned a large war against all the Germans. In the latter case he was not satisfied with the building of a fort 27 miles from his border as the only result of an
entire campaign. As ready as the Roman authors were to exaggerate their praises,
the source from which Dio Cassius took his account would still not have pictured
the building of such a fort as a great deed "in defiance of" the enemy tribes.

No less misleading is the idea that the Romans had intended to create here a
secured crossing of the Lippe. For what purpose would they have needed it?
Could the Germans perhaps prevent them from crossing a little river like the
Lippe wherever they wanted to cross? And could not the Romans without any
question march up on the right or the left bank as best suited them? It is a completely amateurish idea that an army which is far superior to the enemy in the
open field would have needed to protect its crossing point over a river like the
Lippe by means of a fort.

A Drusus who one year builds a great canal in order to be able to attack the
German peoples from the sea and the next year, as a conqueror, accomplishes no
more than building a fort 27 miles from his border would necessarily seem to us to
be precisely a military idiot.

Lieutenant Colonel Dahm (*Archäologische Anzeiger,* 1900, p. 101) has
attempted a very unusual justification for the fort at Haltern. He interprets the
words of Tacitus in *Annals* 2. 7, "*novis limitibus aggeribusque permunita,*" in the old sense, that *limites* means fortifications. Dahm believes that Drusus and Germanicus had wanted to secure for themselves an area of deployment
on the right bank of the Rhine opposite the base camps at Vetera and Mainz, in
order to protect the Rhine crossing under any circumstances. According to him,
the forts of Aliso, Haltern, and Hofheim (in the Taunus) were not isolated posts
but only the "main support points of the positions bounded by the *limites,* the
observation posts, and other fortified installations." And if Haltern was situated
two days' march from the large base camp, and Hofheim only a single day's
march, this was to be explained, according to Dahm, by the fact that the terrain
along the Lippe is very irregular and particularly favorable to the enemy. Fur-

thermore, all the principal operations started from this base, and for that reason, a larger area for the assembling of the army was required there than at Mainz.

I must completely contradict this analysis. The concept of an assembly terrain with a depth of one or two days' march in front of a large fortified place of arms does not exist in military history. The Romans, who dominated the left bank of the Rhine and were able to assemble and prepare crossing equipment at any place they wanted to, could never, according to a recognized law of strategy, be prevented by the Germans from crossing the Rhine. If the Romans wanted a convenient situation, then fixed bridges with bridgeheads were the means — but under no circumstances a cordon with fortifications one or two days' march from the Rhine. To defend such a position would have required an army ten times as large as the Romans had all together on the Rhine. The objectively quite impossible — indeed nonsensical — idea of such a fortified assembly area apparently stems only from the reported false concept of the *limes* as a border fortification intended for defense, associated with the apparent necessity to find a strategic purpose for the fortress of Haltern.

From the passages in Valerius Maximus 5. 5. 3, combined with Tacitus, *Annals* 2. 7, concerning the area where Drusus died and the altar was erected to him, it has already been proven above that they cannot be referring to a place situated so close to the Rhine as Haltern. And the report (*Annals* 2. 7) that the Germans besieged a fort on the Lippe and Germanicus moved up with six legions to relieve it does not refer to Haltern either. In all of world military history, it is impossible to besiege a place if a far superior enemy army is only 27 miles away. Even with armies of approximately equal strength, it is possible only if the besieger has the capability of strongly fortifying his own position very quickly. The Germans were not capable of this. A single day's hard march could have brought the Roman army suddenly on the scene, and each night the Germans, whose strong point was anything but careful observation and watchfulness, would have had to be ready for a sudden attack that would have destroyed the siege army.

The lowest Germanic private who was summoned for such a task would have recognized the uselessness and danger of such an undertaking and would have lost his confidence in the leadership ability of the duke who employed and wasted his strength so foolishly.

We have already seen no less clearly that the report following this one, to the effect that the Romans had built a firm road between Aliso and the Rhine, is not appropriate for the Romans, who would not have made such a big point of a road 27 miles in length. Furthermore, it was right here that Tiberius had already built the road. (See p. 126, above.)

The fugitives from the Teutoburger battle fled to Aliso. From this it can be concluded that the fort cannot have stood so very far from the battlefield. Schuchhardt believes, on the contrary: "Only if we assume the distance to be quite great can we understand how the catastrophe was such a frightful one and why so few escaped." For this reason, he says, the account applies to Haltern. Against this argument we can say that the Romans' withdrawal was cut off by Arminius' position in the mountain pass and that the shorter or greater distance from a place of refuge therefore does not come into consideration. Furthermore, it is clear here that the Germans did not first pursue for a full five or six days and then march back the same number of days to hold their victory celebration, but they remained with their booty. However, if they had not pursued, but had allowed the fugitives to run away, the latter would certainly not have stayed in Haltern but would have hastened directly back to the Rhine. But they were surrounded in Aliso. Let us for a moment assume that Aliso can be sought near Haltern by placing the Teutoburger battle at some other place. One thing is certain, however: if we once assume, with Schuchhardt, that the battle took place in the Dören ravine or somewhere else near the Grotenburg (Teutoburg), then Aliso cannot have been situated near Haltern, 90 miles from the Teutoburg and only one long day's march from the Rhine.

The same thing is also shown by the developments and the length of the siege. Here, so close to the Rhine, the Roman legate Asprenas, who moved up with two legions and who was famous for his energy, would also certainly have made an attempt to liberate the besieged garrison.

Schuchhardt places particular credence in Tacitus' account that in 16 A.D. Germanicus embarked his army on the fleet, sailed into the Ems, and marched up to the Weser, although he was already in position at Aliso with six legions. He says that this is understandable only if Aliso was situated on the lower Lippe, and therefore at Haltern. My correction, that Germanicus did not sail into the Ems but the Weser, seems to him only an expedient to save the position of Aliso at Paderborn — from which we can then conclude that Schuchhardt believes that Tacitus' campaign report would become logical if we accept the location of Aliso at Haltern. This correction is no more valuable than if somebody wanted to object to the expression three times three is eleven, that it would be better to say three times three is ten. The movement into the Ems of an army that is supposed to fight on the Weser is somewhat less illogical if the army previously was in position at Haltern than if it had been at Paderborn, but it is nevertheless still illogical. Koepp also realized this.[9] Since my correction (confusing the Ems with the Weser and dividing up the army) seems too radical to him, he simply gives up any hope of understanding the campaign. If Koepp still sees in this account the most important testimony for the location of Aliso at Haltern, that is obviously not entirely logical. For if the overall campaign has not been reported to us in such a way that we can make logical sense from it, then one cannot use as proof an individual link from the chain, a link in which the very error may indeed exist.

The only reason why Aliso has been sought either at Haltern or at Oberaden is that by chance remains of Roman installations have been discovered at these places. Just as this coincidence has created this confusion, which is psychologically not inexplicable, so on the other hand the lack of traces in the Paderborn area has tended to prevent acceptance of the correct location among many groups of scholars. In reality, the lack of evidence here has just as little significance for the solution of the problem as does the plethora of findings there. After all, there is not the slightest doubt that, in addition to their march camps, the Romans had numerous other base camps and forts in Germany, of which fortune has allowed us to find only a few. The solution as to the location of Aliso cannot be reached through findings — unless an inscription should be discovered — but only through the sources as interpreted from the viewpoint of strategic considerations. The excavations at Haltern and Oberaden do not lose the least bit of their interest, even if we stop calling them Aliso. Even if some kind of fortification should be found at Paderborn, that would still add nothing to the chain of testimony that Aliso was situated there. Almost all contemporary scholars (Mommsen, Knoke, Dahm, Bartels, Schuchhardt, Koepp) are agreed that Varus' camp must have been in the vicinity of the Westphalian Gate, but here too no trace whatever of a Roman camp has yet been found. Just as scholars have not let themselves be led astray by the lack of findings in this place, they need not be deceived by the same lack of findings at Paderborn. And after all, Tiberius' camp at the sources of the Lippe has not yet been discovered either. That this one or that one will still be found is not only possible but also even probable. The legionary camp at Neuss, which was of stone construction and not simple earthworks like the camps and forts in Germany, was, after all, discovered only twenty years ago. And this camp was garrisoned by troops not for just a few years but for generations or perhaps even centuries. The large camps at Haltern were not discovered until nine years ago, and then only by chance; not even the slightest trace of them was to be seen above ground. Four years ago, Pastor Prein found the Camp at Oberaden; shortly before that, Professor Hartmann discovered another camp, 20 kilometers southeast of Lippstadt, at Kneblinghausen bei Rüthen. Whatever the future may still grant us in the way of such discoveries, the decision as to how the discovery fits into the historical picture can never result from the reconstruction of the individual camp or fort, but only from the reconstruction of the strategic context of the campaigns. Anyone who ventures into this field cannot allow himself such errors as to believe that we cannot situate a fort in the rear of the enemy or to confuse forts with fortified camps. He must also avoid the errors of not considering the relationship of the strength of garrison troops to the strength of the field army, having a stronghold besieged while the unbeaten field army is only two short days' march away, and finally, all the types of amateurish concepts that are held by the proponents of the Haltern-Aliso hypothesis.

(Added in the third edition). The excavation of the camp at Oberaden has shown that it is older than the camp at Haltern. It was therefore presumably the base camp of Tiberius when he took position here in order to muster a part of the Sugambri and move them to the other bank of the Rhine. None of these camps comes into consideration in the context of the campaigns we have discussed. The archaeologists who have attempted to construct such relationships have failed in that they did not understand the difference between camp and fort. I have explained this in more detail in a rather long discussion with G. Kropatscheck in the *Preussische Jahrbücher* 143: 135 (1911). Whether a place is a camp or a fort is naturally a very critical point. It is a difference like that between a pistol and a cannon: initially, only a difference of size, which from a practical viewpoint becomes a difference of type. A fort has its inherent purpose (which must be sought and determined), and the garrison is primarily intended to hold the fort and defend it; outside the fort their purpose is normally more of a police nature than a military one. A fortified camp, however, does not exist for its own sake but for the army, which finds protection in it. Anybody who confuses these two functions cannot, of course, arrive at correct strategic conclusions.

Ludwig Schmidt in the *Römisch-germanisches Korrespondenzblatt*, 1911, p. 94, has once again presented the reasons why Aliso must necessarily be sought on the upper Lippe.

NOTES FOR SPECIAL STUDY ON THE LOCATION OF ALISO

1. Stein, *Contributions to the History of the Hansa (Beiträge zur Geschichte der Hanse)*, pp. 24, 25.

2. (Note added in the 2d ed.) Prein, in *Aliso bei Oberaden*, p. 65, has misunderstood this passage in that he repeats it as if the "natural navigability" extends only up to Lippstadt.

3. *Reports of the Commission on Antiquity for Westphalia (Mitteilungen der Altertumskommission für Westfalen)*, Vol. II, 1901.

4. *Reports of the Commission on Antiquity for Westphalia*, Vol. II, 1901, p. 212, note.

5. How deeply rooted these concepts are, even today, can be seen in the excellent monograph by W. Bang, "The Germans in the Roman Service" ("Die Germanen im römischen Dienst"), p. 6, where the author bases conclusions on the point that this number is too small for a German tribe.

6. A principal advocate of Haltern as Aliso is Schuchhardt, writing in Vol. II of the already cited *Reports of the Commission on Antiquity for Westphalia*, 1901, and again in an article "On the Aliso Question" ("Zur Alisofrage") in the *Westdeutsche Zeitschrift*, Vol. 24, 1905. See also "Aliso, Guide Through the Roman Excavations at Haltern" ("Aliso, Führer durch die römischen Ausgrabungen bei Haltern"), 3d ed., 1907. Entering the lists as champion for Oberaden as Aliso is the discoverer Pastor O. Prein, *Aliso bei Oberaden*, 1906, with supplement.

7. Hettner, *Report on the Research of the Upper German-Raetian Limes (Bericht über die Erforschung des obergermanisch-rätischen Limes)*, 1895, p. 25. Noväsium, *Bonner Jahrbücher* 111: 18. Forts between 20,000 and 23,000 square meters (that is, 2 hectares) for a single cohort have been confirmed many times, says Dragendorff in "Archaeological Explorations in Germany" ("Archäologische Forschungen in Deutschland"), *Deutsche Monatsschrift*, March issue, 1906.

8. The camps which A. Schulten identified in front of Numantia are much larger than Caesar's camps in proportion to the number of troops. This can be explained by the fact that those camps of Caesar known to us were always intended to serve for only a short time, whereas in Numantia a very long action was expected from the start.

9. *Korrespondenzblatt des Gesamtverbands der deutschen Geschichtsvereine*, 1906, Column 405. See also Koepp, *The Romans in Germany (Die Römer in Deutschland)*, p. 37.

# Chapter VII

# Romans and Germans in Stalemate

The result of the Teutoburger battle and Germanicus' campaigns was the establishment of a sort of equilibrium between Romans and Germans. The Romans were not capable of overcoming the courageous, freedom-loving barbarian tribes in their broad territories of forest, mountain, and swamp on the borders of the world empire. The Germans were not capable of meeting the Romans in open battle and going on the offensive against them.

Nonetheless, the expansion of the Roman Empire had still not ended. For more than a century longer this expansion continued, and for a century beyond that they still contemplated expanding and fought to accomplish it. If the Germans were too brave and their land too inaccessible, the Romans succeeded in subjecting that part of Britain inhabited by the Celts, and in the plains north of the lower Danube, in present-day Hungary and Rumania, a large new province, Dacia, was founded. Finally, at the beginning of the second century, the fight against the Parthians was also resumed on the broadest scale, and Mesopotamia was conquered.

The Romans allowed a century and a half to slip by before they avenged Crassus' defeat and Antony's failure for the same reason that they finally gave up the idea of subjugating the Germans. We cannot assume that the Parthians would have been strong enough to withstand a full-scale attack with all the resources of the Roman Empire. But for the new "Alexander campaign" a new Alexander was needed. Mark Antony had wanted to be the new Alexander. He did not succeed, not because he lacked the necessary qualities or because it would have been inherently impossible, but because the one approach he made, based on a special plan, failed as a result of unfavorable circumstances, and he renounced a second attempt. The Romans might have been able to try moving forward step by step and first limiting themselves to the conquest of Mesopotamia. Even that was such a large undertaking that only the emperor himself could take it in hand. Consequently, it required an emperor who himself was a great and energetic warrior and who was so sure of his authority and had the empire in such a state of law and order that he could leave the capital for years on end to devote himself entirely to the war on this most distant border. Neither the emperors of the Julian-Claudian house nor those of the Flavian were so gifted or in such a position. Not until Trajan (98-117 A.D.) did the Roman Empire have a head in whom all those conditions were to be found.

Trajan was commander of the Roman legions on the upper Rhine, with his headquarters in Mainz, when he received his call to the throne of Caesar through adoption. One would think that, if he wished to wage war, to increase the fame of Rome, and to ward off future threats to the empire, he would have been most interested in finally carrying out the subjugation of the Germans. But he was not willing to risk that. Appian tells us that the Romans had not conquered the northernmost part of Britain because the land would have been worthless. This reason may also have been advanced whenever the question of whether it was advisable and necessary to incorporate Germany into the empire was discussed in the Roman headquarters. Trajan, too, preferred to consider Dacia, and finally he turned against the Parthians. He did add Armenia and Mesopotamia to the Roman realm, but while engaged in this war, he died. Immediately there again came into play the alternation between the inner constitution of the Roman state and the conduct of war. His successor, Hadrian, who did not have a secure title to the throne, was not in a position either to continue the war against the Parthians himself or to entrust it to a general. He made peace and gave up Trajan's conquests. The Romans no doubt reached and crossed the Tigris many times thereafter, but each time they held out there for only a short time.

The plan to establish the imperial border at the Elbe was never again taken up, and so Tiberius' recall of Germanicus remained the critical turning point in world history. From that day on, the Romans renounced their great offensive against the Germans and limited themselves principally to guaranteeing and protecting their border. This border defense, however, was by its nature a completely new challenge to the art of war.

When Tiberius put a stop to Germanicus' continuation of the war, the legions did not return completely to the left bank of the Rhine but continued to hold a few areas and strongholds on the right bank.¹ They even advanced somewhat. The warm corner between the Rhine and the Main and the silver deposits which were discovered on the Lahn were so attractive that they finally occupied and settled this region. In doing so, they extended themselves beyond the great natural bulwark of the Rhine and now had to provide an artificial system of border protection. In the salient angle, the Wetterau was also drawn into this area and as an adjunct to it the angle between the Rhine and the Danube, with the Odenwald and the Schwarzwald.

It was then a question of protecting this border.

Even if the Germans were not in a position to attack the Roman Empire, protected continuously as it was by the ever-ready legions, still this did not make them in any way peaceful neighbors. The Romans needed a standing army not only to be able to defeat and repel the Germans in large open battles but also for daily protection against pillaging border violations. Barbarian nations could not give international guarantees against violations, even if they wanted to, since they were not able to exert sufficient control over their own warlike bands.

It is extremely difficult to guard a border for hundreds of miles against a continuously bellicose enemy. An incursion can take place at any spot and on any day. If the border troops are distributed equally along the border, then they are equally weak everywhere and can be overrun by an assembled force. If they are held together at a few points, then long stretches are unobserved and open.

On the lower Rhine, the Romans protected themselves by entering into a long-term alliance with the Germans across the river — the Batavians, the Canninefates, and the Friesians. The sons of these tribes entered the Roman service in large numbers and received Roman pay. That provided a guarantee of good behavior, even on the part of their relatives who remained at home. The few difficult disturbances which this relationship experienced now and then were overcome.

Farther upstream, more or less along the present Prussian Rhine province, the river remained the border, but the Romans saw to it that a broad stretch of land on the right bank remained uninhabited. No German was allowed to settle there. If the Germans had only one day's march to make through this deserted area before crossing the Rhine and entering Roman territory, such an undertaking could not easily be accomplished if the Roman patrols and observation points were relatively alert. Of course, particular attention had to be paid to that portion of the bank of the Rhine opposite the mouths of the tributaries flowing from the east, on which the Germans could suddenly move up by boat.

Between Bonn and Coblenz, somewhat below Neuwied, the border jumped over to the right bank and the *limes* began there, crossed the Main 14 miles upstream from Frankfurt, and extended to the Danube at Kehlheim, at the mouth of the Altmühl, upstream from Ratisbon. Hence, the angle between the Rhine and the Danube was cut off and protected.

The individual parts of this *limes* were built at different times and in quite different ways. On the Neckar an older line is still recognizable, extending a long way, and then a new one was built farther out in front of it. Wherever a large stream, a bend of the Main or of the Neckar, formed the border and offered protection, the *limes* installation stopped.

As a result of recent investigations, we can trace quite accurately not only the course but also the history of this border protection, which partly still exists today — the "paling" or "devil's wall," as it is called in popular terminology. Therefore, to use the expression of a perspicacious researcher, the monumental stiffness of this great work is dissolved, and the interest that is everywhere inherent in its development comes alive.

Under Tiberius and his immediate successors, continuous lines of fortification against the Germans were not yet erected. Vespasian moved on the upper Rhine across the Black Forest up to the Neckar in order to establish the shorter connection between the Rhine and the Danube. The occupation of these areas did not cause any difficulty, since they were almost uninhabited. At the Neckar line, however, they came close to the Germans, and Vespasian's son Domitian occupied the Wetterau after a war with the Chatti. There consequently arose the need to protect a long land border which was made particularly difficult by the form of the salient angle that the border had in the Wetterau.

Domitian took possession of this area and laid out a complete system of forts for its protection. Perhaps in his time or somewhat later there developed what we call the *limes* in the narrower sense, the continuous fortification that connected the forts with each other. This first *limes* was a line of interlocking hedges (*vineae*).

Under Hadrian this *limes* was replaced by a palisade, and it was not until a few generations later that this palisade was completed or replaced by an earthen wall and ditch. It was probably at the beginning of the third century that the last part was added, a high stone wall on the stretch north of the Danube at the Raetian border. In doing this, the line, which previously had conformed more closely to the terrain, was now laid out as straight as possible for better observation and signaling.

As we have still been able to determine at a few spots, the Raetian wall was no less than 2½ meters high.

Hereafter we make the distinction between the *limes* of the upper Rhine, which extended from Neuwied on the Rhine and bent around the Wetterau to Lorch in Württemberg, east of Stuttgart, and the Raetian *limes*, which extended in a west-east direction from that point to the Danube not far from Ratisbon.

As the observer can recognize even today, the upper Germanic line consists in general of an earthen bank with ditch, and the Raetian one of a wall of cut stones placed one above the other. On the former there are small watchtowers about five minutes apart, and close behind the wall at distances of no more than 9 miles apart, are permanent forts of varying size, the average one suitable for a garrison of perhaps one cohort. The forts were originally earthworks, and the watchtowers were of wood. Then they changed over to stone construction. Along the Raetian wall the forts are often situated not directly behind the wall but from 4 to 5 kilometers in the rear. As considerable as the differences between the upper Germanic and the Raetian *limes* are, we are still not justified in concluding that the installations had different purposes. Rather, the differences are to be explained partly by the nature of the ground. It was soft dirt in the one case, therefore calling for earthen walls and ditches, and rocky in the other area, calling for stone walls. Furthermore, the differences are due to the subjective concepts of different commanders as to their suitability for the purpose. Occasionally, remains of a stone wall instead of an earthen one have also been found on the upper Germanic line.

The concept that was generally held earlier, that the wall had been intended for direct defense, can now be abandoned, since it has been realized that a line more than 300 miles long cannot be occupied. It has also been determined that at places, instead of a dike, a hill was partially cut off, with its vertical face not toward the Germanic but toward the Roman side,[2] or that the dike was erected on the outer side of a swamp rather than the inner side. For those scholars who have now gone so far in the other direction as to deny entirely the military purpose of the installation and to see in it only a line for customs collection, that concept is too extreme. Trade with the poor Germans cannot possibly have been so great as to justify such a gigantic undertaking as this wall. It is, in fact, a military installation.

In the first place, the wall was a very important obstacle for the particularly dangerous invaders on horseback. Furthermore, according to an

expression by General Gustav Schröder,[3] the wall may also be characterized as an obstacle to a withdrawal. The garrisons of the watchtowers,
probably three men, were not capable of preventing the incursion of pillaging German bands into the Roman culture area. But they observed
any such approach and passed on the signal. All of the watchtowers were
so placed that the terrain in front of them could be observed for at least a
few hundred meters from the towers, and liaison was possible to the rear
with the forts. On Trajan's Column we also see towers depicted on which
a torch is placed, apparently as a signal. On this signal, part of the fort's
garrison immediately moved out to intercept the invaders. The wall
could be very helpful for this, since it held up the flight of the pursued
Germans. They could not get themselves over so quickly, and in any case
they could not quickly move their booty, livestock, or prisoners and carts
across.[4] If the pursuers came from different directions, they cooperated
from the start in catching the invaders at this point. It was no different
in the case of larger warlike incursions, where the garrison of a fort or
even the fort garrisons together were not sufficient, but legions moved up
from a distance, from the large base camps. Their victory could lead to
the destruction of the enemy if they succeeded in pressing him against
the wall.

The wall probably also had a significance for direct border protection
to the extent that for the Roman patrols on their rounds as well as the
troops it guaranteed good security and cover from direct observation.
The Germans who approached the wall could never know if right on the
other side of the place where they intended to cross over a Roman unit
might by chance be lying in wait for them.

Over the entire stretch from the Rhine to the Danube some fifty forts
may have been occupied simultaneously. Counting the lookouts in the
small watchtowers, there were probably at most 25,000 men, and perhaps only 15,000, garrisoning the *limes*.[5] These troops were not Roman
legionaries, but allies, and therefore partially even Germans in the
Roman service. The legionaries were located farther back on the Rhine,
with the main body at the headquarters in Mainz, another part in Strasbourg, and at the start (until 105 A.D.) in Windisch near Zurich. There
may have also been detachments in a few of the intermediate forts. The
legions of lower Germany were stationed in the camps at Bonn, Neuss,
Nijmegen, and especially at Vetera-Xanten, which continuously
remained the headquarters of this province. Upper and lower Germany
were each occupied by a total of four legions, while Raetia did not have
any legions. Consequently, counting all the troops together, the eight

legions and all the allies, the Romans had some 70,000 men stationed on the line from the North Sea, along the Rhine, along the *limes*, and along the Danube as far as Passau.

The system of border protection established by the Romans was not based on direct and absolute defense of the border line itself, but was of an indirect type. Crossing the border was made difficult wherever possible either by moving up to a natural obstacle, a stream, or by building an artificial one, the wall, and creating a cleared area in front of it. It was not entirely impossible for the Germans to cross over these obstacles, but the well-organized system of observation and reporting always enabled the Romans to exact punishment promptly. The Germans had to learn that while they might succeed in pillaging something on the other side, they would have difficulty bringing back their booty as well as themselves.

In a real war, against the offensive of a large army, the wall was not only valueless for protection but was also even dangerous since it caused the available troops, spread wide apart, to be extended in a cordon. But that was unavoidable, since the border had to be defended anyway. With this possibility in mind, the legions were not drawn into the cordon line but were stationed farther to the rear as a general reserve on the Rhine.

As we now know, the Germans could not easily assemble very large armies, and the Romans were not lacking in contacts in Germany who reported large troop movements to them. As a result, the Romans were always in a position to oppose soon enough, with a sufficiently large army, even a large-scale invasion, by having the legions absorb the closest allies.

Protected by the legions guarding the border, the Romans were able to have their refined culture flourish fully in the immediate proximity of the primeval forest and of the bleak wilderness occupied by a people close to nature and bursting with strength. Today we still admire the remains of the Romans' installations, especially in Trier.

Gradually, the Romans felt so secure that in the middle of the second century the number of the Rhine legions could be reduced from eight to four, two each for the commands on the lower and upper Rhine.

EXCURSUS

1. Since 1885, as a result of the systematic study of the Imperial Commission on the Limes, established by the German Empire, the description of the *limes* that Mommsen gave in the fifth volume of his *Roman History (Römische*

Geschichte), 1885, pp. 140 ff., has been partially confirmed and partially modified, and especially shifted chronologically. The results of the excavations and studies by the Commission are published in the Limes Journal (Limesblatt) and in an excellent report published each year since 1894 in the Archäologischer Anzeiger, mainly by Director Hettner and Professor Fabricius.

In a lecture which Hettner delivered at the Conference of Philologists in Cologne in 1895 and later published (Trier, Fr. Lintz), everything that had been published up to that time was graphically brought together.

In the most recent period, particular mention should be made of an investigation by Professor C. Herzog, "Critical Observations on the Chronology of the Limes" ("Kritische Bemerkungen zu der Chronologie des Limes"), in the Bonner Jahrbücher 105 (1900), and "Roman Roads in the Limes Area" ("Römische Strassen im Limesgebiet") by Lieutenant General von Sarwey in the Westdeutsche Zeitschrift für Geschichte und Kunst 18 (1899).

See also Fabricius' excellent summary, The Origin of the Roman Limes Installations in Germany (Die Entstehung der Römischen Limesanlagen in Deutschland), (Trier, Lintz, 1912, from the Westdeutsche Zeitschrift) and Fabricius' "The Roman Army in Upper Germany and Raetia" ("Das römische Heer in Obergermanien und Raetien"), Historische Zeitschrift, Vol. 98, 1906.

My description given in this book is based on the summary and military history interpretation of these studies, in which I have left aside details and intermediate steps.

### 2. PALISADES

Colonel Cohausen, in his extensive work on the "Roman border wall," rejected as technically impossible the idea that the limes was formed of palisades. General Schröder, in the Preussische Jahrbücher 69: 508, agreed with him, because in view of the temporary life of wood the fort garrisons would have had to be constantly occupied with repairs and replacements. Nevertheless, remains of what were unquestionably palisades have been found. The continuous maintenance work by the soldiers is no reason for rejecting the idea. We could even say that it was quite helpful for discipline that these garrisons, with little else to do, should have something to occupy them. Here for once we have an example that not only the philologists but also the technical experts can go astray. The identical conclusion of two recognized experts in their field has been contradicted by the actual findings of the archaeologists.

### 3. DOMITIAN'S LIMES CONSTRUCTION

According to the commonly held assumption, Domitian's construction of the limes is proven for us by Frontinus (1. 3. 10), where it is said of him: "limitibus per centum viginiti milia passuum actis non mutavit tantum statum belli, sed subjecit ditioni suae hostes, quorum refugia nudaverat." ("After the roads had been extended for 120 miles, he not only changed the nature of the war, but brought under his control the enemy whose havens he had stripped.") In the Militär-Wochenblatt 102 (1900), Col. 2533, General Wolf opposed the validity of this testimony. He calls attention to the fact that militibus, and not *limitibus* is found in the manuscript that has come down to us. He says that *limitibus* is based only on conjecture and that, from the practical viewpoint, such a large fortification could not have been built during a short campaign. One would have to conquer and subjugate the enemy before being able to turn attention to the construction of fortifications. If the Romans had split up their army, bold and enterprising enemies like the Chatti would have attacked the individual detachments occupied in the construction. The author adds: "We have here an example of how a deficient understanding of a military situation could lead even the most expert scholar of the Latin language into error."

No doubt here it is not a question of this point of difference. Even Lieutenant General von Sarwey has accepted the word *limitibus*, and it is undoubtedly the right one. Frontinus' whole chapter treats of the discovery of the most correct strategic system for every occasion, *"De constituendo statu belli"* ("On Establishing the Nature of War"). He explains that Alexander and Caesar had good reasons for always resorting to the decisive battle, whereas Fabius Cunctator was right in doing the opposite. Pericles evacuated the countryside and waged war on the sea. Scipio liberated Italy from Hannibal by moving to Africa himself. In this context, it is said of Domitian: "Imperator Caesar Domitianus Augustus, cum Germani more suo e saltibus et obscuris latebris subinde impugnarent nostros tutumque regressum in profunda silvarum haberent, limitibus per centum viginti milia actis non mutavit tantum statum belli, sed et subjecit ditioni suae hostes, quorum refugia nudaverat." ("When the Germans attacked our forces repeatedly from glens and unsuspected hiding-places, as is their custom, and had a safe retreat into the depths of the forests, the Emperor Caesar Domitianus Augustus, after the roads had been extended for 120 miles, not only changed the nature of the war, but brought under his control the enemy whose havens he had stripped.") If we read *militibus*, there is thus created the picture of a very normal campaign; there can be no question of this constituting a special *"status belli."* If we read *limitibus*, we eliminate this difficulty, but if we retain the normal interpretation of *limes* as a border fortification, then the expression *"refugia nudaverat"* ("havens he had stripped") is hard to explain. I would therefore like to propose that the *limites*, as in Tacitus 2. 7, be conceived of as "routes" rather than "borders." With this interpretation, the whole paragraph takes on a precise meaning and definite coherence. The Chatti could not be pinned down in the remote recesses of their forests; therefore, Domitian laid out 180 kilometers of roads through their territory. He thereby not only changed the *"status belli"* but also subjected to his domination the enemies whose refuges had thus become accessible to him.

If this interpretation also eliminates the testimony for the building of the wall by Domitian, that does not really change anything in this matter, since the conquered area had to be protected and the findings have confirmed the building of the forts in Domitian's time.

Naturally, the army was not divided up for the purpose of building roads, forts, and barriers, but the works were carried out piece by piece under the protection of a sufficient number of assembled troops.

(Added in the second edition.) In his study of the *limes* in the *Bonner Jahrbücher* 114: 109 (see p. 129 above), Oxé proposes changing the number 120,000 to 120 feet (instead of *"limitibus per centum viginti milia actis,"* he suggests "*limitibus ped. CXX actis*"), and he would have the number refer not to the length but to the breadth of the roads. This is a truly classical example of the mistakes to which philological scholarship without military knowledge can lead. Oxé writes: "One cannot possibly assume that a practical officer like Frontinus, when he describes a *limes*, would overlook the figure for the width, the most important item in the whole description and the one that is the most common in professional literature." On the contrary, we can say that in the first place it would hardly be understandable if the Romans, for whom a quick decision was necessarily important, would have taken on themselves the tremendous task of laying out roads 120 feet wide in the wilderness, when a width of 30 feet, or even 20, would have served all necessary purposes. But even if we consider that 120 feet as applying not to the road proper but to the open break in the forests, to deter sudden attacks, the width of the cut is of very little importance in comparison with the length of the installation. During the campaign in enemy territories, the emperor laid out 180 kilometers of roads; that was an accomplishment and was the means for subjecting Germanic tribal areas to the Romans. Only a technician with no military understanding would have accepted the idea of recording for following generations the width of the roads rather than their length. Least of all, however, are we justified in making such an unnecessary and worthless change in a source manuscript that is completely unobjectionable in this respect.

Vieze, in *Domitian's War Against the Chatti (Domitians Chatten-krieg)*, Program of the 8th City *Realschule* in Berlin, Easter, 1902, still holds to the translation of *limites* as "border fortification."

4. A very unusual basis for the withdrawal of the Romans into a simple border defense against the Germans has been put forth by Max Weber in the *Pocket Dictionary of Political Science (Handwörterbuch der Staatswiss-enschaften)*, 1: 180. He believes that the owners of the large provincial estates had required from the army "primarily protection and observation of their land, and consequently *defensive* missions." This calls for the remark that owners of large estates were not protected against barbarians in any other way than were other men. As a result, for them as well the best protection against the Germans would have been their subjugation — provided, of course, that it was possible.

NOTES FOR CHAPTER VII

1. In my opinion, Tacitus, *Annals* 11. 19, stands in contradiction to the indications that the Wetterau was not given up in 16 A.D. either, but, even if at first it was still without a Roman settlement, it remained a Roman occupation area. Tacitus says of Claudius: "adeo novam in Germanias vim prohibuit, ut referri praesidia cis Rhenum juberet." ("He so strongly forbade a new campaign in the Germanies that he ordered the garrisons to be withdrawn to the near side of the Rhine.") A possible explanation for this statement is that it refers only to lower Germany. This explanation is not acceptable, however, and all the less so when *Germania*, Chapter 29, "protalit magnitudo populi Romani ultra

Rhenum ultraque veteres terminos imperii reverentiam" ("The greatness of the Roman people expanded the respect of the empire beyond the
Rhine and beyond the old borders") stands in opposition to it, and also
when Seneca says: "Rhenus Germaniae modum faciat." ("The Rhine
should mark the border of Germany.") Germanicus fought against the
Chatti not only in lower Germany but also right here in the Wetterau.
See Herzog, *Bonner Jahrbücher*, 105 (1901), p. 67. I do not venture to
decide how this contradiction is to be clarified.

2. At any rate, this is claimed by General Schröder, *Preussische
Jahrbücher* 69: 511. But I have never found this point confirmed.

3. *Preussische Jahrbücher* 69: 514.

4. A quite similar system of watchtowers along the borders and of signaling by fires is to be found with the Swiss up to the eighteenth century.
A very interesting account of this system, based on documents and topographical research, is to be found in E. Lüthi, *The Bern Chuzen or
High Watchtowers in the Seventeenth Century (Die bernischen
Chuzen oder Hochwachten im 17. Jahrhundert)*, 3d ed., Bern,
1905, A. Francke. When the Freiburgers made a pillaging incursion into
the Bern area in 1448, that was reported to the capital by the high
watchtower on the Guggershorn. The Bern territorial guard assembled at
once but did not move directly against the Freiburgers. Instead, they
blocked their retreat, defeated them, and took away their booty.

Between Hirschberg and the Riesengebirge, near Arnsdorf, there are
also the remains of such a stone watchtower on a hill from which one can
observe the various crossings over the mountain. It perhaps stems from
the period of the Hussites.

5. Mommsen, *Römische Geschichte* 5: 108, note, estimates the
auxiliaries of the upper German army in the period of Domitian and Trajan at some 10,000 men. The Raetian *limes* was considerably shorter
and more weakly occupied than the upper German *limes*. The Raetian
troops, who, according to Mommsen 5: 143, were at the most 10,000
strong, also had to garrison the Danube line from Ratisbon to Passau.
For this reason, Mommsen believes that the forts were probably only
very weakly garrisoned in times of peace. Nevertheless, they still had to
be able to defend themselves against a sudden attack and to send troops
in pursuit of strong robber bands. According to Mommsen, the lower
Germanic auxiliaries were perhaps even less numerous than those in
upper Germany.

# Chapter VIII

# Internal Organization and Life in the Imperial Roman Army

While it is not our task to present what is known of the ancient forms and relics of the Roman military system, we must still seek to understand the principal aspects of the routine life of this great organization.

The Roman army received its definitive form through a comprehensive, systematic set of regulations proclaimed by Augustus, the *constitutiones Augusti*. Although they are not available to us, we can distinguish them in a general way from citations in various passages.

During the civil wars, the number of legions was constantly increased. Caesar left behind him more than forty, the Triumvirate added a few more, and their opponents, the Republicans, had twenty-three. Octavian and Antony together had more than seventy-five legions in 36 B.C. In the older republic only Roman citizens were mustered into the legions. This basic principle had not only been gradually abandoned but also had been reversed, so to speak: acceptance into the legions brought with it the granting of Roman citizenship. Even Caesar's legions had consisted of a minority of soldiers who were Roman citizens by birth, and this same point applies even more definitely to the legions of the Triumvirate. Many of these legions can have had only a very superficial Roman flavor. Vergil bluntly calls the veterans who were settled in Italy barbarians.[1] When Augustus became the unchallenged single ruler, he returned to the older principles and was able to apply them in a truly ingenious way to the conditions of the world empire that was built around the city of Rome and the Latin people as nucleus. He did not go so far as to separate uncompromisingly troop units of citizens and those of noncitizens, but in keeping with the political situation of the nation, the army, too, was organized in various national contingents. If they had continuously assigned Romans and non-Romans to the same troop units indiscriminately, the Latin element in each individual unit would have been so weak that it could neither assimilate nor dominate the others. Under such loose procedures, the military competence of the troop units would necessarily have suffered.

It appears then that Augustus first reduced the number to eighteen. It was increased to twenty-five by the time of his death and to thirty-three by the time of Septimius Severus. Whereas in the period of the civil wars only lightly armed troops and cavalry had stood, in general, beside the legions as auxiliaries, now a distinction was also made within the heavy infantry between the legions with a definite Roman character and the auxiliaries, who were organized by national groupings in cohorts. The principle that service in a legion automatically led to the granting of Roman citizenship was retained. Consequently, those assigned to the legion were in no way exclusively citizens by birth. We may assume, however, that the noncitizens who were so assigned were always to some extent already Romanized and particularly that they knew the Latin language, so that they did not detract from the overall Roman stamp of the unit.

Under the Julian emperors, the occidental legions were still composed principally of natives of Italy. From the time of Vespasian that situation gradually ended.[2] The Italians then were assigned principally only to the Praetorian Guard in Rome. The legions were filled from the provinces in which they were stationed; even the Germans, to judge from the evidence of the inscriptions, were enlisted in them in increasing numbers.[3] In one of the inscriptions that has come down to us, a Praetorian speaks just as Vergil had spoken of the "barbarian legions." And so it was, according to their blood, but by spirit, custom, and language the legions were now recruited from the national groups of the empire that were already Romanized and were becoming completely so in the service, despite their barbarian origins.

The Roman aspect of these legions was further assured by the fact that only a small proportion of centurions was appointed from the legions themselves. Most of the centurions were taken from the imperial guard, the Praetorians, who were Italians.[4] Furthermore, as a result of very frequent transfers of centurions from one legion to another, which we can discern from the inscriptions, particularly gravestones, the unified spirit of the officer corps of the entire army was maintained and nourished. No doubt, individual Roman citizens also served with the auxiliary troops, but the majority of these troops consisted of Roman subjects who were not yet Romanized. Arms, combat methods, and discipline were the same as in the legions. The officers and noncommissioned officers were Romans, and the duty language was Latin. The vernacular was probably the native one.[5] The difference between these auxiliaries and the legions was therefore only a relative one which disappeared more and more with the passage of time. These auxiliary cohorts formed the bridge to the lightly armed support troops and cavalry organized on a national basis, as well as to the pure barbarians. The relationship of the pure barbarians to the Romans was more that of allies than of subjected peoples; they came to the Romans with their own weapons in their own organizations, under their native leaders. Here, too, there were still various degrees of transition.

Tacitus tells us in *Agricola,* Chapter 28, of a cohort of Usipetes who mutinied in Britain, killed their centurion and the Roman soldiers, "qui ad tradendam disciplinam immixti manipulis exemplum et rectores habebantur" ("who were mixed with their maniples to instill discipline and were considered as an example and instructors"), and tried to escape to their homeland on three ships. In this case, then, the Romans had tried to force the obstinate Germans completely into the forms of the Roman military system.

On the other hand, the Batavians, who rebelled under Civilis, although they also appear as cohorts, were apparently organized on a purely national basis. Just after this revolt, however, the Romans became more careful. They no longer left the Germans together in units from the same district but mixed them up, employed them far from their home area, and, instead of commanders from their own princely families, assigned them Roman officers. The present-day English army in India offers analogies to these Roman auxiliaries.

Of great importance for the character of the Roman army was the organization of the larger bodies of troops. Each legion had attached to it a larger or smaller number of auxiliary cohorts, but the cohorts were not normally of greater strength than the legion itself and were usually considerably smaller. Even if this system was not applied with absolute uniformity, since we have found in Raetia, for example, auxiliaries without legions, the organization described above may be regarded as the truly basic one. Let us understand how different everything would have been if the peregrine cohorts had been grouped together in large numbers or had all been treated as a single unit. In that case, the Roman and non-Roman elements would have stood facing each other as two forces with equal rights; the Roman element would have been overcome by the superior number of the barbarians. By placing the legions in the middle, without completely closing them to the Romanized barbarians, and by grouping around those units the auxiliaries who were still in the barbarian stage or not far from it, they gave the Roman element the dominant position in the whole organization. The cohorts, divided up as individual units and of disparate membership, had no other tie but to the legion. From the innermost Roman nucleus of the legion, the process of Romanization necessarily proceeded gradually farther and farther into the outer circles.

The size of the legion remained on the old basis of some 6,000 men at full strength. With the cavalry that was attached to it and the auxiliaries, we may estimate the total strength at an average between 9,000 and 10,000 men.

Legally and in principle the universal military obligation remained in force as previously. From a practical viewpoint, however, the filling out of the army depended on volunteers and recruiting. Once a soldier enlisted, his service obligation lasted twenty years, or in the case of the Praetorians, sixteen years, but the obligation was often extended much longer. We hear of men who, already physically exhausted, were still retained under the colors, even in some cases where their formal discharge had already been granted them. They were then given the privilege of being excused from work details and were probably also taken out of the legion and grouped together in their own small units, *vexillationi* (detachments). The reason for this probably was not that it would have been difficult to muster recruits or that it would have been too much trouble to train them, but the strong effort to economize on the benefits that were due to veterans.

At times, it probably also happened that voluntary recruiting did not suffice to fill the ranks and that it was then necessary to resort to the draft. The man selected for service was allowed to arrange for a substitute, which, of course, would indicate that there were actually men who were ready to follow the recruiter. The only difference is that by taking the detour as "substitute" they won a bonus that the state, at the discretion of the authorities, imposed on this or that more well-to-do young man.

Slaves were forbidden on pain of death to enter the service.

These conditions are made very clear to us in the correspondence between Pliny and Emperor Trajan. As governor of Bithynia, Pliny inquired of the emperor if he should punish two slaves found among the recruits who had already taken their oath but had not yet been assigned to a troop unit. The emperor replied that it should be determined whether they enlisted voluntarily, were drafted, or had been turned over as substitutes. If they were drafted, that was the fault of the authorities; if they were substitutes, the guilt lay with those who had turned them over; and if they had enlisted voluntarily, they were to be punished. The fact that they had not yet been assigned to a troop unit did not come into consideration.

The concept of the "military height," which has played so large a role in recent times, also existed with the Romans. During the imperial period it was known as *incomma*. As to what height it was, our scholars have expressed remarkably different opinions on the subject. One scholar believes he can interpret from a humorous puzzle that "five Roman feet (1.48 meters) was considered to be a quite respectable height, even for a soldier"[6] — which would make the Romans appear to be a dwarf people, for it is still 6 centimeters shorter than the smallest German or French soldier. Another scholar believes that the height amounted on the average to 5 feet, 10 inches (1.725 meters), which would exceed even the required height for the Prussian Guard.[7] Actually, the passage in question (Vegetius 1.5) states only that this height was required for the first cohort. This would be consistent with the fact that in a later passage we find the height given as 5 feet, 7 inches (1.651 meters).[8] When the number to be levied was only small, they naturally took the best-looking ones, and the "long fellows" became a kind of sport for the commander. We hear of Nero that he drafted for himself a new legion of nothing but 6-footers (1.774 meters),[9] named it the Phalanx of Alexander the Great, and intended to move with it to the Caspian Gates.

Only a very few units were stationed in towns or even only villages. Only Rome had a rather large garrison, but the entire Guard Corps of the Praetorians with the city cohorts was still no stronger than 12,000 men, and it also had a few other stations outside Rome. In all of Gaul, only the capital, Lyons, had a garrison, of 1,200 men. Otherwise, the inner provinces of the empire were without garrisons. The legions were stationed in large fortified camps near the borders. Not far from this fortified camp, but far enough so that a ring of open land surrounded the wall, there soon developed a civilian settlement, the *canabae*, from which in time there developed a city.[10]

The auxiliary cohorts were stationed mostly in the smaller and larger forts directly along the border.

Although they were in the service until the age of forty or fifty, soldiers were forbidden to marry. If they founded a family, they were not allowed to have it in the camp. Since it was not a question of a *"justum matrimonium,"* the authorities took no consideration of this when the troops were moved to another location.

The marriage prohibition also extended to the centurions. Even the highest commanders, whenever they left Rome to take over a command, were supposed to leave their wives at home.

The higher officers, the tribunes and legates, came from the aristocratic families of Rome and of the Roman provincial cities. They were not yet military men in the exclusive and specific sense of the word, but, as in the times of the republic, they were officials and magistrates who exercised every kind of higher function of a judicial, administrative, and military type. The only qualification that was required was the high status, the aristocratic mentality, which can do everything because it is confident of being able to do so. When in his time Lucullus had gone off to Asia to assume command of the army against Mithridates, having supposedly understood nothing about warfare up to that time, he prepared himself while on the way through sessions of instruction and readings.[11] He fulfilled his assignment brilliantly. It is true that Marius spoke to the Roman people in a very deprecating manner about this kind of commander,[12] and in Caesar's writings, too, we do not often find his tribunes praised. In this regard, Augustus found a balance between the Roman social structure and military needs by creating the new position of the camp prefects. As the name implies, originally they were probably post commandants in the large base camps, but very soon their numbers were no doubt increased, as were their functions. The supervision and control of the service administration, of which the more or less amateurish tribunes were not capable, were placed in the hands of the camp prefects. For they were professional soldiers, they came from the ranks of the centurions, and they were the feared supervisors of the discipline. Later, in the third century, they moved completely into the position of the legates and became commanders of the legions.

The backbone of the army remained, as under the republic, the position of the centurion, whom we have described as a kind of first sergeant in the position of company commander (Vol. I, pp. 431, 456). Whereas in the period of the republic the centurions came exclusively from the ranks, now educated young men also came into the army by requesting an appointment as centurion from the emperor and advanced to the position of staff officer. The first type of centurion was called *"ex caliga"* ("from a soldier's boot") and the other *"ex equite Romano"* ("from a Roman knight").

Consequently, the officer corps was no longer so strictly divided into two classes as previously. Anybody entering the army as a private could advance to centurion or even to camp prefect, those entering as centurion could advance to tribune, and the young men of the foremost families, especially senators' sons, entered as tribunes and advanced to legate, corresponding to our generals. Each legion had a legate as permanent commander, perhaps as early as Caesar's time (1. 456). In time, perhaps under Augustus or possibly not until Hadrian, the tribunes also became permanent commanders of the cohorts, a situation that actually would have been required by the military principle as early as Marius' time. The legions continuously had six tribunes, whereas they had ten cohorts, and we are told expressly by Vegetius that the cohorts were commanded partly by tribunes, partly by *praepositi* (Vol. I, p. 436, note 2). It can therefore be assumed that here too the balance between backgrounds was provided for from a practical viewpoint by holding four positions as cohort commanders for promoted centurions. The *praepositi* were therefore probably in an intermediate position between the centurion class and the camp prefects.[13] The men of the military hierarchy whom we would call noncommissioned officers, to include first-class privates, were called *principales* in the imperial army. The most capable, better educated, and bravest of the privates were selected and promoted in accordance with a very definite scheme. The most important assignments were, as in the republic, the *signifer* (standard bearer), the *optio* (second-in-command to a centurion), and the *tesserarius* (keeper of the tablet), who also replaced the centurion as commander or were leaders of small units. From the ranks of the *principales* came not only the centurions but also the administrative officials of the army and the staffs of the higher officers, and finally also the imperial civil officials.[14]

The pay of the legionaries, which under the republic had amounted to 75 denarii per year plus subsistence (*frumentum*), which was reckoned at 45 denarii, had been doubled by Caesar. Augustus increased it toward the end of his reign to three times the original, or 225 denarii (195 marks). How generous this pay was can be deduced from the fact that the auxiliary troops, who lived under exactly the same conditions, did not receive more than a third of that (75 denarii). The Praetorians, however, who did not live in camp but in Rome and a few other comfortable posts, received more than three times as much as the legionaries, 750 denarii, or 650 marks, in addition to their subsistence.

In addition to the regular pay, there were donatives when a new emperor assumed power and on other special occasions, and a premium at the time of discharge that amounted to no less than 3,000 denarii (2,600 marks) for the legionaries and 5,000 denarii (4,300 marks) for the Praetorians. Instead of cash, there was also a gift of farmland, but whether a man who had been a soldier from his eighteenth to his fortieth or forty-fifth birthday could still become a contented small farmer is subject to some doubt. These special gifts, too, were received only by the Praetorians and legionaries, and not by the auxiliaries.

Domitian raised the annual pay of the legionaries to 300 denarii, Commodus to 375, and Septimius Severus to 500. How extensive these increases actually were cannot be determined accurately. Since under Septimius Severus the denarius had only half as much silver as under Augustus, the seemingly great increase in pay may actually have been not much more than an apparent one. It is probable, however, that the purchasing power of the currency had increased so that the actual compensation of the soldiers had indeed been significantly raised, a point that is only natural in view of the emperors' dependence on their soldiers.[15]

The centurions, who under the republic had received only twice the pay of the soldiers, received five times as much under the emperors and therefore rose still farther above the common level than previously.

As had already been the case under the republic, so too under the emperors soldierly pride was stimulated by a whole system of external awards and honors. They were awarded spears of honor, standards, shields, decorative medals to be worn on the chest as well as on the horse's harness, bracelets and necklaces, crowns and wreaths.[16] Entire units, too, were distinguished in this way or by the award of special titles of honor.

The legions and cohorts had definitely assigned doctors and hospitals (*valetudinaria*) with their own administrators and nurses (*qui aegris praesto sunt:* who served the sick).[17]

Horse doctors, too, are mentioned.

In each cohort, under the supervision of the standard bearer, there was a savings bank and also small insurance funds for emergencies, particularly a burial fund. The soldiers were obliged to put a portion of their pay, and especially of their donatives, in the savings account, at least until it reached a certain amount. Pescennius Niger once ordered that the soldiers were to carry absolutely no gold or silver money with them whenever they went to battle, but they were to turn it in to the savings fund and withdraw it at the end of the campaign.

A paid army cannot be administered without a very accurate system of bookkeeping. In the Egyptian papyri there are, in addition to so many other documents, a few dealing with the military. In pages from the years 81 to 87 A.D., there are very carefully recorded in Latin accounts for individual soldiers, commands, leave, and other similar items by the clerk of a century.[18]

Each evening all the trumpeters and buglers assembled at the commander's tent in the camp and blew, as we may directly translate it, the tattoo. Then the night sentries took their posts.[19]

The discipline remained that of the ancient Roman type and severity; whenever it may occasionally have loosened up, each time there was soon a commander who tightened it again. Tacitus reported (*Annals* 11. 18) that Corbulo, when he brought the undisciplined legions back to the old customs under Emperor Claudius, had a soldier executed because he was working on the wall without wearing his sword, as prescribed; another one was executed because he had only a dagger.

The centurions, like our officers in the eighteenth century, always went about with their stick, the vine branch, in hand and used it mercilessly. In the widespread mutiny of the legions after Augustus' death, the soldiers beat to death, in addition to many other officers, a centurion to whom they had given the nickname "*cedo alteram*" — "give me another one" — because, whenever he had broken a stick on the back of a soldier, he used to call for another one. In the army of Frederick the Great, the arbitrary right of superiors to administer punishment was restricted to some extent by the fact that the company commander, coming from the aristocracy, had a kind of patriarchal relationship to his men and was also responsible for their care and partially for their replacement. In the case of the Roman centurion, these mitigating factors were missing. He was nothing more than a superior, he himself supervised the daily duties, and he was all the stricter in that he himself had come from the ranks of the privates.

But it was not simply through the means of disciplinary punishment and the abstract concept of military honor that the Roman army and with it the Roman nation were held together. The political wisdom of this dominant people had made Rome not only the political but also the religious center of the world empire. No doubt they allowed the subjugated peoples to retain their national deities, but everywhere there arose, beside the native gods, the temples and altars on which sacrifices were offered to the Roman gods and simultaneously to the majesty of the emperor. In the Roman camps, the situation was similar but still somewhat different. There was no altar for the Roman deities there. In the legions, they honored the old Capitoline gods, Jupiter, Juno, and Minerva; among the auxiliaries, the native gods were honored, but special worship was conducted among all the troops to the genius of the emperor. As the auxiliaries gradually lost their original national character, received replacements from various sources, and became Romanized, they accepted Roman gods. Mars especially won many worshipers. Numerous other gods or personifications, such as Victoria, Fortuna, Honos, Virtus, Pietas, Disciplina, the Spirit of the Locality, the Spirit of the Drill Field, and the Spirit of the Camp all had their altars.[20] Only infrequently, and not until the third century, do we also find an altar dedicated to the city of Rome. This difference between the civilian and the military religion was the expression of the political position of the army within the nation: the army belonged not so much to the nation as to the emperor, as indeed the army actually gave the emperor his position.

There never took place a theological formulation of the concept of the divinity or the spirit of the emperor, a determination of how this godliness applied to a person of flesh and blood. Some emperors claimed this godliness for themselves, for their own person. The better and wiser ones — Augustus, Tiberius, and the emperors of the second century — let the personal aspect fade into the background, but beside the sacred standards, in the circle of the gods of the military deities, there was also included the likeness of the emperor. The army commander enjoyed honors that were normally attributed to godliness, and the soldier's religion represented the bridging pinnacle of soldierly discipline and soldierly honor.[21]

The imperial Roman army, which assured the civilized world of its day a peace that was for centuries only seldom interrupted, was only a very small one in comparison with the levied armies that we know from Greek history and from the Roman Republic, as well as in comparison with modern standing armies. We may estimate Augustus' twenty-five legions, with the support troops that were constantly in service, even in peacetime, at no more than 225,000 men; the empire had a population between 60 and 65 million souls.[22] The ratio was therefore something over one-third of 1 percent, whereas in the tensest years of the Second Punic War Rome had about 7½ percent of its population under arms, and in

Germany and France before 1914 considerably more than 1 percent were under arms, even in peacetime. Thanks to their organization and discipline, as the Romans themselves said with pride,[23] that small fraction of the service-qualified men was able to maintain peace for the empire, while the great mass of people went about the work of business and agriculture and needed only to pay their taxes in order to be freed of any danger of war.

We must leave aside the question of whether the later increase of the legions from twenty-five to thirty-three meant an actual increase of the army corresponding to the increase of the population, since with the constant extension of Roman citizenship there may also have taken place a shift of auxiliaries into legions. Domitian is supposed to have planned at one time to reduce the army, for reasons of economy, but he had to give up the plan since he would then have become too weak in comparison with the barbarians.[24]

With what parsimonius concern the troops were treated can be recognized from a few passages in the correspondence of Pliny with Trajan. Between the provincial governor and his officials and then between the governor and the emperor himself, there was a haggling, so to speak, over each man, and letters on this subject went back and forth between Bithynia and Rome.

The organization and tactics of the legions remained essentially as before. The fact that the strength of the cohorts was changed and double cohorts (*milliariae*) were created did not have any influence on tactics. The reforms that one or another of the emperors, especially Hadrian, introduced were entirely in the area of regulations, without changing anything in the system of tactics. The field artillery, as we may call it, appears to have experienced a broader development. The catapults and ballista, which were originally used only in sieges, had now been converted for use in combat in the field as well. (See Vol. I, p. 247, the battle of Mantinea, in 207 B.C.) It is possible that Caesar had already provided such weapons for his legions on a regular basis. In a few battles, they are mentioned in his descriptions of his own troops as well as those of his opponents.[25] Tacitus reports on this subject in the battle at the dike of the Angrivarii. According to a later report,[26] every legion was supposedly assigned under the regulations fifty-five mobile ballista and ten onagri. The former engines shot large arrows, were pulled by mules, and required a crew of eleven men, while the latter were drawn by oxen and projected heavy stones. In sieges these weapons were very important. In a battle, however, they can hardly have had a telling effect, since their projectiles, while possessing a strong capability for penetration, were not effective at much longer ranges than the hand weapons. It was therefore easy to avoid them either by drawing back or by pressing forward into close combat.

We do not have particular information about the Romans' drill. But the Greek tacticians of that period have no doubt said so much about the organization and commands that we can form a picture of the drill. We may apply that to the Romans all the more confidently in that it is very similar to the modern forms. This point is explained by the fact that it is a question of such simple laws and basic principles, partly mathematical and partly psychological, that they necessarily call for similar actions on a practical basis in every period and with every people.

The units were drawn up in ranks and files, and were aligned. They had a lead guide and a file closer, and they had distinct movements for turning, wheeling, marching to the rear, and facings. Let us give a few of the commands verbatim:

| | |
|---|---|
| Take arms! | *age eis to hopla!* |
| Fall out! | *ho skeuophoros apochōreitō!* |
| Attention! | *siga kai proseche tōi paraggellomenōi!* |
| Shoulder arms (spear)! | *anō ta dorata!* |
| Order arms (spear)! | *kathes ta dorata!* |
| Right face! (to the spear) | *epi dory klinon!* |
| Left face! (to the shield) | *ep' aspida klinon!* |
| Forward march! | *proage!* |
| Halt! | *echetō houtōs!* |
| Right dress! | *zygei!* |
| Cover down! | *stoichei!* |

The exactness of all drill depends on the division of the command into two parts, the preparatory command and the command of execution. This technique was also already known by the men of antiquity. In the authors on tactics, Asclepiodotus and Aelian, we find not only the indication that the commands had to be short and clear but also that the special indication had to be given before the general one: consequently, not "Face — to the spear!" but "To the spear — face!" Otherwise, in their eagerness, some would face to the right and others to the left.

According to army regulations, the Roman soldiers were supposed not only to drill but also to fence, shoot, do gymnastic exercises, swim, and maneuver. Maneuver is called *decursio* and is explained as "divisas bifariam duas acies concurrere ad simulacrum pugnae" ("the battle lines, divided on the two sides of the field, charge each other in a mock battle"). It therefore corresponds exactly to what we understand by that word. Three times a month a practice march (*ambulatio*) with full field equipment was to be made, 10 miles out and 10 miles back.[27]

As in modern standing armies, the discipline was based on drill. But the number of new recruits was very small; the great majority of the legions consisted, after all, of older men. In the armies of the eighteenth century, where a similar condition existed, it was customary to send most of the older men on leave, except for a short maneuver period during the year, and to assign those who were present to guard duty. This system of leaves could not be used for the Roman soldiers, who had the constant duty of border protection. Consequently, as had already been the case in the republican period, the soldiers were kept busy with construction. Not only the *limes*, its towers and its forts were built and maintained by the soldiers themselves, but also the great roads in the border provinces, where even today we can often make out from inscriptions which troop unit built them. Augustus expressly forbade using the soldiers for private undertakings, but they were used for the construction of temples and other public buildings.

A striking example of how very much men always remain basically the same, and how the same institutions always produce the same results, is provided by a document from Roman army history that has come down to us by chance and gives us the picture of a troop inspection.

When the French conquered Algeria, they discovered a large inscription in a relatively deserted region called Lambaesis, where there had long been a legion camp. The inscription was recognized as a speech by Emperor Hadrian which he delivered to the troops on the 1st of July, 128 A.D., after inspecting them there. The commanding legate, Catullinus, had the words carved in stone as an eternal reminder of how well he and his legion had performed in the emperor's inspection. The French colonel honored this souvenir of his far-removed military comrade by a parade in which he had his regiment pass in review before the stone inscription. Since that time, frequent efforts have been made to fill in the missing pieces and words from the context. In this manner, a text has been reconstructed which, to be sure, is not complete but is legible in its main parts. Together with my old school friend Wilhelm Möller and in accordance with the *Corpus inscriptionum latinarum (Corpus of Latin Inscriptions)*, I had it printed in the *Militär-Wochenblatt* in 1882, with the addition of a translation which seeks to show as strongly as possible the similarity of tone to modern forms. I believe that whoever h~~

some contact with the interior life of our army will necessarily feel what we might call the humor of world history in reading how the mixture of recognition and criticism, praise and restraint, authority and good will, the regulation, the greater wisdom of the superior, and instruction have all belonged since time immemorial to the ingredients of a maneuver critique.

The inscription reads as follows:[28]

(Concerning the
legion in general)

. . . et is pro causa ves-
[tra] legatus meus quae excusa
[nda] vobis aput me fuissent
omnia

In his report my legate has explained the particular situation of the regiment (of the division):[29]

mihi pro vobis ipse di[xit: quod]
cohors abest, quod omnibus annis
per vices in officium pr[ocon]sulis
mittitur, quod ante annum ter-
tium cohortem et qua[ternos] ex
centuris in suplementum compa-
rum tertianorum dedistis, quod
multae, quod diversae stationes
vos distinent, quod nostra memo-
ria bis non tantum mutastis castra sed et nova fecistis: ob haec
excusatos vos habe[rem si miles]
diu exercitatione cessasset. Sed
nihil aut cessav[isse videtur, aut
est ulla causa cur . . . a vobis
excusationem accipiam. omnia
strenua fecistis, cum et . . .

one battalion is missing; one command is designated for administration, with annual rotation of this assignment; three years ago, one battalion and one-fourth of the companies had to be transferred as replacements to the sister regiment, the third;[30] the regiment is divided among many separated garrisons; in the most recent past, it has not only changed its base camp twice but has also been obliged to build and fortify a new one. All these reasons would serve as an excuse for the regiment if there had been no maneuvers for larger units for a long time. The results of the inspection show this excuse to be superfluous, and I can express to the regiment my complete satisfaction . . .

vide[antur attendi]sse vobis; primi ordines et centuriones agiles [pro mune] re suo fuerunt.[31]

The staff officers (or the legate?) have carefully supervised the training of the troops. The captains, junior officers, and noncommissioned officers have been enthusiastic in the performance of their duties.[32]

Eq(uites) leg(ionis.)
[Exe]rcitationes militares quodam modo suas leges [ha]bent, quibus si quit adiciatur aut detrahatur, aut minor [exer]citatio fit aut difficilior; quantum autem difficultatis [additur, t]antum gratiae demitur. Vos ex difficilibus difficil[limum fecistis], ut loricati iaculationem perageretis . . . laud]o, quin immo et animum probo . . .

The Cavalry
Military training forms an organic whole; if something is added to it or something omitted, then the training is insufficient or it is too hard; if the difficulty is too great, there is a loss in the perfection of the execution. But the regiment has not been satisfied simply with the difficult; instead, it has accomplished the most difficult tasks, that is, it has trained cuirassiers as marksmen (it is not my intention to criticize this completely), but even praise the spirit that lies behind it (while . . .

[Catullinus, leg(atus) meus, cl(arissimus) v(ir), copiis omni]bus, quibus praeest, parem curam suam exhib[et; . . . prae]fectus vester sollicite videtur vobis attendere. Congiarium accipite viatoriam in Commagenerum campos . . .

(Auxiliary Troops)
His excellency, General Catullinus, shows equal concern for all of the arms under his command. . . the colonel has carefully supervised the training of his unit. I grant the unit a special additional subsistence allowance for the march back to Commagene . . .

Eq(uites) coh(ortis) VI Commagenorum.
Difficile est, cohortales equites etiam per se placere, difficilius post alarem exercitationem non

The Cavalry of the Sixth Commagene Battalion
It is inherently difficult for the battalion cavalry to make a good impression,[33] and even more diffi-

displicere: alia spatia campi, alius iaculantium numerus, frequens dextrator.[34] cantabrius densus,[35] equorum forma, armorum cultus pro stipendi modo. Verum vos fastidium calore vitastis, strenue faciendo quae fieri debebant; addidistis, ut et lapides fundis mitteretis et missilibus confligeretis; saluistis ubique expedite. Catullini leg(ati) mei c(larissimi) v(iri) |insignis cura] apparet, quod tales vos sub . . .

cult for it not to show up poorly if it has been preceded by the drills of the cavalry regiments; the space, the number of troopers, the intricate wheelings,[34] the closed mass, the excellent remounts, the splendid equipment corresponding to the higher pay — everything is different. This is all the more reason for recognizing that the squadron has overcome this difficulty through its hard work, proved itself competent in the prescribed exercises, carried out in addition combat with the catapult and the missile and showed unusual skill in its vaulting. It gives testimony of the careful attention of his excellency, General Catullinus, that he . . . you . . .

|quas] alii |per] plures dies divisis[sent, e]as uno di peregistis; murum lo[ngi] operis et qualis mansuris hibernaculis fieri solet, non [mul]to diutius exstrucxistis, quam caespite exstruitur, qui modulo pari caesus et vehitur facile et tractatur et sine molestia struitur ut mollis et planus pro natura sua vos lapidibus grandibus, gravibus inaequalibus, quos neque vehere neque attollere neque locare quis possit nisi ut inaequalitates inter se compareant; fossam glaria duram scabramque recte percussistis et radendo levem reddidis-

(The Maneuver)

The regiment has accomplished in one day things that normally require several days; it completed a very extensive field fortification, of the type normally used for winter base camps, in a period of time that was not much longer than what is needed when strips of turf are used, which, cut into equal sections according to their type, can easily be obtained and handled, whereas in this case large, heavy stones and rocks were used, which can neither be transported, nor lifted, nor built up without matching up the unevenness between them. The tis. Opere probato introgressi castra, raptim et cibum et arma cepistis, equitem emissum secuti magno clamore revertentem per |spatia excepistis. . . .

ditch, which the regiment had to lay out in hard, rocky ground, was correctly dug, and the sides were smoothed off by hewing. After the completion of this work, the camp was occupied, a meal was quickly cooked, and the troops again formed up. When the cavalry that had been sent out in advance then came dashing back, they were taken in through the intervals and with a loud hurrah . . . .

fecistis et manibus non languidis id . . . non ad signum miseritis[36] quod iam hostis . . . mittendi saepius et instantius hostis ultra.[37] non audeat castra . . . tarde iunxistis . . . erumpetis.

. . . the enemy no longer dares to approach the camp . . . rallied too slowly . . . sortie.

Catullinum leg(atum) meum cl(arissimum) v(irum)| laudo, quod convertuit vos ad hanc exercita|tionem, quae veram di|micationis imaginem accepit, et sic exercet, |ut probare et lau|-dare vos possim; Cornelianus prefectus ves|ter officio suo sa|tisfecit. Contrari discursus non placent mihi. Ne temere, Augustus est auctor. e tecto transurrat eques et pe|rsequatur caute; si non videt| qua vadat aut si voluerit ecum[38] r|etinere nequit, non potest quin sit obnoxius caliculis tectis . . . si vultis congredi debetis concurrere . . . iam adversus hosti facienda . . .

His excellency, General Catullinus, had planned the maneuver (general concept) in such a way that the combat situation corresponded closely to a wartime situation; this point I must commend. The execution by the troops also deserves high praise. Colonel Cornelianus showed himself equal to the demands of his position. I cannot approve his attacks in an extended line(?) The regulations of Emperor Augustus prescribe that the cavalry not advance carelessly out of its cover and that it pursue cautiously; if the rider cannot see where he is going or cannot bring his horse to a halt whenever he

wants to, he will plunge into pit-
falls. . . . The attack must be
made in closed formation.

To this general order of Hadrian, I would now also like to add Tacitus'
account of the great soldiers' rebellion at the time of Tiberius' accession
(*Annals*, Book I).

It is impossible to arrive at a more lifelike picture of the Roman army
in its wonderful blend of common and superior qualities than in the
account of this internal movement that has come down to us from Tacitus' masterly hand. The relationship of the soldier to the dynasty, of the
Roman to the provincials, of the Roman military nation, with the emper-
or as its head, to the Roman civilian nation, which was still represented
in the senate, all of this becomes as lifelike for us in the words that we
find here as did the army of the Roman Republic in the speech by the
centurion Ligustinus. It is not only because of the Roman army that we
want to repeat the full text of Tacitus' account. It is also because, in the
continuation of this work, we shall have occasion time and again to refer
to it when similar, indeed completely identical, events come to our attention in the armies of other periods and other peoples.

Tacitus reports:

This was the situation in Rome, when an uprising broke out among the
Pannonian legions — not from any special causes, but only because the
change of emperor gave promise of a lack of punishment for the rebellion
and the prospect of gain in a civil war. Three legions were together in the
summer camp under the command of Junius Blaesus. Upon receiving
news of Augustus' death and Tiberius' accession to power, he had
stopped the usual military exercises because of the mourning observance
and the celebration for the new emperor. This was the first cause that the
soldiers became boisterous, assumed a hostile tone, and lent their ears to
the arguments of the worst ones, and finally longed for revelry and idle-
ness, being weary of military discipline and work. In the camp there was
a certain Percennius, formerly the head of the theater claque and now a
private soldier, a fresh gossip, clever in stirring up trouble as a result of
his theatrical ability. Gradually, in nightly gatherings, he stirred up the
simple souls who were concerned about the lot of the soldiers after
Augustus' death, or when the time was appropriate and the more sensible
soldiers were not present, he assembled the worst ones about him. Finally, when other associates in the uprising were also ready, he began as
speaker to ask the following questions:

Why did they obey like slaves the small number of centurions and the still smaller number of tribunes? When would they ever be able to demand relief if they were not willing to go to the new prince, still uncertain in his position, with requests or with weapons? They had sinned enough from cowardice for so many years, since they had thirty to forty campaigns behind them and were now old men, most of them affected by wounds. And for the discharged men, too, he went on to say, their service was not ended, but, retained under the colors, they had to bear the same difficulties under another title. And if a man survived so many hardships, then he was sent off to distant lands where, under the name of fields, he was given boggy swamps or rough mountainous terrain. The service itself, he said, was in truth oppressive and miserable; a man's life and limb were valued at ten asses a day, and from that they had to provide clothing, weapons, and tent and from this amount also had to buy themselves out of mistreatment by the centurions and military labor details. Alone under the sky, their lot would continue always to be blows, wounds, hard winters, plague-filled summers, horrible war, or miserable peace. There was no other resort than to enter the service under specific conditions: that each one receive 1 denarius as pay; that the period of service end after sixteen years; that they not be held any longer under the colors, but that the bonus be paid in cash in the camp itself. After all, were the Praetorian cohorts, who received 2 denarii as pay and were sent home after sixteen years of service, exposed to more dangers? He did not wish to put down guard duty in the city, but only *they* had to face the barbarian enemies from their very tents.


The crowd, thoroughly stirred up, shouted its approval. Some bitterly showed the welts from their blows, others their gray hair, and most of them their worn-out clothing and exposed limbs. Finally, they became so enraged that they undertook to join the three legions into one. Restrained from this action by jealousy, because each one thought his own legion should have that honor, they had another idea and placed the three eagles and the field standards of the cohorts together. At the same time, they brought up pieces of turf and erected a stage, so that the position would be more obvious. During this activity Blaesus came up, reproached them, and restrained a few individuals, crying aloud: "Better to dip your hands in my blood; it is less of a sacrilege to kill the legate than to fail your emperor. I will either guarantee the loyalty of the legions alive or, murdered, hasten their remorse."

Nevertheless, the turf was piled up. It had already reached chest height when, finally overcome by Blaesus' firmness, they gave up the undertaking. With great skill of speech, he said to them: "Soldiers must not bring their wishes to the attention of the ruler by mutiny and conspiracy; such reforms would neither have been demanded from the old emperors by your predecessors nor by you yourselves from the god-like Augustus. It would be very untimely to add to the cares of a new ruler." If, nevertheless, they wished to wrest for themselves in peacetime what not even the winning side had demanded in the civil wars, why would they use force in violation of the spirit of obedience and the law of military discipline? They should appoint representatives and give them their charge in his presence. They shouted: "Blaesus' son, the tribune, is to become our spokesman and demand for the soldiers their discharge after sixteen years of service." They would then take up the next step after the first had succeeded. After the departure of the young man it was quite peaceful. In the meantime, the soldiers boasted that the appointment of the legate's son as spokesman for the common cause proved sufficiently that they had accomplished by pressure what they would not have gained through moderation.

Before the beginning of the revolt, a few maniples had been sent to Nauportus for road and bridge construction and other necessary work. As soon as they had learned of the unrest in the camp, they moved out with their colors. After they had plundered the closest villages, including Nauportus itself, which was the equivalent of a country town, they pursued the centurions, who were defending themselves as best they could, with mockery and insults, and finally with blows. Most of all they hated the camp prefect, Aufidienus Rufus, whom they pulled from his wagon, loaded with baggage, and pushed along in front of the column, sarcastically asking if he didn't like such a heavy load and such a long march. For Rufus, long a common soldier, then a centurion, and now camp prefect, grown gray through years of work and hardship, wanted to restore the former strict concept of service, and that all the more uncompromisingly because he himself had experienced it.

As a result of their arrival in the camp, the rebellion flared up again; roaming about, they devastated the surrounding area. Blaesus ordered that a few of those who had the most booty be beaten with rods and imprisoned, as an example for the others, for at that time the centurions and the more loyal soldiers were still obedient to the legate. When those mutineers were seized, they resisted, throwing their arms around the knees of those standing nearby. They called now to individuals by name and now to the century to which each one belonged, the cohort, and the legion, while shouting that all the others could expect the same treatment. At the same time, they heaped insults on the legate, swore by heaven and the gods, and did everything possible to stir up bitterness, sympathy, fear, and hate. Now everybody rushed up. They broke into the jail, removed the fetters from the prisoners, and gathered into their ranks the deserters and condemned criminals.

The violence now became more extreme and the revolt gained new leaders. A certain Vibulenus, a private soldier, was lifted up on the shoulders of his fellows in front of Blaesus' tribunal and spoke as follows to the raging crowd, who listened tensely to his speech:

You have, it is true, restored light and breath to these innocent, pitiable men, but who will give life back to my brother, who will give my brother back to me? He who was transferred to you from the army in Germany for the common good was strangled by this man last night by means of his gladiators, whom he maintains and arms to the detriment of the soldiers. Answer, Blaesus, where have you thrown his corpse? Even the enemy does not begrudge one a grave. Once I have stilled my sorrow by embracing him and shedding my tears, then you may have me murdered also. But just let us be buried by these men here, since we have been killed not because of crimes but for the sake of the welfare of the legions!

These words he emphasized with sobbing as he beat his hands against his breast and face. Then he pushed aside those who were carrying him on their shoulders, sprang down, and throwing himself at the feet of the individuals, he aroused such consternation and animosity that some of the soldiers tied up the gladiators in Blaesus' service. Others bound his other servants, and still others ran off to look for the corpse. And if it had not quickly become known that there was no corpse to find, that the slaves on the torture rack denied the murder, and that the man had never had a brother, the mob would have been close to murdering the legate. Still they drove out the tribunes and the camp prefect and plundered their baggage. They killed the centurion Lucillius, whom they had given the nickname "Give me another one," because when he had broken one rod on a soldier's back, in a loud voice he called for another one and still another. The other centurions were able to hide, except that Clemens

Julius, who because of his good sense appeared to be useful, was held to carry out the demands of the soldiers. In fact, the eighth and the fifteenth legions even drew swords against each other because the eighth demanded the death of a centurion named Sirpicus and the fifteenth protected him. The ninth legion intervened between the two, asking for moderation and threatening the more obstinate soldiers.

News of this uprising forced Tiberius, as reserved as he normally was and inclined to conceal sad events as much as possible, to send his son Drusus with the leading statesmen and two Praetorian cohorts but without any specific instructions. Drusus was to take action according to the situation. The cohorts were reinforced to an unusual degree with specially selected men. Included were a large part of the Praetorian cavalry and the nucleus of the Germans who at that time formed the emperor's life guard. The Praetorian Prefect Aelius Sejanus, who was highly regarded by Tiberius, was assigned to his father Strabo as an official partner to give guidance to the young Drusus and to indicate to the others what they had to fear or hope for. As Drusus approached, the legions moved out to meet him, ostensibly to render honors. However, they met him not smartly, as was customary, with shining equipment, but covered with dirt, with a general attitude that was supposed to show sorrow but actually revealed more defiance.

As soon as Drusus was inside the wall, they posted sentinels at the gates and armed patrols at specified places in the camp. The rest of the men gathered in a large crowd around the tribunal. Drusus stood there, holding up his hand to request silence. Whenever the men looked at one another in the crowd, they raised a wild, threatening shout. On the other hand, when they looked at Drusus, they shuddered. Now a dull murmur, then shrill shrieking, and then sudden silence — with alternating moods they showed fear or they became frightening. Finally, after this tumult subsided, Drusus read aloud his father's proclamation, as follows:

The brave legions with whom he had fought so many wars were particularly close to his heart. As soon as his spirit had recovered from his present sadness, he would present the demands of the legions to the city fathers. In the meantime he had sent his son to grant without delay what could be approved immediately. The remaining points would be brought before the senate, which by the law had to approve benefits and punishment.

The assemblage replied that the centurion Clemens would present their demands. He began with the discharge after sixteen years of service and then with the benefits to be granted after their service was completed. They were to receive 1 denarius of pay daily, and the veterans were no longer to be retained under the colors. When Drusus pointed out the legal requirement for a decision by the senate and his father, he was interrupted by shouting.

Why had he come if he had no authority to raise the pay or to lighten the burdens or to grant any kind of benefit? On the contrary, by the gods, every person was authorized to fight and to kill. Previously, Tiberius had frustrated the legions' wishes in the name of Augustus, and now Drusus was resorting to the same pretenses. After all, would it always be only the sons of emperors that came to them? This was something completely new, that the emperor should refer to the senate only the advantages for the soldier. The senate should also be called on whenever there was a question of an execution or a battle. In other words, did rewards depend on higher authorities while punishments were purely arbitrary?

Finally they left the tribunal. As they encountered a Praetorian soldier or a friend of Drusus, they threatened him with their fists, to stir up quarrels and open combat. They felt the most bitterness against Cneus Lentulus because they believed that this man, outstanding for his age and his combat record, was supporting Drusus and detested the sacrilegious conduct of the soldiers. Not long afterward, as he was walking off with Drusus and wanted to go back into the camp to protect himself from danger, they surrounded him and asked where he wanted to go, to the emperor or to the city fathers? And would he there oppose the best interests of the legions? At the same time they attacked him, throwing stones. When he was already bleeding from being hit and his death seemed certain, he was saved by one of Drusus' units which hastened to the scene.

The threats and potential dangers of the night were alleviated by a fortuitous event: suddenly, in the clear sky, the moon was seen to turn dark. The soldier, ignorant of the reason, took it as an indication of the present situation, comparing the darkening of the moon with his complaints. Whatever they set out to do would go well, provided that the moon goddess again became bright and clear. Consequently, they raised a great din with the banging of metals and sounding of trumpets and horns. As the moon became brighter or darker, there arose jubilation or lamenting. When gathering clouds covered it, since they thought it was buried in darkness, they wailed (as frightened spirits are inclined to superstition) that they were doomed to eternal misery since the gods loathed their sacrilege. Drusus, realizing that he must take advantage of this mood and cleverly utilize the opportunity offered by chance, sent men around in the tent area. The centurion Clemens was called up, as well as other reasonable men who were still in favor with the crowd. They mixed in with the night watch, the camp sentries, and the gate guards, holding up some hope and then playing on fear.

How long are we going to besiege the emperor's son? When will this bickering end? Are we to shelter Percennius and Vibulenus? Will Percennius and Vibulenus distribute the reward to the warriors, will they give land to the retirees? Are they, in the end, to take over the leadership of the Roman people instead of a Tiberius and a Drusus? Let us, rather, as the last ones to be at fault also be the first ones to repent! General wishes are slow to get attention; special pardon will be granted as soon as it is deserved.

When spirits were shaken by these words and the men became mistrustful of one another, the young soldiers moved away from the veterans, one legion from the other. Then the spirit of obedience gradually returned. They moved away from the gates and took the field standards, which had been gathered in one place at the start of the mutiny, back to their proper places.

At daybreak Drusus called for an assembly. Although he was inexperienced in speaking, he showed inherent dignity, denouncing the earlier attitude and praising the present one. "He would not let himself be influenced by fear and threats," he said; "when he saw them return to moderation and when he heard them imploring, he would write to his father, recommending that he receive their requests graciously." At their request, the same Blaesus, together with Lucius Apronius, a Roman knight from Drusus' cohort, and Justus Catonius, senior centurion, were sent to Tiberius. The commanders were of different opinions. Some advised that they should await the return of the emissaries and in the meantime appease the soldiers. Others believed they had to use stronger medicine: there should be no moderation in dealing with the crowd; if they were not trembling, they would terrify others; if kept intimidated, they could be held down without punishment. When they were still fearful from their superstition, the commander must reinforce their fear by removing the leaders of the mutiny. Drusus was more inclined to toughness; he had Vibulenus and Percennius called before him and executed. Many reported that they were buried in the commander's tent, while others said that their bodies were thrown outside the wall as an example.

Thereafter the most prominent instigators of the uprising were sought out. Some of them, walking around outside the camp, were killed by the centurions or the Praetorian soldiers; a few were delivered up by their maniples, as a proof of their loyalty. The soldiers' troubles were increased by the early winter. Because of the continuous and heavy rainfalls they could not leave their tents, could not assemble, and indeed could hardly protect their colors, which were torn loose by wind and storm. Their fear of the gods' anger also continued. "It was not for nothing that the stars faded from the sight of the mutineers, storms broke out, and there was no other amelioration of the troubles except that they should leave the unholy and defiled camp and each one, absolved through sacrifices, should return to his own winter camp." First the eighth and then the fifteenth legion marched off. The ninth had cried out that they should wait for Tiberius' answer, but now, abandoned by the departure of the others, it voluntarily bowed before the threat of necessity. Drusus, without awaiting the return of the emissaries, went back to Rome, since everything now was relatively quiet again.

During almost those same days and for the same reasons the Germanic legions rebelled. Since they were more numerous, their uprising was all the more violent. They also had hopes that Germanicus, unwilling to tolerate the leadership of another, would place his dependence on the legions. Two armies were posted along the Rhine. One of them, called the Upper one, was under the command of the legate Caius Silius, and the Lower one was commanded by Aulus Caecina. All were under the command of Germanicus, who at that time was busy with the collection of tribute in Gaul. The soldiers under Silius watched in an indecisive mood the progress of the other mutiny, while the soldiers of the Lower army worked themselves into a rage. The start of the uprising took place with the twenty-first and fifth legions. The first and twentieth were swept along, for they were billeted in the same summer camp on the border of the Ubii, with little or nothing to occupy them. At the news of Augustus' death the crowd of common soldiers, who had recently been levied in Rome and were therefore not accustomed to discipline and uninclined to work, incited the aroused spirits of the others, saying: "The time was come when the veterans could demand a prompt discharge, the younger soldiers increased pay, and all of them relief from their misery, and they could avenge the harshness of the centurions." It was not just a single man who spoke this way, as in the case of Percennius and the Pannonian legions, and not to the sober ears of soldiers who were hesitant in the face of stronger armies. Rather, the mutinous cry rang out from many voices. "The Roman power lay in their hands; it was through their victories that the commonwealth was expanded; it was from them that the emperors received their surnames."

The legate did nothing to stop the growing rebellion; he had lost his courage because the mutineers were so numerous. Suddenly, the raging soldiers fell with drawn swords on the centurions, who as the traditional objects of the soldiers' hate, became the first sacrifices to their rage. They assaulted the overwhelmed centurions with blows, sixty against one, according to the number of centurions. These victims, beaten, badly cut up, and in some cases already dead, were thrown out in front of the camp or into the Rhine. Septimius, who had fled to the tribunal and had thrown himself at Caecina's feet, was demanded so urgently and so long that he was finally turned over to the mob to be killed. Cassius Chaerea, who at that time was a young man of bold courage and who was later to make a name for himself by murdering Caius Caesar, cut his way with his sword through the rebellious and armed men. No tribune, no camp prefect was able to give commands from that time on. Night watches, sentries, and whatever other duties were required for the daily routine were determined by the soldiers themselves. Anyone looking more deeply into the soldiers' mood found in it an outstanding indication of deeper unrest, which was not to be quieted, for they rose up together and not sporadically, and not at the instigation of a few. They remained quiet, too, all at the same time. All of this occurred so unanimously and consistently as if they were being led by a single chief.

In the meantime, Germanicus, who was in Gaul collecting taxes, as we have said, received word of Augustus' death. He was married to Agrippina, Augustus' granddaughter, and had several children by her. He himself was the son of Drusus, Tiberius' brother, and the grandson of Augusta. Nevertheless, he was tormented by the hidden hate of his uncle and his grandmother, which, because unjust, was all the more bitter. Drusus was held in high regard by the Roman people, and it was believed that if he had acceded to the throne, he would have instituted freedom. Consequently; there was the same preference for Germanicus and similar hopes. That young man had a spirit of citizenship, unusual cordiality, and a completely different manner of speech and countenance than the proud, withdrawn Tiberius. The situation was further aggravated by womanly animosity resulting from Livia's stepmotherly hate for Agrippina. Agrippina was also somewhat too irritable, but still her uprightness and love for her husband gave her strong spirit a better direction.

As for Germanicus himself, the nearer he was to the throne, the more energetically he supported Tiberius. He had the neighboring Sequani and the Belgian towns do homage to Tiberius. After that, on hearing of the legions' uprising, he hastened off and met them outside the camp, with their eyes cast down as if from remorse. When he went inside the wall, the soldiers raised their voices in confused complaints. A few of them, grasping his hand as if to kiss it, put his fingers into their mouths so that he could feel their toothlessness, while others showed him their legs, bent with age. Germanicus ordered the crowd that was standing around him in disorderly groups to line up in ranks. Their answer was they could hear him better that way. He then said that they should bring up the colors so that he could at least distinguish the cohorts. They obeyed with some hesitation. Beginning with a tribute to Augustus, he went on to speak of Tiberius' victories and triumphs, with particular praise of the great things he had accomplished in Germany with those legions. He then pointed out Italy's harmony and Gaul's loyalty, saying that nowhere was there disturbance or discord.

They listened to him silently or with moderate murmuring. But when he touched on the uprising, asking "where military order was? where the reputation for the old soldierly discipline? and where they had driven off the tribunes and the centurions?" then they all bared their bodies and showed him their scars and the welts from their lashes. Then with confused shouting, they complained about the expensiveness of leave periods, the paltry pay, and the hard work, pointing out especially the digging and entrenching, the carrying of fodder, building materials, wood, and whatever else was required through necessity or to keep the soldiers occupied. The wildest outcry was made by the veterans who had thirty or more years of service. They begged that he help those who were thus afflicted and not let them die in misery, but provide for them an end of such difficult service and rest without poverty. Others demanded the money left by Augustus, making favorable suggestions for Germanicus and saying that if he wanted the crown, he could count on their support. At this word he sprang quickly down from the tribune as if their treachery defiled him. As he was hastening away, they held up their weapons to stop him and made threats if he did not turn around. "Better to die than to violate loyalty," he cried. He drew his sword in order to plunge it into his breast, but the closest men, seizing his hand, forcibly held him back.

The rearmost part of the crowd, tightly squeezed together, and, almost unbelievably, a few who were closer, cried out: "Go ahead, strike!" A soldier named Calusidius offered him his drawn sword, saying that it was a sharper one. Even the mutineers found this despicable and wicked; there was a pause during which Germanicus was led off to his tent by his friends.

Here they took counsel as to countermeasures, for it was reported that the mutineers were planning to draw the army of upper Germany to their support by sending emissaries. The city of the Ubii (Cologne) was said to be marked for destruction, and then the robbing crew would fall upon Gaul with their plundering. Their fears were increased by thoughts of the enemy's reaction because, aware of the Romans' uprising, they would break through as soon as the banks of the Rhine were abandoned. If they planned to arm the support troops and allies against the defecting legions, a civil war could be feared. Toughness would be dangerous and compliance would be disgraceful. Whether they gave nothing or everything to the soldier, the commonwealth would still be in danger. After they had weighed all these points one against the other, it was decided to draw up a proclamation in the name of the commander: "Retirement will be granted after twenty years of service. Whoever has served sixteen years will be separated but still retained under the colors, excused from all work except combat against the enemy; the requested legacy will be paid out and doubled."

The soldiers, noting that for the time being these steps were only planned, pressed for implementation. The retirements were expedited by the tribunes, and the distribution of the money for everybody was postponed until the winter camp. The fifth and twenty-first legions did not march off until they were paid while still in the summer camp. Germanicus and his friends raised the money from their travel funds. The legate Caecina led the first and twentieth legions back into the city of the Ubii. This was a shameful march, since they carried along, between the field standards and the eagles, the money forced from the commander. Germanicus traveled off to the upper army, where the second, thirteenth, and sixteenth legions took the oath without hesitation. The fourteenth hesitated for a while; it was then offered a bonus and retirement without having demanded those benefits.

Among the Chauci the *vexillarii* of the revolting legions which were garrisoned there began an uprising that in the meantime was subdued to a certain extent by the prompt execution of two soldiers. The camp prefect, Menius, had ordered this execution more as a frightening example than as a matter of appropriate justice. Later, fleeing from the swelling tumult, he was found, and when concealment did not offer him security, he sought protection through boldness, saying: "It is not the prefect that you are profaning but the commander, Germanicus, and Emperor Tiberius." At the same time, he frightened back those who were opposing him, seized the colors, and turning toward the river, he cried: "Anyone stepping out of ranks will be considered a deserter." And so he led the troops, still tumultuous but not willing to take further risks, back into the winter camp.

In the meantime, the representatives of the senate met Germanicus, who had already returned, at the altar of the Ubii. At that same place two legions, the first and the twentieth, were spending the winter, together with the veterans who were recently discharged but still under the colors. Timidly and confused by a sense of guilt, they feared that the representatives had come at the command of the city fathers to cancel what had been won by the uprising. And as it is normal for the common man to look for a scapegoat, even with false charges, they accused Munatius Plancus, former consul and head of the visiting group, as the author of the senate's decision. Toward midnight they began to demand the colors that were kept in Germanicus' dwelling. They stormed the entrance, forced open the doors, pulled Germanicus from his bedroom, and forced him, under threat of death, to turn over the colors. Then, as they ran through the streets, they encountered the emissaries, who, having heard the noise, were hastening to Germanicus. The soldiers heaped abuse upon them, with the intention of killing them and especially Plancus, whose dignity had prevented him from running off. Thus threatened, he had no other refuge than the camp of the first legion. There he embraced the field standards and the eagle in order to protect himself through religion. If the eagle bearer, Calpurnius, had not driven away the violent pursuers, an emissary of the Roman people, in a Roman camp, would have sprinkled the altars of the gods with his own blood, something most rare, even among enemies. It was not until daybreak, when the commander and the soldiers became recognizable and all learned of the happening, that Germanicus walked into the camp, ordered that Plancus be brought to him, and took him up on the stage. Condemning the riotous behavior as a fateful sign of the anger not of the soldiers, but of the gods, who were once again stirred up, he explained why the emissaries had come. With eloquent reproaches he spoke of the rights of emissaries, of Plancus' hard and undeserved ordeal, and of the disgrace the legion had brought on itself. While the assemblage was more confounded than pacified, he sent

the emissaries away under the protection of cavalry from the auxiliaries.
In connection with this terrifying incident, everybody reproached
Germanicus "for not having gone to the Upper army of Germany, where
he would have found obedience and support against the mutineers. There
had already been enough and more than enough compromising through
the discharges, and the donatives and mild measures. Or if he held his
own life in such little regard, why did he leave his small son and his preg-
nant wife among the barbarians, men who violated every human right?
He should at least return his wife and son to the grandfather and the
commonwealth." After a long delay, and while his wife refused, proving
that, "being of Augustus' breed, she was not too unaccustomed to dangers," he finally embraced her and their son and midst many tears persuaded her to leave. The convoy of women moved off sorrowing, with the
commander's fleeing wife holding her small son at her breast. Around her
were the weeping wives of their friends, who also had to leave at the same
time. And those who remained behind were no less sorrowful.

The appearance of the commander, who did not seem as self-confident
as usual and who seemed to be in a conquered city rather than his own
camp, as well as the moaning and handwringing, attracted the ears and
eyes of the soldiers. They came out of their tents, saying: "Why such a
sorrowful tone? What is there so sad that has taken place? Noble women
without a single centurion or a single soldier to protect them, nothing
that is proper for the wife of a commander, nothing in the way of the
usual escort! They are moving into the land of the Treveri under foreign
protection." Then there was a wave of shame and pity, together with
memories of her father Agrippa, her grandfather Augustus, and her father-in-law Drusus. She herself, they said, was a prolific mother and a
very proper wife. They thought also of the young boy who was born in
the camp and who had been growing up under the eyes of the legions.
They called him by the soldiers' expression "Little Boots" (Caligula)
because he was normally dressed in this kind of footwear in order to win
the approval of the crowd. Still, nothing had such a strong effect on them
as their jealousy of the Treveri. Opposing this move, they asked that she
turn back and remain there. Some of them ran out in front of Agrippina,
while most of them returned to Germanicus. He, overcome with sorrow
and anger, addressed the crowd pushing toward him in the following
terms:

My wife and son are no dearer to me than my father and my fatherland. Only, the emperor will be protected by his high position,

while the Roman Empire will be protected by its other armies. My wife and children, whose lives I would willingly offer up for your fame, I am now sending far away from you raging men so that whatever sacrilege is still to take place here will be atoned by my blood alone, so that the murdered great-grandson of Augustus, the sacrificed daughter-in-law of Tiberius will not make you still more guilty. During these last days what foolhardy and shameful things have you not done? What name shall I give to this mob? Am I supposed to call you soldiers? You who surrounded the son of your emperor with a wall and weapons? Or are you to be called citizens? You who so rejected the dignity of the senate? That which is even respected by the enemy, the inviolability of emissaries, the common law, you have violated. The sainted Julius quieted his mutinous army with a single word when he called them *quirites* (citizens), those who were refusing the oath to him. The deified Augustus struck fear into the hearts of the legions at Actium with his countenance and glance. It is true that I am not yet their equal, but I am their descendant. Even if the warriors of Spain or Syria treated me disrespectfully, that would still be unusual and improper. And now, you the first and you the twentieth legion! The first awarded field standards by Tiberius, and you the twentieth, veteran of so many battles with me, heaped with so many awards, a fine gratitude you show to your army commander! Am I to send this report to my father, who is hearing nothing but good news from all the other provinces? Am I to tell him that his young warriors and his veterans are not satisfied with retirement or with money? That here centurions were killed, tribunes driven away, and emissaries locked up? That the camps and the rivers are spotted with blood and that I am living from day to day an uncertain life among raging men?

Why then on the first day you were assembled did you wrest from me the iron that I was ready to plunge into my breast, oh thoughtless friends? He who offered me his sword acted better and more kindly; at least I would have fallen without knowing of all the disgraceful acts of my army. You would have chosen a leader who, it is true, would have left my death unpunished but would have avenged the deaths of Varus and his three legions. For, after all, may the gods not allow that the Belgae, who are offering themselves for that purpose, should win the fame and the prize that they had helped restore the Roman name and had overcome the peoples of Germany! May your spirit, taken up into heaven, godly Augustus, and your image, father Drusus, and your memory help these warriors who are overcome with shame and a thirst for fame to blot out that spot of disgrace and turn their civic hate toward the ruination of our enemies. And you, whose countenance and whose hearts I see transformed, if you want to restore the emissaries to the senate, obedience to your commander, and my wife and son to me, then flee from this infection and separate the mutineers; this will be the guarantee of your penitence, this the tie of your loyalty.

With humble recognition that his reproaches were just, they begged him to punish the guilty, to excuse those who were misled, and to lead them against the enemy. He should call back his wife and have his son come back to the legions and not deliver them over to the Gauls as hostages. He declined to have Agrippina return because of her approaching childbirth and the winter weather; his son would return, and the rest they themselves should carry out. With their attitude reversed, they ran around and dragged the worst mutineers, bound, to the legate of the first legion, Caius Petronius, who pronounced on each one a special judgment and punishment in the following manner: the legions stood as in an assembly with drawn swords, and the accused was presented on the stage by the tribune. If they shouted guilty, he was thrown down and killed. The soldiers slashed him gladly, as if they were thus freeing themselves. The commander did not object, especially because he ordered nothing, and the wicked and hateful aspects of the deed fell on their shoulders. The veterans followed this example. Shortly thereafter, they were sent to Raetia, under the pretense of protecting the province against the threatening Sueves. In reality, they were sent to get them out of a camp that aroused grim feelings no less as a result of the harshness of the cure than from the memory of the crimes. Then he held a muster of the centurions. Called for by the commander, each one gave his name, rank, fatherland, number of years of service, and what he had accomplished of an outstanding nature in battles and what prizes of war he had received. If the tribunes and the legion recognized his efficiency and good conduct, he retained his rank; anyone who was unanimously blamed for greediness or cruelty was separated from the service.

When the uprising was quelled here, there was still as much to be done because of the defiance of the fifth and twenty-ninth legions. These legions, which were spending the winter 280 miles from there, at Vetera, had been the first to stir up the mutiny. They had committed the most despicable acts of violence. Neither frightened by the punishment of their comrades nor inclined to peace, they became more firmly fixed in their fury. Germanicus therefore prepared to send weapons, a fleet, and allies down the Rhine, determined to fight them if they refused obedience.

Although Germanicus had assembled an army ready for revenge against the mutineers, he believed that he must still allow a delay to see if they themselves, after the recent events, would have a change of heart. He sent a message to Caecina, saying that "he was coming with a strong army and if they did not punish the criminals before his arrival, he would have them all cut down indiscriminately." Caecina secretly read this aloud to the eagle and standard bearers and the loyal men in the camp. He warned that they should let the shame of the uprising be borne by the mutineers and should save themselves from death, for in peacetime the merits of a situation were taken into account, but if war broke out, the innocent were killed with the guilty. These men sought out those who were considered to be reliable. When they found the majority of the legionaries to be loyal, they agreed with the legate on a time when all the evildoers and instigators of the uprising would suddenly be cut down by the sword. At a given signal, they dashed into the tents and killed the unsuspecting victims. Nobody except those involved in the plan knew where the killing was to begin and where it was to end.

Of all the civil wars that have ever taken place, no other has yet presented such a drama: Not in battle formations and not from opposing camps but from the same tents where they had been united by day at their meals and by night in sleep, they were divided into opposing sides and took up the fight. Cries, wounds, and blood were obvious, but the cause was hidden; the rest was determined by chance. A few of the loyal men were also killed, since the mutineers learned who was to be murdered and had seized their weapons. No legate or tribune was in charge, and the revenge was left up to the crowd until they were satiated. Soon Germanicus entered the camp, calling out midst his tears that that was no remedy but a blood bath, and he ordered the corpses to be burned. The still aroused spirits were seized with a desire to march against the enemy, as penitence for their wild deeds. In no other way could they pacify the spirits of their comrades than by receiving honorable wounds in their sinful breasts. Acceding to the emotions of the soldiers, Germanicus had a bridge built and had 12,000 legionaries, twenty-six allied cohorts, and eight cavalry squadrons, whose good conduct had remained unsmirched during this uprising, cross over the river.

Thus wrote Tacitus. The last words form a link with the great Germanic war, which here follows directly and which has been studied and explained by us in the preceding chapters.

## EXCURSUS

### 1. LEVY

When news of the destruction of Varus' legions reached Rome and Augustus had new units formed, Dio Cassius recounts (56. 25) that the resources of the Roman people were almost exhausted. No volunteers had been found, and Augustus had therefore caused lots to be drawn. He had punished with confiscation of their property and defamation one out of ten men above thirty-five years of age and one out of five of those younger, and finally a few were even executed. This passage is often cited, but there is really not much to be done with it. Not quite 18,000 men were to be levied. Nevertheless, from a population of 5 million, that is still so many that they cannot be assembled so quickly simply through the beating of the recruiter's drum. From the point of view of political economy, however, that is only a very small accomplishment, especially since freedmen and peregrines were not entirely rejected. A single year-group of young Roman citizens probably numbered some 40,000. It therefore seems quite incredible that they should have called up citizens over thirty-five years of age, from whom a fortune could be confiscated and who therefore were well-to-do people, at least to the extent that it was a question of forming replacement legions and not something like the formation of a temporary home guard to oppose an incursion of the Germans into Italy. From the whole account it would be easiest to draw that conclusion, since otherwise absolute arbitrariness prevailed on the part of the officials. But the text of the account does not say that, and furthermore, in the case of such a small requirement among so many militarily qualified men, selection by lot is no practical solution. In practice, the levy probably took place as a result of agreements between the recruiting officers and the district authorities, who, as was customary in Germany in the seventeenth and eighteenth centuries, indicated the young men who seemed to them to be "dispensable." These men, though they were declared qualified and available through a procedure of subjective evaluation, quite often had no military inclination. As Suetonius recounts in *Tiberius*, Chapter 8, they preferred to seek shelter among the slaves of the great landowners, whom Tiberius once had inspected on this account.

Suetonius, in *Augustus*, Chapter 24, recounts: "equitem Romanum, quod duobus filiis adulescentibus causa detrectandi sacramenti pollices amputasset, ipsum bonaque subjecit hastae." ("He set up for public auction a Roman knight and his property because he had cut off the thumbs of his two young sons in an effort to shirk military service.") This account, as it stands, is incomprehensible, since a Roman nobleman, a well-to-do man, if he ever had occasion to be in the situation of freeing his sons from military service, had other means than to cut off their thumbs. One possible explanation would be that the sons wanted to enter the army against the father's will (as centurions, with the emperor's approval), and that the father, in the heat of passion of a strong family conflict, resorted to mutilation in order to assert his will. However that may be, a single story of this kind should not be used as an example of the Roman system of conscription.

In his report to the senate, as described in Tacitus, *Annals* 4. 4, Tiberius says: "dilectibus supplendos exercitus: nam voluntarium militem deesse, ac si suppeditet, non eadem virtute ac modestia agere, quia plerumque inopes ac vagi sponte militiam sumant." ("The armies had to be supplemented by levies, for there were no volunteers. If the supply of manpower was sufficient, the recruits did not act with the same prowess and self-control, because for the most part the poor and the vagabonds took up military service voluntarily.")
Pliny gives us proof (*ep.* 10. 39) that is was possible to present a substitute. Whether this was already the case in Augustus' time may be doubtful, and when Varus' legions were to be replaced, it may also have been difficult to find substitutes.
It is obvious from Tacitus, *Annals* 14. 18, *Hist.* 4. 14, *Agricola*, Chapter 7, that the levy was often used for impressing men into service.

2. TOTAL STRENGTH OF THE ARMY
Tacitus, *Annals* 4. 5, recounts that, according to a report to the senate from Tiberius in the ninth year of his reign, the auxiliaries were of about the same strength as the legions, "apud idonea provinciarum sociae triremes, alaeque et auxilia cohortium, neque multo secus in iis virium; set persequi incertum fuit, cum ex usu temporis huc illuc mearent, gliscerent numero et aliquando minuerentur." ("At suitable points in the provinces there are triremes of the allies, alae and auxiliary cohorts. Their strength does not differ much from the legions, but this is an indefinite topic to pursue, since they go here and there according to the need of the moment and they increase and sometimes decrease in number.") Nevertheless, we are probably to understand that as meaning that the legions and the auxiliaries reached equal strength whenever the auxiliaries were especially increased in numbers, that is, when there was a threat of war. In periods of complete peace they were weaker. This point is also in agreement with the individual counts that have been possible (see page 159 n.5 above). Vegetius 2.1, says: "in auxiliis minor, in legionibus longe amplior consuevit militum numerus adscribi." ("A smaller number of soldiers is accustomed to be enrolled in the auxiliaries and a by far greater number in the legions.") But not much is to be concluded from that, since we do not know from which author this reference is drawn, and consequently to which period it belongs.

NOTES FOR CHAPTER VIII

1. *Eclog.* 1. 71.
2. W. Bahr, *De centurionibus legionariis (on the Centurions of the Legions)*, Berlin dissertation, 1900, p. 45 f.
3. Bang, *The Germans in the Roman Service ( Die Germanen im römischen Dienst)*, p. 78.
4. This is a very significant piece of new knowledge which we owe to Domaszewski's careful study of inscriptions, *The Hierarchy of the Roman Army (Die Rangordnung des römischen Heeres)*, 1908.

5. This results from the very nature of the situation and is also evident from a citation in Hyginus, *de mun.*, Chapter 42, which I find on page 60 in Domaszewski's *Hierarchy*. It was probably the same as in the present-day Austrian army (before 1918), where the regiments, in addition to their German army language, had their own national regimental language. As the Romanization of the provinces progressed, the national character of the cohorts gradually faded out. It may also have happened that cohorts stationed very far from their home area received other replacements and changed their character as a result. We must agree with Mommsen, when he emphasizes in *Hermes* 19: 211, that the national character of the cohorts can be concluded from their designations with certainty only at the time of their creation.

6. Seeck, *History of the Fall of the Ancient World (Geschichte des Untergangs der antiken Welt)* 1: 390, 534.

7. Marquardt, *Roman Political Administration (Römische Staatsverwaltung)* 2.542, 2d ed.

8. In the year 367, *cod. Theodosianus*. Cited in Marquardt. In Germany, it was not until 1893 that the minimum height was lowered to 1.54 meters. In 1870, the following regulation was still in force: "The smallest height is 1.57 meters, but men under 1.62 may be selected only if they have a particularly strong body frame and if the yearly replacement figure cannot be met without resorting to this expedient." The smallest height for the Guard is 1.70 Meters.

In France, Napoleon set the height at 1.59 meters in 1801, but then he lowered it to 1.54 in 1804. In 1818, it was raised again to 1.57, and in 1872, after some variations, it was lowered again to 1.54. The Roman foot was 0.296 meters and was consequently shorter than the old Prussian one, which was 0.314.

9. Suetonius, *Nero* 19.

10. Schulten, "The Domain of the Legion" ("Das Territorium legionis"), *Hermes* 29: 481.

11. Cicero, *Acad*. 2. 1. 2.

12. Sallustus, *Bell. Jug*. 85. 12.

13. The matter is perhaps somewhat more complicated. The references to the promotion of the centurions are not easy to understand. One theory after another has been advanced on this subject, but no solution has been found that clarifies the whole situation. Theodore Wegeleben's study, "The Hierarchy of the Roman Centurions" ("Die Rangordnung der römischen Centurionen"), Berlin dissertation, 1913, Ad. Weber, publisher, has superseded Domaszewski's study, to be sure, and has thrown

some light on the subject through its comprehensive comparison of the inscriptions, but some points have still remained doubtful. Wegeleben's conclusion is that the centurions were of equal rank among themselves, with the exception of the six centurions of the first cohort, of whom the three highest ones, of the *primus pilus*, of the *princeps*, and of the *hastatus*, stood so high that they were no longer referred to as centurions at all. This higher position in the first cohort was not just a position of honor. It was also based on the practical organization, since this cohort was 1,000 men strong, while all the other cohorts had about 480 men (Wegeleben, p. 37). We are not told how that was balanced off in the formation of the legion. Either the six centurions of the first cohort or the three highest ones were designated as the *primi ordines*. Also unclear is the meaning of *praepositus* (see Grosse, *Roman Military History [Römische Militärgeschichte]*, p. 143). The remark in Wegeleben, p. 60, concerning the receipt of commands is probably not correct; it is contradicted by Polybius 2. 34.

14. We have just recently been enlightened on the situation of the *principales* by the work of A. von Domaszewski, which is as thorough as it is valuable. *The Hierarchy of the Roman Army (Die Rangordnung des römischen Heeres)*, 1908.

Vegetius 2. 7, speaking of the responsibilities, says: "Campigeni, hoc est antesignani, ideo sic nominati, quia eorum opere atque virtute exercitii genus crescit in campo." ("The *campigeni*, that is *antesignani*, were so named because the kind of training in the field depended on their hard work and ability.") I have not found an explanation of this passage in Domaszewski.

15. The history of the Roman military pay was first set forth in Domaszewski's essay, "The Military Pay of the Imperial Period" ("Der Truppensold der Kaiserzeit"), *Neue Heidelberger Jahrbücher*, Vol. 10, 1900. But Domaszewski, in judging the pay increases in the imperial period, failed to take into account the simultaneous debasement of the money. Consequently, he exaggerated the significance of the numerical increase. I consider it impossible that on the occasions of donatives the centurions were excluded and only the soldiers benefited, as Domaszewski believes, p. 231, note 2. In that case, depending on the amount of the donative (under Marcus Aurelius it was once 5,000 denarii for the Praetorians, or five times their annual pay), the privates would often have been better off than the officers.

16. P. Steiner, "The Military Decorations" ("Die *dona militaria*"), *Bonner Jahrbücher* 114: 1 f.

17. In Polybius' camp description, there is no mention of a hospital, whereas there is in Hyginus. See W. Haberling, *The Ancient Roman Military Doctors* ( *Die altrömischen Militärärzte*), Berlin, 1910.

18. Premerstein, "The Bookkeeping of an Egyptian Legionary Unit" ("Die Buchführung einer ägyptischen Legionsabteilung"), *Klio*, Vol. III.

19. This is reported by Polybius 14. 3. 6. We may assume that the Romans also retained this custom in later periods.

20. Tertullian says: "Religio Romanorum tota castrensis signa veneratur signa jurat, signa omnibus deis proponit." ("The religion of the Romans was completely military. It venerated the standards, swore by the standards, and preferred the standards to all the gods.") Cited in Harnack, *Christian Armies* (*Militia Christi*), p. V.

21. Alfred von Domaszewski, "The Religion of the Roman Army" ("Die Religion des römischen Heeres"). Special reprint from the *Westdeutsche Zeitschrift für Geschichte und Kunst*, Vol. 14, Trier, 1895. The very important point of the difference between the military and civilian forms of religion has not been mentioned in this article. See also Hirschfeld, "On the History of the Roman Emperor Cult" ("Zur Geschichte des römischen Kaiserkultus"), *Sitzungsberichte der Berliner Akademie*, Vol. 35, 1888.

22. Beloch, in *The Population of the Greco-Roman World* (*Die Bevölkerung der griechisch-römischen Welt*), estimated some 54 million. In a later article, however, in the *Rheinisches Museum*, Vol. 54, 1899, he reached a somewhat higher estimate for Gaul than in his book. I myself have gone even higher. See Vol. I, p. 493. The higher estimate for Gaul tends in turn to lower somewhat the figures for the other countries.

23. "Venio nunc ad praecipuum decus et ad stabilimentum Romani imperii salutari perseverantia ad hoc tempus sincerum et incolume servatum militaris disciplinae tenacissimum vinculum, in cuius sinu ac tutela serenus tranquillusque beatae pacis status adquiescit." ("Now I come to the principal glory and support of the Roman Empire — the most stubborn bond of military training, safely preserved and intact by its wholesome persistence up to the present time. In its bosom and guardianship the cheerful and calm state of a blessed peace rests.") Valerius Maximus 2. 7.

24. Suetonius, *Domitian*, Chapter 12.

25. *Bell. Gall.* 2. 8; 7. 41, 81. *Bell. civ.* 3. 45, 51, 56. *Afr.* 31. Schambach, *Some Observations on the Roman Use of Missile Weapons,*

*Especially in Caesar's Time (Einige Bemerkungen über die Ge-schützverwendung bei den Römern, besonders zur Zeit Cäsars)*, 1883. Mühlhausen in Thüringen Program. Fröhlich, *Caesar's Methods of Waging War (Kriegswesen Cäsars)* 1: 77. Attempts have recently been made to reconstruct these weapons. During the excavations on the Lippe, an unusual wooden instrument was discovered, which some believe to be the *pilum murale*. G. Kropatschek has added an interesting study on that subject in the *Jahrbücher des Archäoligischen Instituts* 23 (1908): 79.

26. Vegetius 2. 25.

27. Cited in Marquardt 2: 567.

28. In addition to the eighth volume of the *Corpus inscriptionum latinarum*, the inscription is treated by Sebastian Dehner in a Bonn dissertation, "Hadriani reliquiae," 1883, and by Albert Müller, *Maneuver Critique by Emperor Hadrian (Manöverkritik Kaiser Hadrians)*, Leipzig, 1900. I have adopted quite a few of the insertions suggested by these two authors, but not all of them. The translation from the *Militär-Wochenblatt*, 1882, No. 34, has been significantly changed in some places and filled in in others.

(Added in the second edition.) Recently, many more small fractions of the inscription have been found, but in general they have concerned only the heading and the date. The address is directed *"at pilos"* ("to the *primi pili"*). Héron de Villefosse, *Festschrift zu Otto Hirschfelds 60. Geburtstag*, Berlin, 1903.

29. Legion is to be interpreted as "division" to the extent that it contains all the combat arms.

30. *compares*, actually "comrades." The legion in Lambaesis had the name III Augusta. There were also two more legions that had the number "three": the III Gallica and the III Cyrenaica. Consequently, men had been transferred to one of these two units.

31. Others choose to read: *"agiles et fortes more suo,* which would mean something like "ready and eager, as is proper."

32. I choose this expression because these three classes formed one stratum.

33. I choose this expression by way of analogy with our divisional cavalry. Each cohort of auxiliary troops was permanently assigned a small cavalry detachment.

34. *"frequens dextrator"* has been explained in the most varied ways, and I will not claim that my translation is beyond doubt the right one. It fits the sense and the context with respect to the previously stated

number of skirmishing sharpshooters and the later closed attack. "*dextratio*" means the movement of going around from right to left. Thus, the word *dextrator*, which does not appear anywhere else in the sources, may well have been used for a specific turning movement on parade.

35. An expression that is not definitely clarified, perhaps a specific type of attack.

36. I have not translated "*ad signum miseritis*" since the generally accepted interpretation, "no help was sent to a field standard that was already captured," does not seem acceptable to me.

37. The proposed insertion, "*ultra scamna*," likewise seems unacceptable to me since it would presuppose that the enemy had actually already penetrated into the camp (*scamna* are the places in the camp for the tents of the legates and tribunes).

38. Instead of *equum*.

# Chapter IX

# Theory[1]

As with all other areas of the mind and of nature, Greek philosophy also sought to consider warfare on an intellectual plane. In the first volume, we have treated only the first of these theoreticians of warfare, Xenophon, who laid the groundwork for such study. We postponed any further development to this point, in consideration of the status of the sources, which have been retained only from the Roman imperial period.

The philosophers had no small opinion of the value of their theories. We have one small passage that states unhesitatingly by way of introduction that Alexander was indebted to the teaching of Aristotle for being able to conquer the world[2]. All the individual tactical formations which the king had learned from his teacher and which led him to victory are enumerated. When Hannibal left Carthage and took refuge at the court of King Antiochus, the traveling philosopher Phormio is supposed to have wanted to show him how he should have gone about defeating the Romans.

What we have actually received from the Greek writers on tactics is hardly up to the level of this claim — or we might also say, turning it about, that it is actually at the level of this wisdom. It is astonishing how inadequate this literature is, and all the more so when we consider that two men of the first order, Polybius and Posidonius, wrote about tactics. Even though their works have not come down to us, still the later works of Asclepiodotus, Onosander, Aelian, and Arrian, which we do have at hand, go back to the other two. But they do not have the slightest grain of good sense. The most astonishing point of all is that, although Polybius had already experienced and described the victory of the Roman echelon tactics over the phalanx, and Posidonius had lived at the time of Caesar and the other well-known authors had lived under the emperors, in the writings of these authors on tactics there is not a single word concerning the legion and its peculiar battle formations. There is nothing but the gray theory, copied from book to book through the centuries, which still continues to treat of the sarissa phalanx — an empty type of schematic that is based on a normal army of 16,384 men. This number is used because it lends itself to being divided in half time and again and thus allows creation of nice subordinate units of equal size, from which tactical formations can be built. It is not necessary to go any further into this matter, or even to point out the positive errors and misinterpretations of the details.[3]

Of the Romans, no less a person than M. Porcius Cato the Elder wrote a work, *de re militari*. If it seems quite natural that precisely the first prose writer in Latin to take the stylus in hand wrote about warfare, it is all the more astonishing that he had so few successors and that it was those Greek theoreticians who held the field in the imperial period and were able to dedicate their writings to the Roman emperors. A lost manuscript by Celsus and a composition by Frontinus, who was a very highly regarded general at the turn of the first century A.D. and from whom we have a collection of examples of military history, are the only theoretical products of a military nature of the Roman literature of that period which are worthy of note. It is, of course, very possible that the best product has been lost to us, that is, the constitutions that Augustus drew up for the army and which Trajan and Hadrian revised or expanded. These constitutions were first of all what we would call regulations in the broadest sense. They contained the rules for levies and recruiting, organization, performance of daily duties, drills, rations, and administration. But perhaps the practical instructions and rules were also supported by theoretical explanations and general rationale, so that the regulation was at the same time a manual of collected military knowledge, and, in fact, may have been so thorough and so comprehensive that for that very reason, since, after all, the military art did not make further significant progress, the writings in this area, too, had nothing new to add and therefore carried the work no further.

At the most, there was still room for technical explanations and studies, such as, for example, the instructions of the architect Vitruvus on the construction of missile weapons. Finally, we might also mention in this connection a description of the Roman camp installation that has come down under the name of Hyginus.

Cato's work and the emperors' constitutions have been lost to us. But a considerable amount of material from them has come down to us indirectly in the writings of Flavius Vegetius Renatus, composed in the

midst of the confusion of the *Völkerwanderung*, probably under Theodosius the Great, or perhaps not until the time of his grandson, Valentinian III, in the fifth century. Vegetius was not a practical soldier and
had no insight into the matters about which he wrote. In fact, he could
not possibly have had such knowledge, for the Roman army in the forms
in which we have come to know it had ceased to exist for a long time.
Vegetius regrets the fall of the old Roman Empire and of the old Roman
military might. By taking excerpts from the old authors, he writes his
book in order to show how things were in the time of their ancestors and
how his contemporaries had to proceed in order to renew the old splen-
dor. He had no idea that there were various epochs in the times of the
ancestors, which also varied most significantly from one another, and he
assembled his excerpts in keeping with more or less definite viewpoints,
without regard to chronological sequence.⁴ That fault detracts significantly from the historical value of his book, but it has done no great
harm to the effect of his book on later generations and the use made of it,
since it is only in our time that we have reached the point of really recognizing its errors. It was read throughout the Middle Ages. In Charlemagne's time, the work was edited for the needs of the Frankish army. In
the testament of a certain Count Everard de Fréjus, from the time of
Louis the Pious (837), the name Vegetius is mentioned. During the siege
of the Château Gaillard, Gottfried Plantagenet had the work of Vegetius
thoroughly examined, in order to find the best means of attack. There
are no less than 150 copies in existence dating from the period between
the tenth and fifteenth centuries. During the Renaissance, the book was
reprinted time and again. The Austrian Field Marshal Prince von Ligne
declared it to be a golden book; he wrote: "Vegetius said that a god
inspired the legion, and as for me, I find that a god inspired Vegetius."

The valuable elements of the book probably stem principally from
Cato and the constitutions of Augustus and Hadrian, which are cited.
The work does not have a higher philosophical value, and it has not had a
real influence on the art of war and its development. Consequently, the
book is now read only from the viewpoint of ancient history. But it is
quite understandable why it was so highly regarded for such a long time
and continuously studied. The practical soldier has a great need to arrive
at a certain basic understanding of his profession, and even if Vegetius
does not go deeply into the subject, one still finds in his work a series of
tenets basically and clearly expressed, which are very useful for military
reflection or discussion. It may be doubtful whether it is right for one to
build golden bridges for the enemy or whether it is more advisable to

harm the enemy in small actions by ruses rather than expose oneself to the risks of a battle. In any case, many military men have operated with these tenets. Certain truths can be grasped without the need of a classical authority: that no soldier should be sent into the field without proper training; that he who can correctly estimate his own strength and that of the enemy will not easily be beaten; that the unexpected strikes fear in the heart of the enemy; that he who does not look after the sustenance of his unit is necessarily defeated without a blow being struck. But the commonplace expressions also have to be formulated at some time, and commonplaces that are nicely clothed in general theoretical reflections and mixed with a certain erudition are suitable for making a book popular.

Even the doctrinary-fantastic trivialities in which Vegetius sometimes indulges himself, such as, for example, his seven battle formations, one of which has the form of a spit, have not been held against him. That theory sounded scholarly. The scholars even researched and theorized enthusiastically about these wonderful seven formations, while practical military men naturally paid as little attention to the spit as to the "hollow wedge" or the "tongs."

In considering from which countries and peoples the best recruits came, Vegetius decided in favor of the temperate zone and, supported by the authority of the most scholarly men, as he says, he also gave his reasons for this (1. 2). He believed that the nations that are close to the sun are dried out by the excessive heat, and while they are more intelligent, they have less blood and therefore less steadfastness and reliability in hand-to-hand combat, since anemic as they are, they fear wounds. The northerly peoples, however, although, of course, mentally weak, are full-blooded and therefore warlike. One should therefore draw recruits from the most temperate zones, where they have enough blood to scorn wounds and death and also a reasonable amount of sense, which is of no small usefulness in guaranteeing well-being in camp as well as in battle.

In spite of such aberrations, Roman military writings show the practical, sober mentality of this people. The Greek writings do not belie the speculative mentality of the Greek people either in the poetic garb that Xenophon gave to his teachings in the *Cyropaedia* or in the systems of the later writers. The less we have been able to praise the military results of Greek philosophy, the less we wish to ignore the manner in which Hellenes were able to connect the study of techniques with the general ideas. A native of Alexandria, Hero, who wrote a book on the construction of missile weapons in the period of the Ptolemies, introduced his work with the following words:[5]

The most important and most necessary part of philosophical study is that which treats of the serenity of the soul, with which most of the studies of the practical philosophers have been concerned and are still concerned to the present day, and I believe that the theoretical study of this subject will never come to an end. But the study of mechanics stands higher than the theoretical study of the serenity of the soul, for it teaches all men the knowledge of how to live in serenity through the practice of a single and limited part of its content. By that, I mean the part that treats of the so-called construction of missile weapons. Through this we are put in a position where we neither need ever in peacetime to tremble before the attacks of opponents and enemies nor even to tremble at the outbreak of a war, thanks to the universal wisdom which resides in these machines. For this reason, we must at all times maintain this part (mechanics) in order and pay the closest attention to it; for precisely in periods of the most absolute peace are we able to hope that it will continue to be guaranteed if we give proper attention to weapons construction and in this knowledge assert our peace of soul. And if those who contemplate evil are aware of our careful attention to this, they will not risk any attack. But if we become negligent, any attack, even if it is insignificant in itself, will succeed if the said machines are not on hand in the cities.

The modern artilleryman, too, and with him the minister of war and every advocate of military preparedness, may well weigh these words of ancient wisdom.

NOTES FOR CHAPTER IX

1. In connection with this chapter, I again refer the reader to the basic facts in the introduction to Köchly and Rüstow's *Greek Military Authors* (*Griechische Kriegsschriftsteller*), Part II, and particularly to Jähns' *History of the Military Sciences* (*Geschichte der Kriegswissenschaften*), Vol. I, from which I have taken several citations.

2. Köchly and Rüstow, *Greek Military Authors*, Part II, second section, p. 213.

3. It is also unnecessary for us to go into purely theoretical suggestions, even if they should have led to important experiments, such as Rüstow treats in his *History of the Infantry* (*Geschichte der Infanterie*) 1: 54, since no positive result came from them.

4. Johann Gustav Foerster, *De fide Fl. Vegetii Renati*, Bonn dissertation, 1879, shows Vegetius' inextricable confusion in many places.

5. As a supplement to the translation in *Greek Military Authors* by Köchly and Rüstow, 1: 201.

# Chapter X

# Decline and Dissolution of the Roman Military System

It has been customary to regard the war with the Marcomanni, in the reign of Marcus Aurelius, as the prelude to the Germans' overthrow of Rome. The Marcomanni, inhabitants of Bohemia, reinforced by other Germanic and even non-Germanic peoples, crossed the Danube, overran the Roman border defenses, stormed the cities, moved as far as Aquileia, and threatened Italy. Emperor Marcus Aurelius pawned the crown jewels in order to raise money. On one occasion he himself, with his army, was caught in a very precarious situation, from which he was saved only by a sudden thunderstorm that has been discussed extensively in the legend. It required a total of sixteen years before the Romans finally overcame their attackers.

However much this war may have stirred up the Roman world, it was not a harbinger of what was to come; it fits directly into the series of border wars, as they had already been fought under Augustus. The Germans were initially successful because the Romans were engaged with all their forces in the east, in a war with the Parthians. Even if we cannot say that troops from the Danube were pulled out directly for this purpose, that war was nevertheless the reason why sufficient reinforcements could not immediately be made available.

A plague that raged for many years increased the critical situation and the difficulties of the Romans. When German tribes, becoming aware of this favorable opportunity, now broke across the border simultaneously at many places, to the Romans that movement appeared to be the result of a great alliance of the barbarians and to historians of following ages, a prelude to the *Völkerwanderung*.[1] Actually, however, this war belongs in the period of the preceding ones, and not that of the coming events. If the Roman army was once placed in great danger by the Germans, the same thing had already happened to Drusus and Germanicus. The war with the Marcomanni lasted so long not because it would have been so difficult for the Romans to drive the invaders back across the Danube, but because the Germans had taken a huge amount of booty, and especially prisoners, which the Romans wanted to recapture from them. This war constitutes an overture for the future only to the extent that in the meantime there appeared in the east a counteremperor, creating a situation that paralyzed Marcus Aurelius' forces on the Danube. Nevertheless, he was finally able to defeat completely the bold attackers, and if we are to believe our sources, he almost succeeded in pushing the border of the Roman Empire out across Bohemia. But then Marcus Aurelius died (180 A.D.), and his youthful son and successor, Commodus, was not the man to carry his work to its conclusion. The Danube remained the border.

Even the difficult periods of confusion and civil wars that shook the whole Roman Empire after the fall of Commodus did not yet break up the Roman military state. The Severi — Septimius, Caracalla, and Alexander — were still capable of drawing up great war plans and even entertaining ideas of victory in the east. Mesopotamia fell once again into their hands. But the fall of this dynasty in 235 A.D. brought on the crisis.

Whereas it had always been possible up to that time finally to create a stable regime, often for a very long time, even if at times midst strong uncertainties, now that no longer succeeded. The Severi had no doubt again formed a cohesive dynasty, but they had fallen through force. Now we are entering an epoch in which it was no longer possible to achieve a peaceful continuation of the imperial dignity. Emperors who had just been placed on the throne fell again within a very short period, murdered, and first in this province and then in that one counteremperors were raised up, who fought among themselves. Large portions of the empire remained independent for years under the rulers they had set up.

This is not the place for a thorough presentation of the final reasons for this weakening. Simply let it be said that it was in no way a progressive process of decay. On the contrary, a significant factor was undoubtedly the progressing national unification which gradually eliminated the old superiority of the city of Rome, a dominance that had held everything together. As long as the provinces were still barbarian, they had no possibility for an independent form: what would have become of them if they broke loose from the empire? A movement of this kind that had started in Gaul after Nero's death had subsided again in its own lack of purpose.

Thus, the city of Rome had given its imprint to world empire and for generations had held the governing power. Now not only Italy but also Africa, Spain, Gaul, and Britain were Latinized and full of Roman culture; the east was similarly infused with Greek culture. More and more the officer corps, the body of civil officials, the knightly class, and even the senate were filled with Latinized provincials.[2] But it was precisely this progress that made it all the more difficult to hold together the regions that had been welded through force, from the Caledonian Mountains to the Tigris, from the Carpathians to the Atlas. The subjected countries and cities now felt themselves similar to and on an equal footing with Italy and Rome. Caracalla, by granting Roman citizenship equally to all the subject peoples, also gave legal recognition to this situation.

And neither was the Roman Empire up to that time in any way in an economic decline, as some have continued to believe here and there. All the countries around the Mediterranean formed a unified economic area with an industrious and energetic population. For 200 years internal peace was interrupted only infrequently, and ships passed not only through the entire Mediterranean but even the Black Sea and the ocean, undisturbed by that evil enemy of trade, piracy.

Slavery declined, since the foreign wars seldom brought in any more prisoners. The large landowners were obliged to divide their large estates again into small lease holdings or settlements of *coloni*. Instead of the masses of slaves, without families, more and more families settled in the country, raised children, and increased the population. Outstanding families, too, began to move from the city to the country where they created new small economic and cultural centers. Whereas formerly it was mostly only cities with sea traffic that had had an important position, now in many areas such cities also sprang up on the rivers in the interior. Generation after generation added to a road net that constantly became tighter and tighter. The huge system of administration that held the whole together functioned in an orderly way. The military burden, as we have seen, was not only not heavy but actually light.

If we ask about the spiritual and moral status of the Roman population, we certainly may not speak of a degeneration. Following directly on the last great representatives of antiquity proper — Seneca, Pliny, Tacitus, and the great jurists — were the great fathers of the church. We are now in the period of the development of the Christian Church. What a fullness of spiritual and moral forces this one word conjures up before our eyes!

Even the civil war did not show anything of a senile nature in the people. A series of men of the highest importance and ability, Decius, Claudius, Aurelian, Probus, and Diocletian, were raised to the imperial throne one after the other. Rome was still in no way poor in great personalities, statesmen as well as generals. These emperors were no worse than their predecessors.

The reasons for the fall of the empire are not to be sought in any of these areas. It is not in the nature of a thriving, progressive economic system that it should suddenly and definitely change about to the opposite situation, nor did the character of the Roman people change so much that the nation fell. Rather, it was a great political shift that was taking place and found its strongest expression in that strongest instrument of politics, the army.

What the Roman World Empire in all its glory was never able to create was a secure superior authority, resting on itself. The Roman Empire did not have the character of the modern hereditary dynasties; from the very beginning, it contained an inherent contradiction between the principle of heredity and the original one, the claim of the army commander, as the one on which Caesar had based his authority. Indeed, for a long time it was doubtful whether one of his generals, Antony, or his blood relative, Octavian, would be his successor. This inner cleavage was never overcome and could not be overcome. The hereditary right placed the scepter into the hands of incapable and intolerable men; the raising of a man to power as a result of popular uprising in the capital, or by the senate, by the Praetorians, or by the legions, always had a character of arbitrariness and usurpation. The one type of usurpation was in conflict with the other. It is surprising enough and a strong testimonial for the political sense of the Roman people that after the Julian dynasty had died out they were still successful for more than a century and a half, through understandings and compromises, principally between the army and the senate, time and again to establish a recognized emperor and a secure order. When that no longer succeeded, the crisis arose that finally led to the downfall.

The salient point is the change in the army.

As we have seen, the unity of the army was originally guaranteed by the fact that the legions, its nucleus, were composed of Roman citizens, to which the various provincial troop units were attached. Then the manning of the legions had gradually gone over to the provinces, and the Italians limited themselves to the Guard of the Praetorians. After they had served their apprentice years in the Guard, however, they provided the largest number of the centurions for the legions, and the legions accepted that just as the provinces accepted Rome's hegemony in general, because the empire was based on this authority. On one occasion, as early as Tiberius' reign, it had been pointed out during an uprising in Gaul that basically the Roman plebeian had become unwarlike and the strength of the Roman armies lay in the noncitizens.[3] Still the imperial concept was originally based on Rome, and political ideas are stronger than purely military ones. Now, however, the continuation of this domination for generations had Romanized the provinces themselves; the inner basis for Rome's hegemony had ceased to exist, had eliminated itself. The enthroning of Emperor Septimius Severus signified the rising of the provinces against the domination of the Italians. The emperor had the Italian centurions executed, eliminated the Italian Praetorian Corps, and replaced it with selected men from the legions.

If the Romanization of the provinces had been completely carried out, this shift would not have meant a weakening of the army, but rather a strengthening. But beside and beneath the Romanization of the provinces an element of barbarianism and of tribal individuality was still alive, and this caused the unity of the army to slacken. With the upheavals, Illyrians or Africans, orientals or occidentals, feeling their national pride, sought to gain the dominant role and allowed no further condition of stability to exist for long.

For the army, the numerous changes of emperor, following each other closely, always meant a condition of illness, a high fever that within a short time undermined the strength of one that was even still healthy. The legions were conscious of their right to choose the Emperor and in doing so also to set their conditions. In spite of and after every disruptive period, the great task of the Roman heads of state was to maintain and restore discipline once again. That was only possible if at least between the individual mutinous movements there were quite long intervals in which the strong arm of a fixed authority could make itself felt. That had been accomplished each time in the first two centuries. Now came a time when blow followed on blow; the soldiers lost their feeling of dependence on the emperors, and instead the emperors were dependent on them. The continuous alternation of imperial proclamations and the murders of emperors, the permanent civil war, and the shifting from one master to another destroyed the cement which until then had held together the strong wall of the Roman army, the discipline that was the base of the military value of these legions. Emperors who tried to maintain the discipline and restore it — Pertinax, Posthumus, Aurelian, and Probus — were murdered because of that attempt.

The civil war, in conjunction with a natural process which coincidentally set in at the same time, also brought about an economic catastrophe that sucked the Roman military system into its maelstrom and finally swallowed it up. An important element for every type of higher civilization is the valuable metal which, when pressed into money, puts in motion the economic forces of the social body. Ancient civilization and the Roman nation would not be conceivable without a large stock of gold and silver, just as little imaginable as they would be without a large stock of iron. In particular, a large standing army can be maintained only on the basis of a money economy. The legions on the borders, which defended against the barbarians all around the empire, were maintained by the taxes paid by the inner provinces. Now, in the third century, there developed a lack of valuable metals. How that came about cannot be learned directly from the sources. The natural wear and tear of valuable metals from constant handling, shining, misplacing, hiding, fires, and shipwreck has never been small. Pliny reports — a point confirmed by coins that are still found there in our days — that very much gold and silver had drifted away to India and China, with which countries a significant but almost entirely one-sided commerce existed. We already find Tiberius complaining in his day that the Romans were giving away their money to foreign peoples for jewels, and under Vespasian the imports from the east amounted to no less than 100 million sesterces (22 million marks) annually.[4] Therefore, in the two centuries from Augustus to Septimius Severus, something like 4 billion marks of valuable metals could have drifted from the Roman Empire to India and East Asia.[5] In Chinese chronicles, one can reportedly read that an ambassador of Emperor An-Tun arrived in the Celestial Kingdom; perhaps it was a Roman merchant during the reign of Antoninus Pius.

Much valuable metal also flowed into the barbarian lands, especially to the Germans, as pay and later as tribute. Such metals did not return. There are numerous indications that none of these losses was replaced, because the mines on the Mediterranean coast that had been known and worked up to that time were exhausted from the viewpoint of the then existing technology. Even our period would, of course, not be nearly capable of conducting its entire trade with the available supply of metals. We have understood how to support the supply of metal money by various forms of credit, paper money, bank notes, exchange, and checks.

Nevertheless, we would perhaps still be in difficulty now (I am speaking of the period before 1914) were it not for the unexpected large new gold discoveries in South Africa.

Let us not go into the matter of whether the Romans would have been capable, from a purely technical viewpoint, of discovering the modern means of exchange that substitute for currency. The Carthaginians at one time supposedly had a type of leather money, and among the Romans there existed certain beginnings of a banking system, with payment and remittance offices, which were subjected to governmental control under Hadrian.[6] But to apply such methods and organizations on a broad scale, to assure the cashing of papers of credit, and to prevent forgery, these activities require technical prerequisites that antiquity did not yet have and that have even required centuries for us to create. However that may be, completely aside from the technical prerequisites, there was missing the much more important, in fact indispensable, political situation for usable credit money, that is, stable political conditions fostering confidence. At the very moment when the Romans would have had a most urgent need for such conditions, they lost them. The emperors' struggle for the dominant position, which was at the same time a question of life and death, consumed all their strength and required their full attention. No other solution was found than a constant debasing of the currency. Under Augustus the silver denarius was pure, under Nero it contained 5 to 10 percent of alloy, under Trajan 15 percent, under Marcus Aurelius 25 percent, and under Severus, around 200 A.D., 50 percent. Under Gallienus, sixty years later, the *antonianus*, which had replaced it, normally had only 5 percent of silver.[7] The denarius, which under Augustus was worth 87 pfennigs based on our system, sank to 1 4/5 pfennigs under Diocletian. The minting of gold had already slowed down considerably under Marcus Aurelius; under Caracalla the pieces were made smaller, and then the production became so irregular that gold completely lost its character as currency and was only accepted by weight.[8] All the relationships of property and law that were based on money were upset and were dissolved. The money shortage of the changing emperors became ever more pressing after the decline had once started.[9] The taxes based on the old relationships and institutions brought in no further income. Heliogabalus had once demanded that they be paid in gold, but there was not enough gold available either.[10] His successor, Alexander Severus, lowered the taxes to one-third of the previous requirement in order to make them collectable.[11] Maximinus Thrax placed a tax on all income and gifts allocated to the public games, confiscated the adornments of the public squares and the dedicatory offerings on the temples — not only those of gold or silver, but even of bronze — in order to have them minted into coins.[12] Aurelian made an attempt to put the fiscal system in order with such forcefulness that it created a great uprising in Rome, but neither he nor his successors were capable of solving the problem.

Even in our day, we have been able to understand the situation of the Roman fiscal system of the third century whenever chance has happened to bring to light a treasure that was buried at that time. These treasures have often amounted to many thousands of almost completely worthless alloys and small coins. Silver or gold that might have been hidden was no longer at hand in the chests of the Roman citizens. But in the German area the treasures that have been found consist of the good old coins; the barbarians knew how to distinguish between real money and false, and they demanded the real thing for their pay or tribute.

The fiscal catastrophe slowed and stiffened the thriving economic life of the Roman World Empire; the arteries of this gigantic body became bloodless and dried up. In the course of the third century, the money economy almost died out and the civilized world slid back again into a barter economy. We would be arriving at a false understanding if we conceived of money economy and barter economy as absolute opposites. This they are not, and even in the most highly developed money economy certain remnants and elements of a barter economy remain. The economic existence of the civilized world slid back into the barter economy in the third century, to remain there for eleven or twelve centuries as is normally accepted; however, this barter economy never completely gave up cash money and the use of it. It is only a question of such an extensive rise of the one element and a retreat of the other that for purposes of simplicity we may use the expressions "money economy" and "barter economy."

The civilized world's move backward from a money economy to a barter economy in the third century can be more easily understood if we realize that the economic elements of the Roman Empire needed a huge mass of valuable metal in order to function normally. Almost the entire army was stationed on the borders. Only a very small part of the taxes paid by the provinces was used in the provinces themselves; a portion went to Rome, often to be kept there for a long time in the treasury, and the larger part went to the field camps to be paid to the soldiers. Only very gradually could this money flow back into the provinces as reimbursement for goods and services. Trade was carried out with silver and gold on a cash basis. The soldier demanded silver and gold for his pay, and these coins were gathered by the emperors in Rome in their treasury or were divided among the plebeians to keep them quiet. The annual pay of the army, in addition to rations and other supplies, may well have amounted to some 50 million denarii under Augustus; the emperor boasted in the *Monumentum Ancyranum* that he had divided up among the citizens a total of 919,800,000 sesterces (254,950,000 denarii = some 25 million marks). The transporting of money from the provinces that had no garrisons, such as, for example, Aquitania, Sicily, and Greece, to the Rhine, the Danube, and Rome must have gone on continuously, and the tradesmen who provided the soldiers, the court, and the Roman citizens with their needs brought it back again. Under the slow conditions of this transportation and of the settlements for sales, there had to be a considerable fund of cash on hand in even the smallest town and the last village that had to pay taxes, if the whole system was not to break down.

In the third century, the supply of money had become so small that the system collapsed. It was precisely the means through which temporary help had been provided, the apparent increase of money by the debasement of the coins, that necessarily brought on the final crisis, since the uncertainty of the value both destroyed the regular administration and paralyzed trade. Even before the real invasions of the barbarians began, in the second half of the second century the Roman subjects had begun to hide their cash from the tax collectors in the ground, as is evident from the treasures that have been found in recent centuries.

After Diocletian (284-305) had succeeded with very statesmanlike skill in reestablishing a stable regime for a time, he also sought most forcefully to restore order to the fiscal and economic system. By a sweeping regulation of prices, proclaimed in all the cities of the empire by being hewn in stone and which, for that reason, has for the most part come down to us in numerous pieces of the inscriptions, he attempted to establish legally the balance between money and goods, a relationship that had been completely lost. But all the death sentences that resulted still were not able to prevail against the power of natural economic laws. While much remains here to be clarified by the scholars, it is sufficient to take note of the progressive changeover to the barter economy.

The state, unable to collect taxes in cash, more and more expanded the substitute system of services and goods, which had always existed to some extent. The guilds were merged into definite hereditary corporations, in order to carry out the public works. The bakers baked the bread, the sailors transported the grain, the miners prospected, the fishers fished, the country people provided supplies and made wagons available, the city councilors arranged the public games and heated the baths. As payment the officials received specified rations and portions from the public stocks, grain, cattle, salt, oil, clothing, and only pocket money in cash.

What effect did this economic change have on the army?

I find that the first trace of the downward trend already existed under the very emperor who had ascended the throne as the leader of the provinces against the domination of the Italians, Septimius Severus (193-211). It is reported that he increased the soldiers' allocations of grain and allowed them to live with their wives. To be sure, his action has been regarded as a simple attempt to win favor and as an example of laxity, but this emperor was a very experienced and competent soldier and statesman who did not make such a fateful concession without very strong, in fact, compelling, reasons. These reasons become clear if we do not isolate the two provisions but consider them as inherently related. True, the emperor under whom the alloy in the silver denarius had already reached 50 percent raised the pay on his accession to the throne, but he was hardly in a position to compensate the soldiers regularly in cash. For that reason, he increased their payment in kind and made it possible for them to take advantage of these larger allocations by allowing them to consume these provisions with their families.

This is in agreement with a recently discovered inscription from his reign in which a soldier refers to himself as a tenant of the legion's acreage.[13] We hear that Alexander Severus decreed that the land apportioned to the border soldiers would pass to their heirs only if the latter, in turn, were soldiers.[14] Consequently, the legionaries, who were previously held closely together in the camps and forts, lived under constant discipline, and were even prohibited by law from having a wife, now lived, as had already long been the case in the Egyptian legions,[15] spread about outside the garrisons with their wives and children in their huts, cultivated their land, and assembled only from time to time for their service. However restricted this development may have been under the Severi, it definitely became the common situation in the generation following them.

And with this change the basic nature of the Roman legion was eliminated.

The man whom we have regarded as the characteristic type of the Roman military, the centurion, disappears from the inscriptions at the end of the third century; in the later law books, he appears as an office official. At the same time, the collectors, the tax officials, also disappeared, and as we have seen, both these changes are most closely connected.[16]

The name "legion" remained for a long time. Whereas Septimius Severus had thirty-three legions, the governmental manual from the beginning of the fifth century, the *Notitia dignitatum*, lists some 175 of them, but as this number already shows, these are small troop units of a completely different type. As under the earlier emperors, there was still a levy, insofar as form was concerned, but it was actually a recruiting procedure, and men were also often impressed for the legions. In the broad empire there was no lack of healthy and strong young men. The population that was available was much larger than in Augustus' time, but the military organization that made soldiers out of recruits and guaranteed the quality of the old legions had disappeared.

The ancient Roman army had been constituted from two significantly different components: the more or less Romanized legions and the provincial auxiliaries that were also gradually becoming Romanized,[17] whose quality was based on their military discipline; and the complete barbarians, whose military value rested on their untamed savagery. This military quality was affected neither by the lost authority of the highest commander nor by the new economic conditions.

In previous sections of this work (Vol. I, p. 509), we have raised the question as to how the military quality of a Roman legion might have compared with that of a horde of brave barbarians of equal size, and we came to the conclusion that the Roman discipline could not bring them to much more than about the same capability. The superiority of the Roman armies was much more strategic than tactical in that their commanders were capable of producing numerical superiority at the decisive point. If that is true of the best disciplined Roman legions, then it is clear that units lacking in discipline could not stand up to the barbarians. We know from Caesar's accounts — and he himself points this out repeatedly — what a difference there is between old and new troops. From the time of the Severi on, the Roman legionaries, who lived as farmers and assembled only for duty, no doubt still fought, but they were no longer the legions of Germanicus and Trajan. The Roman legions before Caesar's time had also been assembled only for war, but they had very often failed to live up to their task and had become hardened only during the war itself. At their first meeting with the Cimbri and the Teutones, things went badly enough for them, and we know with what fear they moved out against Ariovistus. It was not until they became full-fledged professional soldiers that they developed their full capabilities. Now, as they gave up this characteristic and again took on more the character of militia, the comparative capabilities shifted over not only to the side of the enemy but also, within the imperial army itself, to the barbarian auxiliary troops — and this all the more so in that the latter had increased their natural value even more as a result of their Roman service and their being equipped with Roman protective weapons and cutting arms. It was no longer the legions but the barbarians, and consequently principally Germans, who were now the best part of the army, and with dashing speed this stream overflowed the entire Roman military system. For in the civil wars that the Roman emperors were now waging against each other, the one who was able to lead the most barbarians into battle had the greatest prospect of winning, claiming the throne, and saving his own life. Competing with one another, the emperors took into their service not only individual soldiers of fortune but also entire tribes. They equipped them and led them into the very heart of the Roman Empire in order with their help to gain or retain the throne.

In the fourth century, the Roman army presents a completely different appearance from the description we have given earlier. It seems that Diocletian established a system based on the changes that were caused by the altered circumstances, and Constantine completed the new order. The troops were now composed of four special groups, the *palatini*, *comitatenses*, *pseudocomitatenses*, and *limitanei*. The old life guard of Praetorians, which was recruited from Italians, had already been eliminated by Septimius Severus. It had been replaced by a new guard corps, composed of men provided by the legions, so that transfer to this guard constituted a reward for the deserving soldier in a provincial legion. This reform had not had any real military significance; it is important only from the political viewpoint, as a symptom of the disappearance of the old dominant position of Rome and Italy over the provinces.[18] If we now find troops called *palatini*, that is nothing significantly different from the former guard. But now, in addition to this guard, there were special troops, called *comitatenses*, because they were to escort the emperor. This was an innovation to the extent that, as we know, in the earlier period almost the entire army was stationed on the borders. Now, however, the emperors could not get along without rather large bodies of troops directly available, even if in doing so they weakened the borders and sacrificed them to the incursions of the barbarians, a situation for which they were criticized by the authors.

Of course, troops were still stationed on the borders, and they were called *limitanei* or *riparienses*. But the protection that these troops could provide was small, for they were not disciplined units but rather what we would today call "border guards," farmers whose military obligation is served through their use in border defense. We have already seen above how little could be expected from such militia against Germanic warriors — so little, in fact, that it is precisely in this point that we find the explanation of the fourth category of troops, the *pseudocomitatenses*. Since the *limitanei* alone could probably be effective only against robber bands, a few regular units were also stationed on the border. Since they, of course, did not escort the emperor but did have an organization similar to the *comitatenses*, they were given that remarkable name.

The breaking up of the army into these different types of units explains the huge increase in the number of legions. The old legions were disbanded; some of the men were settled in the area of their old garrison as *limitanei*, others remained together as *pseudocomitatenses*, and still others were transferred into the *comitatenses* or the *palatini*. All the fractions and new organizations continued to be called by the name of "legion;" but now the simple name *numerus*, meaning "number," was more often used to indicate a troop unit, especially one in the field army.

If we could imagine that in the units of *palatini, comitatenses*, and *pseudocomitatenses*, or even in only the first two of these groups, the old Roman discipline had been maintained, and if it were also true that the Roman army had been greatly enlarged in total numbers, then its new form, in which we now find it, would in no way appear to be a change for the worse. We would then be able to say that the old Praetorians lived on in the *palatini* and the legions in the *comitatenses*, and that this professional and field service army had been supplemented and reinforced by the border militia of the *limitanei*.

But this was not the case. The total strength of the Roman army units, especially if we consider the half-effective military quality of the *limitanei*, had been decreased rather than enlarged. We can no longer consider the units called legions to be the same well-trained and disciplined legionaries of the classical period, but rather as more or less trained and useful groups of mercenaries. The more barbarians among them, the better the situation was. It is said that Emperor Probus divided 16,000 Germanic recruits among the legions so that they could take advantage of their barbarian strength while not making it too obvious who it was that brought about victory. The strength inherent in their characteristics was supposed to provide that which discipline was no longer capable of.

With the disappearance of Roman discipline there had also disappeared the peculiar Roman combat technique, the skillful combination of throwing the javelin with the use of the sword, a method that is possible only with a very well-trained unit.[19]

Now the Romans, too, utilized as their battle formation the Germanic square, the boar's head.

The barbarian auxiliaries, who had formerly constituted a supporting force in the Roman army organization, now formed its cadre and its strength.

In the hierarchy, too, the basic point can be recognized: the more barbaric, the more capable; the more Roman, the less capable. The carved dedications reveal that after the middle of the third century the service of Mars and Hercules came to the fore and the Capitoline gods receded. Hercules was the Germans' god Donar (Thor).[20]

Formerly, the Roman commanders had been senators. Even throughout the first centuries of the empire we have the peculiar phenomenon that, while the army in the strictest sense of the word was composed of professional soldiers, the highest commanders themselves retained the character of government officials. Now the legate with senatorial rank disappeared, and a full-time soldier was commander of the legion, and sometimes he was no longer a Roman but a German.[21] Now there was necessarily a definite separation of civilian authority from the officer corps right up to the highest positions, something that had not previously been the case. Up to the present time, it has been customary to understand this change as a sort of intentional chess move by Emperor Gallienus against the senate, but we must turn this point around. It was less a matter of a decrease in the functions of the senators than of holding the civilian authority in the hands of the Romans, since the troop leadership was beginning to slide over into the hands of the barbarians.

The army of the Roman nation was becoming Germanic. The Roman legions were not finally defeated and overthrown by the barbarians, but they were replaced by the sons of the North. The acknowledgment of this fact opens the gate through which we enter that epoch of world history that is called the *Völkerwanderung*.

## EXCURSUS

1. THE CHANGES IN THE POPULATION

The dominant theory on the social-economic conditions in the Roman Empire is to a certain extent twofold. On the one hand, there was undeniably a high degree of flowering of civilization; the ruins of the mighty construction works of that period remain persuasive witnesses to that fact today. On the other hand, the old sources contain so many complaints about decline that one cannot avoid recognizing them and speaking of continuing decay, especially a constant decrease of the population. The first sense of order was brought into this confusion by J. Jung in the *Wiener Studien* 1 (1879): 185 and by Max Weber's *Roman Agrarian History* (Römische Agrargeschichte), 1891. However, neither these scholars nor Eduard Meyer, in his otherwise very valuable article "Economic Development of Antiquity" ("Wirtschaftliche Entwicklung des Altertums"), *Conrads Jahrbücher für Nationalökonomie*, 1895, seem to me to have gone far enough in their correction of the source material.

If we look more exactly at the individual source passages which supposedly prove the decline of the population, we see that it is a question of either local or temporary phenomena, which do not prove anything for the entire empire and the different centuries.

When Pliny reports (*hist. nat.* 7. 45) how Augustus, because of a shortage of young men, once had to resort to levying slaves, or when in the *Life of Marcus Aurelius* (*Scr. Hist. Aug.*, Chapter 11) the expression *"Hispanis exhaustis"* appears once, no conclusion can be drawn from these points. It is a question of fortuitous temporary difficulties; for example, under Marcus Aurelius Spain was very much affected by the plague.[22]

If in 92 A.D. Domitian prohibited the conversion of grain fields to vineyards and even ordered the elimination of half of all the vineyards in the provinces (Suetinius 7), this action in no way points to an unfavorable development of social and agricultural economy but rather to a development that was too lush. A momentary increase in grain prices was the occasion for this action. It has been believed that the reason for his orders lay in the increasing intemperance, the preference of the farmers for viniculture, and the habit of depending on the importation of grain from abroad. Therefore, an antiluxury law was passed that was supposed to bring the people back to the simpler agricultural customs and social traditions of their ancestors.

As early as in Strabo's time (6. 1), Sicily was pictured as having a decreased population and a shortage of inhabitants. We hear similar reports on Greece, and especially Euboea, and on the immediate environs of Rome itself, the ancient Latium that was once so fruitful. But those areas were only very small pieces of the whole large Roman Empire, and there were special reasons in these cases. The decline of agriculture in the immediate environs of a very large city and its replacement by the raising of livestock have also been observed elsewhere; Eduard Meyer, in his work referred to above, cites present-day Dublin as an example. Sicily had suffered very much during the wars of the slaves but still exported a considerable amount to Rome. Italy had also declined in the last century of the republic as a result of large-scale raising of livestock and the pursuit of agriculture with slaves, but in the first century A.D. its population grew and spread again through the families of small farmers.[23] If we consider that in a period between 300 and 400 years long the great area of the Celts, upper Italy, France, Britain, the Rhine and Danube areas, as well as Spain and North Africa, and finally also Dacia were Latinized from central Italy, all of this is in no other way imaginable than as a result of very large emigration. The legions carried out the process of Latinization on the borders, but very few troops or none at all were stationed in the interior. The small number of officials sent out from Rome to the provinces is hardly to be considered, and agricultural colonization took place at best in only a few places. The Latinization must have been carried out principally by the settling of merchants and artisans in the cities. In the long run, the cities, not the farm areas, establish the standards for the language of a country. Cities change the character of their language quite easily and quickly. This change progresses from above downward; even a number of immigrants who are not too numerous, who possess superiority in capital and technical skill, supported by political hegemony, are sufficient to denationalize a region. This is the explanation for the extremely fast incorporation of the entire Occident by the Latin race. While an undercurrent of proletarian elements from Italy and the entire world continuously moved toward Rome, a main current was moving from there into the provinces. From the blending of the masses of people in Rome, so many able and industrious persons were continuously improving their lot that they were able to go into the provinces as representatives of the superiority of the capital city, prospered there, and created a new economic and social life while at the same time Romanizing these regions. By chance, we have learned that in the first century no fewer than 500 Roman knights (rich merchants) were living in Cadiz and Padua.[24] The direct ancestors of the people who represented and spread the Latin culture in Gaul, Spain, and Africa had perhaps themselves come from these provinces to Rome and had been Latinized there. The existence of this double stream of population movement could not be subject to any doubt. On the one hand, a strong emigration from Rome into the provinces must necessarily be assumed — for without it the rapid Latinization could not be explained — and on the other hand, this loss was continuously replaced, and Rome remained a very large city and probably even grew.

If then a constant and very strong movement, a continuing pushing, took place, it is only natural that it also caused many a painful point of friction, and a number of areas declined for more or less fortuitous reasons, while the whole still grew.

In particular, we are in no way to conclude from the frequently repeated complaints about the lack of agricultural workers and the deserted farmlands that the total population declined. Even from present-day England with all its economic opulence, we hear the complaint that broad stretches of land necessarily lie untilled because of a shortage of labor; in our East Elbe area, one-half of some districts would lie fallow today if we did not bring in annually a few hundred thousand foreign farm hands from the east. At the same time, the population of the German Empire increases by no less than 900,000 souls annually (before 1914). If, then, Pliny was already complaining about a shortage of farm labor, if from Hadrian's time on efforts were being made forcibly to keep the settlers on their lands, if Pertinax (193 A.D.) permitted and encouraged the occupying of untilled land,[25] and if we find legislative regulations concerning fallow lands since the time of Aurelian (270-275 A.D.)[26] — all of these things are no proof whatever of a decline in the population.

We have not received any kind of number that would indicate the change of the population under the emperors.[27] The fact that no decline, but rather a significant increase, took place is to be concluded from the following considerations and evidence.

Appian (about the middle of the second century) gives evidence of a highly developed flowering of the economic life (Introduction, Chapter 7). This evidence is confirmed by the great works of construction, especially the roads, which in part are still in existence today and in part are attested to by numerous inscriptions.[28] The building of roads over a period of centuries must be the most certain existing measure for a rising standard of living. No royal whims and no military purpose can constantly explain such great projects, if they are not backed up by strong economic forces and purposes.[29]

An improving standard of living, in turn, is absolutely irreconcilable with a continuous decline of the population. It is true that in France today we have an example of an improving standard of living with a population that is almost at a standstill. But even if the population of the Roman Empire in the 265 years from Augustus to Alexander Severus had increased only as slowly as that of France in the nineteenth century, it would still almost have tripled, for France continued to have an average annual increase of 0.04 percent, which leads to a doubling of the population in 174 years. The population movement in antiquity and the Middle Ages probably differed significantly from that of modern times in its lack of constancy. Even in the peaceful periods of the Roman Empire, we very often hear complaints about plague and famine, which hardly play any role in the population history of the present-day civilized world. For this reason, the increase during antiquity was certainly not very strong in general, despite economic prosperity, but it requires only a scarcely noticeable annual minimum of increase to bring about a doubling in two and a half centuries. Without exaggeration, we may certainly estimate an increase from 60 to 90 million souls.[30]

I do not consider it impossible that the increase may have been considerably greater, but even if it had amounted to double this it would still have been extremely small in comparison with the natural reproductive capacity of the peoples. This explains for us the laws of Augustus and later emperors fostering marriage and the raising of children. We could perhaps completely exclude these laws from consideration, since after all they applied to only a specific small stratum of the population, particularly the city of Rome.[31] Completely aside from that, however, the increase in population according to our estimate was indeed so small that contemporaries were hardly able to recognize any increase at all. The imperial laws on marriage do not in any way force us to the conclusion that absolute stability or even a decline had occurred, but they simply presuppose that among the Roman citizens, or only in certain parts of the citizenry, the increase remained far behind the normal growth rate. An actual decline may even have taken place from time to time, but neither the complaints of the authors nor the cited laws prevent us from assuming a slow general increase.

We have positive proof of the fullness of the population in Africa from Herodian 3. 4. The existence of a number of large cities, especially Carthage, is absolutely certain in this respect, but for the year 237 A.D. Herodian also adds expressly that there were many farmers. Heisterbergk, in *The Origins of the Tenant Farmer System (Die Entstehung des Kolonats)*, 1876, pp. 113 ff., has strongly confirmed the credibility of this testimony by numerous comparisons.

I find evidence for Spain in Jung, *The Romanic Regions of the Roman*

*Empire (Die romanishcen Landschaften des römischen Reichs)* 1: 43. He cites a geographer from the beginning of the fourth century who writes concerning Spain: "A broad, large country, rich in men who are experienced in all trades. It exports oil and lard, ham and draft animals to every region of the world, possesses all kinds of goods, and is outstanding in everything."

No one disputes the fact that Gaul and upper Italy were flourishing and rich in population under the emperors. In those countries the literature shows such a highly developed urban civilization that it is unthinkable without general economic prosperity.

Diodorus 1. 31 reported the population of Egypt as 7 million, and Josephus 2. 385, gave the figure as 7½ million, in addition to Alexandria; consequently, with Alexandria included, there were at least 8 million. Even if this figure may be subject to certain doubts (see Vol. I, p. 250, Note 2) — and, as I gladly concede to Seeck, *History of the Fall of the Ancient World (Geschichte des Untergangs der antiken Welt)* 1: 505, a sure conclusion can never be drawn from such numbers that provide chance comparisons — nevertheless we do have here at least some possible evidence not only against a decline, but also for a very significant increase. The recently discovered papyri confirm that Egypt under the emperors was very strongly populated. Erman and Krebs, in *From the Papyri of the Royal Museums (Aus den Papyrus der Königlichen Museen)*, 1899, p. 232, determine from a tax declaration that in the reign of Marcus Aurelius no fewer than twenty-seven persons were living in one-tenth of a house in Fayum. Wherever the population is so densely packed, it is necessarily very numerous.

All the preceding points should apply significantly only to the period up to the great economic change occurring from the middle of the third century on. For the time being let us ignore how the decline to barter economy influenced the change of population. In any case, the effect was probably not very fast or strong in either one direction or the other.

2. SUPPLY OF VALUABLE METALS

A special study of a still more detailed nature on the disappearance of valuable metals in the third century would be extremely helpful. In our basic work, the monumental *History of the Roman Monetary System (Geschichte des römischen Münzwesens)* by Mommsen, this aspect has been somewhat neglected in comparison with the debasing of the currency itself.[32] I want to make this comparison at least, which has convinced me that it was also actually — and perhaps principally — a question of too small a supply of valuable metals, because the mines produced no more or at least their production had greatly declined.

No doubt the production of the ancient mines was at times very great. In Greece, much money must have been in circulation in the fifth century, and the ancient authors can hardly say enough about Spain's richness in silver. In the first century, the poet Statius names in first place among the taxes collected "quidquid ab auriferis ejectat Iberia fossis Dalmatico quod monte nitet." ("Whatever Spain puts out from its gold-producing trenches shines on the Dalmatian mountain.") But over several centuries the production of valuable metals in any one place is not so easily maintained. It is reported to us specifically that the Attic silver mines in Laurium had already fallen off strongly in the last centuries before Christ and finally were exhausted.[33] Concerning Spain we have no direct evidence; the statement in Marquardt (*Römische Staatsverwaltung* 2: 260) that the Spanish silver mines were already producing but little at the beginning of the first century seems to be based on an error. At any rate, I have not succeeded in finding a source for it, and all other indications point to the fact that Spain still had a very rich mining industry in the first two centuries of our era. The Romans also succeeded, for example in Dacia, in discovering completely new veins, which were then energetically worked. But then there came about such a decline that Hirschfeld, in his *Studies in the Area of Roman Administrative History (Untersuchungen auf dem Gebiete der römischen Verwaltungsgeschichte)*, p. 91 (2d edition, under the title *Die kaiserlichen Verwaltungsbeamten bis auf Diocletian*, p. 180), can say that in no other area was it so precipitate and so striking. The *Notitia dignitatum* mentions only a single imperial mining official, and that was for Illyria. In the *Codex Theodosianus* there are only a few small provisions concerning mining and mining production (Book X, Title XIX). In Spain under the Visigoths, we hear no more at all about silver mining and find at most a reference to the panning of gold on the Tagus.[34] It was not resumed until the time of the Moors, perhaps in other places.[35]

There is still mention under Macrinus (217 A.D.) of gold and silver statues (Dio Cassius 78. 12), and it is reported that there was so much gold in the national treasury at the time of Gallienus' death (268 A.D.) that each soldier could immediately be given twenty pieces of gold (*Scr. Hist. Aug. Gallieni* 15). We have other similar reports, but, of course, none of these is proof that the money supply was sufficient for the economic needs of the huge empire.

If the fiscal system was again put in a certain degree of order under Constantine, that can probably be explained on the one hand by the fact that economic life had by then assumed other forms which did not require so much cash, and on the other hand that the confiscation of the temple treasures actually did increase the supply for circulation.

### 3. THE CHANGE OF THE SYSTEM OF RATIONS UNDER SEPTIMIUS SEVERUS

Herodian 3. 8. 4 reports of Severus: "He gave the most money (*chrēmata pleista*) to the soldiers and made many other concessions that they did not have before. In fact, he was the first to increase their pay (*sitēresion*). He also permitted them to wear gold rings and to cohabit with their wives. All this he considered not in keeping with military moderation, readiness for war, and good order."*

*Sitēresion* can also have the very general meaning of "compensation," and the passage could be understood in such a way that the first-mentioned *chrēmata pleista* refers to the donatives and that *sitēresion* refers to the pay, which was raised from 375 to 500 denarii.[36] This increase in pay, which Caracalla then even increased to 750 denarii (which had been the pay of the Praetorians under Augustus), seems to contradict completely my concept of the developing shortage of money and the consequent spread of the system of providing rations in kind. But with respect to the evidence, the text in Herodian, that Severus "was the first" to increase the *sitēresion*, eliminates the possibility of a reference to the pay, which had already been increased manifold since Augustus and again a short time previously by Commodus. I may therefore be allowed to hold fast to the idea that the pay increase is included in the *chrēmata*. On the other hand, the fact that the Severi also gave the soldiers very much money in cash still does not eliminate the possibility that at the same time a pressing shortage of money was already making itself felt in the economic body. For it was only through the use of the most extreme force, through mass executions and confiscations, that Severus collected the means for the pay increase, and even then only with the help of a further debasement of the coins, which, as must not be forgotten for one moment, already reached 50 percent under this emperor.

Domaszewski observes, and certainly correctly,[37] that the numerous findings of buried treasure from the second half of the second century were not the result of the barbarian incursions but of the barbaric regime in the interior. "Men hid their money from the tax collector in the bosom of the earth."

My concept is confirmed by Dio Cassius 78. 34, where Macrinus gives the soldiers not just money but also promises to restore to them the full *trophē* (rations) which he had taken away from them. Macrinus certainly did not decrease the rations necessary for the individual man; therefore, it is no doubt a question of a larger allowance, a family allocation. Since this emperor appears in general as a counterreformer after the Severi, we may conclude that he made an effort to eliminate the whole system based on increased rations in kind and family life, which had proven to be pernicious.

It is also expressly reported of Alexander Severus (*Vita*, Chapter 15): "annonam militum diligenter inspexit." (He carefully inspected the rationing of the soldiers.")

Scholars still differ among themselves on the meaning of *gynaixi synoikein* (to live with their wives), as they do in general on the history of marriage for Roman soldiers. I have adopted the solution that seemed to me the most probable one. It still appears particularly strange to me that up to Hadrian's time the foreigners from the provinces, according to the rights granted them by Roman law, should have been allowed a regular marriage and were therefore better treated than the *cives*. In Egypt, the legions had special privileges. See G. Wilmanns, "The Roman Camp City in Africa" ("Die römische Lagerstadt Afrikas") in the *Comm. in. hon. Theodor Mommsens*, 1877, pp. 200 ff; P. Meyer, *The Roman Concubines (Das römische Konkubinat)*, 1895; P. Meyer, *Zeitschrift der Savigny-Stiftung* 18: 44 ff.

#### 4. ARMY STRENGTH AND RECRUITING IN THE FOURTH CENTURY

The sources indicate that Diocletian increased the Roman Army several-fold, even fourfold. Lactantius strongly criticizes the emperor for the increase in the military burden. Mommsen felt authorized to conclude, from the *Notitia dignitatum* and all the other evidence, that the total strength of the Roman army in the fourth century amounted to something between 500,000 and 600,000 men, whereas, for the beginning of the third century, when Severus had increased the number of legions to thirty-three, Mommsen arrives at a strength of some 300,000.[38]

The bases for these numbers are very uncertain, however, as Mommsen himself points out. It is not clear what part of the troop units mentioned in the *Notitia* were actually on hand and how strong the individual units were. Likewise unclear is the question as to what extent the *limitanei* are in general to be considered as soldiers. Nowhere can I find an absolutely reliable number which we could use as a starting point and a control figure for the others. The army strengths given by the historians for Constantine's battles are worthless. But we must consider from the start that it is impossible to feed large armies on a barter economy basis — we shall often have occasion to speak of this point later in this work. The sequence of military actions, as well as the single figure for the army strength which we have and which can be considered as reasonably reliable, points to the fact that the armies of that period were not larger but considerably smaller than in the period of Augustus and Tiberius.

In a document in which Emperor Valerian places the later Emperor Aurelian in command of a large army, all his individual troop units are listed.[39] They include 1 legion, 4 Germanic princes, 300 Iturean archers, 600 Armenians, 150 Arabs, 200 Saracens, 400 Mesopotamians, and 800 heavy cavalry. Nevertheless, it can only have been a quite small army, where such insignificant contingents are specifically listed.

Of the greatest importance is the fact that at Strasbourg in 357 A.D. Julian, with no more than 13,000 men, is reported to have defeated the Alamanni, who supposedly had a strength of 35,000 men.[40] These figures probably go back to Julian's own accounts. We shall treat the battle itself in the next book; at this point, we are concerned only with the strength estimates. The 35,000 Alamanni we can eliminate at once; this is the usual exaggeration. There was never a time when 13,000 Romans were able to defeat 35,000 Germans in open battle, and most certainly not in the fourth century. The question is whether we may accept the 13,000 Romans. The tendency to understate one's own strength in order to have the glory of the victory shine all the more brilliantly is, after all, much too frequent. Moreover, 13,000 men under the command of a general who had available not only the forces of all Gaul but supposedly also of Britain and Spain, and not in a chance engagement but in a decisive battle clearly foreseen and prepared for, for which there was nothing to prevent his assembling all the available troops — under these conditions 13,000 men seems to be much too small a figure.

But even if we assume that Julian actually did state too small a number, we may still conclude from this figure that it was no longer armies of 60,000 and 80,000 men that fought the great decisive battles of that day. Even underestimates and exaggerations must still take into account the prevailing contemporary notions, and Julian could not give a number so distorted that his contemporaries would immediately have realized that. If he wanted to boast, he could, of course, have increased the strength of the Alamanni even more. Without considering his figure of 13,000 men as absolutely credible, I still believe that from this figure we may conclude with certainty that smaller forces were engaged in this battle, and therefore also in this whole epoch, than in the wars of Caesar and Germanicus.

It could still be said in objection to this that we are dealing here with an exceptional case, since Julian complained very bitterly that his cousin, Emperor Constantius II, had purposely made it difficult for him because of his jealousy and suspicion and had supported him poorly. Not only is the justification for these complaints subject to strong doubts,[41] but, even if they were correct, Julian still had at his own immediate disposal the richest and finest provices, and Ammianus (16.11) attributes no more than 25,000 men to his rival Barbatio in Raetia.

The small sizes of the armies in this period are confirmed by the consideration that without this presupposition the Germans in the Roman army could not possibly have attained such outstanding importance. While it is true that we have no measure as to how large the entire population of the German tribes in this period can be estimated, still there cannot already have been hundreds of thousands in the Roman service. Consequently, if they were giving the characteristic stamp more and more to the Roman army, then this army cannot have been very large.

I will not risk stating specific numbers, but it seems certain to me that there can be no likelihood of an increase of the army by Diocletian in comparison with its strength under the Severi. Even the estimate of 300,000 men for the beginning of the third century is already too high. It is very questionable whether the increase in the number of legions by Septimius Severus meant any increase of the army strength at all, and in any event we cannot assume that the number of the auxiliaries was also increased. It seems to me not at all impossible that the Severi with their thirty-three legions still had a total of not more than 250,000 men.

This decrease in our accepted figures for the army strength also necessarily changes our concept of the nature of the recruiting in the fourth century. Vegetius, as well as the legal sources, reports to us that the landowners were obliged to furnish the recruits. This appears as a completely new institution whose origin, as Mommsen states (p. 246 of the work cited above), remains in the dark; it was probably introduced in connection with the similarly new institution of the settlement system, the agricultural serfdom. This provision of recruits has been referred to as one of the actual burdens based on the possession of large estates.

If I understand the new form of recruiting correctly, it is a direct reflection of the new social-politial conditions in the process of simple continuing development of the older arrangement. The older Roman local administration was based on the cities, and the farm population was subjected to them. The estate owners lived in the city and administered their land holdings from there, coming to their property only for purposes of inspection or vacation. Gradually, however, these estate owners had moved from the city to the country and had freed their property politically from the city communes and developed them into independent administrative districts, in which they themselves were the highest authority.[42] This process was hastened by the barter economy; the master, no longer in a position of drawing sufficient lease currency from his property, moved there himself so that he could consume directly the produce of his lands.

In the older system of recruiting, we have imagined that the recruiting magistrates, together with the authorities of the commune, selected a few men from the large number of those available. In the new system the local authorities were the landowners. Consequently, for recruiting purposes, the cities dropped almost completely from the picture, because their citizens, from the decurions down, were already otherwise hereditarily obligated to the state for duties of various types. The number of recruits to be provided was minimal. We may not make an actual estimate, since we have no sure reference point either for the size of the population or for the strength of the army. Only by way of example, for purposes of clarification, let us just assume that the population of the entire empire amounted to 90 million souls and that its standing army, aside from the barbarian auxiliaries, was 150,000 men strong. With a system calling for twenty years of service, about one-fifteenth of the total, or 10,000 men, would have been necessary each year as replacements. But even if we take 20,000 or 30,000 men and

compare that with the fact that the German Empire today (1900), with a population of 54 million souls, each year finds some 250,000 young men fit for service
and inducts them, we can see that the provision of recruits as such cannot have
been a particular burden for the Roman population, even if we estimate the population and the army strength quite differently, making the former smaller and
the latter higher.

A system of recruiting that calls up only one out of thirty or forty qualified
young men automatically becomes more of a voluntary system than a levy. Consequently, we can agree completely with Mommsen, when he says: "If already in
the pre-Diocletian period replacements for the army were regularly provided
through voluntary enlistment, then this holds true even more completely for the
later period."[43] The imperial proclamations contained in the *Codex Theodosi-
anus* (Book VII, Title XIII, *de tironibus* |"On Recruits"|; Title XX, *de
veteranis* |"On Veterans"|; Title XXII, *de filiis militarium apparitorum et
veteranorum* |"On the Sons of Soldiers' Servants and of Veterans"|), in a num-
ber of points do not allow a complete and sure interpretation. Nevertheless, they
leave no doubt that the provision of recruits by the landowners also had for
practical purposes more the character of voluntary enlistment. The sons of veterans were considered to have an hereditary military obligation, and efforts were
made to attract others into the service through special tax privileges that also
applied to the man's parents and wife. If there had been an equal recruiting
demand each year, it would probably have caused few difficulties, but naturally
these requirements were very unequal and sporadic, after heavy losses or in times
of great danger. Under these circumstances there was probably a shortage of volunteers, despite the adequate total numbers of men. Therefore, the recruiting
developed, as in the eighteenth century, into a more or less forced impressment,
and as a result those who were selected attempted to escape service by self-muti-
lation

In general, however, we may hold to the point that voluntary enlistment prevailed. It is necessary to establish this fact from the military viewpoint, since
otherwise it would not be understandable how the Roman units could still have
accomplished anything at all. Levied or impressed soldiers are only competent in
very well-disciplined troop units with strong cadres. This was obviously no longer
the case with the Roman legions of this period. Only if the men came of their own
will with a good attitude and the animal instincts for the warrior's life could they
be employed as usable troops. Consequently, in keeping with the situation, men
were inducted voluntarily from the practical viewpoint, but for purposes of form
the designation by the landowners was retained, both to simplify the business of
recruitment and to save expense for the state. It also served especially as a means
of shifting the obligation for designating recruits into a monetary contribution,
something which happened very often and was on some occasions permitted but
often directly ordered. In 406 A.D., at a time of great emergency, the state conducted the recruiting directly and offered at first 3 and then 10 *solidi* (gold
pieces) of bounty. Even slaves were promised freedom if they were willing to
have themselves inducted, and they were given 2 additional *solidi* as travel money (*pulveraticum*: dust money).[44] Estate owners were assessed 30 *solidi*, sometimes 25, as substitute compensation for a recruit position, and several
landowners would share in this obligation.[45]

5. CONCERNING VEGETIUS' ACCOUNT

For the history of the Roman military system in the fourth century, I have completely disregarded the description which Vegetius gives in the twentieth chapter of his first book. In the *History of the Infantry (Geschichte der Infanterie)* 1: 52, Rüstow has given credence to Vegetius' work, as have many others. If we look more closely at Vegetius' account, however, we must conclude from it that the entire alleged description is an impossibility. Vegetius states that up to the time of Gratian the Roman infantry was equipped with body harness and helmets but that this protective gear was abandoned thereafter because it had become too heavy for the undisciplined soldiers. How was this Roman infantry supposed to look without protective armor? Were the Romans perhaps now used only as light troops? That is impossible, for the training of a competent archer, slinger, or *peltast* was still more demanding than that of a hoplite. But there is no such thing as hoplites without protective armor. I consider the entire description only as a further proof that Vegetius was an impractical literary writer, who composed his work only from scholarly sources and hearsay. The only possible conclusion from this description is that at that time there were no more real Roman soldiers at all, but the nation had only barbarians in its service. What Vegetius reports is some kind of empty talk that reached his ears. Even the individual details of his description confirm this point. With anger and sadness, he reports how the unprotected Romans were inferior to the Goths. But this vulnerability was not based, for example, on the assault of the Goths with spears, swords, or axes but on the effect of their hail of arrows. On the other hand, he does not relate the lack of armor to the Roman hoplites but to the archers, who, since they could not carry a shield, necessarily had to have a helmet and harness. We can see how all the concepts and facts are mixed together here. For this reason, the entire description is to be rejected as worthless.

6. (Added in second edition.) In this edition, the two chapters on the imperial Roman army and its final dissolution have been supplemented significantly on the basis of numerous studies made by Alfred von Domaszewski. Nevertheless, I find myself obliged to disagree with this competent author's opinion on the decline of the army. Domaszewski sees the reasons for the fall of the Roman Empire not in large physical needs and changes, but in the personal errors of a few emperors, particularly Septimius Severus and his successors. He writes that Augustus disarmed the citizenry for the security of the emperor and that as a result of this military system the nation finally collapsed.[46] This point can be countered by the fact that it was not the ruler who disarmed the citizens. On the contrary, the disarming of the citizenry that had been taking place gradually since the Second Punic War necessitated and caused the creation of a professional army, and this professional army finally established the ruler. It was not simply for his personal security that Augustus maintained the professional army, and neither was it for the landowners and the lessees of the estates, as Max Weber believes,[47] but for the sake of the nation. For how would they have been able to retain domination of the subjugated provinces and protect the borders of the civilized world against the savage Germans with a citizen army?

Domaszewski sees the deteriorating effect of the Augustinian military system in the constant increase of the military burdens, which he believes drained the substance of the nation. We have seen (p. 170 above) that the increase in the military burden was perhaps not as great as the amounts of money would make it appear. Even if we should simply accept the pay increases as absolute, still they were not a result of the military system but rather of the *political* structure of the state, which made the selection and continuing existence of the head of state dependent on the army and thus gave the army the opportunity and capability to exert stronger and stronger pressures. The comparison that Domaszewski also makes, and rightly so, between the English and Roman armies demonstrates this point. In England, we see nothing in the way of adverse effects of the military system, and that is, of course, because the political structure of the English nation is a different one. Domaszewski calls the pay increases that Septimius Severus and after him his son Caracalla established (from 500 to 750 denarii per year) "criminal" and "outrageous." Through this laxness, he claims, the greed of the soldiers, among whom the barbaric element was now definitely the dominant one, was given free vent, and the army, once so proud, from which every trace of discipline had vanished, had now become the terror of its own country and a joke to its enemies.[48] Septimius Severus himself, according to Domaszewski, was an incompetent general who assured himself of the loyalty of the soldiers only by a constant bribing of the army, extravagant donatives, and equally extravagant pay increases. He goes on to say that Caracalla, by following his father's example, had stamped an entire century with the financial bankruptcy of the empire.[49] And the imperial authority had collapsed because the ruinous actions of the Eastern dynasty undermined its foundations.[50]

Against these points it can be argued that, first of all, Septimius Severus, as Domaszewski himself shows,[51] reestablished his control over his mercenaries and again put a limit to their greed. If Severus was still successful in doing so, as Augustus had been, then the historical problem lies in the question of why such control was no longer possible at a later time. It is possible that the pay increase that Caracalla granted in order to bind the troops to his cause and win their favor after the assassination of his brother actually did exceed the economic resources of the nation. But when Domaszewski cites this as the reason why the nation then collapsed "beyond hope of redemption," we must ask: Why "beyond hope of redemption"? Earlier emperors, too, distributed huge sums during political crises to win the loyalty of the soldiers, as even Tiberius did after the execution of Sejanus. A world empire does not collapse as the result of such an isolated mistake that an Emperor at some time gives or promises to the soldiers more than the national treasury can afford. It has been possible time and again to restore the discipline in mercenary armies, even after the most difficult disruptions, whenever an unrivaled commander stood at the top and the war treasury was regularly able to provide the necessary sums. Consequently, it was not the individual acts and mistakes of the emperors of the Severian dynasty but the fact that these two conditions, for the reasons developed above, could no longer be fulfilled — therein lies the cause for the disappearance of the Roman discipline and with it the fall of the Roman Empire.

Max Weber has propounded his own viewpoint on the fall of the Roman Empire in his work *Roman Agrarian History (Römische Agrargeschichte)* and, in extension thereof, in an article in the *Wahrheit* (Vol. 6, No. 3, Stuttgart, 1896), "The Social Reasons for the Fall of Ancient Civilization" ("Die sozialen Gründe des Untergangs der antiken Kultur"). Weber places particular emphasis on the fact that the expanse of the Roman world had been greatly extended through the incorporation of large inland areas — Spain, Gaul, Illyricum, and the Danube countries — and that as a result, the center of gravity of the population had shifted to the interior. The ancient civilization had attempted to change its theater of operations and to become an inland civilization from a coastal civilization. "It spread over a huge economic area which even through centuries could not possibly be adapted to the exchange of goods and the financial needs as this had been the case along the Mediterranean coast." According to Weber, the exchange of goods in the interior was so difficult and insignificant that everything necessarily bogged down in the almost immobile barter economy.

The correct portions of this antithesis between coastal traffic and inland traffic, coastal civilization and inland civilization, are helpful, but it is also clear that this contrast is exaggerated in such a way as to obscure the truth. Ancient civilization was, to be sure, based primarily on sea trade but by no means exclusively so. A city that played such a role as Thebes in Greek legend and history, and the second city in Italy after Rome, Capua — these were both inland cities. From the opposite viewpoint, however, the so-called inland areas incorporated in the Roman Empire (and it should be noted that this already occurred as early as the third century B.C. and not just under the later empire) still have so much coastal development that, if we deduct these coastal areas on the one hand and add Britain with its extensive coastal development on the other, a point overlooked by Weber, there can be no argument at all for a displacement of the center of gravity of the population into the interior. And least of all if we consider that these countries are, after all, criss-crossed by navigable streams which in their penetration of the interior were utilized in ancient days, even to the smallest streams, and which hardly need to take second place to the trading advantages of the sea. In addition, the excellent Roman military roads, which I have already cited above (p. 223 n.29) in evidence against Weber's viewpoint, were also used for transportation of goods.

Furthermore, Weber views the movement to the country of the large estate owners, all of whom formerly lived in the cities, not as an expansion and strengthening of the economic life as I have pictured it above, but rather as a weakening influence because the cities had lost in that process, and the new country seats, where the products of the estates were now consumed on the spot, meant the shift from a money economy to a barter economy. "The national financial policy had a reinforcing effect on this collapse of the cities. It, too, became more and more a barter economy, and the treasury tended to become an *Oikus*, which covered its needs as little as possible in the market place and as much as possible from its own means, thus limiting, however, the development of money fortunes."

This concept raises the question as to why the fiscal policy shifted to a barter economy. After all, a money economy has immeasurable advantages over a barter economy, specifically in the case of the fiscal procedures of a bureaucracy. Wherever we find a bureaucracy in world history, it is always concerned with moving from a barter economy to a money economy. Just as feudalism and a barter economy go together, so do bureaucracy and a money economy. Wherever and to what extent we find the opposite situation, most surely it occurred only as a matter of necessity. How then is the Roman bureaucracy supposed to have come to a remarkable preference for a barter economy? It is obvious that Weber did not sufficiently test the relationship between cause and effect, that it was not the bureaucracy that restricted the money economy by creating or fostering a barter economy, but that, on the contrary, the money economy, which for some reason or other had become restricted, forced the bureaucracy to slide over into a barter economy. All of these observations are so obvious and so clear that I did not consider it necessary in the first edition to go into the subject and expressly refute Weber's concept. Now, however, I must go back and pick up this point, since Weber has again taken up his theory in modified form in the article "Agrarian History" ("Agrargeschichte") in the third edition of the *Handwörterbuch der Staatswissenschaften* by Conrad and Gen., and in it has directly rejected and argued against my conclusions as described above.

Weber holds fast to the antithesis of the thriving commerce of the coastal lands and the skimpy commerce of the inland areas.

He believes (p. 180) that trade during the period from the Gracchi to Caracalla had no doubt grown considerably, as was only natural, but had still not increased so very much in relationship to the expansion of the civilized area. He writes: "In the coastal regions the provision of food and clothing for the slaves in the large *Oikoi* was covered more or less by the market. The slaves or tenants of the large landowners in the interior lived, of course, in a barter economy; only the upper class with its small numbers had needs that called for the purchase of goods, and these were covered by the sale of excess quantities of their produce. This trade was but a thin web stretched over the underlying barter economy. On the other hand, the masses of the large capitals were not accommodated by private trade, but by the national production (*annona*)."* Weber supports this description (*Agrargeschichte*, p. 224) with a series of citations from the Roman agrarian authors, from Cato, Varro, Columella.

First, it should be noted that all of these citations are erroneous. In Weber's view, they are supposed to prove that routes of communication were of no particular value. Actually, they prove the opposite. Cato (*de re rust.*, Chapter 1) holds that an estate should, where possible, be situated at the foot of a mountain, facing southward, in a healthful area where workers are available, there is good water, an important city is nearby, or the sea, or a navigable river, or a good, widely used road. Here then is a direct reference to the value of connecting roads. If Weber seeks to diminish its importance by saying that Cato called for them more in connection with the possibility of bringing workers for the harvest, we can reply that there is not even the slightest reference to this relationship in the text. It is a gratuitous addition by Weber.

Referring to Varro, Weber tells us that he estimates the return from an estate near the sea as 5:1 in comparison with one in the interior. Actually, with regard to a specific estate in the Alba region that very profitably raised fowl, fish, etc., and shipped them to Rome, Varro says (3. 2) that it would be five times as profitable if a site on the seashore could be found for it ("secundum mare, quo loco vellet, si parasset villam": "if he had acquired a villa along the sea, where he wanted it"). Since the Alba estate was situated on the Appian Way a scant 13 or 14 miles from the gates of Rome, it is clear that the sea is mentioned here not as a better means of transportation but because of the raising of fish.

Finally, referring to Columella, Weber states that, while he names the sea and large rivers as advantageous for trade, he considered the proximity of large roads to be undesirable because of the necessity for putting up vermin-infested vagabonds. It is true that in the passage cited by Weber (I, Chapter 5) Columella mentions these well-known disadvantages of close proximity to the great military roads. In another passage, however, (I, Chapter 3) he names as the factors that, after fertility and healthful location, come into consideration for an estate: the road, the water, and the neighbor. He then describes in detail the advantage of a good road: "ad invehenda et exportanda utensilia, quae res frugibus conditis auget pretium et minuit impensas rerum invectarum, qui minoris apportentur eo quo facili nisu perveniatur. Nec nihil esse etiam parvo vehi, si conductis iumentis iter facias, quod magis expedit quam tueri propria." (". . . for importing and exporting necessities, this increases the price of stored produce and diminishes the expenses of imports, which are brought in at a lower cost where they arrive with slight effort. It is also important to transport, if you should make the journey with hired pack animals, because this is more useful than to look after your own.")

Concerning Weber's description, it should be remarked further that a "national production" (annona) existed only for Rome. While it is true that in the municipal cities the grain trade was not left completely free to private speculation but was supervised by the local authorities, it was undoubtedly principally private business, and even for Rome this private enterprise was in no way completely excluded.[52]

It is also untrue that the tenant farmers of the interior lived purely from a barter economy. Certain small business and cultural needs existed for them, just as for the serfs of the Middle Ages. A few crockery and iron utensils and instruments and a few bright-colored scarfs and adornments can hardly have been completely missing in the poorest hut, and in the great majority of cases these were not produced on the estate but were procured from the city. This can be concluded from the existence of the many small and medium-sized cities that were presumably concerned with small-scale agricultural production and paid for these products with manufactured goods. As the Middle Ages show, this kind of economic relationship can also exist in a predominantly barter-oriented period. We must remember, however, that this is not a question of absolute opposites but only of relative differences and that in the later Middle Ages, when the cities were thriving, that element of the economy based on money was constantly growing and was already playing a considerable role. From the Roman tax system, we can conclude with certainty that this factor of money economy was at least as strong in the Roman Empire as in the late Middle Ages, and probably even much stronger. The taxes on commerce and the individual and land taxes are not imaginable without the idea that the tenant farmer disposed of a portion of his produce to traders or at the city market. In this connection, we must remember that in no way were the tenant farmers limited to turning over to their masters simply natural produce or working for them, but they also paid lease money. In the first century A.D., the tenants in Italy were still exclusively money lessees, and if in the second century a system of leases based on a portion of the produce appeared, that situation was perhaps already a result of the scarcity of cash currency. On the other hand, in Africa, which after all belongs to the coastal civilization just as much as Italy does, the lease based on produce held true from the start. However that may have been, the existence of a tax to be paid to the state necessarily calls for an active commerce. There is no question but that year after year large amounts of money streamed from all the provinces to Rome and into the army camps and then gradually back into the provinces again in exchange for products. This is not possible without a very active commerce in the interior areas as well as the coastal regions.

Whether the partial movement of the aristocratic families from the cities to the country meant in general an increase or a decrease in trade does not depend on this fact alone, but on the nature of the economic life in general. The aristocratic domains in the country mean just so many small new centers of culture. In many respects, this movement economized means of production, stimulated new powers of productivity, and created new commercial needs, so that the cities did not at all necessarily need to lose what the country gained. There is still no proof that this occurred in the Roman Empire.

Finally, Weber himself seems to have dropped the idea that the bureaucracy as such tended to favor a barter economy and restricted money trade. In place of a direct effect he has substituted an indirect one. Bureaucracy, Weber explains, crushed capitalism. In his view, the ancient capitalism had been built up on a political base; masses of slaves, taken as prisoners of war, and business connections with the state, tax leases, and delivery of products. According to Weber, first the empire had brought peace, thereby putting an end to the influx of slaves, and second it had created the hierarchy of officials, who had taken over business matters from the capitalists and managed them themselves. And so, in spite of the increase of the money economy up to the period of Marcus Aurelius, small traders and artisans had replaced the merchant princes, just as tenant farmers had replaced the slave plantations in the country.

Now it is quite clear, after all, that these are no symptoms of economic collapse; on the contrary, we could see in this respect great progress and gain. Weber arrives at the opposite conclusion with this sentence (p. 182): "The bureaucratic organization killed not only every political initiative of the lower classes but also the economic ones, for which there were, of course, no corresponding opportunities."

It is not very easy to follow this train of thought. One *salto mortale* follows another: the bureaucracy, by killing the political initiative of the citizens, also killed their economic initiative; the bureaucracy, by limiting capitalism, killed economic initiative in general; the elimination of the citizens' economic initiative forced the money economy into a barter economy; the final result of this chain, however, is the collapse of ancient civilization.

Is it true that the bureaucracy killed the political initiative of the Roman subjects? At most, after all, that of the Italians — the huge majority of the inhabitants of the empire had, of course, already been deprived of participation in politics by the republic that had subjugated them.

Is it true that the limiting of capitalism, from which its best opportunities, through the tax lease and grain speculation, were taken or reduced, actually strangled the economic sense in general? Weber himself speaks of the small traders who had multiplied, and the numerous thriving cities that grew up in these centuries speak clearly enough against him. It is also not true that the opportunities of large-scale capital had been so completely eliminated by the bureaucracy. Even if the bureaucracy had deprived the capitalists of the tax lease and furnishing of products for the capital city and for the army (and even this took place only very gradually), they still had room enough for their activity. We have seen how extensive the movement of money must have been, flowing continuously back and forth between the provinces on the one hand and the capital city and the military camps on the other. Small traders alone could not have taken care of that. Rome was the center of a mighty commerce in money, and the banking business was as lucrative as it has ever been in the world. The goods that the provinces had to produce and send to the large cities and the camps in order to obtain cash that was then taken from them year by year in the form of taxes cannot possibly have been produced, assembled, shipped, exchanged, sold, and paid for without the participation of large-scale entrepreneurs as well. Moreover, a portion of the mines always remained private property, and even more were operated privately.[53] That all of these businesses, like the construction of the large cities with their temples, amphitheaters, and water systems, the trade in salt, wine, oil, and fruits, the production of and commerce in mass and luxury goods in fabrics, metals, leather, stone and wood, the construction and renting of multiple-dwelling houses — that all of these things could not have offered any opportunities for profit or that the Roman people were lacking in the necessary economic initiative and energy for these activities is a purely doctrinaire interpretation which not only is not supported at all but also directly contradicts the facts. It sounds like the last echo of that argument by the "Nothing-but-free traders," who reject any interference by the state in the political economy, national railroads, and social politics, because this presumably stifles the economic sense of the individuals. The many rich families we encounter in Latin literature certainly did not owe their riches simply to the inheriting of estates. I believe it is not too bold to turn Weber's thesis around and say: because the imperial authority took politics out of the hands of the citizens and the Roman masters did likewise to the provincials, those who were thus deprived were pushed all the more strongly into economic activity, and the economic liveliness of the period developed that attitude of mammonism which evoked the condemnation and the warnings by Jesus and his apostles and their successors.

Weber's attempt to explain the collapse of the Roman nation and antique civilization has turned out to be as unsatisfactory as all the earlier explanations and those just recently offered by Seeck and Domaszewski.

It might be asked whether Weber has presented any valid points against my concept.

First of all, he has interpreted my explanation very incorrectly in his expression (p. 60) "that the appearance of barter economy in the late Roman period was the result of the beginning of exhaustion of the mines." The unproductiveness of the mines is, of course, only one of the various factors that were working together, in my opinion, and I do not consider this, but rather the political conditions, as the truly decisive factor. Nevertheless, I do believe that the decline of the mines was in fact a very significant factor; it is therefore appropriate to clarify it in view of Weber's objections.

First, Weber seems to doubt to some extent the fact of the decline of available supplies of valuable metals themselves, but he does not discuss the evidence which I cited. To whatever extent lower productivity of the mines had taken place, he believes that this condition did not result from their having been exhausted from the viewpoint of the existing technology but rather that this was the result of the changed economic conditions: instead of the slave labor existing in the classical period, they had now entered a period of small tenant farmer economy, and under this economy they could not continue to work the mines. This admission would really be sufficient for my purposes, for after all it is important to me only to establish the fact that the organization of the Roman Empire required huge masses of valuable metal in order to function, and that these supplies were becoming exhausted; the reason why this took place is not important. Nevertheless, this question is of such far-reaching importance to universal history that I wish to add something further, and all the more so because Weber obviously greatly underestimates its importance. On page 181 he speaks of a "collapse of the ancient money economy extending over generations." In reality, however, barter economy governed the civilized world not for just a few generations but for much longer than a thousand years. In Western Europe, it dominated almost completely, and in the Eastern Roman Empire, while it is true that they again approached a money economy somewhat more closely for a while, in no way was this on the same level as in antiquity.[54] That phenomenon cannot be peremptorily put aside.

Why then the declining productivity of the ancient mines, a point which Weber also admits as at least a possibility?

Weber himself stresses the great importance of supplies of valuable metals for economic life. While he correctly warns against exaggeration of its role, as if the valuable metal as such already had a productive effect, he still considers it to be very important. Even though he does not expressly say so, he would no doubt admit that it was fundamental especially for the Roman Empire with its legions paid in cash. Are we really supposed to believe that the Romans had renounced obtaining an element which was so important for their existence simply because the old work organization no longer functioned as a result of the decline in the number of slaves?

But not even this fact is correct. Neuburg, in his "Studies on the History of Roman Mining" ("Untersuchung zur Geschichte des römischen Bergbaus"), *Zeitschrift für die geschichtliche Staatswissenschaft*, Vol. 56, established the fact that in the later imperial period free wage workers were employed extensively in mining,[55] even some who were at the same time co-owners. In addition, slaves and civil prisoners were used, and as the first group gradually disappeared, the Christians provided new contingents for the second category. Neuburg finds no other explanation for the decline than in the decline of the population, a concept that is no longer espoused. Naturally, mining never completely collapsed; it seems to have held up relatively well, particularly in the northern part of the Balkan Peninsula. A very strong decline is undeniable, and to recognize that this decline cannot have been based on the system of labor would hardly have required Neuburg's findings. We need only cast a glance at the Middle Ages, which after all had as little available in the way of slave masses as did the third century. From the tenth century on, however, the newly discovered mines were worked with continuously increasing success; the Germans especially did this in the Harz, in the Erzgebirge, in the Fichtelgebirge, and in Bohemia. And this success was not supposed to have been possible for the Romans?

Furthermore, I later became aware that Montesquieu, in his *Considérations sur les causes de la grandeur des Romains et de leur décadence,* Chapter 17, had already recognized the disappearance of valuable metal, the failure of the mines, and the effect of this fact on the decline of the army and, through it, on the collapse of the empire.

Weber's idea shows to some extent the correct historical instinct when at least one of the basic causes at which he arrives is of a political and not an economic nature: the organization of the empire. But he seeks the effect in a false place, in the development of the bureaucracy and of the limiting of capitalism by the bureaucracy, a limiting which he then extends generally, even to the destruction of the economic sense. Actually, both the development of the bureaucracy and the limiting of capitalism were so moderate and within such borders that we can consider it only as fortunate. The error lay rather in the inherent impossibility of the empire to adapt to the concept of freedom and to envelop it with institutions which would simply guarantee human dignity, first to the Roman citizens and finally to the whole mass of inhabitants of the empire. Everything depended on the personality of the emperor. Simply to place confidence in the right of heredity proved impossible and also contradicted the nature and origin of the imperial position. For this reason, early in the imperial period, Augustus had to sacrifice his natural grandson, since he was incapable, and placed another man in his position as adopted son. But now they had the eternal uncertainty of the law at the central point of the nation. Hardly any succession to the throne took place without the spilling of blood, whether it was against the ruling emperor or a rival of his successor, or in open civil war. This uncertainty of the imperial succession was the organic flaw in the nature of the empire. It made it impossible to overcome the emerging economic difficulties (monetary crisis), as well as the political ones (the rise of sectionalism), dissolved the discipline in the legions, forced acceptance of the services of barbarians, and thereby finally brought on the collapse of the empire.

Martin Bang, in *The Germans in the Service of Rome (Die Germanen im römischen Dienst),* Berlin, Weidmann, 1906, has treated the inscriptions relating to Germans in the Roman service. He has arranged them systematically and has shown what conclusions are to be drawn from them. If in doing so he has very effectively assembled the testimony of the Romans on the ability of the Germans (p. 16), he has nevertheless underestimated them in that he holds fast to the old legendary gigantic numbers (see p. 6, Note 36; p. 93). But we give full credit to the Germans only when we consider side by side with their accomplishments how few they actually were. Bang's designation of the coming of the Germans into the high positions of the Roman nation as "a break with prejudices" is also incorrect. It was actually something different.

On page 60, Bang states that it was only with Marcus Aurelius that the period began "in which the Germans were made eligible for service in a systematic manner and in large numbers for the purposes of the empire." This had already happened in the time of Caesar and Augustus, Tiberius, and Germanicus. The change that perhaps started already under Marcus Aurelius and did not gain full force until the third century was no new system but a practical shifting of weight. The Germans, who had formerly been secondary troops in the Roman army — but along with the Roman subjects also free men from the start — moved into the highest positions because the legions had lost their discipline and with it their strength.

NOTES FOR CHAPTER X

1. For example — and certainly correctly — L. Schmidt in *Hermes* 34: 135, on the war with the Marcomanni.

2. Dessau, "The Source of Officers and Officials of the Roman Empire During the First Two Centuries of Its Existence" ("Die Herkunft der Offiziere und Beamten des Römischen Kaiserreichs, während der ersten zwei Jahrhunderte seines Bestehens"), *Hermes* 45 (1910).

3. Tacitus, *Annals* 3. 40.

4. Tacitus, *Annals* 3. 53.

5. Nissen, "The Trade Between China and the Roman Empire" ("Der Verkehr zwischen China und dem römischen Reich"), *Bonner Jahrbücher*, Vol. 95.

6. Mitteis, in his "Studies on the Ancient Banking System Based on Papyrus Finds" ("Untersuchung über das antike Bankwesen auf Grund der Papyrusfunde"), *Zeitschrift für Rechtsgeschichte, Römische Abteilung*, Vol. 19, establishes the fact that indications of a specific exchange of checks, which would, of course, be a very important point, are very weak.

7. According to B. Pick in the *Handwörterbuch der Staatswissenschaften* 5: 918, 2d edition.

8. Mommsen, *Roman Monetary System (Römisches Münzwesen)*, pp. 755, 777.

9. Based on an inscription found recently in Africa, an attempt has been made to clarify this with reductions of the army strength and the pay. Domaszewski, *Rheinisches Museum* 58: 383. Mamea lowered the strength as well as the pay of the *principales*, but, of course, this action did not go far toward solving the matter. The soldiers and their good will were only too strongly needed both within the empire and beyond it.

10. To be sure, the gold coins were reduced in weight but not in the same way the silver coins were alloyed. From this point, too, we may conclude that there was practically no more circulation of gold coins; otherwise, they would certainly not have passed up the convenient solution of using alloys in these coins as well. A shortage of gold is referred to directly in a source document, *vita Aureliani*, 46, cited by Mommsen in *Geschichte des römischen Münzwesens*, p. 832.

11. In accordance with the verbatim text, the passage in *Scrpt. Hist.*

*Aug. Vita Alexandri (Writers of the Augustan History, Life of Alexander)*, Chapter 39, must be understood as meaning that the tax was reduced to one-thirtieth. But the correction and interpretation proposed by Rodbertus, according to which it was one-thirtieth of the value of the cadaster, whereas previously one-tenth was required, at least has the advantage of providing something possible and credible from a practical viewpoint. See M. Weber, *Römische Agrargeschichte*, p. 194.

12. Seeck, *Preussische Jahrbücher* 56: 279.

13. On 1 October 205, the soldier C. Julius Catullinus, of the Fourteenth Legion, dedicated an altar to Jupiter, and on it he referred to himself as *"conductor prati Furiani lustro Nert. Celerini primi pili"* ("tenant of the field of Furianus Nert. Celerinus, primus pilus, for a five-year period"). This inscription was found on the Schaflerhof, south of Petronell, near Vienna, and was published in the *Berichte d. Ver. Carnuntum in Wien, für das Jahr 1899*, p. 141. According to this, then, ground belonging to the legion (*pratum*) was regularly leased out to the soldiers. In various other places, inscriptions from the same period that also contain the word *lustra* (periods of five years) have been found. The editor, Bormann, has already related this, and certainly correctly so, to the permission that Septimius Severus gave the soldiers to live with their wives.

In the *Militärdiplom*, No. 90, *C.I.L.* III, supplement, p. 2001, the text apparently speaks of the sons of *"milites castellani"* ("soldiers of a fort") (only the letters . . . *lani* remain). Since it is a question only of the sons of centurions and decurions, Seeck (in *Paulys Realenzyclopädie*, under *castellum; castellani*) believes that this refers to a special type of soldier higher in grade than the privates. I prefer to reconcile the inscription with the context indicated above. Mommsen places it between the years 216 and 247.

14. *Vita*, Chapter 58.

15. Premerstein, *Klio* 3: 28.

16. Biedermann, in his *Studies on Egyptian Governmental History (Studien zur ägyptischen Verwaltungsgeschichte)*, 1913, establishes in detail (p. 108) that the old Egyptian administrative organization disappeared toward the middle of the third century.

17. It is generally assumed that the auxiliaries had been increased as early as the second century because at that time they still had fewer demands than the legions. Under Augustus, for example, they received only a third of the pay of the legions and had no claim on the large donatives. At the same time, the demands of the legions were continuously

increasing, while their military efficiency was declining. Domaszewski, *Heidelberger Jahrbücher* 10: 226. This assumption is contrary to the possibility that I expressed on p. 171 above that the auxiliaries had been organized into legions. Both theories are mere possibilities. And it is, of course, also imaginable that they existed side by side and that now one and now the other actually took place.

18. I do not believe it necessary to attribute any significance to Caracalla's military frivolities, which are reported in Dio Cassius 77. 7 and in Herodian 4. 8. 2. 3.

19. Petersen, in *The Marcus Aurelius Column, Text (Die Markus-Säule, Textband)*, p. 44, says of the legionaries shown on the relief: "Their shield is seldom a normal *scutum*, their lance never shown as a *pilum*," and on page 45 he continues: ". . . often they have trousers." These are unusual phenomena which I do not know how to explain. It has also struck me in Tacitus' account of the German war how little reference is made to the unusual aspects of the Roman combat with the *pilum*.

20. Von Domaszewski, *Die Religion des römischen Heeres*, p. 49. See also p. 113.

21. Bang, in *Die Germanen im römischen Dienst*, p. 91, believes, of course, that he can establish that the highest military grade to which a German rose in the pre-Constantine period was a *dux in Pannonia Secunda Savia* (leader in Pannonia Second-Savia), a Batavian, and he rejects other sources. Nevertheless, Ritterling has already contradicted him in the *Deutsche Literatenzeitung* 17 (1908) and has stated that Bang had gone too far.

22. Just as little is to be concluded from the inscription *C.J.L.* X, 1401, which does not prohibit moving to the country but only selling at a profit buildings for demolition.

23. Hartmann, *Archäologisch-epigraphische Mitteilungen aus Oesterreich*, 1894, Heft 2, p. 126.

24. Strabo 3. 5. 3; 4. 5. 7.

25. Herodian 2. 4. 6.

26. Hartmann, *Archäologisch-epigraphische Mitteilungen aus Oesterreich*, 1894, Heft 2, p. 131.

27. The last census that has come down to us is a result of the count taken under Claudius in 48 A.D. (Tacitus, *Annals* 11. 25). A total number of Roman citizens amounting to 5,984,072 (count of individuals) was recorded. The census in 16 A.D. had shown 4,937,000, but nothing is to be concluded from this increase, since we do not know to what extent it is

based on increase in the population or on extension of the right of citizenship. See Eduard Meyer, *Handwörterbuch der Staatswissenschaften*, article entitled "The Population" ("Bevölkerungswesen").

28. In the *History of the Roman Imperial Period (Geschichte der römischen Kaiserzeit)* by H. Schiller, the building inscriptions are shown for each emperor. See especially in that work 2: 378 (Severus); 2: 753, 772, 798, 871; 3: 151.

29. Max Weber, in his so very commendable *Römische Agrargeschichte*, has, of course, expressed the opinion that the Roman roads had only military and not economic significance. This is true, however, only in comparison with modern mass transportation. After the establishment of internal security, they would certainly not have built so many roads for military purposes in the interior, and we can read in *Panegyriki* VIII: "Even the military road is poor and uneven, and this makes difficult the transportation of produce as well as public transportation." Cited by Jacob Burckhardt in *Constantine*, third section, p. 85.

Wilhelm Weber, too, in his *Studies on the History of Emperor Hadrian (Untersuchungen zur Geschichte des Kaisers Hadrian)*, 1907, p. 204, says of the road construction under this emperor in Africa that it is hardly likely they served military purposes, but that it is likely that their purpose was "to divide overland trade among as many roads as possible, covering the entire country and thus not favoring any single city."

30. On the basis of a comparison with the population at the end of the sixteenth century, Beloch estimates some 100 million. *Zeitschrift für Sozial-Wissenschaft* 2 (1899): 619.

31. Augustus' speech as reported in Dio Cassius 56. 7.

32. Recently, Kurt Fitzler has also contributed to this subject in his *Quarries and Mines in Egypt (Steinbrüche und Bergwerke in Aegypten)*, 1910.

33. The passages are assembled in *Paulys Real-Enzyclopädie* under the headings *Metalla* and *Montes*.

34. *Lembke, Geschichte von Spanien* 1: 235.

35. Schäfer, *Geschichte von Spanien* 2: 241.

36. Domaszewski, *Heidelberger Jahrbücher* 10: 230 f.

37. *Rheinisches Museum* 58: 230, note.

38. "The Roman Military from the Time of Diocletian" ("Das römische Heerwesen seit Diocletian"), *Hermes* 24: 257.

39. *Vita Aureliani,* Chapter 11. To be sure, the source value of this reference is small, since the writing is fraudulent.

40. Ammianus 16. 12.

41. H. Schiller, *Geschichte der römischen Kaiserzeit 3:* 303 ff., discusses this very accurately, and we could perhaps even go one step further toward a skeptical attitude.

42. On the struggle between city and country that develops from this, I find an interesting citation from Frontinus, *de controv. agr. (On Land Disputes)* in Heisterbergk's *Origin of the Tenant Farmer System (Entstehung des Kolonats),* p. 116.

43. *Hermes* 24: 245.

44. *Codex Theodosianus* VII, Title XIII, 16 and 17.

45. The provisions in the cited titles of the *Codex Theodosianus.* It is not necessary to go into the details here. As far as I have conducted the study for my own illumination, as in general for many of the points in this chapter, I have been fortunate to enjoy the advice and support of my colleagues, Messrs. Otto Hirschfeld and Emil Seckel. I should like to take this opportunity to express my thanks for this assistance.

46. *Neue Heidelberger Jahrbücher* 10: 240.

47. *Handwörterbuch der Staatswissenschaften* 1: 180.

48. *Die Rangordnung des römischen Heeres,* p. 196.

49. *Rheinisches Museum* 53: 639.

50. *Rheinisches Museum* 58: 218. It is, of course, somewhat in contradiction to these judgments when Domaszewski, in *Neue Heidelberger Jahrbücher* 10: 235, calls Septimius Severus a "great statesman."

51. *Neue Heidelberger Jahrbücher* 10: 233, 235.

52. Hirschfeld, *Philologus* 29: 23 ff.

53. Hirschfeld, *The Imperial Officials (Die kaiserlichen Beamten),* 2d edition, p. 158. Neuburg, see below.

54. See below the chapters on the military system and strategy under Justinian, which show how the mighty nation was not capable of assembling pay for rather large armies. See also Part 3, Book II, Chapter 7, "Byzantium."

55. This fact has recently been established for Egypt in the study by Kurt Fritz Fitzler, *Quarries and Mines in Ptolemaic and Roman Egypt (Steinbrüche und Bergwerke im Ptolemäischen und Römischen Aegypten),* Leipzig, 1910.

# BOOK II

## The *Völkerwanderung*

# Chapter I

# The Roman Empire with German Soldiers

We have called the first book of this second part of our work "The Conflict Between the Romans and the Germans," and now we call the second book "The *Völkerwanderung*" (Migrations of the Peoples). According to traditional and still accepted opinions, such a parallel arrangement would be incorrect, and a subordination of the second title to the first would seem to be called for: for is not the *Völkerwanderung* precisely the critical point and the decisive factor of the "conflict between the Romans and Germans?"

No, it was not actually that way. The struggle between the Romans and the Germans in the sense of actual combat, of military history, had already ended in the third century. With the end of this century there was no longer a Roman military system, a Roman army, that would have been capable of fighting with the Germans. There was no doubt still a Roman nation, the Roman World Empire, and it continued to live for another century in almost its full development, and after the loss of its western provinces for a full thousand years in its eastern half. But the military forces that enabled this political system to endure were no longer Roman. As early as the fourth century, it was no longer the legions that defended the nation, but rather it continued to live by repelling those barbarians who were threatening and pressing it with other barbarians it took into its service. The struggle that was waged was no doubt still a fight between Rome and the Germans but it was no longer a fight between Romans and Germans; the warriors doing the fighting were Germans and other barbarians, Huns or Slavs, against their own kind.

The Roman Empire's system of barbarian mercenaries, after the collapse of its own former military system as we got to know it in the previous book, led to the migrations of the peoples.

The name *Völkerwanderung* has often been disputed in recent times, particularly because this type of migration was presumably in no way peculiar only to the fifth and sixth centuries, but fills the whole course of world history. The Crusades and the settling of America by Europeans would have just as much claim to be placed under this heading as do the movements in the period of transition from antiquity to the Middle Ages. That is completely correct; still, it seems desirable to retain this name, once so widely accepted, in its specific meaning. Even if there does exist a constant, never completely ending migration of peoples, each period has its own peculiar phenomena and forms, and wherever possible it is good to have specialized names for all of them. Consequently, we retain the old expression. In addition to the press of the Huns and the following movement of the Slavs, it denotes principally the settling of German tribes on the soil of the Roman Empire.

Formerly, there existed the idea that this settling was to be regarded as a continuing broad-scale action of conquest and subjugation: presumably, the age-weakened Roman Empire was finally overrun by the energetic young Germans. The discussion in our previous book has shown us that this was not the case: the Roman legions were not so much conquered by the Germans as they were replaced by them. Instead of a continuing struggle between Romans and Germans, we are to visualize a transitional form that leads from the Roman World Empire into a number of Germanic kingdoms on Roman soil. This transitional form shows us a Roman Empire whose soldiers were no longer Romans, but Germans.[1]

Ever since the time of Caesar, in fact from the Second Punic War on, foreign mercenaries, at first sharpshooters and cavalry, formed a part of the Roman army. The barbarian element even penetrated very strongly into the legions. Augustus' political wisdom had found ways and means to restore and retain the Roman character of the legions. It probably remained this way up into the third century, even though the proportion of barbarian auxiliaries increased at times and possibly even continuously. We are told that Marcus Aurelius bought the assistance of Germans against the Germans ("*emit et Germanorum auxilia contra Germanos*"). Caracalla was accused by his successor of having spent as much on the presents he gave the barbarians as on the pay of the entire army.[2]

In the civil wars of the third century, however, the barbarian element increasingly won the upper hand. Gallienus defeated the Goths with the help of the Herulian Naulobatus, on whom he bestowed the consular insignia.

The Roman legions continued to exist in name, but their character changed. They declined to a weak militia. Besides such degenerate legions (*limitanei*), there existed a few others that retained their military efficiency by adopting the system of the barbarian mercenary units. The Joviani and the Herculians of Diocletian are examples. The system of the old, genuine Roman legions was based on discipline. Their ranks were filled not only by volunteers who were led into the service of Mars by a natural warrior instinct but also by drafted recruits, who initially brought with them only the necessary physical qualifications. Their military training and the strictness of the centurion made useful soldiers of them. This strong point was now destroyed, and only the first-named factor, the natural warlike tendency, remained. Even among a civilized people there are always a certain number of men who, as Tacitus says of the Germans, would rather earn their living through blood than through work and who are possessed of a strong military pride or simply of physical courage. The number of such men, however, is always very small; they are not sufficient to form armies of the size that Augustus or the Severi commanded. They were sufficient to provide continuously a few troop units of predominantly Roman character, but the character of the well-trained legions was lost. Their appearance and combat methods were similar to those of the barbarians, whose fighting quality, of course, also derived from their natural personal courage and esprit de corps.

The transition from the ancient Roman military system into the new forms developed gradually, but in the end it was completed quite rapidly. It started toward the middle of the third century, and toward the end of the century, under Diocletian, it was already completed. The Roman element that still existed was no longer Roman in the old sense. For the most part, barbarians already composed the army that Constantine led out for the conquest of Italy and with which he defeated Emperor Maxentius at the Milvian Bridge and captured Rome. Zosimus tells us that he assembled troops from the subject barbarian peoples — Germans, Celts, and Britons.[3] If these troops carried the cross as their symbol, it was less from Constantine's concern to have troops who did not fear the Capitoline gods — for this could not have been the case with the Germans and the Celts — than a concern for the Roman citizenry itself, among whom there was a strong Christian faction which Maxentius suppressed and Constantine was attempting to win over. Like a Germanic warrior king, Constantine surrounded himself with a retinue of *comites*, who, as a kind of new nobility, displaced the old classes of senators and knights.

Throughout the fourth century, we often find Roman and German elements side by side. In the harangue with which the army commander Julian encouraged the zeal of his men before the battle of Strasbourg, he admonished them "to restore to the Roman dignity its former honor" (*"Romanae majestati reddere proprium decus"*), and he branded the enemy as barbarians (Ammianus 16. 12. 31). But this army which was addressed in this manner did not simply contain a fraction of Germans, as the battle account states, but the Germans apparently formed its real strength; Cornuti, Bracciati, and Batavians are mentioned. In the attack they shout the *baritus,* and it is this same army that shortly afterward selected Julian as emperor by raising him on a shield in the German manner.[4] When the Visigoths had crossed the Danube and the flood of the real migration of the peoples was beginning, the Roman historian describes for us how in the first great battle the "barbarians" sang the heroic songs in honor of their ancestors whereas the "Romans" shouted out the *baritus.*[5]

An unusual piece of evidence showing the extent to which the Roman army was already Germanized in the fourth century has recently been provided us by the diggings of the archaeologists. The angle between the Danube and the Dobrudscha was covered by three lines of defense emplaced in various periods. It has now been established that the oldest of these lines was a low earthen wall facing southward; it was probably erected by the barbarians against the Romans. The second line, a higher earthen wall, has completely the character of our Germanic *limes* and was probably also built at the same time by the Romans. The third line is a stone wall that can definitely be attributed to the fourth century. But the fortifications that belong to it and are tied in with it have completely the character of the early medieval fortifications on German soil. They could hardly have been built by the Germans themselves; their inclination toward hard work was at that time still very small. But the leaders who ordered the installation and planned it in detail were already Germans. They no longer lived under the military traditions of Rome but, as in all military systems, so too in fortifications, they turned toward the concepts that they brought from their homeland and then developed with the extensive means and in accordance with the examples they saw on Roman soil.[6]

In this period, the word *barbarus* was the technical term for a soldier; the military budget was apparently called *"fiscus barbaricus."*[7]

We should not be misled by the fact that during this time the sources continue to speak of the Roman system, Roman fame, and Roman courage. Even Procopius, although he himself recounts on every occasion that it was the barbarians who were principally responsible for the Roman victories, continues to speak in the sixth century of the victories of "Roman courage" over the barbarians because the victories were won under the imperial banner.[8]

And so, from the end of the third century on, the Roman armies were composed of units of mercenaries of various types. They were largely — and perhaps already principally — pure barbarians, Germans, who were brave in combat but were very hard to control outside of combat, particularly in peacetime. If the disciplined legions had already mutinied often enough, now the emperor and the empire were completely dependent on the good will of these bands. The Germans serving the emperors of the first two centuries had always had the feeling of being only auxiliaries. The idea of rebelling never occurred to them, since the punishing and avenging legions stood close by. The national Roman units, which were now still called legions, were very weak in numbers, and themselves contained barbarians, had only much too similar attitudes to those of a unit of foreign mercenaries. Nothing prevented the German warriors who would today take the emperor's pay from taking up arms tomorrow against their former commanders if they found that their contract was not fulfilled in some small point or other, or that their demands were not satisfied.

It is obvious that a military force of this character came nowhere near the old legionary army in strength, efficiency, and readiness. Even if an emperor like Constantine succeeded, as it appeared, in completely restoring the unity and authority of the imperial power, this was still only in appearance, for the firm foundation of ancient times, the discipline in the army, was lacking.

Let us observe in passing the continuing importance of this weakening of the Roman Empire for our spiritual life. In order to find a substitute for what was now missing in military power, Constantine formed an alliance with the great federation of bishops, the Christian Church. The Roman emperor would hardly — or better expressed, never — have permitted this sovereign power to exist beside his own if he had still had in his legions the ancient support. The legions would also have given him the force to suppress this new power of the church, so confident and independent. That the church victoriously survived the persecutions from Decius to Diocletian was due to her martyrs but also no less to the weakness of the nation which no longer had at its disposal its ancient military power.

Living space opened up for the church as the ancient civilization sank. There was no longer any question of the effective border defense that had guarded the *limes* for so long. The Germans also stormed across the Rhine and the Danube, sailed on their ships from the Black Sea all the way across the Mediterranean and into the ocean, and nowhere was it possible to defend against their plundering raids. Unmercifully, they slaughtered those inhabitants whom they did not carry off into slavery. Even today more than sixty French cities show traces of their having been burned down in that period — midst scornful laughter, as the Romans recounted of Chnodomar, king of the Alamanni[9] — and of how, destroyed, they were built up again, tightly pressed together and surrounded with walls. In the preceding peaceful centuries, the cities were open and were often widely spread out, but now they were built with narrow streets and as small a circumference as possible, in order to be able to defend themselves better. In the thick towers and walls that were now built and have survived for thousands of years until broken down again by the pickax of modern traffic or archaeological diggings, remains of columns, statues, friezes, and beams have been found, often bearing inscriptions that identify the period of their erection and still showing traces of the fires set by the barbarians. Far beyond the gates of these fortified cities, however, are to be found remains of the destroyed temples and amphitheaters that allow us to guess the extent of the former open cities.[10] More numerous in its population and richer in all the resources of civilization than at the time of Augustus, the Roman Empire had become too weak to defend its civilization, since it had lost its own standing army, its well-disciplined legions. It was in vain that a patriotic rhetorician like Synesius, for example, complained at the time of Arcadius:[11]

Before we tolerate having the Scythians (Goths) roam about, armed, in the country, we should call all the people to arms with sword and lance — it is shameful that this highly populated nation should entrust the honor of warfare to foreigners, whose victories shame us even while they are useful to us — these armed men will no doubt wish to play the master with us and then we who are militarily untrained will have to fight against seasoned warriors. We must awaken again the ancient Roman spirit, fight our own battles, carry on nothing in common with the barbarians, drive them from every official position as well as from the senate; for inwardly they are ashamed, after all, only of those dignities that have always been held in the highest esteem by us Romans. Themis and Ares must hide their faces if they see these barbarians clad in skins commanding men in the Roman uniform or, laying aside their sheepskins, quickly donning the toga and thus taking counsel together with Roman magistrates and deciding the affairs of the Roman Empire! When they take the seat of honor right next to the consul, ahead of noble Romans, when, as soon as they leave the curia, they slip back again into their skins, making fun of the toga among their comrades, they joke that in the toga one cannot draw his sword. These barbarians, previously useful servants of our house, now intend to rule our nation! Woe to us if their armies and leaders rise up and are joined by a stream of their numerous countrymen who are spread throughout the entire empire as slaves.

In this same mood that naive writer and antiquarian, Flavius Vegetius Renatus, set to work, studied the ancient authors, and described what the Romans had really had earlier by way of a military system on which their greatness rested, what kinds of military regulations they followed, which now had to be recreated and had to serve as an example in order to save the empire and to renew its ancient might. In doing this, he created a book that has served as a manual for military men through centuries and thousands of years, but collapsing empires can no longer be saved either by speeches or by books.

The German mercenary units in the Roman service did not yet constitute the same force that brought about the end of the Roman Empire in the west. Such mercenaries, removed from their homeland, adapt to the political and social customs of the nation they serve, or, if they remain foreign to them, they are still too temporary and too rootless an element to find a lasting hegemony themselves. As dangerous as the rebellious mercenaries after the First Punic War had become for the city they served, Carthage, they were still defeated in the end, and Hannibal waged the Second Punic War with just the same kind of units. What we call the *Völkerwanderung*, with all its immeasurable consequences, originated in the fact that it was finally no longer only large units of individual warriors that entered the Roman military service, but entire peoples who moved with wives and children and all their possessions onto Roman soil and as a Germanic people constituted the Roman army.

There is a great difference between the military service of individuals, no matter how numerous they may be, and the service of an entire people, who retain their social structure and political organization. The possibility that the one type could nevertheless shift over to the other resulted from the character of the Germanic people. This people was so completely warlike and was governed so exclusively by warlike instincts, drives, and passions that it provided an inexhaustible source for recruiting; more than that, the entire people, just as they had formerly moved out to war against their neighbors, were ready to fight in any kind of unfamiliar form for any purpose. The Germans did not set out on the *Völkerwanderung*, as one might think, because the old areas had become too small for their growing numbers; rather, they set out as military units, greedy for pay, booty, adventures, and honors. In a few individual cases, scarcity of land may no doubt have driven some peoples to move on; in other cases, pressure from other enemies was the motive. Even so, these two reasons would only have given impetus to individual moves or border wars. The factor that was decisive for world history is that the German tribes were large bodies of warriors who moved out as such for war, pay, booty, and domination. It was not to look for land, to become farmers and live as farmers that they came into the Roman Empire — often they left their homeland empty behind them — but for the sake of the military actions in which they wanted to participate.

In the shifts from service to enmity and enmity to service that characterized the relationship between Rome and the Germans in the third, fourth, and fifth centuries, a few border areas on the Rhine and on the Danube, as well as Britain, were conquered by the Germans in the true sense of the word. While the local populations were not completely driven out, they were so extensively reduced and suppressed that the new masters could gradually absorb their remnants. In Italy, most of Gaul, Spain, and Africa, the Germanic king commanders, as the real possessors of power, also found legal justification for their positions but without completely separating their provinces at once from the empire. Even Odoacer, after eliminating the Western Roman emperor in Rome, ruled Italy not as a sovereign king, but as a Germanic prince whom the Eastern Roman emperor had designated as his viceroy for this part of his empire, and with all his power, Theodoric the Great, the Ostrogoth, did not conceive of his position in any other way.[12]

Only gradually did this form, this fiction, fade away, and there arose the independent Germanic kingdoms on Roman soil in Gaul, Spain, Africa, and Italy, the kingdoms of the West and East Goths, the Burgundians, the Franks, and the Vandals.

Of all the battles and engagements of this period, there were only two in the fourth century — Strasbourg and Adrianople — for which we have reports of any validity from the military history viewpoint. For lack of sources, I have nothing to recount on the campaigns of Constantine the Great, the battle at the Milvian Bridge,[13] and the battle of the Catalaunian Fields in the fifth century. Not until the sixth century do we again have more detailed and reliable information, on Belisarius and Narses.

## EXCURSUS

### THE FALL OF EMPEROR GRATIAN

Ranke conceives of the uprising in 383 against Gratian, who otherwise was held in high regard, as a rebellion of the legions against the promotion of the Germans and the preferences shown them. Nothing seems more natural than that we should encounter this conflict somewhere or other in the history of the Roman Empire. The self-confident legions, which, as Ranke says, had always determined who would occupy the throne, necessarily opposed the idea that the foreign barbarian mercenaries should be placed above them. Nevertheless, the difference between the legions and the barbarian auxiliaries must not have been felt to be very deep, since the sources never report any conflict arising from such jealousies. At best, the account by Herodian (8. 8) of the fall of the two emperors, Balbinus and Pupienus, in 238 might be interpreted as evidence of such conflict. In this account, express mention is made of the opposition between the Praetorians, who were hostile to the emperors, and the Germans, who protected them, but that is, after all, only a secondary factor in the confusion. The conflict arose from the fact that the double imperial position was the work of the senate, whereas the Praetorians claimed the designation of the emperor as their prerogative. But the Germans defended the emperor chosen by the senate because this conflict was inconsequential to them and they had once recognized him as their military leader.

The question of conflict is of still greater significance in the case of Gratian's fall. If it were true that the reason for the uprising against Gratian is to be sought in the Roman troops' envy of the favored Germans, then toward the end of the fourth century there still must have been in existence the old legions, or at least troops with a definite Roman national spirit, in contrast to the barbarians. But our sources for the happenings in 383 make no mention of them. Scholars have time and again allowed themselves to be misled by the schematics of the *Notitia dignitatum*, by Vegetius, and by the phraseology of the authors to the effect that the ancient Roman military system had survived into the fifth century. If that had been the case, then it would not be understandable that the legions should have been content with the military preference shown the Germans without ever having reacted strongly against it.

If we now examine the documentary evidence, however, we find that it contains absolutely nothing about an uprising of the legions against the Germans. The whole conflict is an hypothesis that can be traced back to Heinrich Richter's

book, so excellent in many respects, *The Western Roman Empire, Particularly under Emperors Gratian, Valentinian II, and Maximus (Das weströmische Reich besonders unter den Kaisern Gratian, Valentinian II,
und Maximus).* On the basis of a few sources, particularly Zosimus and Synesius, Richter portrays with great perspicacity and persuasiveness how strongly
the Romans resented the barbarians clad in skins with long hair and beards
occupying the most important posts and the foremost seats in the curia. But he
himself adds that we know of these complaints only from the mouths of the
heathen-philosopher authors, who at that time represented only limited circles.
Their complaints, which by the way came from the Orient, do not permit any
conclusion concerning the troops stationed in the west, and we cannot arrive here
at a conclusion based purely on an analogy.

The passage in question is found in the author who continued the work of
Aurelius Victor, Chapter 17, where it is said of Gratian:

cunctis fuisset plenus bonis, si ad cognoscendam reipublicae gerendae
scientiam animum intendisset, a qua prope alienus non modo voluntate,
sed etiam exercitio fuit. Nam dum exercitum negligeret, et paucos ex Alanis, quos ingenti auro ad se transtulerat, anteferret veteri ac Romano mili-
ti, adeoque barbarorum comitatu et prope amicitia capitur, ut
nonnunquam eodem habitu iter faceret, odia contra se militum excitavit.
Hoc tempore cum Maximus apud Britanniam tyrannidem arripuisset et in
Galliam transmisisset, ab infensis Gratiano legionibus exceptus, Gratianum fugavit, nec mora exstinxit. ("He would have been full of all good qualities, if he had paid attention to learning the science of government, to
which he was nearly unsuited not only by his attitude but also in practice.
While he neglected the army and preferred to the old Roman military a few
Alani, whom he had won over with huge amounts of gold, he aroused the
hatred of the soldiers against him. To such an extent was he taken with his
retinue of barbarians and nearly by their friendship, that he sometimes
journeyed in the same costume. When at this time Maximus had secured a
tyranny in Britain and had crossed into Gaul, he was received by the
legions hostile to Gratian. Maximus put Gratian to flight and killed him
immediately.")

These words could very well be interpreted in the sense accepted by Richter
and Ranke if we had other proof of the continuing existence of legions in the old
sense and of their opposition to the Germans. But they can also be interpreted
differently.

According to our author, the troops favored by Gratian were not Germans, but
a special race, the Alani. The *vetus romanus miles* (old Roman legionary) that
was opposed to them is in no way necessarily the Roman legionary, but could just
as well refer to other barbarians who were in the imperial service earlier. Gibbon,
too, understood it in this general sense. Even the term at the end, "*ab infensis
Gratiano legionibus*" ("by the legions hostile to Gratian") is not conclusive,
for there is no doubt that the name "legion" was still used for troop units. The
question is: what kind of men composed these so-called legions at that time?
Whether they still bore the specifically national Roman character, and whether

in this passage a contrast with the barbarian auxiliaries is meant? But this interpretation is not to be inferred from the words of the author. If it had actually been a question of the opposition of "Romans on this side, Germans on that," then it would be completely incomprehensible why the Germans did not finally fight for Gratian. Richter himself (page 567) states this reservation on that point: "Even the other Germans may have felt a certain amount of hostility," that is, against the Alani. Whatever the reasons for the dissatisfaction with Gratian may have been, there was in any event no uprising of the Roman element against the German, based on the favor shown the Germans at the court and in the army. The Germans would not have abandoned the game so easily. The troops who first went over from Gratian to Maximus as the two emperors confronted each other near Paris were Numidian cavalry.

In order to understand the rebellion against Gratian, for which there seems to be so little basis, we must realize first of all that in general mercenary troops that are not very strictly disciplined can be held under control in peacetime only with great difficulty. The slightest motive suffices to create unrest among them; finally, they mutiny just from a pure desire for action.

Furthermore, Gratian does not seem to have had his finances in good order, so that he either drastically decreased the number of his soldiers or did not pay them promptly.

If in 383 Maximus, as representative of the legions, had defeated Gratian as representative of the Germans, then the victor would undoubtedly have continued to build up his principal support energetically in the five years of his reign. But we hear not the slightest mention of such action. If there had existed any possibility at all of breathing new life into a truly Roman military system, no one would have been in a better position to make this attempt than Gratian himself, who once won a vaunted victory over the Alamanni (Lentienses) and had felt the danger of the German allies in his own family. He had hastened with all his energy from Gaul to the aid of his uncle Valens so that, with the assembled forces of the entire empire from the ocean to the Tigris, they might drive the fearful Visigoths out of Roman territory, a plan that was ruined by the victory of the barbarians at Adrianople.

Consequently, in the report on Gratian's fall I find no basis for abandoning my concept that the Roman military system had already disappeared a hundred years earlier. Constantine the Great was the Emperor who established the empire on a new base, not only through his alliance with the church but also through his definitive acceptance of the barbarization of the military system. Christianity and the Germans were still more closely related than has heretofore been assumed. The reproach made to Constantine by his nephew Julian (Ammianus 21. 10), that he had brought barbarians into the high offices (quod barbaros omnium primus ad usque fasces auxerat et trabeas consulares: because he had been the first of all to raise barbarians to the fasces and the consular robes) is not just incidental but strikes to the heart of his policy.

HEREDITARY MILITARY OBLIGATION

In the fourth century, the son of a veteran was considered to be obligated to serve, and for that he enjoyed special privileges. The first of these provisions comes from the year 319. (See Mommsen, *Hermes* 24: 248.) The practical significance of this provision, except perhaps for the *limitanei*, was naturally very small; it is to be regarded as a final, actually ineffective expedient to avoid a purely barbarian army. The military tradition of the family was supposed to provide that which the discipline was no longer capable of.

THE BATTLE ON THE FRIGIDUS
We know nothing about the battle on the Frigidus (394) in which Theodosius defeated Arbogast and Eugenius.

Guldenpenning, in the book published jointly by him and Ifland, *Kaiser Theodosius der Grosse*, extracted and assembled the most likely facts from the sources on pages 221-227. They are nothing but twaddle. The troops named or referred to are barbarians on both sides.


NOTES FOR CHAPTER I

1. Robert Grosse's *Roman Military History from Gallienus to the Beginning of the Byzantine Thematic Constitution (Römische Militärgeschichte von Gallienus bis zum Beginn der byzantinischen Themenverfassung)*, Berlin, 1920, has unfortunately very little to offer, despite all the energy that went into it. I have not been able to draw anything from it for my account. See my review in the *Historische Zeitschrift*, 1921.

2. Dio Cassius 78. 17.

3. Zosimus 2. 15. 1. "He collected his forces, which included subjugated barbarians, Germans, and other Celtic nations, and some assembled from Britain."*

4. Ammianus 20. 4.17. A source of little value, Nicephorus Callistus, also reports this of Valentinian I. But the description in Symmachus, *orationes* 1. 10, to the extent that this rhetorician is to be trusted, excludes that possibility.

5. Ammianus 31. 7. 11.

6. Schuchhardt, "Anastasius' Wall at Constantinople and the Dobrudscha Walls ("Die Anastasiusmauer bei Konstantinopel und die Dobrudschawälle"), *Jahrbücher des Archäologischen Instituts* 16: 107.

7. Brunner, *Deutsche Rechtsgeschichte* 1: 39; (2d edition, p. 58).

8. This point is correctly observed by Dahn in *Procop von Cäsarea*, p. 391.

9. Ammianus 12. 12. 61.

10. Lavisse, *Histoire de la France* 1: 2. *Les Origines, la Gaule indépendante et la Gaule Romaine*, by G. Bloch, Paris, 1901, p. 299 f. Ad. Blanchet, in *The Roman Walls of Gaul (Les enceintes Romaines de la Gaule)*, 1907, rejects, on the basis of the broadest

research, the theories that would place the construction of these fortifications as late as Diocletian's period, in the fourth century or even later.

11. According to the citation by Dahn, in *Könige der Germanen* 5: 26.

12. Mommsen, *Ostgotische Studien, Neues Archiv für ältere deutsche Geschichte* 14: 460. L. Schmidt, *Geschichte der Vandalen*, 1901, pp. 65, 72, 122.

13. The study on the battle at the Milvian Bridge by F. Trebelmann in the *Abhandlung der Heidelberger Akademie*, 1915, is very valuable topographically, but from the military history viewpoint it misses the mark just as much as Seeck's account does. Both authors are still entangled in the concept of massive armies. They even believe the sources to the effect that Maxentius had superior forces — and even several times as many — to those of Constantine. Since it is naturally impossible to construct any reasonable account with such preconceptions, Seeck grasps the expedient of having both commanders lead their armies by dreams and portents rather than strategic considerations. I do not see why both Constantine and Maxentius should not have been capable of interpreting their dreams and signs in the same way as had previously been done by Themistocles, Pausanias, and Mardonius. The account by Landmann in Dölgner's *Constantine the Great and His Times (Konstantin der Grosse und seine Zeit)*, 1913, is reasonable, but in view of the lack of sources, it is without any conclusion of importance to military history.

# Chapter II

# The Battle of Strasbourg (357 A.D.)

After the Alamanni had broken through the *limes* in the second half of the third century and had taken possession of the land on the right bank of the Rhine, in 350, taking advantage of a Roman civil war between the Emperors Constantius and Magnentius, they had also occupied Alsace, the region between the Rhine and the Vosges Mountains. Julian, who was appointed Caesar by Constantius and charged with the government of Gaul, decided to drive the Alamanni back across the Rhine, and not simply that but also, through a powerful defeat, to prevent them from returning. Instead of attacking them suddenly and driving off all who were on the near side of the river, he contented himself with a few harassing attacks, while standing fast at the border with his main army and establishing a fortified camp near Zabern, at the exit of the pass through the Vosges. The Alamanni from the far side of the Rhine immediately came to the aid of their compatriots in Alsace. That was exactly what Julian was hoping for. As soon as he learned that a rather large number had crossed the Rhine and was assembled near Strasbourg, he moved out against them.

We have two sources that give us detailed reports on the battle: Ammianus, who himself served as an officer under Julian, and Libanius, a rhetorician, who was personally close to the commander and wrote a funeral oration for him that has come down to us. The accounts of both Ammianus and Libanius are probably based on the same original source, that is, Julian's own memoirs.

Libanius strongly emphasizes the excellent planning with which the commander prepared for the battle. He points out that Julian could have prevented the barbarians from crossing the river but did not want to do so, since he did not wish to fight simply a small detachment. But, Libanius goes on to say, Julian was also careful not to allow all of them to cross, for, as he later heard, their entire strength in service-qualified men had been assembled. Fighting against a few would have been too little for him, while a battle against the full force appeared too dangerous and unwise.

From this enlightening rationale we may draw a conclusion as to the relative strengths. Ammianus tells us that Julian's army was 13,000 strong, and we have already explained in another connection (see page 227) that this number may perhaps be somewhat too small but was at any rate not very far from the true figure. If we say between 13,000 and 15,000, we shall be on sufficiently safe ground.

The strength of the Alamanni was given by the Romans with their usual exaggeration and is not worth repeating here. We can conclude with certainty from Julian's strategic plan that he considered it important to attack them while they were somewhat weaker than his own forces, but not so very much so. The result shows that he estimated correctly; we may therefore assume that the strength of the Alamanni was between 6,000 and 10,000 men.

Somewhat at odds with Julian's strategic ideas, as reported by Libanius, is Ammianus' account to the effect that the Roman commander, marching out from Zabern, halted at midday and intended to postpone the battle until the next day, until the enthusiasm and the urging of his soldiers persuaded him to move forward at once. By hesitating for even half a day, he would have enabled the enemy to increase his strength considerably. The distance from Zabern to Strasbourg amounts to at least 18 miles. The situation may therefore have been that the commander wished and intended to fight the battle at once, but in order to stimulate the spirit of his troops after the hard march under the August sun, he had it appear that the decision was made by the troops themselves, since he gave the impression that he wanted the camp to be drawn up.

The location of the battle cannot be determined with certainty. Only this much is clear, that not only the advantage in numbers lay on the side of the Romans but also the strategic advantage that they themselves, in case of extreme peril, had their fortified camp at Zabern behind them, whereas the Alamanni had the waters of the Rhine. The Germans, in their warlike stubbornness, perhaps estimated in precisely the opposite way that the impossibility of retreat would raise their own strength to its highest point.

The Germans were led by seven kings (princes: *principes* in the old sense). The most prominent one was Chnodomar, who commanded the cavalry on the left flank. In the previous years, he had moved irresistibly through Gaul and had mocked the Roman cities, which he had burned down after pillaging them. The Romans describe him to us as he dashed about at the head of his cavalry, on a foaming steed, in shining armor, trusting in the mighty strength of his arms, carrying a spear of gigantic length, with a red ribbon binding his hair, always a courageous warrior and now an excellent commander.

The right flank of the Alamanni, consisting of infantry, rested on a few terrain obstacles, which Ammianus at one point referred to as *"insidiae clandestinae et obscurae"* ("secret and hidden traps"), and in another place as "ditches" that were filled with armed men. Libanius speaks of an aqueduct and thicket of reeds and a swampy place where they had set up an ambush. The left flank of the Romans hesitated when it noticed these difficulties. Julian himself is supposed to have moved it forward, either simply by shouting his command or by leading up a small cavalry detachment of 200 men to support it. It appears that, in view of the terrain, no cavalry at all was initially allocated to this flank and that now, however, a certain flank protection became necessary before they reached the actual enemy position. But then the enemy was immediately thrown back and pursued.

Both sides had the bulk of their cavalry on the other flank, where there was open ground. There the Germans under Chnodomar's command charged forward, swinging their weapons with their right hands and screaming savagely, with their long hair flying and rage flashing from their eyes: "tela dextris explicantes involavere nostrorum equitum turmas, frendentes immania, eorumque ultra solitum saevientium comae fluentes horrebant et elucebat quidam ex oculis furor." ("Extending their weapons in their right hands and monstrously gnashing their teeth, they enveloped the *turmae* of our cavalry. The flowing hair of these extraordinary maniacs was bristling and a frenzy shone from their eyes.") Light infantry were mixed in with the cavalry. The Roman cavalry could not stand the appearance of the charging enemy and it turned tail.

Our sources report that the commander now personally threw himself in front of the fleeing troops and by his power of persuasion led them back to their task. They also tell us — differing from each other, of course — what he said, and Libanius compares him with Telamon Ajax

and Ammianus with Sulla, who is supposed to have similarly turned his
men around in a battle against Mithridates. Such an act by a commander
is very often found in military history, but the larger the armies
involved, the more certain it is that the reports are false. This could only
have been true in the case of very small detachments at best. Troops
which are already in flight and are sorely pressed by the enemy can no
longer be stopped with mere words, least of all cavalry. If a large number
of mounted men, overcome with fear, has once taken to flight, it does not
stop until forced to do so by some physical obstacle or exhaustion. In the
"Military Letters" of Prince Kraft Hohenlohe(1: 78), we can read a critical description of how powerless a commander is to stop a cavalry unit
overcome by panic, even if no real enemy is in pursuit. The men do not
hear him, and the mass dashes, unstoppable, miles to the rear. In cases
where fleeing troops have again been brought to a stop and have been
turned around for a new attack, it has always been only with the help of
fresh, newly deployed units. The more complete sources for modern history enable us to distinguish with certainty the truth and the fiction in
such an account, and these parallels can profitably be applied here.
Habsburg authors tell us how Grand Duke Karl, in the battle of Aspern,
restored his wavering battle line by seizing the colors of a battalion —
how with a lightning glance at one, an electrifying look at another, and a
magic glance at a third he is supposed to have changed everything
around. A closer comparison with the reports of his times has revealed
that at the same time the entire Austrian reserve, seventeen grenadier
battalions, moved into the battle line, a point that the authors, with
their courtly propensities, did not consider worthy of mention in comparison with the heroic deed of the illustrious commander.

If we look more closely at our Roman sources, we can recognize from
them that something quite similar took place in the battle with the Alamanni. Ammianus expresses himself in only very general terms concerning the return of the cavalry into the fight. In a later author, Zosimus (3.
4), we even find the positive report that they could not be persuaded to
take up the battle again. That it really happened this way is also to be
seen from the continuation of Ammianus' account, where it is said that
the Alamanni cavalry, after their victory over the Roman horsemen, fell
upon the enemy infantry. They would not have been able to do that if
they had still had to carry on the cavalry fight.

From numerous battles of antiquity we know how dangerous a cavalry
attack from the flank was for the infantry. We can see from this that
Chnodomar had his men under control and understood how to lead them.

But we also recognize now that the ancient Roman tactics still existed and that Julian was enough of a general to be able to confront the threatening danger. For if Ammianus has told us previously that Julian had drawn up the larger part of his army forming a front against the barbarians, we now hear that, when the Alamanni cavalry turned against the Roman infantry, the Cornuti and the Bracciati shouted out the *baritus*. That no doubt means that these units were only now moving into the battle and consequently had previously been drawn up in the second or third echelon or in reserve and were now moved up against the enemy's flank attack. That is the same picture we have on Caesar's right flank in the battle of Pharsalus: an infantry unit previously placed in readiness for such a move counters the flank attack of the enemy cavalry. This procedure must have been retained in the Roman tradition, and even if that had not been the case, Julian was a cultured man who was familiar with Caesar's *Commentaries*.

In Caesar's case, this same flank decided the outcome with its counterattack. The Strasbourg battle turned out somewhat differently in that the reinforcements in this area only brought the fight to a stalemate. In the meanwhile, however, the Romans had already been victorious on their other flank. Despite the flight by the cavalry, the numerical superiority of the Romans' right flank no doubt remained considerable and finally overcame the Alamanni with the aid of the victorious left flank, which came to its assistance.

According to Ammianus, the Romans had 243 men killed, including four high-ranking officers. This number seems to be in contradiction to the account, which pictures the battle as extremely fierce and bloody. It is not impossible, however, that the casualties might be accurate (some 1,500 dead and wounded as we normally estimate). The Roman cavalry, which did not receive the enemy shock action at all, may have escaped almost entirely without losses, and when the infantry then withstood the flanking attack, the battle was lost for the Alamanni and may have ended quite rapidly.

King Chnodomar and his entire retinue fell prisoners to the Romans. A large part of the German army was lost on its flight in the waters of the Rhine.

EXCURSUS

1. W. Wiegand attempted to analyze militarily the battle with the Alamanni in the *Beiträge zur Landes- und Volkskunde von Elsass-Lothringen*, Vol.

III, 1887. He provided useful information by his careful selection and analysis of the source material but missed the mark objectively as a result of his completely dilettantish approach. It is not worth the trouble to discuss the false conclusions and relationships sentence by sentence. The author seeks principally to establish that the battle took place between Hurtigheim and Oberhausbergen, almost 10 miles west of the Rhine, in the Strasbourg area. This cannot be reconciled either with the sources or with the strategic situation. Why should Julian already have halted after a march of no more than 16 kilometers and wanted to postpone the battle until the next day? After a march of almost 18 miles, it would be more appropriate to ask whether the troops might not be too tired for a battle. Wiegand himself acknowledges (page 36) that Ammianus pictures the river as close behind the back of the Germans. He seeks to eliminate this objection by assuming that the Ill River at the time formed an arm of the Rhine which would have been only 8 kilometers behind the Alamanni line. This assumption is possible, but the distance would still be too great, since Ammianus says of the fleeing troops (16. 12. 54): "ad subsidia fluminis petivere, quae sola restabant, eorum terga jam perstringentis." ("They approached the river, already close in their rear, which remained their only source of aid.") Why should the Alamanni have gone any farther toward the Romans than to have enough space for freedom of movement? If they remained closer to the Rhine, either they gained one more day, during which more men could come to join them, or the Romans would go into the battle tired from a very stiff day's march. More than 12 kilometers from the Rhine, even the German forces which crossed the river during the day would hardly have been able to arrive in time for the battle. Wiegand's statement that, on the Rhine plain itself, the Romans would have been able to attack downward from the ridge (page 27) is not correct; the plain is broad enough. And the Alamanni, if they wanted a terrain feature on which to rest their flank, were no doubt able to find one closer to the river. The only disadvantage associated with this lay in the fact that, in case of defeat, they had little room for movement to withdraw to the right or the left and would have to go directly into the river. But it is in precisely this way that the sources portray the situation for us. If the battle had taken place at a full 7 miles or even only 8 kilometers from the river bank, the pursuit to that point would have been slowed, at least for the infantry, and a large portion of the Roman cavalry was driven from the battlefield and hardly on hand once again for the pursuit.

2. Ammianus describes the formation of the Romans as follows (16. 12. 20): "steterunt vestigiis fixis, antepilanis hastatisque et ordinum primis velut insolubili muro fundatis." ("They stopped dead in their tracks, and the *antepilani*, *hastati*, and *primi ordines* were extended like an impregnable wall.") It is difficult to say how the individual expressions in this passage are to be understood. The *primi ordines* are the most outstanding centurions, perhaps the commanders of cohorts, but was that still true in this period? It is difficult even to find a place for *hastati* and *antepilani* in the fourth century (see Vol. 1, p. 291). In any case, Marquardt's interpretation (*Römische Staatsverwaltung* 2: 372, Note 1), that it was a question of a formation in three echelons, with the *hastati* in the first, the *antepilani* in the second, and the *primi ordines*, that is, the *pilani*, or *triarii*, in the third, is incorrect. As we have seen from the development of the battle, the rear echelon was formed by the Cornuti and the

Bracciati; the *primi ordines* are not *triarii*, and the *antepilani*, as second echelon, would not have been named first of all. Ammianus probably intended to describe the solidity of the formation for us with the greatest possible pomp and along with the *primi ordines*, the most experienced officers in the first rank, used the expressions *antepilani* and *hastati* only rhetorically as a reference to former periods.

3. In Ammianus' account, the strategic movements that precede the battle have little credibility and are hardly understandable. For our purpose, however, it is not necessary to go into these details.

4. Ammianus describes very graphically how at the beginning of the battle the Germans demanded that their princes dismount and fight on foot so that in case of a defeat they could not leave the private soldiers in the lurch and save themselves. As soon as Chnodomar heard this shout, he supposedly sprang from his horse and the others followed his example.

I cannot, however, give credence to this account. After the defeat, Chnodomar fled on horseback. If he had fought on foot, he would have had to be at the head of a wedge formation (*Keil*). It is hard to see how he and the 200 men of his retinue could have reached their horses again for the flight. And even if that might not be completely impossible, the cavalry under any circumstances still needed a leader. If it was not Chnodomar, it must have been one of the other princes. It is completely impossible that Chnodomar, who is pictured as a very heavy man, could have fought on foot among the horsemen. As the account stands, to the effect that all the princes fought on foot, it therefore seems impossible, and we must pass it up without trying to determine further how much of it is true.

5. Koepp, *Die Römer in Deutschland*, page 96, says that it is not worth the trouble to try to determine what the strength of the Alamanni might have been, since no reliable figure has come down to us and the reference points for an estimate of our own are completely inadequate. That can be said with a certain degree of correctness, and after all it appears that Koepp is not as far from my own concepts as he might seem. He, too, states that the lowest figure given in the sources, between 30,000 and 35,000 Alamanni, is too high, perhaps even several tens of thousands too high. He also assumes that the figure of 13,000 for the Roman army is moderately reliable. The limitation that I have added, that the figure is possibly too small by a few thousands, since it goes back to Julian himself (and we know from experience that the commanders of all periods show a certain weakness in this respect [see Vol. I, p. 551]), can hardly be challenged. Koepp, too, probably does not believe that the Alamanni were fewer than 6,000 men, so that the overall difference between us is that they were possibly a few thousand men stronger than I assume. In no way do I claim that this is completely impossible, but it is certainly highly improbable. It is unlikely that the Romans could have conquered an army of these wild Alamanni considerably superior in strength; it is all the less likely when their cavalry was already defeated; and in the third place it is improbable because it is expressly reported that Julian attacked his opponents before they were completely assembled, when he still believed he could be sure of defeating them. One could now be content with pointing out these relationships without finally arriving at a definite number, as I have done, even if only on a basis of supposition. On this point there can be a variety of opinions. But it is always better to specify positively such a figure,

which may only be approximate, than to take the opposite position and state the figures contained in the sources, which are certainly false, adding an expression of doubt. For despite this expression of doubt, the reader still retains an indefinite, half-subconscious picture of a great mass and with it, consequently, that basically false concept which has made the nature of the Völkerwanderung appear in a greatly distorted light right up to the present day. I have stated clearly enough that I have no truly positive proof that the Alamanni only had between 6,000 and 10,000 men in the battle of Strasbourg and that it is a question only of a supposition based on a certain probability. I have also left no doubt concerning the motive for not being satisfied with generalities but arriving at specific numbers. As I explained in the examination of the numbers involved in the battle of Pharsalus (Vol. I, p. 542), I take this position not simply to state something concerning facts about which we know nothing with certainty. Rather, I do so for the sake of the clarity of understanding that is awakened in the reader only if we give him a positive figure, even on a basis of supposition, and particularly here, where it is important to combat universally accepted concepts that are based on the false figures in the sources and to drive them out of the area of plausible concepts in the study of history. The necessity of stressing this point time and again can be determined from the fact that as recently as in the 1906 edition of Philologus, page 356, a scholar like Domaszewski has Emperor Gallienus blithely destroying 300,000 Alamanni who had invaded Italy.

# Chapter III

# The Battle of Adrianople
# (9 August 378)

The West Goths, pressed by the Huns, a people emerging from the
depths of Asia, appeared on the lower Danube and requested that they
be allied to the Roman Empire. The Romans gladly accepted the proposal and allowed the barbarians to cross the river, hoping to be able to
defend this border of the empire all the better with these strong arms.
Within a short time, however, quarrels broke out between the new allies
over the provisions that the Romans were supposed to deliver. The
Goths, plundering and murdering "like wild animals," drove into the
Roman provinces in the area of the Balkan Peninsula. They were joined
by other bands: a large portion of the East Goths from the far side of the
Danube, Goths who had already been in the Roman service for quite a
long time, and escaped slaves, especially Thracian mine workers.

The Eastern emperor, Valens, was involved in a war with the Persians.
The first troops he sent, aided by West Roman troops which had been
sent by Emperor Gratian, drove the Goths back into the Dobrudscha
area but were not able to overcome them completely. As the Goths now
received further reinforcements from the Alani and even from Huns from
the far side of the Danube, the Roman generals did not dare risk a battle.
The Eastern troops moved back to Constantinople, and the Western
troops toward Illyricum.[1] Only an elite unit, 2,000 men composed of 300
from each regiment, under the energetic General Sebastianus, remained
in the field in Thrace and tried to capture individual bands of plundering
Goths.[2]

On receiving this news, Valens made peace with the Persians and
moved out with the troops that had thus become available, while the

Western emperor, his nephew Gratian, marched toward him from Gaul with his army.

The Goths assembled south of the Balkans near Beroea (Stara Zagora), where the road from the Schipka Pass ends. The task of the two Roman emperors was first to join forces and then to engage the Goths in battle with their united strength. The Goths' task was to prevent the junction of the two Roman armies and to defeat one or the other individually.

Gratian marched up on the large road that leads along the Danube and then through present-day Serbia via Philippopolis along the Maritza toward Adrianople and on farther to Constantinople. Consequently, the Goths could very easily have taken position halfway along this route, somewhere in the area of Philippopolis, in order to separate their opponents. But this maneuver would hardly have succeeded. The Romans had not yet forgotten their skill in erecting fortified camps. Furthermore, the two Roman armies, covering their moves carefully and based on the strong cities of that territory, would undoubtedly have moved around the Goth army and joined forces, without offering the enemy an opportunity to attack. If the Goths had taken position so close to the mouth of a pass as to block it completely, the Romans would still have succeeded, via detours of one kind and another, in bypassing them, and they might perhaps also have succeeded in attacking the Goths simultaneously from two sides. An attempt by the Goths to keep the Romans apart in this manner would therefore have been only too welcome for the Romans and all the more so in that the Goths would not have been able during that time to spread out in the countryside and would therefore have been obliged to spare the land from their pillaging forays.

In the leader of the Goths, Duke Fridigern, we recognize an intellect wise in strategy when we see how he went about his task under these circumstances and led his people to victory.

He did not take position between the two Roman armies; he left the highway along the Maritza completely open and even moved still farther eastward from Beroea to Cabyle (Jamboli).[3] But when Valens now marched on from Adrianople through the Maritza valley toward Philippopolis, he received the astonishing report that the Goths had appeared behind him near Adrianople and were threatening the road to Constantinople. It even appears that Goth cavalry were seen behind the Roman army on the Maritza road, so that it was easy to believe that the Goths intended to cut the emperor's communications with Adrianople.

On receiving this report, Valens turned about, but the Goths on the

Fig. 4 AREA OF THE BATTLE OF ADRIANOPLE

Maritza road may have been only reconnaissance patrols. Valens came back to Adrianople without any fighting.

Now Valens could have calmly remained here and awaited the arrival of the second Roman army. In this case, the Goths, with their move forward, would have won nothing, to be sure, but they would also have lost nothing. They could never directly prevent the junction of the Roman armies, and if they did not want to risk a battle against the two emperors at the same time, they could take up their withdrawal to the lower Danube just as easily from the Thracian plain as from their position near Beroea. But the move into the rear of the enemy gave them still other opportunities. They now cut the line of communications over which the enemy moved up his supplies, and they were in a position to pillage the widely cultivated area of Thrace right up to Constantinople, an area which had been less affected by the depredations of war. There could not have been any stronger incentive to lure the emperor into a premature battle before the arrival of Gratian than this operation by the Goths in his rear. Indeed, it is not impossible that the battle was even inevitable because the Goths in their position blocked the supplies for the Roman army.

Our sources claim that Valens allowed himself to be lured into the battle because of jealousy of his nephew Gratian, who had just won a victory over an Alamanni tribe, the Lentienses. The flatterers presumably pushed the emperor into his rash action. It is, of course, only natural that after the defeat, dismayed and angry, people asked how the emperor could have brought on the battle without awaiting the second army, which was already in Upper Moesia (Serbia). Who can know if the decision was really influenced by an impulse of envy? Who can claim, even if we assume that we have in Ammianus a report from the emperor's most intimate circle, that he can recognize the motives in their most personal aspects? Nevertheless, it is clear that Valens, who had called for the assistance of his nephew, now, when the latter was already close by, did not after all go into the decisive battle without him unless he believed either that he was forced to do so or that he was certain of victory. I consider the account of the jealousy motive to be pure camp gossip.

We hear that it was reported to the emperor that the Goths were no stronger than 10,000 men. The motive for the decision to take up the battle is no doubt more logically found in this report than in the supposed jealousy of the other emperor and the flattery of the courtiers. Was the emperor with a larger army supposed to look on passively as the barbarians laid waste a thriving province before the gates of his capital?

But now Fridigern employed still another means to lure the emperor into battle. He sent a Christian priest (it has been asked whether this was Ulfilas himself) into the Roman camp and had him offer the emperor peace if the province of Thrace, with its cattle and grain, was turned over to the Goths. In addition to the public message, the priest had a secret letter from the duke, in which the latter called upon the emperor to move out with his army so that the Goths would be overawed and would be inclined toward peace.

If Valens had not actually been aware of a sure superiority, the Goth's stratagem would after all have been too crude to lure him to the premature battle before Gratian's arrival. As the men in the Roman headquarters saw the situation, Fridigern's message did not seem so unnatural, however; in fact, we may even ask if it was not at least halfway honestly intended. After all, the Goths had no higher degree of ambition than to be well-paid and well-fed mercenaries of the Romans, and later on leaders actually did agree to conditions quite similar to those Fridigern offered here. What is missing from the account, however, is how the emperor could have been inclined to conclude such a peace. The Roman authority, as well as the personal prestige of the emperor, would have been irremediably damaged if, instead of punishing the barbarians and avenging the suffering they had caused the territory, the Romans had evacuated a province to them. If Valens felt too weak to act, he could, of course, await the assistance of Gratian.

In fact, we now also see that Valens rejected the peace offering and instead marched out against the Goths. Everything points to the fact that Valens felt certain of victory, regardless of whether he intended to fight in any case or to force the Goths to a treaty by the array of his superior might.

When Valens then moved out against the Goths on the following morning, emissaries from Fridigern appeared two more times during the march. To be sure, the Romans did not really trust these men since they were private Goths and were not distinguished men, but they finally acceded when Fridigern proposed an exchange of hostages. While the two armies were already drawn up facing each other, General Richomer reportedly said he was ready to undertake the dangerous mission, after another man had declined it. He was supposedly already on his way to the Goths when the Roman troops at one point of the line started the battle without command, and the general battle then developed.

This account does not seem very likely. It is understandable enough that Fridigern might have sent one more emissary, whether it be to incite the Romans even more strongly to attack through his own simulation of fear or to gain some time while negotiating. For cavalry detachments under Alatheus and Safrax, which had probably been sent out foraging and were not yet in position, actually returned just at the beginning of the battle. We must ask, however, why Valens agreed to the exchange of hostages.

While he did not wish to gain peace by surrendering a province, Valens may have desired negotiations in order to attract the Goths and hold them fast until Gratian should arrive. But that would have been done with greater security from his fortified camp. The emperor perhaps feared that the Goths would slip away from him and now, since they could no longer escape from him, he accepted the exchange of hostages not with the intention of ceding Thrace to the barbarians as a reward for their atrocities but in order to reassure them, keep them assembled, and meanwhile wait for Gratian. Nevertheless, the question still remains as to why he did not halt sooner.

One might perhaps also conclude that, although Valens had felt sure of victory until then, he realized at the last moment that he had underestimated the Goths and that they were much stronger than he had believed. But such a change of attitude would not have been so completely ignored in our sources and would most of all have called immediately for commands to hold up any further advance of the troops. In view of the short range of the weapons, they actually had to be within a few hundred paces of each other if troops were to be able to start the battle without command. At that moment, however, the Roman headquarters must have known for some time what the strength of the enemy was. A deployed army moves slowly; if the commander cannot personally see the enemy during the deployment, he sends officers forward to observe. It is completely impossible that several hours before the battle began Valens did not already have an idea of the strength of the Goths as accurate as can be obtained by the estimates of experienced officers. At most, the cavalry of Alatheus and Safrax might still have provided the Romans with a surprise at this moment, but nowhere in the sources is there the slightest trace of a connection between the arrival of these horsemen and the decision to negotiate. Consequently, we cannot doubt that the Roman headquarters believed they were completely certain of victory right up to the last moment. Otherwise, they would undoubtedly have brought the troops to a halt somewhat sooner and would have taken advantage of the negotiations to allow the troops to move back into the camp and await the arrival of the West Romans. If Valens nevertheless accepted the enemy's proposal for the exchange of hostages at the last moment, or rather when it was already too late, there can be no other explanation but that, after he had presumably been debating with himself from the very start whether he should wait for Gratian, his nerve now failed him as he saw the Goths drawn up for battle.

Our sources tell us practically nothing about the tactical aspects of the battle. We only hear that in their first attack the Gothic cavalry tore apart the Roman horsemen (they were partly Arabians whom Valens had brought from Syria) and that the Roman army was then almost entirely destroyed in a great slaughter. The emperor himself disappeared, and nobody knew how he had fallen.

It would not be permissible to conclude from the extensiveness of the defeat that the Goths had a greatly superior strength. We need not only simply to remember Cannae but also to keep in mind generally that in antiquity a defeated army normally suffered very heavy losses and was easily destroyed completely.

Even if we must give up hope of gaining any tactical insight from this battle account, and though the political-military relationship remains unclear, it is still of great interest from the military history viewpoint, primarily because it once again shows us a German prince as an original strategist, but also because of the strength estimate, the report that the Goths were only 10,000 men strong, which lured the Roman Emperor into his attack.

Ammianus, who preserved this report for us, added that it was erroneous, but he does not tell us the actual strength of the Gothic army. Since he only speaks at the beginning of his account of the huge masses that had crossed the Danube, and another author of that period, Eunapius (Chapter 6), estimated their strength at almost 200,000 men fit for military service, modern scholars have regarded those 10,000 men as some kind of advance detachment. but no such reference appears in Ammianus; in fact, the context completely eliminates this interpretation. It reads that the Roman patrols were sure that what they had seen did not amount to more than 10,000: "incertum, quo errore procursatoribus omnem illam multitudinis partem, quam viderant, in numero decem millum esse firmantibus." ("The scouts asserted that their whole party, which they had seen, numbered 10,000. |How they made such a mistake is uncertain.|") This report persuaded the emperor to attack them. If the report were to be understood as meaning that the patrols had seen with their own eyes only 10,000 of an unspecified large number, then neither the phrase "*incertum quo errore*" nor the emperor's sudden decision would make any sense. The report can only have stated that of the presumed large mass of barbarians the number of those in position here at Adrianople amounted to no more than 10,000.

But, says Ammianus, this report was erroneous. If it was what we may believe, then this error must still have been within certain limits. This army which Valens attacked, thinking that he had 10,000 men facing him, cannot actually have been 200,000 men strong, or even 100,000.

And the idea that here Valens had imagined he was intercepting an enemy raiding force, while the main army of the Goths was somewhere else, but that he had in fact unexpectedly come upon the latter, is not tenable. Fridigern's sending of emissaries proves that they were not dealing simply with a raiding party; Ammianus' entire account would then have had to read differently, and the error would necessarily already have been realized during the approach march. After all, by the negotiations that they initiated, the Goths provided the Romans doubled time and opportunity for a withdrawal. The Roman emperor cannot have been made aware of his error before the actual start of the battle.

It is therefore clear that Valens went into the battle with the idea that the enemy — the main enemy force under command of their Duke Fridigern, who was personally on hand and was sending emissaries — was around 10,000 men strong. They were actually stronger than that, Ammianus assures us, but this difference cannot possibly have amounted to three times as many or even twice as many; for even a strength of 20,000 instead of 10,000 is already a difference that the Roman generals would have noticed during the approach march. It is most unlikely that, if such an observation had been made, voices would not have been raised, advising that it was now preferable to await the arrival of Gratian. And if such voices had been raised, it is certain that some reference to them would have appeared in the sources and would have come down to us in Ammianus' thorough account. For after a disaster nothing is pointed out more energetically than the warning cry of somebody who was right. We find nothing of this kind, not even a positive statement that the Goths were very much stronger than 10,000 men, but instead only the very general expression that the report was erroneous. Consequently, the error can in no way have been a significant one. It probably had to do principally with that part of the cavalry that did not join the Goths until the start of the battle. Accordingly, we may say that they were perhaps 12,000 men strong, or at the very most, 15,000.

This result is confirmed by an expression in Ammianus' account that the Romans, as they moved forward, had seen the enemy's round wagon barricade: "hostium carpenta cernuntur, quae ad speciem rotunditatis detornata digestaque exploratorum relatione adfirmabantur." ("The wagons of the enemy forming a circle were seen, and the information from the report of the scouts was confirmed.") In the same manner, Ammianus describes the Goths' wagon barricade in the campaign of the preceding year as circular in form ("ad orbis rotundi figuram multitudine digesta plaustrorum": "a great number of wagons arranged in a circle") (31. 7. 5). Without precisely drawing up a definite limit, we may still say that such a wagon barricade can only enclose a very moderate-sized army. It would require many days to draw up tens of thousands of wagons in a single circle, and with any kind of terrain obstacles it would simply be impossible. The same would apply to moving out of this position; the army would have lost all freedom of movement. During the establishment of the camp itself, however, in view of the large size of the circle, each individual would be so far removed from his wagon, the possessions in it, and his cattle that there would be not only complete disorder but also no possibility of using the installation. If an army of several tens of thousands intends to secure its position behind its wagons, it would have to form several wagon barricades. Ammianus indicates, however, that in each case it was a question of only a single one.

We find a further confirmation of our conclusion in the marches of the Goths. They moved from Cabyle to Adrianople. Today two roads lead over the mountain that stands between these two towns, on the right and the left of the river Tundscha, not in the river valley itself but in many places quite distant from it.[4] The easterly road was used by General Diebitsch in 1829, and this march in August, in the same season as that of the West Goths, is described for us by Moltke in his history of this war (page 359):

On the far side of Papaskjoi (Popowo) the terrain becomes more mountainous, with deeper ravines. The rocks in this region are for the most part bare, with no soil covering them, and the march over this rocky area reflecting the heat was extremely difficult. The Turks had destroyed all the wells that provide the traveler such comfort in these regions, and the troops suffered from a critical shortage of water. Finally, after a march of 18 miles, they arrived at the small town of Bujuk Derbent, where they spent the night and rested on the following day. The VII Corps had already halted in Kutschuk Derbent. In this barren rock desert the Russians suffered more distress than on their march over the Balkans. The heat was unbearable, and more and more men were affected by fever. The Bujuk Derbent (or large pass) forms a defile that is very hard to cross.

Speaking of the second, westerly, road, Moltke says (page 358) that it is much less difficult. But it runs along the right bank of the Tundscha, which joins the Maritza near Adrianople and can only be crossed on bridges (page 361).

From these road conditions, which must have been similar in their basic features at that time, it results that the Goths had only one road available for their operation, that is, the easterly one, on the left bank of the Tundscha via Bujuk Derbent. They were in a position neither to divide their forces and use both roads simultaneously nor to move out with their whole army on the westerly road. Some 14 to 18 miles north of Adrianople, the passes lead out from the truly mountainous area into hilly terrain that gradually changes into the rolling plain in which the city is situated. The points where the two roads lead out of the mountains are about 9 miles apart, and between them flows the Tundscha. A corps on the westerly road would have been exposed to a flank attack if the Romans by some chance learned promptly of their march, or it could have encountered the main enemy army immediately on moving out of the pass. Then it would have had the deep Tundscha in its rear, separating it from the other part of the army. This obstacle would have been very inconvenient, even if the Roman army was not yet at hand. According to Ammianus, the Goths moved to the road between Adrianople and Constantinople and would therefore first have had to cross the Tundscha with the corps on the westerly road.

Consequently, if Fridigern had marched on both roads, he could not have known whether he would not immediately run into the Roman army as he came out of the pass, and his right column would have been overpowered before the left one could come to its aid. But if they marched on a single road and Valens was already there, the forward elements would have had to enter the fight before those to the rear, who were one or two days' march behind, could support them. Only if the army was so small that a single road sufficed and the column was not more than one day's march long could the Goths risk their march forward. Only under these circumstances could they count on having their army deploy quickly enough to be ready for battle in case the Romans moved up.

A small army cannot accomplish what a large army can, but a large army also cannot do everything a small army can.

According to Moltke (page 359), in 1829 Diebitsch used the easterly road for his advance on Adrianople in order to avoid the necessity of crossing the river near that city and also to have his right flank protected by the river against any possible moves from Philippopolis. In 378, the Goths were in exactly the same situation. They wanted to bypass Adrianople to arrive on the road to Constantinople. When they moved out from Cabyle, Valens was either still at Adrianople or had just moved out in the direction of Philippopolis on the road in the Maritza valley. If by some chance he learned very early of the approach of the Goths, he could also already be in position before them at the mouth of the pass on the westerly Tundscha road and put them in grave danger both here and at the river crossing. On the other hand, by using the easterly road, the Goths could be quite sure of debouching without difficulties from the Romans.

We may assume that the Goths, as they moved forward, did not take with them their entire train, which must have become gigantic as a result of their booty in valuable objects, cattle, and slaves. They probably left it behind, with a security force, farther to the northeast, somewhat distant from the present theater of operations. It is also possible that individual bands were not with the main army; a group of Alani observed Gratian's army and skirmished with it. But a certain number of servants and especially very many women and consequently also children probably accompanied the march of the main force in any case. Hence, even if it did not number as many as 15,000 warriors, the column was still certainly 30,000 souls strong, and therefore with its wagons on a single road a full day's march in length.

Let us now turn back again to the results of the battle. We do not learn from our sources what it was that favored the Goths — in other words, why their cavalry proved to be so unquestionably superior to the Romans, and why thereafter the Roman infantry was no longer able to carry on the battle, as it had done at Strasbourg. At Strasbourg a considerable numerical advantage on the side of the Romans is well attested to; at Adrianople we may assume that the difference on one side or the other was in any case not great. When it was reported that the enemy was only 10,000 men strong, Valens believed he was sure of victory. His army, therefore, was probably a few thousand men stronger, and Ammianus also expressly states it was numerous and efficient.

Since we cannot discern direct military reasons for the absolute defeat of the one side, we are inclined to suppose that the inner political weakness of the Roman Empire, in other words treachery or at least a lack of good will, came into play.

When Emperor Julian had suddenly died in Mesopotamia and the army chose first Jovian and then Valentinian as emperor, Valentinian had overlooked the point that Julian, though without children, had not departed this life without heirs. There still existed a branch of the lineage of Constantine, a cousin of Julian named Procopius, who defended his right and was finally defeated, but for whom so much sympathy had been shown in the new capital, Constantinople, that there remained continuing tension with the new imperial family.[5] Furthermore, Emperor Valens was a confirmed Arian, and when the first generals he had sent out against the Goths came back defeated, they told him to his face that their defeat was caused by the fact that their master did not recognize the true faith.[6] As he was marching out of Constantinople, a priest confronted him and demanded the return of the churches that had been taken away from the true believers. He said that if the emperor did not give them back, he would not return from the war.[7] It was said in Constantinople, however, that because he had been reproached in the amphitheater, he had sworn that when he returned, he would level the capital.[8] These stories have been passed down from clerical authors and are not exactly credible in their details. And the fact that one of them, Socrates, states positively that the cavalry treacherously failed to participate in the battle could hardly be regarded as a real bit of evidence from a reliable source, since there is nothing in Ammianus concerning treachery. Nevertheless, it is certain that the reigning Emperor Valens was doubly challenged and uncertain in his position of authority. Consequently, it may not be so completely off the track to consider that the outcome of the battle of Adrianople, which was of such immeasurable importance, was not determined on a purely military basis but was influenced by political motives, motives of internal Roman politics.

## EXCURSUS

The critical basis for understanding the battle is established in an article by Walther Judeich in the *Deutsche Zeitschrift für Geschichtswissenschaft*, Vol. VI, 1891. Recently, the battle has been treated by Ferdinand Runkel (Berlin dissertation, 1903). Our principal and almost only source is the account by Ammianus, whose battle descriptions, however, although he himself was an officer, "were written more in a romantic style than a military one," to use Wietersheim's expression. Judeich's treatment is unacceptable in its military rationale and often completely inaccurate. However, it does have the great merit of establishing clearly and correctly the geographical relationships involved and in doing so in confirming that Ammianus had misunderstood his source and how he had done so, and the way this error is to be corrected. We only need to go a little further than Judeich himself did, in the same direction.

There is a contradiction in Ammianus' account. He has the emperor, after marching out from Constantinople, establish his headquarters first in Melanthias (between 14 and 18 miles from the capital) and then going to Nike, 16 miles in front of Adrianople. From here General Sebastianus hastens to Adrianople "*itineribus celeratis*" ("by forced marches"), an expression which, since it is only a question of one day's march, is at least confusing.

Immediately thereafter, however, Ammianus has the emperor leaving Melanthias for the second time, and just after that we learn that the enemy intended to block his supply route and that he countered this attempt by sending out archers and cavalry. Three days later, the barbarians marched to Nike; Valens learns that they are only 10,000 men strong, and he marches to Adrianople to join battle with them.

If the barbarians were already at Nike, which is situated between Melanthias and Adrianople, how is Valens, who was on the march from Melanthias, supposed to have come to Adrianople? And how are the barbarians supposed to have been able to cut off his supply route as long as they were in position in front of him?

It is clear that Ammianus did not have any accurate concept of the geographical relationships of the theater of operations. His guilt is less serious than it seems, however; we can cite modern parallels in order to show that such cases are not at all unheard of.

In his account of the operation that led to the terrible defeat on the Marne in February 1814, Johann Gustav Droysen has the Silesian army making the same march on two consecutive days, and in the prelude to the battle of Leipzig, Treitschke places Merseburg to the northwest of Leipzig. As a native Saxon and long-time resident of Leipzig, he must have known, as our philologists are wont to argue, that Halle is situated to the northwest of Leipzig, and Merseburg, which is only 14 miles from Leipzig, is almost directly to the west. But the error is there, and it is impossible, as our unmethodical workers in ancient history love to do, to interpret it away in some clever fashion. Instead, it is simply to be noted and corrected. Precisely the same thing applies to the passage we are considering from Ammianus.

First of all, it is clear that Valens could not send his advanced troops forward via Adrianople while he himself remained with his main body at Melanthias, 120 miles to the rear.

According to Eunapius (page 78) and Zosimus (4. 28), Sebastianus did not simply form the advance guard of the army under Valens' personal command but had already been waging successful guerrilla warfare against the Goths for a long time with 2,000 specially selected men. This account is very highly probable, since after all it is hardly to be assumed that in the long period before the emperor's arrival absolutely nothing had been done to ward off the pillagers. For this reason, I have had no hesitation in combining Ammianus' account with those of the two Greeks concerning the actions of Sebastianus mentioned in the text above.[9]

Whatever may be the case, it is natural that Valens stopped only as briefly as possible in Constantinople and then moved forward quickly in order to protect the country and give support to Sebastianus. The report of the first moving out must therefore be the correct one, and the oversight lies in the second one. There is no simpler correction than that this second move, instead of being from Melanthias, actually took place from the location already reported as having been reached, that is, from Nike and naturally on the route the other Roman army was following, that is, via Adrianople toward Philippopolis. That Valens actually was engaged in this march and already had left Nike behind him is attested to by the fact that the Goths were going to Nike. If Valens had still been there, there would necessarily have been an immediate collision of the two forces.

If now, instead of that, Valens quickly marched to Adrianople in order to fight, he cannot have come in the direction from Nike, which would, of course, have led him away from the Goths, but this can be understood in no way other than that he was already beyond Adrianople and turned about. This is the point that Judeich correctly recognized and that was not clear to Ammianus himself.

Now the cutting off of the supply route also becomes clear; such a blocking can only be done from the rear, not from the front. And likewise reversed; while Valens is in Adrianople, General Richomer, who has been sent by Gratian, joins him there. How could he have done that if the Goths were in front of Adrianople?

I want to quote completely the chapter of Ammianus in question; reading it in context, one easily realizes how simply the correction fits into it. (See Appendix 1 for Latin text.)

As luck would have it at this time, Valens was finally roused from Antioch and made the long journey to Constantinople, where he stayed a very few days. He was confronted by a slight uprising of the populace when he placed Sebastianus, a general of acknowledged diligence, in charge of his infantry forces, a post previously held by Trajan. Sebastianus had just been sent from Italy at Valens' request. After setting out for Melanthias, an imperial villa, Valens began to pamper the soldiers with money, food, and flattering speeches. When he had come to the way station Nike by a march under sealed orders, he learned from a report of his scouts that the barbarians, overloaded with rich booty from the Rhodopean region, had retreated not far from Adrianople. They had learned of the Emperor's campaign with a large army and were hastening to join their people manning fixed positions near Beroea and Nicopolis.

In an instant, as the ripeness of the opportunity at hand demanded, Sebastianus with 300 troops selected from different units was determined to hasten to perform a service for the state, as he promised. When he was sighted near Adrianople after forced marches, the gates were forcefully barred against him and he was forbidden to approach. The defenders feared lest he had been captured by the enemy and would come as their agent. The ruin of their city would result, such as occurred when Actus, a *comes*, had been captured treacherously by Magnentius' soldiers and the passages of the Julian Alps were opened. Nevertheless, after recognizing Sebastianus, although it was late in the day, they permitted him to enter the city. His troops were cared for with food, so far as their supply allowed, and with rest. On the following day, Sebastianus vehemently rushed out of the city in secret, and at dusk masses of Goths pillaging near the Hebrum River were suddenly spied. For a short time he remained hidden by embankments and shrubs. In the dead of night he stealthily attacked them in disarray, and so greatly leveled them that they all perished, except a few whose swiftness of foot had saved them from death. Sebastianus brought back a countless amount of loot, as no city or level field yielded.

Subsequently, Fridigern was aroused to the situation and feared lest this general, successful as he had often heard, would destroy his freely dispersed masses intent on plundering. After concentrating his forces, he quickly retreated not far from the town of Cabyle so that, encamping in an open area, neither a lack of food nor unsuspected ambushes might trouble them. While this occurred in Thrace, Gratian, after informing his uncle with what diligence he had defeated the Alamanni, sent in advance his army's baggage and packs, and proceeded by land along the Danube with a troop of battle-ready soldiers. He reached Bononia and entered Sirmium, staying there for four days. Although taken with intermittent fevers, he continued to descend the Danube to the Camp of Mars. Here he was attacked by a sudden onslaught of the Alani and lost a few men.

At the same time, Valens was aroused by twin reports: he had learned that the Lentienses had been overcome, and Sebastianus in frequent dispatches exaggerated his accomplishments. In haste to equal with some outstanding deed his young nephew, whose abilities incensed him, he moved his camp from Melanthias. Valens led a motley body of troops, neither to be despised nor lazy. In fact, he had attached to them a good number of veterans, among them Trajan, until recently *magister armorum*, and other rather distinguished men found themselves back in uniform.

Since he had learned from careful reconnaissance that the enemy planned to close with strong forces the routes through which the supplies necessary for his campaign were transported, Valens suitably countered this attempt by very quickly sending foot archers and a *turma* of cavalry to retain these useful passes. In the next three days, while the barbarians, fearing an attack from the difficult terrain, advanced slowly in the direction of Nike, a way station 15 miles from the city of Adrianople, the Roman scouts asserted that their whole party which they had seen numbered 10,000. (How they made such a mistake is uncertain.)

The emperor was struck with ardent daring and hastened to meet them. Consequently, marching in a battle-ready square, he approached the outskirts of Adrianople, where impatiently waiting for Gratian after strengthening the rampart of his camp with a palisade and a trench, he received Richomer, a commander in the imperial bodyguard. He had been sent in advance with a letter stating that Valens should await a short time a partner in battle, and he should not rashly commit himself to a sudden battle alone. Valens deliberated what should be done after calling a council of war with his various commanders. Although one faction headed by Sebastianus urged going to battle right away, Victor, a Sarmatian *magister equitum* but a cautious delayer, proposed that the imperial colleague be awaited, so that with the added reinforcements of the Gallic army the flaming commotion of these barbarians might be snuffed out more easily. Many felt the same way. Nevertheless, the fatal destiny of the emperor prevailed, as well as the flattering views of the courtiers, who urged that they swiftly rush to battle, lest Gratian become an equal partner in a victory almost won already, as they supposed.

NOTES FOR CHAPTER III

1. It is curious that the West Roman troops were fighting in the Dobrudscha and when they were returning to Illyricum, they encountered

the Taefalae. Is it possible that they had previously left the Taefalae behind them? These bands probably did not cross the Danube until the Roman troops had already moved farther eastward. Perhaps the East Goths under Alatheus and Safrax also did not come across the Danube until now, although Ammianus recounts this earlier. In any case, the reinforcements that moved to join the Germans must have been very significant.

2. Here I believe it is permissible to combine the accounts by Eunapius and Zosimus with that of Ammianus. See Excursus.

3. Constantine Joseph Jirecek, *The Military Road from Belgrade to Constantinople (Die Heerstrasse von Belgrad nach Konstantinopel)*, 1877, p. 145.

4. In addition to the *Generalkarte* of the Balkans, published by Artaria in Vienna in 1897, there is now available a still better Bulgarian map (1:420,000), which I have used. It is based on surveys made by Russian officers during the war of 1877-1878. The map of European Turkey published by the Turkish general staff, although it bears the title "Drawn up by the General Staff of His Majesty, through Allah's Grace all-powerful and all-protecting," is only a scarcely changed reproduction of the Austrian *Generalkarte*, according to Hardt von Hartenthurm in the *Mitteilungen des königlich-kaiserlichen militärischen geographischen Instituts*, Vol. 18. See *Austria-Hungary and the Balkan Countries (Oesterreich-Ungarn und die Balkanländer)*, by L. v. Thalloczy, Budapest, 1901.

5. Socrates 4. 38.

6. Theodoret 4. 33.

7. Sozomenos 6. 40.

8. Socrates 4. 38.

9. Ludwig Schmidt, *History of the German Tribes (Geschichte der deutschen Stämme)*, page 172, Note 4, opposes this by stating that Ammianus had Sebastianus arrive in Thrace only shortly before the emperor ("*paulo ante*"). This does not seem to me to be sufficient counterproof.

# Chapter IV

# Army Strengths

It is very difficult to estimate correctly the strength of a large mass of people; to count an army accurately is not as easy as one might think, even for its commander. If he is satisfied with adding up the reports by his subordinate commanders, that is, of course, very simple, but the question arises whether these reports are reliable. An organization with controls and the keeping of rosters of the sick, wounded, men on leave, discharged men, and noncombatants cannot be created out of hand and easily maintained. Procopius of Caesarea, who has passed down to us an account of the military deeds of Belisarius, recounts (*bell*. **Pers**. 1. 18) that the Persian kings had a special way to count their warriors. Whenever the army was marching off to war, it passed, man by man, before the king, who sat on his throne and had many baskets beside him. Each warrior, according to this account, threw an arrow into a basket, and the baskets were then sealed. When the army returned from the war, it again passed before the king, and each warrior took an arrow out. In that way they found out how many losses the army had suffered. This little story, less fantastic than the enclosures into which, according to the Greek legend, Xerxes had his millions of soldiers driven, illustrates quite well the difficulty of a reliable strength report. It may therefore serve to prepare us for the task we now face, estimating the strength of the German armies of the *Völkerwanderung* from the reports of our sources.

We are not lacking in accounts of this.

Trebellius Pollio gives the strength of the Goths who invaded the Roman Empire in 267 as 320,000 men under arms. According to the same author, when the Iuthungi (a part of the later Alamanni) had penetrated into Italy, they told Emperor Aurelian that they had 40,000 mounted men and 80,000 on foot. Emperor Probus, Aurelian's successor, himself wrote to the senate that he had killed 400,000 Germans in the campaign of 277.

When the Burgundians appeared on the Rhine, in about 370, they were 80,000 men strong, according to Hieronymus.

We have already heard concerning the West Goths that, according to Eunapius, they were supposed to have been 200,000 warriors strong when they crossed the Danube in 376.

Procopius (3. 4) tells us that the East Goths were of the same strength when they marched into Italy, and Vitiges with 150,000 men besieged Belisarius in Rome.

Zosimus says that in 404 Radagaisus led 400,000 into Italy; Marcellinus puts this number at 200,000; and Orosius states that there were 200,000 Goths alone in this army composed of various peoples.

According to Jordanes, the Franks appeared in Italy in 539 with 200,000 men under King Theudibert, but they fell back without fighting when confronted by Belisarius. Procopius says (*bell. Goth.* 2. 28) that Frankish emissaries even claimed that the army had 500,000 fighting men.

Attila's army in 451 was put at 500,000 by Jordanes, and at 700,000 in the *historia miscella*.

Consistent with the strengths of the German armies, which could still be multiplied in various ways, is the statement of Zosimus (2. 15) that Constantine led an army of no fewer than 90,000 men on foot and 8,000 cavalry into Italy. He defeated Emperor Maxentius at the Milvian Bridge, even though the latter had no fewer than 170,000 infantry and 18,000 cavalry.

The accounts given in the sources are consistent with the numbers given.

Ammianus writes of the Alamanni (28. 59): "They are a huge people; ever since their first appearance they have been weakened by every possible defeat, but a new generation of youth always grows up so rapidly that one might believe they had been untouched by any loss for centuries." Immediately after that, Ammianus describes the mass of the Burgundians similarly, and later (31. 4) that of the West Goths, whom he calls as numerous as the sands on the seashore. Around 320 Nazarius writes the same thing about the Franks.[1]

We must now compare these numbers with another series of figures that provides a very different picture.

We ourselves have already found that at Strasbourg the Alamanni had a strength somewhere between 6,000 and a maximum of 10,000 and the West Goths at Adrianople perhaps between 12,000 and an absolute maximum of 15,000.

Emperor Zeno, according to his contemporary Malchus, once made a treaty with the East Goth Theodoric Strabo, the rival of the great Theodoric, by which Strabo, with 13,000 men whom he was to provide, was to enter the emperor's service and receive pay and rations for his men. The overall context indicates that these 13,000 men formed the main army of the East Goths.

Socrates Scholasticus, the church father, tells us how the Burgundians, sorely pressed by the Huns, accepted Christianity and through the power of their new God conquered with their strength of 3,000 men the 10,000-man army of the Huns.

When Gaiseric crossed over to Africa with his Vandals, he had a census taken of his people, according to Victor Vitensis (1. 1), resulting in a count of 80,000. But the author adds that only the ignorant believed that that was the number of armed warriors. Actually, according to Vitensis, the elderly, children, and slaves were included in this figure. When Emperor Justinian less than a hundred years later sent Belisarius to wrest Africa back from the Vandals, the army he gave him was no stronger than 15,000 men, and not even all of these were actually used. Five thousand cavalry sufficed to inflict on the Vandals a defeat from which they were never able to recover.[2]

To this series of figures we may also add that instead of the 98,000 men about whom we have heard above, another contemporary gives Constantine hardly 25,000 at the Milvian Bridge.[3]

It is obvious that the two series of figures we have drawn up are mutually incompatible. If in the fourth and fifth centuries there were armies of many hundreds of thousands, then corps of strengths between 10,000 and 25,000 men could not win decisive victories like those at the Milvian Bridge and Adrianople. Historians have always been aware of this impossibility, but, since a choice finally had to be made, they accepted not the second but the first series of figures.[4] They believed that the figures of the second group could quite easily be explained away. The panegyrist who gives Constantine fewer than 25,000 men is precisely a panegyrist. The church father who gives the Burgundians only 3,000 warriors wants to prove that the God of the Christians is strong even among the weak. The bishop who claims that Gaiseric was lying about his supposed 80,000 warriors was very hostilely inclined toward the Vandals. The 13,000 East Goths of Theodoric Strabo were only a small part of that people. Finally, the 10,000 Goths who were reported to Emperor Valens were not the main army but only a corps. Furthermore, Ammianus expressly adds that the report was false.

For our part, we have already decided in favor of the opposite interpretation.

The more exact critical consideration of the sources has shown us that the report that the Goths were only 10,000 men strong at Adrianople did not refer to a single corps but that the Romans went into the battle believing that the entire Gothic army opposing them was of that strength. The further development of events has shown us that, even if this belief was erroneous, the extent of the error does not in any case surpass a very narrow limit.

This conclusion has been doubly confirmed for us by the strategic conditions of the campaign. We have been able to determine the route on which the Goths marched and have realized that under the conditions obtaining on this route an army of hundreds of thousands could under no circumstances have been able to move up. In fact, it would have been impossible even for an army that significantly exceeded a figure between 10,000 and 15,000. This same point applies to the wagon barricade with which the army surrounded itself.[5]

Our principal source for the battle of Adrianople, Ammianus Marcellinus, even if he is not absolutely free of errors, is still very well and thoroughly informed, and a truthful man.

The army strength we have found, confirmed by that of the battle of Strasbourg, may therefore be considered to be unquestionably certain within the limits we have established. This is also decisive for all the others. If figures in world history have often been passed down to us with such uncertainty, they do have the advantage of providing the opportunity to be checked one against the other. The fantastic figures that have often been introduced into history fall away as soon as we have found a single reliable one to compare with them. If the Goths at Adrianople were at most 15,000 strong, then this point eliminates all the figures in the hundreds of thousands attributed to the armies of the *Völkerwanderung*. For it is beyond doubt that the West Goths were one of the most numerous and most powerful of the migrating German peoples. Neither the East Goths nor the Vandals, nor the Burgundians, nor the Lombards, neither Radagaisus nor Odoacer can have been significantly stronger; in fact, for the most part, they must have been considerably weaker.

It is possible that parts of the West Gothic people did not take part in the battle; one group had even remained north of the Danube. But these were replaced by those East Goths who had joined their related tribe.

Now we are obliged to look more closely also at the other figures of the second group that history has until now left aside relatively unheeded. The 13,000 men with whom the East Goth Theodoric Strabo was supposed to enter the service of Emperor Zeno cannot possibly have been only a small part of the Gothic people.[6] This interpretation is nothing but a product of the governing concept concerning the great masses of Germans. The treaty was the result of the heavy pressure on the emperor, who tried to play the two rival Gothic leaders off against each other. When he now made a treaty with one of them, that one was at the moment by far the stronger of the two. If he had provided only for a small part of the Goths, the mass would immediately have joined forces with the other Theodoric and would have continued the war instead of letting themselves be pushed aside. Only by pacifying the decisive majority with their leader could the emperor hope to call back to order these barbarians, who were in the middle of the country and were pillaging it to their hearts' content. If we now consider once again the undoubtedly correct number of 13,000 which appears in the source, we shall not only not consider them to be some detachment but rather, on the contrary, we may entertain the suspicion that here we have an early example of that phenomenon we shall encounter time and again in the *Landsknecht* period: namely, that the condottieri state the numbers of their mercenaries much too high in order to pocket the pay for the imaginary additional number themselves.[7] It is very possible that this Theodoric, since for a long time not all the Goths followed him, actually had only 6,000 to 8,000 men, even though the treaty was for 13,000.

Considered in this way, this figure not only serves as a repeated, source-based refutal of the concept of the hundreds of thousands in the German armies, but it also is completely compatible with the 12,000 to 15,000 West Goths that we estimate for the battle of Adrianople.

After Theodoric the Amalian assumed the leadership of the East Goths, he fought for several years in Italy with Odoacer, and the armies marched back and forth. On one occasion, the East Goth assembled his entire people at Pavia. If he had had 200,000 warriors, the entire mass would have amounted to some one million souls. The historians have had no trouble with this and have consoled themselves with the point that the sources actually do not say that they were all in the city, but in a fort near the city.[8] Anyone who wants to get an idea of what it means to feed 200,000 men in one place for several weeks, even with all the modern means of transport, roads, railroads, money, organization, and suppliers, should read the memoirs of Engelhard, Director of the Ration Division, concerning the feeding of our army before Metz in 1870.[9]

Let us now turn to the Burgundians. Now that the report that they had been 80,000 men strong has been eliminated, we must test whether perhaps the other figure, that they had numbered only 3,000 warriors when they adopted Christianity and defeated the Huns, may be regarded as correct.

Jahn, in his *History of the Burgundians (Geschichte der Burgunder)*, worked with that first figure and drew his conclusions from it. Binding,[10] who was more careful, does not venture to go beyond the sentence: "It is a difficult thing to arrive at a clear idea of the strengths of the Germans in comparison with the Romans in the Romanic-Germanic Kingdoms." Without a clear idea of the strengths, however, wavering between 80,000 and 3,000 warriors, much will remain unclear, both in the events and in the conditions of the Burgundians. The source value of the latter report, 3,000 men, is certainly very weak. The tendency of the church father Socrates Scholasticus to have the Burgundians appear as weak as possible in his account is perfectly obvious, and the writer himself is not definitely informed concerning either the people or the period of the event. He closes his account, which has no historically related context, with the sentence that the Arian Bishop Barbas died about the same time, in the thirteenth consulate of Theodosius, in the third of Valentinian, that is, in 430. The expression "about the same time" is in any case false, or it must be very broadly interpreted, since the Burgundians had already adopted Christianity much earlier, soon after 413.[11] In view of this chronological vagueness, we are at least permitted to assume as a hypothesis that the event took place even a few years later, specifically after the great defeat of the Burgundians by the Huns, in 435. Socrates himself says that they had previously had to endure much from the Huns and many of them had been killed.

If we now assume that it really is a question of an event after 435 about which Socrates has either heard or read, then the figure 3,000 takes on a realistic aspect. If we were dealing only with the fantasy of an author of legends who wanted to celebrate the victory of the few Christians over the much more numerous pagans, we would have to ask why he did not choose the opposite procedure and multiply the figure for the opponents by a suitable number. This procedure is so very much the predominant one with the prejudiced authors of that period as in all other periods that the opposite procedure seems curious. If the Burgundian people were really, let us say, 10,000 warriors strong, who would have found anything unusual if Socrates had these 10,000 defeating 30,000 or 40,000 Huns? The fact that he gives the Burgundians only 3,000 men, however, hardly leaves any other explanation than that there was a positive report in support of this number. The Burgundians were not a group of peoples but a single tribe. Twice they suffered defeats — in about 290 by the Goths and in about 435 by the Huns — which in the sources are described as downright annihilation.[12] That the second defeat, under King Gunther, must have been quite decisive is also attested to by the impression that it left behind and that lives on through the centuries. When this people moved into the region, a part of which still carries their name today, our source says that it was the "remnants" (*reliquiae*) of the people who moved into the new area. Taking all these points into consideration, we must say that we have no positive reason for challenging the figure 3,000; if it was more than 3,000 men, the difference was in any case not so very great. Certainly the highest limit to which we might go is 5,000.

Our study forms an interesting analogy with the one on the *bellum gallicum*. There, too, it happened that the figures Caesar gave for the strengths of the Gallic and Germanic armies were not in agreement with one another. Of course, on the one side there was only a single number, while all the others were given on the other side. Scholars believed that they had to trust this great majority, and in order to reconcile the figures they resorted to the expedient of altering the text in that one passage. Objective analysis of the tactical and strategic events has shown us that it was precisely in the opposite way that Caesar allowed the truth to slip out, so to speak, in that one passage (Book V, Chapter 34), and that we are to seize this point definitely and reject all the others as intentional exaggerations (see Vol. I, page 512).

In their concepts of army strengths, men are the same in all periods of history. When Diebitsch crossed the Balkans in 1829, an officer sent out on reconnaissance reported back to the Osman Pascha that "one could more easily count the leaves in the forest than the men in the enemy army." Actually, Diebitsch had 25,000 men. This is what Moltke tells us in his history of the Russo-Turkish campaign of 1828-1829, pages 345 and 349.

When the West Goths crossed the Danube, Ammianus portrays to us their size by recalling the march of Xerxes, saying that it was as if those olden times were returning, when the Persian king could no longer count his troops individually but at Doriscus had them counted by units; that never since then had such immeasurable masses been seen, which spread out through the provinces, covering the plains and the mountains. Now since we have proven that the mass of Goths which made such an immeasurable impression on Ammianus and his contemporaries amounted to no more than 15,000 warriors, and perhaps 18,000 with all their detached units, perhaps we may still accept, from our own viewpoint, the author's comparison with Xerxes' march. We may then conclude that the warriors of the King of Kings, too, can have been neither 2,100,000, nor 800,000, nor 500,000, nor 100,000, but only 15,000 to 25,000 men. Our philologists are a trusting group, but since Ammianus is no longer counted among the classical authors, critical doubt is more permissible in his case than with Herodotus. If we first become somewhat accustomed to incredulity in considering Ammianus, then we are already less fearful of commiting a sacrilege by judging Herodotus also and his contemporaries by the analytical and psychological standards of human beings of other periods.

Proceeding from our conclusions, we now also want to return to the figures that we have found for the earliest Germanic periods and to establish a connecting link between the two periods. It has been assumed that a great increase in the number of Germans took place in these 400 years and that it was specifically this increase in population that gave impetus to the great displacements of the *Völkerwanderung*. We have seen that that is completely false. Even in the period of the migrations, the Germans were not very numerous, and this is only natural, since their economic conditions had remained the same. From start to finish, the Germans were principally warriors and not farmers. If they had significantly developed economically in this period, they would necessarily also have created cities. But they were still without cities, as at the time of Arminius, and they continued to cling only loosely to the soil, because they were primarily raisers of livestock and hunters and only to a slight degree farmers. Since the production of food can have increased but little, the population, too, cannot have expanded significantly. The size of the entire race was able to multiply as a result of the expansion of their territory up to the Black Sea, but the individual tribe, the density of population, cannot have risen importantly; it still cannot have gone far above 12 souls per square mile. The natural increase, small as it was with barbarian tribes — the high fertility rate was balanced by an equally high mortality rate — did not tend to produce a higher level of civilization but continuously pressed outward: wars with neighbors, war against Rome, but primarily service in the Roman army consumed the excess.

For our estimate of individual armies and tribes, we now find a disturbing factor in the uncertainty of the concept "tribe." For the earliest period we were able to reckon from the number of tribes between the Rhine and the Elbe that on an average each tribe had about 2,000 square miles. In such an area, the individual was able to travel to the site of the general assembly in one day, and the assembly, consisting of some 6,000 men, still provided for a unified discussion and decision. It is not said, however, that in that period there were not already individual tribes that had a considerably larger territory and population. In those cases, the unity was represented by the assembly of the princes and the *hunni*. This unity, however, was a very loose one. It was always possible that one or several clans under their *hunni* or a whole group under the leadership of a prince might break away and go their own way; in like manner, larger units could also be formed again from several smaller tribes or fractions of tribes. It was also that way in the period of the *Völkerwanderung.* A part of the East Goths under Prince Wedemir joined the West Goths; a part of the Rugii joined the East Goths; the Vandals broke up into two parts, the Silingae and Asdingae, and when they crossed over to Africa, there were also Alani and Goths with them.

For this reason, it is impossible to arrive at any kind of average or normal figure for the various tribes we encounter. Only this much is certain, that we may never exceed 15,000 warriors for any of the migrating tribal armies. A figure of 15,000 warriors, together with women and children, presupposes a total of at least 60,000, and with their slaves around 70,000 souls. Such a mass is already too large to move as a unit; it has to be divided into various subgroups or move on various routes. Since the warriors can only temporarily be separated from their families and wagons, the greatest attention and prudence are required of the leadership to assemble almost all of them for a battle. In most cases, the armies were probably only a half or a third as strong.

We have estimated the population of the Roman Empire toward the middle of the third century as 90 million people (page 223, above). That is a minimum figure; it could well be assumed to be as high as 150 million. Is it imaginable that such a large population would be overcome by attacks of barbarian hordes that were no stronger than 5,000 to 15,000 men?

I believe that there can be no conclusion of greater importance in world history than that this was really the case. The legendary exaggerations in the army strengths have hidden the realization from us until now. Indeed, in the vague feeling that there was still a puzzle here, scholars have even groped for an explanation in the opposite direction and have sought to explain the defeat of the Romans by the decrease in their population. But that is not the way it was. The Roman Empire was full of people and full of strong arms when it nevertheless was defeated by the very small barbarian armies. This point sheds light on world history both before and after this period.

In the first volume, we became convinced that even the best veteran Roman legion, with all its discipline and tactical ability, could not do more than prove itself about the equal of a German band of the same strength. Marius and Caesar were able to conquer the Germans only as a result of very great numerical superiority. But numerical superiority alone is still not sufficient for victory. This point we now recognize. Even in the fourth and fifth centuries, the Roman Empire could still easily have provided masses of armed men who would have been ten times more numerous than the barbarian invaders. We should perhaps also ask whether such armies could have been fed with the resources of the barter economy that had now set in, but we may leave that point aside. It is sufficient for us to realize that, once the standing army, the disciplined legions, had disappeared, hastily assembled levies of citizens and farmers could by no means stand up against the barbarians. We can hardly imagine the terrifying impression that the fury of these Goths, Alamanni, Franks, Vandals, Alani, Sueves, and Lombards made on the peaceful Roman population. The ancient civilization sank into ashes, and the people were butchered. The Goths cut off the farmers' hands that drove the plow, the right one, and the Lombards defiled the nuns on the altar, the Romans tell us. But the men, fathers and brothers, were unable to protect either their property or their family honor or their own body. A few Roman nobles with their drafted farmers tried to block the passes of the Pyrenees when the West Goths approached.[13] The inhabitants of Auvergne defended themselves courageously against King Euric for a while.[14] When the Vandals had already taken Africa and were threatening Italy, Emperor Valentinian published edicts that called on the Romans to defend themselves, proclamations that have come down to us in the legal collections. The first one states first of all the promise that Roman citizens were not to be drafted forcibly into the army, but they were nevertheless considered as obliged to help build walls and to guard the walls and the gates. Soon thereafter there was a second edict, informing the public that the fearful Gaiseric had sailed with a fleet from Carthage; that help would not be wanting, since the emperor had seen to it that Aetius and Sigiswuld were approaching with their armies; but that, since it could not be known where the enemy would land, the citizens, in view of the trust placed in their strength and their courage to defend their property, would be allowed without violating the normal citizenly order, to take up arms themselves and defend their land and property with loyal steadfastness and mutual support.[15] When Belisarius was besieged in Rome by the Goths, the citizens voluntarily took up arms and offered him their support. Belisarius gladly acknowledged their good will but did not incorporate them into the combat troops, since he was concerned that they might be overcome with fear in the middle of battle and infect the whole army. Consequently, he assigned them to a position where they had only to make a demonstration, in order to give the appearance of a troop unit and thus divert a part of the enemy army.[16] These attempts are about the only ones of which we hear where Romans still dared or were even only levied to fight against the Germans. It was realized from the start that, confronted by the wild assault of a Germanic wedge or a Germanic cavalry mass, any Roman unit, no matter how superior in numbers, would disperse. "The thicker the grass, the easier to mow it," Alaric replied to the Romans who were hoping to frighten him off with their large mass.[17]

The fear felt by Caesar's legions, which did not want to move out against Ariovistus, finds its delayed justification, so to speak, in the events of the *Völkerwanderung*. All the events of the following centuries are time and again to be observed from the viewpoint of the inestimable superiority of professional warriors over undisciplined peoples' levies, as the *Völkerwanderung* has once again taught us in the figures for its army strengths that we have now established.

## EXCURSUS

### 1. THE *NOTITIA DIGNITATUM* AND ARMY STRENGTHS

There has been preserved for us from the time of Honorius an unusual original source, a kind of national manual of the Roman Empire, the *Notitia dignitatum*. From this source, Wietersheim, in his *History of the Migrations of the Peoples (Geschichte der Völkerwanderung)*, 2d edition, 1: 34, has estimated that the total army of both halves of the Roman Empire had a strength between 900,000 and 1,000,000 men. It remains unclear as to what extent the records were complete. Mommsen, in *Hermes* 24: 257, is more cautious; nevertheless, he also estimated the Roman army at that time at many hundreds of thousands. If that were correct, the *Völkerwanderung* would be completely inexplicable. But since the innumerable legions and other troop units listed in the *Notitia* do not actually appear in the wars and battles, this means that they existed only on paper. They probably continued to copy down and carry on the books troop units from the old rosters that had disappeared long before. The *limitanei* (see page

218, above) no doubt still existed, but they were no longer real soldiers but border guards who could not be used in battle.

In one of his passages, Dahn has come quite close to the correct concept of the relationship of the Germans to the Romans. In Volume III, page 58, he cites how the Goths once boasted that they watched over the quiet and security of the Romans: "By evacuating a part of your territory, you have won defenders for yourselves" — and adds: "Actually, caution and mistrust, and probably also the lesser military ability of the Italians, were the reasons for this indulgence" (that is, exemption from military service). If we widen the little crack that is created by the expression "probably also" to a broad and deep ditch, then we arrive at the truth.

Quite a few smaller figures, too, which have previously been considered as credible, will now have to be questioned or rather discarded. For example, that Theodoric, when he married his sister Amalafrida to the Vandal King Thrasamund, also gave 1,000 Doryphori and 5,000 capable soldiers with her (Procopius, *bell. Vand.* 1. 8). Such an escort would have been stronger than the corps of Belisarius' army that destroyed the whole Vandal Empire thirty years later.

2. THE VANDALS

After the figure of 80,000 warriors with which Gaiseric is supposed to have crossed over to Africa has been reduced, both on the basis of objective analysis and the positive source testimony of Victor Vitensis, it would be desirable to find an acceptable explanation for the eighty Thousands, and I think that can be done. The sources report that the king counted his people when he was planning to cross the sea. This occasion was hardly a fortuitous one: it was a question of determining the number of ships necessary for the journey. For this reason, it was not just the warriors who were counted but, also, as Victor says, the total number of persons and therefore undoubtedly the women as well, although they are not mentioned. This point has been correctly observed by Schmidt, in his *Geschichte der Vandalen*, page 37. If then each of the detachments had 1,000 souls, they included no more than some 200 warriors, in fact certainly even fewer, since the figure "1,000" was presumably rounded off upward and the Vandals also had very many slaves. In Procopius (1. 5) this is indirectly attested to by another account which gave the total number as only 50,000; this figure may mean that the eighty Thousands were estimated at a total of 50,000, or each individual group at something like 625 souls actually present. If now on this basis each of the detachments did not count many more than 100 warriors, then it is clear that we are dealing here with about the same thing as the ancient Hundreds. Mommsen (*Ostgotische Studien, Neues Archiv* 14: 499) expressed the supposition that the *chiliarchoi* (commanders of 1,000 men*) of which Procopius speaks was nothing other than a translation of the Latin title *tribunus;* the detachments themselves were called *lochoi*. In contradiction to this notion is a passage in Victor Vitensis 1. 10: "Fuit autem Vandalus de illis, quos millenarios vocant." ("One of those whom they call *millenarii* [commanders of 1,000], however, was a Vandal.") Accordingly, I would not consider it impossible that Gaiseric, before crossing to Africa, not only counted his army and his people but also reorganized them. The ancient clans (Hundreds) must have become very unequal in size. Besides the Vandals, the mass also included Alani, Goths, and probably other individual soldiers. It is therefore no doubt imaginable that Gaiseric, by dividing up and reorganizing his people, created more or less equal units and called them Thousands according to the total number they approached and perhaps also as a deceptive measure (in which, of course, he was more successful vis-à-vis following generations than with respect to his own contemporaries), although according to the ancient concept these were still only Hundreds.

Procopius describes the battle with the Vandals (2. 3): "The *chiliarchoi (millenarii)* held each flank of the Vandals, and each commanded his own *lochos*."* Later, we shall realize even more clearly that Procopius had only a very limited understanding of military matters, but a battle formation in which "the colonels who were leading their regiments stood on each flank" is after all not simply unmilitary but nonsensical. Nevertheless, it is probably clear what is meant; Procopius intends to say: on the flanks were stationed the Thousands, the people's levy, in contrast with the king's retinue, which stood in the center, and behind it the allied Moors.

If we assume that the ancient Hundreds had in many cases become very small as a result of divisions or losses, these groups may still have retained a certain cohesiveness within the new Thousands, a condition that proved itself again in the colonization, wherein such groups retained their identity and were settled together. When the Vandals moved out of Carthage to face Belisarius, Procopius recounts (1. 18), they came "deployed for battle with no order at all except by *symmoriai*, and these were small."* These *symmoriai* may have been such clan- and settlement-groups within the Thousand.

Eight thousand to 10,000 warriors, or even fewer, were a strong enough military force to found the empire in Africa and to conquer for it Sicily, Sardinia, and other islands, particularly since Gaiseric found allies among the barbarians in Africa itself, the desert tribes, which had previously been held in check by the legions. They moved out together with the Vandals to plunder Rome, and in the last battle the Moors, as subjects or allies of Gelimer, still fought against the reestablishment of Roman hegemony in Africa.

Brunner, in the second edition of *Deutsche Rechtsgeschichte* 1: 62, is now willing to concede that the figure 50,000 may have been too high after all, but he holds that my reduction to between 8,000 and 10,000 warriors goes "much too far." This kind of argumentation, which avoids facing the problem objectively, seems to me much too cheap.

(Added in the third edition). That the women were necessarily included in the total figure for the people is explained again by L. Schmidt in the *Byzantinische Zeitschrift*, 1906, p. 620.


NOTES FOR CHAPTER IV

1. G. Kaufmann, *Deutsche Geschichte* 1: 89.

2. I cannot understand how Schmidt, in *Geschichte der Vandalen*, p. 130, can interpret the remark by Procopius 2. 7, that Belisarius with 5,000 horsemen defeated the enemy, as meaning that the Guard was

5,000 men strong and these are to be added to the 15,000 men that Procopius 1. 11 gives as the army strength.

3. *Panegyriki* 9 praises Constantine for having accomplished more with fewer troops than did Alexander, who had supposedly had 40,000. *Panegyriki* 8. 3. 3, says he defeated Maxentius "vix enim quarta parte exercitus contra centum milia hostium" ("with scarcely a quarter of his army against 100,000 of the enemy").

In 313 against Licinius, he is also said by Anon. Bales. to have had 25,000 men.

4. A very energetic addition to the analysis of the figures reported by Procopius is given by H. Eckhardt in the Königsberg Program (1864), "On Agathias and Procopius as Sources for the War with the Goths" ("Ueber Agathias und Procop als Quellenschriftsteller für den Gotenkrieg"). In the final analysis, however, he still holds that, everything considered, a figure of 200,000 men for the East Goths is quite believable (page 11).

5. The number of Cimbrian warriors who crossed the Brenner Pass in 101 and descended into Italy is given by the Romans as 200,000. Judging from the length and the type of route they took, I have felt justified in estimating that they were at most 10,000 strong. See Vol. I, page 513. *Preussische Jahrbücher* 147 (1912): 199.

6. The passage reads: Malchus, ed. Bonn, p. 268: "They established peace on condition that the emperor supply pay and food for 13,000 men whom Theodoric chose."*

7. That this ruse was also common with the Romans, particularly in this period, is amply documented in A. A. Müller's "Excurs zu Tacitus 1. 46," *Philologus* 65: 306. Among other passages, Zosimus 2. 33; 4. 27. Also in Libanius.

8. See Dahn, *Könige* 2: 78, where the source passages are also indicated. *Hist. misc.*, p. 100, and *Ennod. v. Epiph.*, p. 390.

9. Recently published in *Beihefte zum Militär-Wochenblatt* 11 (1901).

10. *History of the Burgundian-Roman Kingdom (Geschichte des burgundisch-römischen Königsreichs)*, p. 323.

11. A very thorough treatment of this, as of the whole question, is to be found in Jahn, *Geschichte der Burgunder* 1: 337. See also Wietersheim-Dahn 2: 212.

12. The passages are quoted in Jahn 1: 345.

13. Orosius 7. 40.

14. Sidonius Apollinaris 7. 7, "viribus propriis arma hostium publico-

rum remorati: sibi adversus vicinorum aciem tam duces fuere quam milites." ("They held back the forces of the public enemy with their own
strength. They were their own generals as well as soldiers against the
army of the enemy at hand.") Cited by Dahn 5: 93.

15. *Constit. novellae Valentin.* III, title V:

"Ex illa sane parte totam sollicitudinem omnemque formidinem vestris animis auferendam, ut hujus edicti serie cognoscat universitas, nullum de Romanis civibus, nullum de corporatis ad militiam esse
cogendum, sed tantum ad murorum portarumque custodiam, quoties
usus exegerit." (New Orders of Valentinian III, Title V: "Indeed, from
that side all anxiety and every fear ought to be removed from your
minds, and that in consequence of this edict all should know that no
Roman citizen and no member of a guild is to be forced into military service, but only to the guarding of walls and gates as need requires.")
According to Section 3, everyone was also obligated to participate in the
construction and repair of the walls.

Title IX (440): "ut Romani roboris confidentia et animo, quo debent
propria defensare, cum suis adversus hostes, si vis exegerit, salva disciplina publica servataque ingenuitatis modestia, quibus potuerint, utantur
armis, nostrasque provincias ac fortunas proprias fideli conspiratione et
juncto umbone tueantur: hac videlicet spe laboris proposita, ut suum
fore non ambigat, quidquid hosti victor abstulerit." ("that, with confidence in Roman strength and the spirit in which they ought to defend
their own, with their own hands against the enemy if violence demands
it, with public discipline intact, and with the moderation of nobleness
preserved, they should make use of what weapons they could, and they
should guard our provinces and their own property with faithful unanim-
ity elbow to elbow; that clearly in this proposed expectation of hardship
it should not be in doubt that whatever the victor takes away from the
enemy will be his own.")

Cassiodor's grandfather is supposed to have repelled the Vandals when
they were plundering Sicily and Bruttium. *Var.* 1. 4. 14, cited by
Schmidt in *Geschichte der Vandalen*, p. 71.

16. Procopius 1. 28.

17. Zosimus 5. 40.

# Chapter V

# The Peoples' Armies in the Migrations

The warlike, nomadic life of the German tribes could not help but produce a strong effect on their social conditions and their political organizations. In their homeland each clan lived in its village under its *hunno* or elder, who himself belonged to the freemen of the community. Over the tribe, which consisted of a group of such clans, stood one or several princely families from which a duke was chosen for war. They had been able to get along with this simple institutional arrangement, but for military expeditions, as they were now carried out, that organization no longer sufficed.

Even in the most ancient period, it had often happened that from a princedom or a duchy there had developed a kingdom, which had either become hereditary or had then been dissolved. Now a continuing monarchical head was indispensable. The strategic tasks they faced were always very closely related to the politics, the relationships with other German tribes as well as with the Roman Empire, the Roman emperor, or the various emperors and pretenders who were competing with one another for the throne. If a German people entered the service of the ruler in Rome or Byzantium as a unit, as an army, the king formed the link by being named, as a German prince, the Roman commander. The king of the East Goths, Theodoric the Great, moved into Italy at the direction of Emperor Zeno as his *Magister militum praesentalis* (Master of the Soldiers at the Emperor's Court).[1]

There are, however, noteworthy differences in the character of these newly formed monarchies.

The Vandal Gaiseric, who reigned for a half century, after only a few years rejected the fiction that he was only a kind of viceroy of the emperor in Africa. Assuming the position of sovereign master, he was strong enough to establish the kingdom of his dynasty completely independently. He proclaimed an order of succession which, to be sure, was not based on the right of primogeniture but did establish a definite seniority and was actually observed. The last king, Gelimer, was his great-grandson.

Theodoric the East Goth was certainly no less powerful than Gaiseric, but he left no son, not even a son-in-law. He passed the crown to his grandson by his daughter under her regency. But when the young king Athalaric also died before coming of age, Amalasuntha was not able to maintain her position, and in the war with Emperor Justinian that now broke out, the East Goths reverted to a purely elective kingship.

The West Goths also continued with an elective kingship, which was interrupted for only a few generations by a hereditary dynasty.

The development with the Franks, however, was completely different. The kingdoms of the Vandals and the Goths had been founded by a conquering people; the kingdom of the Franks was founded by a conquering king. The mass of Germans in the Frankish kingdom was immeasurably larger than in all the other kingdoms, but the largest number either remained completely in their old locations or moved forward only a few days' march into the former Romanic area. The Merovingian monarchy was no army kingship like that of Alaric, Gaiseric, or Theodoric but originated when the prince of a single tribe, Clovis the Salian, succeeded in having himself recognized as king by many other related tribes and in addition conquered a large Roman area. Here it was impossible from the start to fall back again to an elective kingship, for there was no general army assembly. The armies that chose Vitiges, Totila, or Teias as king included such a large part of the East Goth warriors that the election could also be regarded as an expression of the will of the people. The armies that assembled around a Frankish king represented, ever since the founding of the Frankish kingdom, only a small portion of the overall Frankish people. And since the male succession of the Merovingians also continued unbroken for centuries, a hereditary dynasty took shape that was strong enough to survive even the repeated partitions of the kingdom and the civil wars.

The institutional changes spread throughout the entire political and military system of the Germans from the top down.

We have estimated the West Goths at a strength between 10,000 and 15,000 men. Such a mass, when it is not simply making a short campaign but is constantly in the field and moving through enemy territory, requires a more refined organization than simply by Hundreds. The king or duke cannot have his commands conveyed directly to a hundred *hunni;* there is needed an intermediate link that is not established simply on a temporary basis but functions continuously. Likewise, it is impossible for the Hundred to form the smallest unit. The Roman centurion had under him a whole series of junior officers, corporals, and first-class privates; even a modern company composed of only 100 men necessarily has at least two officers and ten to twelve noncommissioned officers. But the German Hundred was, of course, much more than a Roman century; frequently, it not only was probably much larger but it also included, most importantly, all the households. The Roman centurion had to be concerned only with the service of his men. Weapons, pay, and rations were provided for the soldiers by the quartermaster, and the century had at most responsibility for apportionment, supervision, and maintenance. The German Hundred had for the most part to take care of its own rations — the army command hardly had at its disposition a quartermaster establishment with its controls — and not only for the men themselves but also for their entire families. Even with the most merciless plundering of the land, this is completely impossible without a very extensive communal economy. The agrarian communism under which they had lived in the homeland was now not sufficient. They not only had to take their booty on a communal basis, then being able to divide it up, but they also had to provide continuously for very great stocks of supplies on a common basis. If they had left the individual family on its own to provide for itself, the entire army would soon have dispersed and would have become a prey for the enemy. Plunder had to be divided continuously, first among the Hundreds and then from them to the individuals. Small detachments had to be sent out, and what they brought back had to be considered as the property of all and distributed accordingly, so that a main body of the army was always maintained assembled. For this service beyond the Hundred and within it, the *hunni* needed their subordinate leaders.

Consequently, whereas we find in the original Germanic political organization no other division except into Hundreds, now the king commanded or governed large units or territories through high officials whom he appointed, the *comites* or counts; above them, but not actually so in the organization, were dukes, *duces*, who were distinguished only by their rank and the extent of their power.

At a lower level, however, in the case of at least one people, we find indications that seem to point to a kind of real military hierarchy. In the compilation of laws of the West Goths, much of which has come down to us, we find leaders of Thousands, *thiuphadi (millenarii)* as seniors of the *hunni (centenarii)*, and leaders of ten (*decani*) as the latters' subordinates.

If we also find a leader of five hundred (*quingentenarius*), that position should not be considered an intermediate command between the *millenarius* and the *centenarius* but rather a distinction that had arisen because quite a number of the Thousands had become much smaller than others.

This buildup from the Ten to the Hundred to the Thousand and above them perhaps still another unit under a count or a duke is not to be conceived of as a completely uniform organization like the squad, company, regiment, and corps, but among them was one organization that necessarily had and retained a completely different character from all the others. That was the original and basic organization, the Hundred.

Even with us, of course, the company is significantly different, to a much higher degree a spiritual unit, than, for example, the squad or the battalion. This point applies even more so to the Germanic Hundred. The Ten is simply an auxiliary member of the Hundred; the Thousand is a grouping of Hundreds for purposes of army command. But the Hundred has its own independent existence. One can have these or those Hundreds assigned together to a Thousand; one can divide the men of the Hundred into Tens in one way or another. A Hundred, however, cannot be so readily torn apart or constituted. The latter is hardly conceivable, for the Hundred is at the same time the product of nature, the clan. Dividing a Hundred is more easily done, but in any event it is an extremely significant and not a simple act, for the Hundred is not only a military and natural unit but also an economic one. A Thousand is too large and a Ten too small to practice the communal economy that the military expedition requires, and there can only be *one* intermediate unit, *one* organization for this function. The common property in cattle, wagons, supplies, and weapons that were carried along could only have belonged to the Hundred. Consequently, the leader of the Thousand was the superior of the *hunno* only in the military and legal areas, and the leader of Ten was only the *hunno's* agent and instrument. Neither the Thousand nor the Ten was a group that could, for example, come to an effective expression of its common will. Despite the Thousand above it and the Ten below it, the Hundred remained, even in the *Völkerwanderung*, primarily what it had always been.

Dahn has already observed that when the Goths settled in Spain, as in Italy, the families or clans apparently still played a significant role.[2]

They exercised important functions in the law and in those events where relatively independent groups formed themselves into very firm organic units on a small scale on occasions such as the suspension of hostilities, subjection to a conqueror, and the offering of resistance to enemies. The later West Gothic laws still permit us to recognize the ancient significance of the *hunno* in that they threatened him with death if he should desert the army, whereas the *thiuphadus* is not mentioned at all, and the *decanus* escapes with a fine of 5 *solidi*.

It is further provided that the fines that are received, including those of the *thiuphadus* and the *decanus*, are to be divided among the Hundred. Therefore, this last unit is the real corporate body.

We find the Thousand only among the truly migrational peoples, the Goths and the Vandals. Perhaps the same name does not have the same meaning in both cases;[3] in any event, it is best explained by the military needs of the migrations. It is not necessary to assume on that account an ethnographic distinction between East and West Germans.

However clear the distinction may be between the Hundred and its superior and subordinate units, we must still assume that from a practical viewpoint these divisions and this nomenclature soon became confused among themselves. It is a natural result of war that units which are originally of equal strength soon become very unequal. After a half-year of war in 1814, fourteen militia battalions of the Silesian army were formed into four battalions. Thus, modern organization time and again undergoes this equalizing influence; it is possible that the same thing sometimes happened in the German armies. The Thousands that Gaiseric counted when he moved his people to Africa were, as we have sought to explain above, such organizations.

This leads us to the point that, as important as the Hundreds still were during the migrations, their days were numbered. The very same conditions that gave them new life at the same time pushed them toward their dissolution. The organizational will from above limited them, and numerous individual Hundreds disappeared under the many influences of the war and the migrations, and most important of all, the head of the whole system, the *hunno*.

Except for the few families of the princes, the ancient Germans had no nobility; the *hunni* belonged to the mass of freemen. In the *Völkerwanderung* we recognize among the Germans a much more extensive nobility. We can imagine a double root for this new class: those serving the king, and the *hunni* families. A large part of the nobility no doubt came from those in the service of the new monarchies: the court, army leadership, and the administration established offices which brought distinction and wealth and became hereditary. We shall have much more to say about this subject later.

But the monarchy of the period of the *Völkerwanderung* was itself too young to have a new class spring up so soon from it, one that could base its position on its ancestors. This nobility must have had elements of greater age and greater independence, and those could only be the old heads of clans. Even in the ancient period, after all, the princely families and the *hunno* families tended to merge with each other, even though they were perceptibly different. Whenever a small group of Hundreds under the son of a princely family broke away from its previous tribal unit, and whenever a Hundred became very large and divided up, several new *hunno* families sprang up. However, the oldest one in distinction and wealth claimed a superior position, and so similar conditions were created here and there.[4] The *Völkerwanderung*, and before it the successful raids into the Roman area, tended to raise the *hunno* families above the mass, bringing them closer to the princes. In this way, a nobility was created from them which the ancient period did not yet have.

The communal economy of the clan could not be conducted in any other way than by being placed completely in the hands of the head, the *hunno*. In the ancient period, when clan members returned from a campaign, they divided up the booty. The *hunno* was present under the jealous observation of all his contemporaries, and after the division, life went on as previously. Now a much larger part of the booty was not divided up at all but remained in the hands and under the administration of the chief, who doled it out according to his judgment and the need for it. Under conditions of continuing warfare, control and complaints were difficult to exercise, and each individual was all the more at the mercy of the discretionary judgment of the *hunno* in that nobody was any longer in a position to live from his own means. In the homeland they had practiced little cultivation of the soil and had lived principally from their herds. Now, often for years at a time, no crops at all were grown, and except for the draft animals, only a few of the animals from the herds could follow along on the lengthy moves. "Migrating," says Ratzel in his *Politische Geographie*, page 63, "brings many losses: the Boers, who had moved in 1874 from the Transvaal to the west, had taken with them 10,000 cattle and 5,000 horses, which by the time they arrived in Damaraland in 1878 had melted away to 2,000 head of cattle and 30 to 40 horses."

When Theodoric the East Goth settled in Raetia the remnants of the

Alamanni who were fleeing from Clovis, he ordered that they should exchange their cattle with that of the inhabitants of Noricum as they marched through that territory (*"itineris longinquitate defecti. . . . ut illorum provectio adjuvetur"*: "wearied by the length of the journey. . . . their march should be aided").[5]

It is completely impossible that the Vandals drove along with them, from the Danube and over the Pyrenees to Africa, large herds of milk cows and small animals. It is similarly impossible that the West Goths could have done so from the Black Sea through the Balkan Peninsula and Italy and across the Alps to Gaul and Spain. Of course, the countries through which they moved were rich enough to feed a few thousand German families, but only, after all, if the military commanders concerned themselves to some extent with orderliness and allocation of the food. They had to distribute rations to the individuals and at the same time be concerned that sufficient supplies were held out for days and weeks to come, perhaps often months. The most important booty that the Germans could take among the unwarlike Roman population, aside from foodstuffs and valuable objects, was the population itself; they were enslaved and taken along. From the thickly populated, defenseless regions, they could have taken along hundreds of thousands — if they had been capable of feeding them. But what would have become of the mobility and combat effectiveness of a German army if it had wanted to take along, let us say, in addition to its 10,000 men and 30,000 women and children, some 40,000 or 30,000 slaves?[6] We can imagine that the *hunno* took for himself as many slaves as he needed to be able to care for his community. The individual freeman, however, preferred to see his booty transformed into jewelry, precious stones, gold, and weapons; but beyond that, as long as they were migrating, he had to continue living in his previous simplicity.

The conditions of the migrations consequently caused the authority, power, and possessions of the *hunno* to rise greatly above those of the mass. No doubt his property was basically the property of the community, the whole clan, but the *hunno* exercised such exclusive disposition of it that this kind of distinction gradually faded away and was eliminated. The *hunno* was rich, he became richer and richer, and he left his wealth to his own family.

In the ancient period, the *hunni* were undoubtedly elected, but very soon the choice of the people often remained with the same families and in this way gradually developed into a hereditary claim and finally even a hereditary right. Since these *hunni* families had now become the economic masters and almost the providers for their community, on the death of such a chief it had become quite impossible to pass over his family and choose a man from the masses. Quite automatically, the position went over from father to son, and under these conditions the family no longer belonged to the common freemen of the community but held a special position. It was a noble one. The people, who previously had had only a princely nobility, now also had a lower class of nobles.

Of the migrating tribes, it was the Vandals, as we have seen, who, for special, more or less fortuitous reasons, developed the strongest monarchy. Twice the *Optimates,* that is, the higher nobility, rose up against Gaiseric, but he defeated them and reduced them to submission (442 A.D.).

The Bavarians (Marcomanni), Alamanni (Swabians, Hermunduri, and Juthungi), and Franks (Chamavi, Chattuarii, Batavians, Sugambri, Ubii, Tencteri, Marsi, Bructeri, and Chatti) made only a very short migration into the neighboring territory or no actual migration at all but simply expanded beyond their former boundaries. In doing so, they in no way drove out the Romanized Celtic or even Germanic inhabitants from the territories they took over on the banks of the Rhine and the Danube up to the Alps, the Vosges, the entrance to the English Channel, but in many cases these inhabitants remained among the conquerors and gradually became Germanized or re-Germanized. We find later, particularly in Bavaria but also in the other indicated areas, that large properties, often still recognizable as Romanic villages, were dependent on outstanding Germanic families.[7] We must think of the procedure associated with the conquest in this way, namely, that Romanic villages requested the protection of a Germanic prince or *hunno* and in return became his subjects and paid him tribute. This form of dependence and of utilization of unfree labor was already common among the Germans in the earliest period. We need not assume that it was only and exclusively the few princely families that now gained a large property of tribute-paying tenant families (Liti, Aldioni, Barschalki); the leaders of the Hundreds were also in a position to provide protection and could take advantage of the opportunity to become masters in this way. This class of masters was able to develop all the more strongly because the Bavarians and the Alamanni still had no unified princely organization at the time of the occupation of the south German areas. In the battle of Strasbourg, Ammianus was able to speak of seven kings (*reges*) and ten *regales* who led the Alamanni. The kings were obviously what Tacitus called *principes*, princes like Arminius. We will have to pass over what is to be understood by the word *regales*. In any case, it was not until later that the position of duke as the permanent highest authority was raised above the other nobles of the country among the Alamanni and the Bavarians; in the case of the Alamanni it quickly disappeared again, and with the Bavarians it was perhaps first established by the Franks when they subjugated the Bavarians. The Bavarian code of law as well as that of the Alamanni recognizes a nobility with increased tribute; among the Bavarians there were later, in addition to the duke's family, five families of the higher nobility.

On the island of Britain, the relationship of the natives to the conquering Germans was similar to that among the Bavarians and Alamanni; a portion of them remained as subjugated people among the Germans and were gradually assimilated. The old princely families rose to the position of the small monarchy, and the former *hunni* (elders) became the high nobility, the earls.

On the left bank of the Rhine, too, among the Franks, large land holdings were formed in conjunction with the occupation,[8] but the rising monarchy of the Merovingians held them down, so that, contrary to the situation of all the other Germanic tribes in this period, no nobility developed here. The king governed solely through his counts; the *hunno* or *tunginus* sank to the position of village magistrate.

In the original German state, we find occasion for the development of both a monarchy and a high nobility. Both appeared in the *Völkerwanderung:* with the rule that the stronger the monarchy, the weaker the nobility, up to the extreme of the latter's complete nonexistence in the Frankish kingdom; the weaker the monarchy, the more powerful the nobility. Among the Bavarians and the Alamanni there was no monarchy at all, among the Anglo-Saxons petty monarchies, and among the West Goths elected kings.

Under either of these developments one thing gradually disappeared everywhere: the basic cell of the ancient Germanic political system, the clan, the Hundred. The new class of the nobles, in the manner in which it was formed and while it was still being formed, was already breaking away from the native soil on which it had grown up. It is natural that the high positions that the king now established were filled in no small part precisely by members of these noble families, so that the nobility based on royal service and that springing from the people blended with each other. Even if the Hundred now elected a new leader or the departing one or even the king designated one, the relationship was not quite the same as before. The new *hunno*, without ancestors in the position and without much property, started over again from the bottom; he was again still more of a simple official, and the Hundred itself, no longer in the patriarchal relationship of trust with its leader, became a looser organization.

The leader who had separated himself from his clan left behind a dismembered trunk. When he went, he did not go alone but took with him a number of particularly capable people who joined him as his retinue and entered his service. The wealth acquired in war made this kind of following possible, while political ambition produced it. A military organization, such as the formation in Thousands and the lower division into Tens, diminished the strength of the Hundred still further, and all the more so if it was no longer under the leadership of an ancestral chief but rather of an appointed one.

Finally, the settling and expansion over the broad territories that were captured had a completely destructive effect on the system of the old Hundred; all the conditions of its existence were changed.

The Hundred no longer lived in one location together. The community ceased to exist. In the Romanic areas the people spread out among the Romanics. In the Germanic areas they began to reject the military life and turned more and more toward cultivation of the soil. The large clan villages broke up into smaller ones, where each person could have his fields nearby. New noble families could no longer spring up from the roots of the clan leadership. The Hundred now existed only as a division of a district, and it finally died off.

In the most ancient period the clan was the community, taking possession of its land in common, living together, working and trading together, fighting together. There was no questioning of actual relationships; they could be extremely distant. Now as the communal life ended, and particularly the common ownership of the land shifted over to private ownership, specific limits had to be established for the functions of the clan that still remained: welfare, guardianship, and wergeld. In the various tribes they were worked out differently; in some cases the fifth degree of relationship was established as the limit of the clan, in others the sixth or even the seventh.

In later sources, we still read at times of the ancient grouping of the clan in battle. In *Beowulf* the entire clan was supposed to be punished if one of its men was found to be a coward,[9] but with the end of the *Völkerwanderung* the last trace of the clan as a troop disappeared, except for the word itself (in case, that is, the word "troop" is etymologically the same as "Dorf").

# EXCURSUS

THE HUNDRED IN THE *VÖLKERWANDERUNG*

It has been very well explained by Karl Weller in "The Settling of the Alamanni Territory" ("Die Besiedelung des Allemannenlandes"), in the *Württembergisches Vierteljahrheft für Landesgeschichte*, Neue Folge 7 (1898), that the unit of the Hundred showed a special toughness in the *Völkerwanderung*. While it is true that the author has a false point of departure in that he still believes in an original Thousand district, by having the latter disappear and the old subordinate unit, the Hundred, take its place, he causes the strength and significance of the Hundred to show up all the more strongly.

And from the same work I also take, once more somewhat contrary to the opinion of the author himself, a very strong proof for the identical aspect of the Hundred and the clan.

Weller points out that in the original sources of the eighth century there still appear no small number of Alamanni localities ending in "-ingen" as the principal centers of important marks. These are the original marks, which also appear as Hundreds, for example, *Munigisinga*, *Munigises huntare*, Münsingen; *Muntarihes huntari*, Munderkingen; *centena Eritgauvoia*, Ertingen; Pfullichgau, Pfullingen. The places ending in "-ingen" are the settlements of a clan that was named for its leader, a Munigis, Muntarih, an Erit, a Phulo.[10]

Now we cannot possibly assume (as Weller, of course, does) that both the district and a town among several within the district had been named for the same man. If there had been several clans within a Hundred, they would after all have been equal, and we would not be able to find again and again that both the whole district and a clan in it had the same name. Rather, this double use of a name clearly shows the original identity: each Hundred district originally had only *one* town; they had the same name because they were the same thing. The other places are offspring villages that were founded later. In harmony with this concept is the observation by Weller (p. 31) that in the regions settled later by the Alamanni, Alsace and Switzerland, the Hundred districts played a much smaller role than in the areas on the right of the Rhine. The reason is that in the meantime the Hundred unit had already become much looser and less important.

Furthermore, the nature of the Alamanni Hundreds is shown very clearly by the fact that the names we find on the upper Danube are repeated in almost the same sequence in Uechtland in Switzerland:[11] Waldgau, Baargau, Ufgau (Uf-Afa), Schwarzenburg (Swerzagau), Scherli (Scherragau), Eritgau (Eriz), Munisiges Huntari (Munsingen). This phenomenon can hardly be explained in any other way than that the old Hundreds split up, the one part remaining in place while the other migrated and carried the old name over to the new settlement.

Brunner, in *Deutsche Rechtsgeschichte*, first edition, 1: 117, believes himself justified in concluding from the fact that most of the Alamanni Hundreds are formed from names of persons, that the divisions did not occur until their subjection by the Franks. He believes that the name was that of the leader "under whom the naming of the Hundred became a permanent arrangement." But the Hundred, after all, cannot have been nameless until then. True, it might be possible that the Hundreds did not have individual names for a long time but were known by the name of the current chief and that finally one of the names was retained. Procopius, too (*bell. Vand.* 1. 2) was of the opinion that the German clans were named for their leaders. That would make no difference for our concept. For Brunner, however, this interpretation is not possible, since, of course, he considers the ancient, original Hundred to be only a group of persons that banded together according to need. If that were correct, then the division of the territory into Hundreds must have been an organization systematically directed from above at some later time, and therefore presumably by the Franks. The Hundred of the ancient period and the Hundred of the Alamanni-Frankish period would consequently have had nothing to do with each other.

Now that is certainly not only very improbable, but this concept leaves unexplained the appearance of the identical name for the Hundred and its main locality. If it is assumed that the Hundreds among the Alamanni were first created by the Franks and named for the first *hunno* they appointed, how is it supposed to have come about that the principal locality of the newly created district had the same name?

The situation is completely different if the district originally had only the one locality (inhabited by Alamanni); in other words, if the Hundred with its leader together settled in *one* location. With this fact we have with a single stroke an explanation for the identical name of the Hundred and the locality as well as the development of this name from that of a person. From this fact it follows that since the identical nature of the village and the clan is conceded, then the Hundred and the clan were also identical.

In his second edition, page 161, Brunner modifies his concept somewhat. He now concedes that "Alamanni Hundreds may, after all, reach back before the time of the Frankish subjugation." They are supposed to have originated from a "rooting" of the original group of military men. He seems to find no conclusion from the fact that the Hundred and a locality within it had the same name, since, to be sure, the same names appeared quite often in the clan — this phenomenon, consequently, was a pure coincidence. But we can hardly believe that such a coincidence would be repeated time and again.

Several of the Swabian districts initially had the name *Baren*, for example, *Perichtilinpara, Adalhartespara*. Baumann, in *Counties in Württemberg Swabia (Gaugrafschaften im württembergischen Schwaben)* and *Studies in Swabian History (Forschungen zur Schwäbischen Geschichte)*, p. 430, claims to relate that word to *Barra*, bar, that is, court of justice. Brunner does likewise in *Deutsche Rechtsgeschichte* 2: 145. Hermann Fischer, in *Swabian Dictionary (Schwäbisches Wörterbuch)*, relates *pâra* to "*â*" in connection with the present pronunciation and identifies it with *baren*, gesture. From that he derives the meaning "administrative district" (*Amtsbezirk*) or " court district" (*Gerichtsbezirk*). On this point my colleague, M. Roediger, writes me as follows:

> If the stem a in *para* is originally long, it could be the same word as the Middle High German *bâra, bâre*, New High German *Bahre* (barrow) and therefore be related to *beran*, to carry, to bring forward. *bâra* means something that bears or produces, that is, in our combinations, the fruitful (bearing) earth, a productive piece of land. The meaning "administrative district," "court district" was not originally included in this word.

If the word *para* points to the fact that it was not a court district but an economic unit that constituted the system of the Swabian district during the period of immigration, that is a new argument for my concept. It is the Hundred, which has not yet broken up into smaller villages and which, under the leadership of its chief for whom it is named, takes possession as a unit of an area that borders on the neighboring Hundreds, under the overall direction of the princes.

THE NOBILITY OF THE CLAN LEADERS

Naturally, we do not have sources that recount in so many words the develop-ment of noble families during the *Völkerwanderung*, but the individual facts and events leave no doubt about this process.

Nowhere do the sources have technically precise expressions distinguishing the status of high officials or officers from the nobility. Instead, we constantly find the use of general, broad expressions such as "The First Ones," "The Wisest Ones," "The Most Noble Ones," "The Most Respected Ones" of the people, a manner of expression that reveals quite strikingly the transitional status and the merging of official position and class. The following passages I have assembled partly on my own and have taken partly from Dahn's *Könige* 2: 101; 3: 28, 50; 5: 10, 29. *primates et duces Visigothorum* (chieftains and leaders of the Visi-goths), Jord., c. 26. *primates* (chieftains), c. 48; c. 54. *optimates* (nobility), Ammianus 31. 3; 31. 6. "The well born ones, nobles,"* Malchus, p. 257. "*generis tua honoranda nobilitas*" ("Your nobility is of a kind to be respected"), King Theodahad writes to one of his counts, *Cass. Var.* 10. 29. "Leaders of tribes; the first in rank and birth,"* Eunapius, p. 52. "Most notable men,"* Procopius 1. 2; 1. 3; "elders,"* 2. 22; "the best men, the noblest men,"* 2. 28; 3. 1; "notable men,"* 1. 13; "If there was any pure blood among the Goths,"* 1. 13; "foremost men,"* 1. 7; 1. 12. Vitiges is chosen as king, although "not of a distinguished fam-ily,"* Procopius 1. 11.

The number of leaders of the Goths with equal status who are named in the period when there was no king is quite large, as Dahn (5: 21) correctly points out: Muthari, Gaina, Saul, Sarus, Fravitta, Eriulf, Alaric.

Sarus, who became noted for his constant opposition to the Balti, still had only 200 to 300 men, according to Olympiodorus, p. 449 (cited by Dahn 5: 29).

These leaders cannot have been simply the old princes, *principes*, in the sense of Tacitus' account.

Nor can they have been simply a nobility that developed from service at court.

Nor can they have been simply the leaders of purely temporarily formed mili-tary units. The group at whose head they stood necessarily must have been a very firm, basically organized one.

Consequently, there remains no other possibility but that they were the heads of clans (if not, in some cases, simply officers on the strength of imperial appoint-ment). Where their body of troops appears larger than even the largest clan can be assumed to have been, several clans had placed themselves under a single head in a way similar to that in which the entire people had princes or dukes. And so Sarus in his own right was only the *hunno* of a clan of 200 to 300 men, but he was temporarily recognized as leader of a much stronger opposition grouping. The nucleus of each such higher position, however, always remained the position of leader in a clan. It is impossible to conceive of Sarus' 200 to 300 men as simply his retinue; that would be far too many. Perhaps a king like Chnodomar had a retinue of 200, but not so a simple Hundred leader.

THE *THIUFADUS*

There is a question as to whether the *thiufadus* was the commander of 1,000 men or of 10. Grimm changed the *tiufadus* appearing in the sources to *thiufadus* (*thiu* abbreviated from *thusundi*) because one cannot imagine a commander over ten men. See Diefenbach, *Wörterbuch der gotischen Sprache* 2: 685. As we have seen, the second possibility is incorrect under any circumstances. But the matter is not completely clear.

In the military regulations of the West Gothic kings Wamba and Erwig, which we shall treat below (Book IV, Chapter 4), the *centenarius* and the *decanus* have disappeared, while the *thiuphadus* still exists, but as a man who belongs to the *"viliores personae"* ("more common people"), who are subject to lashings. If the *thiuphadus* had really been a leader of 1,000 warriors, he had slipped very far, for a man who commands 1,000 is still a highly placed person; even if the figure 1,000 should not be even distantly approached from a practical viewpoint, such a strong decline still seems very strange. But the older West Gothic regulations (reproduced below in Book IV, Chapter 1) seem to permit hardly any other explanation, and in the long run this would only tend to confirm our concept, especially in connection with the disappearance of the *centenarius*. The complicated organization of the migrations period, with its units of 10, 100, and 1,000 and a count or duke above them, became more and more superfluous after a tribe had settled. The Hundred in its old sense disappeared. The Thousand (which, from the start, was considerably smaller than this number) became smaller and smaller as a result of the multiple divisions accompanying the step-by-step process of settling. For a certain time, the designations "Hundred" and "Thousand" may have existed side by side, meaning approximately the same thing. How far such names often differ from their original meaning is shown by the word "division," which in Napoleon's army meant either a large subdivision of the army composed of several regiments (as in present-day terminology) or the tactical formation of the army. This double sense even led to a disastrous misunderstanding in the great attack of the Erlon Corps at Belle Alliance. The West Gothic *tiuphad*, in slipping to a lower status, became similar to the *tunginus* in the Frankish kingdom, a village justice, and it is not impossible that the *thiuphadia L. Vis.* 9. 2.5, which Dahn explains away in a somewhat artificial manner in *Könige* 6: 209, note 8, came into the picture because it was actually already identical with the *centena*, although in other passages the regulation retains the traditional organization of the chain of command.

Zeumer, in *Neues Archiv* 23: 436, points out that Chapter 322 of the *cod. Euric.* still names the *millenarius* as the judge in a matter of civil right, a position that is omitted in the corresponding *Antiqua* 4. 2. 14. In the meantime, the position had already changed.

NOTES FOR CHAPTER V

1. Mommsen, "Ostgotische Studien," *Neues Archiv* 14: 504.

2. *Könige der Germanen* 3: 3; 4: 61.

3. In the case of the East Goths, the *millenarius* appears only a single

time, and Mommsen ("Ostgotische Studien," *Neues Archiv* 14: 499) has seen fit to explain the word completely differently; he relates it to *millena*, "hide" — hardly correctly.

4. There possibly even exists an etymological trace leading back from the monarchy to the leader of the Hundred. Ammianus 25. 5. 14, reports that among the Burgundians the kings had been called *hendinos*, and Wackernagel has felt justified in relating the word to "Hundred." Other scholars, however, have explained it differently.

5. Dahn, *Könige der Germanen* 3: 161, from Cassiodorus. Later, Theodoric quite generally prescribed that the soldiers might exchange their ruined carts and exhausted animals on the march with the landowners through the intermediary of a royal official, the Sajo. But the soldiers were not to put pressure on the citizens, and they were to be satisfied if in exchange for larger and better animals they received, for example, smaller but healthy ones (Dahn, *Könige* 3: 88, from Cassiodorus, *Var.* 5. 10).

6. Dahn, in *Könige der Germanen* 6: 82, believes that, while the migrating armies of the Germanic tribes were accompanied by women, the latter could not possibly have followed the campaigns in the same numbers.

Where then are the Goths supposed to have left their wives and daughters?

7. "Walsians, some of whom already had German names, appeared individually in Ratisbon as late as the ninth century, around Ebersberg as late as the eleventh, and in the Salzburg region as late as the twelfth and thirteenth centuries." Riezler, *Geschichte Bayerns* 1: 51. Many Romanics settled in the Tyrol in particular.

The *Tegernseeer Gründungsgeschichte* reports that only 1,000 Bavarian knights had conquered the territory. While the legend has no validity in itself, it does reflect the continuing idea that here not only was a territory occupied but a people was subjugated.

8. Waitz, *Deutsche Verfassungsgeschichte* 2: 169; 2d edition, 2: 1, 282.

9. Brunner, *Deutsche Rechtsgeschichte* 1: 85.

10. Kluge, in "Clan Settlements and Clan Names" ("Sippensiedelungen und Sippennamen"), *Vierteljahrsschrift für Soziale und Wirtschaftliche Geschichte*, Vol. 6, Issue no. 1, p. 73, sees in the suffix "-ingen" no proof that it was a question of a clan settlement. He believes the suffix denotes only a general relationship; consequently, for example, Sigmaringen can also mean "among Sigimar's people."

11. According to E. Lüthi, "The Deployment of the Alamanni," ("Der Aufmarsch der Allemannen"), *Pionier,* Organ der schweizerisch-permanischen Schulausstellung in Bern, 23. Jahrgang, No. 1, 28 February 1902. Lüthi, *On the Fifteen Hundredth Anniversary of the Alamanni in Western Switzerland (Zum 1500 jährigen Jubiläum der Allemannen in der Westschweiz),* Bern, A. Francke, 1906, p. 21.

# Chapter VI

# The Settling of the Germans Among the Romans

If the entry of complete tribes into the Roman service is the decisive factor that determined the decline of the ancient world and the eventual formation of new, unique political systems, the Romanic-Germanic, it is still impossible to designate a specific beginning for this movement. From the earliest times, the Romans made alliances with barbarian tribes on their border, the terms of which called for their defending both themselves and the Roman Empire in their region against enemy attacks. From the treaties with tribes in their own native territory, the next step was the settling of such a tribe in a border area, and then movement farther into the interior, assignment of an area to them, and finally settling among the Romans.

It has been customary to regard as the beginning of the *Völkerwanderung* in this sense the reception of the West Goths into the Roman Empire when, pressed by the Huns, they appeared on the Danube, entered the empire as allies, but then defeated the Roman army and the Roman emperor himself in the battle of Adrianople. There is nothing absolutely new in all of this, neither in their reception, nor in the conflict, nor in the victory of the Goths. Nevertheless, the decisive point is here. The similar events that preceded this did not have any direct, continuously ongoing after-effects; setbacks eliminated their influence, and so they were only precursors.

The Roman Empire never again recovered, however, from the defeat at Adrianople. Although Thedosius once again reestablished the external authority of the imperial dignity and the empire lasted generations longer, the Germanic movement that ended with the establishment of independent German kingdoms on Roman soil was henceforth in full swing and, while perhaps delayed, was never again pushed back.

The conflict with the West Goths arose over the food supply. Whether the Roman officials who were accused of insufficient deliveries were actually so guilty is a point we have left aside, for even for the most far-sighted and careful officials it must have been an extremely difficult task to furnish provisions on a regular basis for a whole people, with women, children, and slaves, and the Goths were hardly very modest in their demands.

We cannot recognize clearly from the sources how Theodosius, as successor to Emperor Valens, who was killed at Adrianople, finally managed to get along with the Goths. He is supposed to have won victories over them, but these cannot have been very significant. The Goths remained within the borders of the Roman Empire and again entered the emperor's service. Certain areas, from which the inhabitants had already been driven by the previous pillaging raids or now had to vacate by order of their officials, were assigned to the Goths. We must imagine that the Goths lived here, in the middle of a Roman region, in the same manner as their ancestors: in flimsy district villages (unless they remained in their wagons or used Roman farmhouses), principally from their herds, with little cultivation of the fields, supported by Roman provisions of grain. Their number was, of course, not so very great. It was hard to provide for them continuously in one spot, but when they were spread in a number of smaller groups, it was not impossible to shelter them and provide them the additional foodstuffs.

Nevertheless, it naturally was not long until this foreign object in the body of the Roman Empire again began to make itself felt. New conflicts broke out. How would it have been conceivable that these Germanic warriors, who considered it more honorable to achieve their gains by bloodshed rather than by work, would have left untouched the fine things of the world all about them, toward which they had but to stretch out their hands?

Under Alaric the West Goths marched to Italy and burned Rome; from Italy they moved under Ataulf to Gaul. When they arrived there, the Vandals, Alani, and Sueves had already moved through that defenseless land and settled in Spain.

Concerning the manner in which the German areas of domination were established in the former Roman provinces in the course of the fifth century, we learn most from the Burgundians, whose *Notices of the*

*Chronicles*, as well as the articles of a book of laws, the *lex Gundobada*, have come down to us.

After the Burgundians, who had originally come from eastern Germany, had first settled on the left bank of the Rhine in the area of Worms, where under King Gunther they suffered their legendary defeat by the Huns, a few years later (443) they were assigned by Aëtius new areas in Sapaudia, that is, Savoy. "Sapaudia Burgundionum reliquiis datur cum indigenis dividenda" ("Sapaudia is given to the remnants of the Burgundiones to be divided with the natives"), we are told by the chronicler Prosper Tiro.

Fourteen years later (456 or 457) another chronicler, Marius von Avenches, who was familiar with this region, reports: "eo anno Burgundiones partem Galliae occupaverunt, terrasque cum Gallicis senatoribus diviserunt." ("In this year the Burgundiones occupied part of Gaul and divided that land with the Gallic senators.") Still another, later chronicler, Fredegar, recounts that the Burgundians had come at the invitation of the Romans themselves, who in this way had wished to get rid of their tax burden.

According to these accounts, on both occasions — when they first settled in Savoy and again when they extended their area beyond Lyons and across the Rhone — the Burgundians did not come as conquerors but were settled in agreement with the Romans. We are told exactly the same thing about the Alani at that same time,[1] and in the same way the West Goths had already been settled on the Garonne in 419.

The specific provisions under which the settling was to take place have not been preserved for us, but they were related to the forms of the Roman billeting procedure that is mentioned in the sources. Like that procedure they were also called *"hospitalitas"*; King Gundobad (473-516) says in his Book of Laws (Title 54): "At the time when our people received one-third of the serfs and two-thirds of the tilled land, it was prescribed by us that whoever had received land and serfs from us or our ancestors was not permitted to demand either a third of the serfs or two-thirds of the land from the locality where he was assigned a living area." He also says that this order was disregarded by quite a few; for that reason, it was thereby commanded that the land that had been unrightfully taken from the inhabitants would be returned, so that the previously maltreated Romans would enjoy security.

In a very similar vein, we find in the West Goths' Book of Laws a provision that a division between a Goth and a Roman, once carried out, was not to be changed subsequently; neither was the Roman to claim the two-thirds belonging to the Goth, nor the Goth the third belonging to the Roman.

Finally, we hear that Odoacer deposed the last Roman emperor because the Germans were demanding a third of the land and the Romans would not approve that. Burgundians and West Goths took two-thirds; Odoacer's people, therefore, seem to have been modest enough to demand only one-third.

This is the significant content of the historical source from which we have to form a picture of how the intersettling and establishment of the Germans among the Romans took place, by which the whole course of later history was determined.

With respect to the agricultural organization in the Roman Empire, three types of property come into consideration: small farmers who till the soil principally by their own labor and that of their own family, perhaps assisted by a man or woman slave; medium landholders, who no longer do the work themselves but have slaves to do the farming, being occupied themselves with their daily tasks of direction and supervision, or, if they live in the city, turn the supervision of the farming over to a manager; and finally, the large landowners, who perhaps cultivate their property in the second manner described above or have managers exercise supervision, but who for the most part have divided their property among tenants, the half-free serfs tied to the soil who work as small farmers, turn over a part of their produce to the master, and, according to need, also work for him as socage-tenants. Of these three types, the first no doubt still existed only very infrequently; most of the previously free owners had gone over into the status of tenants, in doing which they lost, to be sure, their full freedom but in return gained a strong economic support and a patron for protection under the law in the form of their rich master. The second type, the fairly large undertaking carried out by slaves, even if still existing here and there, was in any case also infrequent, except for citizen farmers in the cities. By far the largest mass of land and soil belonged to the large landowners using tenant labor.[2]

It is clear that the only type of property that lent itself to a division with the Burgundians was the third. The tenant farmer could not divide his land, for then he would have retained no usable land at all. A Burgundian would have been just as little inclined to content himself with a small piece of land that was not even a complete tenant farmer's share, at least in the sense that he would then have supposedly become a farmer on this acreage. After all, he was called into their territory not to be a farmer but specifically to be a warrior and defend the area. Even seventy years later, the Burgundian king Sigismund himself in a letter to Emperor Anastasius referred to his people as imperial soldiers (*milites*). The Germans had practiced very little agriculture up to that point, and the men had had little to do with it; they had lived principally from their herds and hunting. Consequently, they had been ready at any moment to take to the field en masse. As farmers they could no longer have done that; in many seasons, the farmer cannot leave his land at all and at other times only for brief periods, if his farm is to thrive. But the Burgundians were much too small in number to have been able to accomplish something if they marched out with only those who could be spared; when they went into the field, they had to have the maximum possible strength.

But they were also much too small in number to fill the large territory, which they did not do immediately in 443, to be sure, but nevertheless did occupy in the course of the next generation, in such a way as to have a Burgundian farmer installed beside a Roman on each of the previous farms, or at any rate on a very large part of them. Jahn, in his *Geschichte der Burgunder* 1: 389, estimates, on the basis of the fabulous numbers previously considered as credible, that in 443 they had moved into the territory with 93,900 men (281,700 souls). But because in our estimate we have gone down to between 3,000 and 5,000 men, a completely different prerequisite for the settling process is also created.

Finally, there comes into consideration the fact that the Burgundians only occupied their land in gradual stages. Quite the same applies to the West Goths, who had initially settled on the Garonne and then gradually took over all the land up to the Loire and the Rhone, in the south also across the Rhone to the Alps, and finally the largest part of Spain. It is impossible to assume that people who were content with having a farm assigned to them and had settled down there should again have moved off en masse within a few years in order once again to take over a similar share of land somewhere else. On the contrary, in their war with Justinian the East Goths once said they were ready to evacuate all of Italy and be satisfied with the land north of the Po:[3] testimony enough that, although they had already been in the country for fifty years, they had not settled themselves as farmers.

Did the division of land then perhaps apply to the medium-sized properties that were cultivated with the help of a number of slaves? Even that is hardly imaginable. The medium landowners were principally city dwellers. According to the still existing regulations for administration and taxes, these landowners were burdened with a property tax that would immediately have been lifted if their property had been taken from them.[4] But not only from the viewpoint of the Roman but also from that of the German, the idea that such medium properties were divided is hardly acceptable.

The Burgundian who was supposed to take over such a property would have been in an embarrassing situation. He was completely lacking in knowledge as well as personal characteristics for doing the farming himself; neither the direction of the daily work, nor the advantageous sale of his produce, and least of all the necessary accounting was in his nature. He would have had to employ a manager, but even the supervision of such a manager would have been beyond his abilities and interests. The new master would undoubtedly already have failed in trying to effect the necessary reorganization of his two-thirds share of the property. The only possible form of utilization of a rather large property by a barbarian was the division into tenant holdings, a form of agriculture with which, according to Tacitus' report, they had always been familiar in their homeland. But tenant farming is not appropriate for a small property of the medium category. Even the common freeman in ancient Germany had seldom had a tenant, for that meant, of course, that he allowed this hand to establish a family which in lean years would have had to be fed along with his own, and lean years were not infrequent. A large-scale farm has at its disposal so many supplies that it can count on other things in this respect. Three or four tenants are also not in a position to provide for an owner's family. The number must be much larger. Consequently, a medium-sized farm is worked by having the serfs not in a position of tenant farmers but as farm hands. Farming with tenant farmers is in every respect a large-scale activity.

Accordingly, the only type of farm suitable for sharing with the Germans was the large property with tenant farmers.

We have cited above from the Burgundian Book of Laws the title calling for the Romans to give up two-thirds of the land and one-third of their serfs. In the continuation of that passage, it is further stated that to each partner belonged one-half of the farmhouse, the gardens (vineyards), the forests, and the cleared woodlands. This threefold different measure for the division — two-thirds, one-half, one-third — must have been instituted for specific reasons and calls for an explanation.[5] It might possibly be somewhat as follows:

The two-thirds of his farm land that the Roman owner gives up is principally tenant farmer land. The third he keeps is partly tenant farmer land but principally the land he cultivates himself, and with it he keeps half of the forest, garden, and vineyards. In order to be able to continue cultivating this part, he must keep two-thirds of his serfs, for the serfs are not only the farm workers but also the house servants and all kinds of artisans whose number cannot be decreased, or need not be decreased simply because most of the cultivated land has been given up.

What then did the Burgundian do with his two-thirds of the cultivated land but only one-third of the slaves? We might well assume that he brought along so many slaves himself as to be able to fill a possible shortage in the number necessary for working in the fields. But there is also the possibility of a completely different arrangement.

We have seen that in accordance with the prerequisites and the purpose of the land division only the large properties lent themselves to that purpose.

It is completely impossible that all the Burgundians would have shared property, each with a Roman large landholder. As few as they were, they were still too numerous for this, especially at the time of the first settling in Sapaudia.

The Germans with whom the Romans had to share were consequently only the prominent ones and the leaders. The passage of that chronicler to the effect that the Burgundians had shared with the "senators," that is, according to the vernacular of the period, with the aristocracy, the large landholders, is to be understood quite literally.

Now we have at hand the material for filling out the apparent discrepancy that the Romans were to give up two-thirds of their farm land but only one-third of their slaves. A number of tenant farmers' houses were included, which were turned over unoccupied. The common Burgundian freemen moved into these farmhouses.

The method of settling and of dividing the property which the sources report was in no way suited to the common mass of the Germans: a small piece of property could not satisfy them, and they were not capable of dealing with a larger one. Indeed, the German was still completely untutored and undeveloped from the agricultural viewpoint. The transition from the semi-communism of the clan system in which he had previously lived into an individual type of economic management could take place only very gradually, and all the more slowly in that at first every impulse in that direction was lacking. The dominant idea could be no other than to retain the warrior status in which they lived, rather than to give it up as soon as possible.

It was a question of fitting the Germanic organization into the Roman civilization. It was impossible to have these wild warriors continue to live in their previous manner amidst the Romans. What we have now gleaned from the sources, however, gives us a graphic and understandable picture of the new condition. The Roman landowners, who had previously supported the barbarian mercenaries with huge provisions of food and taxes and yet, whenever a conflict broke out, had to be prepared to be plundered by them most unmercifully, shed a part of this burden by turning over their land.

The Germans spread out in moderately large groups on the large properties; their leader acquired possession of half of the house, the farmyard, the garden, the vineyards, and the forest and of two-thirds of the cultivated land with the tenants' houses located on it. In the empty farmhouses or those vacated for this purpose, he established his fellow clansmen or his subordinates with their families, who worked the farm to the extent that they understood how to do so and insofar as their energy prompted them. But they continued to regard the warrior life as their principal occupation, and they also expected that activity to be their principal means of livelihood. If there was no campaign in a given year, they had to get along with the produce of the farm or their savings. If there was war, the commander did not give any cash payments, but he did provide rations and promised booty.

The warrior status included not only personal courage and ability to use weapons but also the capability of moving out on order. Such moving out, unless it was only in the most immediate area, called for supplies and equipment that the individual could not provide for himself. He needed many more rations than he himself could carry; he needed replacement weapons; he needed care in the event of sickness or being wounded. The individual was not in a position to provide the wagons and the draft animals necessary for all of this. Even a man who had to be considered as belonging to the medium-sized property owners was incapable of that. For these purposes, a continuing organization possessing the necessary means is needed, such as had been previously provided by the clan organization.

If the Cherusci and their allies had once besieged the fort of Aliso for weeks or months, the detachments from the individual regions must have been supplied and fed there by their fellow clansmen, for even a campaign of five or six marches and as many weeks necessitates very large supplies. This organization was also active on the moves of the migrations.

From the sources we can fairly well conclude how the Germans now met this requirement after their settling.

We observe that the property allocated to the leaders was not turned over so simply as completely free property. The parcel was, to be sure, passed on to one's heirs, but it could not be sold at will or divided up, and it remained in the male line of descent as long as such heirs existed, with the exclusion of the daughters. In some expressions of the Burgundian Book of Laws, the idea of a common family property seems to be suggested.[6] The individual shall not sell his parcel arbitrarily, unless he has another piece of property. Whoever is granted a piece of property by the king is obligated in return to serve loyally and fully (Title I, Section 4).

From this I believe I can conclude that the newly created Germanic large property owners had certain obligations of support with respect to their fellow tribesmen who settled on the farms. Of course, we do not find any kind of regulation calling for this in the Burgundian Book of Laws or elsewhere, but such a regulation was perhaps on the one hand superfluous and on the other difficult to formulate juridically. Wherever the concept of the ancient clan survived, no matter how weakened, a traditional patriarchal-communistic spirit was also still alive. Each of the groups settled on a Roman estate retained something of the nature of an ancient clan, and if it was called up for war service, no special regulation was needed, by Germanic standards, to indicate that the leader, to whom a large part of the estate and its slaves were assigned for his direct disposition, had to carry out the mobilization with these means. There was no specific law covering this.

We cannot say to what extent and for how long this factor was actually effective. Certainly we may not completely deny it. But in addition there now also existed the public administration, which the Germans soon took completely out of the hands of the Romans. The Germanic king placed in charge of each region a count with his officials, who provided rations for the army with the provisions turned over by the Roman population. Among the West and East Goths we see how the Roman tax system was maintained, but the citizens were allowed to fulfill their obligation with the delivery of foodstuffs instead of cash. In the West Gothic law, we find regulations concerning the delivery of grains, supply stocks, and prescribed punishments for dishonest administrators.[7] We also find the depots often mentioned among the East Goths.[8]

The gradual expansion of the areas of the Burgundians and the West Goths now ties in very well with our concept. The common man did not consider himself to be permanently settled on his farm; rather, he occupied it just as temporarily as he had previously on the Rhine or far away in eastern Germany. He had no objection to moving into another area as

soon as the king and his leaders required it. In this process it was the king
who gained, increasing his power and his income, as well as those men
who, as younger sons of the foremost families already settled on estates
or thanks to the favor of the king, now also moved into the ownership of
a large estate. Finally, the Burgundian kingdom may have covered
between 43,000 and 54,000 square miles, divided into some thirty counties or districts. Consequently, there were not more than some 200 warriors, on the average, in each such county.[9]

Of these warriors, however, a large number were no longer in the status
of a common fellow clansman but were in the service of one of the new
lords or of a royal count. The gigantic possessions that the Germans
acquired as they settled were for the greatest part of benefit to a very
small class. We might ask why the common freemen put up with this situation. But the whole mass of warriors could not suddenly all be made
great lords, and many of them participated indirectly in these properties
by entering the service of the new landowners and thereby still maintaining their warrior status. For it was precisely warriors that the lords wanted to have in their service. In this process the concept and cohesiveness
of the ancient clan crumbled.

In the idea that has previously been entertained, that fully two-thirds
of the entire lands of the Romans were taken over in order to settle Germans on them, there lay a property revolution never seen elsewhere in
history. And we have now moved back from this concept.

In the place of a gigantic shifting of all property relationships, there
has appeared a new method of army administration suited to the conditions of a barter economy. We do not even need to assume that even in
those places where the land was actually turned over, the individual
owners who were arbitrarily dispossessed had to sacrifice their property.
The basic expression, "two-thirds of the cultivated land, half of the farmhouses, one-third of the serfs," did not hold true for the entire property
of the Roman, which after all, could have been of various types and scattered through many districts. Rather, in each case it held true only for
the property or the village designated for settling.[10]

In the division of the land, as we now picture it, special considerations
might well have been taken, so that only the properties of very rich
owners were chosen and the burden to some extent was divided equita-
bly. Hence, the sacrifice was easily tolerated.

A medium landowner who had two-thirds of his land confiscated
would not only have been that much poorer, but he would also have been
ruined; his whole social status would be changed. A large landowner who

gave up one-third to two-thirds from two estates remained in the same social status.

After the end of the civil war, when Octavian settled his veterans in Italy, he arrived at no other solution than to drive out masses of civilian inhabitants from entire regions and divide the confiscated land among his soldiers. The assignment of land to the barbarian Burgundians and Goths was probably far less painful.

Roman authors have left us statements to the effect that the Romans were better off under the control of the barbarians than previously, because under the Roman administration the tax burden had become unbearable. If this portrayal is based on the truth, it could very well be explained by the fact that not only was the direct turning over of the land not very extensive but also that the taxes now consisted almost entirely of contributions of produce, which could be raised in the immediate area. The contribution of produce at great distances increases the burden so very much that it finally becomes impossible. But in view of the insufficient supply of valuable metals, it would have been difficult to provide cash instead. Furthermore, if one was now secured against the plundering raids of the neighboring barbarians and their compatriots as a result of the peaceful arrangement, then his condition was indeed improved.

A realistic picture of how the Roman aristocrats felt about their Germanic "guests," the *hospites*, who now lived beside them on a permanent basis on their estates, is provided by a poem from the time of King Gundobad. The bishop and poet Sidonius Apollinaris sent the poem to one of his friends in order to apologize for not having written any real wedding poem for him. Its translation reads as follows:

> How shall I, even if I am otherwise quite able to do so, compose for the wedding feast while I sit here among the crowd of long-hairs, listen to Germanic words, and have to praise with a serious countenance the songs sung by the gluttonous Burgundian who has salved his hair with rancid butter? Need I say how this strangles my poetry? Fleeing from the barbarian lyre, Thalia, since she sees the seven-foot gentlemen around her, may know no more about the six-footer (hexameter). Happy may one consider your eyes and ears and happy your nose that early in the morning are not assailed by ten devices (cookpans or gurglings?) belching out their odor of garlic and onions. You are not pounced upon even before daybreak like an old uncle or the husband of a child's nurse by a number of giants

that could hardly be satisfied even by the kitchen of Alcinous. But now the muse becomes silent and curbs her few jocular verses so that this might not simply be called a satire.

Well may the cultivated Roman joke, but we still take delight in the seven-foot giants who sing their songs at the feast. We would gladly give up all the poetic skill of Sidonius Apollinaris if the poet had condescended to indicate a single one of those Germanic songs that he mocks, or even one of the accounts by his guests of the death of their King Gunther or of their participation in the great battle against Attila on the Catalaunian Fields.

To this point, we have looked principally only at the division of land and the settling of the Burgundians and West Goths. That does not mean that the same kind of developments took place among the other Germanic tribes.

Up to now, it has been assumed that things went quite differently with the Vandals. From the beginning they took a political stance different from that of the Romans. The Burgundian kings were willing to have their land assigned to them by Aetius and considered themselves to the end as soldiers of the emperor, and still after the fall of the West Roman Empire soldiers of the emperor in Constantinople — or at least referred to themselves as such. The West Goths also long considered their kingdom as a part of the Roman Empire. Gaiseric, on the other hand, took Africa by force and soon had it turned into a full monarchy of his own. Then instead of assigning his people throughout the entire land, he held them together in the Zeugitana, the area closest to his capital Carthage, while completely driving the Romans out, according to the account of our sources, Procopius and Victor Vitensis. If we consider this further, however, we see that it is at least not impossible that the experience of the Vandals was very similar to that of the other Germanic tribes. Their area was much larger than even that of the West Goths, but their number was probably smaller; they probably numbered no more than 8,000 to 12,000 warriors. Consequently, it is only natural that they did not spread out along the entire North African coast. The fertile Tunis area sufficed to feed them, and they were better prepared for military purposes by remaining together there. The officials whom the king installed for the administration of the individual more distant territories were assigned only quite small detachments to support them. The question is whether the Zeugitana was really completely cleared under the conquerors or whether there was a division of property here too, so that the

Romans remained with a certain amount of property. The statements of our two source authors shed little light on this subject, for both are very hostile toward the Vandals and do their best to paint their cruelty and hardness in the blackest colors. But it is also not impossible that they are right.

In the division of properties undertaken by Odoacer in Italy and in which the East Goths later participated, it seems particularly curious that the Romans here had to give up only a third, whereas the West Goths and Burgundians took two-thirds. With the interpretation that we have now given to this regulation, however, the difference loses its significance: the importance of the impact, after all, does not depend so much on the segment that is separated from the individual estate but rather on the overall area that is claimed. If in Italy less was taken from each estate, we still do not know whether all the more estates may not have been designated for the division.

For this reason, it appears that more important than the varying ratio of division was the other difference, the fact that the East Goths, as the sources state, had to pay property taxes. The Burgundians and West Goths did not do so, since, of course, the allocation was their pay, so to speak.[11] But Theodoric also gave his warriors a cash payment, which to be sure was not regular pay but an annual gift. On one occasion, he expressly emphasized that he did not keep the income from taxes for himself like some kind of miser but passed it on to his compatriots.

We do not have a reliable contemporary report concerning the experience of the Lombards in Italy. According to the later account provided by Paulus Diaconus, it appears that they simply drove out and exterminated the Roman aristocracy and took over their positions.

Originally, the Germanic tribes on Romanic soil were nothing but armies. Their first place of settlement was regarded as a kind of billets. Then the army commanders, the Germanic kings, also took over the civil administration; they governed the land through the counts whom they appointed to replace the former Roman officials. The division of the land was not the truly fundamental and determining aspect of these changes; it was a partial liberation from the burden of taxes and the providing of foodstuffs and billets. The determining and decisive point is that, thanks to and assisted by the Germanic war methods and military system, the entire Germanic political system with all its legal and social concepts gradually replaced the Roman organization or was injected into it.

A sequential development of the more modern period in history may provide a parallel to this Germanic-Romanic political formation: I refer to the administrative organization of the Prussian state. Just as the Burgundians and Goths were originally nothing but the army, which in order to take care of its needs also took the civilian administration and a part of the property in hand, so too it was the original supply authorities of the army that eventually provided the Prussian administration. In the place of the Roman national and communal authorities there appeared the Germanic count appointed by his king for a district that corresponded more or less to that of an ancient Germanic tribe. The commissars for marches, billeting, and rations of the Brandenburg army during and after the Thirty Years' War became the district councils (*Landräte*), the councils of war (*Kriegskammern*), and the General Directorate (*Generaldirektorium*). From the collecting of supplies, provisions, and taxes for the maintenance of the army there arose a system of administrative services for the entire country — from the Brandenburg-Prussian army there grew the Prussian state.

## EXCURSUS

REFERENCES
The basic work on the settling of the Germans is still Gaupp's *The German Settlements and Land Divisions in the Provinces of the West Roman Empire (Die germanischen Ansiedlungen und Landteilungen in den Provinzen des römischen Westreichs)*, 1844.

Other important works are: Binding, *History of the Burgundian-Romanic Kingdom (Geschichte des Burgundisch-romanischen Königreichs)*, 1868.

Albert Jahn, *Die Geschichte der Burgundionen und Burgundiens*, two volumes, 1874.

G. Kaufmann, "Critical Discussion of the History of the Burgundians in Gaul" ("Kritische Erörterungen zur Geschichte der Burgunder in Gallien"), *Forschungen zur deutschen Geschichte*, Vol. X.

Of the great work of Felix Dahn, *The Kings of the Germans (Die Könige der Germanen)*, particularly valuable for our purpose are the third volume (1866), which contains the "Organization of the East Gothic Kingdom in Italy" ("Verfassung des ostgotischen Reiches in Italien"), and the fifth (1870) and sixth (2d edition, 1885) volumes, which contain the history and organization of the West Goths.

The latest work is that of R. Saleilles, "Concerning the Settling of the Burgundians on the Estates of the Gallo-Romans" ("Sur l'établissement des Burgundes sur les domaines des Gallo-Romans"), *Revue bourguignonne de l'enseignement supérieur*, 1891, No. 1 and 2, which also gives a detailed list of references.

The *lex Burgundionum* or *lex Gundobada* has recently been published by Binding in the first volume of the *Fontes rerum Bernensium*, 1883.

Gingins, "Concerning the Settling of the Burgundians in Gaul" ("Sur l'établissement des Burgundes dans la Gaule"), *Memorie della Academia di Torino* 40: 1838, claimed to prove that it was not individual properties but regions by *pagi* that were divided between the Burgundians and the Romans. That is certainly incorrect, and it is not necessary to dwell on it. Nonetheless, there is still a certain grain of truth in this concept, for the opposite idea, that everywhere the estates were divided and in this way the Burgundians were spread out individually over the entire territory, has been shown to be false. The common Burgundians remained together in groups, and since they became Arians, they remained separated from the Romans for a long time. Gingins reports on page 224 that a part of the city of Arbois was called the "town of the Faramans." This point is quite correctly connected with the fact that a group of Burgundians was settled here together; *Faramanni* are the men of the clan, the fellow clansmen.

MANCIPIA

My concept presupposed that the *mancipia*, the serfs, who were divided up, included the tenant farmers. It is certain that *mancipia* can mean not only actual slaves but also tenants. Title VII of the *lex Burgundionum* uses the expressions *servus*, *colonus*, *originarius*, and *mancipium* interchangeably. Other passages are also cited in Waitz, *Deutsche Verfassungsgeschichte* 2: 173 ff. Eichorn has consequently translated simply by "tenants" (*Kolonen*) the *mancipia* whom the Romans had to turn over to the Burgundians. Nevertheless, a special proof that this was really so is needed, since in this case the *mancipia* could also mean the actual slaves, as this has been interpreted by the more recent scholars. I think the explanation is as follows. If the expression *mancipia* in the *lex Gundobada* excluded the tenants, then division of property would apply exclusively to properties cultivated on a large scale, of which the Burgundians received two-thirds in order to cultivate them with one-third of the slaves on hand. It is impossible that two-thirds of all the tenants' farms were also given up and assigned to the Burgundians, since the tenant would then not have had the means of economic survival. The divided estate, however, would not possibly have been sufficient. The number and size of such enterprises was certainly not great in comparison with the tenant farms. Turning over half the house, the farmyard, and the garden without the food provided by a rather large number of tenants would have given the Burgundians empty barns. Consequently, the expression *mancipia* here must necessarily include the tenants.

The edict of Theodoric the East Goth, section 142, allows the masters to remove from the estate, and to sell if they so desire, "*rustica mancipia, etiamsi originaria sint* (tenants)" ("rural slaves, even if they were born on the land").

Dahn 4: 96 explains this by pointing out that the Goths brought many slaves along with them (a fact that is also proven elsewhere), whom they partially wanted to settle on the tenants' farms. They therefore arranged that they might deal with the former tenants as they wished.

DIVISION OF THE LARGE ESTATE

That only the Burgundian aristocracy shared with the Roman aristocracy is also confirmed by the fact that in the Burgundian law, as in the West Gothic, the forests were especially emphasized in connection with the division of property. The possession of forests was not normally associated with ownership of smaller properties.

Dahn, *Könige* 6: 168, says: "The status of the common freemen (West Goths) branched out into three levels: the highest one moved upward in continuously fluid motion toward the ruling nobility, a declining small minority held an insignificant middle position, and by far the greatest majority sank to the position of 'lesser ones', 'lower ones,' 'small ones', that is, impoverished people at or below the level of the serfs."

Certainly, these men whose status was lowered were never owners of medium-sized lands.

DIVISION OF THE HOUSE AND FARMYARD

Curiously enough, in Title 45 of the *lex Burgundionum* the house is not mentioned as a subject for division; the same applies in the *lex Visigothorum*. It has therefore been concluded that the Roman did in fact retain his whole house and that the German built one for himself. That may make sense, since the continuous sharing of a house that we may imagine as a rather strong castle necessarily would have created many inconveniences. To be sure, the division of the house is precisely specified in the Roman billeting regulations, but that was always only something of a temporary nature. Certain though it is that the division of the land was related to the existing methods of billeting, nevertheless it was also something quite different, not only because the land is now part of the division but principally because it is now no longer a question of a temporary situation but of a permanent one.

But it seems to me that almost more difficult than the division of the house was the division of the farmyard with its stables and barns. The Germans regarded the farmyard as a definitely specified place. *Lex Bajuvariorum (Law of the Bajuvarians)*, XI, Section 1: "Si quis in curte alterius per vim contra legem intraverit." ("If anyone forcefully entered the courtyard of another contrary to the law.") *Lex Alamannorum (Law of the Alamanni)* (lib. III), C, Section 3: "Si in Curte aliena ingressus fuerit." ("If he entered the courtyard of another.") *Lex Visig.* 8. 1, Section 4: "Quicumque dominum. . . . intra domum vel curtis suave januam incluserit." ("Whoever enclosed an owner . . . inside a house or the gate of his own courtyard.") Because of this, for a long time I have hesitated as to whether we could assume that a division of the farmyard actually took place with the Burgundians. The passage in Title 44. 2, reads: "quoniam sicut jam dudum statutum est, medietatem silvarum ad Romanos generaliter praecipimus pertinere, simili de curte et pomariis circa faramannos conditione servata: id est ut medietatem Romani estiment praesumendam." ("since, just as it was established long ago, we generally order that half of the forests belongs to the Romans with a similar arrangement observed for the courtyard and the orchards near the *faramanni* |tribesmen|, that is, the Romans think that their half must have preference.") I have considered whether we might not be able to understand the word *curte* here in the collective sense, as the total of all the tenant farmyards, half of which were to be vacated. But despite all the violations of correct Latin forms in this law, such an interpretation still seems to me out of the question. We must continue to assume that the master's farmyard was meant here and was really divided up. But then the house is also included.

### THE TWO *HOSPITES*

Gaupp, Binding, Jahn, and Kaufmann are all agreed in accepting in each case, along with a Roman *hospes*, *one* Burgundian who shared his property with him. In opposition to this viewpoint, Saleilles has sought to explain that several titles of the *lex Gundobada*, especially Title 67, can be understood in no other way than that several Burgundian *hospites* shared with *one* Roman. This is in agreement with our concept. Title 67 reads: "Quicumque agrum aut colonicas tenent, secundum terrae modum vel possessionis suae ratum sic silvam inter se noverint dividendam. Romano tamen de silvis medietatem in exartis servata." ("Those who hold a field or farms know that a forest must be thus divided mutually according to the established size of the land or of their property. Nevertheless, half of the forest is reserved for the Roman in cleared-off fields.") Binding considers the second sentence to be interpolated.

Titles 13 and 31 seem to indicate the opposite. Title 13 reads: "Si quis tam Burgundio quam Romanus in silva communi exartum fecit aut fecerit, aliud tantum spatii de silva hospiti suo consignet et exartum, quem fecit, remota hospitis commotione (communione) possideat." ("If any Burgundian or Roman in a common forest cleared off a field or will have cleared it off, he would return to his guest another part of the field of equal size, and the part which he cleared he would possess without dispute with his guest.") Title 31 reads: "Quicumque in communi campo nullo contradicente vineam fortasse plantaverit, similem campum illi restituat, in cujus campo vineam posuit." ("Whoever planted a vineyard perchance in a common field without another's objection should reserve a like space for him in whose field he placed the vineyard.") In both titles, it is apparently assumed that there are only two co-owners of the *communis campus*. The explanation no doubt is that there was not yet any idea of common Burgundians who could clear forests or lay out vineyards. At most, it was the outstanding men who rose to this high degree of agricultural capability. The common member of the clan (*faramannus*), who was settled with twenty or thirty others in a village and with them had a claim to half of the common pasture land and the common forest, would indeed not have been anxious to occupy a parcel for himself, lay out a vineyard, and satisfy the Roman co-owner with a similar piece of land. On the other hand, the Roman would have been still less interested in sharing with all the Burgundians.

The fact that the need arose at all for such provisions, which also existed in a similar way among the West Goths, was no doubt due less to the agricultural enthusiasm of the Germans than to the needs of the Romans, who sought to offset their loss of fields by means of new clearings in the forest, which remained common property.

### *BURGUNDIONES, QUI INFRA VENERUNT* (BURGUNDIANS WHO CAME LATER)

Title 107, Add. II, Section 11, of the *lex Burg*. reads: "De Romanis vero hoc ordinavimus, ut non amplius a Burgundionibus, qui infra venerunt, requiratur, quam ad praesens necessitas fuerit, medietas terrae. Alia vero medietas cum integritate mancipiorum a Romanis teneatur: nec exinde ullam violentiam patiantur." ("We in fact issued this order concerning the Romans: that not more land

should be required by the Burgundians who came later |*qui infra venerunt*|
than there was need for at present. This is half of the land. The other half in truth
with all its slaves should be held by the Romans, and thereafter they should suffer no violence.'') The Burgundians "*qui infra venerunt*'' can probably not be
any others than later immigrants. But what then is the *terra*, half of which is
supposed to be given to them without serfs? Half of a tenant parcel? Impossible,
for the many reasons already given. Half of a large estate? That would have been
very much, but without any slaves it would not have been of much use to the
immigrant. Did the count in whose area he wanted or was supposed to settle
decide on the property he was to be assigned, based on the man's own agricultural abilities? Did the count therefore seek a rather large piece of property for a
well-to-do man who arrived with his own farmhands, cattle, and equipment, and
a tenant parcel for a newcomer who owned almost nothing? But that would have
been unbearably arbitrary and would also have completely freed precisely the
richest Romans from this burden.

I think we can imagine it somewhat along these lines. The Burgundians who
came later were either individuals — and probably this was true in most cases —
who had lived for a while as mercenaries in the Roman service in Italy or Constantinople, or they were entire clans or parts of clans. The individuals were not
settled one by one; either they entered the service of a Burgundian noble, or they
sought out their clan and their family and were taken in by them. Our paragraph
does not treat of these cases; rather, it refers to entire groups which moved in
from Germany. They were then assigned an estate from the possessions of a rich
Roman, and each Burgundian family then received, as in the case of the earlier
divisions, a tenant farm or a corresponding parcel of the master's land as their
own property. The displaced tenants were moved somewhere else by the master.
The half that the Roman was supposed to give up means ''a half at most,'' and
not an absolute half, for that would, of course, depending on the number of settlers that might perchance arrive and the extent of the estate, have led to intolerable inequalities. At the time of the initial settling, it was always two-thirds of
the property that was actually turned over and the possible excess went to the
*hunno* or other leader of the group, who, as we have seen, had to use it for certain military needs and in doing so won for himself a high position in the econom-
ic-social scale. This advantage was no longer provided to the late arrivals. If they
were called up for war, the burden of equipping them fell on the count.

ROYAL GIFTS AND *HOSPITALITAS*
Title 54 of the *lex Burg*. prescribes that anyone who had received land and
serving men through the generosity of the king was not also allowed to claim "*ex
eo loco, in quo ei hospitalitas fuerat delegata*'' ("from that place in which
hospitality had been assigned to him") the two-thirds of property and one-third
of slaves. To what extent could anyone who had been given an estate by the king,
no matter where he lived, still be a *hospes* anywhere else? Two interpretations
seem possible.

It could be that the meaning of *hospes* had already changed very much, so
that it did not mean a person actually billeted in a place but rather one who, like
a billeted person, had a claim to certain produce. In this way there was avoided
the complication of having the owners first deliver their produce to a central

point and then having it distributed to the Hundreds from there. The Hundred leaders or subordinate leaders went directly to those obligated to furnish the produce, but under some circumstances they misused this right by demanding land from them.

The other and probably more likely interpretation is that here *hospitalitas* means a billeting in the old sense, which had taken place before the person received his gift of land from the king. While taking possession of the land, he nevertheless retained his right to billets where he had had them and derived from that his claim to a division.

Incidentally, it also follows indirectly from this provision that it was not the entire area that was divided up but only certain selected estates; for the title assumes, to be sure, that the Romans were unjustly forced into the division of property. That cannot have been, for example, individual selected people, for the same conditions or relationships that brought about this selection in their cases would certainly also have protected them against the illegal taking of their property. This provision is understandable only if there were whole classes or groups of such Romans who did not need to share their property.

Heinrich Brunner, even in the second edition of his *Deutsche Rechtsgeschichte*, does not, in my opinion, arrive at a clear picture of the nature and the procedure of the "taking of land" by the Germans. He holds fast to the idea that the residences of the old and new inhabitants were mixed together like the squares of a chess board, even though the number of Germans was much too small for this. On the other hand, Brunner now also accepts the point (p. 74, Note 4) — and emphasizes it with a new and valuable piece of evidence — that it was not the tenant farms that were divided. In addition to the large estate, which probably bore the principal brunt of the measure (p. 74), medium-sized estates were also supposedly involved in the division of property (p. 76, note). But is *each* Burgundian supposed to have received in this way two-thirds of an estate? In that case, their number would have had to be much smaller than even I assume. But it seems that Brunner actually claims to conclude from the wording of the law "*populus noster . . . duas terrarum partes accepit*" ("our people . . . received two-thirds of the land") that *each* Burgundian received such a parcel of land.

I have not been able to determine to whom the wording (p. 76) applies, "as if the *jus hospitalitatis* (right to hospitality) raised *all* the Germans to estate owners, who were able to live a life of ease on the contributions received from their assigned tenants."

NOTES FOR CHAPTER VI

1. Prosper Tiro, anno 440: Deserta Valentinae urbis rura Alanis . . . . partienda traduntur. (The uninhabited countryside of the city Valentina is handed over to be divided up by the Alani.)

Prosper Tiro, anno 442: "Alani, quibus terrae Galliae ulterioris cum incolis dividendae a Patricio Aëtio traditae fuerant, resistentes armis subigunt, et expulsis dominis terrae possessiones vi adipiscuntur." ("The

Alani, to whom the territory of Farther Gaul had been handed over by the patrician Aëtius to be divided with the inhabitants, suppressed the armed resistance of the natives. They acquired the property by force, after the owners of the land had been driven off.")

2. Here we may pass over whatever else there still was in the way of lease conditions, etc. See Brunner, *Rechtsgeschichte* 1: 199.

3. Procopius 3. 2.

4. Hartmann has drawn attention to this in his *History of Italy in the Middle Ages (Geschichte Italiens im Mittelalter)* 1: 109. The liability of the curiae naturally did not carry over to the Germans. Of course, the argument disappears as to whether and where the taxes were shifted as a result of the division.

5. The idea that an original 1/2: 1/2 division of the cultivated land was later changed to 2/3: 1/3 has been rejected with good and convincing reasons by Kaufmann in *Forschungen zur Deutschen Geschichte*, Vol. X.

6. Gaupp, p. 352, note.

7. *Lex Visig*. 9. 2. 6.

8. Dahn, *Könige* 3: 162, Note 4.

9. The *lex Burg*. carries the signature of thirty-one or thirty-two *comites* (Binding, *Fontes rerum Bernensium*, p. 95, Note 16). But it is no doubt not necessary that all of these *comites* were active administrators of counties. Binding, in his *Geschichte des burgundisch-germanischen Königreichs* 1: 324, assumes that there were at least thirty-two counties.

10. If in *lex Visig*. 10. 1. 16 it is assumed that a Goth has taken by force the third belonging to a Roman and he is supposed to return it if the situation has not existed for fifty years, that can after all only apply to estates of absentee landowners. A Roman who had been robbed of his entire property by the Goth with whom he was supposed to share would certainly have taken up the fight for his rights either immediately or never. On the other hand, a high Roman may have realized for many years that one of his estates had illegally been taken from him but then finally, after the sense of legal security had become firmer among the new masters, he might have again made his claim.

11. Gaupp, p. 404.

# BOOK III

# Emperor Justinian and the Goths

# Chapter I

# Justinian's Military Organization

Whereas our information on the history of the second and third centuries is very scant, we have been given the possibility of more thorough knowledge and consideration of the fourth century, from the battle of Strasbourg to the battle of Adrianople, by Ammianus Marcellinus. The fifth century is again weak in source material, but in the sixth once again there appears a historical author in the grand style, Procopius of Caesarea, to whom, together with his follower Agathias, we owe the history of the wars of Belisarius and Narses and the account of the fall of the Vandals and the East Goths.

Procopius was Belisarius' secretary and took part in a large portion of the wars in the retinue of the commander. Not only is he admirably informed, but he also patterned himself on and imitated the great exemplars, Herodotus and Polybius. His analytical ability is small, but that does not greatly detract from his source value; the same thing, of course, not only applies to Herodotus, but even in the case of Polybius we have found his analytical powers considerably less than had formerly been generally accepted. If now, however, even aside from this weakness, Procopius misses quite a bit and as a source does not give us quite so much and such clear-cut material as we might hope, that does not, for the purposes of our study, stem from a lack of truthfulness (which, of course, is also not completely to be excluded) or a partisan bias.[1] But, even if the rhetoric that made Tacitus an almost useless source author from the military viewpoint has disappeared, the tendency remains for the author to force himself to paint impressive pictures, even at the expense of objective events, instead of letting the facts speak for themselves. In reading Procopius, we are reminded quite often of Herodotus' accounts, and if the situation remained that way, he would be a much more valuable source than the Father of History. For the latter, after all, took his information only from popular legend, whereas Procopius learned from personal observation and the direct presence of the key persons, the generals. But in the final analysis we are more often closer to the truth in Herodotus than in Procopius, because Herodotus limits himself to the actual event, while Procopius feels obliged, according to the degree of his insight, to create relationships and to present pictures — we might even say tableaux. I might compare the two accounts with a natural and a stylized picture of a plant or animal: the former reproduces nature as well as the artist is capable of doing; the latter, forced into specific forms, allows nature to be perceived only indirectly. As close as Procopius was to the events and as highly as his work is to be valued, he still may be used as a source only with extreme care and prudence.[2]

The transition of the ancient imperial legions into mercenary units, which we can observe and deduce in the fourth century but which, because of the status of the sources, could only be recognized as if through a veil, lies clearly before our eyes in the bright light of history, thanks to Procopius' account in the sixth century.[3] The commanders and generals, as has been appropriately remarked, were now at the same time condottieri in the sense of a later period: they had troops around them who had been recruited on the strength of their own names; they were called *hypaspists, buccellarii*. They cannot really be called "life guards," since their number often amounted to several thousand men. A "guard" is also not the sense of this organization, which depended rather on the fact that the mercenary system was more easily administered when the leader was at the same time the entrepreneur, the middleman for the business of military service. The truly personal retinue of the commander was formed by the *doryphori*, who at the same time could be called staff, adjutants, aides, and life guard. In addition to the corps of *hypaspists*, whose national composition is not clear, we find in Justinian's armies national units of the most varied type: Huns, Armenians, Isaurians, Persians, Herulians, Lombards, Gepids, Vandals, Antes, Slavs, Arabians, Moors, Massagetae.

The active armies were quite small. Belisarius had 25,000 men when he won his victory over the Persians at Daras in 530. He landed in Africa with no more than 15,000 men, and of these 15,000, the 5,000 cavalry included in that total were sufficient to defeat the Vandals in the open field. Even smaller was the army with which Belisarius moved to Italy in order to destroy the East Gothic Kingdom eleven years after Theodoric's death: there were no more than 10,000 to 11,000 men. Including all the replacements in the course of five years, there were no more than some 25,000 men who actually toppled Gothic hegemony in Italy in 539, and Narses had hardly that many when he crossed the sea to fight Totila after the Goths had risen again. He may have had some 15,000 men in the decisive battle at Taginae.

A contemporary author, Agathias (5. 13), estimated that the total Roman army must have been 645,000 men strong but that only 150,000 men were actually available under Justinian.[4] The first estimate may be based on some kind of ancient roster of the type of the *Notitia dignitatum* and is of no value to us; the second one does not appear unreasonable if we remember that we have estimated the army of Augustus at some 225,000 men and that of Severus at perhaps 250,000 men (see above, pp. 170, 228), and that half of the empire had been lost. But if we compare the strengths of the armies that actually appeared in the field, the sizes of which have been reliably reported to us and are consistent among themselves, we realize that, in the sense of a real standing army, 150,000 men is already much too large a number. If there is an original estimate of any kind at the base of this, it cannot be understood in any other way than that all of the border guards, the *limitanei*, who were unsuitable for the actual operations, were included.[5]

Most characteristic of the composition of the armies of this period, the variety of peoples that made them up, and the designation of units not according to numbered legions or some other scheme but after the leaders to whom they belonged, is Procopius' account (4. 26) of the mobilization of the army with which Narses was supposed to strike the decisive blow against Totila and with which he actually did so. It reads as follows:[6]

Narses moved out from Salona and marched against Totila and the Goths with the entire Roman army, which was of a mighty size; for the emperor had placed at his disposal correspondingly rich resources. For that reason, he was now able on the one hand to assemble a very splendid army and to provide satisfactorily for his other military needs; on the other hand, he was also capable of paying to the soldiers in Italy all the back pay that the emperor had for an unduly long time allowed to accumulate instead of paying them the agreed salary from the national treasury, as was the custom. He even had so much as to be able to change the minds of those who had gone over to Totila, and, appeased by these jingling attractions, they were won back for the empire. Consequently, whereas

Emperor Justinian had initially fought this war without any real enthusiasm, he now finally made very significant efforts. For when Narses observed that they should move to Italy, he showed a degree of ambition appropriate for a commander, and he explained to the emperor, when he was summoned by him, that he would comply with his wishes only if he received sufficient forces at his disposal. In this way, he received from the emperor money, men, and equipment commensurate with the dignity of the Roman Empire, and with tireless energy he assembled a splendid army: he drew numerous soldiers from Byzantium and also called to his colors a large number from Thrace and Illyricum. In like manner, Johannes joined him with his own troops and those he had inherited from his father-in-law, Germanus. Furthermore, the king of the Lombards, Auduin, was persuaded by rich presents from Emperor Justinian and the treaty of alliance to select 2,500 brave warriors from his own retinue and send them to support Narses, providing them also with more than 3,000 men as squires. Narses also had more than 3,000 men from the Herulians, who with others were commanded by Philemuth; numerous Huns; Dagisthaeus, released from prison for this purpose, together with his retinue; many Persian deserters under Kabades, son of Zames and grandson of the Persian king Kabades, who, as I have recounted earlier, with the help of Chanarang had escaped the persecution of his uncle Chosroes and had at that time gone over to the Romans; also Asbad, a young Gepid of outstanding courage, with 300 of his compatriots, who were also courageous warriors; the Herulian Aruth — who from his youth had been raised in the Roman style and had married the daughter of Mauritius, son of Mundus — himself a brave fighter, who had numerous Herulians of equal courage with him; and finally Johannes, who was nicknamed "The Glutton" and who has already been mentioned frequently, with a band of capable Roman warriors. Narses himself was of a very generous nature and had an open hand for anyone asking help. Since he was richly outfitted by the emperor, he was all the freer to follow his generous tendency. Because there were already many officers and soldiers who honored him as their benefactor, they all pressed forward with true enthusiasm to serve him as soon as his appointment as commander-in-chief against Totila and the Goths became known, partly because of a sense of obligation for previous favors and partly with the natural expectation of earning rich rewards with him. Most devoted to him were the Herulians and the other barbarians, whose favor he had assured himself through special generosity.

In this description we feel hardly a touch of Roman participation, but we need only to substitute a few names in order to believe that we are reading how Wallenstein, once again called to the emperor, moved his great army against Gustavus Adolphus.

The direct military performance, the battle feats of these colorful bands, left nothing to be desired. Their basic weakness, in addition to their small number — this army of Narses, pictured as so formidable, was, as we have already said, no stronger than 25,000 men all together — was their lack of discipline.

From the moment when the ancient Roman army began to be transformed into a barbarian one, complaints were heard about the demands of the soldiers and the damages they caused the country. Emperor Pescennius Niger (died 194) commanded, as we may freely translate it, that the "soldiers should be satisfied with their issue bread" (*"buccellato jubens milites et omnes contentos esse"*: "commanding the soldiers and all the rest to be content with biscuit")[7] Aurelian (died 275) did likewise ("Nemo pullum alienum rapiat, ovem nemo contingat. Uvam nullus auferat, segetem nemo deterat, oleum, sal, lignum nemo exigat, annona sua contentus sit.")[8] ("No one should carry off another's chicken, touch a sheep, steal a bunch of grapes, thresh grain, and demand oil, salt, and wood. He should be content with his rations.") In the armies of the sixth century, hardly any notice was taken of such small points as a soldier's taking a hen, a sheep, or a few bunches of grapes, or his demanding oil, salt, or wood.

Procopius considers it a half-miracle and an extraordinary accomplishment of Belisarius that the Romans marched into Carthage in good order, "whereas otherwise the Roman troops never march into their own cities without disorder, even if there are only 500 of them." But after the conquest of the Vandals' camp the same army indulged in such undisciplined conduct and forgot to such a degree any respect for its commander that Procopius felt obliged to express the fear that not a single man would have escaped if the enemy had attacked. Later, Prince Germanus' army behaved with just as little restraint and sense of obedience. Belisarius trembled because of the lack of discipline of his troops in Naples, and Narses, after his victory, had first of all to send his Lombard auxiliaries home.[9]

The garrison that Belisarius had left in Rome, Procopius recounts (3.

30), reproached their commander, Konon (548), for having enriched himself from the contributions, to the detriment of the troops. They murdered him and sent several priests as emissaries to the emperor to tell him they would desert to Totila and the Goths if they were not granted amnesty and if their back pay was not forthcoming by a specific date. The emperor approved and fulfilled their demand.

Actually, a very large number of the soldiers with whom Belisarius had conquered Italy deserted to the Goths when, after he was relieved, the Roman domination again collapsed and Totila established the Gothic kingdom.

When Totila was besieging Centumcellae (549), he had the announcement made to the Roman garrison that they could not expect any help and relief from the emperor and that he was offering them free movement back to Byzantium or admission to the Gothic army on an equal status with his own soldiers. The mercenaries declined to desert, since they had their wives and children in the Roman Empire and did not want to be separated from them. They could also not agree to the immediate surrender because they had no firm reason for it, since they wished, after all, to remain in the emperor's service. They agreed, however, that they would send to the emperor and explain their situation; if no help came by a certain date, they would surrender the city.

Imperial mercenaries, themselves mostly Germans, deserted not only to the Germans but even to the Persian king. Two such instances are reported by Procopius (b. Pers. 2. 7; 2. 17). As long as they were in the Roman Empire, the Germanic warriors could always hope to find a connection with their compatriots or even further contact with their homeland; their desertion to the Persians shows how these mercenaries cut every tie with their national or social background.

On the other hand, the Goths of Vitiges and Totila were also ready, on occasion, to re-enter the service of the emperor. It was as his warriors, after all, that they had conquered Italy, and even Theodoric had always recognized a certain subordination to the emperor. The emperor could not do anything better with the captured Vandals and Goths than to send them to Mesopotamia to fight for him there against the Persians,[10] and Persian deserters fought in Italy against the Goths.

The strongest expression of this warriorhood, torn as it was from any natural roots in the soil and depending on itself alone, is the fact, unique in world history, that the Goths, when they realized they could no longer stand up to Belisarius, offered him, the enemy commander, their royal crown. It makes little difference if one says that it was not so much the royal crown of the Goths as the imperial crown of the west that was offered to Belisarius. The idea that the imperial commander would not only desert to them but that the Goths could also simply accept him as their master and entrust themselves to his leadership shows that they had not the slightest glimmer of a political concept. Belisarius, of course, was not only loyal but also wise enough to tell himself that such a position of leadership, built in the air as it was, could have no durability, that he himself would find no benefit in it. He profited from the offer by taking from the Goths their last firm position.

The armies of ancient Carthage had already had a composition similar to those of Justinian. Hannibal's army was composed of Africans, Spaniards, Balearics, and Gauls, and it also happened that a part of his Numidian cavalry deserted to the Romans, and those Gauls, who did not want to follow him when he went back to Africa, he felt obliged to have executed. If these were only rare incidents and the great Carthaginian normally had firm control of his barbarians, that is a result not only of his personality but also of other conditions. What kind of expectations would the barbarians who might have left him have had? A small portion would have found employment as Roman auxiliaries, but most of them would quickly have been sent home by Rome. For at that time Rome still fought its wars with its own forces, and the senate knew very well what it would have meant if instead of its own legions it had sent only barbarians into the field. Consequently, we can say: indirectly, it was the national Roman legions that forced the barbarians in the Carthaginian camp to stand by their duty and remain loyal to the colors of the commander whose fame they had once followed. The internal situation of the one army reacted on that of the other, the enemy. After the fourth century A.D., and after the disappearance of the legions, everything changed. The barbarian mercenaries now felt that they were the masters. Woe to the prince or the general who might have dared to incur their displeasure by his strictness!

Almost more dangerous than the unreliability and lack of discipline of the soldiers was the insufficient obedience of the subordinate leaders, over whom the commander had no power to enforce his will, since the troops, of course, did not normally belong directly to the commander but rather to their leaders, whether they were their national chiefs or the condottieri who had recruited them with their own resources. Time and again Procopius tells us how Belisarius, both in Mesopotamia and in

Italy, was unable to carry out his war plans because subordinate commanders refused to obey him.

In the armies of classical antiquity, we find a basic and definite separation of the combat branches: we have the hoplites, the heavy infantry that constitutes the nucleus of the armies, and in addition the light infantry, archers or slingers. Besides the infantry there was the cavalry, armed principally with cold steel and less frequently as mounted archers. Justinian's armies had the same weapons and also battle-axes or other national types of weapons in the various contingents, but no longer combat branches. The entire infantry, like the cavalry, had been armed with the bow; missile weapons and close-combat weapons, light and heavy infantry, all were now combined. Indeed, infantry and cavalry were no longer completely separate; the infantry mounted on horseback, and the cavalry fought on foot. The predominant and decisive arm, however, was formed by the mounted men. Even when Belisarius planned to make a sortie out of besieged Rome, he wanted to use only mounted men for that purpose. For, as Procopius recounts (1. 28), most of his infantrymen had provided themselves with mounts from horses taken as booty and preferred to serve on horseback. The remaining group of infantrymen was too small to form a proper phalanx. Only on the special request of two leaders did Belisarius finally also take this infantry along into the battle. At Taginae, however, Narses placed dismounted cavalrymen in the center of his formation.

Procopius knows that antiquity valued the weapon of cold steel more highly than the arrow and preferred the close-combat fighter to the marksman. He is not willing to recognize this preference (*bell. Pers.* 1. 1), since the archer of his time had become quite different: he was mounted, fully armored, carried in addition to the bow and arrows a sword and perhaps also a spear, and finally, according to Procopius, the shooting of arrows was now much stronger, since the marksman pulled the string back to his ear and not just to his chest. In another passage (1. 18) he recounts that, while it was true that the Persians shot much faster than other peoples, their shooting was too weak, with a loose string, so that, contrary to the Roman arrows, they caused no injury to an armored man. This whole observation is to be rejected as factually incorrect; it belongs in the same category as the soft swords of the Gauls that had to be bent straight again after each blow, which Polybius recounts to us (see Vol. I, p. 306). The Asiatic archers have always been famous,[11] and it is not to be assumed that since the days of Cambyses the Persians and Parthians had become less skillful than any other people in the art of shooting, which had always been their national sport. Dio Cassius reports expressly (40. 22) that the arrows of the Persians also pierced shields and body armor. An illustration of Chosroes II shows the king hunting and pulling the string of his bow back behind his ear.[12]

Procopius' observations reflect the camp conversations of soldiers who were more boastful than perspicacious or historically educated; the real problem is not touched on at all in these accounts. Even the best marksman with the best bow, whether Persian or Roman, could only seldom and at very close range have penetrated a suit of protective armor. In the *Introduction to Archery*, which stems from this very period,[13] it is prescribed that one should not shoot directly at an enemy line (unless he aims at the horses' legs), but obliquely, for each man in line protected himself from the front with his shield; consequently, it was not so easy to penetrate. The real question is therefore: How did it happen that all the heavily armored warriors adopted the bow? This combat arm, called *cataphractes*, is by no means entirely new; as far back as Darius and Xerxes their warriors were of this same type. How does it happen that, defeated for such a long time, this combat method gained the upper hand more and more from the founding of the Parthian kingdom on? We shall discuss this subject later in a separate chapter.

Justinian's reign was distinguished not only by the broad, active power that the empire under him once again showed externally but just as much by the great defensive works that were erected. We are familiar with the *limes*, which protected the ancient empire in places where there were no natural obstacles forming the border. Justinian fortified the borders that he won again to a completely different degree and in a different manner. Connected lines played no significant role. But this emperor built border forts and fortified villages in such numbers and such size that their ruins astonish us. These forts were not just quarters for the troops; at the same time they were to serve as refuges for the entire surrounding population and their belongings. There were not many regular troops on hand to occupy them, but the border guards themselves, the *limitanei*, who also cultivated the fields, were supposed to be capable of defending themselves and the empire behind these strong, high walls. Starting from Ceuta in Morocco, the line of these fortified places stretched all across Africa for protection against the barbarian tribes; in Mesopotamia and Asia Minor, we find them facing the Persians, and north of the Danube and along the Black Sea providing protection against Germans, Slavs, or Huns. Between this system of fortifications and the composition, armament, and tactics of the army there existed an interrelationship that we shall likewise have occasion to discuss later.

## EXCURSUS

THE HERULIANS

Procopius, in *bell. Pers.* 2. 25. 266, says of the Herulians in the Roman service that they wore neither a helmet nor armor but only a shield and a thick coat. Their private soldiers even had to go into battle without a shield, which was then awarded to them if they proved their manliness by a brave deed.

The Herulians with their thick coat here appear better outfitted than the ancient Germans (see p. 49, above). I cannot, however, give any credence to the story of the young soldiers. As long as these serving men had no shield, they would probably not have been combatants but simply followers of the actual warriors. The awarding of the shield then meant that a serving man in whom they had confidence was accepted among the warriors.

(Added in the third edition.) A. Müller in *Philologus* (1912): 102, and Maspero in the *Byzantinische Zeitschrift* (1912): 97, have recently devoted their studies to Justinian's military organization. Maspero distinguishes between *phoideratoi (foederati)*, *symmachoi* (allies), and *stratiōtai* (soldiers). The old name of the *foederati* was now applied to the barbarian soldiers of fortune who were individually recruited for the Roman service and were assigned under Roman leaders but formed special corps. *Symmachoi* are the same thing as the earlier allies; they came under their own leaders on the basis of a treaty with their people. *Stratiōtai* were recruited or levied within the empire itself. Müller systematically studies the entire military system. When he states at one point that Justinian, without feeling ashamed and without fearing the consequences, did not give the soldiers their pay and bases this on the *hist. arcana*, that is a strong misjudgment both of the value of this source and of the character of the emperor and the empire. Justinian would certainly have done nothing more gladly than to pay his soldiers promptly — but where was it to come from?

In the Justinian army, the regiment was called *katalogos;* according to Müller, the subordinate unit, the *lochos,* was equated by Procopius to the legion; a new indication of how low the significance of this word had sunk.

NOTES FOR CHAPTER I

1. A. Auler, *de fide Procopii in sec. bello Persico Justiniani I imp. enarrando (On the Reliability of Procopius in Describing the Second Persian War of Emperor Justinian I)*, Bonn dissertation, 1876.

2. Belonging to the same period as Procopius are two theoretical documents that do not offer much in themselves but are important as controls, extension, and even refutation of Procopius. One is a writing by Urbicius (Orbikios) and the other an anonymous work, *Peri stratēgikēs*

*(On Generalship)*\*. For discussion of both, see Jähns, *Geschichte der Kriegswissenschaften* 1: 141 ff. and Rüstow-Köchly, *Griechische Kriegsschriftsteller* 2: 2.

3. *De Justiniani Imperatoris aetate quaestiones militares scripsit Conradus Beniamin (Military Questions from the Age of Emperor Justinian I by Conrad Benjamin)*, Berlin dissertation, 1892, W. Weber.

4. Mommsen, *Hermes* 24: 258.

5. Justinian also sought to maintain the institution of the "border guards" (*Grenzer*), and he organized new ones in Africa. The edict covering this was even transcribed into the code and has come to us in that way. Mommsen, *Hermes* 24: 200. But the salary that was allocated and promised to these men, in addition to the land given to them, could not be paid to them; there was too much demand elsewhere for liquid currency. Finally, Justinian seems to have deprived them of their character as soldiers as well as their pay. Procopius, *hist. arc.* 24, as cited by Mommsen in *Hermes* 24: 199. Others consider this as applying only to the east.

6. Taken from the translation by Coste in the *History Writers of the Earliest German Period (Geschichtsschreiber der deutschen Vorzeit)*.

7. Spartian, Chapter 10.

8. Vopiscus, Chapter 7.

9. Dahn, *Procop von Cäsarea*, p.395.

10 Procopius, *bell. Pers.* 2. 17; 2. 18. *bell. Vand.* 2. 14.

11. See Vol. I, p. 67. Luschan, "On the Ancient Bow" ("Ueber den antiken Bogen"), *Festschrift für Benndorf*, 1898. Jähns, *Trutzwaffen:* the entire very informative chapter on the bow, third phase. See also my Vol. III, Book 3, Chapter 8: "English Archery" ("Das englische Bogenschiessen"). The same account appears again there.

12. Reproduced in Diehl, *Justinien et la civilisation byzantine*, p. 209.

13. Köchly and Rüstow, *Griechische Kriegsschriftsteller* 2: 2, 201. It is from the anonymous document.

# Chapter II

# The Battle of Taginae (552)

We intend to study this battle by taking Procopius' complete report (4. 29-32) and inserting our analytical and explanatory remarks paragraph by paragraph.[1]

The Goths under Totila came from Rome, and the Byzantians under Narses from Ravenna. They met face to face in the Apennines and encamped opposite each other, no farther apart than two trajectories of an arrow, on a plain surrounded by hills. There follows Procopius' verbatim account:

There was a hill there of small circumference that both armies would gladly have held, for the Romans had a strong interest in shooting at the enemy from above, and the Goths, in the hilly terrain that I have already described, could attack the Roman army from the rear only if they moved forward on a country road that ran along right beside this hill. Consequently, this point was necessarily of the greatest importance to both sides: for the Goths so that they could envelop the enemy during the battle and shoot at him from two sides, and for the Romans so that they could prevent this. Narses acted before the enemy by selecting fifty men from an infantry regiment and sending them out before midnight to take and occupy this point. They arrived there without encountering any of the enemy and established a defensive position. A stream flows along in front of the hill close to the country road that I just mentioned and directly opposite the point where the Goths had set up their camp. The fifty men halted there, closely pressed together to the extent that the narrow space allowed, forming a phalanx.

Hardly had Totila become aware of them, at daybreak, than he prepared to drive them away. He immediately sent out a squadron of cavalry with the order to drive them off as quickly as possible. The cavalry charged upon them with much noise and shouting in order to overrun them in their first assault; but the fifty men, shield to shield in close formation, awaited the attack that the Goths, getting in each other's way in their rush, now attempted. The wall of shields and spears of the fifty men was so thick and tight that it brilliantly repulsed the attack. At the same time, with their shields they made a great noise, scaring the horses while their riders recoiled from the spear points. The horses, which became wild as a result of the close quarters and the noise of the shields and could move neither forward nor backward, reared up, and the riders could do nothing against this tightly formed band that neither wavered nor yielded, while they vainly spurred their horses on against them. The first attack was therefore repulsed; a second one had no better success. After several attempts they finally gave it up, and Totila sent forward a second squadron with the same mission. When this one, too, was driven off like the first one, a third squadron took its place. In this way Totila sent out a whole number of squadrons, but when he was able to accomplish nothing, he finally abandoned the effort. For their courage the fifty men gained undying fame from this battle, but above all two men distinguished themselves in this fight, Paulus and Ausilas, who sprang out in front of the phalanx and showed their bravery in the brightest light.

This preliminary encounter we shall discuss later. Now Procopius reports the speeches that the two commanders made to their soldiers, and he continues:

The armies, however, stood ready for battle, drawn up as follows. Each of them had a straight front that they tried to make as long and as deep as possible.

This expression ("They made the front of their phalanx as deep as possible and long"*) appears very questionable: one can make a phalanx deeper, but then it becomes less long; one can make it longer, but then it becomes less deep. But to make it at the same time as long as possible and as deep as possible cannot be done, unless the author intended to say that they actually formed up all the available troops. Even if we relate the expression "as much as possible" only to the depth of the formation, translating according to the specific wording, the sense and the error of logic remain the same.

"On the left flank of the Romans Narses and Johannes stood fast by the hill (*amphi to geōlophon:* near the hill*)."

According to the account above of the battle for the hill, we would expect to find it in about the middle between the two armies. Later, we hear that the Romans inclined their left flank forward from here. Consequently, the hill must have been situated closer to the Roman camp, and in fact, since the two armies were encamped only two arrow trajectories apart, very near. It is in this point that we find the explanation for the Goths' inability to drive off the fifty men.

> and with them the flower of the Roman army: for, in addition to the normal soldiers, both leaders had a select retinue of *doryphori*, *hypaspists*, and Huns. On the right flank stood Valerian, Johannes the Glutton, and Dagisthaeus with the other Romans; on both sides there were about 8,000 archers from the infantry regiments. In the middle of the phalanx Narses placed the Lombards, Herulians, and other barbarians, and had them dismount so that they would fight on foot and would not have the possibility of withdrawing quickly if perchance during the battle they should become faint-hearted or insubordinate.

Are we really supposed to believe that it was mistrust that caused Narses to have the barbarians fight on foot? These very troops later repelled all the assaults of the Goths. Was Narses really supposed to have such a poor knowledge of his troops? Or were these Germans men who, if they were really cavalry, could be commanded to fight on foot, and that without any practical reason? The story is so incredible that we must assume either that they were professional infantrymen whom Procopius turned into dismounted cavalry because of some misunderstanding or that there was some clear and practical reason for this formation which Procopius' source did not understand himself or failed to mention because of some colorful campfire story.

> Narses advanced only the extreme left flank of the Roman front, composed of 1,500 cavalry, in a slight angle. Five hundred of these men were ordered to hasten as fast as possible to any point where

the Romans might be losing the battle; 1,000 men had the mission of enveloping the enemy infantry as soon as it entered the action, so that it would be attacked simultaneously from two sides.

A reserve that has the mission of providing support everywhere where there is an emergency should not be placed on the most extreme flank, especially when it is curved forward. Such a reserve can be stationed only behind the center. We can, however, understand how this was meant. The hills surrounding the valley must have been so steep and high that no envelopment of the Roman army was possible. The only place where one could have accomplished this was on that country road that led between the single hill and the surrounding hills, that is, on the right of the hill from the Goths' viewpoint, up onto the heights. Behind this ravine-like route leading upward, Narses placed the 1,000 horsemen who were to fall on the flanks of the infantry attacking his front, and behind these 1,000 cavalry he held 500 more in reserve, maintaining them under his direct command. The forward inclination of the flank was only very slight; consequently, the 500 horsemen were so placed as to be able to come also to the aid of the center in case of emergency.

Totila drew up his entire army correspondingly. He rode along in front of his lines, encouraging his soldiers and by word and gesture stirring their courage. On the other side Narses did the same thing; he had golden arm rings, chains, and bridles carried along on poles in front of him and showed the soldiers these and similar things that were supposed to strengthen their courage for battle and danger. For a while the armies stood passively facing each other as each awaited the attack of the enemy.

Then a brave warrior named Kokas sprang forward from the Gothic army and approached the Roman line of battle, shouting out whether somebody might not be willing to face him in individual combat. This Kokas was one of the Roman soldiers who had earlier deserted to Totila. Immediately, one of Narses' *doryphori*, an Armenian named Anzalas, who was also mounted, moved out to face him. Kokas drove forward first against his opponent, aiming his lance at the latter's midriff, but Anzalas turned his horse aside quickly so that he avoided the attack. Since he had thus moved to the flank of his adversary, he pierced him with his spear in the left side. His opponent fell dead to the ground, whereupon the Romans raised a gigantic shout. Nevertheless, both armies stood still. But

Totila rode out alone into the space between the two, not to challenge anybody to individual combat, but to gain time. For, since he had received a report that the 2,000 Goths who had not yet joined him were already nearby, he did not want to start the battle before their arrival, and he did the following: first he wanted to show the enemy what kind of man he was. He was wearing equipment completely decorated with gold; from his helmet and his spear there floated purple plumes of great beauty, appropriate for a king. Riding on a splendid horse, he manipulated his weapons expertly in the open space. First he had his steed make the most graceful turns and jumps. Then at full speed he threw his spear high into the air, and as it fell spinning, he grasped it in the middle. He caught it in skillful alternation, first in the right hand, then in the left, thus showing his agility; he jumped down from his horse to the rear and to the front, as well as on both sides, and sprang up again like one who had practiced the skills of the riding ring ever since his youth. He spent the whole morning in this activity. Then, to delay the start of the battle still longer, he sent a herald to the Roman army to ask for negotiations. But Narses rejected that request, saying that there had been a long time for discussions, that Totila had shown himself eager for battle, and that now, in the middle of the battlefield, he was seeking to have a discussion — Narses was not going to be deceived by all of this.

Why, then, did Narses not attack, since he was not deceived by the expedients of the Goth, who only wanted to gain time? The individual combat between Kokas and Anzalas and the knightly exercises of the Gothic king in view of the two armies make splendid reading. It is also entirely believable that Totila was seeking to gain time, since he was expecting 2,000 more cavalry. But gaining time for one side means losing time for the other. If we are not to consider the entire account as a fable, we must assume that Narses had a tactical reason for remaining on the defensive and leaving the initiative for the attack to his opponent, something that Procopius has neglected to tell us.

In the meantime the 2,000 Goths had arrived. When Totila learned that they were in his camp, he went to his tent, since the time for the noon meal had arrived; the Goths gave up their formation and likewise fell back. When he arrived, he found the 2,000 already there and ordered that all the soldiers should take their noon meal.

Here again the question arises as to why Narses did not take advantage of the unusually favorable moment when the Goths broke up their battle formation and moved back to their camp to attack them with his deployed forces? Did this movement actually take place directly in front of the Roman lines?

All the questions that we have brought up to this point can be clarified by one and the same concept. Consequently, they point in common to this solution as to the lost link of the entire sequence, a link that simultaneously fills all the lacunae. That is, we must assume that Narses had an excellent defensive position and was definitely counting on the fact that Totila would necessarily have to attack him in it. For this reason, he had the infantry in the center, consisting of or reinforced by dismounted horsemen; for this reason, his willingness to await the attack; and for this reason, the quiet observation of the equestrian skills of the Gothic king. The latter, however, had for his part intentionally spent the morning with little skirmishes and feints in order to allow his reinforcements to arrive but had held back his main body at such a distance that, in case of an enemy attack, he would still have been able to take up an orderly withdrawal. That would have been practicable, since he was the stronger in cavalry.

> He himself put on another set of armor and had all his men prepare for battle. Then he immediately led his army against the enemy, hoping to take him by surprise and defeat him. But the Romans were in no way unprepared, for Narses, correctly anticipating what actually took place later, had commanded, in order to prevent a surprise attack, that nobody was allowed to cook, to take a midday rest, to remove any piece of his equipment, or to unbridle his horse. Nevertheless, the soldiers did not go entirely without food and drink; they ate in their ranks, without for even one moment taking their eyes from observation of the enemy advance. Furthermore, the battle formation was changed: Narses had his flanks, on each of which 4,000 dismounted archers were stationed, swing into a crescent formation.

It is no doubt possible that Totila hoped that when the main body of the Goths, instead of attacking, moved back into their camp, the Romans would also withdraw from their position. He could hardly have expected, however, that Narses would be so unobservant directly in the face of the enemy as to allow himself to be attacked by surprise. While it is true that this kind of thing has sometimes happened, for example, at Murten in 1476, that incident was not calculated, and there were also special circumstances.

The crescent-shaped swing forward of the Roman archers is probably explained by the fact that they moved forward somewhat on the hills that surrounded the plain. It cannot have been very far, for such an extended horn, too isolated, would have been sacrificed to an attack by the enemy.

All the Gothic infantry was stationed behind the horsemen so that, if the latter should be defeated, the fleeing troops would have had a supporting force behind them and would be able to go back again to the attack together with the infantry.

If the entire Gothic infantry really had no other purpose than to serve as a reserve, it follows that they must have been very weak and that the Gothic army therefore consisted very predominantly of cavalry.

All the Goths had strict orders not to use the bow or any other weapon except the lance in this battle. In this way Totila was defeated by his own lack of wisdom, by throwing his army against the enemy at the beginning of this battle when it was not equal to its opponent in respect to its arms or otherwise — how he came to do this, I do not know. As for the Romans, as each opportunity offered itself in the battle, they used now the bow, now the lance, and now the sword, and in this way were able to profit from every opportunity; they fought partly mounted, partly on foot, at one place surrounding the enemy, at another awaiting his attack and successfully opposing the first shock with their shields. The Gothic cavalry, on the other hand, leaving their infantry far behind them, charged out wildly with blind trust in the weight of their lances, and when they encountered the enemy, they reaped the fruits of their thoughtless charge; for, since they had directed their attack against the middle of the enemy formation, they came completely unsuspectingly directly in the middle between the 8,000 archers, for the latter, as already mentioned, had gradually swung about. Under fire from both sides, they were immediately brought into confusion and lost numerous men and even more horses before they had yet reached the enemy. Roughly received, they finally found themselves in hand-to-hand combat with the foe.

What we hear in this passage about the tactical fundamentals and the weapons of the Roman troops shows that we are in a completely different world from that of the ancient Roman legions. We shall discuss this later. Suffice it to remark here that the losses that the Gothic horsemen suffered at the hands of the enemy archers cannot, after all, have been so very great. The Romans were shooting down from the hills surrounding the battlefield; no archers can have been stationed on the plain itself, for they would have been immediately overrun by the wild charge of the Goths. Although the advantage of shooting down from the heights was very effective, it can still have been principally only the horsemen and steeds on the two flanks of the attacking columns that were dangerously affected. The plain must not have been so very narrow, and arrows are not effective at a very great range. (See Vol. I, p. 89, Note 6.) Not only the Gothic horsemen but also their mounts were armored (Procopius 1. 16), and they dashed by the position of the Roman archers at their greatest speed — to the extent that the heavy equipment permitted, we must add.

In another passage (1. 27), Procopius claims that the Gothic cavalry were not at all familiar with the use of the arrow but used only sword and lance.

> Whether in this battle we should have more admiration for the Romans or their barbarian allies I cannot say, because the spirit and courage they both showed in repelling the enemy attack were really quite equal. It was already becoming dusk when both armies suddenly went into motion, the Goths in flight, the Romans in pursuit. The attack of the Goths had completely failed; they gave way before the press of the Romans and turned tail, staggered by the large number and the excellent order of the Romans.

The Gothic cavalry directed a tightly formed charge against the enemy infantry, which, by all appearance, had some kind of advantages in the terrain, not mentioned by Procopius but which we may conclude from the points mentioned above: namely, that first Narses had his horsemen who fought here dismount, and that second he remained strictly on the defensive. That this battle lasted from midday until evening is no doubt a very strong exaggeration. The reserve that the Goths had was not brought into the battle. They based the battle exclusively on the expectation that the mighty charge of their massed cavalry would break open the Romans' center. When that did not happen, the battle was already decided against them. Such an attack, without support by fresh forces, does not become stronger a second time, but weaker, and it is therefore already decided at the first encounter. Under such circumstances a battle lasting for hours is not conceivable. If the cavalry with its shock action has succeeded in penetrating into the infantry, it then holds the superior position and will no doubt soon disperse the infantry. If they have not penetrated and are themselves also threatened and shot at from both flanks, they can hardly accomplish anything from this purely frontal attack. As Procopius describes the battle as a struggle lasting for hours, we fail to see a real reason why fortune finally favored the Romans. But the description of the battle becomes obvious and clear if we set aside the exaggeration and concentrate on the fact that the "large number and excellent order" of the Romans carried the day and repulsed the attack of the Goths. ("All received the onslaught of the charging enemy and repulsed it most stoutly. It was already about dusk and each army suddenly moved — the Goths in retreat and the Romans in pursuit. The Goths did not resist their enemy rushing headlong at them, but yielded when they attacked and turned to flight, panic-stricken at their mass and battleline."*)

It is not clear whether there took place the flanking attack that Narses planned to make on his left flank from the ravine with the 1,000 horsemen. It was, of course, intended for the Gothic infantry, and they did not participate in the battle. Since this force was held back, it would not be illogical to assume that Narses finally sent his cavalry against the flank of the Gothic horsemen and possibly decided the outcome of the battle by this very action.

They no longer thought of resisting but fled as if they feared ghosts or some higher power was fighting against them. When they got back to their infantrymen shortly thereafter, the panic increased and spread more and more, for they did not move back in an orderly withdrawal, in order to reassemble and reenter the fight or attempt a new attack or something similar, but in such disorder that in their wild dash to the rear they overran men of their own infantry.

For this reason, the infantry did not open up its ranks to let them through, nor did it hold fast and thereby provide them security, but everybody fled with them helter-skelter, and in doing so, as in a night battle, they caused each other many deaths and wounds. The Roman soldiers profited from this panicky fear and mercilessly cut down everyone who was still standing but not daring either to defend himself or to look up. To some extent they even exposed their throats to the knife. And their fear did not subside but if possible even increased. In this butchery 6,000 of them died; many surrendered to the enemy, who first granted them quarter but then later killed them. In addition to the Goths, most of the old Roman soldiers who had previously left the Roman army and, as already mentioned earlier, had gone over to Totila and the Goths, also perished. Those in the Gothic army who had not died or fallen into the hands of the enemy sought to escape by stealth, on foot or horseback, as luck, circumstances, and local conditions permitted.

The tactical action that is to be derived from this account may be expressed as follows. When the Gothic attack was brought to a standstill, Narses ordered his whole line of battle to go over to the attack, drove the enemy horsemen back on their infantry, and finally drove them all to disorderly flight.

The sequence of the battle also gives further testimony that the Gothic infantry must have been very insignificant. It was completely useless. It neither moved forward to support the cavalry nor received and protected the cavalry when it was defeated. Furthermore, the special mission that might have been called for by the structure of the enemy formation — that is, by climbing the encircling hills to attack one of the advanced flanks of the enemy archers and thus affect the result of the whole battle by a success at this point — was not taken up by the Gothic infantry. It may very well be that this was no fully qualified combat unit at all but consisted only of old men, partial invalids, and youngsters, so that the Gothic army in this battle was really formed exclusively of horsemen. It is also not entirely impossible to interpret the account as meaning that the Goths may have had a considerable fighting force of infantry but that it did not enter the battle because the decisive action resulting from the cavalry attack came so quickly. The flood of retreating Gothic horsemen, energetically pursued by the Romans, swept the infantry along with it before the foot soldiers had moved up into the actual battle line.

If this were the case, Procopius' principal error lies in his statement concerning the length of the battle, which, of course, is exaggerated in any case. That the real battle lasted even only a half-hour and in this time the Gothic infantry supposedly did not move up also seems hardly believable. In that case, we would have to conclude that Totila was a very incompetent commander.

Procopius himself explains that he did not have good information concerning the personal fate of Totila. He says that one report had him killed during the flight, while another indicated he was hit by an arrow and fatally wounded in the battle itself and his fall filled the Goths with such terror that, already inferior to the Romans, they had taken flight. We must leave aside the question of whether Totila received his fatal wound in the battle itself or while fleeing. In any case, that cannot have had a direct effect on the outcome of the battle, since, once the hand-to-hand combat has begun, the mass of men can no longer notice the fall of their leader.

Whether the statement that 6,000 Goths were killed is correct we must also pass over; these statements, to be sure, are mostly very exaggerated.

It is clear that the Romans had a great overall numerical superiority; we may estimate their total strength at some 15,000 men.

NOTE FOR CHAPTER II

1. According to the translation by Coste in the *History Writers of the Earliest German Period (Geschichtsschreiber der deutschen Vorzeit)*.

Nissen claims that the name reads not "Taginae" but "Tadinae."

# Chapter III

# The Battle of Mount Vesuvius (553)

Despite their defeat at Taginae, the Goths continued the war under a newly elected king, Teias. For two months the armies stood facing each other, separated only by the small river Dracon (Sarnus), with its steep banks, not far from Mount Vesuvius. Since Narses had previously assembled all of his troops for the battle, we may conclude that it was the Goths who avoided battle and now intended to conduct the war with delaying tactics. They could hope for some incident or other in the Romans' unreliable mercenary army and for the intervention of the Franks. Narses made no attempt to maneuver them directly out of their position, but a treacherous act enabled him to bring under his power the fleet that was bringing provisions to the Goths. If we look at the map, we might believe that the Roman commander had also surrounded the Goths and cut off a possible withdrawal by them. Procopius does not say that expressly, but he does show the Goths, after they had first withdrawn onto Milk Mountain (*mons Lactarius*), preferring death in battle to starvation. As well known as it is and often repeated, I would still like to consider the account of this battle as not useful from a military viewpoint. It reads (4. 35):

Mount Vesuvius rises up in Campania; at its base are brooks with potable water that form a river named Dracon, which flows by Nuceria. At that time, both armies set up their camps on the banks of this river. The Dracon is, to be sure, only a small river, but it is not passable for cavalry and men on foot, since it flows in a deep and narrow bed and its banks are unusually steep. Whether this was caused by the nature of the soil or the force of the water I cannot say. The Goths occupied the bridge leading over the river and had their camp close to it. The bridge was fortified with wooden towers and engines of every type, to include also so-called ballista, so that the Goths could harass their enemies with shots from above. There could be no thought of a hand-to-hand fight, since the river, as already noted, separated the opponents. They just approached the bank as closely as possible and shot at each other. There also occurred a few individual combats, when a Goth would cross the bridge and shout a challenge. In this way, the armies remained facing each other for two months. As long as the Goths were able to control the sea and bring up provisions by ship, they were able to hold out, since their camp was not far from the sea. But the Romans soon took possession of the enemy ships as a result of the treachery of a Goth who had command of the entire fleet, and furthermore countless ships now came for the Romans from Sicily and the other parts of the empire. Narses also had wooden towers erected on the river bank, which necessarily completely discouraged the Goths. Consequently, the Goths, who were already suffering from lack of provisions, became greatly dismayed and moved back onto a nearby mountain that the Romans called in Latin *Mons Lactarius*. Because of the unfavorable terrain, the Romans could not follow them there. But the barbarians were soon to regret having moved back to that position, since they had to suffer much greater shortages than before and had no means at all of obtaining anything for themselves and their horses. Consequently, it seemed better to them to seek death in open battle than to die of hunger.

We ask: Was it then impossible for the Goths to withdraw?

They moved forward unexpectedly and suddenly attacked the enemy. The Romans defended themselves in keeping with the circumstances, that is, not drawn up in ranks and columns, by squadrons or regiments under normal command, but mixed up among themselves, without even being able to hear the commands that were given. Nevertheless, they defended themselves well enough, with all their strength. The Goths had driven their own horses away and all were drawn up on foot, their front facing the enemy, in a deep phalanx. When the Romans saw that, they likewise dismounted and took up the same formation.

Why did the Goths drive away their horses? Procopius gives no reason. But why did the Romans then also dismount from their horses? That the

Goths came on foot could have been for the Romans a double reason for at least part of them to attack from the flank with cavalry.

Everything clears up if we assume that the Goths were surrounded by the Romans with field fortifications. The Goths tried to break through them — consequently on foot — and the Romans likewise defended them on foot.

Now I come to the description of a highly remarkable battle and the heroic courage of a man who was in no respect inferior to any one of the so-called heroes. It is of Teias that I wish to speak. The Goths were spurred on to courage by their desperate situation; the Romans opposed them with all their strength, even though they noticed their despair, since they were ashamed to yield before their weaker opponent. On both sides they violently attacked the nearest enemies, the one side seeking death while the other struggled for the laurels of victory. The battle began early in the morning. Teias stood with a few companions in front of the phalanx, recognizable from afar, protected by his shield and wielding his lance. When the Romans saw him, they believed that when he fell the battle would be immediately ended, and therefore the very bravest men, forming a very large group, moved forward against him in close formation, all of them thrusting and throwing their spears at him. But he caught up all the spears with the shield that covered him and with lightning-like movements he killed many men. Each time that his shield became full of spears, he handed it to one of his weapon bearers and took another. In this way he had fought continuously for a third of the day.

The Goths are supposed to have formed a deep phalanx ("The Goths dismounted from their horses, and at first all on foot formed their front into a deep phalanx."*), and Teias allegedly fought all alone with a few companions in front of this phalanx, holding his own for many hours? That is a poem but not a battle. What then did the entire deep phalanx of Goths do this whole time? Were they afraid to move up? The Romans, however, supposedly were unable to overpower the few men? That is possible in battles such as those fought before the walls of Troy but no longer possible after men had learned how to form phalanxes. Even the strongest and bravest Gothic king with his companions would necessarily have been overcome by an ancient Roman maniple, even if it was composed of nothing but recruits. We must eliminate either the two opposing phalanxes, in the technical sense of the word, or the individual combat by King Teias. The solution might be that when the Goths attempted to break through the Roman lines, the king personally, among others, distinguished himself through his bravery, was killed in the process, and had his death embellished by the legend.

Then it happened that twelve spears were caught in his shield so that he could no longer move freely and could no longer repel the attackers with it. He loudly called for one of his weapon bearers, without giving up his position or yielding even a finger's breadth. Not for a moment did he allow his enemies to advance farther. He neither turned in such a way as to cover his back with his shield nor did he bend to the side, but he stood as if planted in the ground, behind his shield, dealing out death and injury with his right hand and pushing back his opponents with his left — and so he called out loudly the name of his weapon bearer. The latter moved up with the shield, and he immediately took it in place of the one laden with spears. At this moment his chest was exposed for only a second; a spear struck him, and he fell dead to the ground. A few Romans put his head on a pole and showed it to both armies, to the Romans to arouse their zeal even further and to the Goths so that they would give up the battle in despair. But the Goths did nothing of the kind, and they fought on until nightfall, although they knew that their king was dead. When it became dark, the opponents broke away from each other and spent the night under their arms. On the following day they rose up early, took the same formation, and fought again until nightfall. Neither side yielded even a foot, although many died on both sides; they bitterly continued the fearful slaughter, the Goths in the full realization that they were fighting their last battle and the Romans because they refused to be defeated by these opponents. Finally, the barbarians sent a few of their leaders to Narses and had them tell him they felt that God was against them — they had the impression that an invincible power was opposing them — and now, aware of the true situation as a result of the events, they wanted to change their minds and give up the battle, not in order to become subjects of the emperor but to live in freedom among other barbarians. They asked the Romans to grant them a peaceful withdrawal and, giving reasonable consideration to their request, give them for their travel expenses the monies that they had previously saved for themselves in the forts of Italy. Thereupon Narses took the matter under consideration. But Johannes, Vitalian's nephew, persuaded him to grant this request and no longer to fight with men for whom death had no terror and not to put to the test the courage of their despair, which could still prove fatal not only for them but also for their opponents. "The man of wise moderation," he said, "is satisfied with victory, but extreme efforts could easily lead to losses." Narses approved this view, and it was agreed that the remaining barbarians with all their belongings should immediately evacuate the whole of Italy and under no circumstances bear arms against the Romans again. In the meantime, 1,000 Goths broke out of their camp and moved to the city of Ticinum and the villages on the far side of the Po, led among others by Indulf, of whom I have spoken earlier; the remainder all gave their oath to the treaty.

In the same way, the Romans also took Cumae and all the other towns, and thus ended the eighteenth year of this Gothic war that Procopius has described.

So much for Procopius: impressive, but not very satisfying historically. Why and how did the 1,000 Goths separate themselves from the others? How did they move from Vesuvius to Pavia? We may be allowed to assume that at one point a rather large unit of the Goths succeeded in breaking through the ring of the Romans' encirclement and that it was not the whole army but only the larger part of it that finally capitulated.

Agathias starts his historical work in direct continuation of that of Procopius, and he recounts: "When Teias, who followed Totila as chief of the Goths, again took up the war against the Romans with all his force and took position facing Narses, he was struck in the head and himself died in the battle. The remaining Goths, whom the Romans were attacking incessantly, being hard pressed by the continuous attacks and completely surrounded in a position without water, finally made a treaty with Narses, agreeing to occupy their own lands ("They would inhabit their own land without fear."*) and saying that they would willingly be subject to the Roman emperor thenceforth." No historian has yet discovered how to reconcile these two reports.

# Chapter IV

# The Battle on the Casilinus (554)

Of almost less military value than Procopius' description of the battle of Mount Vesuvius is the account given by Agathias of the defeat of the Franks on the Casilinus. From the start even the strategic context is erroneous.

The Franks had already intervened many times in the Gothic-Roman war, with the ulterior motive of thus gaining an advantage for themselves. Now that the Goths were disposed of, there appeared a Frankish army under the two Alamanni dukes, the brothers Buccelin and Lothar. Narses was still busy with the siege and capture of the cities and fortified places occupied by the Goths. It is clear that, on hearing of the invasion by the Franks, he could have done nothing better than to march against them at once, in order to defeat them and drive them back across the Alps. We should not be misled by the fable-like figure given for the strength of the Franks (75,000 men). From the start we can have no doubt that such a supporting army, sent across the high mountains, taken not even from all of the Frankish kingdom but only from a part of it, was considerably weaker than the total of the East Goths in their own country, whom Narses had just conquered. With their morale raised by their victories and the deaths of the two brave Gothic kings, the Roman fighting forces must have been capable of overcoming the Frankish invaders as well, if they had attacked them with their assembled strength.

If Narses had done that and had conquered the Franks, no stronghold in Italy would have offered him any further resistance. Instead, he sent against the new enemy only a part of his army, under the Herulian Fulcaris, with orders, according to Agathias, to hold up the enemy and attack him only if there were good chances of success. This error was atoned for seriously: Fulcaris was defeated, and since he did not dare face Narses again after his defeat, he himself sought death in the battle. Agathias places the blame for the defeat on the carelessness and foolhardiness of the Herulian, but if it is correct, as he goes on to say, that Narses himself from the start regarded the enemy as being of superior strength, then the real guilt obviously lies with the commander. One explanation might be that Narses, on the contrary, underestimated the strength of the Franks and that the statement that he had cautioned Fulcaris to be careful was a later addition intended to absolve the overall commander himself, because he sent out an insufficient force.

Despite Fulcaris' defeat, Narses continued the siege of Lucca with which he was occupied, but when he finally captured the city, he took no further action than to divide up his troops in winter quarters in various cities. If we can imagine Caesar in this situation, we cannot doubt that he would even then have assembled his troops from all sides and gone directly after the Franks with the largest possible numerical superiority. But according to Agathias, Narses, considering that it was winter and believing that the Franks were especially competent in the cold season to which they were accustomed in their homeland, divided up his troops in various cities in winter quarters and sat patiently by, with the Roman troops secure behind the walls of their cities, while the Franks moved through all of Italy to the Strait of Messina and plundered the land most fearfully. Indeed, the Franks did not even consider it necessary to keep their forces assembled but divided them into two armies. Many of the Goths, feeling new courage, joined them.

We can hardly believe that Narses would expose to this misery the empire that was entrusted to him, without having pressing reasons therefor. If the Franks were particularly suited for the conduct of war in winter, the Roman troops, after all, were likewise composed of Germans.

Perhaps a clue to the true sequence of events is that a few units, when called on to move forward, pointed out that they had not received their pay. But this leads us only to a mere surmise. Suffice it to say that it was not until spring, when the Franks were returning from the southern part of the peninsula, that the army that Narses had assembled in the meantime blocked their way along the Casilinus (Volturno) River near Capua. According to Agathias, Narses had 18,000 men; although it was only half of their army, the Franks are said to have had 30,000 men — a number that naturally deserves no credence at all.

Immediately before the deployment for the battle, a conflict over a disciplinary matter arose between the commander and the contingent of Herulians under Sindual, as a result of which this unit refused to participate. But when Narses cried out before the army that whoever wanted to participate in the victory should follow him and then marched forward, the Herulians, after all, considered it shameful to remain behind, since that could be interpreted as cowardice on their part, and so they reported that they would come. Narses sent them the reply that he could not wait for them, but he would leave a place open for them in the battle formation.

Agathias recounts the battle itself as follows:

When Narses had reached the place where he planned to fight, he immediately drew up his army in a phalanx, placing on both flanks the cavalry with javelins and round shields, their bows and swords slung on, and a few also with long lances. The commander himself was on the right flank and with him was Zandalas, chief of his household, with that portion of the household servants that was capable of combat. On the two flanks were stationed Valerian and Artabanus, who had orders to keep themselves concealed in the edge of the forest so that they could charge the enemy unexpectedly when he attacked and could take him from two sides. The entire space in the center was occupied by the infantry. At the front of the line were stationed the forward fighters, covered in iron from head to toe, forming a protective wall, and behind them the other ranks were drawn up in close formation all the way to the rear. The light infantry and slingers moved about behind them and waited for an opportunity to make use of their long-range projectiles. A place was assigned in the middle of the phalanx for the Herulians, and it was still empty, for they had not yet marched up. Two Herulians who had deserted to the enemy a short time previously, since they knew nothing of Sindual's later decision, urged the barbarians to attack the Romans as quickly as possible, "for you will find them in complete disorder and confusion," they said, "because the Herulian regiment is obstinately refusing to take part in the battle, and the others are very much shaken by their failure to do so." In the hope that this assertion would prove to be correct, Buccelin was easily persuaded and led his army forward. Eager for combat, they all rushed toward the Romans, not at a steady pace and well ordered, but as if they could not move forward fast enough, ready and aggressive, as if they intended to throw the enemy army back on its

heels in their first assault. Their battle formation had the form of a
wedge, so that it resembled a Greek delta: out in front, where it
came to a point, the shields were pushed tightly together like a roof
so that it looked like a boar's head. The flanks were formed in echelons of sections and platoons and sloped very sharply so that they
gradually spread out to a greater width, and an empty space was
created in the middle, and one could see the bare backs of the soldiers in their ranks. That is, they had divergent fronts so that they
were placed facing the enemy toward both sides and could fight
covered by their shields, while this very type of formation was supposed to provide automatically for protection from the rear.

Everything went according to the desires of Narses, who was
favored both by fortune and by his ability to take the necessary
measures in an outstanding manner. For when the barbarians, with
their fearful shouting, clashed with the Romans in the first assault,
they broke through the middle of the forward fighters and came
into the empty space into which the Herulians had not yet moved.
The point of their wedge cut through the ranks all the way to the
rear, without causing any great loss; a few men even went on farther, as if they intended to storm the Roman camp. Then Narses
gradually bent and extended his flanks, so that they reached
around toward the front, and he ordered the mounted archers on
both flanks to shoot at the rear of the enemy. That was done without difficulty, for since the enemy was fighting on foot, it was an
easy task for the mounted men to shoot from a distance at the
extended lines, which could not defend themselves from the rear.
And it seems to me that it was very simple for the horsemen on the
flank to shoot over the men who were close in front of them into the
backs of the ranks on the opposite side. In this manner, the backs of
the Franks were assailed from all sides, since the Romans on the
right flank shot at one of the inner sides of the wedge, while those
on the left flank covered the other. And so the arrows flew from all
sides and hit everything that was in the middle without the barbarians' knowing where the missiles were actually coming from or
being able to defend themselves against them. For, since they stood
with their front against the Romans and were looking only in this
one direction, were fighting with the heavily armored men directly
in front of them, and could hardly see the mounted archers farther
back, and finally were being shot not in the chest but in the back,
they had no idea where their wounds were coming from. Further-

more, most of them had no time at all to think about this, because almost every shot was fatal. For since it was always the ones in the last rank who fell, the unprotected backs of the next rank became visible, and because this happened very often, their total mass melted away fast. In the meantime, Sindual and the Herulians had arrived and moved against those who had broken through the middle and had gone farther forward. The Herulians attacked immediately; but the Franks were considerably shaken, believed they had fallen into an ambush, and turned in flight, accusing the two deserters of treason. Sindual and his men, however, did not let up, but they pushed forward until their opponents were either cut down or thrown into the swirling stream. So when the Herulians had thus taken their place and the empty space was filled, forming a closed phalanx, the Franks, as if caught in a net, were slaughtered. Their battle formation was completely broken up, and they pulled together into individual little groups that did not know which way to turn.

The Romans struck them down not only with their arrows, but now the heavy infantry and the lightly armed troops also attacked, with spears, rods, and swords. The cavalry completely outflanked them, attacked them in the rear, and cut off every possible line of retreat. Anybody who escaped the sword found himself forced by the pursuit to jump into the river and be drowned. From all sides there rang out the wails of the barbarians, who were being slaughtered in the most miserable way. Their leader Buccelin and his entire army were wiped from the face of the earth, and in the process the imperial deserters also died. None of the Germans saw their home and hearth again, with the exception of five men, who in some way or other had escaped the general disaster. How can it not be said that the Germans suffered here the punishment for their misdeeds and that a higher power had conquered them? That whole great mass of Franks and Alamanni and whatever others had marched with them into the war — all were destroyed; on the Roman side only eighty men had fallen, those who had to withstand the enemy's first shock. In this battle almost all the Roman regiments fought with distinction. And of the allied barbarians the most outstanding were the Goth Aligern, for he too participated in the fight, and the Herulian colonel Sindual, who was outdone by no one. But everybody praised and admired Narses, who had won such great fame through his skillful leadership.

So much for Agathias. I cannot suppress the suspicion that this entire account is a free fantasy, developed from the single expression "boar's head."

Obviously, Narses was numerically greatly stronger, especially in cavalry; his battle line overreached that of the Franks on both flanks. Whether both of the most extreme flanks were initially hidden by the forest is of little consequence. The Franks risked the battle on their ability to overrun the enemy center with their boar's head, their strong and deep infantry column, and break through, thereby bringing the decision in the battle.

If this column had been pointed, the point would have been immediately surrounded; if it had also been quite hollow, it would have had no pressure from the rear (see pp. 41 and 49 of this volume concerning the Germanic wedge). Although, in other words, it certainly did not have the two weaknesses that Agathias attributes to it, of being both pointed and hollow — it still did not penetrate. It may be that the contingent of Herulians, arriving at the last moment, reinforced the Romans' wavering center and brought the drive of the Franks to a standstill.

At the moment that happened, the Roman cavalry, armed with javelins and bows, had dashed out against the two flanks of the assault columns and worked them over with their missiles, and probably quite soon also from the rear. We are reminded of the battle of Cannae.

The idea that the cavalry kept shooting in a high arch over the flank of the enemy formation that was closest to them and into the backs of the troops on the other wing we can reduce to the fact that in the attack from all sides many Franks were naturally hit in the back. With a hollow wedge such as that described by Agathias, the Roman marksmen, since they could not move up quite close to the enemy directly in front of them, were necessarily several hundred paces distant from the opposite wing of the enemy wedge and consequently could not have exerted any effect with arrows and javelins.

If anyone is inclined to take offense at my skepticism over a source description, I request he give me a reason why he is willing to lend more credence to this description by Agathias than to the accounts of Cannae and Zama (Naraggara) by Appian.

# Chapter V

# Strategy

When Justinian ascended to the throne in 527, the entire west was alienated from the empire, some of it already for more than a century, the rest for a half-century. Justinian won back Africa and Italy and came close to subjugating Spain again as well. Large portions of Italy still remained under Byzantium for centuries thereafter. The sudden development of the power of the east seems all the more surprising and all the greater when we remember what accomplishments of a cultural type, the *corpus juris* and the Church of Saint Sophia, adorned this very regime.

Justinian's wars, in three varied theaters of operations — Mesopotamia, Africa, and Italy — offer a greatly varying appearance: against the Persians, a pushing back and forth without any great or final decisive result; the Vandals defeated in a single blow, simply by an advance guard; against the East Goths an eighteen-year war with the most extreme shifts of fortune; and a final complete victory of the Byzantians in a great battle.

Previously, the victories of Belisarius and Narses were incomprehensible, since scholars knew of the small size of the armies they commanded and still believed in the mighty masses of the Vandals and Goths. Taking their figures from the Byzantine historian, they wrote that Vitiges was supposed to have besieged Belisarius in Rome with 150,000 men. What were these same Goths doing, where had they stayed, when Vitiges surrendered two years later to Belisarius, who did not have as many as 25,000 men when he surrounded Vitiges in Ravenna?

Now that we have clarified the strengths of the Vandal and Gothic armies, it appears less miraculous that the Vandals hardly dared to enter battle against an army of 15,000 men than that the Goths could have held out for so long against 25,000.

Here again, as always, it is politics that determines the conduct of war and also prescribes the directions of strategy.

When Belisarius crossed the sea to conquer Italy, he first landed in Sicily (end of 535) with only a quite small army. He then captured Naples, Rome and Spoleto without having waged an open battle. It was only then that the Goths appeared with a large army, surrounded him in Rome, and besieged him there for an entire year. From a purely military viewpoint, this action could not be explained: if the Goths were so strong as to be able to besiege the enemy army, there must have been some special reason why they did not oppose him earlier and prevent the loss of the large cities.

It is true that Justinian was also threatening the Goths in Dalmatia with other troops at the same time, and from the other side an attack by the Franks seemed imminent, but that is still not a satisfactory explanation for the complete inactivity of the Goths during a whole year.

Justinian risked sending Belisarius to Italy with such a small army because the East Gothic kingdom was severely shaken internally. King Theodahat, who was first only coregent, had seized power for himself by having Amalasuntha, Theodoric's daughter, murdered. The Byzantians appeared as the avengers of a legitimate heiress to the throne, and Theodahat was not even a warrior type who would have accepted battle bravely and energetically. Not until the Goths had gotten rid of him, to avoid going down to defeat with him, and had established Vitiges as elected king following his selection by the army in accordance with the ancient custom, and he had strengthened his position by marrying a daughter of Amalasuntha, did they appear in the field. Then the insignificant resources of the Byzantians immediately became apparent as Belisarius with his army was besieged in Rome.

But, as we know, the Goths were not very numerous either and were not capable of besieging a city like Rome. Belisarius held his own, and when it was realized in Constantinople that the Goths possessed more national fighting strength than the Vandals, reinforcements were sent. These appeared in the rear of the Goths besieging Rome, and, with the consent of the inhabitants, they took the fortified cities that lay behind them. This obliged Vitiges not only to lift the siege of Rome but also finally to withdraw to Ravenna, since he did not feel capable of dealing with the united forces of the Romans in the open field.

The situation suddenly reversed itself: this time, without there having been an open battle, Vitiges was encircled and besieged in Ravenna by Belisarius.

In Ravenna, after the amazing incident of Belisarius' having been offered the crown himself, Vitiges finally surrendered. Belisarius took him to Constantinople, as he had done only a few years earlier with the Vandal king, Gelimer. It seemed that after a four years' struggle, but without any real battle, the Goths were finally subjected to the Byzantians.

Soon, however, a turnabout occurred. The Goths rebelled again, elected another king, and within a short time, under Totila, they again captured all of Italy and Sicily and even established a fleet. For a number of years Totila reigned in the full brilliance of success. It was not until the Greek fleet had defeated the Goths and Justinian sent Narses over with a significant army in the eighteenth year of the war that the decisive battle of Taginae took place, in 552. This battle was followed by two encounters in the next year, the one at Mount Vesuvius, where Totila's successor, Teias, was defeated, and the other on the Casilinus, where the Franks under Buccelin were beaten.

During this period, Rome had changed hands five times: Belisarius had taken the city in 536, Totila in 546, Belisarius again in 547, Totila in 549, and Narses in 552.

Consequently, we see that the events of the first phase of the war, namely, great successes and shifts of fortune without a tactical decision, were repeated throughout the whole war. Not until the very end did there occur what had naturally been expected at the start of the war: the attempt, with the maximum possible assembly of one's own forces, to attack the enemy and defeat and destroy him — the battle.

The reason is that the internal weakness of the Gothic kingdom was matched by that of the Byzantians. Justinian, by making peace with the Persians, had no doubt been able for a moment to launch a considerable force first against Africa and then against Italy, but only for a brief moment. In comparison with the size of the countries and cities that were being fought over, the forces on both sides remained small.

The surprising restoration of the Gothic power under Totila was made possible by the fact that a large number of the Roman mercenaries, dissatisfied with the regime and especially the pay of the Byzantians, deserted to the Goths. In the same manner, the Italian cities, which had initially welcomed the Byzantians, had soon become disillusioned with the new administration and its tax demands and had found that under a Gothic king their life was no worse, and perhaps even better.

The strategy of the Gothic war was therefore determined by the fact that on both sides only very small forces were available in comparison with the broad region that was being disputed. The Goths were able to occupy the numerous fortified Italian cities either not at all or only in a very insufficient way. The inhabitants maintained a position that was not so much a neutral one but rather, having little love for either side, they shifted easily from one to the other under the alternating pressures, or at least did not oppose the transfers.

When Vitiges moved up against Belisarius, the latter felt himself so much weaker that he was not willing to accept open battle but preferred to be besieged in Rome. Ten thousand reinforcements — it was probably about this number — were sufficient to reverse the situation. Consequently, the war was conducted and decided simply by sieges and capitulations of cities.

Then when Totila came into power, he leveled the walls of the cities that he captured. Other rulers act in the opposite way and seek to secure the possession of their countries by building fortifications.

A modern scholar has stated the belief:[1] "The entire great superior force of the Gothic national army was smashed against the walls of Rome; that accounts for their hate for all city walls, which they everywhere demolished." But Totila acted in no way from simple hate; rather, he was a strategist who knew what he was doing. The Vandal Gaiseric, when he captured Africa, had razed the walls of the cities. These Germanic kings did not have enough troops to occupy satisfactorily all the cities of their broad territory; the inhabitants were not to be trusted, and by opening the gates to enemy troops, they caused the cities to become strong points for the enemy.

The modern period has shown us on one occasion a quite similar situation. That is, when the Allies arrived at the Rhine in the fall of 1813, Gneisenau urged that they continue the advance without delay and not let themselves be frightened off by the famous triple belt of fortifications in France. He pointed out that these numerous fortifications now could only work to Napoleon's disadvantage because he no longer had enough troops. If he should occupy them, he would have no army left in the open field; if he should withdraw his garrisons, the fortresses would promptly fall into the hands of the Allies. If it had been possible for Napoleon quickly to destroy a large part of his fortifications and reinforce his field army with their garrisons, that would have been a strategic advantage for him at that particular moment. When we see that Totila did that, we recognize in him a commmander of strategic insight.

The Gothic war therefore dragged back and forth as long as political factors were dominant. By this I mean political factors in the broader sense: not simply the partisanship of the inhabitants of Italy but also the inability of the Byzantine administration to exact obedience from its own mercenaries. The war was decided when Justinian for the second time sent over a truly significant force and, on the Gothic side, the destruction of the fortifications had brought things to the point that they believed they had made available and assembled sufficient forces for the open battle. This decisive battle went against the Goths, and with it their defeat was sealed.

Justinian's mighty military successes were not based so much on an unheard-of development of new forces but rather on a fortunate and clever organization of the existing ones, which were small enough in comparison with the great expanse and the material resources of the empire and accomplished so much only because the opposing side was even weaker. In the midst of all the great victories, it happened once that a band of Huns and again a band of Slavs crossed the Danube and swept through the Balkan Peninsula as far as Greece, plundering and murdering. The empire did not have the troops to defeat them.

A special condition of the successes in the west was the fact that in the meantime the empire was enjoying peace in the east. Before Belisarius went to Africa, peace was made with the Persians. The Germans, too, were well aware of this situation, and King Vitiges, in his dire situation, sought to push the Persian king, Chosroes, to attack again. With the greatest sacrifices, especially payments of money, Justinian was obliged to pacify the Persians again before he could send Narses with enough troops for the last decisive blow against the Goths. The entire army, however, that could be assembled even after such limitations in the other area, was, to repeat once again, still no stronger than 25,000 men.

Justinian was confident of being able to defeat the Vandals and the Goths, who were encamped in their territory only as a thin and narrow layer of foreign warriors. From the very start, no such objective could have been considered against the Persians. The Persians also had mercenary troops just like the Romans, especially Huns, and the Roman mercenaries indeed deserted to them quite often. Nevertheless, their nucleus was a nation occupying its own soil, and that formed their strength. This situation, then, called for a completely different strategy.

In the history of warfare, we have already often encountered situations that cause the opponents to be less interested in mutual destruction than in simple attrition, even by directly avoiding large-scale decisive actions. Pericles first did this in the greatest style in the Peloponnesian War, and later Fabius Cunctator did likewise. Extensively argued and carried to an extreme of one-sidedness that is even in contradiction to the nature of warfare, Procopius now shows us this kind of strategy developed in a speech by Belisarius (*bell. Pers.* 1.18).

The Roman commander is speaking to his soldiers when they press him to attack the enemy, who is already retreating, and to do battle with him:

> Where are you rushing, Romans, or what passion has so inflamed you that you want to expose yourselves to unnecessary danger? Men consider as a true victory only that one in which one suffers no loss from the enemy. This advantage is now offered you by fortune and the terror that has overcome the army of our enemies. Is it not better to enjoy the advantages at hand than to seek far more distant ones? The Persians, driven on by great expectations, had undertaken a campaign against the Romans; now, with all their hopes shattered, they have taken to their heels.
>
> If we force them against their will to give up the idea of their retreat and to enter battle with us, even if we carry the victory, we shall have from it absolutely no further advantage. For what does it matter if one defeats a fleeing man? But if we should perhaps have the worse of it, we would deprive ourselves of the victory we now have; we would see it not so much snatched away by the enemy but would rather be trifling it away ourselves and necessarily exposing to the enemy for further plundering the land of the emperor without defenders. This too deserves to be considered by you, that God stands by men in emergencies but not in self-sought dangers. Furthermore, it happens that men who have no escape show themselves involuntarily very brave, whereas with us there are many circumstances that are unfavorable for a fight. For most of us have marched here on foot, and all of us have empty stomachs. I hardly need to add that quite a number have not yet even arrived.

In consonance with this speech, Procopius also shows Belisarius restricting the pursuit of the beaten Persians after his victory at Daras (*bell. Pers.* 1. 14), since the victory was sufficient for him, and the Persians, driven to the extreme, might turn about and throw back the unwary pursuers. ("They feared lest the Persians in flight would, if cornered, turn on them in their senseless pursuit, and they thought it sufficient to preserve their victory intact."*) In the same manner, the contemporary anonymous theoretician warns against completely encircling the enemy, even when one is twice as strong as he is, since, seeing every avenue of flight shut off, he might rise to new heights of bravery.[2] About a half century later, Emperor Mauricius, who mounted the throne as a great victorious commander, advises in his *Art of War (Kriegskunst)* avoiding open battle wherever possible, even when the prospects are good, and preferably wearing down the enemy by small actions.[3] Procopius (1. 17) also has Belisarius' Persian opponents stating the same principle. Alamundarus, a Saracen prince, speaks to the Persian king as follows: "In war one should not rely on luck and chance, even if one is very much stronger than the enemy, but should preferably seek to lie in wait for the enemy by means of ruses and stratagems. He who moves directly toward danger is not at all sure of victory." ("Men without perpetual confidence in their success do not begin a war with battle immediately, even if they should boast that they excel the enemy in every respect. Rather, they take pains to circumvent the enemy with deceit and strategems, for there is danger from their opponent. Victory does not travel a steady course."* )

We shall meet these viewpoints again. They played a large and sometimes fateful role from the sixteenth to the eighteenth century and into the nineteenth, and they will still occupy our attention to a large degree. Certain it is that neither Alexander nor Hannibal nor Caesar waged war according to these principles. None of these commanders believed that a victory that one won against men who were already fleeing was no real victory; none of them believed that he had to be primarily concerned about suffering no losses himself. Alexander did not restrain his men when they were pursuing the Persians but drove them on and on until their horses fell from exhaustion. Hannibal based his battles on the complete encirclement of the Romans. Caesar was victorious by cutting off the withdrawal of Vercingetorix in Alesia, as he did to Afranius and Petreius at Ilerda; after he was victorious at Pharsalus, he did not let up until he had forced the entire enemy army to capitulate. The highest principle of these commanders was: defeat and destruction of the enemy, even if with Hannibal this principle was limited to the tactical decision and could not be extended to the strategic operation with the ultimate purpose of deciding the war.

Whether Belisarius always acted so completely in an opposite way to these great conquerors, according to the principles developed above, remains a question that cannot be answered so quickly. The bases of the strategy that aims at the destruction of the enemy are clear and easy to formulate in their simplicity. But the principles of the strategy of attrition contain a polarity that cannot be resolved with a simple formula.

Even Frederick the Great, who took great pains in this area, did not arrive at a completely clear and comprehensive theoretical expression of his concept. For this reason, we cannot judge Belisarius strictly on what Procopius has him say or what is offered by other theoreticians of his period. His actions are not reported to us surely enough in their motives and their details to allow us to draw completely reliable conclusions. Belisarius' fame rests on his success against the Vandals and the East Goths; he defeated and subjugated those two warlike peoples and took their kings, Gelimer and Vitiges, as prisoners to Constantinople. In neither war did the events ever result in a large battle, but no conclusion concerning Belisarius' strategy is to be drawn from this; it was precisely the Vandals and the Goths who prevented such a battle. It was not until Totila accepted battle that Narses finally waged the battle of annihilation against the East Goths.

Procopius says that Belisarius fought two real battles against the Persians. The first time, in 530, the Persians wanted to prevent the construction of the fortress Daras, north of Nisibis in Mesopotamia, where the mountainous terrain blends into the plain. Belisarius received their attack in a well-prepared defensive position and repelled them with heavy losses, but neglected to pursue them (*bell. Pers.* 1. 14). If his victory was as great as Procopius describes it, the failure to pursue would undoubtedly have been a grave error; a pursuit across the Mesopotamian plain would necessarily have produced the greatest possible results. But it is perhaps to be doubted whether the battle was so important and whether it was not a question simply of an extended skirmish; according to Procopius, the Persians were twice as strong as the Romans, 50,000 against 25,000. Procopius states later (1. 16. 1) that the Persians did not even give up their position near Daras and could not be prevented from making raids into the Roman territories in the north (Armenia) and the south (Syria).

The incursion into Syria led to the second battle, at Kallinikon (Nicephorium), on the Euphrates. Belisarius followed the withdrawing enemy army without intending to attack it, but he was pushed into doing so by his excited troops and was beaten.

From these events we must conclude that the Persians in this theater of operations enjoyed a quite considerable superiority, either qualitative or numerical, so that the Romans never had a chance for a lasting, large-scale success. These kinds of politico-military counterbalancing relationships are the native soil on which the ideas of the strategy of attrition grow.

NOTES FOR CHAPTER V

1. Dahn, *Procop von Cäsarea,* p. 412.

2. Köchly and Rüstow, *Griechische Kriegsschriftsteller* 2: 2, 167. Chapter **XXXIV**, p. 4.

3. Jähns, *Geschichte der Kriegswissenschaften* 1: 155. See Vol. IV, pp. 194, 207.

# BOOK IV

## The Transition to the Middle Ages

# Chapter I

# The Military Organization in the Romanic-Germanic Nations

The Germanic peoples moved into the Roman provinces as armies and not as farmers looking for land. As holders of the power, they created new political arrangements and established new political organizations in which they themselves represented the armed power. Their warriorhood was based on the strength of their warlike nature, which they brought with them from their barbarian origins, on the cohesiveness of the clans, and on the savage personal courage of the individual.

In rightful recognition and estimation of these military values, for a time attempts were made here and there to retain the valuable treasure of this warriorhood by intentionally keeping the Germanic and the Romanic separated from one another instead of having them blend quickly together, by isolating the Germanic and seeking to preserve it from the poison of the Romanic and its civilization. When the Romans became aware for the first time of the danger that threatened them from these barbarians; when the Goths and the Franks swept through the empire by land or sea, and the legions no longer had the power to drive them back and to protect the interior regions; and when it was seen that the only help that still existed against the barbarians had to be sought among the barbarians themselves, in the second half of the third century, then the Romans sought to draw as closely as possible to them those barbarians whose services were needed. Emperor Gallienus himself married a German, Pipara; Emperor Aurelian made it possible for his officers to marry Germans. Constantine the Great began to confer the high honors of the republic, even the consulate, on Germans, an act for which he was later reproached by his nephew and successor, Julian. Under Julian's successor, Valentinian, however, we find an effort in the opposite direction: marriage between Romans and Germans was specifically forbidden (in the year 365).[1]

When the West Goth Ataulf founded his kingdom, he himself married the daughter of the Roman emperor, Placidia. But his successor forbade his people to marry Romans, and this prohibition lasted for almost a century and a half.[2] The practical feasibility of carrying out such a separation within the same nation was facilitated everywhere by the fact that the Romans and Germans, even after the Germans were Christianized, formed separate ecclesiastic communities; all of the Germanic tribes, with the exception of the Franks, became Arians. Particularly the East Goth Theodoric seems to have specifically bent his efforts toward keeping his people as the warrior class within the Roman sphere; the Goths continued to live on foreign soil according to their own law; no Goth was allowed to hold a civilian office and no Roman was allowed to be a soldier.[3] When Theodoric's daughter Amalasuntha wanted to have her son Athalaric educated, the Goths remonstrated with her, saying: she was not raising the young king correctly, for reading and writing were something different from bravery; anyone who learned to fear the schoolmaster's rod would become no warrior; Theodoric had never had Gothic boys go to school and he himself had won a great kingdom without understanding anything of reading and writing.[4]

The idea that the German was a soldier, a professional warrior, was maintained with the utmost strictness. In Theodoric's kingdom, only the Goth had a military obligation, but this was absolute for him. A document on this subject has come down to us showing how a veteran with honorable service who could no longer bear arms had to submit a special request for release from military service, and his request was approved by royal order only after a long and detailed investigation of the reasons for his being excused. The annual present that the king regularly gave his warriors from the tax receipts would not be given to this man who was no longer militarily qualified.[5]

As we have already seen above, the West Goths, probably during the period when they were living in Thrace after their victory at Adrianople (378-395), refined their military organization following the Roman pattern.[6] A number of Hundreds were formed into a Thousand under a *millenarius* or *thiuphadus* (tribal leader), and they were subdivided below into Tens under a *decanus*. When they settled on both sides of the Pyrenees, all or many of the Thousands were divided and Five-

Hundreds were created. The numerically based military organization, however, was now intermingled with and gradually pushed aside by the geographic-political, the division into provinces with *duces* at their head and counties, headed by *comites*.

A people that now no longer lived together in close proximity but was spread afar over the land could no longer be so easily assembled for military service. Severe punishments were threatened for those who were slow to obey. In order to be able to feed the army, grain depots were established; anyone who did not receive his rightful share could complain, and the responsible officials then had to reimburse him fourfold.

At the same time, in addition to the general people's army there developed another warrior group which we meet in the Book of Laws of King Euric (466 to 484), a son of that King Theodoric who was killed in the battle of the Catalaunian Fields.

We have seen how the mercenary system in the Roman Empire had led to a condottiere system: the generals were the leaders of bands that were in their personal service. This kind of private soldiers, as they were also called, had the name *buccellarii*, a word that supposedly derives from *buccella*, meaning "biscuit" or a "bit," and therefore actually "bread men" — apparently, initially a nickname which, as is so often the case, lost this special flavor and became part of general speech usage. This word and meaning we find now in Euric's law. Scholars have identified the *buccellarii* with the German retainers and have also seen them as an expression of the penetration of the German system into the Roman. Greek authors sometimes use the expression *paides* (boys), which an alert observer has recognized as a translation of the German word *Degen*. For this word has nothing to do with the weapon *Degen* (sword), but is related either to the stem of *gedeihen* (to thrive) or, in keeping with a more recent concept, with the stem of the Greek word *teknon* (child), and therefore means in any case the "ones who have just grown up" or "young fellows." There is undoubtedly here a certain relationship of this form with the ancient system of retainers, but it is still only a distant one. The Germanic retainer in the ancient real sense was personally much closer to his master; he was his table companion, he increased in prestige with his master, and in cases where the master became king, he became a prominent person. The extension of the group of military followers, which moved downward, results in the common soldier (*Kriegsknecht*), who assumes mercenary service and with whom the real concept of the retainer, the personal friendly relationship to the master, disappears.

Nevertheless, we may certainly say that wherever we find *buccellarii* in the service of Germanic leaders, they still enjoyed some reflection of the highly esteemed concept of the personal obligation of loyalty of the retainer to his master. Euric's law prescribes that the *buccellarius*, as a free man, had the right to choose another master, but in this case he was obliged to give back whatever he had received from his previous lord. It was reported of Theudes, who long administered the West Gothic kingdom as viceroy and later (531) made himself king, that he had no fewer than 2,000 men in his retinue.[7] These 2,000 men were, of course, mostly Goths. We may estimate the total number of Germans in the West Gothic kingdom at certainly no more than 20,000 warriors. Consequently, if a single one of them had 2,000 men in his service, we can see the important position assumed by this form of military service.

In the Goths' later Book of Laws, the word *buccellarius* is no longer used, but the concept was expressed by *"in patrocinio constitutus"* ("placed in patronage").[8] The lack of a truly technical expression for a phenomenon referred to with such a definite circumlocution points to what is also confirmed by the events — that is, that a significant development in this direction did not take place among the West Goths.

The sharp separation between Germans and Romans resulted in a simple and smoothly functioning military organization among all the Arian tribes. We can probably imagine the conditions as quite similar among the East and West Goths, the Vandals, and the Burgundians. But the conditions among the Franks were different from the start. No division of the lands ever took place there, and no attempt was made to retain the military strength by a continuing separation between the two elements of the population. The Franks did not become Arians but entered directly into the Catholic Church. The question then is whether perhaps the Frankish kings, by considering their Germanic and Romanic subjects from the start as one group, also placed their military organization and their military obligation on a broader base.

Passages in our sources show that the Frankish king was authorized to require military service of all his subjects. This has been interpreted to mean that, contrary to the situation in the other countries, in the Frankish kingdom a general military service was actually required of all freemen and those who were half free. This interpretation is proof of the extent to which pure book learning can lead even truly great scholars astray. The individual burgher and farmer who was supposed to be stationed for months in the field at a great distance and at his own expense; armies of many hundreds of thousands, even if only parts of the kingdom were supposed to be levied and only one man from each square kilometer; finally, these masses unaccustomed to warfare for many centuries and in every respect unfit for military service — in considering these points, we are reminded of the armies of millions of men of Xerxes and Darius Codomannus, which so many philologists still cannot tear from their hearts. The concept of the mass levy and the general military obligation is attenuated to some extent if we consider that only the landowners were obligated. If we eliminate .the tenants, there would remain very few for the Romanic areas; but if we include them, which has to be necessary because of the division of the burden between the Romanic and Germanic areas, we may make the following calculations. Let us assume that for a campaign across the Pyrenees the areas south of the Seine were levied, with the provision that every three farms should provide one warrior. The area covers some 152,000 square miles; on every 22 square miles we estimate as an average, since large forests and mountains must be removed from our calculations, only three to six villages with a total of ninety farms. Each of these areas provided thirty warriors, and so the levy amounted to about 210,000 men; and if we estimate one man for every square kilometer, the result is a full 400,000. As many as this in a partial levy! Since, however, in "very special cases" the entire country was supposed to be levied for a campaign,[9] and the half-free and other dependent persons were also supposed to be included as lightly armed troops,[10] we could certainly not arrive at a number less than one million.

Clearly, we must look for a completely different basis. Military service in the form of the general obligation of subjects to their lords had no other significance in the Frankish kingdom than with the Romans: here, too, it never completely disappeared. Even Emperor Valentinian III once levied his subjects against the Vandals with urgent edicts, and Roman citizens helped Belisarius in the defense of Rome. As the Romans did here, so too the Germanic kings probably also on occasion levied the otherwise unwarlike inhabitants of a region. For instance, it is reported how the Burgundian King Gundobad in a war with the West Goths, probably in 507, had a fort in the Limousin razed by the Romans, that is, by a levied militia from the nearby Burgundian border region.[11]

Totila did the same thing once by calling up, for a task that he thought did not require Goths, farmers from the neighboring region and assigning only a very few Goths to serve with them.[12]

Nevertheless, the real army was composed of the warrior class of quality soldiers, and this could not have been any different with the Franks either.

The Frankish kingdom was composed of Germanic and Romanic areas. Let us look first at the Romanic regions. Here there immediately occurs to us the question as to what conclusions are to be drawn from the fact that the Franks, unlike the more southerly tribes, did not participate in a division of lands with the Romans.

The settling of the Burgundians, Goths, and Vandals has been explained by us in this way, that the private individuals were given farmhouses in small groups but that the truly decisive factor was the placing of the Germanic leaders and most prominent men in the class of the Roman large-estate owners. As a result of this new characteristic, the Germanic lesser nobility and counts were now in a position to provide their tribal and military colleagues with the indispensable economic support, either through a continuing effect of the ancient clan grouping or by taking these colleagues directly into their service. Even without a division of the lands, it could have been a quite similar situation with the Franks. Clovis did not find it necessary to undertake a land apportionment, since the majority of his people did not migrate at all but remained in place. He only needed to give each count a certain number of warriors whom the count, in view of their rather small number, was easily able to settle on the lands, castles, and farms formerly belonging to the emperor or otherwise public or confiscated properties.

Therefore, the real difference between the Frankish settlement and those of the other peoples lies in the fact that with the Frankish settlement there was not such a strong Germanic large-estate owner class created at first, the settling was considerably thinner, and the ancient clan unit lost its importance even faster. The warrior group that lived in each county as a kind of fraternity under the command of the count consisted principally of Franks, who, as professional warriors, did not cease to cultivate the military qualities of a physical and spiritual nature. It was not impossible, however, for Romanics, too, to be admitted into this fraternity.[13] The warrior spirit had not so completely died out among these Celtic peoples as to prevent the appearance time and again of individuals possessing the natural characteristics of warriors and heroes.[14] All in all, none of the Romanized territories was capable any longer of opposing the invasion of a Germanic tribe of a few thousand men, but this does not mean that there was a lack of brave men. The Germanic kings appointed as counts over the districts of their kingdom not only their own compatriots but also prominent Romanics who had entered their service.[15]

The Germanic warriors had no objection to serving under their command; they were, after all, long accustomed to fight under Roman leadership. Nor was it impossible that the count, whether he be German or Romanic, would take Romanics among his warriors, if their conduct assured their colleagues that they were as capable as the others in bravery and ability to control their steeds and use their weapons.[16] Not isolated in camps or barracks and not living in the constant constraint of military discipline but rather in the middle of civilian life, the Germans who were settled on the lands became a Germanic-Romanic warrior class. Even serfs moved into this class in increasing numbers.[17] A serving man of whose personal bravery and usefulness the count had become convinced was to this extent still more valuable to him than a freeman, namely, that this serf was completely dependent on his will and could never leave him. Once he was accepted among the warriors, if he possessed the other essential qualities, he became completely imbued with the spirit of his class.[18]

In the case of the Franks, we do not have direct and fully reliable testimony that free men-of-war in any number had a position of personal dependence, as did the *buccellarii* among the West Goths. Nevertheless, as we shall see below, we can adduce proof that this was actually the case, although at first the monarchy was still so strong here that this private relationship did not take hold politically and legally.

The military system of the Merovingian kingdom was based on the king's calling up the men of the warrior class through his officials, according to need and under threat of being outlawed. When our sources use the word *leudes*, people, they are referring to this warrior class;[19] with the same meaning we also find the expression *fideles*, the loyal ones. Even the king's court and the officials were included under these meanings, and by extension this also no doubt applied at times to the entire people. Especially in the purely Germanic areas of the Frankish kingdom, the class distinction between warriors and the rest of the people naturally became noticeable only very gradually.

We have found that in the Frankish kingdom of the Merovingians, just as in the Gothic kingdom of Theodoric, there existed a class of professional warriors who were obligated to obey the king's call to arms. Nevertheless, there is a large difference; in Italy, these professional warriors were the Goths, who lived completely to themselves, without intermarriage with the Romans; here there was no doubt as to who was a warrior and who was not. In the Frankish kingdom, this applied neither to the Romanic nor the Germanic part. In the former area, there were also Romans who belonged to the warrior class; in the latter area, the levy can have applied to only a small portion of the entire male population. The warrior class, which derives from nature in the East Gothic kingdom, is therefore only conceivable in the Frankish kingdom in conjunction with the official power of the counts appointed by the king to govern the counties. In the Romanic area, the count also accepted Romans as warriors if they seemed to him to be capable; in the Germanic area, he limited the levy to the number that he could provide for or that he believed to be necessary.

It has been very difficult for modern scholarship to recognize the character of the Merovingian military system. At one moment it seemed that there were retinues, at another a truly applied general military obligation, then an obligation for all who owned estates, and then one applying only to those possessing royal grants. This difficulty lies in the circumstances of the Frankish warrior class, which are so uncertain from the social, political, and administrative viewpoints. One of our foremost scholars, Paul Roth, once pointed out that in our principal source, the extensive chronicler of the Merovingian period, Gregory of Tours, the expression *leudes* appears only three times. He concludes that if this were the technical expression for a warrior class, it would necessarily have appeared much more frequently in the works of such an author. This observation is as psychologically fine as it is correct. But as we see, the word *leudes* was not a technical expression in the strict sense of the word. There was a warrior class but still there was no sharply defined word for it. That is no contradiction, since the class itself was not sharply defined. On the one hand, it merged with the class of officials and the court and on the other, with armed serving men, and finally, in the purely Germanic areas, with the totality of freemen.

Historical scholarship sometimes appears to move in circles. There was a time when scholars refused to believe in the migration of whole peoples but regarded the bands that took possession of the Roman provinces as large retinues of individual warlords. The sources proved that concept to be erroneous. It was really the entire peoples who moved out, abandoned their ancient homeland, and sought a new one. But now by determining how small these populations were and realizing that the idea of migrating millions was legendary, we have introduced a picture that is objectively again more similar to the former concept, although not so from the political and legal viewpoints.

The *leudes*, the warrior class in the Frankish kingdom, were also regarded as retainers. And again it was pointed out that this legal form was inappropriate; the levy for war was a call by the king on his subjects and not on retainers, possessors of royal lands, or estate owners. But the

subjects to whom the levy was actually directed were a narrowly limited class of warriors insofar as their number was concerned, a group that could be considered quite similar to a large retinue.

And so scholarship has moved not in a circle but in a spiral. While turning back closer to the old point of view, the more recent work has in the meantime led it upward and therefore above the former idea.

## EXCURSUS

BUCCELLARII

The translation of the word *paides* (boys) in Agathias 3. 16 and Malalas by *Degen* stems from Seeck, "The Germanic Retainer System on Roman Soil" ("Das deutsche Gefolgschaftswesen auf römischem Boden") in the *Zeitschrift der Savigny-Stiftung* (1896): 109, and Pauly, *Real-Enzyclopädie*, under *buccellarius*. But Seeck goes somewhat too far in equating retainers and mercenaries, although he correctly points out that even the ancient retinue system already had various classes. See Brunner, *Deutsche Rechtsgeschichte* 2: 262.

The first mention appears under "Honorius" in Olympiodorus, p. 7.

Emperor Leo prohibited them; *codex Justinians* 9. 12. 10: "omnibus per civitates et agros habendi buccellarios vel Isauros armatosque servos licentiam volumus esse praeclusam." ("We desire that the freedom of having private retainers, Isaurians, and armed slaves be forbidden to all throughout the cities and lands.")

According to Zeumer, *Leges Visigothorum antiquiores*, p. 13, the title in the *codex Eurici* reads:

Si quis buccellario arma dederit vel aliquid donaverit, si in patroni manserit obsequio, apud ipsum quae sunt donata permaneant. Si vero alium sibi patronum elegerit, habeat licentiam, cui se voluerit commendare, quoniam ingenuus homo non potest prohiberi, quia in sua potestate consistit; sed reddat omnia patrono, quem deseruit. Similis et de circa filios patroni vel buccellarii forma servetur: ut, si ipsi quis eorum obsequi voluerit, donata possideat. Si vero patroni filios vel nepotes crediderint reiinquendos, reddant universa, quae parentibus eorum a patrono donata sunt. Et quidquid buccellarius sub patrono adquesierit, medietas ex omnibus in patroni vel filiorum eius potestate consistat; aliam mediaetatem buccellarius, qui

If anyone gives arms to a *buccellarius* or grants him something, and if he remains in allegiance to his patron, that which was given would remain in his possession. If in truth he selects another patron for himself, he would have the freedom to commit himself to anyone he wished, since a free man cannot be restrained because he is under his own power. But he should return everything to the patron he left. A similar procedure should be observed in regard to the sons of a patron or a *buccellarius*. If the son wanted to pledge allegiance, he would get possession of his donations. If in truth they believe that they ought to leave the service of the patron's sons or grandsons, they would return everything that was given to their parents

adquaesivit, obtineat; et si filiam reliquirit, ipsam in patroni potestate manere iubemus; sic tamen, ut ipse patronus aequalem ei provideat, qui eam sibi possit in matrimonium sociare. Quod si ipsa sibi contra voluntatem patroni alium forte elegit, quidquid patri eius a patrono fuerit donatum vel a parentibus patroni, omnia patrono vel heredibus eius restituat.

by the patron. And whatever a *buccellarius* acquires under a patron, half of it would be under the control of the patron or his sons. The *buccellarius* who acquired it would possess the other half. And if he leaves behind a daughter, we decree that she remain under the control of the patron. Nevertheless, we also decree thus that the patron should provide for her a man of equal status, who can marry her. But if she perhaps chooses for herself another man against the wish of the patron, she should restore to the patron or his heirs whatever was given to her father by the patron or by the parents of the patron.

Among the Burgundians I have not found direct mention of *buccellarii* or anything similar, but it might be appropriate to quote the following passage here. In *Passio S. Sigismundi* the king says: "qualem se . . . suis optimatibus praebuerit . . . lectio succedens docebit." ("The following text will demonstrate . . . what sort of man he proved to be . . . to the nobles.") Jahn, in *History of the Burgundians (Geschichte der Burgunder)* 1: 101, note, sees the fulfillment of this proclamation in the sentence: "patriae exercituique suo videbatur esse sollicitus" ("He seemed concerned for his fatherland and his army"). According to him, *exercitus* is the retinue of the *optimates*. If Jahn's interpretation is correct, which I would like to believe, we have here an institution corresponding to the *buccellarii*.

This is also supported by the fact that we find Arian bishops mentioned in the cities and Arian tombstones have been found. Kaufmann, from whose study in the *Researches in German History (Forschungen zur deutschen Geschichte)* 10: 383 I take these facts, has interpreted them as meaning that the Germans had lived in the cities as citizen farmers. This they most certainly did not do; they did not even have an inclination to become farmers and still less to become burghers. But they lived for the most part in the cities as retainers and serving men of the counts.

GENERAL MILITARY OBLIGATION. *LEUDES*

The interpretation by Waitz that the military obligation in the Frankish kingdom had a land-based character and was related to ownership of real property is refuted by Roth in the two works *History of the System of Benefits (Geschichte des Benefizialwesens)* (1850) and *The Feudal System and the Organization of Retainers (Feudalität und Untertanenverband)* (1863). See Brunner, *Deutsche Rechtsgeschichte* 2: 203, and Richard Schröder, *Manual of German Legal History (Lehrbuch der Deutschen Rechtsge-*

*schichte).* p. 151. But Roth's concept, which has also been accepted by later researchers, that the general obligation was not only considered as a theoretical right but was also used in a practical way, is, for the military and statistical reasons given above, not tenable. In his *Benefizialwesen*, pp. 200 and 202, Roth actually goes so far as to state that at least in the case of the kings' internal quarrels themselves, "the general levy was used not only from a legal viewpoint but also in fact." If we estimate as the area of a king referred to here 65,000 square miles and only four or five service-qualified men to each square mile, that would already give armies of 300,000 men, and if there were seven militarily qualified men, a number that might correspond more closely to the actual situation, a total of 450,000 men. But if we now reduce the actual levy so much as to arrive at numbers that are conceivably possible, a levy of landowners or other well-to-do people without any military training still remains a military impossibility. Since the disciplined units of a standing army were missing, militarily it is absolutely necessary, above all in the Romanic areas, to assume the existence of a class of warriors in which the military qualities were developed and fostered. This assumption is then not only reconcilable with the sources but, as soon as one has found the correct interpretation, is also to be read directly from them.

Gregory of Tours tells us, 5. 27 and 7. 42, how members of his church were punished because they did not obey the command to move out. 5. 27 reads:

Chilpericus de pauperibus et junioribus ecclesiae vel basilicae bannos jussit exigi pro eo quod in exercito non ambulassent. Non enim erat consuetudo, ut hi ullam exsolverent publicam functionem.

Chilpericus ordered that bans be enforced against the poor and the young men of the church and the basilica because they had not marched in his army. In fact, it was not the custom that they should perform any public duty.

7.42 reads:

edictum a judicibus datum, ut qui in hac expeditione tardi fuerant, damnarentur. Biturigum quoque comes misit pueros suos, ut in domo S. Martini, quae in hoc termino sita est, hujusmodi homines spoliare deberent. Sed agens domus illius resistere fortiter coepit, dicens: S. Martini homines ii sunt; nihil quicquam inferatis injuriae; quia non habuerunt consuetudinem, in talibus causis abire. At illi dixerunt: Nihil nobis et Martino tuo, quem semper in causis inaniter profers, sed et tu et ipsi pretia dissolvetis, pro eo quod regis imperium neglexistis. Et haec dicens ingressus est atrium domus.

A decree was issued by the judges that whoever had been reluctant to join in this campaign should be punished. The Count of Bituriges sent his "boys" with orders that they should plunder men guilty of such an offense in the house of St. Martin, which was located in this district. But the manager of that house began to resist stoutly with the words: "These are men of Saint Martin. You should do them no harm because they are not accustomed to go on campaign." The others replied: "That is nothing to us or to your St. Martin, whom you always bring up vainly in such cases. You and the

others will pay the price because you
disregarded the king's command."
With these words one of them
entered the courtyard of the house.

From these two passages Roth has concluded, p. 186, that there was a general
military obligation. The levy cannot have been the result of a special service obligation of the churches. This is contradicted by the wording; furthermore, such a
service obligation of the churches is not reconcilable with the sources. It is also
not a question of the exceptional case of a general levy against an invasion, for
the levy is concerned with a war of aggression against the Britons. Consequently,
we have here, Roth concludes, the general military obligation of all free men,
without regard to nationality, "for who would claim to see only Franks or even
*leudes* in the *pauperes ecclesiae* (poor of the church)?" As long as one imagined among the *leudes* either retainers or estate owners, that was not possible,
but as we have now characterized the *leudes*, nothing more stands in the way of
this interpretation. It is to be presumed from the start that the church of Tours
had taken into its service for its own protection a number of Franks armed with
battle-axes. But in the opinion of the king and his count this service did not
relieve them of their levy responsiblity, and they were to be called up. In no way
does the concept of the *leudes* call for their being property owners, and even the
church of Tours, while presumably promising and giving its private warriors
good pay and rations, had given them no property. The chronicler of Saint Martin could therefore very well refer to them as *pauperes* (the poor) and may also
be correct in saying that it was already no longer the "custom" to call them up
for foreign wars.
   Waitz, in *Deutsche Verfassungsgeschichte* 2: 527, cites other passages
from Gregory, from which it can be seen that the author understands by
*pauperes* only people of a low class, but in no way those receiving alms. In one
account, Gregory 10. 9, they are even shown to have horses.

MILITARY SERVICE OF THE SERFS *(LITI)*
   According to Roth, *Geschichte des Benefizialwesens* p. 406, Waitz,
*Deutsche Verfassungsgeschichte* 4: 454, and Brunner, *Deutsche
Rechtsgeschichte* 1: 239 (2d edition, p. 356), even the *liti* had a military obligation in Saxony. Nevertheless, the sources cited in support of this do not prove
it. The information in the *Vita Lebuini (Life of Lebuinus)* that the *liti* were
also represented in the territorial assembly is rightly considered by Brunner as
fictitious. The privilege of Corvey that forbade the counts to levy *(in hostem
ire compellunt*: They compel them to join the army) for campaigns the freemen
as well as the *liti* of the monastery *(homines tam liberos quam et lutos qui
super terram ejusdem monasterii consistunt:* free men as well as the *liti*
who are on the land of the same monastery) does not prove that the *liti* were levied as warriors; they may have been called up as wagoners for the train.

*BEATUS AVITUS* (SAINT AVITUS)
   One of the important differences between the Frankish nation and the other
Germanic-Romanic states is that in the former the two national elements never
remained so sharply separated as in the latter and that, while there did exist a

warrior class in the Frankish kingdom as in the other countries, nevertheless this class was not so exclusively limited to the governing Germanic people but also included Romanics. Among the East Goths and the Vandals, it is clear and beyond any doubt that only they and not the Romans living in their area were considered as militarily qualified and obligated to bear arms. Among the West Goths, we must distinguish between the various periods. When the kingdom was established and during its early generations, the situation can hardly have been different from that among the related peoples. In the seventh century, the sharp distinction between the races no longer existed. To the question as to when and how soon this transition took place, we have as evidence the life of a certain Saint Avitus that has been reproduced in the *AA. SS. Bolland.*, 17. June, 2d edition, Vol. IV, p. 292 (*Beatus Avitus, Eremita in Sarlatensi apud Petrocovios dioecesi:* Saint Avitus, Hermit in the diocese of Sarlatensis among the Petrocovii). It reads as follows: (See Appendix 2 for Latin text.)

Saint Avitus, coming from a notable family tree sprouting its roots to the depths, produced in good time ripe fruit far and wide with his odoriferous sweetness. Of high origin from birth, he flourished in the manner of a curial family from the seed and status of princes. In the village of Linocasium of the province Petragorica his auspicious birth took place. It is said that scarcely past weaning he had to begin his education under parental pressure. Thus, after he had crossed the finish line of boyhood in first place, now as an adolescent with youthful flower, he reached the forked road of Pythagorean literature in which lies the border between two life-styles. In a wise selection he chose the right branch, preferring to be forced into the detachment of this life, rather than by living for public acclaim and by pursuing the course of pleasure, only to be condemned in the final judgement.

At this time Alaric, the common enemy of Christianity, held the rule of the Goths. With the tyrannical rage of a cruel mind and the brutality of animal savagery, he waxed proud in the power of the kingdom he had acquired, and he was accustomed to conquer his neighbors on all sides with the arm of his own strength. Aroused by his confidence in the expectation of gain, Alaric decided to enter the kingdom of the Franks (obviously to attack them). He saw that his persistent desire, as it is the case for the powerful, was strengthened by the common practices of his whole kingdom, and through his agents the weighty mass of his people was smelted into the unitary body of his army. All of military rank and powerful in strength would receive the king's reward, the willing as well as the unwilling, and were summoned by heralds with the urging of public opinion.

Thus, Saint Avitus, a most energetic athlete of God and already in possession of a triumph in the gymnasium of philosophy, was ordered against his will to secular military service by virtue of his rather large wealth and the equestrian rank of his family. As if he were another Martin about to receive a military reward, he was named among the others as one who would fight against the enemy army of the Franks. Avitus was not an inattentive listener of that passage of the Gospel where it is commanded: "Therefore render to Caesar the things which are Caesar's, and to God the things which are God's." On the outside he was girded with a swordbelt and enshrouded in secular arms. On the inside, in truth, secretly performing the service of Christ, he gave his assent to the earthly king with the intent of being his soldier.

The battle in which Avitus was taken prisoner was Vouglé, in 507. If we could trust our source unconditionally, then the West Goths at that time already had a warrior class that also included prominent Romanics. The text of this life story, however, stems from a much later period, so that, even if it is based on older accounts, we cannot trust the details of the ideas we meet here. Nevertheless, the fact remains that the young Avitus, although an educated, prominent Roman, took to the field and became a prisoner. It is questionable whether we can conclude much from this. It is not impossible, however, that by that time, among the West Goths as with the Franks, prominent Romans, by entering the service of the Germanic king, were already moving into the warrior class that was obligated to obey the king's call to arms. But it is also possible that the pious author invented the obligation that forced Avitus to take up his sword and that the young man willingly volunteered and was accepted by the king or a count in his retinue. This possiblity is particularly supported by the pay that he received. It is not to be assumed that King Alaric II really paid his army. Either this point was also added by the author or the reference is to the gift that the lord made to his retainers.

Consequently, we can conclude with certainty from this account only the fact that at the beginning of the sixth century there were at least individual Romans serving in the West Gothic kingdom.

FROM THE *LEX VISIGOTHORUM* (LAWS OF THE VISIGOTHS)

The provisions of the *lex Visigothorum*, concerning the military organization (which Oldenburg, basing his text on the research by Zeumer, attributes to King Euric [466-484], *M. Germ. LL. I*, tome 1 [quarto]), read as follows (IX, Title 2, 1-4): (See Appendix 3 for the Latin text.)

### I. Old Law

If the commanders of an army are bribed and permit a man to return home from a campaign, or do not compel him to leave his home.

If a *thiufadus* (*millenarius*) is bribed by a man from his own unit (*thiufa*) to permit him to return home, he would render to the count of the city in whose district he was stationed what he had accepted ninefold. And if he receives no bribe from that man, but thus sends him home while he is healthy, or does not force him to leave his house for the army, he would pay 20 solidi; a *quingentenarius* in fact would pay 15; and a *centenarius* 10. If, of course, he is a *decanus*, he would be compelled to pay 5 solidi. The solidi should be divided among the unit (*centena*), where they are enrolled.

## II. Old Law

If the conscription officers of the army venture to carry off anything from their houses, while they draft the army for military service.

If servants of the lord, i.e., conscription officers of the army, when they draft the Goths to go into the army, take or venture to carry off anything from their property without their consent, whether they are at home or absent, and it is possible to prove this before a judge, they would not delay to restore it to him from whom they took it elevenfold. So, however, it is also laid down, that each of these should receive fifty lashes publicly in the marketplace.

## III. Old Law

If the commanders of an army after deserting the theater of war should return home or should permit others to return.

If a *centenarius*, abandoning his unit (*centena*) in the army, deserts to his home, he will be executed. But if he flees to a holy altar or perchance to a bishop, he would pay 300 solidi to the count of the city in whose district he was stationed, and would not fear for his life. Nevertheless, the count of the city should inform the king, and so by our order those solidi should be divided among the unit (*centena*) which had been assigned to him. Afterwards, however, the *centenarius* should in no case be placed in command again, but he should be one of the *decani*. If a *centenarius* without the knowledge and consent of the army commander or the *thiufadus* (*millenarius*) is persuaded through a bribe by someone, or is asked and permits him to return home from his unit (*centena*), or relieves him from going on campaign, he would be compelled to pay as much as he had accepted from him ninefold to the count of the city in whose district he was stationed. Just as we stated above, the count of the city should not delay to make a report to us, so that by our command the sum may be divided among those in whose unit (*centena*) he had been assigned. But if the *centenarius* receives no bribe from him and thus dismisses him to go home, that *centenarius*, just as it has been recounted above, would pay to the count of the city 10 solidi.

## IV. Old Law

If the commanders of an army either should return home after deserting the campaign or should scarcely compel others to join the army.

If a *decanus* deserting his unit (*decania*) flees the army for his home, or is unwilling to leave his home and to set out on campaign when he was healthy, he would pay 10 solidi to the count of the city. But if he perchance gives a bribe to someone, he would pay 5 solidi to the count of the city in whose district he was stationed. The count should make a report to us so that by our command the solidi may be divided among the men in whose unit (*centena*) he had been assigned. But if anyone who had been enrolled in his unit (*thiufa*) deserts the army for his home without the permission of his *thiufadus, quingentenarius, centenarius,* or *decanus,* or is unwilling to set out from his home on campaign, he would receive 100 lashes in the public marketplace and would pay 10 solidi.

(*The following Section V certainly dates from Leovigild (568-586), and Section VI probably does also.*)


## V. Old Law

If the conscription officers of the army permit someone in good health to stay at home after receiving a bribe.

If anyone perchance ransoms himself from the servants of the lord who draft men to go on campaign, he would be compelled to pay ninefold as much as he receives from him to the count of the city, and those whom he asks not to force him to go on campaign while he was healthy, and who release him from service, even if they receive no bribe from him, would pay to the count of the city in the stead of the man exempted 5 solidi. In fact, the *thiufadus* should inquire through his *centenarii,* and the *centenarii* through the *decani,* and if they are able to find out whether through personal plea or bribe they deserted to their home or were unwilling to set out from home on campaign, then the *thiufadus* should inform the count's commander and he should write to the count of the city in whose district he was stationed, so that he may not delay to render the punishment which has been laid down in law concerning those men, who in their own behalf request exemption from military service or who ransom themselves, and to discharge completely all fines collected to the *thiufadi,* the *centenarii,* the *decani,* or the servants of the lord. But if he exacts the fine, conceals it, and does not report it, he would pay all which he exacted ninefold; and if, bribed or asked to take a bribe, he hesitates to exact the fine, he would pay double the amount of the fine from his own purse to those who had been about to divide this payment mutually. But if after exactment of the fine he does not report to the king so that he may give the order to divide this sum in the unit (*thiufa*) to which it was owed, or the count of the city should pretend that he perchance does not hand over the fine, he would not delay to pay the sum to them elevenfold.


## VI. Old Law

Concerning the men who receive rations for distribution and venture to defraud.

We determine the following to be the proper procedure: that whoever has been appointed as the collector of rations throughout all the cities and castles, whether count of the city or dispenser of rations, should order that the produce which he is going to give to them be furnished in a fresh condition, and he should not delay to deliver it to them undiminished. But if it happens that the count of the city or the *annonarius* through his own negligence should defraud the payment of their rations (not in possession of them or perhaps unwilling to distribute them), they would register a complaint with the count of the army that the managers were unwilling to hand over to them their rations. And then that commander of the army should not delay to send his man to us so that the time might be calculated from which the rations were not paid to them according to normal practice. Then the count of the city or the *annonarius* should restore to them without his consent four times the amount from his own means for as long a time as he had withheld their usual rations. In a similar way, we order that this procedure be observed concerning the men who have been enrolled in a *thiufa*.

NOTES FOR CHAPTER I

1. Although the law of Valentinian I is contained in the *Codex Theodosianus* 4. 14, Heinrich Richter has sought to interpret away this content in his work, *Das weströmische Reich,* p. 681, Note 150. But his interpretation, considering among the *barbara conjux* (barbarian wife) and the *gentiles* (foreigners) only barbarians outside the border of the Roman Empire, is juridically untenable. That Valentinian himself gave Merobaudes a Roman as his wife, and Theodosius gave Fravitta the Goth and the Vandal Stilicho his own nieces were exceptions such as the most powerful people sometimes make for themselves.

2. According to Zeumer, "History of the West Gothic Laws" ("Geschichte der westgotischen Gesetzgebung"), in the *Neues Archiv für ältere deutsche Geschichtskunde* 24: 574, Leovigild (569-586) legally permitted the *connubium* (intermarriage) between Goths and Romans; but he says that, in fact, the prohibition had already been violated and disregarded many times previously.

3. Mommsen, *Ostgotische Studien* 497: "As only the Goth can be a soldier in Theodoric's state, so too can he alone be an officer. The exclusion of Romans from the military offices counterbalances the exclusion of the Goths from positions as civil magistrates."

4. Procopius, *bell. Goth.* 1. 2.

5. Dahn, *Könige* 3: 5: 36.

6. In this third edition, this paragraph has been reworked on the basis of the study by Eugen Oldenburg, *The Military Organization of the West Goths (Die Kriegsverfassung der Westgoten),* Berlin dissertation, 1909.

7. Procopius, *bell. Goth.* 1. 12.

8. The *Codex Eurici*, Chapter 310, uses the expression *buccellarius* four times; the corresponding *Antiqua* 5. 3. 1 uses the circumlocutions *"quem in patrocinio habuerit"* ("whom he had in patronage") and *"in patrocinio constitutus"* ("placed in patronage").

9. Waitz 2: 531. 3d edition, 2: 1: 215.

10. Waitz 2: 528. 3d edition, 2: 1: 213.

11. Binding, *History of the Burgundian-Romanic Kingdom (Geschichte des burgundisch-romanischen Königreichs)* 1: 196, Note 671.

12. Procopius 3. 22.

13. Brunner, *Deutsche Rechtsgeschichte* 1: 302, argues that the Romans were already referred to as subjects in the oldest existing version of the *Lex Salica* but still did not form any part of the army. This text is from the time of Clovis. Under Clovis' sons, however, in later texts and a supplement, note is taken of the fact that Romans can also be in the army.

14. Roth, *Benefizialwesen*, p. 172, has assembled examples of military accomplishments by Gallo-Romans. But when he concludes from this that, contrary to the effeminate Italians, the Gallo-Romanic population can still be generally designated as warlike, that is concluding too much. Roth especially praises the Aquitanians. Why is this particular group supposed to have been especially brave? The preference for the one area shows us the error of the whole concept: these are no more than individual events preserved by chance, which have given a false picture. Quite similar things may have happened in Italy without, as a matter of chance, being described. The refining process of civilization and the inevitably accompanying softening had affected the population of Gaul in the course of four and a half centuries no less than it had the Italians.

15. Proven by Roth with numerous examples, p. 173.

16. Roth, *Benefizialwesen*, p. 180.

17. Gregory 4. 47 and elsewhere. Waitz 2: 533.

18. The Burgundians, too, already had other than free men as warriors. The *Lex Gundobada*, Title X, reads: "Si quis servum natione barbarum occiderit lectum ministerialem sive expeditionalem, sexagenos solidos inferat, multae autem nomine XII.

Si alium servum Romanum sive barbarum aratorem aut porcarium XXX sol. solvat."

("If anyone should have killed a barbarian slave selected for service at court or for military service, he would pay 60 solidi, and 12, moreover, as a fine.)

("If anyone should have killed another slave, Roman or barbarian, farmer or swine-herd, he would pay 30 solidi.")

In this case, then, we have the barbarian military serving man (*Kriegsknecht*); the common servant (*Knecht*) can also be a Roman, but this is not possible for the military serving man.

19. Fredegar, Chapter 56, says: "universos leudes, quos regebat in Auster jubet in exercitu promovere." ("He ordered all the men (*leudes*) whom he ruled in Auster to join the Army.") Chapter 87 says: "jussu Sigiberti omnes leudes Austrasiorum in exercitu gradiendum banniti sunt." ("By order of Sigibert, all the men (*leudes*) of the Austrasians were summoned to go on campaign.") The statistical reckoning that we made above will explain sufficiently that "men" in general cannot be meant by these *leudes*; the word *universi* necessitates a very limited meaning. It shows that the mass of the entire people cannot be intended, since that would lead to huge numbers, but some kind of limited group must be meant. See Vol. III, pp. 22, 33, 534, the decree by Charles the Bold of 3 May 1471 and the proclamations of Emperor Maximilian, where all men were always called up but always only a small selection was intended (as cited by Meynert in *Geschichte des Kriegswesens* 2: 27 ff.).

# Chapter II

# Changes in Tactics

Up to this point we have observed that in all periods of world military history national military systems and tactics are always most closely interrelated.

The hoplite phalanx developed in a different direction under the Macedonian kings than in the Roman republic of aristocratic officials, and the latter moved to the cohort tactics only in close relationship with constitutional changes. On the other hand, in keeping with their nature, the Germanic Hundreds fought in a different manner than the Roman cohorts.

Was it possible for these Germans to retain the combat methods they had developed amongst the primeval forests when all their living conditions of an economic, social, and cultural nature were now completely changed? Or what kinds of new forms developed here?

The ancient Germans are extolled as competent in both the combat arms, infantry and cavalry; among one people the latter might be more outstanding, whereas with another the former enjoyed greater fame. Ariovistus was strong because of his "double-fighters," a mixture of infantry with mounted men. In the critical year of his battles in Gaul, the seventh, Caesar reinforced his troops with Germanic horsemen whom he took into his pay, and with their help he conquered Vercingetorix. The same horsemen played an important part in his victory at Pharsalus and no doubt also in the other decisive battles of the civil war. When in 213, under Emperor Caracalla, the Alamanni come to our attention for the first time, they are famous as a people who know how to fight wonderfully well on horseback (*"gentem populosam, ex equo mirifice pugnantem"*: "a populous nation fighting marvelously on horseback");[1] indeed, in the battle of Strasbourg they were victorious with their cavalry. In like manner, it was the cavalry that brought about the decision in favor of the Germans at Adrianople. The Spaniard Isidorus, who lived under the hegemony of West Goths, reported of them that, although good infantrymen, they were particularly competent in the use of the javelin in mounted combat. Vegetius praised the horses of the Burgundians and the Thuringians as full of stamina (*"injuriae tolerantes"*).[2] Procopius says flatly of the Vandals that they had not learned to fight on foot but were exclusively cavalry. ("They were neither javelin-men nor archers, and they did not know how to enter battle as infantry. Rather, they were all horsemen and used thrusting spears for the most part, and swords."*)[3] From the prisoners taken from this people, Justinian formed five regiments of cavalry ("He established five *katalogoi.*'") and sent them to eastern garrisons.[4] Even 200 years earlier, they were also mentioned by another Greek author, Dexippus (around 270), as a people consisting predominantly of horsemen.[5] And we have seen that the East Goths fought preferably as cavalry, not with bow and arrow but with sword and lance; not only the men themselves but also their horses were armored.[6]

The Franks were also outstanding as horsemen. As far back as Plutarch (*Life of Othos*, Chapter 12) and Dio Cassius (55. 24), these authors say of an important group of the later Franks, the Batavians, that they were especially good cavalry ("the best horsemen of the Germans,*" "They are most excellent at riding horses*"). The *Notitia dignitatum* names the Batavians and the Franks as cavalry; an *ala* of Canninefates, likewise a group of the later Franks, is attested to in inscriptions,[7] and in the writings of Gregory of Tours, they often appear as mounted men.[8] But when they invaded Italy during the Gothic War (539 and 552), they were mostly on foot; only the king's life guard was mounted.[9]

We have found as a characteristic peculiarity of the Byzantine armies of this period that they did not really have combat branches; infantry and cavalry, cutting and thrusting weapons, and bows were all mixed together. The armored horsemen also carried a bow, and they fought on foot as well. In other words, the real warrior was the man on horseback; an actual infantry no longer existed.

Archers on foot form an arm that cannot hold its own against horsemen when isolated and in the open field. When covered by their own cavalry or using fortifications or terrain obstacles, however, foot archers can accomplish very much, even against cavalry. At that time, first of all in the writings of Urbicius,[10] there arose the idea, which we shall meet in practical use in a later period, of protecting the archers against the shock action of cavalry by means of portable obstacles, "Spanish riders," but archers always remained only a supporting arm, and the horseman was valued more highly.

In the case of the infantryman with a close-combat weapon, it is not a question simply of the courage and skill of the individual but primarily of the tactical unit of which he is a part. With the horseman and the marksman, the tactical unit no doubt also plays its role, but the warrior has individual significance in addition to the unit. The infantryman with his close-combat weapon, in situations where he is not a member of a larger unit of an effective tactical body, can have only little value. Aristotle already knew that in his day when he wrote in his *Politics* (4. 13): "Without a tactical formation the heavy infantry is unusable, and since in ancient times they did not yet have this insight and skill, the power remained with the cavalry." Frederick the Great, using quite similar words, said in his *Reflections on Tactics (Réflexions sur la tactique)* of the year 1758,[11] "that the infantry is only strong as long as it is massed and in good order; that, as soon as its formation becomes loose and breaks up, a weak unit of cavalry falling on them at this moment of disorder would be sufficient to destroy them" ("que l'infanterie n'a de force que tant qu'elle est tassée et en ordre, et que lorsqu'elle est séparée et presque éparpillée, un faible corps de cavalerie qui tombe sur elle dans ce moment de dérangement, suffirait pour la détruire").[12] The Roman legions were closely formed infantry of this type, and we do not find that they ever allowed themselves to be ridden down by cavalry.

In Justinian's armies, we no longer find close-formed tactical units of infantry of this type with close-combat weapons. The infantry we encounter are archers or dismounted horsemen, or men who mount on horseback as soon as they have a horse. The center against which the Gothic cavalry charged in the battle of Taginae was apparently based on some kind of terrain obstacle, which was also perhaps artificially strengthened.

Belisarius once said to his men that the Persian infantry was formed of poor farmers who were brought along to undermine walls, to plunder the dead, and to serve the soldiers.[13] The situation was no doubt not quite as bad as this, and the Roman infantry may have enjoyed a somewhat higher status. But in general the armies of Justinian and Chosroes were very similar, and the judgment concerning the Persian infantry still gives a certain reflection of the reputation of the branches with the Romans as well.

The military power of the ancient Germans, as we have previously been convinced, was based not only on the savage courage of the individual but just as much on the cohesion of the clan under its *hunno*. Grouped in a massive wedge or boar's head, the German infantry launched its attack. As little as we may seek among the Germans the concept of real military discipline, nevertheless the natural cohesiveness of the clans gave them the same thing that was provided by discipline among the civilized peoples, the tactical unit, the singleness of will in a large group of warriors. This organization disappeared with their settling among the Romans and was lost forever.

From the start, the peoples who were settled in their new kingdoms were divided into two groups. One group consisted of men who left their old clan unit and entered the direct service of either the king or one of his counts. They were quartered right at the court or nearby and were fed there, in some cases having no family and in others having a small piece of land assigned to them with their family. The other group lived on in the clan units, presumably now very diminished in size. The first group was no doubt principally in the cities, while the second was in the country, either with a leader who had become a large estate owner as a result of the property division, or even without such a leader. The clans, which formerly were seldom smaller than a hundred men strong and often counted several hundred, were now broken up into individual groups much smaller in size, which no longer had a way of life in common and could no longer develop a unified spirit.[14] The men at the court and at the direct disposal of the count had found there a new focal point of a completely different kind. Even the relationship to their leader of the groups that were still living in the country with their clans had become completely different. The old *hunno* had lived with and among his compatriots and had developed a natural authority in this communal life. The new estate owner became an aristocrat whose way of life differed more and more from that of his common fellow countryman. If they now still formed a battle wedge of the old type, it nevertheless no longer had the old solidity and the old value.

There could be no question of perhaps retaining the tactical unit or reestablishing it by expedients such as drills. The prerequisites for this were missing. The authority that the Germanic kings or their counts or the old *hunni* exercised over their compatriots was not of this type.

There was already missing even the physical prerequisite, the closely knit life in common of a rather large group. The few hundred men of the warrior class, Goths, Burgundians, or Franks, who lived in a Romanic county could no doubt seek to maintain their skill through constant practice with their weapons but not in the creation of a drill discipline.

We shall have occasion to explain this point again when we arrive at the period of reestablishment of tactical units in the continuation of this work. But now we are entering a period where this pole of military efficiency, on which the value of the Roman legions was principally based, gradually disappears almost entirely and all the attention is devoted solely to the other pole of the development, the personal courage and skill of the individual warrior.

The old battle wedge with the long spear, the *framea*, the battle-ax, the javelin (*ango*),[15] or whatever other close-combat weapon the individual preferred, could still have been replaced by a relatively efficient infantry armed with the bow. We have found that this was actually the case with the Byzantines. But although the Byzantine army did consist principally of Germans, the very special preference for the bow in this army must be attributed to the high command. Among the independent Germanic peoples, Vandals as well as East Goths, we find it specifically stated that, although they were not unpracticed in the use of the missile weapon, they preferred sword and lance. The same thing also applies to the Franks, among whom we find only rare mention of the bow.

What was lost to the infantry added to the growth of the cavalry. For it was neither courage, nor competence with their weapons, nor warlike spirit that declined but only one specific combat branch, the infantry, for which the conditions of the period were unfavorable. Vegetius (3. 26), with all his lack of practical knowledge, had already remarked that the cavalry of his time left nothing further to be desired.

For the Germans who had settled among the Romans, the cavalry was necessarily the arm to which they devoted all their care and attention, not in the specifically cavalry-related sense, but in the sense of the man who moves into the field on horseback, knows how to control his horse and to fight from his mounted position, but is also ready, if the circumstances call for it, to dismount and fight on foot. The warrior was not so much a cavalryman as a man on horseback; expressed in another way, he was a cavalryman for the reason that he could do everything in conjunction with his mounted situation. This period was not capable of forming tactical units. The whole military system was based on the individual, the person. The man who can only fight on foot with a close-combat weapon is very insignificant if he is not a member of a tactical unit, while the man who fights on foot with bow and arrow can only provide a support weapon. The man who fights on horseback is superior to both as an individual combatant.

Once it is effective, such a relationship with its natural momentum pushes the scale all the farther in its direction. The best men aspired to cavalry service; the kings no longer paid any attention to infantry in the old sense of the word.

The economic factor also worked directly toward the same end. Italy and Gaul, despite their tremendous decline since the third century, and despite all the murdering and plundering incursions with which the Germans had time and again plagued the Roman provinces, were certainly not more sparsely, and perhaps even considerably more densely, populated and better developed agriculturally than at the time of the founding of the Roman world monarchy. At that time, Caesar and the Triumvirate had made it possible to move through the countryside with armies up to 60,000 and 70,000 men strong; but that was practicable only with the backing of strong financial means and an organized supply system. Now the world had fallen back into a barter economy, and the Germanic kings did not have the administrative organization of Rome at their disposal. The warriors were not assembled in legions but were spread throughout the entire country, so that they could be fed. It had become very difficult to accomplish anything with masses, but the most outstanding warrior was no harder to feed than the mediocre one. The cavalryman was an artist of military handwork to a much higher degree than the infantryman. It was never difficult to assemble a few hundred tolerably useful foot soldiers from a district, but it was very difficult to assemble a few hundred or even only 100 or 50 really useful cavalrymen with appropriate horses. That count who brought to the king the best warriors, not the most, served the king best. The mounted man was more than the man on foot in every respect; if the number of horses was not too large, they could be fed off the land and whenever it was necessary, the man dismounted and fought on foot.

Already in his day, Caesar had accomplished very much through his cavalry, but the nucleus of his army still remained the legionary, the heavily armored infantryman with the close-combat weapon. The ratio of cavalrymen in his army probably varied between 5 and 20 percent.[16] In the Germanic-Romanic countries, the cavalry won the upper hand completely, but this cavalry was not entirely the same as that of Caesar. The same thing applies here that we have already said about Justinian's army: the specific aspect of the combat branch was wiped out. These Frankish or Gothic horsemen were not so much cavalry as they were warriors on horseback. They also fought on foot without feeling out of their element. There was only one identifying feature: each individual had to be a strong, brave man, competent in the use of his weapons.

In the first chapter of this book, we observed the difference between the settling of the Franks and that of the other peoples: the Franks did not participate in any division of the land. Now we recognize once again that the practical significance of this difference was not really so very great. The levy of warriors from each individual district was determined not so much by the number of available men as by the possibilities for equipping and feeding them and utilizing them in combat operations. Furthermore, the number of Goths, Burgundians, and Vandals who were settled in the Roman provinces was only very small. Consequently, the claim to private lands by the West Goths and the Burgundians must have been made principally for the reason that they were originally limited to a very small area; in the case of the Vandals, because they willingly limited their settling to a single province of their broad kingdom for political-military reasons. Similar reasons may have played a role with Odoacer and the East Goths; at least we find that there were very few Goths in lower Italy. When the Franks founded their large kingdom under Clovis, the majority of this people remained in those areas that they had always occupied or from which the earlier generations had either completely driven the Romans or where they had at any rate completely subjugated them. In the Romanic districts over which Clovis now placed his counts, the imperial domains or the communal estates or the confiscated possessions of individual well-to-do Romans sufficed to provide for the few men whom the king gave to each count.

As with the Gothic, Vandal, and Burgundian armies, so too were the Frankish armies only small ones. It would not have been difficult to assemble much larger units from the purely Germanic areas, but they would not have been capable of feeding them without giving up completely any orderly organization and destroying the agriculture of the area. They could move strategically to distant areas only with units of moderate size, and it was a question not of the total number of available service-qualified men but rather of the number that could be used operationally. That is the reason why Theodoric the Great remained superior to the Frankish kings, Clovis and his sons. Clovis certainly had more warriors, but the East Goths, even with their widespread area in conquered Italy, continued to form together a constantly mobile army. This army could, in accordance with the will of the king and his commanders, and utilizing the resources of the rich countryside, be moved and assembled for battle wherever it was needed.

Let us again trace the thread that has led us from one theme to the other: the dominant cavalry, the coming into prominence of the individual warrior, the decline of the tactical unit — all these factors lead to the smallness of the armies. But if we first know that in the battles of this period the deciding action was produced by small units of especially brave men, it is also clear why Clovis, in the broad Romanic areas that he conquered, needed to settle only a very few Franks and consequently did not need to effect any division of the lands.

The dissolution of the clan organization and the settling of the warriors throughout broad areas loosened the cohesiveness of the ancient battle wedge and thus decreased and finally destroyed its value without, however, causing any decline in the individual warrior's courage or skill with weapons. But since there remained only the factor of personal courage, it led to the kind of combat in which the individual can be most effective, that is, by being mounted on horseback but without giving up the capability of fighting on foot when the circumstances demanded it.

Army strengths, military organization, and tactics mutually influence and limit each other. By establishing how small the armies of the *Völkerwanderung* and of the East Goths were, we have indirectly also arrived at a standard of measure for the Franks: their armies too were only small ones. That means that the warriors of which they were formed were quality fighters. The way was now prepared for the military system and the tactics of knighthood.

NOTES FOR CHAPTER II

1. Aurel. Victor., Chapter 21.

2. *Ars veterinaria* 6. (4.) 6. The horses of the Thuringians were also praised by Jordanes 1. 3. 21.

3. *De bell. Vand.* 1. 8.

4. Procopius, *de bell. Vand.* 2. 14.

5. Schmidt, *Geschichte der Vandalen*, p. 39.

6. Procopius, *bell. Goth.* 1. 16; 1. 28; 1. 29. *bell. Pers.* 2. 18.

7. Brunner, *Zeitschrift der Savigny-Stiftung* (1887): 6.

8. For example, 3. 28; 4. 30; 8. 45; 9. 31.

9. Procopius 2. 25. Agathias 2. 5. Whether Procopius' statement here is entirely reliable must be considered doubtful, since he completely denies that the Franks used both the spear and the bow, weapons which many other sources indicate they had. Waitz, *Deutsche Verfassungs-*

*geschichte* 2: 528; 2d edition, 2: 213. If Procopius' report is at all correct, there may have been some unusual circumstance or other, as in 552, when the invaders were principally Alamanni, whom we elsewhere find to be specifically famous as cavalry.

10. Jähns, *Geschichte der Kriegswissenschaften* 1: 142.

11. *Oeuvres* 28: 163.

12. Napoleon used very similar expressions in his regulations for the training of dragoons, as cited by Kerchnawe, *Kavallerie-Verwendung*, p. 3, note.

13. In Procopius, *bell. Pers.* 1. 14, Belisarius describes the Persian infantry as follows: "All the infantry is nothing else than a crowd of pitiful rustics who come to the army for no other purpose than to undermine a wall, to strip the dead, or to perform other services for the soldiers."*

14. The reader's attention is called to the citation already analyzed above, Procopius, *de bell. Vand.* 1. 18, where it is recounted how the Vandals came neither in order nor formed for battle, but "They went in *symmoriai*, and these were small — about thirty, or in fact, twenty men."* Those could have been such diminished clans.

15. The *ango* has some similarity to the Roman *pilum*, and so it can be considered as a javelin.

16. Rüstow, in *Heerwesen Cäsars*, p. 25, assumes that on the average the cavalry was one-fourth as strong as the legionary infantry, thus forming 20 percent of the army. Marquardt, in *Römische Staatsverfassung* 2: 441, agrees with this point. Fröhlich, *Kriegswesen Cäsars*, p. 40, rightly avoids considering this relationship as an average. Of the numbers reported in the sources, 20 percent is not an average but the maximum.

# Chapter III

# The Decline of the Original Germanic-Romanic Military System

The kingdoms of the Vandals and the East Goths did not last long. Gaiseric's kingdom fell victim to the first attacks by the East Romans, whereas Theodoric's successors fought for at least eighteen years, because the Vandals had already lived a half-century longer in the new situation and had exposed their Nordic military strength to the sun of civilization during that period. The West Goths, who were likewise already strongly threatened, finally survived the crisis and maintained their kingdom and their independence principally because of their geographical situation rather than any greater inherent strength. But after 150 years, when a new and strong enemy, Islam, approached, they were defeated with a single blow and immediately collapsed completely.

The sources enable us to trace the decline of their military organization, but what we find there need not be considered as something specifically applicable to the West Goths. It was rather the natural and inevitable course of the development that would necessarily have applied in common to all the Germanic-Romanic states if some had not already collapsed previously and the other still surviving one, the Frankish kingdom, had not produced a different and completely new political form.

Indications of the dissolution began to be apparent very soon after the settling, and they have already been touched on above in the first chapter. The Goths, spread throughout the vast countryside, could not be assembled for military service. The king, the dukes and counts, the large estate owners, and finally the highly placed clergy all maintained their own military forces, the *buccellarii*. For a while the two types existed side by side: the general people's levy of the Goths and the private mercenaries of the members of the ruling class. But the extreme degree to which the former had sunk can be recognized from the fact that the former Thousand leader, the *thiufadus,* now belonged among the persons of lower status and was liable under the law to physical beating if he did not perform his duties properly. Many Goths lost their warlike nature; on the other hand, Romans, among whom there were naturally always some suitable to be warriors, entered the military service.

We are informed of the sequence of this development by the attempts at reform that were undertaken shortly before the collapse of the system and that led to laws under Kings Wamba (672 to 680) and Erwig (680 to 687), statutes that have come down to us.

Wamba's law of the year 673 begins with emotional complaints that during an enemy raid so many men had avoided their duty of defending the country and nobody had helped his fellow man. From then on, however, every man, clergy as well as layman, was to help out with his body of men (*virtus*) up to a distance of 150 kilometers as soon as called upon. Anybody who did not do this was liable to the sternest punishment: exile, dishonor, compensation for damages, and confiscation of his fortune.

Erwig's law of the year 681 likewise began with complaints about men who preferred to be rich rather than strong, cared more about their fortune than their skill with weapons, and imagined they could enjoy the fruits of their work if they ceased to be victorious. Therefore, the law was intended to obligate those who refused to be guided by their own advantage, and every person was to obey the call to arms, whenever and wherever it might be. Any prominent man who did not do so would be subject to the judgment of the king; his entire fortune could be taken from him and he could be sentenced to exile. But the common man, from the *thiufadus* downward, was subject to 200 lashes; and with this, as a symbol of dishonor, he was to have his head shaved and pay a fine of one pound of gold or, if he did not have that much, he was to become a serf. The man who was called up was not only to come in person but also to bring with him a tenth of his serving men, well armed.[1] If it should be discovered that he brought fewer than the prescribed tenth part, the number missing would be turned over to the king, who could give them to anybody he pleased. It was especially indicated to the royal officials that the punishments under this law applied also to them, and punishment was established for bribery.

In both laws, the case of excuse as a result of illness was provided for;

the illness was to be verified by an appropriate witness, and if the master was really incapable of moving out himself, still his men were to be sent. A later code has the very characteristic supplement, no doubt added afterward, that the illness had to be verified under oath by an inspector of the diocesan bishop; otherwise it would not be believed.

The most important difference between these two laws is that the first one refers only to the case of defense of the country, whether it be against a foreign enemy or in case of a rebellion. The second law mitigates the first one to the extent that it removes the punishment of dishonor and of the ban on bearing witness that are included in the first one, but in return it considers and regulates not only the call-up for direct defense of the country but the call-to-arms in general.

Dahn regards the laws as a real army reform whose most important feature, in addition to the more severe punishment and control, lies in the extension of the military obligation to the serfs.[2] Literally speaking, that is correct; from the practical viewpoint, however, the completely unorganized extension of the obligation to innumerable masses signals the bankruptcy of the law.

In places, the wording of the laws seems to apply to the entire people; this interpretation would necessarily have meant the assembling of huge masses of men. But then again the requirement concerning the men to be brought along and the serving men shows that the lawgiver was thinking not at all of the great masses but had in mind principally only the large landowners. Whoever takes to the field, it says, whether he be duke, count, *garding* (that is, a member of the king's retinue), Goth, or Roman, freeman or freedman or servant of the king, was supposed to bring along a tenth of his men. Why would they have needed the mass of armed servants if they had counted on even only a respectable fraction of the nation? A similar situation applied to the extension of the military obligation to the clergy: perhaps they were not supposed to fight themselves, but to provide their military force.

The situation was apparently such that the original warrior class of the Goths had in the course of 250 years become civilized and had shed its warlike inclinations. In the atmosphere of civilization, their warlike nature melted away along with their barbarianism.

The idea that there was still a warrior class continued to exist but it was no longer realistic. In some way or other, it was gradually replaced by a class of large estate owners, each with a group of fighting men. Whereas the lawgiver apparently and literally was calling on a mass of people who were neither inclined to fight battles nor capable of doing so, in reality he was calling on the good will of an aristocracy. There was no question of any kind of organization to maintain the army in the field. In the ever more apparent recognition that the old Gothic warrior had died out and the individual citizen or farmer was not capable of suddenly moving into the field and to distant places, the lawgiver ordered the great lords, clergy as well as laymen, to provide men and to bring along their serving men. These landowners would at least have been in a position to equip and feed their men, but subjects and men serving at their discretion are still not useful warriors. Even if it were thinkable that the strictness of the law and a very energetic administration actually assembled the numbers of men and regulated the readiness of the weapons and the quantity of accompanying food supplies, the main point was still missing: the guarantee of military competence.

This weakness is apparent from the fact that they sought to replace the lack of any useful organization and of any real military system by a wave of patriotic and moralistic expressions and an increase of threats of punishment that were necessarily all the less effective in that their very enormity betrayed the fact that they could not be carried out.

Certainly, the warlike vigor was not completely extinguished in the grandsons of Fridigern and Alaric, just as it had not fully died out among the Romanics either. Indeed, wars were constantly being waged, both internally and externally. The institution of the *buccellarii*, the warrior retinue of the individual leaders, must have continued to exist, but there was no longer on hand a real, powerfully functioning army organization.

It is no wonder that thirty years after the proclamation of this law the West Gothic kingdom collapsed as the result of a single blow, just as the kingdom of the Vandals had previously fallen.

## EXCURSUS

THE TEXT OF THE LAWS

The laws of Wamba and Erwig are found in the older versions of the *lex Visigothorum* as chapters 8 and 9 of Title 2 in Book IX, directly after the older provisions shown on p. 395 above, which I, like Zeumer, believe justified in dating more than 200 years earlier. In Zeumer's octavo edition, which reconstructs the basic text as a code of King Reccessvind (649-672), the two later laws are therefore not included. They are included in Zeumer's new edition of the *Leges Visigothorum* in the *Mon. G. LL.*, Sec. I, Tome I, quarto. Zeumer was also the first to determine that the second law was promulgated neither by Wamba, as the Madrid and Lisbon editions claim, nor by Egika, as Dahn assumed, but by Erwig. (See Appendix 4 for the Latin text.)

In the Name of Our Lord.
King Flavius Gloriosus Wamba

What must be observed if a revolt occurs within the territory of Spain.

A most beneficial initiation of action induces Our Glory to decree that, just as the authority of laws is spread abroad in terminating the troubles of people, so in war a brotherhood, maintained by levy and supported by mutual aid, should remain capable of conquest. In fact, there is no doubt that our peace benefits everyone, if by calling out on the trumpet of law it binds the attention of all to a good purpose. We know, of course, that what was not well ordered in the past runs askew, and thereafter set in order with the help of Our Lord, should proceed to the better. Therefore, Our Clemency abhors and irksomely endures the practice of the following and usually harmful custom, because frequent damage to the fatherland occurs through the carelessness of some. In fact, as many times as an attack of the enemy is launched against the provinces of our kingdom, and while the military necessity of waging war arises for our men who are adjacent to foreign peoples on the border, some so scatter themselves at the quickest opportunity, relying on change of location, malicious hate, and even pretense of their incapacity, that in that struggle of fighting the one does not expend fraternal aid to the other, and whoever at this time has to be in charge of the public service, deprived of his brothers' help, either retreats or, if he desires to attack boldly in defense of the nation and the fatherland, in the misfortune of impending danger he is destroyed by the enemy.

Thus, we determine by the present decree that from the day and time noted on this law if any hostility of the enemy should be provoked against our territory, whether a man be a bishop or even established in an ecclesiastical order, whether he be a duke or count, *thiufadus* or *vicarius*, *gardingus* or any individual, who is where the hostility occurred either as a result of this very enterprise or another reason, and who is assembled in the vicinity, or whoever, coming into this province and territory is situated within one hundred miles; then, immediately when the need arose, if he is summoned by his duke or count, *thiufadus, vicarius*, or anyone, or by whatever means he learns, and if he is not present to defend our nation and country with all the strength which he possessed, and desires to go elsewhere and to excuse himself by some ruses or vainly sought pretexts, so that he may not be on hand and ready in support of his brothers for the defense of the country, and the advancing army of the enemy afterwards inflicts some damage or captivity on the people and provinces of our realm, whoever is slow, fearful, or restrained by malice, fear, or alarm, and delays to go out for the benefit and defense of his nation and country and to oppose the enemy of our nation with the complete exertion of his strength; if any of these be a priest or cleric and he does not have the means from which to make amends from his own resources for the losses of property inflicted on our land by the enemy, according to the decision of the prince he should be subjected to a rather severe exile. This provision alone must be observed among the bishops, presbyters, and deacons. Indeed, every provision of this law must be discharged among the clerics not holding office according to the command set down below concerning the laity.

Whoever of the laity, in fact, whether a noble or a more common, poorer individual, did such as listed above, we lay down in the present law that proof of his rank should be lost and he should be reduced straight away into a condition of the lowest servitude, and that the power of the prince will remain sure to decide whatever he wanted about the life of this man, for it is just that whoever refuses to defend steadfastly the nobility of his own nation and the state of his country, and that which the benefit of an honorable nation procures, should be punished by the provision of this law, as well as whoever has been charged with notably higher crimes and is found base and worthless. We determine the following, however, must be observed concerning the property of transgressors, laymen as well as clerics who are without office: that thereafter whoever perchance committed this offense should then make amends for all the damages to our land and to those who endured them; and that the man whose spiteful and cowardly action neither repelled an enemy on the offensive nor showed himself a man in battle with the enemy, should rightly feel remorse that he lost the rank of nobles and the resources of their estates.

Now if anyone within the territory of Spain, Gaul, Gallaecia, or in all the provinces which belong to the sway of our realm stirs up or desires to stir up a revolt in any part against the nation, the fatherland, our rule, or the rule of our successors, provided that this was known in the neighboring areas of the site according to the number of miles noted above, or also anyone is especially summoned by the priests, clerics, dukes, counts, *thiufadi*, *vicarii*, or anyone according to the command written above, or by whatever means he learned it, and, after his loyalty has been appealed to, he does not hasten immediately to the defense either of the king or of the nation and of the country or the faithful of the present king, against whom the revolt was stirred up, and he does not show himself present in their support to destroy the revolt which had arisen: if he is a bishop, a cleric, or perchance an officeholder in the palace, a member of an order, anyone of rank, or perchance an inferior involved in the crime of this disloyalty, he not only would be constrained to exile, but he will be subject in all respects concerning his property to the judgment and power of the royal decision — whatever the king would have desired to do or to decide thereafter. This law will only render exempt those of the upper classes who are so burdened by infirmity that they cannot in the least advance or set out in the company of the loyal according to the above command, and who, in truth, even if hampered by disease, will direct, nevertheless, all their force in support of the bishops, clerics, and their brothers sincerely for the service of the royal power, the nation, and the fatherland of those loyally toiling. But if they do not do this, they would be punished by the above provision in an equal manner with transgressors. Nevertheless, that individual will then be safe from the punishment noted above, provided that he proved his case through a suitable witness that he was so incapacitated by illness that he had not had the strength to set out and to be present in time. We decree that the severe judgment of this law should refute the vice which had remained with evil consequences from past times to the present, and that harmonious and unanimous acquiescence should procure the peace of the people and the defense of the country.

The law was dated and ratified on the first day of November in the second happy year of our reign.

## IX. King Flavius Gloriosus Ervigius

Concerning men who do not join the army on the appointed day at the determined place and time, or deserted; and what fraction of the servants of each ought to set out on the same campaign.

If they are undoubtedly proven lovers of the fatherland who voluntarily expose themselves to dangers for its deliverance, why, rather, should they not be called deserters, who cease to be its defenders? Now when must such men as these be supposed as voluntarily potential saviors of the land, who even after being summoned do not rise up for the deliverance of the fatherland? Yet either they defer themselves from departure for war, or, what is worse, they either delay without regard to the summons or contrary to the command they set out on the campaign without their equipment. While some of them eager to cultivate their fields withdraw the masses of their slaves, and for the sake of looking after their own welfare they take with them not even a twentieth of their household. But they desire to become richer by profit rather than by the safety of their own body, while they protect their property and deprive themselves of protection with greater attentiveness to their household affairs than practice in arms; as if they will enjoy the objects of their labor and would keep them, if they cease to be victors. Therefore, we must take measures of punishment against such men whom the interests of their own advantage do not induce. Whence we command to all the people of our kingdom in a general comprehensive decree that on the day and time established and decided in advance, where either the prince determined to assemble the army or a duke or count ordered that the army would set out on public service, whoever receives the summons of any of these, or, even not summoned, hears nevertheless by some inquiry, or it becomes known to him by some decree at which site the army about to go on campaign assembles, he should not dare to reside at home further, or about to start on campaign he should exhibit neither any sort of delay nor excuse; but at the determined sites and times, according to what either the order of the prince announced, or the summons of the duke, count, *thiufadus, vicarius,* or anyone in authority mentioned, the individual should show himself on hand at the determined site and time, as it was stated. Now in fact, whoever, if summoned or even if not summoned, and, however, aware if he learns by some inquiry, fails to be present at the determined sites and times: if he is a person of higher station, that is, duke, count, or even *gardingus,* by the order of the king he would be deprived of his property and deported by the banishment of exile, so that what his Princely Highness elects to decide about the property of this man stands in the control of his power. Indeed, inferiors and more common individuals, obviously the *thiufadi* and all the recruiting officers of the army, and men who are forced into the army, if they either delay to join the army, or at least come to the established site and time and failed to set out, or withdraw themselves by deserting the public force with a contrivance of deceit, they would not only be beaten with 200 strokes of the lash, but also disgracefully multilated by shaving their heads, and in addition each would be compelled to pay a pound of gold, and it would remain immediately within the judgment of the Princely Power to decree to whom he grants it. But if he does not have the means from which to pay this indemnity, then it would be permitted to the authority of the king to subject a transgressor of this sort to eternal servitude, and the Royal Authority would undoubtedly have the power to command what he decided concerning him and his property. Of course, by a provision of this law we determine that those remain innocent whom the order of the prince acquitted, whom either minority of age or old age still restrained, or even whom the severe weight of illness kept back. Nevertheless, if an individual who was burdened with sickness is able to prove by a legitimate witness that he was unable to go off in the army because of the weakness of illness, he who was burdened with sickness would not delay, however, to set all the manpower of his property in the public service with his duke or count according to the disposition of this law.

Now in fact it remains, because we made mention earlier of the general departure of all, that we should establish rules concerning the strength of the participants and supplies. Therefore, we determine by special decree that, whoever the individual is, whether duke, count, *gardingus*, whether Goth or Roman, also freeborn or manumitted slave, or also slaves of the state, whoever of these is about to join the army should come with the intention of taking a tenth of his own slaves with him on the military campaign. So that this tenth of the slaves may not be unarmed, but may appear equipped with varied armament, we thus also decree that each should be diligent in presenting to his prince, duke, or count some part of the men which he brought with him to the army armored with cuirasses or breastplates, the majority indeed equipped with shields, broadswords, short swords, javelins, and arrows, and some also with sling equipment and other weapons, which each had at the recent request of a noble or his lord. If anyone, however, comes to the departure of the army without this tenth of his own slaves, the whole tenth of his slaves would be diligently investigated and counted, and whatever number of slaves it was found that an individual had brought with him to the military campaign below this established and apportioned tenth of his slaves must be reduced to the control of the prince to lie within the prince's authority to grant this same body of slaves to anyone whom he selected. Certainly, whoever of the palace staff starts on the campaign of the army in such a manner that he is not steadfast in the service of the prince and does not endure hardship with his brothers on duty, he would learn that he must be punished according to the judgment of this law, unless a clear display of weakness proved him sickly. In fact, if any freeborn man setting out on the same military campaign should have scarcely followed his duke, count, or even his patron, but should have extended himself through the patronage of several different ones, so that he may not remain on duty with his superior and may not show that any public service was performed, a departure of this sort must not be put down to his credit, but he would know that what was decreed in this law concerning the more common and lower individuals, according to the command above, bears against him.

Therefore after having commanded and arranged the above provisions, it remains that we should put a check on the greed of those whom we direct to perform the work of our service. And therefore no duke, count, *thiufadus*, or anyone commanding the assembled people should dismiss from departure for war anyone of his troops after receiving a bribe or any favor to his basest inclination. Nor should he forego the summons, which ought to be made at the departure of the army, and the distribution of arms, as if he injects this at the time of the summons from which he takes any of these men to do military service. For example, whoever does such things for these reasons, as it has been stated, and either takes something offered by someone, or demands anything from someone, and certainly if he is one of the dignitaries of the palace, he would repay the man from whom he received any such thing fourfold, and he would know that he would pay to the prince a pound of gold for this offense alone by which he ventured to enrich himself. Lesser individuals, in fact, stripped of office and the rank of noble birth, are to be brought within the control of the prince to be subject in all respects to his power to decide what he preferred concerning these men and their property.

*(Instead of the foregoing passage from line 5, page 424 to line 17, page 425, later codices read as follows)*

But if he does not have the means from which to pay this indemnity, then it would be permitted to the power of the king that a transgressor of this sort be sentenced to eternal servitude, and he would be a slave for whom the king selected. It would also be permitted to grant and to give away his property, otherwise divided, in one collected mass of his possessions, so that the same transgressor may not return again to the status of a freeman by some indulgence, or may not receive the rights of his property by restoration. But if the master of the property, certainly that is the very man who had received the property of the transgressor which had been given away, should be marked by the accusation of a crime and should fall from the status of his original rank, whence the property should come again into the power of the prince, then by an irrevocable decree it will be maintained that, even if the man who had received the property earlier does not deserve to have it, after transferring the property to other loyal men, it should profit them; only provided that the property does not pass later into the control of that man who was tardy in his departure for war and was once deprived of his rank and property. Of course, all the dukes and nobles of the palace will be held liable to a sentence of this sort, who were found to be transgressors of this ruling. They will also deserve a sentence of this kind of punishment, who either desert from a war or were stationed in the departure for war and are found to have hurried off elsewhere without the permission of their superior. Nevertheless, among individuals of greater as well as lesser rank it must be observed at this same period of departure that, if any should be subject to a severe illness and should in no way have the strength to depart, he would desire that the bishop of this locale or district ought to come immediately to examine the troublesomeness of his illness, so that he may call forward that bishop as the examiner of his affliction, in whose district or province he happened either to have fallen ill or to have lingered, or happened to come to from the district of others; for we must not otherwise believe him, unless either by the proof of the bishops in whose districts he is known to have fallen ill he is supported by their testimony under oath, or by the oath of those whom the same bishops ordered in turn to be examiners he is confirmed. Let these bishops, however, have this duty in such matters: to examine diligently the illnesses of these men, either themselves or through their subordinates, to see either if they in no way are able to depart, or if after a few days they should clearly be able to participate in waging war, that is, before the army will advance to battle at the determined locale. Because the bishops saw the illnesses of such men, we entrust to their judgment whether they stayed at home to recover their health or, after regaining their health, it is expedient that they have to march on campaign. Just as under the testimony of these bishops either we should feel pity for their illnesses, so that they may retire from the campaign, or we should curtail their offense, if they feigned illness, so that we may oblige their duty; so, nevertheless, we decree that if anyone sees himself so wearied by infirmity that he was in no way capable to depart for battle, he should not delay to direct the manpower of his property into public service with his duke or count according to the provision of this law. But if, however, he feels by his continued improvement that soon he should have recovered his bodily strength, according to what is prescribed by the ordinance of this law, he would not delay to advance with all his manpower where he knew he had been summoned or where he will have learned afterwards that the army had hastened. [For the sake of better English, the translation deviates slightly from the Latin text without altering the sense. *Translator's note*].

NOTES FOR CHAPTER III

1. Some of the codes call for half of all the serving men instead of a tenth.
2. *Könige der Germanen* 6: 222, 2d edition.

# Chapter IV

# The Origin of the Feudal System

The Frankish kingdom differed from all the other Germanic states principally in the immeasurably greater power of the monarchy. Clovis, his sons, and his grandsons were despots of the most savage type. And even while the Germanic sense of freedom and obstinacy tended to oppose this despotism, the movement was directed not against the position of the king as such and did not seek, for example, the overthrow of the dynasty, but only intended to limit the power of the king within the system. The great conflict associated with the names of Queens Brunhilda and Fredegunda was really a fight between the monarchy and the nobility that was only set off by the conflict within the dynasty. In Spain, the nobles and the church made the monarchy so dependent on them that they really possessed the throne themselves; the hereditary aspect of the monarchy vanished. The Merovingian dynasty, which created the state and formed the sole unity in its otherwise completely disparate elements, Germanic and Romanic areas and peoples, survived, even if it was at times placed in a tutelary situation. Power stood facing power, and this internal tension worked to the advantage of the military system.

Originally, the Frankish kingdom had no recognized nobility. When Clovis placed his counts in charge of the subjugated areas (presumably mostly from the men of his retinue having an obligation of personal loyalty to him, his *antrustiones*), they were his officials and commanded the *leudes* allocated to them in the name of the king. But a hundred years after Clovis, Chlotar II, in the Edict of Paris (614), the first document to which the name "*magna carta*" can be applied, gave to the Frankish nobles the commitment, in addition to other promises, that the counts were to be appointed only from among the large estate owners of the district.[1] This edict was the reward for their partisanship and decisive support in the dynastic family conflict and for the sentence that bade Fredegunda's son to have the aged Queen Brunhilda dragged to death by wild horses. Among the West Goths, kings were either killed or deposed, and others elected; among the Franks, they were limited in their kingly powers.

In this period, then, a class of large estate owners developed in the Frankish kingdom whose partisanship determined the outcome of civil wars and who intended to be included along with the king in the public power. The sources do not directly indicate the origins of this landed class, but we may arrive at its beginnings somewhat in the following way: in the Romanic areas, it was the continuation of the Roman senatorial class, which had been Germanized partly through intermarriage with Germans who then became heirs, since many prominent Romans entered the clergy, and partly as a result of confiscation and ceding of the property to Germans. Furthermore, the king gave the members of his loyal retinue, that is, principally his counts, extensive grants of lands from the public domain, and the counts used their power to extend their possessions. In the earlier Kingdom of Burgundy and the earlier West Gothic area, the Germanic ownership of large estates had developed from the sharing of the lands with the Romans. In the Germanic areas in this earlier period, when the common man among the Franks still refused to be forced into a subordinate status, the large estate class can probably be explained principally as resulting from the Roman tenant farmers who had remained among the Germans and had become serfs of a German. The numbers of such dependents were also increased by royal grants, which in this case, however, where men suited to be turned over in this way were lacking, cannot have had great significance.

If this class of large estate owners was now so powerful as to swing the balance in civil wars between the strong contenders for the kingship and to force the Edict of Paris from the king, it must have had fighting men at its disposal. Undoubtedly, these large estate owners, when they officially held the position of count, already had their possessions; their possessions had in fact originated with their position as count. In other words, the counts whom Clovis appointed as his officials and to whom he assigned his warriors to be commanded by them had become large estate owners who had their own fighting men. The warriors originally serving the king, or a large part of these warriors, had become the soldiers of private individuals.

As a result of the fortuitous circumstance that has caused a part of King Euric's Book of Laws to come down to us in a Paris palimpsest, we have direct proof of the existence of the *buccellarii*, the private soldiers, among the West Goths as early as the fifth century. We have also seen how in a later period the military system in this kingdom developed for practical purposes into an unorganized recruitment of armed serving men by the large landowners. For the Franks, we do not have direct and completely reliable sources until the period after the Edict of Paris, somewhere toward the middle of the seventh century. But the Paris edict itself is testimony enough that this institution also existed previously in the Frankish kingdom, and to a very considerable extent. Indeed, judging from their accomplishments and success, we must assume that it existed to a much greater degree and with more energetic application than among the West Goths.

Paul Roth, who has done so much to clarify these difficult times and conditions, has expressed the opinion that the accompanying men who appear so often in association with the Merovingian nobles under the name *pueri* (boys) were serfs.[2] A few times, of course, they do carry out activities that lead us to conclude they were simple servants and consequently probably serfs or slaves. But that still does not mean that the word can only refer to men who were not free. In this point, Roth is misled as a result of too narrow a questioning; that is, he asks: bondman or retainer? But for him the retainer is a prominent man. Between the retainer, however, and the man who is not free, we have found the common fighting man, the *buccellarius*, among the West Goths, who is dependent but still free. I believe it is not too bold to suppose that the *pueri* in the books of Gregory of Tours and elsewhere in the Merovingian period were the same as the *paides* (boys) in Agathias—that is, the German *Degen*. Socially, their position was so low that men who were not free could also be designated with the same expression, but legally they belonged to the class of free men and obligated and subjected themselves to a master only through their own free will. And so, of course, even a thousand years later, the word *Knecht* (serving man) meant also an obligated man like the private soldier (*Kriegsknecht*), who, as a free mercenary, takes service wherever he wishes. How could it also be imaginable that Merovingian counts and dukes who wanted to surround themselves with warriors from whom they required the highest courage were supposed to have taken for this purpose only men that were not free, since, after all, the bravest and most effective freemen were available? Anyone who wants to gather fearless fighters around him will only seldom find appropriate material among slaves. Even if our sources do not provide a completely positive and indisputable proof as to whether the Frankish nobility of the sixth century had *"freie Degen"* (free soldiers) about them, still we do not have any evidence to the contrary. The nature of the question requires that men like the Frankish counts, who surrounded themselves with a retinue of warriors and had appropriate candidates for this group among their compatriots, would not have taken for this purpose men who were simply slaves. That at first appearance there is nothing special to notice from a political-legal viewpoint in this situation rests simply on the fact that it was a purely private relationship that was not at odds with the monarchical right of the king and the subject's obligation of the man.

Among those serving the Frankish nobles we find, in addition to the *pueri*, also *amici* (friends), *pares* (equals), *gasindi* (armed retainers), and *satellites* (attendants). In the case of these designations, too, it is doubtful and not directly apparent what they refer to. Even if it is surely a question in part of freemen, it would still be possible, as Roth understands it (p. 157), to find among members of this group protective relationships in the nature of the *clientela*. Now, after we have established that there must necessarily have been free warriors in the retinue of the Frankish nobles, we cannot avoid the conclusion that those names too (not exclusively, to be sure, for they are not technical expressions, but partially) mean members of the warrior retinue, men of a more or less higher social level than the *pueri*.[3]

If the Germanic kings, whether Clovis or Theodoric, placed counts in charge of the districts of their kingdom, nothing was, of course, more natural than that the counts should take not simply bonded servants and rough fellows from the masses but also some reliable and proven comrades and should assure themselves of the loyalty of these men through a personal oath, as was the custom among those peoples.

There can be no doubt that in the Germanic legal concept, a freeman could obligate himself to another in the status of a loyal member of his retinue. Any kind of political idea that only a prince was permitted to have a retinue was foreign to the ancient Germans. From a practical viewpoint, of course, only a very highly placed, very wealthy man could have a retinue of men who were, after all, his companions at meals and whom he had to feed. Now a large number of large estate owners and counts were in this situation. Consequently, we can justifiably designate the *amici*, *pares*, and *gasindi*, whom we find mentioned in the sources, as the retainers of the counts or other prominent men. For even if this was not originally a relationship recognized publicly and legally, nevertheless it was inspired by the same spirit as the ancient retinue system. But the groups with which we are now dealing were much too large to be forced into the concept of the former type of retinue. We do not know whether the forms of the obligation of loyalty of the members of the retinue that were passed down were also applied to these later relationships. And if that were the case, it would still necessarily have been associated in this expanded form with certain changes and variations, so that the question automatically arises as to whether we are dealing with a retinue. Suffice it to say that some warriors committed themselves to an obligation of loyalty more or less in the forms of the ancient royal retinue, toward a man who was not the king.

The sources demonstrate the existence of such warriors from the middle of the seventh century on. However, the very nature of things and the Edict of Paris make it obvious, as we have now seen, that they existed in this form much earlier.

We have adopted the expression "vassal" as a technical indication of those warriors who entered the military profession not as a result of recruitment by the national authority but through a special obligation. This expression has a Celtic origin and means "man." It is therefore nothing other than what is expressed in the sources in Latin as *homo* and in Germanic as *leudes*. It is only by chance that the word with the Celtic root happened to be adopted for this particular meaning.

In our oldest sources, the word *vassus* does not mean what it means today; rather, it refers to an unfree serving man. The word "vassal" seems to have received its later meaning and one we have accepted to the present day as a result of a kind of transformation such as we have, of course, also observed elsewhere. We first encounter it in the meaning of the free warrior in Bavaria. Among the Bavarians, to whom it was a foreign word, there was no connotation of its actually referring to men who were not free; it was also adopted for prominent men, and in its new meaning it moved back across the Rhine under Charlemagne.[4]

For the sake of shorter and understandable terminology, let us henceforth designate as *leudes* that warrior class which Merovingian kings levied directly, and as "vassals" the military class recruited by the large estate owners and called *buccellarii* by the earlier West Goths. The sources do not provide such a sharp distinction between the two expressions. It was not until the second half of the eighth century that the word *vassus*, in the current sense of the free man who is subject to another, gradually came into general use under Charlemagne and Louis the Pious.

But in the sources the word *leudes* is used not only for the king's warriors but also for those of the nobles, and it did not die out until the eighth century.[5] Between these two we still have the expresions *amici, gasindi, ingenui in obsequio* (freeborn men in allegiance), *pueri, satellites*, and others. Consequently, my use of these two distinguishing words, by pushing forward chronologically the word "vassal" and limiting the meaning of *leudes*, is to be understood only as a kind of abbreviation.

The vassal's lord was called the senior, the "old one," from which the French word *seigneur* derived.

We cannot determine directly from the sources when numbers of recruited vassals began to be expanded. Certainly at the start they were only very small. But the Edict of Paris leaves no doubt that by the time of the civil wars, which ended with the execution of Queen Brunhilda (613), it was not the levy of the old *leudes* by the counts but rather the vassals that determined the outcome. How did this come about?

From the tactics of this period, we have concluded that the warriors who were demanded and produced by the characteristics of the period were quality warriors. This type of warriorhood was the only one capable of developing, indeed of surviving, under the conditions prevailing in the Germanic-Romanic states.

It is of the greatest importance that we understand this point clearly. As strong as the Merovingian monarchy was, it was still incapable, for example, of returning to the military system of the Roman emperors of the first two centuries. Neither were the new illiterate masters of the country capable of establishing a bureaucratic administration with its financial controls, nor would the Franks have subjected themselves to discipline, nor can there be in an area of barter economy a disciplined army paid through taxes. An unwarlike general levy is worthless. In this kind of society, there is no other military system than in the form of a special military class, and this system cannot be bureaucratic in large countries but must be feudal.

The lord who leads into the field *his* warriors, with *his* weapons, on *his* steeds, with *his* resources, for *his* purpose, necessarily has completely different men than the count who is sent from the court into a district to govern it for a longer or shorter time and equips his men from the public resources. Even if the latter has the best of intentions, he will not be as effective as the former. If he does not even have the best intentions and complete dedication but somehow is also concerned with his own interests, does not seek out and train his men with the greatest care or maintain horses and weapons in good condition, and is unwilling to spend whatever might be necessary while still carefully supervising his expenditures and economizing, his troops will soon become a joke. No control can enable him to do better, for barter economy as well as warrior quality can be controlled from above only very superficially or not at all. A trained unit and a fund derived from taxes can be determined to be in order by inspections, and when the troops take to the field, everything else is in the hands of the army administration and leadership. But whatever was accomplished by a Frankish military unit under Clovis' successors, a unit in which everything depended on the personal courage of the individual and his personally provided equipment, was never evident until after a campaign had begun. The Byzantine Empire was very far ahead of the Merovingian monarchy in techniques of administration and organization. Nevertheless, as we have seen, Byzantium too had already resorted to the expedient of providing troops through condottieri. The Frankish large estate owner who took to the field with his vassals was a type of condottiere, a permanent condottiere, so to speak. He maintained the warriors and the military organization not only in wartime but also in peace.

Up to this point, the development has been completely analogous to that which we have observed in the West Gothic kingdom. But in the latter kingdom we did not find that a new and useful military organization finally developed from the *buccellarii*. It was only in the Frankish kingdom that this happened, through the addition of a new element that maintained the vassal system in its warriorhood and forced it to retain professional qualities.

The new element was the institution of fiefs.

We have already observed, in connection with the settling of the Burgundians, that the land given by the king, while granted as hereditary property, was still subject to certain reservations and limitations. These now also served as models and starting points for legal institutions. Suffice it to say that there developed among the Franks the practice of granting properties to warriors in return for military service, not as private property on a hereditary basis but with the provision for revocation when the lord was replaced or the subject died, that is, that the property returned to the giver or his successor on the death of either the giver or the receiver. When there was a change of lords, the succcessor could grant the property again to the man already holding it, if he also received from him a commitment of loyalty and military service. In case of the individual's death, the lord could award the property to the family of the deceased if in that family there was a man capable and willing to take to the field and swear allegiance. If these conditions were not met, the lord reclaimed his property. Consequently, the granting of fiefs was the lord's means of providing for vassals without giving up the property permanently and, in doing so, keeping at his disposal warriors residing on his properties and therefore dependent on him, not just for one generation but continuously.

Vassalage and feudalism were two political institutions that did not necessarily accompany one another. It was possible for a person to enter the service of a senior as vassal without being given a fief, and it was possible for a man to receive a fief without being a vassal. The significance in world history resides in the combination of these two concepts, which together made up the feudal system.

We may assume that in the continuous tension both between the Merovingian kings who reigned simultaneously over parts of the kingdom and between the kings and the nobles, there was constant awareness of a strong need for military power in the Frankish Kingdom. When the original warrior class existing at the time the kingdom was founded turned more and more to agriculture, this gave the impulse to a continuation or creation anew of the warrior class in the vassals and gave vassalage a broad, permanent basis as a result of the granting of land when there was a change of lords and when the individual vassal died.

But vassalage in conjunction with the granting of fiefs not only was an appropriate form for a landholder to maintain fighting men, but also was extremely useful in creating rather large organizations of various types. A very large family, as for instance the Pepins or the Arnulfs, or even the union of the two families that resulted from the marriage of Ansegisel with Begga, was not capable of governing directly a property extending across many districts, and we have seen how important the supervision by the master was for the military system based on vassalage. And so there was available the expedient of granting quite large pieces of the property as fiefs on the condition of providing warriors by means of sub-fiefs.

The large landowners also had the need to stand closely together in order to be able to carry on the fight for their rights with the monarchy. The most definite and reliable form for such a union was the procedure of giving their leader the vassal's oath of allegiance. Indeed, they went even further: the lawndowners gave their property to a lord in order to have it given back to them as a fief. While it is true that the right of hereditary succession was retained, eliminating an important characteristic of the system of fiefs, the possibility still remained that the grant would be revoked in case of a breach of loyalty. Therefore, the legal act meant the providing of a bond for the retention of the vassal's loyalty. Then the lord frequently gave in addition a fief from his own property.

The largest property owner in the Middle Ages was the church. So when military power became a condition of land ownership, the church, too, in order to assure its power, its security, and its broad influence, could not escape the practice of granting fiefs in order to maintain vassals on them. As early as the sixth century there was a case of two bishops, the brothers Salonius and Sagittarius, who took to the field and personally engaged in battle; the pious Gregory of Tours was still very upset over this (4. 42; 5. 21). In the seventh century, bishops had their military units, which they sent into the field; from the start of the eighth century on, we find them as the personal leaders, a situation which then soon became public law.

A reasonable picture of the significance of the campaign of a senior with his vassals is provided by a mobilization proclamation of Charlemagne that by chance has been preserved. While it belongs to a considerably later time than we are dealing with here, the years 804-811, similar documents and prescriptions were undoubtedly already promulgated and placed in force during the whole previous period. Thus, we may be permitted to weave it in at this point, where we are concerned with learning the system of mobilization of a feoffment. It is addressed to an Abbot Fulrad, probably of St. Quentin in northern France.[6]

The abbot is informed that the royal assembly will take place this year at Stassfurt-on-the-Bode, in eastern Saxony. The abbot is to be there with all his well-armed and equipped men (*hominibus*) on the 16th of June, ready to move out from there into the field, wherever it might be decided. Each mounted man was to have a shield, a lance, a sword, a dagger, and a bow and arrows. All kinds of tools necessary in war were to be loaded on the carts: axes, hatchets, drills, mattocks, shovels, and hoes. The provisions to be brought were to be sufficient to last for three months after the Stassfurt assembly, and there was to be a half-year's resupply of weapons and clothing. The troops were to move peacefully through the country, taking nothing but green fodder, wood, and water. The leaders were to remain with the carts and horsemen to prevent any illegal acts.

We must pause a bit to consider the requirement that the abbot was to bring a three months' supply of provisions. Since he was to arrive in Stassfurt with provisions for three months and had some 450 miles to march to reach that place, he had to move out with more than a four months' supply of provisions. In a capitulary of the year 811, it is prescribed that those who came from the far side of the Loire should count on having provisions for three months beyond the Rhine; those coming from the near side of the Rhine were to have a three-month supply from the Elbe on. If the campaign was conducted toward Spain, those coming from beyond the Rhine were to reckon their supply from the Loire and those beyond the Loire were to reckon from the Pyrenees. Consequently, in most cases supplies for four months had to be taken along at the start of the march. It is not clear in the sources how the return march was to be provided for. If they did not take a large amount of booty in the war itself, the campaign could not last longer than two months, so that the three months' provisions for the more distant contingents would still suffice for the march home.

The modern ration for a man (omitting the combination with potatoes or rice) amounts to:

| | |
|---|---|
| 1½ pounds of bread | 750 grams |
| smoked meat | 250 grams |
| beans or flour | 250 grams |
| salt | 25 grams |
| coffee | 25 grams |
| | 1,300 grams |

If we omit the coffee and consider that flour weighs one-fourth less than the corresponding quantity of bread, such a daily ration would weigh about 1,100 grams. In the case of fresh meat, about one-half more is allowed than of smoked meat, and consequently 375 grams. The Roman soldier received about 15 kilograms of flour for sixteen days. The Franks may have taken along, in addition, dried fruit, onions, and turnips or something similar,[7] but their ration differed from the Roman one principally in the fact that they were accustomed to much more meat and took their animals for slaughtering alive with them into the field. If we must estimate the weight of a Roman ration as 1250 grams, since we must still add something or other else to the 1000 grams of flour and salt, the Germanic one may have weighed no more than 750 grams, in addition to the fresh meat, or about 90 kilograms for four months. If we add to that the other items in the way of baggage and tools that each man had on the wagon and allow 200 kilograms of net load for each draft animal, whether horse or ox,[8] and also consider that the driver had to be fed, then a wagon pulled by one team was hardly sufficient for three men. If Abbot Fulrad had 100 warriors, he needed for them some fifteen two-team wagons or more than thirty wagons with single teams. Certainly, these vassals carried nothing on their backs; in fact, we can assume that they often took a wife or a son into the field with them, not only for their pleasure but also to care for them in case of sickness or wounds. The abbot himself was a prominent man who had his own requirements, and no doubt many men in his retinue had with them their squires and personal servants, so that the entire train of 100 warriors numbered more than twice that many persons. And since we have still not loaded any casks to take care of the Germanic thirst, the entire train could not have made out with fewer than forty to fifty heavily laden double-team and single-team wagons. Although the wagons gradually became empty, only a few were sent back home during the move, since a long journey and a campaign in which large masses move along simultaneously and compete with each other daily for fodder and water, to say nothing of their actual war losses in the way of animals and tools, continuously require replacements. Since the animals for slaughtering cannot have had very much meat on their bones, let us estimate three animals per week for 200 persons, and therefore a herd of fifty head for four months.

The question arises as to whether a large deduction should be made because they may have taken on new provisions during the move. For example, by using the water route of the Rhine and its tributaries, it would not have been difficult to establish supply depots at the principal crossing points — Strasbourg, Mainz, Cologne, Duisburg — for all the contingents moving up from the west. But we never hear anything about this, for that would have been a matter for the central administration, and provisions were the responsibility of each of the individual contingents. If Abbot Fulrad had wanted to replenish his supplies at any depot, he would have had to pay cash and would therefore have had to exact from his farmers very high tax payments in currency. They were not capable of providing this, and so there was nothing left to do but take along their own supplies in their own wagons, even to such distant points.[9]

The reader will have noticed that our estimate has not included any fodder for the horses. Under modern regulations a horse ration amounts to from 5 to 5.65 kilograms of oats, 1.50 kilograms of hay, and 1.75 kilograms of straw.[10] Consequently, considering only the oats, a horse eats in six weeks more than it can carry.[11] For a rather distant movement, fodder for the saddle horses, and especially for the draft animals, cannot possibly have been taken along. Since it was hardly possible to buy anything en route and nothing was allowed to be confiscated, the animals had to rely exclusively on green fodder and were therefore relatively weak.

If there were something like fifty wagons and carts in the train of a senior with only 100 warriors, the number of necessary animals, since, of course, the saddle horses of all the men also had to be counted, was much larger than the number of persons and far more than double the number of combatants. That would no doubt still be correct even if we assume that the animals for slaughter were a part of the oxen that initially pulled the wagons and were no longer needed for the purpose as the wagons gradually became empty or broke down.

During the period of barter economy, the movement of an army to a distant point was a large operation and a heavy burden. Even if the monastery of St. Quentin was very rich, Abbot Fulrad probably provided considerably fewer than 100 warriors for a campaign to Saxony.

At this point, I invite the reader to cast a final sympathetic glance at the scholarly opinion that would have the Frankish count moving into the field at the head of all the farmers of his district or even all the service-qualified men, from the Thuringians to the Gascons, at his own expense and with his own equipment, first at one border and then at another.

The Frankish kingdom was composed of Germanic and Romanic areas. When Clovis forged these different lands into a kingdom, they could not have been more varied in their social structure: here clans of equal and free warriors with very little inclination for farming; there a small number of large estate owners and masses of dependent peasants and city dwellers. Is it not surprising that in the course of a few generations the social structure in both regions became the same? Scholars should have raised the question long ago as to why no rather great differences are to be observed between the Romanic and Germanic Franks. As we ask this question now, we have already given the answer. In the civil wars Austrasia proved to be the strongest. One is tempted to attribute this superiority to its predominantly Germanic character, but if that were the whole answer, the superiority would necessarily have been still much greater. We must really ask then how Neustria, Aquitania, or Burgundy could contend at all with Austrasia? But they fought with each other so much and so long that their differences in strength can only have been quite small. The reason is that the Franks, including those who remained in their previous areas, very soon began to lay aside their warriorhood and become farmers, once they had become a part of the large kingdom. The new military system was necessarily not associated with a general levy of warriors; instead, it required a process of division and selection. If a warrior class arose above the Celtic-Romanic farmers and burghers who had long since become unwarlike, a class principally recruited from Franks who had immigrated, then the areas of the old Franks differed in precisely the same way. The kings and counts no longer tolerated the old plundering mass migration; for war they summoned from each Hundred as many men as could be fed on an orderly basis, and that was but very few. The German still held out for a rather long time, but those of his former comrades who remained as warriors finally pushed him into a bondage that was perhaps even harder than that of the Romanic tenant farmer on the other side.

The Frankish kingdom was founded as an administrative nation with a universal military obligation that was limited for practical purposes to a warrior class. This warrior class was able to survive only in the status of vassals under the class of large estate owners. This latter group, which bound the warriors to itself through the system of fiefs, became the possessor of armed power and as such took over the administrative positions, the counties, and shortly thereafter also the central administration, the seneschal office, which today is called the ministry. The Merovingian kingdom continued to exist but under the tutelage of the leaders of the new aristocracy. These leading families that had come to power in the subordinate kingdoms of Austrasia, Neustria, and Burgundy fought among themselves for a while until finally one of them partially subdued the others and partially absorbed them through marriages and once again created a unified authority for the principal branch of the kingdom, even if the border countries, Bavaria and Aquitania, still maintained their independence.

The feudalization of the military system in the Frankish kingdom took place through a very slow and gradual development, so that it is difficult to establish any cutoff or starting dates. Very early, soon after the formation of the kingdom, the principle of a general military obligation and the practice of a levy of *buccellarii* or vassals already existed side by side. And while the practical aspect remained dominant, was founded securely and permanently in the system of fiefs, and finally became legally and politically fixed, nevertheless the basic principle, the royal right to a general levy, was in no way abandoned. For a long time the two existed side by side. In the next book we shall have occasion to treat this contrast.

The new warrior class of vassals resulted from the transformation of the old warrior class of the *leudes*, with the distinction that the latter was a warrior class that was called up by the king, whereas the former was composed of the subjects and loyal subordinates of their seniors, the landowners. And just as the *leudes* were the Frankish people in the process of becoming a warrior class, which was not, however, closed to Romanic elements, so were the vassals also a class composed principally but not exclusively of Germanic strains.

The Franks who settled among the Romanics undoubtedly learned the Latin language very soon, not literary Latin but Vulgar Latin, from which the French language later developed, but they still retained their Germanic language for a long time. It is reported that, as late as 698, at the funeral procession of St. Ansbert in Rouen, the mourners expressed their grief in various intermingled languages.[12] The first certain proof that the West Franks no longer understood the Germanic language was the oath that Louis the German swore to his brother Charles in Strasbourg in 842, which he spoke in Romanic so that his brother's warriors could understand him. The first West Frankish king who no longer understood the German language was Hugh Capet.[13]

In Italy, where similar conditions reigned, it was not until the second half of the tenth century that the Lombard language in the south was supplanted by Italian, and in the north it had still not died out around the year 1000.[14] The Germanic language, then, held out in the Romanic areas 300 to 400 years. That was possible because the warriors formed a class that remained a tight group and consequently married principally within itself. The Romanics who were accepted in this class became Germanized. We can observe how in many cases the prominent Romanics in France not only assumed Germanic names but also adopted Germanic customs, their dress, the constant wearing of weapons, the feud, the vendetta, and beer drinking.[15] Court and aristocracy retained a Germanic character and had very little inclination toward Roman literary education. Anybody who learned to read went into the service of the church, not the state.

How completely different the world now appeared than it had three or four centuries earlier, when all the citizenry of the one and unified civilized world led peaceful lives and paid taxes, and from those taxes there was maintained a recruited army, which, organized on the border in strictly disciplined legions, protected and secured the empire on all sides against the barbarians! The Romans could not by themselves have produced the warrior class of *leudes* and vassals; there was no longer present so much of the warrior spirit in the civilian society, the world of civilization. Only through the technique of discipline were they in a position to maintain a Roman army. The Germanic soldiers, warriors by nature, grafted onto the dying Romanism, produced the fruit of a unique warrior class resting on itself and continuing as a result of its own warrior spirit.

Procopius (4. 30) has the Roman commander saying to his troops in his speech before the battle of Taginae: "You are going into battle as the defenders of a well-ordered national system, whereas the men over there are spoilers who have no hope at all of seeing their work continued in their posterity, but they measure their existence and outlook only from one day to the next." A very significant expression! As certain as it is that this harangue was apocryphal, nevertheless the idea was probably not at all so incomprehensible even for the Lombards, Herulians, and Gepids in Narses' army. They took their pleasure in destroying civilization under foot while enriching themselves on it, but they had too strong a consciousness of their own barbarism to create by themselves a new cultural situation. And what became of the creations of Gaiseric and Theodoric?

Even the old Roman Empire with its barbarian soldiers was unable to hold its own, confronted by one crisis after another, so that finally there arose from the mixture of Roman and German elements a new and unique political order. Antiquity continued to live on in the church; the state and the military system remained capable of survival and development in the feudal system, which grew principally from Germanic roots.

At this moment, after having overthrown the West Gothic kingdom, the Arabs crossed over the Pyrenees and intended to subjugate the Franks as well.

Islam had also just pressed and closely besieged Constantinople, Italy was strongly threatened, and the horsemen of the Prophet appeared on the Loire, while beyond the Rhine paganism was already starting up again. Christianity and the Roman-Germanic world were barely holding out within a narrow periphery. There is no more important battle in world history than the battle of Tours, in which Charles Martel stopped the Arabs and threw them back. We know practically nothing about the details of this battle, but one thing we can state: it was the Carolingian vassals, that warriorhood which was developed in the Frankish kingdom and neglected in the West Gothic state, that here saved the future of the Germanic-Romanic and Christian world.

# EXCURSUS

## BISHOP PRAETEXTATUS

Gregory 5. 19 recounts how King Chilperic accused Bishop Praetextatus of Rouen of having given presents to men and having caused them to swear loyalty to Merowech, who rebelled against Chilperic's father. The bishop excused himself by saying that he had only returned gift for gift and had not intended to deprive the king of his crown. From this Roth has concluded, *Benefizialwesen*, p. 152, that at that time it was still unacceptable in the existing social order to promise loyalty to anybody but the king himself. I personally would prefer to conclude the opposite from this account. If by contemporary standards it had been considered a crime to promise loyalty to another than the king, primarily the bishop would have had to answer to this accusation. But he does not go into this point at all. For him, that is something that still has no significance in itself. Rather, his reply was: "*sed non haec causa extitit, ut rex ejiceretur e regno*" ("but this is no reason for a king to be driven from his realm").

## THE MAY-FIELD

In about the year 755, the regular Frankish royal and military assembly, which originally took place in March, was shifted to May. This change has been considered proof that it was not until this time that the armed force of the Franks changed from an infantry army to a cavalry army, a conclusion based on the idea that the postponement was due to consideration of available fodder for the horses. In accordance with our explanation above concerning the march of Abbot Fulrad, we can no longer believe in this relationship; even a contingent of nothing but infantry had so many draft animals that consideration of providing fodder had always been a very important factor. Furthermore, the Franks were always partly cavalry; consequently, a few horses more can have made no significant difference.

But we can probably go one step further and completely reject the idea that this assembly had the character of an army review. It was, in fact, only a kind of parliament to which the prominent men probably came with a military retinue but not at all with their entire military force. An assembly of the entire army, or even of only a considerable part of it in a place that was not so situated that they could move directly into a military campaign, would indeed have been an economic as well as a military monstrosity. See Brunner, *Deutsche Rechtsgeschichte* 2: 127 ff.

## VASSALAGE AMONG THE WEST GOTHS

In my explanation I emphasized strongly the difference between the West Gothic kingdom, where the old military system from the time of the settling remained in force, and the Frankish kingdom, where the new form of feudal vassalage had developed. Nevertheless, I chose my expressions with a certain amount of care, since that difference, though decisive, was still not absolute. Even in the West Gothic kingdom, we find various traces that point to a development similar to that of the Frankish kingdom, but these beginnings never developed into full force. Dahn, *Könige* 6: 141, Note 3, already found it surprising that the *antiqua* (old law) spoke of "*se commendare in obsequium*" ("to commit himself to allegiance"). If we realize, however, that the *buccellarius* and the vassal were basically the same, we may be surprised rather at the fact that we do not find more of such expressions.

In *lex Visigothorum* 5. 3. 4 there is the statement: If a man leaves his patron and goes to another one, "ille, cui se commendaverit, det ei terram; nam patronus, quem reliquerit, et terram et que ei dedit, obtineat." ("The one to whom he committed himself should give him land, for the patron whom he left should keep possession of both the land and anything he gave to him.") From this it appears that the West Gothic leaders not only maintained warriors but also provided them with land.

The word *leudes* appears only once in West Gothic literature, *lex Visigothorum* 4. 5. 5, *antiqua*, apparently simply with the meaning "warrior."

SECULARIZATION

I believe I am justified in completely eliminating the secularization of holdings of the church in connection with the genesis of the legal institution of the benefices. It was undoubtedly a political event of the first importance because of the increased power it brought to the Carolingians. But the fact that it was principally possessions of the church that were granted to the vassals is after all only a fortuitous one and not the reason for the elimination of the right of inheritance. The real reason lies in the purpose of the institution, the concern that these possessions should retain their purpose of providing for warriors and not slip from the control of the lord with the next generation.

As I was correcting these pages, there came into my hands the study by Ulrich Stutz, "The Carolingian Tithe System" ("Das karolingische Zehntgebot"), *Zeitschrift der Savigny-Stiftung, Germanische Abteilung*, 29 (1908): 170 ff., which sheds a new and very interesting light on the relationship of secularization to the development of the system of fiefs. In my opinion, Stutz proves convincingly that the tithe system, which was previously only an ecclesiastical arrangement and therefore enforced with difficulty and incompletely, became a national law in Pepin's reign, and that this was the compensation which was provided the church for the lands taken from it. With this discovery we gain an insight of the greatest significance into medieval political and economic life. Let us clearly recognize that the weakness of the Frankish kingdom and the medieval states in general was the lack of a satisfactory tax system; because the ruler did not have money at his disposal from which to pay his men, he had to fill his military needs with a warrior class that provided for itself from the properties it was granted. In order to have enough of these properties, they had to take over the entire complex of the estates of the church; but what then did the church live from? In return she received the tithes which she had no doubt always claimed but had not been able to collect in a general and regular way and which the political administration now actually made available to her. In other words, the state could neither administer nor use for its purposes a tax like the tithes, for deliveries of produce in kind can only be centralized, stored, accounted for, and controlled to a very small degree; the German, in his concept of the law, did not feel obligated for such a payment to the state and the king. The church, however, had just as much use for the tithes in the feeding and maintaining of its priests, its bishops, and its institutes as it had a claim to such tithes in the minds of the faithful. Now the state and the church joined in that alliance of great importance in world history, which led first to the supporting of Bonifacius by the seneschals, then to the creation of the Carolingian kingdom with the approval of the Pope, and finally to the crowning of Charlemagne as emperor. Beneath all this, however, in the basis of this alliance, we now recognize the inspired political realism, the exchange of the taxes of the church tithes and ecclesiastic land holdings. While the state provided for and guaranteed to its closely allied and befriended church the income of its tithes, which it needed and could use, the state received in turn from the church the estates that had been accumulating for centuries, which for its part it needed and could use.

Let us repeat here that the form of the ceding of the fief upon a change of lord or the death of a vassal had nothing to do with the fact that many of these fiefs 'were originally church property. This form is explained uniquely and exclusively by its purpose, the military one. But the utilization of church properties, not for the creation but for the sufficient expansion of the enfeoffed warrior class, was a happening of the greatest significance. The discovery of the relationship of this fact with the introduction of the national tithe system, so important for posterity, impresses on us the greatness and far-reaching influence of this event.

PROVISIONS AND TRAIN

In view of the great importance of transporting provisions in war, I wish to add a few more points and facts of a more special nature to the discussion above of the mobilization letter from Charlemagne to Abbot Fulrad.

In the first edition (Vol. I, p. 427, and Vol. II, p. 105) [*Translator's note:* 3d ed., English translation of Vol. I, p. 461], on the basis of estimates of Napoleon III, I accepted the load for a horse as 500 to 525 kilograms. But I have now become convinced that that is much too high a figure. According to Balck, *Taktik* 2: 1: 288, a horse today in a one-team ration wagon pulls 425 kilograms, of which 250 kilograms are net load; in a two-team ration wagon, it pulls 432 kilograms, of which 250 kilograms are net load; in a one-team transport pool wagon, it pulls 650 kilograms, of which 450 kilograms are net load. (There is a typographical error in Balck that I have corrected here.) Very close to these figures are the Hessian regulation of 1542, cited by Paetel in his *Organisation des hessischen Heeres*, p. 218, the account of the transport of flour by Maximilian of Bavaria in 1620, cited in Vol. IV, p. 343 of the present work, and the document *On the Provisioning of Armies (Von der Verpflegung der Armeen)*, 1779, cited in Jahns 3: 2186.

If this amount is already somewhat smaller than Napoleon's figures, nevertheless the sources show us that in antiquity not even half this much load was assumed. In the *Cyropaedia* 6. 1. 30, Xenophon estimates 25 talents to a pair of oxen, that is, about 675 kilograms or 338 kilograms per animal, but not as a net load, rather as gross weight. Furthermore, we must consider the regulations for the Roman postal service and the relay horses, information that is plentifully provided to us, especially in the *Codex Theodosianus* (L. VIII, Tit. 5). It is true, if we find prescribed here (Emperor Constantius' decree of 357, *Codex Theodosianus* 8. 5. 8) that a wagon (*rheda*) with an eight-mule team is not to be loaded with more than 500 kilograms, these and similar prescriptions have no significance for us, since it was here not a question of the load but of the speed of the transport. But we also find the regulation (8. 5. 11) that an *angaria* with a four-ox team was not to be loaded with more than 750 kilograms. These plodding vehicles moved in large part on the excellent Roman roads, and ox wagons have always been only load-carrying vehicles, without regard to speed. If we nevertheless find not even 200 kilograms of net load (or even only 150, in consideration of the light Roman pound of about 330 grams) reckoned for each animal, this point, together with Xenophon's figure, may serve as proof that the weight of the wagons, particularly of the wheels (often solid disks instead of spokes), and of the harness, and perhaps also the small average capability of the farm teams, did not permit any greater demands. And even less was possible at the time of Charlemagne in Germany, where there were no Roman roads.

As a draft animal the ox is sometimes stubborn and slow, but he pulls more than a horse.

Instead of wagons or carts with draft animals, the use of pack animals has the advantage that the individual animals can more easily follow the movements of the troops, especially in the mountains, and they can also give way more easily when necessary. In both the Roman and the medieval armies and right up into the nineteenth century, they were used very extensively for this reason. Not only the Roman officers but also the men had pack animals, for the most part mules. Their load was 100 kilograms. If we reckon that each Roman tent group of ten men was allowed one animal by the regulations, it could carry, in addition to the leather tent with its accessories (about 20 kilograms) and a hand mill, a kettle, a few tools, ropes and blankets, and probably some rations as well.

Rüstow, in his *Caesar's Army Organization and Conduct of War (Heerwesen und Kriegführung Cäsars)*, p. 17, is of the opinion that the pack animal could also carry a week's rations for each man. That is obviously impossible. The weekly ration for a man can no doubt not have weighed less than 8½ to 9 kilograms and therefore 85 to 90 kilograms for ten men. Together with the tent, that already amounted to more than the full load. But the other items and tools without the tent would hardly have weighed less than 50 kilograms and probably more.

Along with its advantages, however, the use of pack animals also has great disadvantages. It is impossible to load an animal with more than 100 kilograms.[16] Pulling is easier than carrying, and according to the sources cited above, in antiquity they could count on a load of 150 kilograms per draft animal, and today we assume from 250 to 450 kilograms. The draft animal can rest as soon as it stands still, whereas the pack animal continues to be burdened even during the halts. Furthermore, the pack animal is much more easily injured by his load than is the draft animal.

Consequently, Rüstow is undoubtedly incorrect when, on pp. 17 and 18 of the cited work, he states that the Roman armies carried their entire provisions on pack animals. Fröhlich, in his *Kriegswesen Cäsars* 1: 89, has already proven that to be wrong, not only by the very nature of the matter but also with two direct pieces of testimony (Plutarch, *Pompey* 6, and *bell. Afric.* 9. 1), which specifically mention the train wagons and ration wagons. An account in Sallust, *Jugurtha* 75. 3, in which Metellus intends to make an expedition of 75 kilometers through a desert region and therefore orders "omnia jumenta sarcinis levari nisi frumento dierum decem; ceterum utris modo et alia aquae idonea portari" ("that all baggage animals be relieved of their bundles except grain for ten days;

that in addition only skins and other suitable vessels for water be carried"), proves nothing, since wagons could not be used in the desert. Rather, we can conclude from this how difficult it was to procure the necessary pack animals even for a march of only 45 miles. (The animals would also, of course, have to carry along the whole supply of water.) For this purpose, Metellus arranged a large-scale induction of the natives.

The individual man, in addition to his weapons, can carry only a very small supply of provisions. On the basis of a commission by the Ministry of War, Professor Zuntz and Major Doctor Schomburg in 1896 carried out experiments on the physiological effects and loads for marches, the results of which were reported in the February 1897 issue of the *Militärärztliche Zeitschrift*. Five students from the Army Medical College had volunteered for the experiments. They made the marches principally with three stages of loads: 22 kilograms, 27 kilograms, and 31 kilograms.

According to Balck, *Taktik* 2: 1: 208, the two researchers stated the results of their experiments as follows:

1. With a moderate load (up to 22 kilograms) and not too high a temperature, there were no harmful results from a march no longer than 25 to 28 kilometers; on the contrary, it was observed that the march itself eliminated conditions of fatigue produced by other causes and minor disturbances of the functions of individual organs. It is true that under conditions of very high temperatures and humidity a whole series of minor disturbances were perceived (decline in vitality, considerable dehydration of the body, a high pulse rate and breathing rate, and congestion of the blood). But these symptoms disappeared shortly after the march and in any case were completely gone on the following day, so that no accumulation of these difficulties was observed for marches on several consecutive days.

2. With the second phase of loading (27 kilograms), no disadvantages were noticeable under favorable weather conditions and the same march distances. On the other hand, hot weather with this degree of load caused changes which had not disappeared on the following day. Consequently, the second day's march was started under more unfavorable conditions than the first. In any event, a march of 25 to 28 kilometers is the limit of what an average soldier with a 27-kilogram load could tolerate under relatively hot weather conditions.

3. The 31-kilogram load clearly had a damaging effect on the body functions over the same march distances, even in cool weather.

4. With respect to the question of adapting to the load (training) it was observed that a light load (up to 22 kilograms) caused no further harmful effects, even after a few marches and with a gradual increase of the distance; with the heavy load (31 kilograms), only a very little decline in the harmful effects was noted after a rather long period of practice.

It is apparent from the foregoing that even an increase of a few kilograms above the normal load for the soldier (in our time for the infantryman in Germany, 25.3 kilograms [previously 29]; in France, 27 3/4 kilograms; in England, 27¼ kilograms; in Italy, 28 kilograms; and in Switzerland, 31 kilograms) very strongly limits the individual's capability.[17]

It is therefore completely impossible that the Roman soldiers themselves carried much more than an "iron ration," just as is the case with our soldiers. Moreover, the idea of carrying rations is refuted in the sources by a passage in Polybius 18. 18,[18] where the author praises the Romans for carrying palisade stakes in addition to their weapons; if they had also carried provisions, Polybius would not have left that point unmentioned in this connection.

We cannot allow ourselves to be led astray from this conclusion by a few statements of ancient authors who actually claim the contrary. Some of these passages can also be interpreted differently, and in others we must assume either misunderstandings or exaggeration.

Livy, in *Periocha* 57, states: "Scipio Africanus Numantiam obsedit et corruptum licentia luxuriaque exercitum ad severissimam militiae disciplinam revocavit . . . militem . . . triginta dierum frumentum ac septenos vallos ferre cogebat." ("Scipio Africanus besieged Numantia and restored the army corrupted by licentiousness and luxury to the harshest discipline of military service. . . . he compelled the soldier to carry grain for thirty days and seven palisade stakes.") That was no wartime standard but either a practice march or a special punishment such as the carrying of sand bags today. Furthermore, in Frontinus, *Strategem*. 4. 1. 1, there is only the statement "portare complurium dierum cibaria imperabat" ("he ordered them to carry several days' rations"). Obviously, this is the original and correct passage, and in Livy, as a result of some kind of distortion, the expression "several days" has become "thirty days." At the same time, from this we can see how little we can rely on such individual statements.

Frontinus, *Strategem*. 4. 1. 1, reports: "Philippus, cum primum exercitum constitueret, vehiculorum usum omnibus interdixit, equitibus non amplius quam singulos calones habere permisit, peditibus autem denis singulos, qui molas et funes ferrent. In aestiva exeuntibus triginta dierum farinam collo portare imperavit." ("As soon as Philip organized his army, he forbade to all the use of wagons. He permitted the cavalrymen to have no more than a single servant. He allowed the infantry, however, one servant for ten men to carry the mills and the ropes. While they were departing for summer quarters, he commanded them to carry flour for thirty days on their shoulders.") Whatever the expression *"in aestiva exeuntibus"* ("while they were departing for summer quarters") may mean, in any case it is not reported here that the soldiers carried a sack with 30 kilograms of flour on their backs in wartime marches.

In Livy 44. 2, it is stated: "consul menstruum jusso milite secum ferre profectus . . . castra movit." ("After the consul had ordered the soldiers to take with them a month's supply of provisions, he set out and moved his camp.") This does not, after all, need to be translated that the soldier had to carry his requirements for a month; it only needs to indicate that the consul ordered that provisions for thirty days be carried on the expedition. There is a similar statement in Livy 43. 1. 8.

Vegetius 1. 19 says "pondus quoque bajulare usque ad LX libras et iter facere gradu militari cogendi sunt milites, quibus in arduis expeditionibus necessitas imminet annonam pariter et arma portare." ("Soldiers also ought to be compelled to carry weight up to 60 pounds and to march at the military pace. On difficult campaigns the need to carry rations as well as weapons hangs over them.") If that is supposed to mean "60 pounds all together" (equals 20 kilograms), then that is less than the load that is considered normal today. If Vegetius should mean that the soldier had to carry 20 kilograms in addition to his weapons, then we may reject that simply as a misunderstanding, just as with the testimony of Cicero, who cries out in the *Tusculanae* 2. 16. 37: "qui labor, quantus agminis: ferre plus dimidiati mensis cibaria, ferre, si quid ad usum velint, ferre vallum. Nam scutum, gladium, galeam in onere nostri milites non plus numerant, quam humeros, lacertos, manus." ("What hardship! How great a column it takes to carry more than a half-month's rations, to carry anything they should want to use to build a rampart. Of course our soldiers count shield, sword, and helmet no more in weight than shoulders, arms, and hands.")

Judging from various reports, there can be no doubt that the quartermaster or supply administration for the Romans always made a practice of issuing grain to the troops for half a month and that the troops themselves were responsible for transporting these rations. In order that the soldier under no circumstance would suffer a shortage, a half-month was reckoned as seventeen days.

It is clear that with only *one* pack animal for every ten men, it was impossible even to carry rations for seventeen days but at the most only half of that, by having some of it carried by the men themselves and some loaded on the pack animal. That passage from the Jugurthan War where ten days' rations on pack animals is stressed as something unusual establishes an almost smaller limit for us. Consequently, when we read in Ammianus 17. 9. 2 that Julian stored a portion of the seventeen-day supply that each soldier normally carried ("annona decem dierum et septem, quam in expeditionem pergens vehebat cervicibus miles": "the rations of seventeen days, which the soldiers marching on campaign were carrying on their shoulders") and that as a result a shortage occurred, that cannot possibly be taken literally but must be regarded as rhetorical embellishment.

There are, of course, scholars who reply to all such practical considerations and figures with the stiff answer: "That's the way it's written" and consider the source reports to be unconditionally authoritative. Although Colonel Stoffel has already spoken with the sharpest sarcasm of the scholars who loaded on the Roman soldier a 20-kilogram bag of flour in addition to his weapons, nevertheless we still find again in Nissen, "Noväsium," *Bonner Jahrbücher* 111 (1904): 16: "In addition to his equipment, which weighed more than 15 kilograms, the Roman soldier on the march carried his needs in grain for seventeen to thirty days, that is, a load of 14 to 25 kilograms"; he also carried three or four entrenching stakes, which increased his load by 10 more kilograms. Of what good is the precision with which the author reckons to the third decimal point that the Roman recruit, according to Vegetius, carried 19.647 kilograms on training marches, when in the next breath he makes that terrible estimate of the flour bag and sees the difference between "heavy" and "light" infantry as determined by the load carried? In this connection, see also Vol. I, 3d edition, p. 425.

Not only is it impossible for the soldier himself to carry such very large weights of provisions but also it cannot even be done by the supply train.

In a treatise entitled *The Roman Fort of Aliso near Haltern on the Lippe (Die Römerfestung Aliso bei Haltern an der Lippe)*, Leipzig, Phil. Reclam, Lieutenant Colonel Dahm writes: "An army that replenished its supplies in the depots of Aliso (Haltern), since the Roman soldier carried with him grain for seventeen to thirty days, could maneuver in the area of the Sugambri, the Marsi, the

Bructeri, the Ampsivarii, and the Tubantes for weeks without any resupply of rations." Later, Dahm explained this passage by saying he did not intend to mean that the soldier himself was burdened with a bag of 20 kilograms of flour but that he meant it was in the mule column. Let us just figure out this example.

An army of 30,000 combatants (and the Romans, of course, operated in Gaul and Germany with much larger armies than that) needs in thirty days 1,125,000 kilograms of provisions for the fighting men alone and consequently would have had 11,250 mules for this purpose. Since the mule-leaders and other noncombatants also had to be fed, a total of some 18,000 mules would have been needed, which could not possibly have been fed by grazing along the way. With wagons they would have needed something over half that many animals for the same load. If we add to this the large number of animals in the rest of the train and the cavalry horses, even that becomes such a huge number that we must consider it as out of the question in most situations (see p. 126 above and Vol. 1, p. 461). How were they supposed to have maintained regularly such an unprecedented mass of animals and wagons, which could prove useful only in very rare cases? How could they have put them up in the fortified camps that were customarily erected? Therefore, it cannot possibly be a question of regularly carrying along provisions for thirty days, and least of all with pack animals. If Rüstow believed that the Roman armies were equipped not with ration wagons but only with pack animals, he certainly did not think of the regular transporting of rations for seventeen or especially thirty days by means of this method of transportation.

The fact that Lieutenant Colonel Dahm could have formed such concepts of the Roman supply system, as well as his idea of a fortified "deployment area" 27 miles deep (see p. 144 above), is for me one more proof for the conclusion that training in a modern, practical military service still offers no guarantee of clear and correct insights into the military systems of earlier times. On the other hand, this is an excuse for the numerical concepts and Gulliver-like interpretations of our historians, philologists, and jurists.

The mobilization letter to Abbot Fulrad reads as follows:

In nomine patris et filii et spiritus sancti. Karolus serenissimus augustus a Deo coronatus magnus pacificus imperator, qui et per misericordiam Dei rex Francorum et Langobardorum, Fulrado abbati.

Notum sit tibi, quia placitum nostrum generale anno praesenti condictum habemus infra Saxoniam in orientali parte super fluvium Boda in loco que dicitur Starasfurt. Quapropter precipimus tibi ut pleniter cum hominibus tuis bene armatis ac preparatis ad praedictum locum venire debeas XV. Kalendas Julias quod est septem diebus ante missam sancti Johannis baptiste. Ita vero prepara-

In the name of the Father and of the Son and of the Holy Spirit.

Charles the Fairest, Augustus, Crowned by God, the Great, the Peacemaker, Emperor, Who by the mercy of God is King of the Franks and the Langobards, to Fulrad the abbot:

Let it be known to you that we have issued our general decree in the present year within Saxonia in the eastern part upon the Bode River in a place which is called Stassfurt. Therefore, we command that you ought to come to the aforesaid place in full with your men well armed and prepared on 17 June, which is seven

tus cum hominibus tuis ad predictum locum venies, ut inde in quamcumque partem nostra fuerit iussio et exercitaliter ire possis; id est cum armis atque utensilibus necnon et cetero instrumento bellico, in victualibus et vestimentis, ita ut unusquisque caballarius habeat scutum et lanceam et spatam et semispatum, arcum et pharetras cum sagittis, et in carris vestris utensilia diversi generis id est cuniadas et dolaturias taratros, assias, fossorios, palas ferreas et cetera utensilia que in hostem sunt necessaria. Utensilia vero ciborum in carris de illo placito in futorum ad tres menses, arma et vestimenta ad dimidium annum. Et hoc omnino praecipimus, ut observare facietis, ut cum bona pace pergatis ad locum predictum, per quamcumque partem regni nostri itineris vestri rectitudo vos ire fecerit, hoc est ut preter herbam et ligna et aquam nihil de ceteris rebus tangere presumatis, et unicuiusque vestri homines una cum carris et caballariis suis vadant et semper cum eis sint usque ad locum predictum, qualiter absentia domini locum non det hominibus eius mala faciendi. Dona vero tua quae ad placitum nostrum nobis presentare debes, nobis medio mense Maio transmitte ad locum ubicumque tunc fuerimus; si forte rectitudo itineris tui ita se conparet, ut nobis per te ipsum in profectione tua ea presentare possis, hoc magis optamus. Vide ut nullam negligentiam exinde habeas, sicut gratiam nostram velis habere.

days before the Mass of St. John the Baptist. In fact, you will come to the aforesaid place with your men so prepared that you can go with the army in whatever direction from there we ordered, that is, with arms, implements, and the other equipment of war as well as food and clothing, so that each horseman may have shield, lance, broadsword, short sword, bow, and quivers with arrows, and in your wagons implements of a diverse nature, that is, axes, pickaxes, braces, double-edged axes, hoes, iron spades, and other implements which are necessary in an army. Of course, there should be vessels of food in the wagons from the date of that decree up to the next three months, and arms and clothing for a half year. And in general we command that you will have your men observe that, when you proceed to the aforesaid place in good order, through whatever part of our kingdom your line of march causes you to travel, you should venture to touch nothing else except grass, wood, and water, and every one of your men should proceed together with the wagons and their horsemen, and they should always be with them up to the aforesaid place, so that the absence of the master may not grant an opportunity to his men to commit crimes. Certainly, in the middle of May send your gifts to us, which you ought to present according to our decree, to wherever we are at that time. If perchance your line of march thus puts you in a position that you can present these to us in person while on your journey, we prefer this more greatly. See to it that you should have no negligence thereafter, just as you should wish to have our favor.

REFERENCES

At the very beginning of my studies on the history of the art of war, I formed the opinion that the basing of the medieval military system on the system of vassalage and fiefs was to be attributed to a much earlier date than had commonly been assumed in Germany. In an 1881 article, I happened to state that Charles Martel won the battle of Tours with the vassals who formed the Frankish army. (See my *Historical and Political Essays [Historische und Politische Aufsätze]*, p. 126.) The Carolingian Capitularies, which seem to contradict this concept, will be explained in detail in the next volume.

Boretius, in his *Contributions to the Critique of the Capitularies (Beiträge zur Kapitularienkritik)*, has thrown light on this subject and has established the basic points. But there has still remained much too much of the old misconception. Even the valuable treatment by Brunner in "Cavalry Service and the Beginnings of the Feudal System" ("Der Reiterdienst und die Anfänge des Lehnswesens"), *Zeitschrift der Savigny-Stiftung für Rechtsgeschichte, Germanische Abteilung*, Vol. 8 (1897) is in error in its main point by tracing the cavalry service from the special needs of combat against the Saracens and in turn the feudal system from the special needs of the cavalry service. It was not the cavalry that was the characteristic and primary factor in this military system, but the individual fighter, the quality warrior, in contrast to the tactical body. Roloff correctly develops this point in an article in the *Neue Jahrbücher für das klassische Altertum* (1902): 389.

The strong opinions of Wittich are off the mark.

Of great value is the work by Oskar Dippe, "Vassalage and Obeisance in the Kingdom of the Merovingians" ("Gefolgschaft und Huldigung im Reiche der Merowinger"), Kiel dissertation (Wandsbek, 1889). But even Dippe does not go back far enough for the origins of the vassal system. He believes that the fall of the Merovingian kingdom and with it the rise of a new aristocracy cannot be dated before the death of King Dagobert in 639. It is true that this king, as well as his father, Chlotar II, still exercised strong personal royal power. Nevertheless, that occurred only during a temporary suppression of the challenging aristocrats. It is only natural that the two forces, monarchy and aristocracy, for a time alternated in tipping the scales. We may not say, as Dippe does, that when the monarchy had declined, the aristocracy came into power. Rather, both events are complementary, and while we see that the monarchy is weak, the aristocracy must already be present. Weakness of the monarchy and strength of the aristocracy are only different expressions for the same thing. On this point the Edict of Paris in 614 uses a language that can in no way be misunderstood.

On p. 1, Dippe says: "With respect to the system of fiefs, the question of its origin and its historical importance has already been solved in earlier works; as a definite conclusion from them it is to be noted that the feudal system was the inevitable result of an economic shift that had already begun under the Merovingians to destroy the old Germanic independence of the small farmers."

The shift referred to was no simple economic one but even more of a political one, arising from the military system. It was not the "old Germanic independence of the small farmers" that was destroyed, but as the old Germans became farmers they simultaneously lost both their warrior instincts and their independence.

Guilhiermoz' *Treatise on the Origins of the Nobility in France in the Middle Ages (Essai sur l'origine de la noblesse en France au moyen âge)*, Paris, Alphonse Picard et fils, 1902, 502 pp., is a book worthy of the highest consideration; it is based on the broadest possible study of the sources and a complete mastery of the references. The research is methodical, energetic, and penetrating, and the style is that of French elegance.

In completely different ways we have come to the same conclusions on important points.

Guilhiermoz, too, regards vassalage not as a newly risen institution in the Frankish kingdom, whether it be in the seventh or eighth century, but as the continuation of the system of *buccellarii*. And he too considers the *pueri* of the sixth century to be the German *Degen*.

He refers (p. 21) to the first traces of armed freemen in the service of private individuals as early as the third century in Rome. The statesmen Rufinus and Stilicho, who governed the Roman Empire under the sons of Theodosius, were the first to surround themselves on a standing basis with a rather large number of their own troops, dependent only on them.

Guilhiermoz rejects the explanation of the word *buccellarii* as "breadmen" but does not offer any other meaning in its place. For it turns out that the word was originally applied not to private soldiers but to an imperial troop unit and was later carried over to private soldiers. This point ought to be sufficient to eliminate the usual explanation. The fact still remains, however, that originally it was presumably a nickname, the origin of which we can no longer guess.

Whatever the situation may be with respect to this name, the main point is that this institution appears to Guilhiermoz as a purely Roman one, and if the *buccellarii* sprang from a purely Roman root, so did their successors, the vassals. Even the *antrustiones* of the Merovingian kings, who until now have generally been considered as members of the retinue in the old sense used by Tacitus, are seen by the French author as being only common mercenary soldiers.

On this point Guilhiermoz is directly at odds with Seeck. As we have seen on page 389 above, on the contrary, Seeck recognizes in the appearance of the *buccellarii* the real penetration of Germanic ideas and the Germanic system into the Roman Empire, by regarding the *buccellarii* as members of the retinue.

On this point I would like to hold fast to the compromise viewpoint, as I have pictured it in Book IV above. Military service in return for pay, and the idea that the mercenary owes loyalty to the master to whom he has taken an oath are general human phenomena and not specifically Germanic ones. Consequently, Brunner goes somewhat too far in *Deutsche Rechtsgeschichte* 2: 262, Note 27, when he says: "The position of the West Gothic *buccellarius*, despite its Roman name, is in its important aspect that of the Germanic retainer." For example, there were also Huns among Stilicho's *buccellarii*. Therefore, in this matter Guilhiermoz is theoretically correct. But if Brunner and Seeck have attributed too much of the retainer concept to the common *buccellarius*, Guilhiermoz is at fault in the other direction when he denies the retainer character even to the *antrustiones*, so that Clovis and his sons would have completely eliminated this ancient Germanic phenomenon. The closest companions of the Merovingian kings, that is, the *antrustiones*, were quite unmistakably retainers; therefore, it seems to me there is no doubt that very much of the spirit of the Germanic retinue actually resided in the mercenary system based on Roman legal concepts. Even this spirit is indeed not exclusively Germanic but is also to be found among other peoples. But there is no question that it was particularly strongly developed among the Germans and that through the entire Middle Ages it played a highly important, indeed a leading role. We must therefore conclude that it was also very much alive among the Germans in the fifth century. If the Gaul Rufinus and the German Stilicho were the first Roman statesmen who had *buccellarii* in their service, that is after all no simple accident; the mass of these warriors may not have been significantly different from mercenaries, but the leaders were no doubt filled with the Germanic feel for loyalty to their masters and probably transferred something of this feeling to their men. Indeed, if Guilhiermoz believes he can establish that the cradle of the *buccellarii* system lay in the *scholae* that Constantine I established, then that reminds us again that it was precisely Constantine who Germanized the Roman army once and for all. Relationships of this kind cannot really be proven. There is little to be concluded from the legal forms (the handshake and other similar acts), and the sources and witnesses tell us nothing. The important, continuing development is nevertheless unmistakable, and Brunner (*Deutsche Rechtsgeschichte* 2: 262) may have hit the mark with his expression that the Gallo-Roman system of private soldiery was "equivalent" to the Germanic retinue.

The error in Brunner — and on this point I have come to the same conclusion as Guilhiermoz — is only that he portrays as much too thin the thread that leads from the *buccellarii* to the vassals, so that at times it seems to break completely; the "unfree men" in the retinue of the Merovingian leaders play much too large a role in his work.

With regard to the origin of the granting of land, Guilhiermoz is not ready to deny completely a connection with secularization, but he comes to a conclusion similar to mine to the extent that he places the emphasis on the *purpose* of the grant. And from this institution, too, he draws connecting threads over into the Roman law. He points out that indeed, even in accordance with West Gothic law, the master gave his man "*in patrocinio*" ("in patronage") a piece of property with reservations and limitations. I shall leave it to the legal historians to come to agreement on this point; for our purpose, after all, the legal forms and their origin are not so important. The decisive point is that it was not a half-way fortuitous circumstance, like secularization, but an inherent practical need that produced the institution of land grants, with its innumerable consequences. If it is true that Guilhiermoz, while coming close to my ideas on this point, still has not completely separated himself from the ruling concept, this is due to the fact that his studies did not lead him to the factor that in the final analysis has to be the decisive one, the postulate of the conduct of war. One can say specifically the *tactical* postulate, the relationship that always exists, in every period, between tactics and military organization; that period in history required individual warriors who were quality fighters (not trained tactical bodies); the lord had no other means of keeping these warriors from becoming farmers or burghers than to make their property dependent on the continuation of their service, that is, to give them their land not as private property but only as a fief.

There appeared in 1898 *A History of the Art of War, the Middle Ages, from the Fourth to the Fourteenth Century,* by Charles Oman, M.A.

F.S.A., fellow of All Souls College, Oxford (London, Methuen and Co., 36 Essex St. W.C.), 667 pp. This book, which first came to my attention in 1901, is conceived as the second volume of a general four-volume history of the art of war. The author had already made a name for himself earlier through his studies in the field of medieval military organization. He therefore has felt exactly the same need to fill in historical knowledge as I, and our works will parallel each other. Oman's book is scholarly and has sound basic concepts. We nevertheless have arrived at differing conclusions in those parts that treat the same periods and peoples, and the reasons are so clearly to be seen that I have not considered it necessary to go into detailed explanations.

As far as I can see, the first national economist to notice that there was something to be learned also for economic history from the *History of the Art of War* was Max Weber. But as is usually the case, the first understanding can easily be a misunderstanding.

Weber correctly recognized that there was a class of knights in the Greco-Italian world in the pre-classical period and that this knightly class was also the group responsible for the developing trade and capitalism (see Vol. I, p. 258),[19] whereas Eduard Meyer still assumed that it was first people from the lower classes, without property, who became seafarers.[20] As a result of the ascendancy of military-economic factors, a distinction developed between classes and a system of political leadership arose which Weber designates "city feudalism," since the lords did not live in the country, like the medieval knights, but lived exclusively in the cities and controlled the farmers from there.

The idea of extending the concept of "feudalism" to this ancient knightly class as well is not bad, but it must be treated with care. For to feudalism, as we are now accustomed to use the word, there also belongs the echeloning of ranks of the subordinates, the "military scutcheon," which was not known to antiquity, whereas, on the other hand, the element of capitalism that was inherent in the ancient knighthood is not only foreign to but even the direct opposite of what we understand as "feudalism." Weber even includes the Spartan system as part of feudalism.

But no matter how we express it, the principal point is the origin of this class formation and the explanation of the difference between the ancient and medieval types of knighthood.

Weber traces the formation of a special warrior class from economic and technical foundations. He believes that the great mass of the population, because of the necessity for more intensive work on the land, was no longer available for military service and was helpless in comparison with the technical skill of the professional warriors. Both points are incorrect. In the large nations, whose wars last for months and years, the masses are economically indispensable. But in small countries, where the campaigns of the masses last only a few days, work is no obstacle. And yet the ancient knighthood was formed in small countries. The skill aspect, however, even though not unimportant, is nevertheless of only secondary importance in knighthood; the farmer too can ride well, and in the Middle Ages we hear only very little of a real combat skill (see Vol. III, Book III, Chapter 1). With quite heavy defensive armor it is not so decisive. At least as important is the economic factor of the production of better weapons, both defensive and offensive. The real essence of the matter, however, is not to be found here but in the psychic factors, the warrior's concept of honor, the trust, the courage, which are always very small in the masses as soon as they have progressed beyond barbarism, but which are highly developed in a warrior class. This military spirit cannot be subsumed under the concept of "skill," and least of all a skill to be acquired from external sources, as Weber believes (p. 53, para. 3).

The most important technical factor in this type of development is the training for mounted combat. As explained above (see Vol. I, page 256), this, of course, undoubtedly contributed much to the formation of the Italian knighthood — but only contributed. The Greek Eupatrids, which Weber quite correctly considers as identical with the Roman patrician class, did not yet fight on horseback. Of course, the Homeric war chariot was already of assistance, but that "the introduction of the horse led to the formation of the Mediterranean knightly society," as Weber says on p. 177, is an unacceptable exaggeration.

Incidentally, even less accurate is the statement in the same passage that the *iron* weapon (instead of the bronze) was the decisive factor in the formation of the hoplite phalanx and that the latter led to the formation of the ancient "city-state." The portion of this combination that is accurate loses its validity as a result of the exaggeration.

The erroneous tracing of knighthood from economic-technical bases leads into an incorrect explanation of the difference between the ancient and the medieval knight. Weber traces this difference back to the fact that the ancient culture was a coastal civilization, whereas the medieval was a civilization of the interior. According to him, sea trade created city feudalism, whereas in Central Europe, with its overland trade, feudalism was built much more strongly on a land basis and therefore produced the property-based leaders. That is incorrect both in its assumptions and in its conclusions. We have already shown above in another connection (see pp. 231 ff.) that Weber's antithesis of coastal civilization and interior civilization is false. Ancient commerce was not as exclusively sea trade as Weber believes; even Athens, at the time when the Eupatrid clans became a special class, was not really a sea power. Central Europe, on the other hand, and particularly Gaul, had, in its rivers, trade routes and commercial possibilities that offered almost as many advantages as the sea (which, to be sure, was in no way lacking in these countries). Finally, it is also incorrect that the medieval feudalism developed only or specifically in the countries that got along without sea trade. Spain and Italy, which were situated on the sea as much in the Middle Ages as in antiquity, had in general the same form of feudalism as France and Germany. On the other hand, the Anglo-Saxons on their island in the sea did not develop this feudalism, but the seafaring Normans were its principal proponents. Consequently, with sea and land, sea trade and land trade, both in antiquity and in the Middle Ages, feudalism had — I will not say no effect, for in the final analysis everything has some effect on everything else — only very little connection. These great phenomena of world history cannot be explained so simply, and least of all as a result of simple natural conditions, economic and technical relationships.

I believe that I may refrain from any special argument with W. Erben's "On the History of the Carolingian Military System" ("Zur Geschichte des karolingischen Kriegswesens"), *Historische Zeitschrift* 101: 321, and I simply point out that the author differs from my concept and runs into contradictions with himself. Whereas on p. 330 he considers the Carolingian army "to be composed principally of German peasants," he gives the opinion on p. 333 that the real effect of the general mobilization may have lagged far behind the literal wording of the laws and that neither the number of peasants who actually participated in Charlemagne's campaigns nor the role they played in comparison with and under the leadership of the vassals involved could be accurately recognized. The question is not raised at all as to where in the Romanic areas, which after all formed five-sixths of the Carolingian Empire before the incorporation of Saxony and Bavaria, the German peasants came from, or whether it was the Romanic-Celtic peasants, who had been unaccustomed to war for many centuries, who were mobilized in this case. The author claims that what is new in my work consists only of the fact that I have assigned an earlier date and different reasons for the concept, which is otherwise generally accepted, that is, that the practice of providing personal service shifted to the providing of taxes. He also concedes that these other reasons are the more correct ones. Finally, he claims that it is difficult — indeed, "perhaps impossible" (p. 330) — for the military professional to gain a picture of the organization and accomplishments of the Carolingian "people's levy," the "peasant armies." But despite all this, the literal interpretation of the capitularies should hold true, for "The judgment of the ruler (Charles) and his court, experienced as they were in military and governmental affairs, the basis for the capitularies, fully outweighs all the suspicions of modern objective critics" (p. 334). This is another example of what I earlier called "theological philology" (Vol. I, p. 411) — *credo, quia absurdum* (I believe because it is absurd).

Finally, it appears unmistakable to me that the author basically has taken into consideration the *History of the Art of War* not completely, but only partially. The chapter on the Norman military organization in England and the capitularies of these kings, which are of such great importance for the correct interpretation of the Carolingian capitularies (Vol. III, Book II, Chapter 5), have not been given due consideration.

Of course, the author finally says that he is in complete agreement with the other parts of my book (p. 334). But I cannot see what that can refer to without having the author contradict himself: for I consider it impossible that anybody who has really accepted my concept of knighthood, of its military character and value, can still see peasants in the armies of Charlemagne.

Fehr, in "The Peasants' Right to Bear Arms in the Middle Ages" (Das Waffenrecht der Bauern im Mittelalter"), *Zeitschrift der Savigny-Stiftung für Rechtsgeschichte, Germanische Abteilung*, 35:118, agrees with Erben and believes he is reinforcing Erben's proof by reference to the Capitulary of 811 (Boretius 1: 165: 5), which complains that the *pauperiores* were called up and the well-to-do were left at home. According to him, these *pauperiores* were small farmers. Why farmers? Even in the warrior class there were both rich and poor, and I believe I have proven that the word "populus" applied not to the whole mass of the people but to military men.

NOTES FOR CHAPTER IV

1. The provisions of the edict read as follows: "ut nullus judex de aliis provinciis aut regionibus in alia loca ordinetur; ut si aliquid mali de quibuslibet conditionibus perpetraverit, de suis propriis rebus exinde quod male abstulerit, juxta legis ordinem debeat restituere." (that no judge from different provinces and regions should be appointed in other locations; that if he should have rendered some injury under any circumstances, according to the order of this law he would have to restore what he subsequently gained from his own property.") *Mon. Germ. Leg.* 1. 14, Waitz, *Deutsche Verfassungsgeschichte* 2: 377. *Judex* applies to the official in general, also the count. The indefinite expression *"de aliis provinciis et regionibus"* ("from different provinces and regions") is either the pure bombast of a copyist or intentional because of those owners who had property in several districts. It is not specifically stated that only estate owners were to be named, but this is to be inferred from the prohibition *"de aliis provinciis aut regionibus,"* together with the requirement for wealth: owners of a large mobile fortune without real property hardly came into consideration for the position of count.

2. *Geschichte des Benefizialwesens,* p. 153.

3. On this point I agree essentially with Brunner in his *Deutsche Rechtsgeschichte,* except that he still considers *pueri* too much as unfree men.

The difference between the Frankish monarchy and that of the other Germanic countries was first clearly recognized and sharply defined by Sohm; Sohm's idea was in turn effectively developed by W. Sickel, *Westdeutsche Zeitschrift* (1885): 231 ff.

4. Dippe, *Vassalage and Obeisance in the Kingdom of the Merovingians (Gefolgschaft und Huldigung im Reiche der Merowinger),* p. 44.

5. Examples in Dippe, p. 18.

6. According to the extract in Boretius, *Contributions to the Critique of the Capitularies (Beiträge zur Kapitularienkritik),* p. 154.

7. According to M. Heym, *The German Production of Foodstuffs (Das deutsche Nahrungswesen),* p. 295. *räuchern* (to smoke) is a common Germanic word; this method of protecting meat from spoiling is therefore very ancient. When Pomponius Mela reports that in Germany they ate meat raw, Heym believes that this statement referred to smoked meat. The technique of making cabbage and greens preservable by a spe-

cial procedure is, according to Heym, p. 327, not a native one; *sauer-kraut* is a name that was adopted much later. Nevertheless, it may not be impossible that Abbot Fulrad knew this dish and took some of it into the field with him.

8. See the excursus, "Provisions and Train."

9. (added in the 2d edition.) Consequently, I have not, as Erben states in the *Historische Zeitschrift* 101: 329, admitted the possibility of depots, for example on the Rhine, only missing testimony therefor, but I have expressly argued against the possibility of such depots.

10. Bronsart, *Dienst des Generalstabes*, p. 414, 2d edition. Today it is even more.

11. N.B.: under the then existing conditions; the present-day train horse, on a modern road, pulls more than twice that much.

12. Roth, *Benefizialwesen*, p. 99, Note 224.

13. Petit de Juleville, *Histoire de la littérature française*, 1: 67. Toward the middle of the ninth century, Abbot Lupus of Ferrière en Gâtinais sent his nephew to Prüm to learn German. Consequently, there was no longer the possibility for this at home; but it was still considered advisable to know that language.

14. W. Bruckner, *The Language of the Lombards (Die Sprache der Langobarden)*, Strasbourg, 1895.

15. Roth, *Benefizialwesen*, pp. 98, 100, 101. In a roster of the monks of St. Denis drawn up in 838, we find only eighteen non-Germanic names in a list of 130; furthermore the majority of the eighteen were biblical names. Even in the most southerly part of Gaul, we find the names in the ninth century to be predominantly German. The same situation is shown in the rosters in a sacramentary of the Paris church at the end of the ninth century, published by Leopold Delisle in the *Mémoires de l'Institut de France* 32 (1886): 372.

16. For ordinary service an animal can, of course, be loaded with up to 150 kilograms, but that is hardly possible for war service, where unusually long marches are quite often required, fodder is irregular, and the loss of animals must be avoided as far as possible.

17. Balck, *Taktik* 1: 62. In a handwritten document by Alexander von der Goltz from the period of Frederick the Great, cited in Jähns 3: 2539, we learn that the infantryman at the time had to carry only 52.36 pounds, including 8.8 pounds of bread and sixty live cartridges. This figure appears rather too high still, since in that estimate the empty cartridge case counts for 4 pounds and the rain cover for the musket 1 pound. In 1839, the Prussian infantryman carried 26.4 kilograms, with-

out considering his uniform. In 1913, there was a discussion in the *Militär-Wochenblatt* concerning the lightening of the equipment, in which it was shown that by the regulation of 1 February 1908 the total load of the German infantryman was lowered to between 24 and 24 3/4 kilograms, while the French soldier, as the result of elimination of a few items, had only a 20-kilogram load. See my *Perser-und Burgunderkriege*, p. 56.

18. This has been pointed out by Liers in *The Military System of the Ancients (Das Kriegswesen der Alten)*, p. 226.

19. *Handwörterbuch der Staatswissenschaften* I, article "Agrargeschichte," p. 53.

20. *Geschichte des Altertums* 2: 242.

# APPENDIX 1

# Latin Text: Battle of Adrianople (Passage on pages 282-283)

His forte diebus Valens tandem excitus Antiochia, longitudine uiarum emensa uenit Constantinopolim, ubi moratus paucissimos dies seditoneque popularium leui pulsatus, Sebastiano paulo ante ab Italia, ut petierat, misso, ugilantiae notae ductori pedestris exercitus cura commissa, quem regebat antea Traianus: ipse ad Melanthiada uillam Caesarianam profectus militem stipendio fouebat et alimentis et blanda crebritate sermonum, unde cum itinere edicto per tesseram Nicen uenisset, quae statio ita cognominatur: relatione speculatorum didicit refertos opima barbaros praeda a Rhodopeis tractibus prope Hadrianopolim reuertisse: qui motu imperatoris cum abundanti milite cognito, popularibus iungere festinant, circa Beroeam et Nicopolim agentibus praesidiis fixis: atque ilico ut oblatae occasionis maturitas postulabat, cum trecentenis militibus per singulos numeros lectis Sebastianus properare dispositus est, conducens rebus publicis aliquid, ut promittebat, acturus. qui itineribus celeratis conspectus prope Hadrianopolim, obseratis ui portis iuxta adire prohibebatur: ueritis defensoribus ne captus ab hoste ueniret et subornatus atque contingeret aliquid in ciuitatis perniciem, quale per Actum acciderat comitem, quo per fraudem Magnentiacis militibus capto claustra patefacta sunt Alpium Juliarum. agnitus tamen licet sero Sebastianus et urbem introire permissus, cibo et quiete curatis pro copia, quos ductabat, secuta luce impetu clandestino erupit, uesperaque incedente Gothorum uastatorios cuneos prope flumen Hebrum subito visos paulisper opertus aggeribus et fructetis obscura nocte suspensis passibus incompositos adgressus est, adeoque prostrauit, ut praeter paucos, quos morte uelocitas exemerat pedum, interirent reliqui omnes, praedamque retraxit innumeram, quam nec ciuitas cepit nec planities lata camporum. qua causa percitus Fritigernus et extimescens, ne dux, ut saepe audierat, impetrabilis dispersos licenter suorum globos raptuique intentos consumeret, inprouisos adoriens: reuocatis omnibus prope Cabylen oppidum cito discessit, ut agentes in regionibus patulis nec inedia uec occultis uexarentur insidiis.

Dum haec aguntur in Thraciis, Gratianus docto litteris patruo, qua industria superauerit Alamanos, pedestri itinere, praemissis inpedimentis et sarcinis, ipse cum expeditiore militum manu permeato Danubio, delatus Bononiam, Sirmium introiit, et quadriduum ibi moratus per idem flumen ad Martis castra descendit, febribus intervallatis adflictus: in quo tractu Halanorum impetu repentino temptatus amisit sequentium paucos.

Isdemque diebus exagitatus ratione gemina Valens, quod Lentienses conpererat superatos, quodque Sebastianus subinde scribens facta dictis exaggerabat, e Melanthiade signa commouit, aequiperare facinore quodam egregio adulescentem properans filium fratris, cuius uirtutibus urebatur: ducebatque multiplices copias nec contemnendas nec segnes, quippe etiam ueteranos isdem iunxerat plurimos, inter quos et honoratiores alii et Traianus recinctus est, paulo ante magister armorum. et quoniam exploratione sollicita cognitum est cogitare hostes fortibus praesidiis itinera claudere, per quae commeatus necessarii portabantur, occursum est huic conatui conpetenter, ad retinendas oportunitates angustiarum, quae prope erant, peditibus sagittariis et equitum turma citius missa. triduoque proximo cum barbari gradu incederent leni et metuentes eruptionem per deuia, quindecim milibus passuum a ciuitate discreti stationem peterent Nicen — incertum quo errore — procursatoribus omnem illam multitudinis partem, quam uiderant, in numero decem milium esse firmantibus, imperator procaci quodam calore perculsus isdem occurrere festinabat. proinde agmine quadrato incedens prope suburbanum Hadrianopoleos uenit, ubi uallo sudibus fossaque firmato, Gratianum impatienter operiens, Richomerem comitem domesticorum suscepit ab eodem imperatore praemissum cum litteris, ipsum quoque uenturum mox indicantibus. quarum textu oratus ut praestolaretur paulisper periculorum participem, neue abruptis discriminibus temere semet committeret solum, adhibitis in consilium potestatibus uariis, quid facto opus esset, deliberabat. et cum Sebastiano auctore quidam protinus eundum ad certamen urgerent, Victor nomine magister equitum, Sarmata sed cunctator et cautus, eadem sentientibus multis imperii socium exspectari censebat, ut incrementis exercitus Gallicani adscitis opprimeretur leuius tumor barbaricus flammans. uicit tamen funesta principis destinatio et adulabilis quorundam sententia regiorum, qui, ne paene iam partae uictoriae — ut opinabantur — consors fieret Gratianus, properari cursu celeri suadebant.

*  *  *

# APPENDIX 2

# Latin Text: Beatus Avitus (Passage on pages 399-400)

Beatus Avitus ex nobili prodiens stirpe ad alta pullulando, congruenti tempore maturos fructus longe lateque redolenti suavitate produxit. Hic, secundum schema curialis prosapiae, altorum natalium productus floruit germine ac loci Principum; et in quodam vico nomine Linocasio Petragoricae provinciae felicis nativitatis sumpsit exordium. Vix tempore ablactationis emerso parentum cura urgente, litterarum imbuendus studiis traditur. Transcurso igitur puerilis metae bravio, jam juvenili pubescens flore bivium attigit Pythagoricae litterae in quo utriusque vitae confinio, dextrum ramum praeelegit sapienti comitio; malens in exilio hujus vitae coactari, quam ambitiose vivendo, vel voluptatum latitudinem sequendo, in extremo judicio damnari.

Ea tempestate Alaricus, Christiani nominis publicus inimicus, regnum Gothorum obtinuit: qui tyrannica crudelis animi rabie, et feralis saevitiae atrocitate, adepti regni potentia in superbiam elatus, et qui brachio suae fortitudinis undequaque affines vincere est solitus; spei animatus majoris fiducia, oppugnandi scilicet gratia regnum adire disposuit Franciae; quod suae pertinaciae votum ut firmis roborari videt assensu morum totius regni (argenti) ponderosa massa per executores in unum corpus conflatur: et quisque ex militari ordine viribus potens, donativum regis volens nolens recepturus, per praecones urgente sententia invitatur.

Beatus ergo Avitus, Athleta Dei strenuissimus, jam triumpho philosophicae palaestrae nobiliter potitus, censu majore, equestri gradu natalium, licet invitus, seculari praescriptus militiae, quasi alter Martinus militare donativum recepturus, inter ceteros praenotatur, ut contra hostilem Francorum aciem pugnaturus. Qui non surdus illius auditor Evangelii, ubi praecipitur Reddite ergo Caesari quae sunt Caesaris, et quae sunt Dei Deo, exterius baltheo circumcinctus et secularibus armis obumbratus: interius vero Christi gerens occultum militiam terreno Regi accessit militaturus.

\* \* \*

# APPENDIX 3

# Latin Text: Lex Visigothorum (Passage on pages 400-403)

I. ANTIQUA.

Si hi, qui exercitui prepositi sunt, commodis corrupti aliquem de expeditione domum redire permiserint vel a domibus suis exire non coegerint.

Si thiufadus ab aliquo de thiufa sua fuerit beneficio corruptus, ut eum ad domum suam redire permitteret, quod acceperat in novecuplum reddat comiti civitatis, in cuius est territorio constitutus. Et si ab eo nullam mercedem acceperit, sed sic eum, dum sanus est, ad domum dimiserit vel de domo in exercitum exire non compulerit, reddat solidos **XX**; quingentenarius vero **XV**, et centenarius **X**; si certe decanus fuerit, V solidos reddere conpellatur. Et ipsi solidi dividantur in centena, ubi fuerint numerati.

II. ANTIQUA.

Si conpulsores exercitus aliquid, dum exercitum ad hostem conpellunt, de domibus eorum auferre presumserint.

Servi dominici, id est conpulsores exercitus, quando Gotos in hostem exire conpellunt, si eis aliquid tulerint aut ipsis presentibus vel absentibus sine ipsorum volumtatem de rebus eorum auferre presumserint, et hoc ante iudicem potuerit adprobare, ei, cui abstulerint, in undecuplum restituere non morentur; ita tamen, ut unusquisque eorum in conventu publice L flagella suscipiat.

III. ANTIQUA.

Si prepositi exercitus relicto bello ad domum redeant aut alios redire permittant.

Si quis centenarius, dimittens centenam suam in hostem, ad domum suam refugerit, capitali supplicio subiacebit. Quod si ad altaria sancta vel ad episcopum forte confugerit, CCC solidos reddat comiti civitatis, in cuius est territorio constitutus, et pro vita sua non pertimescat. Ipse tamen comes civitatis notum faciat regi, et sic cum nostra ordinatione partiantur solidi illi ad ipsam centenam, que ei fuerat adscripta. Ipse autem postmodum centenarius nullo modo preponatur, sed sit sicut unus ex decanis. Et si centenarius sine conscientia aut volumtate prepositi hostis aut thiufadi sui de centena sua, ab aliquo per beneficio persuasus aut rogitus, quemquam ad domum suam redire permiserit vel in hostem, ut non ambularet, relaxaverit, quantum ab eo acceperat in novecuplum comiti civitatis, in cuius est territorio constitutus, satisfacere conpellatur; et sicut superius diximus, comis civitatis nobis in notitiam referre non differat, ut ex nostra preceptione dividatur inter eos, in cuius centena fuerat adscriptus. Quod si centenarius ab eo nullam mercedem acceperit et sic eum ad domum suam ambulaturum dimiserit, ille centenarius, sicut superius est conprehensum, det comiti civitatis solidos X.

IV. ANTIQUA.

Si prepositi exercitus aut relicta expeditione ad domum redeant aut alios exire minime conpellant.

Si decanus relinquens decaniam suam, de hoste ad domum refugerit aut de domo sua, cum sanus esset, exire et ad expeditionem proficisci noluerit, det comiti civitatis solidos X. Quod si alicui forte mercedes dederit, reddat solidos V comiti civitatis, in cuius est territorio constitutus; et ipse comes civitatis notum nobis faciat, ut cum nostra iussione dividantur inter eos, in quorum centena fuerat adscriptus. Quod si aliquis, qui in thiufa sua fuerat numeratus, sine permissione thiufadi sui vel quingentenarii aut centenarii vel decani sui de hoste ad domum suam refugierit aut de domo sua in hostem proficisci noluerit, in conventu mercantium publice C flagella suscipiat et reddat solidos X.

V. ANTIQUA.

Si conpulsores exercitus beneficio accepto aliquem sine egritudine domu stare permiserint.

Servi dominici, qui in hoste exire conpellunt, si ab eis aliquis se forte redimerit, quantum ab eo accepit, in novecuplum comiti civitatis cogatur exolvere, et eos, quos rogaverit, dum esset sanus, ut eum in expeditionem non conpellerent, etiam si nullam mercedem ab eo acceperint, illi, qui eum relaxaverint, reddant pro eo comiti civitatis solidos V. Thiufadus vero querat per centenarios suos, et centenarii per decanos, et si potuerint cognoscere, quia per precem aut per redemtionem ad domum suam refugerint aut de domo in hostem proficisci noluerint, tunc thiufadus preposito comitis notum faciat et scribat comiti civitatis, in cuius est territorio constitutus, ut comes civitatis vindictam, que in lege posita est de his, qui pro se rogant aut qui se redimunt, aut thiufadis vel centenariis aut decanis vel servis dominicis, omnia ad integrum inplere non differat. Quod si exegerit et celaverit et in notitiam non protulerit, omnia, que exegit, in novecuplum reddat; et si corruptus ab aliquo vel rogitus exigere distulerit, in duplum de propria facultate satisfaciat illis, qui inter se hanc solutionem fuerant divisuri. Quod si post exactam rem regi notum non fecerit, ut ipse hoc iubeat in thiufa, cui debebatur, dividere, aut comes civitatis reddere fortasse dissimulet, undecupli compositionem eis satisfacere non moretur.

VI. ANTIQUA.

De his, qui annonas distribuendas accipiunt vel fraudare presumunt.

Hoc iustum elegimus, ut per singulas civitates vel castella quicumque erogator annone fuerit constitutus, comes civitatis vel annone dispensator, annonam, quam eis est daturus, ex integro in civitatem vel castello iubeat exiberi et ad integrum eis restituere non moretur. Quod si contigerit, ut ipse comes civitatis aut annonarius per neglegentiam suam, non habens aut forsitan nolens, annonas eorum dare dissimulet, comiti exercitus sui querellam deponant, quod annonas eorum eis dispensatores tradere noluerint. Et tunc ille prepositus hostis hominem suum ad nos mittere non moretur, ita ut numerentur dies, ex quo annone eorum iuxta consuetudinem eis inplete non fuerit. Et tunc ipse comes civitatis vel annonarius, quantum temporis eis annonas consuetas subtraxerat, in quadruplum eis invitus de sua propria facultate restituat. Similiter et de his, qui in thiufa fuerint dinumerati, observari precipimus.

\* \* \*

# APPENDIX 4

# Latin Text: Laws of Wamba and Erwig (Passage on pages 421-426)

IN NOMINE DOMINI.
FLAVIUS GLORIOSUS WAMBA REX.
Quid debeat observari, si scandalum infra
fines Spanie exsurrexerit.

Cogit nostram gloriam saluberrima intentio actionis, ut, sicut in dirimendis negotiis populorum legum est auctoritas promulgata ita in rebus bellicis mutuo suffulta presidio habilis ad expugnandum maneat fraternitas dilectione retenta. Prodesse enim omnibus tranquillitas nostra non ambigit, si cunctorum animos ad bonum propositum classica legis tuba evocando constringit; scilicet, ut que in preteritis non bene ordinata discurrunt, deinceps disposita opitulante Domino in melius proficiscant. Et ideo huius male usitate consuetudinis mores nostra clementia perhorrescit et tediose tolerat, quod per quorundam incuriam frequentia occurant patrie damna. Nam quotiescumque aliqua infestatio inimicorum in provincias regni nostri se ingerit, dum nostris hominibus, qui in confinio externis gentibus adiunguntur, hostilis surgit bellandi necessitas, ita quidam facillima se occasione dispergunt, modo transductione loci, modo livore odii, modo etiam inpossibilitatis dissimulatione subnixi, ut in eo preliandi certamine unus alteri fraterna solacia non inpendat, et sub hac occassione aut qui prestare debuit publicis utilitatibus fratrum destitutus adiutorio retrahatur, aut si adgredi pro gentis et patrie utilitatibus audacter voluerit, casu inminentis periculi ab adversariis perimatur. Adeo presenti sanctione decernimus, ut a die legis huius prenotato vel tempore, si quelibet inimicorum adversitas contra partem nostram commota extiterit, seu sit episcopus sive etiam in quocumque ecclesiastico ordine constitutus, seu sit dux aut comes, thiufadus aut vicarius, gardingus vel quelibet persona, qui aut ex ipso sit commissu, ubi adversitas ipsa occurrerit, aut ex altero, qui in

vicinitate adiungitur, vel quicumque in easdem provincias vel territoria superveniens infra centum milia positus, statim ubi necessitas emerserit, mox a duce
suo seu comite, thiufado vel vicario aut a quolibet fuerit admonitus, vel quocumque modo ad suam cognitionem pervenerit, et ad defensionem gentis vel
patrie nostre prestus cum omni virtute sua, qua valuerit, non fuerit et quibuslibet
subtilitatibus vel requisitis occasionibus alibi se transferre vel excusare voluerit,
ut in adiutorio fratrum suorum promptus adque alacer pro vindicatione patrie
non existat, et superveniens adversariorum hostilitas aliquid damni vel captivita-
tis in populos vel provincias regni nostri amodo intulerint, quisquis tardus seu
formidulosus vel qualibet malitia, timore vel tepiditate succinctus exierit, et ad
prestitum vel vindicationem gentis et patrie exire vel intendere contra inimicos
nostre gentis tota virium intentione distulerit: si quisquam ex sacerdotibus vel
clericis fuerit et non habuerit, unde damna rerum terre nostre ab inimicis inlata
de propriis rebus satisfaciat, iuxta electionem principis districtiori mancipetur
exilio. Hec sola sententia in episcopis, presbiteris et diaconibus observanda est. In
clericis vero non habentibus honorem iuxta subteriorem de laicis ordinem consti-
tutum omnis sententia adinplenda est. Ex laicis vero, sive sit nobilis, sive
mediocrior viliorque persona, qui talia gesserint, presenti lege constituimus, ut
amisso testimonio dignitatis redigatur protinus in conditionem ultime servitutis,
ut de eius persona quidquid princeps iudicare voluerit potestas illi indubitata
manebit. Nam iustum est, ut qui nobilitatem sui generis et statum patrie, quod
prisce gentis adquisivit utilitas, constanti animo vindicare nequivit, legis huius
sententia feriatur, qui notabiliter superioribus culpis adstrictus, degener atque
inutilis repperitur. De bonis autem transgressorum, laicorum scilicet adque etiam
clericorum, qui sine honore sunt, id decernimus observandum, ut qui deinceps
hoc fortasse commiserint, inde cuncta damna terre nostre vel his, qui mala pertu-
lerint, sarciantur; ut recte doleat, et dignitatem se amisisse nobilium et predia
facultatem, cuius maligna vel timida factio nec ledentem reppulit hostem nec se
ostendit in adversariorum congressione virilem. Nam et si quilibet infra fines
Spanie, Gallie, Gallecie vel in cunctis provinciis, que ad ditionem nostri regiminis
pertinent, scandalum in quacumque parte contra gentem vel patriam nostrum-
que regnum vel etiam successorum nostrorum moverit aut movere voluerin-
dum hoc in vicinis loci ipsius partibus iuxta numerum miliorum suprascriptum
nuntiatum extiterit, aut etiam specialiter quisquis ille a sacerdotibus, clericis,
ducibus, comitibus, thiufadis, vicariis vel quibuslibet personis iuxta ordinem
suprascriptum admonitus fuerit, vel ad suam cognitionem quoquo modo pervenerit, et statim ad vindicationem aut regis aut gentis et patrie vel fidelium pre-
sentis regis, contra quem ipsum scandalum excitatum extiterit, non citata
devotione occurrerit et prestitum se in eorum adiutorio ad destruendum exortum
scandalum non exhibuerit: si episcopus vel quilibet ex clero fuerit aut fortasse ex
officio palatino, in quocumque sit ordine constitutus vel quelibet persona fuerit
dignitatis, aut fortasse inferior huius infidelitatis inplicatus scelere, non solum
exilio religetur, sed de eorum facultatibus quidquid censura regalis exinde facere
vel iudicare voluerit, arbitrii illius et potestatis per omnia subiacebit. Illos tan-

tum a superioribus capitulis lex ista indemnes efficiet, qui ita ab infirmitate fuerint pregravati, ut progredi vel proficisci in consortio fidelium secundum superiorem ordinem minime possint; qui vero, et si ipsi morbis quibuslibet fuerint prepediti, omnem tamen suam virtutem in adiutorio episcoporum vel clericorum adque fratrum suorum sinceriter pro utilitate regie potestatis, gentis et patrie fideliter laborantium dirigebunt. Quod si hoc non fecerint, superiori sententia pariter cum transgressoribus feriantur. Persona autem illa tunc erit a suprascripta damnatione innoxia, dum per idoneum testem convicerit, ita se esse pre egritudine inpossibilem, ut nullum habuisset in tempore prestandi vel proficiscendi vigorem; ut vitium, quod ex preteritis temporibus male usque hactenus inoleverat, et severa legis huius censura redarguat, et concors adque unanimis adsensio quietem plebium et patrie defensionem adquirat.

Data et confirmata lex di kalendarum Novembrium anno feliciter secundo regni nostri.

## IX. FLAVIUS GLORIOSUS ERVIGIUS REX.
De his, qui in exercitum constituto die, loco vel
tempore definito non successerint aut refugerint;
vel que pars servorum uniuscuiusque in eadem
expeditione debeat proficisci.

Si amatores patrie hii procul dubio adprobantur, qui se periculis ultronee pro eius liberatione obiciunt, cur desertores potius non dicantur, qui vindicatores eius esse desistunt? Nam quando hi tales voluntarie terram salvaturi credendi sunt, qui etiam admoniti pro liberatione patrie non insurgunt? dum aut de bellica profectione se differunt, aut, quod peius est, vel remorari contra monita cupiunt, ,vel destituti contra ordinem proficiscuntur; cum quidam illorum laborandis agris studentes servorum multitudines cedunt, et procurande salutis sue gratia nec vicesimam quidem partem sue familie secum ducunt; quin potius auctiores volunt fieri fruge quam corporis sospitate, dum sua tegunt et se destituunt, maiorem diligentiam rei familiaris quam experientiam habentes in armis; quasi laborata fruituri possideant, si victores esse desistunt. Consulendum est ergo talibus per disciplinam, quos studia utilitatis propie non invitant. Unde id cunctis populis regni nostri sub generali et omnimoda constitutione precipimus, ut instituto adque prefinito die vel tempore, quo aut princeps in exercitum ire decreverit aut quemlibet de ducibus vel comitibus profecturum in publica utilitate preceperit, quisquis ille sive admonitionem cuiuslibet suscipiat, seu etiam nec admonitus qualibet tamen cognitione id sentiat vel quocumque sibi indicio innotescat, quo in loco exercitus bellaturus accedat, domui ulterius residere non audeat vel qualemcumque remorationem vel excusationem profecturus exhibeat; sed definitis locis adque temporibus, iuxta quod eos vel iussio principalis monuerit, vel admonitio ducis vel comitis, thiufadi, vicarii seu cuiuslibet curam agentis tetigerit, prestum se unusquisque, ut dictum est, definito loco vel tempore exhibeat. Iam vero, si quisquis ille admonitus, vel etiam si nec admonitus, et tamen qualibet cognitione sibimet innotescente non nescius, aut progredi statim noluerit, aut

in definitis locis adque temporibus prestus esse destiterit: si maioris loci persona
fuerit, id est dux, comes seu etiam gardingus, a bonis propriis ex toto privatus exi-
lii relegatione iussu regio mancipetur; ita ut, quod principalis sublimitas de rebus
eius iudicare elegerit, in sue persistat potestatis arbitrio. Inferiores sane vilior-
esque persone, thiufadi scilicet omnisque exercitus conpulsores vel hi, qui conpel-
luntur, si aut in exercitum venire distulerint, aut in loco vel tempore constituto
minime occurrerint vel proficisci neglexerint, seu de expeditione publica quocumque fraudis commento effugiendo se subtraxerint, non solum ducentorum fla-
gellorum ictibus verberati, sed et turpiter decalvatione fedati, et singulas insuper
libras auri cogantur exolvere, quas principalis potestas cui largiri decreverit, sui
maneat incunctanter arbitrii. Quod si non habuerit, unde hanc conpositionem
exolvat, tunc regie potestati sit licitum huiusmodi transgressorem perpetue servituti subicere; ut quod de eo suisque rebus ordinare decreverit, habeat sine dubio
potestatem. Illos sane ab huius legis sententia decernimus permanere innocuos,
quos aut principalis absolverit iussio, aut minoris adhuc retinuerit etatis tempus
aut senectutis vetustas, vel etiam egritudinis cuiusque gravida represserit moles.
Si tamen is, qui egritudine fuerit pregravatus, per legitimum testem probare
potuerit, quia pre egritudinis languore in exercitum proficisci nequivit, omnem
tamen virtutem rei sue ipse, qui egritudine pregravatus fuerit, secundum legis
huius institutionem in publicis utilitatibus cum duce vel comite suo dirigere non
moretur. Nunc vero, quia de generali omnium progessione prediximus, restat, ut
de progressorum virtute vel copiis instituta ponamus. Et ideo id decreto speciali
decernimus, ut, quisquis ille est, sive sit dux sive comes atque gardingus, seu sit
Gotus sive Romanus, necnon ingenuus quisque vel etiam manumissus, sive etiam
quislibet ex servis fiscalibus, quisquis horum est in exercitum progressurus, decimam partem servorum suorum secum in expeditione bellica ducturus accedat; ita
ut hec pars decima servorum non inermis existat, sed vario armorum genere
instructa appareat; sic quoque, ut unusquisque de his, quos secum in exercitum
duxerit, partem aliquam zabis vel loricis munitam, plerosque vero scutis, spatis,
scramis, lanceis sagittisque instructos, quosdam etiam fundarum instrumentis
vel ceteris armis, que noviter forsitan unusquisque a seniore vel domino suo
iniuncta habuerit, principi, duci vel comiti suo presentare studeat. Si quis autem
extra hanc decimam partem servorum suorum in exercitus progressione accesser-
it, omnis ipsa decima pars servorum eius studiose quesita adque discripta, quidquid minus fuerit inventum de hac instituta adque discripta decima parte
servorum in bellicam unumquemque secum expeditionem duxisse, in potestate
principis reducendum est, ut, cui hoc idem princeps prelargiri decreverit, in eius
subiaceat potestate. Quicumque vero ex palatino officio ita in exercitus expeditione profectus extiterit, ut nec in principali servitio frequens existat, nec in wardia cum reliquis fratribus suis laborem sustineat, noverit se legis huius sententia
feriendum; excepto si eum manifesta languoris ostensio conprobaverit morbi-
dum. Nam et si quisque exercitalium, in eadem bellica expeditione proficiscens,
minime ducem aut comitem aut etiam patronum suum secutus fuerit, sed per
patrocinia diversorum se dilataverit, ita ut nec in wardia cum seniore suo persis-

tat, nec aliquem publice utilitatis profectum exhibeat, non ei talis profectio inputanda est, sed superiori ordine, que de vilioribus interioribusque personis in hac lege decreta sunt, in semetipsum noverit sustinere. His igitur ordinatis atque conpositis, restat, ut frenum cupiditati eorum ponamus, quos ad peragenda negotia utilitatis nostre inpingimus. Et ideo nullus dux, comes, thiufadus seu quislibet commissos populos regens accepto beneficio vel qualibet occasione sue pessime volumtatis quemquam ex suis subditis de bellica profectione dimittat, aut admonitiones ipsas, que fieri debent progressione exercitus vel inductiones armorum, sub ista quasi admonitionis occasione interserat, unde quemquam illorum militare presumat. Nam quisquis talia agens pro his, ut dictum est, causis a quolibet aut oblatum quodcumque perceperit, aut ipse quidquam cuicumque exegerit, et quidem si de primatibus palatii fuerit, et illi, a quo tale aliquid accepit, in quadruplum satisfaciat, et principi pro eo solo, quo se munificare presumpsit, libram auri soluturum se noverit. Minores vero persone, ab honore vel dignitate ingenuitatis private, in potestate sunt principis redigende, ut, quod de eis vel de rebus eorum iudicare elegerit, sue subiaceat modis omnibus potestati.

*Instead of the passage from line 11, page 472, to line 21, page 472, later codices read as follows:*

Quod si non habuerit, unde hanc conpositionem exsolvat, tunc regie potestati sit licitum huiusmodi transgressorem perpetue servituti addictum cui elegerit serviturum, res quoque eius alibi separata collatione concedere vel donare; ita ut idem transgressor nec ad statum libertatis quolibet sibi indulgente ulterius redeat, neque rei sue iura quocumque sibi restaurante recipiat. Quod si etiam quidem rei dominus, id est ipse, qui quidem transgressoris reiculas donatas perceperat, culpe cuiuslibet crimine forsitam dinotatus a statu dignitatis pristine cadat, unde res ipsa in principis potestatem iterum veniat, tunc id irrevocabili constitutione tenebitur, ut etiam si ipse eam habere non meruerit, qui eam prius acceperat, in aliis fidelibus transfusa res ipsa proficiat; tantum, ut in illius ultra potestatem non transeat, qui in profectione bellica tardus et dignitate semel exstitit privatus et rebus. Sane duces omnes senioresque palatii ad huiusmodi sententiam obnoxii tenebuntur, quicumque fuerint superioris precepti transgressores inventi. Nec non et illi huiuscemodi damnationis sententiam merebuntur, qui aut de bello refugiunt, aut in bellica profectione constituti extra senioris sui permissum alibi properasse reperiuntur. Id tamen in hac eadem progressione tam in maiorum quam in minorum personis est observandum, ut, si quilibet sub gravi egritudine consistens nullo modo proficiscendi habeat vires, statim loci illius vel territorii episcopum ad sue egritudines inspiciendam molestiam veniendum exoptet; ita ut illum ex episcopis inspectorem sue egritudinis advocet, in cuius territorio vel provincia aut infirmasse ei contigerit aut immorasse, vel ex aliorum territorio advenisse contigerit. Nam non aliter eis est credendum, nisi aut episcoporum testimonio, in quorum territoriis dinoscitur infirmasse, iurisiurandi fuerit attestatione firmatum, aut eorum iuramento, quos iidem episcopi vice sua inspectores direxerint, fuerit conprobatum. Qui tamen episcopi hanc de talibus curam habeant, ut egritudines eorum aut per se aut per subditos diligenter inspiciant, si aut proficisci nullo modo possunt, aut si post aliquos dies possint definite concurrere ad bellandum, id est, antequam exercitus in prefinitis locis ingrediatur ad prelium. Et secundum quod talium egritudines viderint, ipsorum est iudicio committendum, utrum domi sospitatis gratia reparande immorentur, an reparatis viribis illis expediat ambulandum; qualiter sub eorum episcoporum testimonio aut egritudinibus eorum compatiamur, ut concedat, aut vitium, si sub egritudine fingitur, resecemus, ut placeat; ita tamen, ut si se quisquis ille ita viderit infirmitate defessum, ut nullo modo proficisci valeat ad prelium, virtutem rei sue secundum legis huius institutionem in publicis utilitatibus cum duce vel comite suo dirigere non moretur. Sin autem senserit, se continuo meliorari, mox ut corporis reparaverit vires, statim per se cum omni virtute sua, secundum quod legis huius sanctione precipitur, illic non moretur succedere, ubi novit se admonitum exstitisse vel exercitum cognoverit postea properasse.

* * *

# INDEX

Administrative system: Roman, orderly 209; of later Roman armies, suited to barter economy, 326; of Prussia, developed from army administration, 330

Adrana, 107

Adrianople, battle of: one of two battles of fourth century with reliable reports, 255; account of, 269-84; start of, by Romans, without command, 273; importance of outcome of, 280; lasting blow to Roman Empire, 317

Aelian, 172, 201

Aelius Sejanus, 182

Aetius: to defend against Gaiseric, 294; assignment of area to Burgundians by, 319, 328; territory given to Alani by, 335 n.1

Africa, large cities and towns in, 223

Agathias, 341; unreliable as source on wedge, 50; on wedge formation at Casilinus, 51-52; successor to Procopius, 339; account by, of battle of Mount Vesuvius, 367; account by, of battle on Casilinus, 369, 371-74; suspect nature of account by, 374

*Aggeres*, 129

Agrarian organization, Roman, 320

Agricola, 125

Agriculture: decline of, near large cities, 221; organization of, in Roman Empire, 320

Agrippina: relationship of, to Augustus, 186; departure of, from camp, 190, 192

Alamanni, 285, 308, 311; burning of cities by, 252, victory of Gratian over, 257, 272, 283; in battle of Strasbourg, 261-68; crossing of *limes* by, 261; losses of, in battle of Strasbourg, 265; reported dismounted combat of princes of, at Strasbourg, 267; strength of, at Strasbourg, 267, 286; remnants of, settled in Raetia, 307; in battle on Casilinus, 369, 373; as cavalry, 407

Alamundarus, 381

Alani, 256-57; reinforcement of West Goths by, 269, 279, 283; with Vandals, 293, 296; in Spain, 318; settling of, 319

Alaric, 295, 313, 318, 399, 420

Alatheus, 273-74, 283 n.1

Aldioni, 308

Alesia, 143, 381

Alexander, pursuit of Persians by, 381

Alexander Severus, 208

Aligern, 373

Aliso: fort at, constructed by Drusus, 58; purpose of fort at, 58-60, 136; uncertainty of site of, 58-60; risk of wintering near, taken by Tiberius, 62; Roman fugitives from Teutoburger battle besieged in, 78-79, 145; reconstructed by Romans 15 A.D., 101; road built from, to Rhine 113, 139; central point for reconstruction of Roman-Germanic campaigns, 131; location of, dependent on Lippe, 131; aid to, from Vetera, 137; name of, cited in three passages,

*About the Author:*

HANS DELBRÜCK (1848–1929) was the editor of the *Prussian Annals* from 1883 to 1919 and Professor of History at Berlin University from 1896 to 1921. A member of the German delegation to the Paris Peace Conference, Delbrück served as an expert on the question of German responsibility for World War I.

*About the Translator:*

WALTER J. RENFROE, JR. retired as a Brigadier General in the United States Army and as Professor of Foreign Languages at the United States Military Academy at West Point.